T0177971

Lecture Notes in Computer Science

Vol. 60: Operating Systems, An Advanced Course. Edited by R. Bayer, R. M. Graham, and G. Seegmüller. X, 593 pages. 1978.

Vol. 61: The Vienna Development Method: The Meta-Language. Edited by D. Bjørner and C. B. Jones. XVIII, 382 pages. 1978.

Vol. 62: Automata, Languages and Programming. Proceedings 1978. Edited by G. Ausiello and C. Böhm. VIII, 508 pages. 1978.

Vol. 63: Natural Language Communication with Computers. Edited by Leonard Bolc. VI, 292 pages. 1978.

Vol. 64: Mathematical Foundations of Computer Science. Proceedings 1978. Edited by J. Winkowski. X, 551 pages. 1978.

Vol. 65: Information Systems Methodology, Proceedings, 1978. Edited by G. Bracchi and P. C. Lockemann. XII, 696 pages. 1978.

Vol. 66: N. D. Jones and S. S. Muchnick, TEMPO: A Unified Treatment of Binding Time and Parameter Passing Concepts in Programming Languages. IX, 118 pages. 1978.

Vol. 67: Theoretical Computer Science, 4th GI Conference, Aachen, March 1979. Edited by K. Weihrauch. VII, 324 pages. 1979.

Vol. 68: D. Harel, First-Order Dynamic Logic. X, 133 pages. 1979.

Vol. 69: Program Construction. International Summer School. Edited by F. L. Bauer and M. Broy. VII, 651 pages. 1979.

Vol. 70: Semantics of Concurrent Computation. Proceedings 1979. Edited by G. Kahn. VI, 368 pages. 1979.

Vol. 71: Automata, Languages and Programming. Proceedings 1979. Edited by H. A. Maurer. IX, 684 pages. 1979.

Vol. 72: Symbolic and Algebraic Computation. Proceedings 1979. Edited by E. W. Ng. XV, 557 pages. 1979.

Vol. 73: Graph-Grammars and Their Application to Computer Science and Biology. Proceedings 1978. Edited by V. Claus, H. Ehrig and G. Rozenberg. VII, 477 pages. 1979.

Vol. 74: Mathematical Foundations of Computer Science. Proceedings 1979. Edited by J. Bečvář. IX, 580 pages. 1979.

Vol. 75: Mathematical Studies of Information Processing. Proceedings 1978. Edited by E. K. Blum, M. Paul and S. Takasu. VIII, 629 pages. 1979.

Vol. 76: Codes for Boundary-Value Problems in Ordinary Differential Equations. Proceedings 1978. Edited by B. Childs et al. VIII, 388 pages. 1979.

Vol. 77: G. V. Bochmann, Architecture of Distributed Computer Systems. VIII, 238 pages. 1979.

Vol. 78: M. Gordon, R. Milner and C. Wadsworth, Edinburgh LCF. VIII, 159 pages. 1979.

Vol. 79: Language Design and Programming Methodology. Proceedings, 1979. Edited by J. Tobias. IX, 255 pages. 1980.

Vol. 80: Pictorial Information Systems. Edited by S. K. Chang and K. S. Fu. IX, 445 pages. 1980.

Vol. 81: Data Base Techniques for Pictorial Applications. Proceedings, 1979. Edited by A. Blaser. XI, 599 pages. 1980.

Vol. 82: J. G. Sanderson, A Relational Theory of Computing. VI, 147 pages. 1980.

Vol. 83: International Symposium Programming. Proceedings, 1980. Edited by B. Robinet. VII, 341 pages. 1980.

Vol. 84: Net Theory and Applications. Proceedings, 1979. Edited by W. Brauer. XIII, 537 Seiten. 1980.

Vol. 85: Automata, Languages and Programming. Proceedings, 1980. Edited by J. de Bakker and J. van Leeuwen. VIII, 671 pages. 1980.

Vol. 86: Abstract Software Specifications. Proceedings, 1979. Edited by D. Bjørner. XIII, 567 pages. 1980

Vol. 87: 5th Conference on Automated Deduction. Proceedings, 1980. Edited by W. Bibel and R. Kowalski. VII, 385 pages. 1980.

Vol. 88: Mathematical Foundations of Computer Science 198 Proceedings, 1980. Edited by P. Dembiński. VIII, 723 pages. 198

Vol. 89: Computer Aided Design - Modelling, Systems Engineerin CAD-Systems. Proceedings, 1980. Edited by J. Encarnacao. XI 461 pages. 1980.

Vol. 90: D. M. Sandford, Using Sophisticated Models in Res lution Theorem Proving. XI, 239 pages. 1980

Vol. 91: D. Wood, Grammar and L Forms: An Introduction. IX, 3 pages. 1980.

Vol. 92: R. Milner, A Calculus of Communication Systems. VI, 1 pages. 1980.

Vol. 93: A. Nijholt, Context-Free Grammars: Covers, Normal Form and Parsing. VII, 253 pages. 1980.

Vol. 94: Semantics-Directed Compiler Generation. Proceeding 1980. Edited by N. D. Jones. V, 489 pages. 1980.

Vol. 95: Ch. D. Marlin, Coroutines. XII, 246 pages. 1980.

Vol. 96: J. L. Peterson, Computer Programs for Spelling Correctio VI, 213 pages. 1980.

Vol. 97: S. Osaki and T. Nishio, Reliability Evaluation of Some Fau Tolerant Computer Architectures. VI, 129 pages. 1980.

Vol. 98: Towards a Formal Description of Ada. Edited by D. Bjørn and O. N. Oest. XIV, 630 pages. 1980.

Vol. 99: I. Guessarian, Algebraic Semantics. XI, 158 pages. 19

Vol. 100: Graphtheoretic Concepts in Computer Science. Edited H. Noltemeier. X, 403 pages. 1981.

Vol. 101: A. Thayse, Boolean Calculus of Differences. VII, 144 page 1981.

Vol. 102: J. H. Davenport, On the Integration of Algebraic Functio 1–197 pages. 1981.

Vol. 103: H. Ledgard, A. Singer, J. Whiteside, Directions in Hum Factors of Interactive Systems. VI, 190 pages. 1981.

Vol. 104: Theoretical Computer Science. Ed. by P. Deussen. V 261 pages. 1981.

Vol. 105: B. W. Lampson, M. Paul, H. J. Siegert, Distributed Systems Architecture and Implementation. XIII, 510 pages. 1981.

Vol. 106: The Programming Language Ada. Reference Manual. 243 pages. 1981.

Vol. 107: International Colloquium on Formalization of Programmin Concepts. Proceedings. Edited by J. Diaz and I. Ramos. VII, 4 pages. 1981.

Vol. 108: Graph Theory and Algorithms. Edited by N. Saito ar T. Nishizeki. VI, 216 pages. 1981.

Vol. 109: Digital Image Processing Systems. Edited by L. Bolc ar Zenon Kulpa. V, 353 pages. 1981.

Vol. 110: W. Dehning, H. Essig, S. Maass, The Adaptation of Virtu Man-Computer Interfaces to User Requirements in Dialogs. X, 14 pages. 1981.

Vol. 111: CONPAR 81. Edited by W. Händler. XI, 508 pages. 19

Vol. 112: CAAP '81. Proceedings. Edited by G. Astesiano and C. Böh VI, 364 pages. 1981.

Vol. 113: E.-E. Doberkat, Stochastic Automata: Stability, Nondete minism, and Prediction. IX, 135 pages. 1981.

Vol. 114: B. Liskov, CLU, Reference Manual. VIII, 190 pages. 19

Vol. 115: Automata, Languages and Programming. Edited by S. Ev and O. Kariv. VIII, 552 pages. 1981.

Vol. 116: M. A. Casanova, The Concurrency Control Problem f Database Systems. VII, 175 pages. 1981.

Lecture Notes in Computer Science

Edited by G. Goos and J. Hartmanis

164

Logics of Programs

Workshop, Carnegie Mellon University
Pittsburgh, PA, June 6–8, 1983

Edited by Edmund Clarke and Dexter Kozen

Springer-Verlag
Berlin Heidelberg New York Tokyo 1984

Editorial Board

D. Barstow W. Brauer P. Brinch Hansen D. Gries D. Luckham
C. Moler A. Pnueli G. Seegmüller J. Stoer N. Wirth

Editors

Edmund Clarke
Computer Science Department, Carnegie Mellon University
Pittsburgh, PA 15213 USA

Dexter Kozen
IBM Research
Box 218, Yorktown Heights, NY 10598 USA

AMS Subject Classifications (1980): 68C01, 68B10, 68B15, 03B45, 03D45

CR Subject Classifications (1982): F.3, F.4.1, B.2.2, B.6.3, D.2.4

ISBN 3-540-12896-4 Springer-Verlag Berlin Heidelberg New York Tokyo
ISBN 0-387-12896-4 Springer-Verlag New York Heidelberg Berlin Tokyo

This work is subject to copyright. All rights are reserved, whether the whole or part of the material is concerned, specifically those of translation, reprinting, re-use of illustrations, broadcasting, reproduction by photocopying machine or similar means, and storage in data banks. Under § 54 of the German Copyright Law where copies are made for other than private use, a fee is payable to "Verwertungsgesellschaft Wort", Munich.

© by Springer-Verlag Berlin Heidelberg 1984
Printed in Germany

Printing and binding: Beltz Offsetdruck, Hemsbach/Bergstr.
2145/3140-543210

FOREWORD

Logics of Programs, as a field of study, touches on a wide variety of activities in computer science and mathematics. It draws on mathematical foundations of formal logic, semantics, and complexity theory, and finds practical application in the areas of program specification, verification, and programming language design. The Logics of Programs Workshop was conceived as a forum for the informal sharing of problems, results, techniques, and new applications in these areas, with special emphasis on bridging whatever abyss may exist between the theoreticians and the pragmatists.

The workshop was held on June 6-8, 1983 at Carnegie Mellon University. It was the fourth in an unofficial series, which started in 1979 with the workshop in Zürich organized by Erwin Engeler, and continued with the 1980 Poznan workshop organized by Andrzej Salwicki and the 1981 Yorktown Heights workshop organized by Dexter Kozen. Since the 1979 workshop, interest and participation has grown precipitiously: the CMU workshop drew 59 registered participants from 8 countries, as well as many unregistered participants. 38 technical papers were presented, representing the entire spectrum of activity in Logics of Programs from model theory to languages for the design of digital circuits. The contributions of the workshop participants appearing in this volume are unrefereed and are to be considered working papers.

The workshop was held in cooperation with the Association for Computing Machinery, and was made possible through the generous support of the National Science Foundation[1] and the Office of Naval Research[2]. We wish to thank all who helped with the organization of the workshop and preparation of the proceedings, especially John Cherniavsky, Robert Grafton, Magdalena Müller, and Nancy Perry.

Edmund Clarke
Dexter Kozen
Sept. 1, 1983

---

[1] grant MCS-8303082

[2] grant N00014-83-G-0079

CONTENTS

A STATIC ANALYSIS OF CSP PROGRAMS

Krzysztof R. APT

LITP, Université Paris 7
2, Place Jussieu
75251 PARIS
France

Abstract A static analysis is proposed as a method of reducing complexity of the correctness proofs of CSP programs. This analysis is based on considering all possible sequences of communications which can arise in computations during which the boolean guards are not interpreted. Several examples are provided which clarify its various aspects.

1. INTRODUCTION

Correctness proofs of concurrent and distributed programs are complicated because in general they are of the length proportional to the product of the lengths of the component programs. We claim in this paper that in the case of the CSP programs the length and the complexity of these proofs can be substantially reduced by carrying out first a preliminary static analysis of the programs. This analysis allows to reduce the number of cases which have to be considered at the level of interaction between the proofs of the component programs.

The analysis is quite straightforward and contains hardly any new ideas. It is based on considering all possible sequences of communications which can arise in computations during which the boolean guards are not interpreted. In this respect it bears a strong resemblance to the trace model for a version of CSP given in [H 1].

We apply this analysis to three types of problems. The first one consists of determining which pairs of input-output commands (i/o commands) may be synchronized during properly terminating computations. The second one consists of determining all possible configurations in which deadlock occurs. Finally we provide a sufficient condition for safety of a decomposition of CSP programs into communication-closed layers, a method of decomposition which has been recently proposed by Elrad and Francez [EF].

A similar analysis can be carried out for other programming languages which use rendez-vous as a sole means for communication and synchronization. In fact while writing this paper we encountered in the last issue of the Communications of ACM a paper by Taylor [T] in which such an analysis is carried out for ADA programs.

The only difference is in the presentation of this approach. R.N. Taylor presents an algorithm which computes all rendez-vous which may take place during execution of a program and all configurations in which deadlock may arise. His algorithm is also capable of determining which actions may occur in parallel. We on the other hand present the analysis in a formal language theory framework providing the rigorous definitions which can be used in the case of concrete examples. We also link this analysis with a subsequent stage being the task of proving correctness of the programs.

The paper is organized as follows. In the next section we introduce the basic definitions. In section 3 we provide three applications already mentioned above. Section 4 is devoted to a more refined analysis which takes into account the problem of termination of the repetitive commands. Finally in section 5 a number of conclusions is presented.

2. BASIC DEFINITIONS

We assume that the reader is familiar with the original article of Hoare [H]. Throughout the paper we consider programs written in a subset of CSP. We disallow nested parallel composition, assume that all variables are of the same type and consequently omit all the declarations. Additionally we allow output commands to be used as guards. For the reasons which will become clear later we label each occurence of an input or output command by a unique label.

By a parallel program we mean a program of the form $P_1 \| \ldots \| P_n$ where each P_i is a process. For simplicity we drop the process labels. So according to the notation of [H] each process is identified with the command representing its body. The name of the process can be uniquely determined from the position of the command within the parallel composition.

The analysis carried out here can be straightforwardly extended to the full CSP.

Throughout the paper we denote by S,T arbitrary (sequential) commands, by g guards, by b,c boolean expressions, by t expressions and by α,β i/o commands. Labels of the i/o commands are denoted by the letters k,l,m. Finally, we write $[\ \square_{i=1}^{m} g_i \rightarrow S_i]$ instead of $[g_1 \rightarrow S_1 \ \square \ldots \square \ g_m \rightarrow S_m]$.

Consider now a parallel program $P_1\|\ldots\|P_n$. We proceed in two stages.

1°) With each process P_i we associate a regular language $L(P_i)$ defined by structural induction. We put

$L(x:=t) = L(skip) = \{\epsilon\}$,

$L(l:P_j!t) = \{l : \langle i,j\rangle\}$,

$L(l{:}P_j?x) = \{l : <j,i>\}$,

$L(S_1;S_2) = L(S_1)L(S_2)$,

$L(g \rightarrow S) = L(g)L(S)$,

$L(b) = \{\epsilon\}$, $L(b;l{:}\alpha) = L(b)L(l{:}\alpha)$ $(=L(l{:}\alpha))$,

$L([\,\square_{i=1}^{m} g_i \rightarrow S_i]) = \bigcup_{i=1}^{m} L(g_i \rightarrow S_i)$,

$L(*[\,\square_{i=1}^{m} g_i \rightarrow S_i]) = L([\,\square_{i=1}^{m} g_i \rightarrow S_i])^*$

Note that $L(P_i)$ is the set of all a priori possible communication sequences of P_i when the boolean guards are not interpreted. Each communication sequence consists of elements of the form $l{:}<i,j>$ or $l{:}<j,i>$ where l is a label of an i/o command uniquely identified and $<i,j>$ $(<j,i>)$ records that fact that this i/o command stands for a communication from $P_i(P_j)$ to $P_j(P_i)$.

It is important that we associate with assignment and skip statements the set $\{\epsilon\}$ and not the empty language $\emptyset$. Otherwise not all communication sequences would be recorded in $L(P_i)$. The following example clarifies this issue.

Example 1

Let

$P_1 \equiv [b_1 \rightarrow \text{skip} \ \square \ b_2 \rightarrow k{:}P_2!x]$;

$*[l{:}P_2?y \rightarrow \ldots \ ; \ m{:}P_2!y]$

where ... stands for a "private part" of P_1, i.e. a command not involving any i/o commands. Then

$L(P_1) = \{(l{:}<2,1>)(m{:}<1,2>)\}^*$

$\cup \ \{k{:}<1,2>\}\{(l{:}<2,1>)(m{:}<1,2>)\}^*$

If we associated with skip the empty language then the first part of $L(P_1)$ would not be present even though it represents possible communication sequences.

2°) We associate with $P_1\|\ldots\|P_n$ a regular language $L(P_1\|\ldots\|P_n)$. Its letters are of the form $k,l{:}<i,j>$ standing for an instance of a communication between the output command of P_i labeled by k and the input command of P_j labeled by l.

First we define a projection function $[.]_i$ $(1 \le i \le n)$ from the alphabet of $L(P_1\|\ldots\|P_n)$ into the alphabet of $L(P_i)$. We put

$[k,l{:}<i,j>]_i = k{:}<i,j>$

$[k,l{:}<i,j>]_j = l{:}<i,j>$

$[k,l{:}<i,j>]_h = \epsilon$ if $h \neq i,j$

and naturally extend it to a homomorphism from the set of words of $L(P_1\|\ldots\|P_n)$ into the set of words of $L(P_i)$.

We now define

$L(P_1\|\ldots\|P_n) = \{h:[h]_i \in L(P_i),\ i = 1,\ldots,n\}$

Intuitively, $L(P_1\|\ldots\|P_n)$ is the set of all possible communication sequences of $P_1\|\ldots\|P_n$ which can arise in properly terminating computations during which the boolean expressions are not interpreted.

3. APPLICATIONS

1. Partial correctness

Given a parallel program $P_1\|\ldots\|P_n$ we define

$STAT = \{(k:\alpha,\ l,\beta) : k:\alpha$ is from P_i, $l:\beta$ is from P_j,

$\quad\&\ \exists h\ \exists a\ [h \in L(P_1\|\ldots\|P_n)$, a is an element of h,

$\quad L(k:\alpha) = \{[a]_i\}$ and $L(l:\beta) = \{[a]_j\}]\}$.

Intuitively STAT (standing for static match) is the set of all pairs of i/o commands which can be synchronized during a properly terminating computation of $P_1\|\ldots\|P_n$ which ignores the boolean guards.

The set STAT should be compared with two other sets of pairs of i/o commands :

$SYNT = \{(k:\alpha,\ l:\beta) : k:\alpha$ is from P_i, $l:\beta$ is from P_j and $k:\alpha$ and $l:\beta$ address each other (match)$\}$

$SEM = \{(k:\alpha,\ l:\beta)$: in some "real" properly terminating computation of $P_1\|\ldots\|P_n$ $k:\alpha$ and $l:\beta$ are synchronized$\}$.

In the proof systems of [AFR] and [LG] dealing with partial correctness of CSP programs the crucial proof rule is the one that deals with the parallel composition of the processes. First one introduces so called proof outlines for component processes. A proof outline of S is a special form of a proof of partial correctness of the program S in which each subprogram of S is preceded and succeded by an assertion. These assertions are supposed to hold at the moment when the control is at the point to which they are attached. As behaviour of each component process depends on the other processes we ensure the above property by comparing proof outlines of the component processes. Given a proof outline the only assertions which have to be justified using proof outlines ot other processes are those succeeding the i/o commands.

Thus one identifies all pairs of possibly matching i/o commands and checks that the assertions attached to them are indeed justified when the communication takes place. This part of verification of the proof outlines is called in [AFR] the cooperation test and in [LG] the satisfaction test.

If the proof outlines satisfy the test then one can pass to the conclusion stating partial correctness of the parallel program.

We now concentrate on the step consisting of identifying all pairs of possibly matching i/o commands. According to our definition this is the set SEM. But since SEM is in general not computable as a function of the program $P_1\|\ldots\|P_n$, this set is replaced in [AFR] and [LG] by a larger set SYNT being obviously computable. We propose to replace in this analysis the set SEM by the set STAT.

Note that the following clearly holds.

Fact SEM $\subseteq$ STAT $\subseteq$ SYNT

Moreover, the set STAT is obviously computable. Using the set STAT instead of SYNT as an "approximation" for SEM is more economical as less checks in the cooperation (satisfaction) test phase are then needed. Also the proof outlines (and in the case of [AFR] - the global invariant) can be simplified.

As an illustration of the difference between the sets STAT and SYNT consider the following example :

Example 2

Let

$$P_1 \equiv k_1{:}P_2?x\ ;\ldots;k_2{:}P_2!z\ ;\ldots;$$
$$*[b_1 \rightarrow\ldots;\ k_3{:}P_2?x\ ;\ldots;\ k_4{:}P_2!z\ ;\ldots],$$

$$P_2 \equiv l_1{:}P_1!y\ ;\ldots;\ l_2{:}P_1?u\ ;\ldots;$$
$$*[b_2 \rightarrow\ \ldots;\ l_3{:}P_1!y\ ;\ldots;\ l_4{:}P_1?u\ ;\ldots]$$

Then

$$\text{STAT} = \{(k_i{:}\alpha_i,\ l_i{:}\beta_i)\ :\ 1 \le i \le 4\}$$

and

$$\text{SYNT} = \{(k_i{:}\alpha_i,\ l_j{:}\beta_j)\ :\ |i-j| \text{ is even},\ 1 \le i,j \le 4\}.$$

Thus STAT has here 4 elements whereas SYNT has 8 elements.

The difference between STAT and SYNT becomes more evident for longer programs. For example if in the above programs both repetitive commands contained 2k instead of two alternating i/o commands in succession then STAT would contain $2(k+1)$ elements whereas SYNT would contain $2(k+1)^2$ elements.

It is important to note that the set STAT consists of pairs of i/o commands which can be synchronized during a properly terminating computation. The following two examples clarify this issue.

Example 3

Let

$$P_1 \equiv \ldots;\ k_1{:}P_1?x\ ;\ldots\ ,$$

$$P_2 \equiv \ldots;\ l_1{:}P_2!y\ ;\ldots;\ l_2{:}P_2!u\ ;\ldots$$

Then $L(P_1) = \{k_1:<2,1>\}$ and $L(P_2) = \{(l_1:<2,1>)(l_2:<2,1>)\}$ so $L(P_1 \| P_2) = \emptyset$. Thus STAT = $\emptyset$ even though the i/o commands labelled by k_1 and l_1, respectively can be synchronized. On the other hand, since $L(P_1 \| P_2) = \emptyset$, there does not exist a properly terminating computation of $P_1 \| P_2$. Indeed, for any properly terminating computation the sequence consisting of its consecutive communications belongs to $L(P_1 \| P_2)$.

Example 4

Let

$$P_1 \equiv [b_1 \rightarrow \dots \,\square\, b_2 \rightarrow \dots \,;\, k_1:P_2?x;\dots;k_2:P_2!x],$$

$$P_2 \equiv [c_1 \rightarrow \dots \,\square\, c_2 \rightarrow \dots \,;\, l_1:P_1!y;\dots;l_2:P_1!y].$$

Then $L(P_1) = \{\epsilon, (k_1:<2,1>)(k_2:<1,2>)\}$ and $L(P_2) = \{\epsilon, (l_1:<2,1>)(l_2:<2,1>)\}$ so $L(P_1 \| P_2) = \{\epsilon\}$. Thus STAT = $\emptyset$. The i/o commands labeled by k_1 and l_1, respectively can be synchronized but not during a properly terminating computation.

The situation when $L(P_1 \| \dots \| P_n) = \emptyset$ should be compared with the situation when $L(P_1 \| \dots \| P_n) = \{\epsilon\}$. In the first case no properly terminating computation of $P_1 \| \dots \| P_n$ exists. In the latter case the properly terminating computations of $P_1 \| \dots \| P_n$ can exist but in none of them a communication will take place.

In both cases STAT = $\emptyset$ so no cooperation (resp. satisfaction) test will take place in the proof rule dealing with parallel composition. This is in accordance with the fact that partial correctness of programs refers to properly terminating computations only. In both cases above no communication will take place in any such computation.

Finally we consider the following example :

Example 5

Let

$$P_1 \equiv *[k_1:P_2?x \rightarrow \dots] \,;\, k_2:P_2!u,$$

$$P_2 \equiv *[l_1:P_1!y \rightarrow \dots] \,;\, l_2:P_1?z.$$

Then STAT = SYNT = $\{(k_i:\alpha_i,\ l_i:\beta_i) : i=1,2\}$. Note however that the communication between the i/o commands with labels k_2 and l_2, respectively cannot take place as none of the repetitive commands can terminate. In particular no computation of $P_1 \| P_2$ terminates. The tools used so far do not allow us to deduce these facts formally. We shall return to this problem later.

2. Proofs of deadlock freedom

In the proof systemsof [AFR] and [LG] one proves deadlock freedom of the parallel programs by identifying first the set of blocked configurations, i.e. the vectors of control points corresponding to a deadlock. Then for each blocked configuration one shows that the conjunction of the assertions attached to the corresponding control points (and the global invariant in the case of [AFR]) is inconsistent. Thus the length of the proof of deadlock freedom is proportional to the number of blocked configurations.

We now suggest a more restricted definition of a blocked configuration which is sufficient for proofs of deadlock freedom and results in shorter proofs. The control points which are of interest here are those when the control resides in front of an i/o command or at the end of a process. With each control point of the first type we associate a set of i/o commands which can be at this point executed. With the control point of the second type we associate the set $\{\text{end } P_i\}$ corresponding to the situation when the control is at the end of the process P_i.

We define

$$C(k{:}\alpha) = \{\{k{:}\alpha\}\}$$

where $k{:}\alpha$ occurs in the process as an atomic command,

$$C([b_1 \to S_1 \,\square \ldots \square\, b_m \to S_m \,\square\, k_1{:}\alpha_1 \to S_{m+1} \square \ldots \square\, k_n{:}\alpha_n \to S_{m+n} \,\square b_{m+1}; k_{n+1}{:}\alpha_{n+1} \to$$
$$S_{m+n+1} \,\square \ldots \square b_{m+p}; k_{n+p}{:}\alpha_{n+p} \to S_{m+n+p}]) = \{A : A = \{k_i{:}\alpha_i : i=1,\ldots,n\} \cup B$$

where $B \subseteq \{k_{n+i}{:}\alpha_{n+i} : i=1,\ldots,p\}\}$, where $m \geq 0$ and $n+p \geq 1$,

$$C(*[\,\square_{i=1}^{m}\, g_i \to S_i]) = C([\,\square_{i=1}^{m}\, g_i \to S_i]).$$

For other type of commands S $C(S)$ is not defined. Note that a typical set A considered above consists of all i/o guards which occur without the boolean guards together with a subset of those i/o guards which occur with a boolean guard.

Given now a process P_i we define $C(P_i)$ to be the union of all sets $C(S)$ for S being a subprogram of P_i together with the element $\{\text{end } P_i\}$. Each element of $C(P_i)$ corresponds to a unique control point within P_i.

The identification of all blocked configurations depends on the fact whether so called distributed termination convention (d.t.c) of the repetitive commands is taken taken into account. According to this convention a repetitive command can be exited when all processes addressed in the guards with boolean part true have terminated. This convention corresponds to the following definition of a guard being failed : a guard fails if either its boolean part evaluates to false or the process addressed in its i/o part has terminated. A repetitive command is exited when all its guards fail. If in the definition of a failure of a guard we drop the second alternative we obtain the usual termination convention of the repetitive commands. In [H] the distributed termination convention is adopted.

Consider first the simpler case when the usual termination convention is used.

A triple $<A_1,\ldots,A_n>$ from $C(P_1)\times\ldots\times C(P_n)$ is called <u>blocked</u> if

i) $\exists\, i \;\; A_i \neq \{\text{end } P_i\}$

(not all processes have terminated)

ii) $(\bigcup_{i\neq j} A_i \times A_j) \cap SYNT = \emptyset$

(no communication can take place)

Alternatively ii) can be stated as : no pairs of elements from A_i and A_j $(i\neq j)$ match. The notion of a blocked tuple is from [AFR].

Let Init(L) for a formal language L denote its <u>left factor</u> i.e. the set $\{u : \exists\, w(uw \in L)\}$. We now put

$LP(P_1\|\ldots\|P_n) = \{h : [h]_i \in Init(L(P_i)),\ i=1,\ldots,n\}$.

Intuitively, $LP(P_1\|\ldots\|P_n)$ is the set of all possible communication sequences of $P_1\|\ldots\|P_n$ which can arise in partial computations during which the boolean guards are not interpreted.

We now say that a tuple $<A_1,\ldots,A_n>$ from $C(P_1)\times\ldots\times C(P_n)$ is <u>statically blocked</u> if

i) it is blocked

ii) $\exists\, h \in LP(P_1\|\ldots\|P_n) \;\; \forall\, i$

$[A_i \neq \{\text{end } P_i\} \Rightarrow \forall\, \underline{d} \in A_i([h]_i a \;\; \in Init(L(P_i)))$ where $L(\underline{d}) = \{a\}$

$\wedge\; A_i = \{\text{end } P_i\} \Rightarrow [h]_i \in L(P_i)]$

The second condition states that there exists a communication sequence which reaches the vector of the control points associated with $<A_1,\ldots,A_n>$. Reachability is checked by considering the projections $[h]_i$ of the sequence h. If $A_i \neq \{\text{end } P_i\}$ then $[h]_i a$ for all $a \in \{L(\underline{d}) : \underline{d} \in A_i\}$ should be an initial part of a sequence from $L(P_i)$. If $A_i = \{\text{end } P_i\}$ then $[h]_i$ should be a sequence from $L(P_i)$.

If d.t.c. is used then we should add the following condition to the definition of a blocked triple

iii) For no $i_o, i_1,\ldots,i_k$ from $\{1,\ldots,n\}$, where $i_j \neq i_l$ for $j \neq l$: $A_{i_j} = \{\text{end } P_{i_j}\}$ and the processes addressed in the i/o commands of A_{i_o} are all among $\{P_{i_1},\ldots,P_{i_k}\}$.

This condition states that no exit can take place due to the distributed termination convention. Thus the set A_{i_o} should correspond to a repetitive command.

We denote the set of all statically blocked tuples by STATB and the set of all blocked tuples by SYNTB.

We now consider a couple of examples.

Example 6

Consider the processes P_1 and P_2 from the example 2. D.t.c. cannot be used here. It is easy to see that

$$\begin{aligned} SYNTB = & \{<\{k_i:\alpha_i\}, \{l_j:\beta_j\}> : |i-j| \text{ is odd}, 1 \le i,j \le 4\} \\ & \cup \{<\{k_i:\alpha_i\}, \{end\ P_2\}> : 1 \le i \le 4\} \\ & \cup \{<\{end\ P_1\}, \{l_j:\beta_j\}> : 1 \le j \le 4\} \end{aligned}$$

whereas

$$\begin{aligned} STATB = \{ & <\{k_3:\alpha_3\}, \{end\ P_2\}>, \\ & <\{end\ P_1\}, \{l_3:\beta_3\}>\} \end{aligned}$$

Thus SYNTB has 16 elements whereas STATB has only two elements.

Example 7

Let

$$\begin{aligned} P_1 \equiv & \ldots;k_1:P_2!x ;\ldots; k_2:P_2?z ;\ldots; \\ & *[b_1 \rightarrow k_3:P_2!x ;\ldots; k_4:P_2?z ;\ldots], \end{aligned}$$

$$\begin{aligned} P_2 \equiv & \ l_1:P_1?y ;\ldots; l_2:P_1u ;\ldots; \\ & *[l_3:P_1?y \rightarrow \ldots\ l_4:P_1!u ;\ldots]. \end{aligned}$$

This is a structure of the program partitioning a set studied in [D] and [AFR].

Consider first the case when the distributed termination convention is not used. Then SYNTB and STATB are the same as in the previous example.

Suppose now that d.t.c. is used. Then

$$\begin{aligned} SYNTB = & \{<\{k_i:\alpha_i\}, \{l_j:\beta_j\}> : |i-j| \text{ is odd}, 1 \le i,j \le 4\} \\ & \cup \{<\{k_i:\alpha_i\}, \{end\ P_2\}> : 1 \le i \le 4\} \\ & \cup \{<\{end\ P_1\}, \{l_j:\beta_j\}> : j = 1,2,4\} \end{aligned}$$

and

$$STATB = \{<\{k_3:\alpha_3\}, \{end\ P_2\}>\}.$$

Here SYNTB has 15 elements whereas STATB only one. Note that the only staticly blocked pair cannot arise in actual computations either. The only way P_2 can terminate is due to the termination of P_1. Thus if the control in P_2 is at its end then the same must hold for P_1. We note that our analysis is not precise enough in order to deal with this type of situations. The next example gives more evidence to this effect.

Example 8

Let for $i=1,\ldots,n$

$$P_i \equiv *[b_i \,;\, P_{i-1}!x_i \rightarrow \ldots$$
$$\Box\, c_i;P_{i+1}!x_i \rightarrow \ldots$$
$$\Box\, P_{i-1}?y_i \rightarrow \ldots$$
$$\Box\, P_{i+1}?z_i \rightarrow \ldots$$

where the addition and substraction is modulo n.

This is a structure of the distributed gcd program considered in [AFR]. The labels of i/o commands are omitted as they are not needed here.

We have in the case when d.t.c. is not used

$$\begin{aligned} SYNTB = \{<A_1,\ldots,A_n> : \exists\, i\; A_i \neq \{\text{end } P_i\} \\ \wedge \forall\, i[P_{i-1}!x_i \in A_i \rightarrow A_{i-1} = \{\text{end } P_{i-1}\} \\ \wedge P_{i+1}!x_i \in A_i \rightarrow A_{i+1} = \{\text{end } P_{i+1}\} \\ \wedge A_i \neq \{\text{end } P_i\} \rightarrow \{P_{i-1}?y_i, P_{i+1}?z_i\} \subseteq A_i]\} \end{aligned}$$

and

STATB = SYNTB.

Suppose now that d.t.c. is used. Then

$$\begin{aligned} SYNTB = \{<A_1,\ldots,A_n> : \exists\, i\;\; A_i \neq \{\text{end } P_i\} \\ \wedge \forall\, i\,[P_{i-1}!x_i \in A_i \rightarrow A_{i-1} = \{\text{end } P_{i-1}\} \\ \wedge P_{i+1}!x_i \in A_i \rightarrow A_{i+1} = \{\text{end } P_{i+1}\} \\ \wedge A_i \neq \{\text{end } P_i\} \rightarrow (\{P_{i-1}?y_i, P_{i+1}?z_i\} \subseteq A_i \\ \wedge (A_{i-1} \neq \{\text{end } P_{i-1}\} \vee A_{i+1} \neq \{\text{end } P_{i+1}\}))]\} \end{aligned}$$

and once again STATB = SYNTB.

We see that in this example all blocked tuples are statically possible. The reason for it is that recording sequences of communications does not suffice to distinguish between two control points : the beginning and the end of a repetitive command.

On the other hand a simple informal argument allows to reduce the number of blocked triples which can arise in actual computations to one. The argument runs as follows. Suppose that d.t.c. is not used. Then no process P_i can terminate. Assume now that this convention is used. If some process P_i has terminated then by d.t.c. his neighbours P_{i-1} and P_{i+1} must have terminated, as well. Thus no process can terminate as the first one. In other words no process can terminate.

Thus in both cases a blocked tuple $<A_1,\dots,A_n>$ with some $A_i = \{end\ P_i\}$ is not possible. This reduces the number of possible blocked tuples to one being $<A_1,\dots,A_n>$ where for $i = 1,\dots,n$ $A_i = \{P_{i-1}?y_i, P_{i+1}?z_i\}$.

In the next section we propose a more refined analysis which leads to a more restricted notion of static match and staticly blocked configurations. These notions will allow to deal properly with the above examples.

3. Proofs of safety of a decomposition of programs into communication-closed layers

In a recent paper [EF] Elrad and Francez proposed a method of decomposition of CSP programs which simplifies their analysis and can be used for a systematic construction of CSP programs. It is defined as follows.

Suppose that we deal with a parallel program P of the form $P_1\|\dots\|P_n$ where for all $i=1,\dots,n$ $P_i \equiv S_i^1;\dots;S_i^k$. Some of the commands S_i^k can be empty. We call the parallel programs $T_j \equiv S_1^j\|\dots\|S_n^j$ $(j=1,\dots,k)$ the <u>layers</u> of P.

A layer T_j is called <u>communication-closed</u> if there does not exist a computation of P in which a communication takes place between two i/o commands from which one lies within T_j and the other outside T_j. A **decomposition** $T_1;\dots;T_k$ of P is called <u>safe</u> iff all the layers T_j are communication-closed. In other words a decomposition $T_1;\dots;T_k$ of P is safe if there does not exist a computation of P with a communication involving two i/o commands from different layers.

In [EF] also more general types of layers are considered whose boundaries may cross the repetitive commands. Our analysis does not extend to such decompositions. The interest in considering safe decompositions stems from the following observation.

<u>Fact</u> ([EF]) Suppose that $T_1;\dots;T_k$ is a safe decomposition of the parallel program P. Then the programs $T_1;\dots;T_k$ and P are input-output equivalent.

<u>Proof</u> (informal) Obviously every computation of $T_1;\dots;T_k$ is also a computation of P. Consider now a properly terminating computation of P. Due to safety of the decomposition we can rearrange some steps of this computation so that it becomes a properly terminating computation of $T_1;\dots;T_k$. Both computations terminate in the same final state.

Thus both programs generate the same pairs of input-output states. □

As an example of a safe decomposition consider the following program

$$P \equiv P_1?x\|P_2!y\|P_3?u\|P_4!z$$

Consider now the layers

$$T_1 \equiv P_1?x\|P_2y\|\Lambda\|\Lambda$$

and

$$T_2 \equiv \Lambda \| \Lambda \| P_3?u \| P_4!z$$

where Λ stands for the empty program.

The decomposition $T_1;T_2$ of P is obviously safe. Note however that the program $T_1;T_2$ admits less computations than the original program P.

This property holds in general for safe decompositions of parallel programs with more than three components. Consequently the safe decomposition is in general easier to study than the original program.

A natural question now arises how to prove safety of a decomposition into layers of a given parallel program P. We propose a simple sufficient condition for safety of a decomposition. It has been suggested by H. Fauconnier.

We first slightly refine the definition of the set STAT. Let STAT' be defined in the same way as STAT but refering to $LP(P_1\|\ldots\|P_n)$ instead of $L(P_1\|\ldots\|P_n)$. Intuitively STAT' is the set of all pairs of i/o commands which can be synchronized during a computation of $P_1\|\ldots\|P_n$ which ignores the boolean guards. Such a computation can be infinite or deadlocked. Clearly STAT $\subseteq$ STAT' but not necessarily conversely.

Let SEM' be defined by an analogous refinement of SEM.

Theorem Consider a decomposition $T_1;\ldots;T_k$ of a parallel program P. Suppose that there does not exist a pair $(k:\alpha,\ l:\beta)$ in STAT' (of P) such that $k:\alpha$ is from T_i and $l:\beta$ from T_j $(i \neq j)$. Then the decomposition $T_1;\ldots;T_k$ of P is safe.

Proof By definition the decomposition $T_1;\ldots;T_k$ of P is safe if for no pair $(k:\alpha,\ l:\beta)$ from SEM'(of P) $k:\alpha$ is from some T_i and $l:\beta$ from some T_j $(i \neq j)$. Since SEM' $\subseteq$ STAT', the result follows. □

As an illustration of the use of the above theorem consider its two simple applications. First, the above given decomposition $T_1;T_2$ of $P \equiv P_1?x \| P_2!y \| P_3?u \| P_4!z$ obviously satisfies the condition of the theorem thus it is indeed safe.

Secondly, consider the parallel program from the example 2.

Let $T_1 \equiv (k_1:P_2?x;\ldots;k_2:P_2!z;\ldots \| l_1:P_1!y;\ldots;l_2:P_1?u;\ldots)$

and

$$T_2 \equiv *[b_1 \rightarrow \ldots;k_3:P_2?x;\ldots;k_4:P_2!z;\ldots]$$
$$\| *[b_2 \rightarrow \ldots;l_3:P_1!y;\ldots;l_4:P_1?u;\ldots]$$

Then the decomposition $T_1;T_2$ is safe because STAT'(of P) obviously satisfies the required condition of the theorem. Note that here STAT' = STAT.

We conclude by observing that whenever STAT' = SEM' (which is the case for many CSP programs suggested in the literature) then the condition from the theorem becomes equivalent to the safety of the decomposition $T_1;\dots;T_k$ of P.

4. A MORE REFINED ANALYSIS

We now return to the problems signaled in section 3.2. We stated there that our analysis is not sufficiently precise to deal with some type of blocked configurations. We now refine some of the concepts in order to obtain an even more restricted notion of staticly blocked tuple. To this purpose we need three additional types of symbols. One is $\surd_i$ denoting a sucessful termination of the process P_i. This symbol is directly inspired by [H1]. The second new symbol is $\langle i{\downarrow}i_1,\dots,i_k\rangle$ which marks termination of a repetitive command within the process P_i due to the termination of the processes $P_{i_1},\dots,P_{i_k}$. The symbols $\surd_i$ and $\langle i{\downarrow}i_1,\dots,i_k\rangle$ are used only when d.t.c. is assumed. Finally we adopt the symbol $\not{Z}$ which is intended to indicate that a repetitive command cannot terminate. It will be used only when d.t.c. is not assumed.

Consider first the case when d.t.c. is not used. We now refine the definition of $L(S)$ (see section 2.1°) for a repetitive command as follows.

Let $S \equiv * S_1$ for an alternative command S_1. If all guards in S_1 contain a boolean part (distinct from <u>true</u>) then $L(S) = L(S_1)^*$, i.e. the former definition is retained. Otherwise $L(S) = L(S_1)^*\{\not{Z}\}$.

Note that in the latter case S cannot terminate. An occurrence of $\not{Z}$ in a communication sequence will mark the fact that an impossibility of termination of a repetitive command has been ignored. Consequently such sequences will not be admitted. A different possible approach to this problem is by admitting <u>infinite</u> communication sequences. We prefer to use the above approach since it is simpler. All other definitions including that of $L(P_1\|\dots\|P_n)$, STAT and STATB are retained. Note that $\not{Z}$ does not occur in any sequence of the form $[h]_i$ so no communication sequence from $L(P_1\|\dots\|P_n)$ or $LP(P_1\|\dots\|P_n)$ "violates" the impossibility of termination of a repetitive construct.

Let us now return to the examples 5, 7 and 8.

<u>ad Example 5</u>

With the new definitions we have $\forall\, w \in L(P_i)$ ($\not{Z}$ is an element of w) for $i=1,2$. Thus $L(P_1\|P_2) = \emptyset$ and consequently STAT = $\emptyset$. This agrees with our informal definition of STAT.

<u>ad Example 7</u>

According to the new definition $\forall\, w \in L(P_2)$ ($\not{Z}$ is an element of w). Thus by the definition $\langle\{k_3{:}\alpha_3\}, \{\text{end } P_2\}\rangle \notin$ STATB. We have here

$$STATB = \{<\{end\ P_1\},\ \{l_3:\beta_3\}>\}.$$

Note that here $L(P_1 \| P_2) = \emptyset$ for the same reasons as above, so $STAT = \emptyset$.

<u>ad Example 8</u>

We have $\forall w \in L(P_i)$ ($\emptyset$ is an element of w) for $i=1,\ldots,n$. Thus by the definition of STATB if $<A_1,\ldots,A_n>$ is a staticly blocked triple then for all i $A_i \neq \{end\ P_i\}$. We thus have

$$STATB = \{<A_1,\ldots,A_n> : A_i = \{P_{i-1}?y_i,\ P_{i+1}?z_i\},\ i=1,\ldots,n\}.$$

We now pass to the case when d.c.t. is used.

Let S be a repetitive command within the process P_i. Let $\{i_1,\ldots,i_k\}$ be the set of indices of the processes addressed in the guards of S which do not have a boolean part. Note that if S terminates in a computation of $P_1 \| \ldots \| P_n$ then at least the processes $P_{i_1},\ldots,P_{i_k}$ must have terminated at this moment.

We now refine the definition of $L(S)$ by identifying $<i\downarrow>$ with ϵ and putting $L(S) = L(S_1)^*\{<i\downarrow i_1,\ldots,i_k>\}$ where S_1 is the alternative command such that $S = *S_1$. All other clauses for sequential commands remain the same. We now put $L'(P_i) = L(P_i)\ \{\surd_i\}$ and define $L'(P_1 \| \ldots \| P_n)$ and $L'P(P_1 \| \ldots \| P_n)$ by defining first

$$[<i\downarrow i_1,\ldots,i_k>]_i = <i\downarrow i_1,\ldots,i_k>$$

$$[<i\downarrow i_1,\ldots,i_k>]_j = \epsilon \quad \text{if} \quad i \neq j$$

$$[\surd_i]_i = \surd_i$$

$$[\surd_i]_j = \epsilon \quad \text{if} \quad i \neq j$$

and putting

$$L'(P_1 \| \ldots \| P_n) = \{\ h : [h]_i \in L'(P_i),\ i=1,\ldots,n \wedge \underline{A}\}$$

$$L'P(P_1 \| \ldots \| P_n) = \{h : [h]_i \in Init(L'(P_i)),\ i = 1,\ldots,n \wedge \underline{A}\}$$

where the condition $\underline{A}$ is defined as follows

$$\underline{A} \equiv \forall p,j\ (h = a_1 \ldots a_p \wedge a_j = <i\downarrow i_1,\ldots,i_k>$$
$$\rightarrow \forall l \in \{1,\ldots,k\}\ \exists m < j\ \ a_m = \surd_{i_l}).$$

The condition $\underline{A}$ states that if in a communication sequence h an exit from a repetitive command in P_i has been recorded then necessarily all the processes on which termination this loop exit depends have terminated before this exit took place.

The set STAT is defined as before but with reference to $L'(P_1 \| \ldots \| P_n)$ instead of $L(P_1 \| \ldots \| P_n)$. Similarly the set STATB is defined in the same way as before but with reference to $Init(L'(P_i))$ and $L'(P_1 \| \ldots \| P_n)$ instead of

$Init(L(P_i))$ and $L(P_1\|\ldots\|P_n)$, respectively. Also the condition iii) in the definition of a blocked tuple is adopted.

We now return to the examples 7 and 8.

ad Example 7

It is easy to see that the new definition of STATB is more restricted than the previous one considered in section 3, so

STATB $\subseteq \{<\{k_3:\alpha_3\}, \{end\ P_2\}>\}$. We now show that $<\{k_3:\alpha_3\},\{end\ P_2\}\notin$ STATB, i.e. that STATB is empty.

We have

$$L'(P_1) = (k_1:<1,2>)\ (k_2:<2,1>)\ ((k_3:<1,2>)\ (k_4:<2,1>))^*\ \{V_1\}$$

and

$$L'(P_2) = (l_1:<1,2>)\ (l_2:<2,1>)\ ((l_3:<1,2>)\ (l_4:<2,1>))^*\{<2\downarrow 1>\ V_2\}.$$

Suppose that $<\{k_3:\alpha_3\}, \{end\ P_2\}> \in$ STATB.

Then there exists $h \in L'P(P_1\|\ldots\|P_n)$ such that $[h]_1(k_3:<1,2>) \in Init(L'(P_1))$ and $[h]_2 \in L'(P_2)$.

By the form of $L'(P_2)\ [h]_2$ so a fortiori h contains the element $<2\downarrow 1>$. Since $h \in L'P(P_1\|\ldots\|P_n)$, by the condition A h contains the element V_1. But this is impossible because by the above $[h]_1$ does not contain V_1. Contradiction. Thus STATB is indeed empty.

Note that

$$L'(P_1\|\ldots\|P_n) =\{(k_1,l_1:<1,2>)\ (l_2,k_2:<2,1>)\}$$
$$\{k_3,l_3:<1,2>)\ (l_4,k_4:<2,1>)\}^*\{V_1<2\downarrow 1>V_2\}$$

so STAT = $\{(k_i:\alpha_i,l_i:\beta_i),\ i = 1,\ldots,4\}$ in contrast to the case when d.t.c. was not used.

ad Example 8

Suppose that $h \in L'P(P_1\|\ldots\|P_n)$. We prove that h does not contain any element of the form $<i\downarrow i-1,\ i+1>$. Suppose otherwise. Let $<i\downarrow i-1,i+1>$ be the first element of this type in h. By the condition A some earlier element of h must be of the form V_{i-1}. We have $[h]_{i-1} \in Init(L'(P_i))$ and by the form of $L'(P_i)\ V_{i-1}$ must be preceded in $[h]_{i-1}$, so also in h, by $<i-1\downarrow i-2,i>$. Contradiction.

Suppose now that $<A_1,\ldots,A_n> \in$ STATB. Let $h \in L'P(P_1\|\ldots\|P_n)$ be a sequence certifying that $<A_1,\ldots,A_n>$ is a blocked tuple. If for some i $A_i = \{end\ P_i\}$ then $[h]_i \in L'(P_i)$ i.e. by the definition of $L'(P_i)\ [h]_i$ terminates with $<i\downarrow i-1,i+1>V_i$. Thus h contains the element $<i\downarrow i-1,i+1>$ which is impossible.

Thus for no i $A_i = \{end\ P_i\}$. We conclude that similarly as in the case when d.t.c. was not considered earlier in this section

STATB consists of exactly one element $<A_1,\ldots,A_n>$ where for $i=1,\ldots,n$ $A_i = \{P_{i-1}?y_i, P_{i+1}?z\}$.

The same conclusions about STATB in the examples 7 and 8 above were reached in [AFR] by a formal reasoning within a proof system. The above proofs are more straightforward and moreover require only a limited knowledge about the programs under consideration.

As a final remark we observe that the use of the set STAT is not sufficient for the proofs of safety properties (in the sense of [OL])that are more general than partial correctness. In such cases more appropriate set to be used is STAT' in the definition of which one refers to arbitrary, possibly non-terminating or blocked computations.

Observe that in the case of example 8 (independently of the fact whether d.t.c. is used STAT = Ø whereas

$$STAT' = \{(P_{i-1}?y_i,\ P_i!x_{i-1}) : i=1,\ldots,n\}$$
$$\cup \{(P_{i+1}?z_i, P_i!x_{i+1}) : i=1,\ldots,n\}$$

In [AFR] it is proved that a distributed gcd program whose structure is considered in the example 8 computes the g.c.d. of n numbers at the moment of reaching the only blocked configuration, the one discussed above. A proof of this fact within the proof system of [AFR] requires the use of the set STAT' and not STAT in the proof rule for parallel composition.

5. CONCLUSIONS

We have presented in this paper a method of analyzing the CSP programs which leads to simpler proofs of their correctness.

It can be easily automated and in fact such an algorithm for the case of ADA programs has already been described in [T].

It should be however noted that (as indicated in [T]) the algorithms computing the sets STAT, STAT' and STATB arising in this analysis are necessarily exponential. This can lead to inherent problems in the case of longer programs for which such an analysis is especially useful.

One could envisage a still more refined analysis in which one would take into account the boolean guards of the program under consideration. One could then infer for example that the second repetitive command in the process

$$P_i \equiv \ldots *[b \rightarrow S_1] ; *[b \rightarrow S_2]$$

cannot be entered so no i/o command from S_2 can be reached.

Such an analysis, however does not lead to any useful conclusions when applied to concrete examples. Any gain obtained by it is restricted to ill designed programs such as for example the above process P_i.

This leads us to an interesting question about the usefulness of the analysis presented in this paper. How accurate is it with respect to the semantical analysis ?

Consider first the sets STAT and STAT' which are used as "approximations" of the sets SEM and SEM', respectively. It is easy to design programs for which STAT (STAT') differs from SEM(SEM'). However, all such programs seem artificial. We observed that in all examples studied in [H] these sets do not differ and we conjecture that it is always the case for well-designed CSP programs. Of course such a conjecture is difficult to prove because no definition of a well-designed CSP program exists.

The situation changes when we compare the set STATB with the set of blocked configurations which can arise in actual computations. These sets may differ for simple and well-designed CSP programs. One can easily design a program of the form studied in the example 2 which is deadlock free whereas in this case STATB is not empty. An example of such a program is a slightly modified version of the program partitioning a set from [D].

REFERENCES

[AFR] K.R.APT, N. FRANCEZ & W.P. DE ROEVER, A proof system for communicating sequential processes, TOPLAS, vol. 2, N° 3, pp. 359-385, 1980.

[D] E.W. DIJKSTRA, A correctness proof for communicating processes : a small exercise, in : E.W. Dijkstra, Selected writings on computing : a personal perspective, Springer Verlag, New York, pp. 259-263, 1982.

[EF] T. ELRAD & N. FRANCEZ, Decomposition of distributed programs into communication-closed layers, to appear in SCP.

[H] C.A.R. HOARE, Communicating sequential processes, CACM, vol. 21, N° 8, pp. 666-677, 1978.

[H1] C.A.R. HOARE, A model for communicating sequential processes, in : R.M. McKeag, A.M. McNaughton, Eds., On the construction of programs, Cambridge University Press, pp. 229-243, 1980.

[LG] G. LEVIN & D. GRIES, A proof technique for communicating sequential processes, Acta Informatica, vol. 15, N° 3, pp. 281-302, 1981.

[OL] S. OWICKI & L. LAMPORT, Proving liveness properties of concurrent programs, TOPLAS, vol. 4, N° 3, pp. 455-495, 1982.

[T] R.N. TAYLOR, A general purpose algorithm for analyzing concurrent programs, CACM, vol. 26, N° 5, pp. 362-376, 1983.

COMPACTNESS IN SEMANTICS FOR MERGE AND FAIR MERGE

J.W. de Bakker
Mathematical Centre, Kruislaan 413, 1098 SJ Amsterdam
Free University, Amsterdam

J.I. Zucker
Computer Science Department, SUNY at Buffalo, NY

ABSTRACT

An analysis of the role of compactness in defining the semantics of the merge and fair merge operations is provided. In a suitable context of hyperspaces (sets of subsets) a set is compact iff it is the limit of a sequence of finite sets; hence, compactness generalises bounded nondeterminacy. The merge operation is investigated in the setting of a simple language with elementary actions, sequential composition, nondeterministic choice and recursion. Metric topology is used as a framework to assign both a linear time and a branching time semantics to this language. It is then shown that the resulting meanings are compact trace sets and compact processes, respectively. This result complements previous work by De Bakker, Bergstra, Klop & Meyer. For the fair merge, an approach using scheduling through random choices is adopted - since a direct definition precludes the use of closed, let alone of compact sets. In the indirect approach, a compactness condition is used to show that the fair merge of two fair processes yields a fair process.

0. INTRODUCTION

In the last few years we have seen a remarkable increase in the importance of topological tools in denotational semantics. Topology has always played a role in Scott's domain theory (for a recent example see Scott [25]; much information is contained in the comprehensive volume Gierz et al. [15]). An extension of its area of application was initiated by Nivat and his school (e.g. Arnold & Nivat [4,5], Nivat [21,22]) who use metric techniques, especially when dealing with the study of infinite words and infinite computations. Further recent evidence for our observation is provided by papers such as Arnold [3] or Smyth [26].

The present paper is devoted to two case studies concerning the role of *compactness* in semantics. We adopt the metric approach, continuing the above mentioned investigations of Nivat et al., and, furthermore, our own work as described in De Bakker & Zucker [8,9], De Bakker, Bergstra, Klop & Meyer [7], and De Bakker & Zucker [10]. More specifically, we take as starting point the latter two papers, and investigate the role of compactness in the development of linear time and branching time semantics for a language with recursion and merge, and of the definition of fair merge based on an appropriate alternation of random choices.

Before going into somewhat more detail about the aims and achievements of our paper, we make a few remarks on the role of metric topology and compactness in general. Classical denotational semantics - in particular when concerned with sequential programming - has relied primarily on order structures (lattices, complete partially ordered sets, etc.). As a consequence of the vigorous current interest in concurrency, new questions have arisen for which an approach solely in terms of order is not necessarily the most convenient one. Semantics of concurrency requires the preservation of intermediate stages of the computation in order to deal with phenomena such as interleaving, synchronization etc. In the simplest case they appear as *traces*, i.e. (possibly infinite) sequences of elementary actions. Two traces, e.g. abcd, abce, have no natural order relation, but a *distance* can be conveniently defined for them: We take 2^{-3}, or, in general, 2^{-n+1}, where $n \geq 1$ is the first position where the sequences differ. Distances can be defined as well for *sets* of sequences, and appropriate limit considerations can be based on well-known metric tools.

Compactness is a generalization of finiteness. In fact, it can be seen as a direct counterpart of the familiar property of *bounded nondeterminacy* in sequential denotational semantics (see, e.g., De Bakker [6]; Apt & Plotkin [2] discuss the effects of lifting the boundedness condition). More specifically, we shall develop a topological framework in which it is the case that a set is compact iff it is the limit of a sequence of finite sets. Compactness is a desirable property since it is preserved by various operations. For example, continuous mappings preserve compactness, a result which turns out to be quite fruitful below. In many situations, compactness is a direct consequence of the *finiteness* of the alphabet of elementary actions which underlies the model at hand. Our paper does not impose this finiteness condition; more effortis then needed to obtain certain compactness results.

In the first part of the paper, we are concerned with a simple language L which features, besides elementary actions a,b,c,..., fundamental concepts such as sequential composition ($S_1;S_2$), recursion, nondeterministic choice ($S_1 \cup S_2$), and merge ($S_1 \| S_2$, denoting arbitrary interleaving of the elementary actions of S_1 and S_2). In [7] we have provided a detailed semantics for this language based on a combination of cpo- and metric techniques. We distinguish the so-called "linear time" (LT) and "branching time" (BT) semantics for L, adopting a terminology inspired by the model theory of temporal logic. The crucial difference between LT and BT is illustrated by the difference between the treatment of the two programs (a;b) ∪ (a;b) and a; (b ∪ c). In LT, both have as meaning the trace set {ab,ac}. In BT we obtain, respectively, the trees

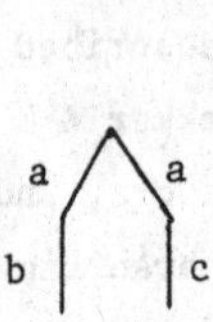

and

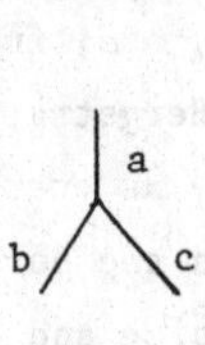

,

thus preserving the difference in the moment of choice between the two cases. Technically, in BT we do not require left-distributivity of ";", over "∪". Moreover, as a consequence of our wish to impose commutativity and idempotence of choice ($S_1 \cup S_2 = S_2 \cup S_1$, and $S \cup S = S$) as a feature of our model, we cannot, in general, use trees. Instead, we need another notion, viz. that of *process* (first described in a metric setting in [8,9]). A process is like an unordered tree, but without repetitions in its successor sets. Also, processes are closed objects: they contain all their limit points, in a sense to be made precise below. In [7] we have used a cpo structure on trace sets for LT, and (closed) processes for BT. What we shall present below is a metric approach for both cases, based on compact trace sets for the first, and on compact processes for the second case. Besides a certain uniformity obtained in using the metric approach throughout, we also circumvent the restriction to a finite alphabet which was imposed at certain essential points in the development in [7] (in particular in theorem 2.10 of that paper). The results of part 1 can be summarized as follows: For each $S \in L$, its LT semantics $[\![S]\!]_L$ is a compact set, and its BT semantics $[\![S]\!]_B$ is a compact process. Moreover, there exists a continuous mapping *trace* which maps $[\![S]\!]_B$ to $[\![S]\!]_L$. An important technical role is played by a theorem of Michael [19] which can be paraphrased (in the context of hyperspaces) as "a compact union of compact sets is compact".

The second half of the paper is devoted to an analysis of *fair merge*. Consider, e.g., two sequences 0^ω and 1^ω (a^ω denotes an infinite sequence of a's). Their fair merge *excludes* all sequences $(0 \cup 1)^*(0^\omega \cup 1^\omega)$, i.e., sequences with, eventually, only zero's or ones. Hence, the resulting set cannot be closed (since it does not contain all limits of sequences of finite approximations), let alone compact. Thus, a *direct* approach based on compactness does not work. In [10] we have instead proposed an indirect approach based on "implementing" fairness through suitable alternation of random choices (continuing an idea of Plotkin [23]; random assignement is also used extensively in Apt & Olderog [1]). What we shall do below is to present a *proof* - not provided in [10] - that the fair merge of two fair processes (defined as in [10]) is again fair. In the argument an essential role is played, once more, by a compactness property of the processes involved.

The organisation of the paper is as follows: You are now reading section 0 which gives the introduction. In section 1 we briefly describe some of the topological notions and results which are necessary for the development below. Section 2 presents the announced result for LT semantics, and section 3 for BT semantics. Section 4, finally, is devoted to the fair merge.

Besides the already mentioned literature, we would like to refer to the papers by Golson and Rounds [16], and Rounds [24], which are also concerned with the use of metric topology in general, and the role of compactness in particular, in the semantics of concurrency. Processes in general have been studied extensively by Milner, e.g. [20]; the *algebra* of processes is pursued by Bergstra & Klop, e.g. [11,12].

1. TOPOLOGICAL PRELIMINARIES

We assume known the notions of metric space, Cauchy sequence (CS) in a metric space, isometry (distance-preserving bijection), limits and closed sets, completeness of a metric space, and the theorem stating that each metric space (M,d) can be completed to (i.e., isometrically embedded in) a complete metric space. Throughout our paper, we shall only consider distances d with values in the interval [0,1]. Explicit mentioning of the metric d is often omitted.

We first present the standard definitions of *continuous* and *contracting* functions:

DEFINITION 1.1.

a. Let M_1, M_2 be two metric spaces. A function $\phi: M_1 \to M_2$ is called continouos whenever, for each CS $\langle x_i\rangle_{i=0}^{\infty}$ in M_1, we have that $\langle\phi(x_i)\rangle_{i=0}^{\infty}$ is a CS in M_2, and $\phi(\lim_i x_i) = \lim_i \phi(x_i)$.

b. Let $\phi: M \to M$. We call ϕ contracting whenever, for each $x,y \in M$, $d(\phi(x),\phi(y)) \leq c*d(x,y)$, for some constant c with $0 \leq c < 1$.

A well-known classical result is Banach's fixed point theorem:

THEOREM 1.2. Let $\phi: M \to M$ be contracting. Then ϕ has a unique fixed point x satisfying $x = \lim_i \phi^i(x_0)$, for any $x_0 \in M$. □

Let (M,d) be a complete metric space. (It simplifies matters to assume completeness from now on; certain definitions or claims made below would, in fact, remain valid without this requirement.) For $X,Y \subseteq M$ we can define the so-called Hausdorff distance $\tilde{d}(X,Y)$:

DEFINITION 1.3. Let $x,y \in M$ and $X,Y \subseteq M$.

a. $\hat{d}(x,Y) = \inf_{y \in Y} d(x,y)$

b. $\tilde{d}(X,Y) = \max(\sup_{x \in X} \hat{d}(x,Y), \sup_{y \in Y} \hat{d}(y,X))$

(By convention, $\inf \emptyset = 1$, $\sup \emptyset = 0$.)

We have

LEMMA 1.4. Let $P_c(M)$ be the collection of all *closed* subsets of M. Then $(P_c(M),\tilde{d})$ is a metric space. Moreover, (if M is complete) $(P_c(M),\tilde{d})$ is complete, and, for $\langle X_i \rangle_i$ a CS in $P_c(M)$, we have that

$$\lim_i X_i = \{x \mid x = \lim_i x_i,\ x_i \in X_i,\ \langle x_i \rangle_i \text{ a CS in } M\}.$$

Proof. For the first part see, e.g., Engelking [14]. The second statement is due to Hahn [17].

Next, we introduce the important notion of *compactness*. Also, the definition of a set being *totally bounded* is given.

DEFINITION 1.5.

a. A subset X of M is called compact if each open cover of X has a finite subcover.

b. Let, for each $\varepsilon > 0$ and $x \in M$, $N_\varepsilon(x) \overset{\text{df.}}{=} \{y \mid d(x,y) < \varepsilon\}$. A subset X of M is called totally bounded if, for all $\varepsilon > 0$, there exists a finite set $F \subseteq M$ such that

$$X \subseteq \bigcup_{x \in F} N_\varepsilon(x).$$

The following theorem characterizes compactness in a number of different ways:

THEOREM 1.6. For any $X \subseteq M$, the following are equivalent:

a. X is compact

b. X is closed and totally bounded

c. X is the limit (in the Hausdorff metric) of a sequence of *finite* sets.

Proof. Standard topology (see [13] or [14]). □

The following properties of compact sets are important in the sequel:

THEOREM 1.7.

a. Each closed subset of a compact set is compact

b. The continuous image of a compact set is compact. I.e., if $\phi: M \to N$ is continuous, $X \subseteq M$ is compact, and $\hat{\phi}(X) \overset{\text{df.}}{=} \{\phi(x) \mid x \in X\}$, then $\hat{\phi}(X)$ is compact.

c. If $X \subseteq M$, $Y \subseteq N$, X and Y compact, then $X \times Y$ is compact in the product topology for $M \times N$.

d. If $\langle X_i \rangle_i$ is a CS of compact sets in M, and $X = \lim_i X_i$, then X is compact.

Proof. a,b,c. Standard.

d. For each i there is a CS of finite sets $\langle Y_{i,j} \rangle_j$ such that $X_i = \lim_j Y_{i,j}$. Then X is the limit of the diagonal sequence $\langle Y_{i,i} \rangle_i$, hence, X is compact. □

The next property of compact sets may be somewhat less well-known. It is due to Michael ([19]). Let, for (M,d) a complete metric space, $(P_{comp}(M),\tilde{d})$ be the space of compact subsets of M, equipped with the Hausdorff metric. (By theorem 1.7c we know that $(P_{comp}(M),\tilde{d})$ is complete.) We have

THEOREM 1.8. Let $X_i, i \in I$, be compact subsets of M, and let $\{X_i \mid i \in I\}$ be compact in $(P_{comp}(M),\tilde{d})$. Then $X \overset{df.}{=} \bigcup \{X_i \mid i \in I\}$ is compact in (M,d).

Proof. See [19]. □

We now specialize our considerations to spaces of sequences and sets of sequences. Let A be a, *possibly infinite*, alphabet with elements a,b,c,... . Let A^* be the set of all finite sequences over A, let A^ω be the set of all infinite sequences over A, and let $A^\infty \overset{df.}{=} A^* \cup A^\omega$. Let x,y,... denote elements of A^∞. The prefix of $x \in A^\infty$ of length n will be denoted by x[n] (with the convention that, e.g., abc[5] = abc; abc[0] is the empty word). The distance d(x,y) for $x,y \in A^\infty$ is defined by

$$\tilde{d}(x,y) = 2^{-\max\{n \mid x[n] = y[n]\}}$$

(with the convention that $2^{-\infty} = 0$).
Let $P_c(A^\infty)$ denote the class of all closed subsets of A^∞. The distance d on A^∞ can be extended to the Hausdorff distance $\tilde{d}$ on $P_c(A^\infty)$ in the manner described above. Alternatively, we might define

$$d(X,Y) = 2^{-\max\{n \mid X[n] = Y[n]\}},$$

where $X[n] = \{x[n] \mid x \in X\}$. We omit the straightforward proof that the two definitions of $\tilde{d}$ are equivalent.

It is known (e.g. Nivat [21]) that, in case A is finite, A^∞ and (hence) all its closed subsets are compact. This is no longer the case for an infinite alphabet A. Only in certain situations - of which we treat the case that we are concerned with subsets of A^∞ which are meanings of statements in some suitable language - can we again establish compactness. The next two sections are devoted to an exposition of this, and a similar, result.

2. LINEAR TIME SEMANTICS

We study the semantics of a simple language L, which features some standard sequential concepts (sequential composition, recursion) together with nondeterministic choice and merge (arbitrary interleaving). In the present section we present the LT semantics for L, in which we do not distinguish between, e.g., the meanings of $\underline{a};\underline{b} \cup \underline{a};\underline{c}$ and $\underline{a};(\underline{b} \cup \underline{c})$. In section 3 we shall deal with its BT semantics. Let $\underline{a},\underline{b},\ldots$ be elements of a, possibly infinite, set $\underline{A}$ of elementary actions. We assume that for each (syntactic) $\underline{a}$ we have a corresponding (semantic) a in the alphabet A. Let $\underline{x},\underline{y},\ldots$ be elements of a set of *statement variables* *Stmv*. The variables $\underline{x},\underline{y}$ will be used in the formation of *recursive* or μ-statements. The syntax for *L* is given, in a self-explanatory BNF notation, in

DEFINITION 2.1.

$$S ::= \underline{a}\,|\,\underline{x}\,|\,S_1;S_2\,|\,S_1 \cup S_2\,|\,S_1 \| S_2\,|\,\mu\underline{x}[S].$$

Here $\underline{x}$ is required to occur only *guarded* (see remark below) in S.

Examples: $(\underline{a}\|\underline{b}) \cup (\underline{a}\|\underline{c})$, $\mu\underline{x}[(\underline{a};\underline{x}) \cup \underline{b}]$, $\mu\underline{x}[\underline{a};\mu\underline{y}[(\underline{b};\underline{y})\|\underline{x}] \cup \underline{c}]$.

Remarks.

1. Syntactic ambiguities should be remedied by using parentheses or conventions for the priorities of the operations.
2. (For the reader who is not familiar with the μ-notation) A term such as $\mu\underline{x}[(\underline{a};\underline{x}) \cup \underline{b}]$ has the same intended meaning as a *call* of the procedure declared (in an ALGOL-like language) by $P \Leftarrow (\underline{a};P) \cup \underline{b}$, or, alternatively, generates the same language of finite *and infinite* words as the grammar $X \to \underline{a}X|\underline{b}$.
3. In a term $\mu\underline{x}[S]$, occurrences of $\underline{x}$ in S may be "guarded", i.e. of the form $\ldots\underline{a};(\ldots\underline{x}\ldots)\ldots$, for some $\underline{a} \in \underline{A}$. We shall consider only terms $\mu\underline{x}[S]$ in which all occurrences of $\underline{x}$ are guarded. In [7] we have dealt, in a cpo setting, with the consequences of dropping this restriction. In language theory, the equivalent notion is the "Greibach condition", see e.g. [21].

We proceed with the development of the LT semantics for *L*. In this, we use a metric (rather than the cpo framework of [7]). Let, for brevity, *C* stand for $P_{comp}(A^\infty)$. We shall assign meaning to statements $S \in L$ as elements of *C*. Due to the presence of recursion, we employ an *environment* component in the defining equations, which serves to assign meaning to the free statement variables in S. Let $\Gamma \overset{\text{df.}}{=} Stmv \to C$, and let γ range over Γ.

We first discuss the definitions of the basic operations on $X,Y \subseteq A^\infty$. We use the obvious fact that, for each $x \in A^\infty$, $x = \lim_i x[i]$. We assume known the definitions of x.y and x‖y for $x,y \in A^*$ (see, e.g., [18]). We give

DEFINITION 2.2. Let $x,y \in A^\infty$, $X,Y \subseteq A^\infty$.

a. $x.y = \lim_i (x[i].y[i])$

   $x\|y = \lim_i (x[i]\|y[i])$

b. $X.Y = \{x.y \mid x \in X, y \in X\}$

   $X \cup Y$ is the set-theoretic union of X and Y

   $X\|Y = \bigcup \{x\|y \mid x \in X, y \in Y\}$.

Remark. Direct definitions - which avoid the use of CS and limits - for x.y and x∥y with $x,y \in A^{\omega}$ are also possible. We omit the proof that definition 2.2a yields equivalent results.

We have the following lemma:

LEMMA 2.3.
a. The sequences $\langle x[i].y[i]\rangle_i$ and $\langle x[i] \| y[i]\rangle_i$ are CS of finite sets.
b. x.y and x∥y are compact.

Proof. a. Left to the reader (who might consult Appendix B of [9] for very similar results).
b. For "." this is trivial; for x∥y it follows from part a and theorem 1.7d. □

The three operations .,∪,∥ are continuous:

LEMMA 2.4. The operations .,∪,∥ are continuous mappings: $A^{\infty} \times A^{\infty} \to P_{comp}(A^{\infty})$.

Proof. Omitted (cf. for techniques of [9], Appendix B). □

We can now prove the central theorem of this section:

THEOREM 2.5. For X,Y compact subsets of A^{∞}, X.Y, X∪Y and X∥Y are compact subsets of A^{∞}.

Proof. For "∪" this is trivial. The proof for "." is simpler than that for "∥", which we now give. Let X,Y be compact subsets of A^{∞}. By theorem 1.7c, X × Y is compact in $A^{\infty} \times A^{\infty}$. By the continuity of "∥" as mapping: $A^{\infty} \times A^{\infty} \to P_{comp}(A^{\infty})$ (lemma 2.4) and theorem 1.7b, we have that $\hat{\|}(X,Y) \overset{df.}{=} \{x\|y \mid x \in X,\ y \in X\}$ is a compact *subset* of $P_{comp}(A^{\infty})$. Thus, $\hat{\|}(X,Y)$ is a compact subset of $P_{comp}(A^{\infty})$ consisting of "points" which are compact subsets of A^{∞}. We can therefore apply Michael's theorem and obtain that $\|(X,Y) = \bigcup \{x\|y \mid x \in X,\ y \in Y\}$ is a compact subset of A^{∞}. □

We are now sufficiently prepared for the main definition of this section:

DEFINITION 2.6. LT semantics for *L*.
The mapping $[\![\ ]\!]_L : L \to (\Gamma \to C)$ is defined by
$[\![\underline{a}]\!]_L(\gamma) = \{a\}$, $[\![\underline{x}]\!](\gamma) = \gamma(x)$,
$[\![S_1;S_2]\!]_L(\gamma) = [\![S_1]\!]_L(\gamma).[\![S_2]\!]_L(\gamma)$
$[\![S_1 \cup S_2]\!]_L(\gamma) = [\![S_1]\!]_L(\gamma) \cup [\![S_2]\!]_L(\gamma)$
$[\![S_1 \| S_2]\!]_L(\gamma) = [\![S_1]\!]_L(\gamma) \| [\![S_2]\!]_L(\gamma)$
$[\![\mu\underline{x}[S]]\!]_L(\gamma) = \lim_i X_i$, where X_0 is arbitrary, and $X_{i+1} = [\![S]\!]_L(\gamma\{X_i/\underline{x}\})$

(In the last formula, $\gamma\{X_i/\underline{x}\}$ denotes an environment which is like γ, but for its value in $\underline{x}$ which is set to X_i.)

We verify that this definition assigns a compact set as meaning to each $S \in L$:

THEOREM 2.7. For each $S \in L$ $[\![S]\!]_L(\gamma) \in C$.

Proof. Induction on the structure of S. If $S \equiv \underline{a}$ or $S \equiv \underline{x}$, the result is clear. If $S \equiv S_1;S_2$, $S \equiv S_1 \cup S_2$ or $S \equiv S_1 \| S_2$, we use theorem 2.5. If $S \equiv \mu\underline{x}[S_1]$ we use the fact - the easy proof of which we leave to the reader - that, for $\underline{x}$ guarded in S_1, $\lambda X.[\![S_1]\!]_L(\gamma\{X/\underline{x}\})$ is a contracting mapping: $C \to C$. From this we obtain that $\langle X_i \rangle_i$ is a CS; an appeal to theorem 1.7d then yields the described result. □

Thus, we have shown compactness of $[\![S]\!]_L(\gamma)$ independent of the finiteness of A. We also observe that, by Banach's theorem, for guarded $\mu\underline{x}[S]$ we have that its meaning equals the (unique) fixed point of $\lambda X.[\![S]\!](\gamma\{X/\underline{x}\})$, in accordance with the intended meaning of the recursive construct $\mu\underline{x}[S]$.

3. BRANCHING TIME SEMANTICS

We follow [7,8,9] in the design of a branching time semantic framework for the language L as introduced in section 2, with the replacement of "closed" by "compact" at certain crucial points as major difference.

Let A be any (finite or infinite) alphabet. Let p_0 denote the so-called nil-process - the role of which will become clear as we go along. The first definition introduces sets of finite *processes* over A, and associated metrics on these sets:

DEFINITION 3.1. For n = 0,1,... we define sets P_n and metrics d_n on P_n:

a. $P_0 = \{p_0\}$, $P_{n+1} = \{p_0\} \cup \mathcal{P}_{finite}(A \times P_n)$

b. $d_0(p,q) = 0$; d_{n+1} is defined as follows: let $p,q \in P_{n+1}$.
Either
(i) $p = q = p_0$. Then $d_{n+1}(p,q) = 0$
(ii) $p = p_0$, $q \neq p_0$ or vice versa. Then $d_{n+1}(p,q) = 1$.
(iii) $p = X \subseteq A \times P_n$, $q = Y \subseteq A \times P_n$. Then $d_{n+1}(p,q) = \tilde{d}_{n+1}(X,Y)$, where $\tilde{d}_{n+1}$ is the Hausdorff metric (definition 1.3) induced by the distance $\bar{d}_{n+1}$ between "points" $\langle a',p'\rangle$, $\langle a'',q'\rangle$ defined by

$$\bar{d}_{n+1}(\langle a',p'\rangle,\langle a'',q'\rangle) = 1, \text{ if } a' \neq a''$$
$$= \tfrac{1}{2}d_n(p',q'), \text{ if } a' = a''.$$

We now consider the set $P_\omega \overset{df.}{=} \bigcup_n P_n$ of all finite processes, together with the metric $d = \bigcup_n d_n$ (with the natural definition of $\bigcup_n d_n$). (P_ω,d) is a metric space which can be *completed* to a complete metric space, say (P,d). We can show that

THEOREM 3.2.

$$P = \{p_0\} \cup \mathcal{P}_{comp}(A \times P).$$

Proof. This is as in [9], but for the modification that

(i) We use compact sets instead of closed sets throughout

(ii) We use the theorem that a CS of compact sets has a compact limit (rather than Hahn's theorem that a CS of closed sets has a closed limit, which was fundamental in [9]). □

Next, we define the three fundamental operations $\circ$, $\cup$, $\|$ for processes. Apart from a cosmetic change in the definition of "$\circ$", these definitions are as in [7,8,9]. Throughout, we distinguish the finite case ($p,q \in P_\omega$) and infinite case ($p \in P \backslash P_\omega$ or $q \in P \backslash P_\omega$). Moreover, we (implicitly) use induction on the *degree* of the processes concerned, where, for $p \in P_\omega$, *degree* (p) is given by: *degree* $(p_0) = 0$, and, for $p \neq p_0$, *degree* (p) = n iff $p \in P_n \backslash P_{n-1}$.

DEFINITION 3.3. Let X,Y range over sets of finite processes.

a. $p_0 \circ p = p$, $X \circ p = \{x \circ p \mid x \in X\}$. $\langle a,q\rangle \circ p = \langle a, q\circ p\rangle$, $(\lim_i q_i)\circ p = \lim_i (q_i \circ p)$

b. $p \cup p_0 = p_0 \cup p = p$, and, for $p,q \neq p_0$, $p \cup q$ is the-set theoretic union of p and q.

c. $p_0 \| p = p \| p_0 = p$, and, for $p,q \neq p_0$, we put

$X \| Y = \{x \| Y \mid x \in X\} \cup \{X \| y \mid y \in Y\}$,

$\langle a,q\rangle \| Y = \langle a, q\| Y\rangle$, $X \| \langle a,p\rangle = \langle a, X \| p\rangle$

$(\lim_i p_i) \| (\lim_j q_j) = \lim_i (p_i \| q_i)$.

Using a combination of the techniques of Appendix B of [9] and the compactness properties of section 1 (but note that we do not need Michael's theorem here), we can justify the above definitions, and prove that the three operations $\circ, \cup, \|$ are continuous. It is now straightforward to define the branching time semantics for L. Let P be as in theorem 3.2., and let $\Gamma = Stmv \rightarrow P$.

DEFINITION 3.4. The valuation $[\![.]\!]_B : L \rightarrow (\Gamma \rightarrow P)$ is given by

$[\![\underline{a}]\!]_B(\gamma) = \{\langle a, p_0\rangle\}$, $[\![\underline{x}]\!]_B(\gamma) = \gamma(x)$

$[\![S_1;S_2]\!]_B(\gamma) = [\![S_1]\!]_B(\gamma) \circ [\![S_2]\!]_B(\gamma)$, and similarly for $\cup, \|$

$[\![\mu \underline{x}[S]]\!]_B(\gamma) = \lim_i p_i$, where p_1 is arbitrary, and $p_{i+1} = [\![S]\!]_B(\gamma\{p_i/\underline{x}\})$.

The proof that, for each $S \in L$, $[\![S]\!]_B(\gamma) \in P$ can now be given exactly as that of theorem 2.7.

Finally, consider the mapping *trace* studied in [7]. We define *trace*: $P \rightarrow C$ by

DEFINITION 3.5.

trace $(p_0) = \{\varepsilon\}$, *trace* $(X) = \cup \{$*trace* $(x) \mid x \in X\}$

trace $(\langle a,p\rangle) = a.$ *trace* (p),

trace $(\lim_i p_i) = \lim_i ($*trace* $(p_i))$.

In [7] it was shown that, for each $S \in L$ without free statement variables and each γ, (*): *trace* $([\![S]\!]_B(\gamma)) = [\![S]\!]_L(\gamma)$, provided the underlying alphabet is finite (and using the observation that $[\![S]\!]_B(\gamma) \neq \emptyset$ for each such S). Inspection of the proof of (*)

shows that it can be taken over, but with an appeal to the finiteness of A (used in [7] to establish that *trace* (p) is a closed set) replaced by suitable use of the above compactness results. Details are omitted.

4. FAIR MERGE

This section is devoted to a study of fair merge of processes. A similar analysis can be made for the fair merge of trace sets; we leave this to the interested reader. As remarked above, a *direct* definition of fair merge in terms of closed (let alone compact) sets seems not possible. Therefore, we use an indirect approach in which we model fair merge in terms of a scheduling mechanism which employs a sequence of random choices determining successively the (finite) number of times the left- and right operand of the fair merge operation should be chosen. (See also [10] for further explanation of this idea.) The indirect definition uses an *extended* domain of processes, viz. P solving the equation

$$P = \{p_0\} \cup \mathcal{P}_{closed}((A \cup \mathbb{N}) \times P)$$

where $\mathbb{N}$ is the set of natural numbers. Note that we have $\mathcal{P}_{closed}(.)$ rather than $\mathcal{P}_{compact}(.)$ in this equation. We shall use $B \overset{df.}{=} A \cup \mathbb{N}$, and b to range over B. Our first definition introduces some terminology:

DEFINITION 4.1.

a. $\Sigma_k\, p_k \overset{df.}{=} \{\langle k,p_k\rangle \mid k \in \mathbb{N}\}$
   A process $\Sigma_k\, p_k$ is called a "sum process".

b. A *basic* process is one of the form $\{\langle a_i,p_i\rangle\}_{i\in I}$

c. A *path* for a process p is a (finite or infinite) sequence (*): $\langle b_1,p_1\rangle, \langle b_2,p_2\rangle,\ldots,$ such that $\langle b_1,p_1\rangle \in p$, and $\langle b_{i+1},p_{i+1}\rangle \in p_i$, $i = 1,2,\ldots$. We say that path (*) *passes through* p_i, $i = 1,2,\ldots$.

d. An "action" b is called "enabled" in a path (*) whenever, for some i and q, $\langle b,q\rangle \in p_i$. b *occurs* is (*) whenever, for some i, $b = b_i$.

c. A path (*) is called *fair* whenever, for all $a \in A$, if a is infinitely often enabled in (*), it infinitely often occurs in (*). A process is called fair whenever all its paths are fair. (Only actions in A are taken into account in the definition of fairness.)

f. Process q is a node of p - also called a subprocess of p - if there is a path from p which passes through q.

g. We call a process p *normal* if each node of p is either a basic node, or a sum node, or p_0.

h. p is called *pure* (or hereditarily basic) if each node of p is a basic node or p_0.

i. p is called hereditarily compact if each basic node of p is compact (as a subset of P).

Remarks.

1. Note that, in clause i, we impose the compactness requirement only for basic nodes.
2. The theory below will be developed for hereditarily compact, normal processes (HCN processes, for short).
3. The set HCN is closed in P.
4. If A is finite then each pure process is heriditarily compact, and hence in HCN.

Fair merge will be defined for all normal processes, and it takes normal processes to normal processes. But to show that fairness is preserved by fair merge, we must also assume hereditary compactness. That is, as we will show, fair merge takes fair HCN processes to fair HCN processes.

DEFINITION 4.2 (fair merge). For p,q finite we define, by induction on *degree* (p) + *degree* (q), their fair merge $p \|_f q$, using a number of auxiliary operations $p \|_x q$, for $x = f;L;R;L,k;R,k$.

a. $p \|_x p_0 = p_0 \|_x p = p$.
   Otherwise, assume $p,q \neq p_0$.
b. $p \|_f q = \{\langle 2k, p \|_{L,k} q\rangle\}_{k \in \mathbb{N}} \cup \{\langle 2k+1, p \|_{R,k} q\rangle\}_{k \in \mathbb{N}}$.
c. $p \|_{L,k+1} q = \{\langle b, p' \|_{L,k} q\rangle \mid \langle b,p'\rangle \in p\}$.
d. $p \|_{L,0} q = \{\langle b, p' \|_R q\rangle \mid \langle b,p'\rangle \in p\}$.
e. $p \|_R q = \Sigma_k (p \|_{R,k} q)$,

and the symmetric cases for c,d and e.

Remark. In order to extend the definitions to infinite processes, we must show that these operations are continuous.

LEMMA 4.3. $d(\Sigma_k p_k, \Sigma_k q_k) = \frac{1}{2} * \sup d(p_k,q_k)$.

Proof. Clear. □

LEMMA 4.4. For finite p,p',q,

$$d(p \|_x q, p' \|_x q) \leq d(p,p').$$

Proof. This is proved simultaneously for all x, by induction on $n \stackrel{df}{=} \max(degree\,(p), degree\,(p')) + degree\,(q)$. For fixed n, prove for x in the following order: L,0; L,k+1; L; R,0; R,k+1; R; f, and use the results of [9], Appendix B. □

LEMMA 4.5. For finite p,p',q,q'

$$d(p \|_x q, p' \|_x q') \leq \max(d(p,p'),d(q,q')).$$

Proof. This follows from lemma 4.4 together with the symmetric result, and the strong triangle inequality (since d is in fact an ultrametric). □

Now we are justified in defining:

DEFINITION 4.6. For p,q infinite, $p = \lim_i p_i$, $q = \lim_j q_j$, p_i and q_j finite, we put

$$p \Vert_x q = \lim_i (p_i \Vert_x q_i).$$

The proofs of the following lemma's are now direct (and omitted):

LEMMA 4.7. The statement of lemma 4.5 also holds for infinite processes. Hence, the operations "$\Vert_x$" are jointly continuous in both arguments.

LEMMA 4.8. The fair merge takes normal processes to normal processes.

LEMMA 4.9. Clauses a,b and e in the definition of fair merge (definition 4.2) hold also for infinite processes, but clauses c,d are changed (for infinite processes) to
c'. $p \Vert_{L,k+1} q = CL\{\ldots\}$
d'. $p \Vert_{L,0} q = CL\{\ldots\}$
i.e. the closures of the sets on the right-hand side above.

LEMMA 4.10. If p,q are in HCN then
a. all the clauses in the definition of fair merge hold for p and q
b. $p \Vert_f q$ is in HCN.

Proof. a. Consider clause c or d of definition 4.2. Let X be the set on the right-hand side of the definition. If p is a sum node, then it is clear that X is closed, since any two points in it are a distance 1 apart. If p is a basic node then it is compact, hence X, being a continuous image of p, is compact and hence closed.
b. Clear. □

The reader should observe the essential role played by the compactness requirement in the proof of part a.

We can now prove the main theorem of this section:

THEOREM 4.11. Let p,q be fair HCN processes. Then $p \Vert_f q$ is fair.

Proof. Let $path_0$ be any infinite path in $p \Vert_f q$. By lemma 4.10 it can be seen that $path_0$ can be (uniquely) represented as the "fair shuffle" of two paths $path_1$ in p and $path_2$ in q. Fairness for $path_0$ now follows by a simple argument: For suppose that a basic action a is enabled infinitely often in $path_0$: Then clearly a is enabled infinitely often in $path_1$ or $path_2$. Suppose without lack of generality a is enabled infinitely often in $path_1$. Because p is fair, a occurs infinitely often in $path_1$, and hence in $path_0$. □

Remarks.
1. Note the role of the closedness property in the first claim of this proof: Without the closedness of the X on the right-hand size of clauses c,d (see proof of lemma 4.10) we would have to take into account the possibility that nodes added by the closure

operation are involved in the formation of $path_0$ rather than $path_0$ being the (direct) fair shuffle of paths in p and q.

2. The reader may wonder whether the above argument would also work with the ordinary merge as defined in section 3, in which case we would not have to concern ourselves with sum nodes at all. In fact, it would not work. The reason is, roughly, as follows. Let p and q be two heriditarily compact pure processes, and let $path_0$ be a path in $p \| q$. Again, by lemma 4.10, $path_0$ can be uniquely represented as a shuffle of two paths, $path_1$ in p and $path_2$ in q. Suppose that a is infinitely often enabled in $path_0$ and suppose, for definiteness, that a occurs only in nodes of p (not of q). It does not follow that a is enabled infinitely often in $path_1$. This is because $path_0$ may be an "unfair" shuffle of $path_1$ and $path_2$ and, from a certain point onwards, may involve $path_2$ only, in which case a, although infinitely often enabled in $path_0$, never gets a chance to be enabled in $path_1$ again past this point.

3. Certain HCN processes are clearly "degenerate" from our point of view, namely those containing infinite paths which, from some point on, contain only sum nodes. We could exclude such processes explicitly from consideration, since we are only really concerned with processes which arise from finitely many applications of the fair merge operation to pure heriditarily compact processes. However the set of these processes is not closed in P. (Whether this is an important consideration is not so clear.)

4. A topic for further research is the combination of the techniques of this section with those of section 3, allowing the definition of the semantics of L extended with the fair merge operation.

REFERENCES

[1] APT, K.R. & E.R. OLDEROG, *Proof rules dealing with fairness*, Proc. Logic of Programs 1981 (D. Kozen, ed.), 1-9, LNCS 131, Springer, 1982.

[2] APT, K.R. & G.D. PLOTKIN, *A Cook's tour of countable nondeterminism*, Proc. 8th ICALP (S. Even & O. Kariv, eds), 479-494, LNCS 115, Springer, 1981.

[3] ARNOLD, A., *Topological characterizations of infinite behaviours of transition systems*, Proc. 10th ICALP (J. Diaz, ed.), 28-38, LNCS 154, Springer, 1983.

[4] ARNOLD, A. & M. NIVAT, *Metric interpretations of infinite trees and semantics of nondeterministic recursive programs*, Theoretical Computer Science 11, 181-206, 1980.

[5] ARNOLD, A. M. NIVAT, *The metric space of infinite trees, algebraic and topological properties*, Fund. Inform. III, 4, 445-476, 1980.

[6] DE BAKKER, J.W., *Mathematical Theory of Program Correctness*, Prentice-Hall International, 1980.

[7] DE BAKKER, J.W., J.A. BERGSTRA, J.W. KLOP & J.-J.Ch. MEYER, *Linear time and branching time semantics for recursion with merge*, Proc. 10th ICALP (J. Diaz, ed.), 39-51, LNCS 154, Springer, 1983.

[8] DE BAKKER, J.W. & J.I. ZUCKER, *Denotational semantics of concurrency*, Proc. 14th ACM Symp. on Theory of Computing, 153-158, 1982.

[9] DE BAKKER, J.W. & J.I. ZUCKER, *Processes and the denotational semantics of concurrency*, Information and Control, 54, 70-120, 1982.

[10] DE BAKKER, J.W. & J.I. ZUCKER, *Processes and a fair semantics for the ADA rendez-vous*, Proc. 10th ICALP (J. Diaz, ed.), 52-66, LNCS 154, Springer, 1983.

[11] BERGSTRA, J.A. & J.W. KLOP, *Process algebra for communication and mutual exclusion* Department of Computer Science Technical Report IW 218/83, Mathematisch Centrum, 1983.

[12] BERGSTRA, J.A. & J.W. KLOP, *The algebra of recursively defined processes and the algebra of regular processes*, Department of Computer Science Report IW 235/83, Mathematisch Centrum, 1983.

[13] DUGUNDJI, J., *Topology*, Allen and Bacon, 1966.

[14] ENGELKING, R., *General Topology*, Polish Scientific Publishers, 1977.

[15] GIERZ, G. et al., *A Compendium of Continuous Lattices*, Springer, 1980.

[16] GOLSON, W. & W.C. ROUNDS, *Connections between two theories of concurrency - metric spaces and synchronization trees*, University of Michigan Computing Research Laboratory Technical Report CRL TR 3-83, 1983.

[17] HAHN, H., *Reelle Funktionen*, Chelsea, 1948.

[18] HOPCROFT, J.E. & J.D. ULLMAN, *Introduction to Automata Theory, Languages and Computation*, Addison-Wesley, 1979.

[19] MICHAEL, E., *Topologies on spaces of subsets*, Trans. AMS 71, 152-182, 1951.

[20] MILNER, R., *A Calculus of Communicating Systems*, LNCS 92, Springer, 1980.

[21] NIVAT, M., *Infinite words, infinite trees, infinite computations*, Foundations of Computer Science III.2 (J.W. de Bakker & J. van Leeuwen, eds), 3-52, Mathematical Centre Tracts 109, 1979.

[22] NIVAT, M., *Synchronization of concurrent processes*, Formal Language Theory (R.V. Book, ed.), 429-454, Academic Press, 1980.

[23] PLOTKIN, G.D., *A power domain for countable nondeterminism*, Proc. 9th ICALP (M. Nielsen & E.M. Schmidt, eds), 418-428, LNCS 140, Springer, 1982.

[24] ROUNDS, W.C., *On the relationships between Scott domains, synchronization trees, and metric spaces*, preprint, Department of Computer and Communication Sciences, University of Michigan, 1983.

[25] SCOTT, D.S., *Domain equations*, Proc. 6th IBM Symp. on Mathematical Foundations of Computer Science: Logical Aspects of Programs, 105-256, IBM Japan, 1981.

[26] SMYTH, M.B., *Power domains and predicate transformers, a topological view*, Proc. 10th ICALP (J. Diaz, ed.), 662-675, LNCS 154, Springer, 1983.

ALGEBRAIC TOOLS FOR SYSTEM CONSTRUCTION

J.A. Bergstra, J.W. Klop
Mathematical Centre, Kruislaan 413, 1098 SJ Amsterdam

J.V. Tucker
Department of Computer Studies, University of Leeds, Leeds LS2 9JT

INTRODUCTION

Computer systems, in all their diversity, often share certain common properties: they are hierarchically organised into levels of abstraction and, at each level, they possess a certain architecture based on their construction from basic subsystems. Of especial interest are the hierarchical and modular structures of concurrent computer systems.

In this paper we consider a variety of computer systems and collect a set of informal principles concerning their hierarchical construction. These ideas are readily transformed into an elementary *formal* account of systems in which levels of abstraction are represented by *algebras* and the relationships between levels are represented by *homomorphisms*.

The algebraic approach to systems is then exemplified in an algebraic theory of concurrent systems based on a set of axioms called ACP - axioms for concurrent processes in part modelled on the calculi of R. Milner.

1. EXAMPLES OF COMPUTER SYSTEMS

1.1. Von Neumann Computer Systems. The term *computer system* usually refers to a configuration of hardware and software such as a computer whose operating system supports a number of languages and software tools. But the idea of the computer system is machine independent and possesses a hierarchical structure organized into levels of abstraction. In the case of the *von Neumann computer system*, this hierarchy is shown in the following figure (adapted from Bell and Newell [10]):

system configuration level
symbolic programming level
register-transfer level
logic level
circuit level
device level

Each level is characterized by a *medium* for processing, *basic components* for this processing, *composition methods* to build systems from the basic components and *rules of behaviour* to explain the operation of the systems constructed in terms of their components (illustrations may be found in Bell and Newell [10]).

The structure of a system at various levels is consistent and high levels reflect the structure of low levels: it is what we may term a bottom-up system built by a process of abstraction. The von Neumann hierarchy may be termed a bottom-up hierarchy in which data stores and data transfer paths are represented at each level of abstraction: see Backus [6].

1.2. Machines and Languages. A machine defines a programming language in which an instruction represents an operation of the machine. Conversely, the language defines a machine by supposing its instructions to specify certain machine operations to be available. This observation initiates the idea of the *virtual machine* that refines the hierarchy of the von Neumann computer system, matching ideas about machine architecture with ideas about programming languages (see Tanenbaum [25], for instance). Actually, virtual machines serve the following purpose: *a level of abstraction is defined by a programming formalism for which an operational semantics is made based on a model of computation*; that these models of computation are called machines reflects that the von Neumann systems compose a bottom-up hierarchy.

1.3. Other Architectures. The processor-channel-store model underlying von Neumann computer systems may be replaced by other models of computation that give rise to *data flow systems*, *reduction systems*, *systolic systems* and *vector systems*. In each case computers, with architectures derived from the models, are under construction and bottom-up hierarchies for the systems can be expected to evolve.

1.4. Distributed Computer Systems. By a *distributed computer system* we have in mind a system based on a network of computers. The hierarchical structure of such a distributed system is unknown and remains a substantial research problem. A notable attempt at a solution is made in the *ISO-OSI Model* which organises into seven levels of abstraction the interconnections of a distributed computer system (see Tanenbaum [26]); the proper specification of these and other independent layers remains a problem, however, and composition principles are unknown.

1.5. VLSI Systems. A VLSI system is a system specially implemented in silicon using VLSI technology. The need for custom VLSI leads to the problem of programming into silicon wherein system descriptions are compiled into circuits. Thus, the following scientific problem is encountered:

VLSI System Hierarchy Problem. To analyse and structure VLSI computation as a hierarchy of levels of computation; and to develop formal many-level specification languages which have regard for verifying system logic and predicting system performance.

The problem asks for a generalisation of the von Neumann and other machine-language hierarchies; and its answers may be as complex in their organisation. The VLSI Hierarchy Problem is of interest to us: in Dew and Tucker [15] the complexity theory of the composition principles is investigated experimentally.

1.6. Software Systems. Within the symbolic level of the von Neumann hierarchy of 1.1 reside *software systems* of considerable complexity. Ideas that determine a hierarchical structure for software systems are emerging from researches into programming languages that support the hierarchical and modular decomposition of programs: the subjects of stepwise-refinement and top-down design of programs, data type specification, data type modules, generic data types immediately come to mind through their popularisation in ADA. (A very useful survey is Wulf [27] and many early research articles are collected in Gries [17].)

Of particular importance is the concept of the *algebraic data abstraction* with which programs may assume a hierarchical structure the levels of which are defined in terms of *the operations allowed on data*. There is a mathematical theory for algebraic data types that programmers may *refer* to and that contains many satisfying results: see ADJ[2,4], Goguen and Meseguer [16].

The algorithmic theory at a fixed level of data abstraction is well understood in conventional terms. But the ideas of a *data type module as a system component* and appropriate *module composition tools* are underdeveloped (Back [5]). And the relation between levels is not well understood: for example, the implementation of a data type specification by a data type module is plagued by problems to do with partial functions.

However in the case of specification languages the study of hierarchies and composition tools is very well advanced as a result of researches of Burstall and Goguen related to CLEAR: see Burstall and Goguen [14].

Since an algebraic structure in the syntax and denotational semantics of programming languages was observed (in ADJ [1]), further research has shown that conventional programming language definitions can be recast in an algebraic (and therefore compositional) mould. The hierarchical implications of this are seen in compilation: see ADJ [3].

1.7. Concurrent Systems. The parallel execution of tasks has led to special developments in software for concurrent systems; for example OCCAM [23] which is based on CSP, first defined in Hoare [19]. In later studies of CSP the modular structure of programs is established by means of composition operators including sequencing, nondeterministic composition and merge; see Hoare, Brookes and Roscoe [20].

Composition operators for concurrent processes have been the subject of long standing research by R. Milner, an introduction to which is Milner [21]. An important idea is that of a *calculus*, called CCS, for the composition operators which describes their effects by means of *laws*.

Hierarchical aspects of system construction are treated only through the simple algebraic idea of encapsulation where an interconnected set of processes is regarded as a single process.

1.8. Functional Programming. In his critique of von Neumann computer systems, J. Backus identified the need for composition tools for program construction and the requirement that such tools constitute a rich set of program forming operators about which a satisfactory *algebraic* theory can be made. Backus' theory of *functional programming* is intended to satisfy this requirement. In particular, it uses operator laws to support algebraic proofs of program equivalence and correctness: see Backus [6,7].

1.9. Knowledge-based Systems. Finally, we notice A. Newell's thesis concerning a *knowledge level* above the symbolic level of the von Neumann hierarchy in 1.1. The new level of abstraction achieves a separation of knowledge and knowledge representation: the latter belonging to the symbolic level. The knowledge level and its structure is described in Newell [22].

2. PRINCIPLES FOR SYSTEM ORGANISATION

From the examples of hierarchically organised systems the following ideas, by no means exemplified in all the systems, can be collected:

2.1. Levels. A *system* belongs to a well-defined category of systems having an autonomous specification; this category we refer to as a *level of abstraction.*

2.2. Composition. Each level of abstraction is characterised by a collection of *basic systems* and a collection of *composition tools* for system construction. The systems of the level are all manufactured by applying the composition tools to basic systems.

2.3. Architecture. The *structure* or *architecture* of each system is defined by the way the system is configured from the basic system components by the composition tools.

2.4. Hierarchy. Two levels of abstraction L_1 and L_2 may be hierarchically ordered: in symbols, $L_1 < L_2$ meaning that L_1 is *below* L_2 and that L_2 is *above* L_1. The relationship between the systems of levels L_1 and L_2 is expressed as follows:

(i) The view from below: the systems of L_2 are *abstractions* or *modularisations* of the systems of L_1.

(ii) The view from above: the systems of L_1 are *specialisations*, *refinements*, or *implementations* of the systems of L_2

We imagine mappings

$$ab: L_1 \to L_2 \quad \text{for abstraction}$$

$$sp: L_2 \to L_1 \quad \text{for specialisation.}$$

Abstraction and specialisation mechanisms are inverse to one another if $ab \circ sp = sp \circ ab =$ identity.

2.5. Hierarchy and System Architecture. A method of abstraction or specialisation must respect system structure or architecture at both levels of abstraction.

2.6. Bottom-up and Top-down Hierarchies. A *bottom-up hierarchy* is a collection of levels of abstraction $L_1,\ldots,L_n$ and structure preserving abstraction operations $ab_1,\ldots,ab_{n-1}$;

in symbols:

$$L_1 \xrightarrow{ab_1} L_2 \longrightarrow \ldots \longrightarrow L_{n-1} \xrightarrow{ab_{n-1}} L_n.$$

Thus in a bottom-up hierarchy system architectures at high levels reflect the structure of systems at low levels.

The concept of a *top-down hierarchy* is characterised in a similar way using specialisations.

3. ALGEBRAIC MODEL OF SYSTEM ORGANISATION

The ideas of the last section may be formalised as follows:

3.1. Levels of Abstraction. A level of abstraction is represented by an *algebra* A whose elements are *systems*. The composition tools for system construction at the level A are the *operations* of the algebra A. The basic components for system construction at the level A are collected in a set G of *generators* for the algebra A.

3.2. Architectures. A notation for system architectures for a level of abstraction A is made as follows: the components or generators G of A are named by a set of symbols X and the composition operators are named from the signature Σ of A. The algebra $T(\Sigma,X)$ of all Σ-terms over X is an algebra of *system notations* for A that represents the system configurations possible by means of applying the composition tools to the basic components. The unique semantic homomorphism $v: T(\Sigma,X) \to A$ formalises the concept of *system architecture* in these two definitions: An *architecture for a system* $a \in A$ is a term $t \in T(\Sigma,X)$ such that $v(t) = a$. Two architectures t_1 and t_2 are *equivalent as A-systems* if $v(t_1) = v(t_2)$.

3.3. Realisations. Let A_1 and A_2 be two levels of abstraction. Then the systems of A_1 are *realisable as systems of* A_2 if there is a homomorphism $\phi: A_1 \to A_2$; the map ϕ may be called a *realisation*. Abstractions (modularisations) and specialisations (refinements, implementations) are instances of system realisations. *We do not allow an algebraic status to these ideas of abstraction and specialisation.*

3.4. Hierarchy. A *hierarchy* is a sequence of levels of abstractions and realisations

$$A_1 \xrightarrow{\phi_1} A_2 \xrightarrow{\phi_2} \ldots \longrightarrow A_{n-1} \xrightarrow{\phi_{n-1}} A_n.$$

Again we notice that it is *not* an algebraic matter that A_1 is the top of a top-down hierarchy of specialisations or, alternatively, the bottom of a bottom-up hierarchy of abstractions.

3.5. System Laws. The development of a theory for a class of systems using these ideas requires a set of properties of the system composition tools to serve as algebraic axioms: an algebraic theory *begins* with the choice of its basic laws. These laws are established by investigating the semantics of the systems *and* by evaluating the mathematics the laws support. Ideally, the axioms should be formally elegant and small in number, to be easy to memorise and to aid calculation. And the set of axioms allows the construction of free objects for the category of all its models to service the concept of system architectures.

3.6. Concurrent Systems. In the sequel a set of axioms for concurrent processes (ACP) is presented. Many general laws for concurrent processes have been found in the course of studies by R. Milner and his collaborators and a number of calculi have been formed: Milner [21], Hennessy [18]. A search for laws relevant to CSP and OCCAM has also started as part of the study of semantics of that attractive syntax for concurrency: Hoare, Brookes and Roscoe [20], Olderog and Hoare [24].

In contrast, the laws of ACP are made to support an exclusively algebraic study of concurrency. The axioms are used as a kernel of properties of composition operators with which further laws may be employed on occasion to prove a result (see 6.1). It is hoped that the theory of ACP will be an interesting instrument to analyse concurrency and will be of use in the analysis of other calculi.

Semantically, the models of ACP represent distinct levels of abstraction of concurrent systems implemented in agreement with the specifications represented by the axioms of ACP. The homomorphisms of ACP algebras represent the abstractions and specialisations between such levels of abstraction for ACP systems.

4. ALGEBRA OF COMMUNICATING PROCESSES

We will introduce an algebraic system for the analysis of communicating systems made from given systems by means of the following composition tools: for communicating systems x and y we allow the operations of

sequential composition	$x \cdot y$
alternative composition	$x + y$
parallel composition	$x \| y$
encapsulation	$\partial_H(x)$

Our analysis will also involve a finite collection of atomic systems and their pattern of communication.

4.1. ACP-algebras. Let A be a finite set, called the set of *atomic actions*. An *ACP-algebra* over A consists of a set P equipped with operators

$$\cdot,\ +,\ \|,\ \llcorner\!\llcorner,\ |,\ \delta,\ \partial_H.$$

All operators are binary, except the constant δ, a distinguished atomic action and the unary H-projection $(H \subseteq A)$ ∂_H. The set P contains A as a subset on which communication '|' restricts as a map $|: A \times A \to A$.

These operations satisfy the following equational axioms, where a,b,c vary over A and x,y,z over P. Often we will write instead of $x \cdot y$ just xy.

$x + y = y + x$	A1
$x + (y + z) = (x + y) + z$	A2
$x + x = x$	A3
$(x + y) \cdot z = x \cdot z + y \cdot z$	A4
$(x \cdot y) \cdot z = x \cdot (y \cdot z)$	A5
$x + \delta = x$	A6
$\delta \cdot x = \delta$	A7
$a \mid b = b \mid a$	C1
$(a \mid b) \mid c = a \mid (b \mid c)$	C2
$\delta \mid a = \delta$	C3
$x \| y = x \mathbin{\|\!\!\lfloor} y + y \mathbin{\|\!\!\lfloor} x + x \mid y$	CM1
$a \mathbin{\|\!\!\lfloor} x = a \cdot x$	CM2
$(ax) \mathbin{\|\!\!\lfloor} y = a(x \| y)$	CM3
$(x + y) \mathbin{\|\!\!\lfloor} z = x \mathbin{\|\!\!\lfloor} z + y \mathbin{\|\!\!\lfloor} z$	CM4
$(ax) \mid b = (a \mid b) \cdot x$	CM5
$a \mid (bx) = (a \mid b) \cdot x$	CM6
$(ax) \mid (by) = (a \mid b) \cdot (x \| y)$	CM7
$(x + y) \mid z = x \mid z + y \mid z$	CM8
$x \mid (y + z) = x \mid y + x \mid z$	CM9
$\partial_H(a) = a \quad \text{if } a \notin H$	D1
$\partial_H(a) = \delta \quad \text{if } a \in H$	D2
$\partial_H(x + y) = \partial_H(x) + \partial_H(y)$	D3
$\partial_H(x \cdot y) = \partial_H(x) \cdot \partial_H(y)$	D4

Axioms of ACP

4.2. Commentary. On intuitive grounds $x\cdot(y + z)$ and $x\cdot y + x\cdot z$ present different mechanisms and an axiom $x\cdot(y + z) = x\cdot y + x\cdot z$ is not included in ACP.

The constant δ is to be interpreted as an action which cannot be performed, hence $\delta x = \delta$; the law $x + \delta = x$ postulates that in the context of an alternative it will never be chosen.

The source of intuition for the $\|$-operation axioms is the arbitrary interleaving semantics of parallelism. The operations $\lfloor\!\lfloor$, left-merge, and $|$, communication merge, are auxiliary operations helpful in obtaining a finitary specification of $\|$. The essential algebraic properties of $\lfloor\!\lfloor$ and $|$ are the *linearity laws* CM4, CM8, CM9. Intuitively, $x \lfloor\!\lfloor y$ is $x\|y$ but takes its initial step from x; and $x|y$ is $x\|y$ but takes its initial step as a communication of an initial action of x and an initial action of y.

4.3. Generators. Let P be a process algebra over A. A *subalgebra* Q *of* P is a subset Q of P containing A and closed under all the operations.

Let $X = \{x_i \mid i \in I\}$ be a subset of a process algebra P over A. The smallest subalgebra of P containing X is denoted by $\langle X\rangle$. The algebra P is said to be *generated* by a subset X if $P = \langle X\rangle$.

4.4. Homomorphisms. Let P and Q be process algebras over A. A *homomorphism* $\phi: P \to Q$ is a map which respects all operations and which leaves atoms invariant. The *image* of a homomorphism $\phi: P \to Q$ is an A-subalgebra of Q, denoted by $\phi(P)$.

4.5. Syntax and Semantics. Let P be an ACP-algebra with atom set A. We define the *communication function* $\gamma_P: A \times A \to A$ for P by:

$$\gamma_P(a,b) = a|b.$$

Given a function $\gamma: A \times A \to A$, one defines ACP_γ as the class of all ACP-algebras P with $\gamma_P = \gamma$. Clearly for ACP_γ to be nonempty, γ must satisfy the requirements C1-3.

Let us now fix a communication function γ that satisfies C1-3. Then ACP_γ contains an initial algebra denoted by A_ω. Let $X_1,\ldots,X_k$ be a set of formal symbols. Now $A_\omega[X_1,\ldots,X_k]$ is the *free* ACP_γ*-algebra over* k *generators*.

According to the thesis of ADJ [1,2] one conceives $A_\omega[X_1,\ldots,X_k]$ as an algebra of *system notations*, finding their semantics as homomorphic images. Indeed, if $p_1,\ldots,p_k$ are processes in P, an ACP_γ-algebra, then there is a unique homomorphism

$$\phi: A_\omega[X_1,\ldots,X_k] \to P$$

mapping X_i to p_i. If we see the p_i as realisations of the X_i, then ϕ extends these realisations to all system notations in $A_\omega[X_1,\ldots,X_k]$.

On A_ω one defines *projection operators* $(.)_n: A_\omega \to A_\omega$ as follows:

$$(a)_n = a$$
$$(ax)_1 = a$$
$$(ax)_{n+1} = a(x)_n$$
$$(x + y)_n = (x)_n + (y)_n.$$

For each $n \geqslant 1$ a congruence relation $\equiv_n$ on A_ω is obtained by

$$x \equiv_n y \Leftrightarrow (x)_n = (y)_n .$$

The algebras $A_\omega/\equiv_n$ are again ACP_γ-algebras. We write A_n for $A_\omega/\equiv_n$.
Clearly, $(.)_n$ induces a homomorphism

$$(.)_n : A_{n+1} \to A_n .$$

The chain $A_1 \xrightarrow[(.)_1]{} A_2 \xrightarrow[(.)_2]{} A_3 \longrightarrow \ldots$ determines a *projective limit* which we denote by A^∞.

5. SOLVING RECURSION EQUATIONS

Consider the algebra $A_\omega[X_1,\ldots,X_k]$ and let E be a system of equations:

$$\begin{cases} X_1 = t_1(X_1,\ldots,X_k) \\ \vdots \\ X_k = t_k(X_1,\ldots,X_k) \end{cases}$$

where the terms t_i are built from the constants and operations of ACP and the variables from $X = (X_1,\ldots,X_k)$. This system generates a congruence $\equiv_E$ on $A_\omega[X_1,\ldots,X_k]$. We will consider the quotient algebra $A_\omega[X_1,\ldots,X_k]/\equiv_E$, also denoted as

$$A_\omega[X]/X{=}t(X) \text{, or } A_\omega(X,E)$$

where $X = t(X)$ is short for the system of equations E. This algebra is also in ACP_γ. In $A_\omega(X,E)$ the X_i are solutions of E. In this way we have a purely algebraic method for solving fixed point equations.

It can be shown that for each system of equations E, there exists a homomorphism

$$\phi: A_\omega(X,E) \to A^\infty .$$

In the case of a single equation this was shown in Bergstra and Klop [11]. The homomorphism need not be unique.

From this observation one concludes that A^∞ solves all systems of fixed point equations, and that $A_\omega(X,E)$ is guaranteed to have a nontrivial structure. The algebra $A_\omega(X,$ is a countable semicomputable structure, whereas A^∞ is uncountable.

Problem: Under which circumstances is $A_\omega(X,E)$ computable?

6. SOME MATHEMATICAL PROPERTIES OF ACP-ALGEBRAS

Consider A_ω, whose domain consists of terms built from A, +, $\cdot$, $\|$, $\lfloor\!\lfloor$, $|$, ∂_H. In fact it can be shown [12] that each term t is equivalent to a term t' built using A, + and $\cdot$ only:

<u>NORMAL FORM THEOREM</u>. *For each closed term* t *there is a closed term* t' *not containing* $\|$, $\lfloor\!\lfloor$, $|$, ∂_H *such that* ACP $\vdash$ t = t'.

6.1. Algebras with Standard Concurrency and Handshaking. A useful intuition about communicating processes is to postulate that $\|$ is commutative and associative. This leads to the following requirements for $\|$, $\lfloor\!\lfloor$ and $|$, called *axioms of standard concurrency:*

$$(x \lfloor\!\lfloor y) \lfloor\!\lfloor z = x \lfloor\!\lfloor (y \| z)$$
$$(x|y) \lfloor\!\lfloor z = x|(y \lfloor\!\lfloor z)$$
$$x|y = y|x$$
$$x\|y = y\|x$$
$$x|(y|z) = (x|y)|z$$
$$x\|(y\|z) = (x\|y)\|z$$

These axioms are not independent relative to ACP, for instance commutativity and associativity of $\|$ are derivable from the other axioms.

In [12] it is shown that A_ω and A^∞ satisfy the axioms of standard concurrency. Moreover, matters are greatly simplified by adopting the *handshaking axiom*:

$$x \mid y \mid z = \delta.$$

Both CSP and CCS adopt this axiom. The handshaking axiom implies that all proper communications are binary.

Let P be an ACP-algebra with standard concurrency and handshaking. Let $x_1,\ldots,x_k$ be processes in P. We make the following abbreviations: X_k^i is obtained by merging $x_1,\ldots,x_k$ except x_i, and $X_k^{i,j}$ is obtained by merging $x_1,\ldots,x_k$ except x_i,x_j. Here we suppose $k \geqslant 3$. Then one easily proves the following generalisation of the ACP-axiom CM1:

EXPANSION THEOREM. $x_1\|\ldots\|x_k = \sum_i x_i \lfloor\!\lfloor X_k^i + \sum_{i\neq j} (x_i|x_j) \lfloor\!\lfloor X_k^{i,j}$.

6.2. Literature. We will catalogue the principal influences on ACP. In addition to work on calculi for concurrency, from Milner's CCS we have adopted the laws A1-5 and the idea of the expansion theorem; Milner's restriction operator is here called the encapsulation operator. (In [13] Milner's τ-laws have been incorporated in the algebraic framework.) From Hennessy [18] we have adopted laws C1 and C2.

The left-merge $\lfloor\!\lfloor$ and projective limit A^∞ first appeared in [11]. The full system ACP, including $|$, was introduced in [12]. Our work on ACP arose from a question in De Bakker and Zucker [8] about the existence of solutions for non-guarded fixed point equations in their topological model of processes (A^∞ is equivalent to their space of uniform processes).

REFERENCES

[1] ADJ (GOGUEN, J.A., J.W. THATCHER, E.G. WAGNER & J.B. WRIGHT), *Initial algebra semantics and continuous algebras*,

[2] ADJ (GOGUEN, J.A., J.W. THATCHER & E.G. WAGNER), *An initial algebra approach to the specification, correctness and implementation of abstract data types* , in R.T. Yeh (ed.): Current trends in programming methodology IV, Data structuring, Prentice Hall, Englewood Cliffs (1978), 80-149.

[3] ADJ (THATCHER, J.W., E.G. WAGNER & J.B. WRIGHT), *More advice on structuring compilers and proving them correct*, in: H.A. Maurer (ed.), Automata, languages and programming, 6th Colloquium, Springer LNCS 71 (1979), 596-615.

[4] ADJ (EHRIG, H.,H.-J. KREOWSKI, J.W. THATCHER, E.G. WAGNER & J.B. WRIGHT), *Parameterized data types in algebraic specification languages*, in: J.W. de Bakker & J. van Leeuwen (eds.), Automata, languages and programming, 7th Colloquium, Springer LNCS (1980), 157-168.

[5] BACK, R.J., *Locality in modular systems*, in: M. Nielsen & E.M. Schmidt (eds.), Automata, languages and Programming, 9th Colloquium, Springer LNCS 140 (1982),1-13.

[6] BACKUS, J., *Can programming be liberated from the von Neumann style? - a functional style and its algebra of programs*, CACM 21 (1978), 613-639.

[7] BACKUS, J., *Is computer science based on the wrong fundamental concept of a 'program'? An extended concept*, in: J.W. de Bakker & J.C. van Vliet (eds.), Algorithmic languages, North-Holland 1981, 133-165.

[8] DE BAKKER, J.W. & J.I. ZUCKER, *Denotational semantics of concurrency*, Proc. 14th ACM Symp. on Theory of Computing (1982), 153-158.

[9] DE BAKKER, J.W. & J.I. ZUCKER, *Processes and the denotational semantics of concurrency*, Report IW 209/82, Mathematisch Centrum, 1982, to appear in Information & Control.

[10] BELL, C.G. & A. NEWELL, *Computer structures: Readings and Examples*, McGraw-Hill 197

[11] BERGSTRA, J.A. & J.W. KLOP, *Fixed point semantics in process algebras*, Report IW 206/82, Mathematisch Centrum, 1982.

[12] BERGSTRA, J.A. & J.W. KLOP, *Process algebra for communication and mutual exclusion*, Report IW 218/83, Mathematisch Centrum, 1983.

[13] BERGSTRA, J.A. & J.W. KLOP, *An abstraction mechanism for process algebras*, Report IW 231/83, Mathematisch Centrum, 1983.

[14] BURSTALL, R.M. & J.A. GOGUEN, *The semantics of CLEAR, a specification language*, in: Proc. on Abstract Software specifications, Copenhagen, Springer LNCS 86 (1980) 292-332.

[15] DEW, P.M. & J.V. TUCKER, *An experimental study of a timing assumption in VLSI complexity theory*, Univ. of Leeds, Dept. of Computer Studies, Report 168.

[16] GOGUEN, J.A. & J. MESEGUER, *An initiality primer*, in preparation.

[17] GRIES, D. (ed.), *Programming methodology*, Springer, Berlin 1978.

[18] HENNESSY, M., *A term model for synchronous processes*, Information & Control, Vol. 51, nr.1 (1981), 58-75.

[19] HOARE, C.A.R., *Communicating sequential processes*, C. ACM 21 (1978), 666-677.

[20] HOARE, C.A.R., S.D. BROOKES & A.W. ROSCOE, *A theory of communicating sequential processes*, to appear in JACM.

[21] MILNER, R., *A Calculus for Communicating Systems*, Springer LNCS 92, 1980.

[22] NEWELL, A., *The knowledge level*, Artificial Intelligence 18 (1982), 78-127.

[23] OCCAM, *The OCCAM programming manual*, INMOS, Bristol 1982.

[24] OLDEROG, E.R. & C.A.R. HOARE, *Specification-oriented semantics for communicating processes*, in: J. Díaz (ed.), Automata. languages and programming, 10th Colloquium Springer LNCS 154 (1983), 561-572.

[25] TANENBAUM, A.S., *Structured computer organisation*, Prentice Hall, Englewood Cliffs 1976.

[26] TANENBAUM, A.S., *Computer networks*, Prentice Hall, Englewood Cliffs, 1981.

[27] WULF, W.A., *Abstract data types: a retrospective and prospective view*, in: P. Dembinski (ed.), Mathematical Foundations of Computer Science 1980, Springer LNCS (1980), 94-112.

PC-compactness, a necessary condition for the existence of sound and complete logics of partial correctness

by

J.A. Bergstra

Mathematical Center, Amsterdam, The Netherlands

J.Tiuryn

Institute of Mathematics, University of Warsaw, Poland

ABSTRACT

A first order theory is called PC-compact if each asserted program which is true in all models of the theory is true in all models of a finite subset of the theory. If a structure has a complete Hoare's logic then its first order theory must be PC-compact; moreover, its partial correctness theory must be decidable relative to this first order theory.

This identifies two necessary conditions that a structure must satisfy if Hoare's logic (or any sound logic of partial correctness extending Hoare's logic) is to be complete on the given structure. We provide an example of a structure that satisfies both conditions, on which Hoare's logic is incomplete but which does possess a sound and complete logic of partial correctness. This logic is obtained by adding a proof rule which incorporates aprogram transformation. The concept of PC-compactness is further studied in detail by means of an examination of various example structures.

KEY WORDS & PHRASES: Hoare's logic, logic of partial correctness, soundness, completeness, PC-compactness.

1. INTRODUCTION

This paper studies general and natural necessary conditions that are true of structures A which happen to have a complete Hoare's Logic for their <u>while</u>-programs. Especially we consider the following conditions:

(I) Th(A) is PC-compact

(II) PC(A) is recursive in Th(A).

These conditions (to be explained in detail below) are quite natural and interesting for themselves.

We show that HL(A) may be incomplete even if I and II are satisfied for A. The new concept of PC-compactness is investigated by evaluating it on various interesting example structures where it will show an unexpectedly irregular behaviour.

If HL(A) is incomplete it is conceivable that some sound proof system HL'(A), properly extending HL(A), can be found which is complete. If so then we observe that also in this more general case the conditions I and II must necessarily be satisfied. (At this stage it will be essential to have a convincing concept of a sound proof system at hand). We infer that given A satisfying conditions I and II but having HL incomplete it is worthwhile to search for a sound and complete extension of HL(A). Applying this on the example mentioned before we succeed in finding such an extension. It is not clear whether conditions I and II imply the existence of a sound and complete logic.

Before discussing connections with the litterature we will briefly consider some technical and definitional matters. Let Σ be a single or many-sorted signature. Mod (Σ) denotes the class of all Σ-structures, $L(\Sigma)$ the corresponding first order language. For $A \in \text{Mod}(\Sigma)$, $\text{Th}(A) = \{p \in L(\Sigma) \mid A \models p\}$, the first order theory of A. For an asserted triple {p} S {q} over Σ we write $T \models \{p\}\ S\ \{q\}$ if for all $A \in \text{Mod}(\Sigma)$, $A \models T$ implies $A \models \{p\}\ S\ \{q\}$.

PC(T), the partial correctness theory of T consists of all asserted triples {p} R {q} with $T \models \{p\}\ S\ \{q\}$. For $A \in \text{Mod}(\Sigma)$, PC(A) denotes PC(Th(A)) and coincides with the set of all asserted programs true in A.

<u>1.1. DEFINITION</u>. T is PC-<u>compact</u> if for all $\{p\}\ S\ \{q\} \in \text{PC}(T)$ there is a finite subtheory $T' \subseteq T$ with $\{p\}\ S\ \{q\} \in \text{PC}(T')$.

On the syntactic side we have for each theory $T \subseteq L(\Sigma)$ a proof system HL(T), Hoare's Logic, proving asserted programs over Σ. HL is sound in the sense that HL(T) $\vdash$ {p} S {q} implies T $\models$ {p} S {q}, for all T and {p} S {q}. For a fixed structure A, HL(A) is an abbreviation of HL(Th(A)), it is complete if it proves all of PC(A). We summarize some facts of prime importance in a proposition.

1.2. PROPOSITION.

(i) *If* HL(A) *is complete then* Th(A) *is* PC-*compact.*

(ii) Th(A) *is* PC-*compact if and only if for each* {p} S {q} *true in* A *there is a sentence* $\phi \in$ Th(A) *such that* $\phi \models$ {p} S {q}.

(iii) *If* A *and* B *are elementary equivalent* (Th(A)=Th(B)) *then* PC(A) = PC(B).

(iv) *If* HL(A) *is complete then* PC(A) *is recursive in* Th(A).

PROOF. (i) follows from the finitary nature of HL. (ii) is obvious, (iii) follows from the fact that {p} S {q} can be written as an infinite conjunction $\bigwedge_{i=1}^{\infty}$ {p} S^n {q}, where S^n denotes a program running n steps of S; {p} S^n {q} moreover is a formula in $L(\Sigma)$. (iv) if HL(A) is complete then HL(A) = PC(A); as HL(A) is recursively enumerable in Th(A) by the nature of a proof system, on the other hand {p} S {q} $\notin$ PC(A) iff $\exists n\, A \models$ {p} S^n {q} iff $\exists n$ {p} S^n {q} $\in$ Th(A) which shows that PC(A) is also co-recursively enumerable in Th(A). Combining both facts PC(A) is recursive in Th(A).

From this proposition we find that conditions I and II are necessary for the completeness of HL(A). It can easily be seen that both conditions are independent. For instance the structure A = $(\omega, S, 0)$ satisfies condition I but not condition II whereas the structure [N,N] satisfies condition II but not condition I (see 3.1.). Consequently the conjunction I $\wedge$ II is a meaningful stronger necessary condition for completeness of HL(A).

We will now briefly discuss results from previous work connected with our topic. WAND [9] presents a nice example of a structure A with HL(A) incomplete. One can show that Wand's example violates condition II. COOK [5] introduces the now familiar concept of expressiveness which constitutes a condition on a structure A sufficient for the completeness of HL(A). In BERGSTRA & TUCKER [3] it is shown that expressiveness is not a necessary cocdition however. Condition II studied in BERGSTRA, CHMIELIENSKA & TIURYN [1]; it is shown that condition II is not sufficient for completeness of HL. Using two-sorted structures this fact is derived more easily in BERGSTRA & TUCKER [2]. Essentially [1] show how to transform examples using two-sorted structures into similar examples using single sorted structures. We take that as a justification for freely using two-sorted structures in this paper.

Four concrete structures will be considered more closely. These examples all are two sorted structures $[M_1,M_2]$ resulting from combining two disjoint (and disconnected) single sorted structures M_1 and M_2 into a two-sorted structure.

[N,B] with N = (ω,S,t,·,<,0) and
B = ({t,f}, ∨,¬,T,F), the booleans.

[N,A] with A = (ω,S,0), in LAMBEK [7]
A is called Abacus arithmetic.

[N,A0] with A0 = (ω,S,<,0), Abacus arithmetic with ordering.

[N,N] two copies of N.

The only essential point of two-sorted structures is that we may use separate variables for both sorts. For clarity it may be useful to have different names S',t',·',<',0' in connection with the second sort.

Each of these structures satisfies condition II. This follows from the following simple fact that can serve as a test for condition II in most (practical) cases:

1.3. PROPOSITION. *Suppose* A *is computable and* Th(N) *is recursive in* Th(A), *then* PC(A) *is recursive in* Th(A).

Concerning condition I, PC-compactness, we will prove the following theorem.

1.4. THEOREM.

(i) Th([N,B]) *is* PC-*compact*. (3)

(ii) Th([N,A]) *is not* PC-*compact*. (3.3)

(iii) Th([N,A0]) *is* PC-*compact*. (3.5)

(iv) Th([N,N]) *is not* PC-*compact*. (3.1)

This behaviour of PC-compactness is rather surprising and the proof of (iii) suggests that [N,AO], though not a pathological structure, might be a rather isolated example of a PC-compact structure of such complexity. Relating these results to proof systems we obtain the following theorem.

1.5. THEOREM.

(i) [N,AO] *satisfies both conditions I and II but* HL([N,AO]) *is incomplete.* (3.7)

(ii) There exists a sound logic of partial correctness HL'([N,AO]) *properly extending* HL([N,AO]) *which is complete.* (3.6)

We will conclude the paper with a listing of four open questions that naturally arise from our results.

2. PRELIMINARIES ON LOGIC

First of all we will need logical information about the structures A,AO and N. The following proposition contains all nontrivial facts that will play a rôle in the proofs of both theorems 1.4 and 1.5.

2.1. PROPOSITION.

(i) Th(A) *has no finite axiomatisation.*

(ii) Each finite $T \subseteq$ Th(A) *has a model that contains a finite S-cycle as a substructure.*

(iii) Th(AO) *is finitely axiomatizable.*

(iv) There is a formula $\phi(x) \in L(N)$ *such that* $\{n \mid N \models \phi(\underline{n})\}$ *is not recursively enumerable.*

PROOF. (i), (ii) and (iii) follow from various results in CHANG & KEISLER [4]; (iv) follows from the fact that all arithmetical relations are definable in N (see SHOENFIELD [8] for more details).

Then we need a simple fact about two-sorted structures of the form [M,M'].

<u>2.2. SEPARATION OF VARIABLES LEMMA</u>. For each $\phi \in L([M,M'])$ there exists a formula ψ equivalent to ϕ which is a propositional combination of formulae in $L(M_1) \cup L(M_2)$.

<u>PROOF</u>. A proof is given in [2]. Note here that $L(M_1)$ and $L(M_2)$ are supposed to use different variables.

In particular ψ can be written in the form $\mathop{W}_{i=1}^{n} (\psi_1^i \wedge \psi_2^i)$ with $\psi_1^i \in L(M_1)$ and $\psi_2^i \in L(M_2)$.

Thirdly we must explain what exactly will be meant by a (sound) proof system for partial correctness. Given a signature Σ a logic of partial correctness L_Σ for Σ is a recursively enumerable set of pairs:

$$\{(\phi_i, \{p_i\}S_i\{q_i\}) \mid i \in \omega\}$$

with $\phi_i \in L(\Sigma)$ and $\{p_i\}\ S_i\ \{q_i\}$ an asserted triple over Σ. We write for $T \subseteq L(\Sigma)$

$$L_\Sigma(T) \vdash \{p\}\ S\ \{q\}$$

if for some ϕ, $T \vdash \phi$ and $(\phi, \{p\}S\{q\}) \in L_\Sigma$. L_Σ is sound if for all T and $\{p\}\ S\ \{q\}$

$$L_\Sigma(T) \vdash \{p\}\ S\ \{q\} \text{ implies } T \models \{p\}\ S\ \{q\}.$$

Note that soundness of L_Σ is a notion not related to any particular interpretation $A \in Mod(\Sigma)$.

We put

$$L_\Sigma(A) = L_\Sigma(Th(A)).$$

$L_\Sigma(A)$ is sound if L_Σ is sound, and complete if $L_\Sigma(A) = PC(A)$.

HL_Σ can be considered as an L_Σ as follows: Let $(\phi, \{p\}S\{q\}) \in L_\Sigma^{HL}$ if ϕ is of the form $\phi_0 \wedge \ldots \wedge \phi_{2(k-1)}$ with k the smallest number of applications of the rule of consequence necessary in a HL-proof of $\{p\}\ S\ \{q\}$ and with ϕ_{2n}, ϕ_{2n+1} the logical information required to pass the n-th application of the rule of consequence in a proof of {p} S {q}.

3. PROOFS OF THE THEOREMS

We will prove the various parts of both theorems 1.4 and 1.5 in the form of a series of propositions that cover individual parts. Th 1.4. (i), however, follows from the results in [2]; as a mather of fact for any finite structure F, [N,F] is expressive and therefore satisfies conditions I and II. All remaining parts require some argument and have a special proposition devoted to them.

<u>3.1. PROPOSITION</u>. Th([N,N]) *is not* PC-*compact.*

PROOF. We will destinguish both copies of N by writing [N,N'] and using the superscript prime on all symbols of its signature.

Now let $\phi(x)$ be a formula in $L(N)$ such that $\{n \mid N \models \phi(n)\}$ is not recursively enumerable (see 2.1. (iv)). Let $\phi'(y)$ be a version of ϕ for $L(N')$, and let z be one more variable for N. Consider the program R:

z := 0; y := 0;

<u>while</u> z ≠ x <u>do</u> z := S(z); y := S'(y) <u>od</u>

It is clear by inspection that

$$[N,N'] \models \{\phi(x)\}\ R\ \{\phi'(y)\}.$$

We will then show that there is no sentence θ true of [N,N'] such that $\theta \models \{\phi(x)\}\ R\ \{\phi'(y)\}$. Indeed suppose such a θ exists. Using the separation of variables lemma θ can equivalently be written as follow:

$$\vdash \theta \leftrightarrow \bigvee_{i=1}^{k} (\theta_i \wedge \theta_i') \text{ with } \theta_i \in L(N),\ \theta_i' \in L(N).$$

Because $[N,N'] \models \theta$ we may choose an i such that $[N,N'] \models \theta_i \wedge \theta_i'$. Clearly $\theta_i \wedge \theta_i' \models \{\phi(x)\}\ R\ \{\phi'(y)\}$. We will derive a contradiction from this fact.

Let $\underline{0} = 0$, $\underline{n+1} = S(\underline{n})$, $\underline{0}' = 0'$, $\underline{n+1}' = S'(\underline{n}')$ and write

$$A = \{n \in \omega \mid N \models \phi(\underline{n})\}$$

$$B = \{n \in \omega \mid \theta_i^! \models \phi(\underline{n}')\}$$

B is recursively enumerable (by construction) and due to the choice of ϕ, A is not recursively enumerable so $A \neq B$. Taking into account that $N \models \theta_i^!$ we see that $A \supseteq B$. So we may choose $n \in A - B$. Then by the completeness theorem there is a model N" of $\theta_i^!$ in which $N'' \models \neg\phi(\underline{n}')$. On the other hand $[N,N''] \not\models \{\phi(x)\}\ R\ \{\phi'(y)\}$ which follows by giving x the initial value n. Indeed because $n \in A$, $[N,N''] \models \phi(\underline{n})$ but after termination of S, y equals $\underline{n}'$ and $[N,N''] \not\models \phi'(\underline{n}')$. This gives the required contradiction.

<u>3.2. PROPOSITION</u>. *If* $[M_1,M_2]$ *satisfies condition I then so do* M_1 *and* M_2.

<u>PROOF</u>. Supppose $M_1 \models \{p\}\ S\ \{q\}$, then $[M_1,M_2] \models \{p\}\ S\ \{q\}$. Choose $\theta \in L([M_1,M_2])$ such that $\theta \models \{p\}\ S\ \{q\}$. Write $\theta \leftrightarrow \bigvee_{i=1}^{n} (\theta_i^1 \wedge \theta_i^2)$ with $\theta_i^j \in L(M_j)$. Choose i such that $[M_1,M_2] \models \theta_i^1 \wedge \theta_i^2$; then $\theta_i^1 \wedge \theta_i^2 \models \{p\}\ R\ \{q\}$ and obviously $\theta_i^1 \models \{p\}\ R\ \{q\}$ which state of affairs we were looking for.

<u>3.3. PROPOSITION</u>. [N,A] *does not satisfy condition I.*

<u>PROOF</u>. In view of the previous proposition it suffices to show that Th(A) is not PC-compact. To see this consider the asserted program

{<u>true</u>} R {<u>false</u>}

with R: z := S(x)

<u>while</u> z ≠ x <u>do</u> z := S(z) <u>od</u>

Clearly $A \models$ {<u>true</u>} R {<u>false</u>}; assume that $A \models \phi$ and $\phi \models$ {<u>true</u>} R {<u>false</u>}. Using 2.1. (ii) ϕ has a model A^* in which a finite S-cycle exists. Choosing as an initial value of x some element in such a cycle one finds that $A' \not\models$ {<u>true</u>} R {<u>false</u>} thus contradicting the assumption on ϕ. It follows that A and [N,A] do not meet condition I.

3.4. PROPOSITION. *If* T *is finitely axiomatizable then* T *is* PC-*compact.*

PROOF. Obvious.

3.5. PROPOSITION. Th([N,AO]) *is* PC-*compact.*

PROOF. From proposition 2.1. (iii) we obtain a sentence $\phi \in L(AO)$ which finitely axiomatizes Th(AO) i.e. for each $\psi \in L(AO)$, $\psi \in Th(AO) \Leftrightarrow \phi \vdash \psi$. So Th(AO) is PC-compact, a promising fact in view of 3.2. We will now use the rather accidental fact that there is an easy interpretation of $L(AO)$ in $L(N)$. Let $L(N) = (S, +, \cdot, <, 0)$ and $L(AO) = (S', <', 0')$ and use variables x_i for N and x_i' for AO. Omitting the superscripts yields a mapping $\Delta: L(AO) \to L(N)$. Now suppose that $[N,AO] \models \{p\}\ R\ \{q\}$; in several steps θ will be constructed such that $[N,AO] \models \theta$ and $\theta \models \{p\}\ R\ \{q\}$.

Step 1. Transform the asserted program {p} R {q} to an equivalent one, $\{p^*\}\ R^*\ \{q^*\}$ by changing the free and bound variables in such a way that variables x_i ranging over N have even indices and variables x_i' ranging over AO will have odd indices. Observe:

$$[N,AO] \models \{p^*\}\ R^*\ \{q^*\}$$

and even

$$\{p^*\}\ R^*\ \{q^*\} \models \{p\}\ R\ \{q\}.$$

Step 2. The interpretation Δ can be extended to asserted programs. Write $\Delta(\{p^*\}R^*\{q^*\})$ for $\{\Delta(p^*)\}\ \Delta\ (R^*)\ \{\Delta(q^*)\}$; this is an asserted triple over $\Sigma(N)$ true in N. Because N is expressive, HL(N) is complete and N is PC-compact; so choose $\psi \in Th(N)$ with $\Psi \models \Delta(\{p^*\}R^*\{q^*\})$ and put $\theta \equiv \psi \wedge \Delta(\phi) \wedge \phi$ (here ϕ is the sentence that axiomatises Th(AO)).

By construction $[N,AO] \models \theta$. In order to prove $\theta \models \{p\}\ R\ \{q\}$ it suffices to show $\theta \models \{p^*\}\ R^*\ \{q^*\}$. Suppose $[\overline{N},\overline{AO}]$ is some model of θ, then $\overline{N} \models \psi \wedge \Delta(\phi)$ and $\overline{AO} \models \phi$. Let Σ be the signature of AO and denote with $\overline{N}_\Sigma$ the Σ-reduct of $\overline{N}$. Because $\psi \models \Delta(\{p^*\}R^*\{q^*\})$, $\overline{N} \models \Delta(\{p^*\}R^*\{q^*\})$ and thus $[\overline{N},\overline{N}_\Sigma] \models \{p^*\}\ R^*\ \{q^*\}$ (this uses the fact that Δ will map AO-variables in $\{p^*\}\ R^*\ \{q^*\}$ to variables different from the N-variables occurring in it).

Because $\overline{N} \models \Delta(\phi)$, $\overline{N}_\Sigma \models \phi$ and consequently $\overline{N}_\Sigma$ and $\overline{AO}$ are elementary equivalent. Using the separation of variables lemma also $[\overline{N},\overline{N}_\Sigma]$ and $[\overline{N},\overline{AO}]$ are elementary equivalent. Consequently $PC([\overline{N},\overline{N}_\Sigma]) = PC([\overline{N},\overline{AO}])$ and a fortiori $\{p^*\}\ R^*\ \{q^*\} \in PC([\overline{N},\overline{AO}])$ which had to be shown.

3.6. PROPOSITION. *There is a sound logic* L_Σ, *with* Σ *the signature of* [N,AO], *such that* L_Σ([N,AO]) *proves all asserted programs true in* [N,AO]. *(I.e.* L_Σ([N,AO]) *is complete).*

PROOF. Using definitions and notations from the preceding proof we can explicitly define L_Σ as follow:

$$L_\Sigma = \{(\psi \wedge \Delta(\phi) \wedge \phi, \{p\}R\{q\}) \mid HL_\Sigma(\psi) \vdash \Delta(\{p^*\}R^*\{q^*\})\}.$$

The completeness as well as soundness are now an immediate corollary to the previous proof.

3.7. PROPOSITION. HL([N,AO]) *is incomplete.*

PROOF. Let $\underline{n} = S^n(\underline{0})$, $\underline{n} = S'^n(\underline{0}')$ where again we use superscripts to distinguish the symbols of Σ(AO) from those in Σ(N). The diagonal of [N,AO] is the set $\{(\underline{n},\underline{n}') \mid n \in \omega\}$. Using the separation of variables lemma one finds that the diagonal is not definable in [N,AO].

Let x_1, x_2 be variables for N and y_1, y_2 be variables for AO. Consider the following programs R_1 and R_2.

R_1:
$x_2 := \underline{0}$
$y_1 := \underline{0}'$
$y_2 := \underline{0}$
while $x_2 \neq x_1$
do $x_2 := S(x_2)$
  $y_2 := S'(y_2)$
od
$x_1 := \underline{0}$

R_2:
$x_2 := \underline{0}$
$y_1 := \underline{0}$
while $y_2 \neq y_1$
do $y_1 := S'(y_1)$
  $x_1 := S(x_1)$
od

It follows that $[N,AO] \models \{\underline{true}\}R_i;R_2\{x_1 = x_2 \wedge y_1 = y_2\}$. In order to prove this fact in HL([N,AO]) we need an intermediate assertion between R_1 and R_2 equivalent to the predicate

$$x_1 = 0 \wedge y_1 = 0 \wedge \exists n(x_2 = \underline{n} \wedge y_2 = \underline{n}').$$

Definability of this predicate entails definability of the diagonal in [N,AO] thus leading to a contradiction.

4. CONCLUDING REMARKS AND OPEN QUESTIONS

We have shown that for some fixed datatype A, HL(A) is incomplete but nevertheless a sound and complete proof system $L_\Sigma(A)$ can be found. Searching for a complete special purpose logic in this fashion competes with more rigorous options like adding extra functions or relations in order to obtain an expressive structure, or with adding second order features to assertion language or proof system.

Various problems remains unsettled, we mention four of these:

(i) Let PRA = $(\omega,S,+,0)$. Is Th([N,PRA]) PC-compact?

(ii) If A satisfies conditions I and II, does there exists a sound logic L_Σ with $L_\Sigma(A)$ complete?

(iii) If A is computable and HL(A) is complete, must A be expressive?

(iv) Let K be the class of all Σ-structures A for which there exists a sound and complete $L_\Sigma(A)$. Can one find a single logic L_Σ which is uniformly complete for all $A \in K$? (If so this would be the logic of partial correctness for Σ).

REFERENCES

[1] BERGSTRA, J.A., A. CHMIELIENSKA & J. TIURYN, *Hoare's logic is incomplete when it does not have to be*, in Logics of Programs Ed. D. Kozen Spr. L.N.C.S. 131 (1981), 9-23.

[2] BERGSTRA, J.A. & J.V. TUCKER, *Hoare's logic for programming languages with two datatypes*, Math. Centre Department of Computer Science Technical Report IW 207 Amsterdam 1982.

[3] BERGSTRA, J.A. & J.V. TUCKER, *Expressiveness and the completeness of Hoare's logic*, JCSS, vol. 25, Nr. 3 (1983), p. 267-284.

[4] CHANG, C.C. & H.J. KEISLER, *Model Theory*, North Holland, Studies in logic vol. 73.

[5] COOK, S.A., *Soundness and completeness of an axiom system for program verification*, SIAM J. Computing 7 (1978), 70-90.

[6] HOARE, C.A.R., *An axiomatic basis for computer programming*, Communications ACM 12 (1967), 567-580.

[7] LAMBEK, J., *How to program an infinite abacus*, Canadian Mathematical Bulletin 4 (1961), 295-302.

[8] SHOENFIELD, J., *Mathematical logic*, Reading, Addison-Wesley (1967).

[9] WAND, M., *A new incompleteness result for Hoare's system*, J. Association Computing Machinary, 25 (1978), 168-175.

THE INTRACTABILITY OF VALIDITY IN LOGIC PROGRAMMING AND DYNAMIC LOGIC*

Howard A. Blair
Iowa State University**

1. Introduction

This is a technical note that sets out a lemma that, as we shall demonstrate, is useful in establishing the intractability of validity of various formal systems of logic, particularly program logics, and is, we feel, of interest in its own right. The lemma, which we state now, and which introduces some intellectual economy into discussions of the complexity and intractability of the validity problem for program logics, is in fact already known in mathematical logic. (See problem 8.11 in [S67].) What is new, as far as we can tell, is our method of establishing it; the lemma is a corollary of a result on the complexity of a validity decision problem in logic programming.

Lemma A: The decision problem for ω-validity for first-order logic (with or without equality) is Π^1_1-complete (provided the logic contains sufficiently many (finite) nonlogical symbols.) (The result also holds for the fragment of first-order logic consisting of all formulas of the form

$$R \to \sim A$$

where A is a variable-free atomic formula, and R is the fixed finite extension of iff-Q to be described below.)

This result (with equality) is derivable from the ω-completeness theorem, which, in turn, is derivable from the Henkin-Orey omitting types theorem. For the details of this tale see any of [M76,thm 30.10], [S67,sec 8.5, and prob. 8.11], [CK73, sec 2.2], [He54], or [O56]. The lemma is also implicit in results given in [Hi 78, thm 5.16]. The interest in this lemma in the present context lies in its

---

*The preparation of this paper was supported under a grant from the DOE administered by the DEP of Argonne National Laboratory.

**Author's current address: University of Connecticut, EECS Dept., U-157 Storrs, Conn. 06268.

utility and accessability. It is subsumed by far more thorough results obtained in the systematic study [MD81]. These results, however, depend upon techniques of mathematical logic that take one significantly afield from the present subject. In a larger context this is all to the good; we nevertheless believe that the lemma as it stands is fairly useful, has a certain simplicity, and has a rather straightforward proof. Of course, one generally cannot expect a magical elimination of the intracacy in the proofs of such results. Rather, we claim that we have backed up the intracacy to a lemma which is not tied to a particular form of program logic.

2. Validity in Logic Programming.

Validity notions, and consequently validity decision problems, arise in several ways in connection with logic programming. Full treatments of these concepts are given in [L82], [B80], [AVE82], [JLL83], [LM83], and [B82]. All them however are based, at least in part, on restricting validity to validity in Herbrand structures in which the logic program is valid. By an ω-structure for a logic we mean a structure in which the universe of individuals is exhausted by the variable-free terms of the logic. This departs from the standard definition of ω-structure in which every individual is the value of a numeral corresponding to each of the natural numbers, and where each numeral is a term in the logic. This departure is justified, we believe, by the simplicity and ease of application of lemma (A). An Herbrand structure is an ω-structure in which distinct variable-free terms name distinct individuals. A formula of a logic is ω-valid if it is valid in all ω-structures for that logic, and similarly for Herbrand validity. A brief example will serve to illustrate how the various points of view on validity come about in logic programming. We employ conventional logic notation rather than the procedural notation popular in the logic programming literature. The following two Horn clauses are intended to define the append relation among lists.

$$\forall L(\text{append}(\text{nil},L,L)).$$

$$\forall X\ \forall L\ \forall M\ \forall N(\text{append}(L,M,N) \rightarrow \text{append}(\text{cons}(X,L),M,\text{cons}(X,N))).$$

We are using lower case identifiers as constant, function, and relation symbols; upper case identifiers are variables. These two clauses are interpreted as a program by attempting to show constructively that various existential closures of conjunctions of atomic formulas are provable from these clauses and logical axioms. For example,

$$\exists L(\text{append}(\text{cons}(a,\text{nil}),L,\text{cons}(a,\text{cons}(b,\text{nil}))))$$

has a proof (by linear resolution) from the two clauses that contains a construction of the list cons(b,nil) that demonstrates such a list L exists. For a complete exposition of linear resolution and its application to logic programming see either [K79a] or [K79b]. Suppose that we seek to 'solve'

$$\exists L(\text{append}(L,L,\text{cons}(a,\text{cons}(b,\text{nil})))).$$

Linear resolution is complete for the Horn clause fragment of logic, [H74] and the application of linear resolution will in this case reveal that no proof by linear resolution is possible, hence no proof is possible. If we are thinking in the context of, say, Lisp, that there is no solution, then it is safe to infer

(1) $\sim\exists L(\text{append}(L,L,\text{cons}(a,\text{cons}(b,\text{nil})))),$

but of course this is not a logically valid inference. The problem is to provide an appropriate notion of validity for logic programming for such inferences to be valid. If we have in mind that the Horn clauses of a logic program are to be interpreted solely as an inductive definition, then the clauses will define a r.e. set of closed instances of the relations present in the clauses. In the preceding example the two Horn clauses define the set of all correct instances of the append relation (with respect to some fixed set of atoms.) Generally, the clauses of a logic program construed as an inductive definition will define a strictly r.e. set. Such a set determines the smallest Herbrand model of the logic program, and validity can be construed as the ordinary notion of validity in this model. The validity decision problem is then equivalent to deciding truth in the natural numbers. Notice that in the preceding example the extremal constraint that one expects as part of an inductive definition is implicitly used when inferring (1). A slightly relaxed view of the extremal constraints associated with logic programs yields yet another notion of validity; the one that leads to the lemma.

To approximate the extremal constraint we can restrict our attention to only those Herbrand models of the logic program which satisfy the "iff version" of it. (cf. [C80], [B80], [AVE82].) For example, consider the following pathological program, with a "useless" clause.

(P) $m(a).$

$n(0).$

$\forall X(n(X) \rightarrow n(s(X))).$

$\forall X(n(X) \rightarrow n(X)).$

The "iff version" is

$$\forall X[m(X) \leftrightarrow X = a]$$
$$\forall X[n(X) \leftrightarrow \exists Y(X = s(Y) \,\&\, n(Y)) \vee X = 0 \vee n(X)].$$

$\{m(a)\} \cup \{n(s^k(0) \mid k \in \omega\}$ is the smallest Herbrand model of (P), and satisfies the "iff version" of (P).

$\{m(a)\} \cup \{n(s^k(a)) \mid k \in \omega\} \cup \{n^k(0) \mid k \in \omega\}$ also satisfies the "iff version" of (P).

The "iff-version" will of course in general not capture the inductive extremal constraint. The constraint restricts the only satisfying Herbrand model to the minimal structure which is not the only satisfying structure of the "iff version". There is controversy over which notion of validity is "natural" or significant for logic programming. It is our view that no particular choice should be singled out as the "right" one. The various concepts of validity should be studied for there intrinsic interest, theoretical utility (as is the case here,) and as their utility for logic programming is seen to arise.

It can be shown (cf. [AVE82], [L82], [B83]) that the union of all of the Herbrand models of the "iff version" of a logic program P (iff-P) is itself an Herbrand model of iff-P. Our latter notion of validity is that a formula is valid with repect to logic program P iff it is valid (in the usual sense) in all Herbrand models of iff-P. Consequently, a variable-free instance of the negation of an atomic formula A is valid with respect to P iff A is not in the set of atomic formulas determining the maximum Herbrand model of iff-P. The decision problem for membership in this set provides a lower bound on the complexity of the validity decision problem for logic programming associated with this notion of validity. [B83] gives a logic program Q for which this is shown to be Π^1_1-complete.

A recursion-theoretic lemma provides the foundation for constructing Q. The intracacy which one would expect to appear at some point in the full proof of lemma (A) occurs in the proof of this underlying recursion-theoretic lemma. Below, we briefly outline the construction of Q. For details, see [B83]. For notation, see [R67].

3. The Proof.

Associate with logic program P an operator T_P: $2^H \to 2^H$ where H is the set of all variable-free atomic formulas in the language of P, defined by

$A \in T_P(I) \leftrightarrow$ there is a variable-free instance

$$B_1 \ \& \ \ldots \ \& \ B_n \to A$$

of a clause in P such that $\{B_1, \ldots, B_n\} \subseteq I$.

If we view the set of all variable-free instances of the clauses in P as production rules, T_P applies these production rules to I^*. T_P is a monotonic and continuous operator on 2^H. Define

$$T_P^0 = H , \qquad T_P^y = \bigcap_{x<y} T_P(T_P^x)$$

for all ordinals y. By a cardinality argument, in the descent from H, T_P reaches a fixed point. (The fixed point occurs at $y \leq \omega_1^{ck}$. The logic program Q we will construct achieves the bound.) By simulating a Turing machine, choose P such that

i) $T_P^{\omega} = T_P^{\omega+1}$

ii) $w(s^m(0),s^n(0)) \in H - T_P^{\omega} \leftrightarrow \langle m,n\rangle \in W_z$.

where $\langle .,. \rangle$ is a fixed primitive recursive pairing function. The choice of P depends on z.

Obtain Q from P by adding the following clauses. (We abbreviate by omitting universal quantifiers.)

$$n(X) \to n(s(X))$$
$$n(X) \to a(Y)$$
$$a(X) \ \& \ w(X,Y) \to a(Y),$$

where n and a are new relation symbols. For each set S of natural numbers define Z_S by

$$Z_S\,(X) = \{y \in \mathbb{N} \mid \langle x,y\rangle \in S \ \& \ x \in X, \text{ for some } x\}.$$

Define, as we similarly did for T_P,

$$Z_S^0 = \mathbb{N}\ , \qquad Z_S^y = \bigcap_{x<y} Z_S(Z_S^x)$$

It follows that

(2) $\quad a(s^y(0)) \in T_Q^{\omega+x} \leftrightarrow y \in Z_{N-W_z}^x$

for each ordinal $x > 0$.

Let X be a set and let $F : 2^X \to 2^X$. Define F-dual by

(3) $\quad F\text{-dual}(Y) = X - F(X - Y).$

Following [R67] define

$$\mathrm{Dom}(X) = \{n \mid W_n \subseteq X\}$$

$$\mathrm{Dom}^0 = \emptyset, \qquad \mathrm{Dom}^y = \bigcup_{x<y} \mathrm{Dom}(\mathrm{Dom}^x)\ , \text{ for all ordinals } x,\ y.$$

$\mathrm{Dom}^{\omega_1^{ck}}$ is Π_1^1-complete (cf. [R67,sec 11.9, and prob 11.63].)
Choose S by

$$x \in S \leftrightarrow (x)_0 \in W_{f((x)_1)}.$$

Then

$$Z_S\text{-dual}(X) = f^{-1}\mathrm{Dom}(X)\ .$$

For each ordinal x define $(f^{-1}Dom)^x$ in the same way as we defined Dom^x.

Lemma B: There exist 1-1 recursive functions f and g such that

i) $W_{f(x)}$ is recursive, and $W_{g(x)} = N - W_{f(x)}$ for every x, and

ii) $Dom^y = (f^{-1}Dom)^y$, for all ordinals y.

Proof: cf. [B83]. []

By lemma B and (2) we can choose Q such that

$$a(s^y(0)) \in T_Q^{\omega_1^{ck}} \leftrightarrow y \in N - Dom^{\omega_1^{ck}}$$

Finally, the fixed point of T_Q reached in the descent from H is the maximun Herbrand model of iff-Q. It follows that the validity decision problem we are considering for logic programming is Π_1^1-complete. We can now prove lemma A.

It suffices to give a finitely axiomatized theory that has a Π_1^1-complete ω-validity decision problem. iff-Q, the iff-version of a logic program, is a finitely axiomatized theory. If iff-Q can be extended to a finitely axiomatized theory which eliminates the non-Herbrand ω-models of iff-Q, the proof will be complete. We have only to give the axioms of the extension.

i) For each pair of distinct function symbols f, g of arities m, n $\geq$ 0, the axiom

$$\sim(f(x_1, \ldots, x_m) = g(y_1, \ldots, y_n))$$

ii) For each function symbol f of arity n, the axiom

$$f(x_1, \ldots, x_n) = f(y_1, \ldots, y_n) \rightarrow$$
$$x_1 = y_1 \ \& \ \ldots \ \& \ x_n = y_n.$$

iii) Axioms for a strict partial order < (a new relation symbol.)

iv) For each function symbol of arity $n > 0$, the axioms

$$x_1 < f(x_1, \ldots, x_n)$$
$$\vdots$$
$$x_n < f(x_1, \ldots, x_n) .$$

As there are only finitely many nonlogical symbols in Q, and as the axioms of the strict partial order are finite in number, the extension adds only finitley many new axioms to iff-Q. It is clear that the axioms pertaining to < enable us to prove all instances of

$$\sim(t = x)$$

where x occurs in term t. Thus all ω-models of the extended theory are Herbrand models. Moreover, each Herbrand model of the extended theory is given by the disjoint union of an Herbrand model of iff-Q and a set of variable-free instances of $x < y$. Consequently, the ω-validity decision problem associated with the extended finitely axiomatized theory remains Π^1_1-complete. This completes the proof of lemma A.

For our application to program logics, it is critical to take note of the fact that in the logic program P that simulates a Turing machine, and from which we derived Q, and hence the extended theory, only unary function symbols occur. The Π^1_1-completeness result attributed to Meyer given in [Ha79] exhibits only a single unary function symbol in the program set of the 'smallest' fragment of dynamic logic displayed for which Π^1_1-completeness of its validity problem holds. Logic program P however contains two unary function symbols, s and 'blank'. Thus our proof of lemma A demands the occurrence of at least two unary function symbols in the first-order logic, however no other function symbols need occur. Of course, the axioms in the extended theory are substantially simplified. We do not see how to push the result down to the occurrence of only one unary function symbol by this approach from logic programming.

4. Applications to Program Logics.

We shall in this section apply lemma A to easily show the well known result that first-order DL has a Π^1_1-complete validity decision problem. We intend in a future technical note to give additional applications.

Consider first-order dynamic logic. In what follows the underlying first-order language is assumed to have at least two unary function symbols.

Lemma C: Let L be the underlying first-order language of first-order dynamic logic DL. Let q be a program which nondeterministically assigns to X any one of the values of the Herbrand terms of L which contain only unary function symbols. Then

$$\forall Y\langle q\rangle(Y = X)$$

is valid in all, and only, the ω-structures for the fragment of DL containing only unary function symbols. (We mean by ω-structure, in the context of DL, a simple universe in which the individuals are exhausted by the variable-free terms (cf. [Ha79]) .))

Proof: Let U be an ω-structure as required by the hypotheses of the lemma, and let i be the value of Y in, say, state s. q, by definition, can reach a state t such that the value of X in t is i. Thus

(4) $\quad t \models Y = X$.

Hence

(5) $\quad s \models \langle q\rangle(Y = X)$,

and

(6) $\quad \models_U \forall Y\langle q\rangle(Y = X)$.

Conversely, suppose (6). Let i be an individual in U. Let s be any state in U for which val(Y) = i. Then (5), and hence (4), and by the definition of q, i is the value of some Herbrand term.

[]

Theorem 1: Let F be any effective fragment of DL containing all formulas of the form

(7) $\forall Y\langle q\rangle(Y = X) \to (R \to \sim A)$,

where A is atomic, and R is the conjunction of the universal closures of the extension of iff-Q. Then F has a Π^1_1-complete validity decision problem.

Proof: Immediate from lemmas A and C.

[]

Corollary: First-order DL has a Π^1_1-complete validity decision problem.

[]

References

[AVE82] Apt, K. R., and M. H. Van Emden. "Contributions to the Theory of Logic Programming," JACM vol 29,no 3, (July, 1982) pp. 841-862.

[B80] Blair, H. A., The Recursion-theoretic Complexity of the Fixed-Point Semantics of Definite Sentences, Ph.D. thesis, Syracuse University, 1980.

[B82] Blair, H. A., "The Undecidability of Two Completeness Notions for the "Negation as Failure" Rule in Logic Programming," Proceedings of the First International Logic Programming Conference, Marseille, 1982.

[B83] Blair, H. A., "The Recursion-theoretic Complexity of the Semantics of Predicate Logic as a Programming Language," Information and Control. (to appear.)

[C80] Clark, K. L., "Negation as Failure," Logic and Data Bases, Gallaire & Minker, eds., Plenum, New York, 1980, pp. 55-76.

[CK73] Chang, C. C., and H. J. Keisler, Model Theory, North-Holland, Amsterdam, 1973.

[Ha79] Harel, D., First-Order Dynamic Logic, Lecture Notes in Computer Science, no. 68, Springer-Verlag, New York, 1979.

[He54] Henkin, L., "A Generalization of the Concept of ω-Consistency," Journal of Symbolic Logic, vol 19, no 3, (Sept. 1954) pp. 183-196.

[H74] Hill, R. LUSH-Resolution and Its Completeness, DCL Memo 78, University of Edinburgh, 1974.

[Hi78] Hinman, P. G. Recursion-theoretic Hierarchies, Springer-Verlag, Berlin, 1978.

[JLL83] Jaffar, J., J-L. Lassez, and J. W. Lloyd, Completeness of the Negation as Failure Rule, Technical Report 83/1, The University of Melbourne, 1983.

[K79a] Kowalski, R. A., "Algorithm = Logic + Control," CACM, vol 22, no 7, (July, 79) pp. 424-436.

[K79b] Kowalski, R. A., Logic for Problem Solving, Elsevier North-Holland, New York, 1979.

[LM83] Lassez, J-L., and M. J. Maher, Optimal Fixed Points of Logic Programs, Technical Report 83/4, The University of Melbourne, 1983.

[L82] Lloyd, J. W., Foundations of Logic Programming, Technical Report 82/7 The University of Melbourne, 1982.

[M76] Monk, J. D., Mathematical Logic, Springer-Verlag, New York, 1976.

[MD83] Manders, K. L., and R. F. Daley, "The Complexity of the Validity Problem for Dynamic Logic," Information and Control. (to appear.)

[O56] Orey, S., "On w-Consistency and Related Properties," Journal of Symbolic Logic, vol 21, no 3, (Sept. 1956) pp. 246-254.

[R67] Rogers, H., Theory of Recursive Functions and Effective Computability, McGraw-Hill, New York, 1967.

[S67] Shoenfield, J. R., Mathematical Logic, Addison-Wesley, Reading, Mass., 1967.

A SEMANTICS AND PROOF SYSTEM FOR COMMUNICATING PROCESSES.

Stephen D. Brookes
Carnegie-Mellon University
Pittsburgh
Pennsylvania 15213
USA.

0. Introduction.

In this paper we describe a semantic model for communicating sequential processes extending the so-called *failures* model of CSP which appears in [B1,2], [HBR] and [R]. We also give a proof system for proving semantic equivalence of processes. This provides an axiomatic characterisation of our semantics.

The failures model of processes represents the behaviour of a sequential process as a set of failures, each of which is a finite piece of information about a possible behaviour of the process. A failure consists of a *trace,* recording a possible finite sequence of actions, and a *refusal set,* representing a set of events which the process *may* decide to refuse at the next step. The idea of using traces to represent process behaviour appeared in [H2], where the inability of traces alone to model deadlock was also noted.

Each failure is essentially a potential result of a nondeterministic decision by the process. This model is well suited to reasoning about the potential deadlock behaviour of a process, since the possibility of deadlock is represented explicitly by the ability to refuse all sets of actions. As described in the above references, the failures model can be given the structure of a complete semi-lattice under the superset ordering, which corresponds to a measure of nondeterminism: if the failure set of process P contains as a subset the failure set of Q, then every possible nondeterministic decision of Q is also possible for P, and we may say that P is more nondeterministic than Q. Since the space of failure sets, under this ordering, has the structure of a complete semi-lattice, we know that limits of chains of processes exists, and every non-empty set of processes has a greatest lower bound. Moreover, applying well-known arguments of fixed point theory (see [LNS] for example), we know that every monotone function on failure sets has a least fixed point; we may therefore give semantics to recursively defined processes, provided that the operations used in constructing processes are all monotone. This is the case for a wide variety of operations whose definitions are suggested by CSP.

The failures model has been used to give a semantics to a language based on Hoare's CSP in [HBR]. However, there are some undesirable aspects to this model. Notably, the behaviour of processes which may *diverge,* or engage in *infinite internal chatter,* is not adequately modelled by a failure set. Internal chatter is the phenomenon of a process continuously engaging in a sequence of actions which are internal or hidden from the environment in which the process is operating: that environment has no control or influence on the process while the process is continuing to perform invisible actions, and the process may never respond to requests from the environment. This type of behaviour arises when, for example, two processes are connected and allowed to communicate along a channel which the outside world cannot affect; the communications which may occur along this channel are hidden from the environment. If there is a potentially unbounded sequence of communications along the hidden link then the two processes may indulge in infinite internal chatter.

Attempts were made to treat divergent behaviour by identifying it with either deadlock (STOP) or wholly arbitrary behaviour (CHAOS), as described in [HBR,B,R], but none of these is satisfactory. It is possible to extend the failures model in a fairly straightforward way which does model divergence more satisfyingly. The new model, whose development first appeared in [B1,R], still enjoys the order-theoretical properties of a complete semi-lattice, and is therefore well suited to provide a semantic basis for a language of processes. Moreover, we find that we can axiomatize the semantics of a language like CSP by giving a set of axioms and inference rules sound and complete for proving semantic equivalence of terms in the language. Thus we will describe a semantics for processes in both the denotational style and axiomatically.

The language with which we are concerned is a derivative of Hoare's CSP [H1]. To begin with, we will discuss a simple sub-language called here FCSP (for "Finite CSP"), whose terms will denote processes with finite behaviour. For these terms the possibility of divergence does not exist, and we will introduce a failure semantics for this language. The associated logical language will contain assertions of the form $P \sqsubseteq Q$ or $P \equiv Q$, with the interpretation that P semantically approximates Q or is semantically equivalent to Q. We will give a set of axioms and inference rules for proving such assertions, and show that the system is both sound and complete; under the given interpretation of assertions, every provable assertion is true and every true assertion is provable.

Next we make the transition to a more general language of processes, by allowing recursive terms. Now terms may denote processes with infinite behaviour. We show how to modify the previous proof system to obtain a new system complete and sound for the larger language. Essentially, we use the well known ideas of *syntactic approximation* of terms, and use the fact that the failure semantics of an infinite process is uniquely determined by its finite syntactic approximants. A new inference rule is added which states this fact and basically allows us to reason about infinite terms by manipulating their finite approximations. Crucial to this work is the fact that all of the process operations in the language are continuous with respect to the nondeterminism ordering. Similar techniques were used by Hennessy and de Nicola [HN] to give a proof system for Milner's language CCS [M].

Bearing in mind our earlier problems with the notion of *divergence,* we have made the proof system sufficiently general to cope with divergent processes, by adding to the language a term $\perp$ (representing divergence) and augmenting the failure set model with a divergence set component. A similar augmentation of the failures model was suggested by Roscoe [R]. The special case of well-behaved (divergence-free) processes turns out to correspond to the sublanguage of all terms in which no recursive subterm has an unguarded occurrence of its bound variable, and in which there is no sub-term $\perp$. As a corollary, the proof system is also complete for the old failures ordering on well-behaved processes.

Throughout this paper we will use P, Q, R to stand for terms in the variant of CSP currently under consideration. We are not necessarily assuming that the universal alphabet Σ is finite, but every term will only use a finite set of events. As usual, refusal sets are finite; we use $p\Sigma$ for the finite powerset of Σ. We will use X, Y, Z to range over $p\Sigma$. Finally, s, t, u range over Σ^* and a, b, c over Σ.

1. A simple subset of CSP.

Let FCSP (Finite CSP) be the language generated by the following syntax:

$$P ::= \text{STOP} \mid (a \to P) \mid P \Box P \mid P \sqcap P,$$

where a ranges over Σ. STOP denotes a process which is unable to perform any event, and represents deadlock. The process $(a \to P)$ must first perform event a and thereafter behaves like P. The combinator $\Box$ is a *conditional choice* operator: $P \Box Q$ can behave either like P or like Q, and the environment of the process can influence this choice by offering an action at the first step which only one of the two is able to perform then. In contrast, $P \sqcap Q$ behaves either like P or like Q but does not allow its decision to be affected by the desires of its environment; this is an *uncontrollable* choice. (The reader familiar with

Hoare's CSP will recognise the connection with guarded commands: the two forms of choice arise when the guards are communications or purely boolean.)

The semantic function $\mathcal{F}$ maps terms to failure sets, and is defined by structural induction as usual, one clause for each syntactic construct of FCSP. This is a *denotational* semantic definition, because the semantics of a term is built up from the semantics of its syntactic constituents.

$$\mathcal{F}[\![\mathrm{STOP}]\!] = \{(\langle\rangle, X) \mid X \subseteq \Sigma\}$$

$$\mathcal{F}[\![a \to P]\!] = \{(\langle\rangle, X) \mid a \notin X\} \cup \{(as, X) \mid (s, X) \in \mathcal{F}[\![P]\!]\}$$

$$\mathcal{F}[\![P \,\Box\, Q]\!] = \{(\langle\rangle, X) \mid (\langle\rangle, X) \in \mathcal{F}[\![P]\!] \cap \mathcal{F}[\![Q]\!]\} \\ \cup \{(s, X) \mid s \neq \langle\rangle \;\&\; (s, X) \in \mathcal{F}[\![P]\!] \cup \mathcal{F}[\![Q]\!]\}$$

$$\mathcal{F}[\![P \sqcap Q]\!] = \mathcal{F}[\![P]\!] \cup \mathcal{F}[\![Q]\!].$$

Note that these clauses capture the intuitive definitions of the syntactic constructs stated above. For instance, $(a \to P)$ must initially perform a because this event does not belong to any of the refusal sets of $\mathcal{F}[\![a \to P]\!]$; and $P \,\Box\, Q$ refuses a set initially only if both P and Q can refuse it, but once an event has occurred it behaves either like P or like Q.

We will use Φ to stand for a failure set. Recall that in [HBR] a failure set is a subset of $\Sigma^* \times p\Sigma$ such that

(i) $\mathrm{dom}(\Phi)$ is non-empty and prefix-closed,
(ii) $(s, X) \in \Phi, Y \subseteq X \Rightarrow (s, Y) \in \Phi$,
(iii) $(s, X) \in \Phi, (sa, \emptyset) \notin \Phi \Rightarrow (s, X \cup \{a\}) \in \Phi$.

These conditions state that (i) the empty trace is always a possible trace of a process, and whenever st is a trace of a process so is s; (ii) if P can refuse X after doing s then at the same time it could refuse any subset Y of X; (iii) an impossible event can always be included in a refusal set. These are intuitively reasonable properties. It is easy to check that our semantic function does indeed map terms to failure sets satisfying these conditions.

The semantic ordering on failure sets is $\Phi_1 \sqsubseteq \Phi_2 \Leftrightarrow \Phi_1 \supseteq \Phi_2$. We will write $P \sqsubseteq Q$ to mean $\mathcal{F}[\![P]\!] \sqsubseteq \mathcal{F}[\![Q]\!]$, where no confusion can arise. In case this relation holds we say that P is at least as nondeterministic as Q, since failures represent consequences of nondeterministic decisions by a process.

Now we introduce the proof system. The logical language is built from FCSP terms and two binary relation symbols $\sqsubseteq$ and $\equiv$. Each formula in the language has the form $P \sqsubseteq Q$ or $P \equiv Q$. The intended interpretation of $P \sqsubseteq Q$ is that P semantically approximates Q, and $\equiv$ is interpreted as semantic identity.

We include axioms on idempotence, symmetry, associativity of $\sqcap$ and $\Box$, distribution of these two operators over each other, and some interactions with prefixing. The inference rules assert monotonicity of the operators with respect to $\sqsubseteq$, and state that $\sqsubseteq$ is a partial order and $\equiv$ the associated equivalence. The following table lists the axioms and rules:

(A1) $$P \sqcap P \equiv P$$

(A2) $$P \Box P \equiv P$$

(A3) $$P \sqcap Q \equiv Q \sqcap P$$

(A4) $$P \Box Q \equiv Q \Box P$$

(A5) $$P \sqcap (Q \sqcap R) \equiv (P \sqcap Q) \sqcap R$$

(A6) $$P \Box (Q \Box R) \equiv (P \Box Q) \Box R$$

(A7) $$P \sqcap (Q \Box R) \equiv (P \sqcap Q) \Box (P \sqcap R)$$

(A8) $$P \Box (Q \sqcap R) \equiv (P \Box Q) \sqcap (P \Box R)$$

(A9) $$P \Box \mathrm{STOP} \equiv P$$

(A10) $$P \sqcap Q \sqsubseteq P$$

(A11) $$(a \rightarrow P) \sqcap (a \rightarrow Q) \equiv (a \rightarrow P \sqcap Q)$$

(A12) $$(a \rightarrow P) \Box (a \rightarrow Q) \equiv (a \rightarrow P \sqcap Q)$$

(O1) $$\frac{P \sqsubseteq Q \sqsubseteq P}{P \equiv Q}$$

(O2) $$\frac{P \equiv Q}{P \sqsubseteq Q \sqsubseteq P}$$

(O3) $$\frac{P \sqsubseteq Q \sqsubseteq R}{P \sqsubseteq R}$$

(M1) $$\frac{P \sqsubseteq Q}{(a \rightarrow P) \sqsubseteq (a \rightarrow Q)}$$

(M2) $$\frac{P_1 \sqsubseteq Q_1 \ \& \ P_2 \sqsubseteq Q_2}{P_1 \sqcap P_2 \sqsubseteq Q_1 \sqcap Q_2}$$

(M3) $$\frac{P_1 \sqsubseteq Q_1 \ \& \ P_2 \sqsubseteq Q_2}{P_1 \Box P_2 \sqsubseteq Q_1 \Box Q_2}$$

Table 1

Axioms for FCSP

Soundness.

In order to prove soundness of the system, it is enough to show that all the axioms are valid and that the inference rules are sound. Each axiom has already appeared in [HBR] and [B1], where proofs of validity were given; similarly all of the operators were shown to be monotonic, so the inference rules (M1)-(M3) are valid. For details the reader is referred to [B1]. We know, therefore, that every provable formula is true. We write $\vdash P \sqsubseteq Q$ when the formula $P \sqsubseteq Q$ is provable. The following theorem states that the proof system is *sound.*

Theorem 1.1: For all terms P,Q

$$\vdash P \sqsubseteq Q \Rightarrow \mathcal{F}[\![P]\!] \supseteq \mathcal{F}[\![Q]\!].$$

Derived laws.

The following laws are derivable, and hence valid. They will be useful in establishing completeness. The first states the connection between nondeterministic choice and the ordering. The second says that nondeterministic choice allows more failures in general than conditional choice, in accordance with our intuition and earlier results on these operators. These laws will be heavily used in establishing the existence of normal forms.

Lemma 1.2:

The following formulae can be derived in the above proof system:

$$\begin{array}{ll} \text{(D1)} & P \sqcap Q \equiv P \Leftrightarrow P \sqsubseteq Q \\ \text{(D2)} & P \sqcap Q \sqsubseteq P \square Q \\ \text{(D3)} & P \sqcap (Q \square R) \sqsubseteq P \square Q. \end{array}$$

Proof. For (D1) we have

$$\vdash P \sqcap Q \sqsubseteq P$$

by (A10). And if we assume $P \sqsubseteq Q$ is provable, we have:

$$P \sqsubseteq Q \vdash P \sqcap P \sqsubseteq P \sqsubseteq Q,$$

by (M2). The result follows by (A1) and (O1).

For (D2):

$$\begin{aligned} (P \sqcap Q) \sqcap (P \square Q) &\equiv ((P \sqcap Q) \sqcap P) \square ((P \sqcap Q) \sqcap Q) && \text{by (A7)} \\ &\equiv (P \sqcap Q) \square (P \sqcap Q) && \text{by (A1)} \\ &\equiv P \sqcap Q && \text{by (A2)} \end{aligned}$$

The result follows from (D1).

For (D3) we have

$$\begin{aligned} P \sqcap (Q \square R) &\equiv (P \sqcap Q) \square (P \sqcap R) && \text{by (A7)} \\ &\sqsubseteq (P \square Q) \square P && \text{by (M3), (A10) and (D2)} \\ &\equiv (P \square P) \square Q && \text{by (A6)} \\ &\equiv P \square Q && \text{by (A2)} \end{aligned}$$

That completes the proof. ∎

Completeness.

We will show that whenever the failures of P include the failures of Q the formula $P \sqsubseteq Q$ is provable. For the proof we use a ***normal form*** theorem. We define a class of normal forms and show that every term is provably equivalent to a unique term in normal form. Moreover, we show that whenever the failures of one normal form include the failures of another, the corresponding formula is provable.

Essentially, a normal form will be a term with a ***uniform*** structure, rather like a nondeterministic composition of a collection of ***guarded*** terms. In order to get uniqueness of normal forms we will require certain closure conditions on the sets of guards appearing at each position in the term; these conditions amount to a ***convexity*** requirement. In addition, we will require that in a normal form every subterm guarded by a particular event be identical and also in normal form. This means that every normal form is itself built up from normal forms in a simple way that facilitates proofs. Formally, these constraints are defined as follows.

Normal forms.

Definition 1.3: A subset $\mathcal{B}$ is ***convex*** iff it is non-empty and

(i) $A, B \in \mathcal{B} \Rightarrow A \cup B \in \mathcal{B}$,

(ii) $A, C \in \mathcal{B} \;\&\; A \subseteq B \subseteq C \Rightarrow B \in \mathcal{B}$.

Note that a convex set is closed under (finite) unions as well as the convex containment relation (ii). We will write con($\mathcal{B}$) for the smallest convex set containing $\mathcal{B}$, and refer to the ***convex closure*** of $\mathcal{B}$.

There are clear connections between this form of convexity on sets of sets of events and the "saturated" condition of [HN], a fact which is not surprising in view of the close connections which can be found between their models and ours (see [B1,2] for example).

Examples.

Example 1. The set $\mathcal{A} = \{\emptyset, \{a, b\}\}$ is not convex, because

$$\emptyset \subseteq \{a\} \subseteq \{a, b\}$$

but $\{a\}$ is not in $\mathcal{A}$.

Example 2. The set $\mathcal{B} = \{\emptyset, \{a\}, \{b\}\}$ is not convex, because it does not contain $\{a, b\}$.

Example 3. The smallest convex set containing $\mathcal{A}$ and $\mathcal{B}$ is the set

$$\mathcal{C} = \{\emptyset, \{a\}, \{b\}, \{a, b\}\}.$$

We have con($\mathcal{A}$) = con($\mathcal{B}$) = $\mathcal{C}$.

Example 4. For any set $B \subseteq \Sigma$ the powerset of B is convex.

Now we can define normal form:

Definition 1.4: A term P is in ***normal form*** iff it has the structure

either $P = \text{STOP}$

or $\quad P = \sqcap_{B \in \mathcal{B}} \Box_{b \in B}(b \to P_b)$

for some convex set $\mathcal{B}$, and each P_b is also in normal form.

Note that although a normal form P may have "disjuncts" P_B and P_C with some initials in common, say

$$P_B = \Box_{b \in B}(b \to P_b)$$
$$P_C = \Box_{c \in C}(c \to P_c)$$

the definition forces these two processes to have identical derivatives P_a for all $a \in B \cap C$. Some examples will help.

Examples.

Example 5. $P = \text{STOP} \sqcap (a \to \text{STOP})$ is in normal form: here $\mathcal{B}$ is the convex set $\{\emptyset, \{a\}\}$ and $P_a = \text{STOP}$.

Example 6. $P = (a \to (b \to \text{STOP})) \sqcap ((a \to \text{STOP}) \Box (b \to \text{STOP}))$ is not in normal form, because the two subterms guarded by a are distinct.

The next result is the basis of our completeness theorem.

Lemma 1.5: Any term P can be transformed using the proof system into a normal form.

Proof. By induction on the length of the term.

The base case, when $P = \text{STOP}$, is trivial; the case when $P = (a \to Q)$ is also straightforward. In the remaining two cases, we must show that if P and Q are normal forms then $P \sqcap Q$ and $P \Box Q$ can be but into normal form. To this end, suppose the two normal forms are:

$$P = \sqcap_{B \in \mathcal{B}} \Box_{b \in B}(b \to P_b)$$
$$Q = \sqcap_{C \in \mathcal{C}} \Box_{c \in C}(c \to Q_c).$$

Write $P_B = \Box_{b \in B}(b \to P_b)$ and $Q_C = \Box_{c \in C}(c \to Q_c)$, so that

$$P = \sqcap_{B \in \mathcal{B}} P_B$$
$$Q = \sqcap_{C \in \mathcal{C}} Q_C.$$

Then it is easily provable that

$$P \sqcap Q \equiv \sqcap_{B \in \mathcal{B}} \sqcap_{C \in \mathcal{C}} P_B \sqcap Q_C.$$

Let $\mathcal{A} = \mathcal{B} \cup \mathcal{C}$, and define the terms R_a for $a \in \mathcal{A}$ by:

$$\begin{aligned} R_a &= P_a && \text{if } a \in B - C, \\ &= Q_a && \text{if } a \in C - B, \\ &= P_a \sqcap Q_a && \text{if } a \in B \cap C. \end{aligned}$$

Using the obvious notation, it is clear that the statements

$$P_B \sqcap Q_C \equiv R_B \sqcap R_C$$

are provable, and hence that

$$\vdash P \sqcap Q \equiv \sqcap_{A \in \mathcal{A}} R_A.$$

To complete the proof in this case we use the convexity laws to replace $\mathcal{A}$ by its convex closure. The following identities are deducible from (D1)-(D3) and show that replacement of $\mathcal{A}$ by $\text{con}(\mathcal{A})$ is valid here:

$$\begin{aligned} R_A \sqcap R_B &\equiv R_A \sqcap R_B \sqcap R_{A \cup B}, \\ R_A \sqcap R_C &\equiv R_A \sqcap R_B \sqcap R_C, && \text{if } A \subseteq B \subseteq C. \end{aligned}$$

Finally we must reduce $P \Box Q$ to normal form. Again it is easy to show that

$$\vdash P \Box Q \equiv \sqcap_{B \in \mathcal{B}} \sqcap_{C \in \mathcal{C}} P_B \Box Q_C,$$

and (using the same notation as above) that

$$\vdash P_B \Box Q_C \equiv R_{B \cup C}.$$

It follows that

$$\vdash P \Box Q \equiv \sqcap_{A \in \mathcal{A}} \Box_{a \in A}(a \to R_a),$$

where $\mathcal{A} = \text{con}(\{B \cup C \mid B \in \mathcal{B}, C \in \mathcal{C}\})$. ∎

The following result states that every true statement about normal forms is provable.

Lemma 1.6: Given two normal forms P^* and Q^*,

$$\mathcal{F}[\![P^*]\!] \supseteq \mathcal{F}[\![Q^*]\!] \Rightarrow \vdash P^* \sqsubseteq Q^*.$$

Proof. Let the two normal forms be

$$P^* = \sqcap_{B\in\mathcal{B}} \Box_{b\in B}(b \to P_b)$$
$$Q^* = \sqcap_{C\in\mathcal{C}} \Box_{c\in C}(c \to Q_c).$$

Write P_B and Q_C for the subterms:

$$P_B = \Box_{b\in B}(b \to P_b),$$
$$Q_C = \Box_{c\in C}(c \to Q_c).$$

Then $P^* = \sqcap_{B\in\mathcal{B}} P_B$ and $Q^* = \sqcap_{C\in\mathcal{C}} Q_C$.

By definition of normal form, the sets $\mathcal{B}$ and $\mathcal{C}$ are convex, and each P_b and Q_c is also in normal form. We will use an induction on the length of the normal forms. The base case, when both P and Q have zero length, is trivial; both terms are STOP. For the inductive step, we argue as follows. First we show that

$$\mathcal{F}[\![P^*]\!] \supseteq \mathcal{F}[\![Q^*]\!] \Rightarrow \mathcal{C} \subseteq \mathcal{B} \ \& \ \forall c \in C \in \mathcal{C}.\ \mathcal{F}[\![P_c]\!] \supseteq \mathcal{F}[\![Q_c]\!] \quad (1).$$

To this end, assume that $\mathcal{F}[\![P^*]\!] \supseteq \mathcal{F}[\![Q^*]\!]$. Let $B_0 = \bigcup\mathcal{B}$ and $C_0 = \bigcup\mathcal{C}$ be the initials of P^* and Q^*. Then we know that

$$B_0 \supseteq C_0.$$

Since P^* and Q^* have unique c-derivatives P_c and Q_c respectively, for all $c \in B_0 \cap C_0$, we must have

$$\mathcal{F}[\![P_c]\!] \supseteq \mathcal{F}[\![Q_c]\!]$$

for all such c. All we need to show now is that $\mathcal{C} \subseteq \mathcal{B}$. If this does not hold, let $X = B_0 - C$. Then $(\langle\rangle, X)$ must be a failure of P^*. By hypothesis, this is also a failure of Q^*. But this happens only if there is a $B \in \mathcal{B}$ with

$$B \cap X = B \cap (B_0 - C) = \emptyset.$$

Equivalently, $B \subseteq C$. But $C \subseteq C_0 \subseteq B_0$, and the sets B and B_0 belong to $\mathcal{B}$ (B by assumption and $\mathcal{B}$ by convexity). Thus we find that $C \in \mathcal{B}$, contradicting our assumption. It must therefore be the case that $\mathcal{C} \subseteq \mathcal{B}$, as required. The truth of (1) has now been established.

Now the inductive hypothesis applied to the terms P_c and Q_c gives

$$\vdash P_c \sqsubseteq Q_c,$$

for all $c \in \bigcup\mathcal{C}$. This implies that, for each $C \in \mathcal{C}$,

$$\vdash P_C \sqsubseteq Q_C.$$

Then, since $\mathcal{C} \subseteq \mathcal{B}$, we may use (A10) and (M2) to show

$$\vdash P^* \sqsubseteq Q^*,$$

as required. That completes the proof. ∎

Corollary 1.7: For all terms P and Q,

$$\mathcal{F}[\![P]\!] \supseteq \mathcal{F}[\![Q]\!] \Rightarrow \vdash P \sqsubseteq Q.$$

Proof. By Lemmas 1.5 and 1.6. ∎

2. Extending to infinite processes.

In this section we modify the language FCSP, adding process variables, recursion and a new constant $\perp$, which is intended to denote a process whose only capability is to diverge. Such a pathological process will turn out to correspond precisely to the terms in which a badly constructed recursion appears. We will be mainly interested in terms without free process variables, so-called ***closed terms***. The semantics we use for this language is based on failure sets but has an extra component called a ***divergence set*** in order to allow us to distinguish between deadlock and divergence.

Let RCSP ("Recursive CSP") be the language generated by the following syntax:

$$P ::= \mathrm{STOP} \mid (a \to P) \mid P \,\Box\, P \mid P \sqcap P \mid \bot \mid x \mid \mu x.P$$

where $a \in \Sigma$ and x ranges over a set of process variables or ***identifiers.***

Let **F** be the domain of failure sets, ordered by $\supseteq$. Now we introduce **D**, the domain of ***divergence sets,*** which is just the powerset $\mathcal{P}(\Sigma^*)$, ordered also by $\supseteq$. The semantics of terms in RCSP will be given via two semantic functions, one for failures and one for divergence. Since terms may contain occurrences of identifiers we will use an ***environment*** in the semantics, which binds each identifier to the failure set and divergence set it is intended to denote. Let Ide be the set of identifiers. Then the domain of environments is

$$U = \mathrm{Ide} \to (\mathbf{F} \times \mathbf{D}).$$

For an environment u which maps identifiers to pairs, we will use the conventional notation $(u[\![x]\!])_1$ and $(u[\![x]\!])_2$ to refer to the components of pairs.

The semantic function $\mathcal{D}$ maps terms to divergence sets, relative to an environment. It is defined in the usual way, by structural induction:

Definition 2.1: The divergence semantic function is:

$$\mathcal{D} : \mathrm{RCSP} \to U \to \mathbf{D}$$
$$\mathcal{D}[\![\mathrm{STOP}]\!]u = \emptyset$$
$$\mathcal{D}[\![a \to P]\!]u = \{\, as \mid s \in \mathcal{D}[\![P]\!]u \,\}$$
$$\mathcal{D}[\![P \,\Box\, Q]\!]u = \mathcal{D}[\![P]\!]u \cup \mathcal{D}[\![Q]\!]u$$
$$\mathcal{D}[\![P \sqcap Q]\!]u = \mathcal{D}[\![P]\!]u \cup \mathcal{D}[\![Q]\!]u$$
$$\mathcal{D}[\![\bot]\!]u = \Sigma^*$$
$$\mathcal{D}[\![x]\!]u = (u[\![x]\!])_2$$
$$\mathcal{D}[\![\mu x.P]\!]u = \mathrm{fix}(\lambda\delta.\mathcal{D}[\![P]\!](u + [x \mapsto \delta])).$$

It is easy to see that all of the operations induced on divergence sets by the above definitions are continuous with respect to the superset ordering and hence that the fixed point used in the semantics of recursion will always exists. The usual fixpoint characterisation as a limit is expressed in:

$$\mathcal{D}[\![\mu x.P]\!]u = \bigcap_{n=0}^{\infty} \delta_n,$$
$$\text{where} \quad \delta_0 = \Sigma^* = \mathcal{D}[\![\bot]\!]u,$$
$$\text{and} \quad \delta_{n+1} = \mathcal{D}[\![P]\!](u + [x \mapsto \delta_n]) \quad \text{for } n \geq 0.$$

Notice also that the only terms with a non-trivial divergence set are those with a subterm $\bot$ or with an *unguarded* recursion, *i.e.* a subterm of the form $\mu x.P$ in which there is an occurrence of x appearing in P without a guard. This fact could be proved by a structural induction, once we have defined rigorously the notion of well-guardedness. Finally, our definition guarantees that whenever a particular trace s belongs to a divergence set then all extensions of that trace are also included:

$$s \in \mathcal{D}[\![P]\!]u \Rightarrow st \in \mathcal{D}[\![P]\!]u, \quad \text{for all } t.$$

Examples.

Example 7. The recursion $\mu x.(a \to x)$ is guarded. Applying the previous definition, we have

$$\mathcal{D}[\![\mu x.(a \to x)]\!]u = \cap_{n=0}^{\infty}\delta_n,$$
$$\text{where} \quad \delta_0 = \Sigma^*,$$
$$\text{and, for each } n, \quad \delta_{n+1} = \{\, as \mid s \in \delta_n \,\}.$$

Thus $\delta_n = a^n\Sigma^*$, for each n, and the intersection of these sets is empty: $\mathcal{D}[\![\mu x.(a \to x)]\!]u$ is the empty set.

Example 8. The recursion $\mu x.x$ is obviously not well-guarded. This process diverges on all traces:

$$\mathcal{D}[\![\mu x.x]\!]u = \Sigma^*.$$

Example 9. The term $\mu x.((a \to x) \Box (\mu y.y))$ is not well-guarded, because of the subterm $\mu y.y$. One can check that the divergence set of this term is Σ^*.

The semantic function for failures is also given by structural induction, and it makes use of $\mathcal{D}$. For the most part, the definition is exactly as in [HBR,B1,B2,R], but extended to make it consistent with the notion that divergence is catastrophic: when a process is diverging we can guarantee no aspect of its behaviour; thus we make the operations (except prefixing) ***strict,*** so that a process constructed from divergent components can diverge too.

Definition 2.2: The failures semantic function is:

$$\mathcal{F} : \mathrm{RCSP} \to U \to \mathbf{F}$$

$$\mathcal{F}[\![\mathrm{STOP}]\!]u = \{(\langle\rangle, X) \mid X \subseteq \Sigma\}$$

$$\mathcal{F}[\![\bot]\!]u = \Sigma^* \times p\Sigma$$

$$\mathcal{F}[\![a \to P]\!]u = \{(\langle\rangle, X) \mid a \not\in X\} \cup \{(as, X) \mid (s, X) \in \mathcal{F}[\![P]\!]u\}$$

$$\begin{aligned} \mathcal{F}[\![P \Box Q]\!]u &= \Sigma^* \times p\Sigma, \qquad \text{if } \langle\rangle \in \mathcal{D}[\![P \Box Q]\!]u, \\ \mathcal{F}[\![P \Box Q]\!]u &= \{(\langle\rangle, X) \mid (\langle\rangle, X) \in \mathcal{F}[\![P]\!]u \cap \mathcal{F}[\![Q]\!]u\} \\ &\quad \cup \{(s, X) \mid s \neq \langle\rangle \ \&\ (s, X) \in \mathcal{F}[\![P]\!]u \cup \mathcal{F}[\![Q]\!]u\} \\ &\quad \text{otherwise} \end{aligned}$$

$$\mathcal{F}[\![P \sqcap Q]\!]u = \mathcal{F}[\![P]\!]u \cup \mathcal{F}[\![Q]\!]u$$

$$\mathcal{F}[\![x]\!]u = (u[\![x]\!])_1$$

$$\mathcal{F}[\![\mu x.P]\!]u = \mathrm{fix}(\lambda\phi.\mathcal{F}[\![P]\!](u + [x \mapsto \phi]))$$

Again we can prove that all operations on failure sets used here are continuous, and therefore the least fixed point of any construction exists and is given by the limit:

$$\begin{aligned} \mathcal{F}[\![\mu x.P]\!]u &= \bigcap_{n=0}^{\infty} \Phi_n, \\ \text{where} \quad \Phi_0 &= \Sigma^* \times P\Sigma, \\ \text{and} \quad \Phi_{n+1} &= \mathcal{F}[\![P]\!](u + [x \mapsto \Phi_n]). \end{aligned}$$

Example.

Example 10. If the alphabet Σ is finite, then the term

$$P = \mu x. \sqcap_{B \subseteq \Sigma} (\Box_{b \in B}(b \to x))$$

is expressible in RCSP. This denotes a process which never diverges, but which can perform or refuse to perform any sequence of events. This is the same process as was called CHAOS in [HBR]. We have, for this term P,

$$\mathcal{F}[\![P]\!]u = \Sigma^* \times p\Sigma,$$
$$\mathcal{D}[\![P]\!]u = \emptyset.$$

We say that P may diverge on s if s is a trace in the divergence set of P. Notice that we have defined the semantics of terms in such a way that the following conditions hold:

$$\text{(i)} \quad s \in \mathcal{D}[\![P]\!]u \Rightarrow \forall t, X.(st, X) \in \mathcal{F}[\![P]\!]u.$$
$$\text{(ii)} \quad s \in \mathcal{D}[\![P]\!]u \Rightarrow \forall t.st \in \mathcal{D}[\![P]\!]u.$$

Intuitively, (i) says that a divergent process is totally unpredictable: we cannot be sure that it will or will not ever stop diverging and allow some sequence of actions. Condition (ii) says that once a process starts to diverge it cannot "recover" by performing a visible action: divergence continues forever. Thus, a pair (Φ, δ) is a reasonable model for a process iff the following conditions hold:

$$\begin{array}{lrl}
(1) & & \text{dom}(\Phi) \text{ is non-empty and prefix-closed} \\
(2) & (s,X) \in \Phi,\ Y \subseteq X & \Rightarrow (s,Y) \in \Phi \\
(3) & (s,X) \in \Phi,\ (sa,\emptyset) \notin \Phi & \Rightarrow (s, X \cup \{a\}) \in \Phi \\
(4) & s \in \delta & \Rightarrow st \in \delta, \quad \text{for all } t \\
(5) & s \in \delta & \Rightarrow (st, X) \in \Phi, \quad \text{for all } t, X.
\end{array}$$

This more general model of processes is thus seen to be derived from the old failures model by adding divergence sets and requiring a kind of *consistency* between failures and divergences. Indeed, the processes with empty divergence sets form a space isomorphic to the failures model. Notice that the limit of a directed set of pairs (Φ_i, δ_i) is the intersection and the greatest lower bound of a non-empty set of pairs is again the union. As with the set of failures, the new model forms a complete semi-lattice with respect to the (pairwise) superset ordering. We will write $P \sqsubseteq Q$ to mean that the failures of P contain those of Q and the divergence set of P contains the divergence set of Q. All of the operations considered in this section are continuous with respect to this ordering. This fact justifies our use of fixpoints in the semantics of recursively defined processes.

Syntactic approximation.

Before we introduce a complete axiom system for the new model, we will need some important results which allow us to reason about a (possibly) infinite process in terms of its (finite) approximations. Beginning with the standard definition of *syntactic approximation* on terms, we define the set of finite approximants of an arbitrary term and show that the semantics of any term is uniquely determined from the semantics of its finite approximants.

The notion of *syntactic approximation* on terms is well known (see, for example, [Gu]). The following presentation is typical of the general style.

Definition 2.3: The relation $\prec$ on terms is the smallest relation satisfying:

$$\begin{array}{ll}
\text{(i)} & \bot \prec P \\
\text{(ii)} & P \prec P \\
\text{(iii)} & P \prec Q \prec R \Rightarrow P \prec R \\
\text{(iv)} & P \prec Q \Rightarrow (a \to P) \prec (a \to Q) \\
\text{(v)} & P_1 \prec Q_1,\ P_2 \prec Q_2 \Rightarrow P_1 \Box P_2 \prec Q_1 \Box Q_2 \\
\text{(vi)} & P_1 \prec Q_1,\ P_2 \prec Q_2 \Rightarrow P_1 \sqcap Q_1 \prec P_2 \sqcap Q_2 \\
\text{(vii)} & P[(\mu x.P) \setminus x] \prec \mu x.P
\end{array}$$

We have used the notation $P[Q \setminus x]$ to denote the result of replacing every free occurrence of x in P by Q, taking care to avoid name clashes.

If $P \prec Q$ we say that P *approximates* Q. An easy structural induction shows that for all P and Q syntactic approximation implies semantic approximation:

$$P \prec Q \Rightarrow P \sqsubseteq Q.$$

A term P is *finite* iff it does not contain any subterm of the form $\mu x.Q$. For any term P, the set of finite approximants is

$$\mathrm{FIN}(P) = \{\, Q \mid Q \prec P \ \&\ Q \text{ is finite} \,\}.$$

It should be noted that FIN(P) is *directed* with respect to $\prec$.

The common notion of *unrolling* or *unwinding* a recursive term is intimately connected with finite approximation. The result of unrolling the term P n times will be denoted $P^{(n)}$. The formal definition is:

$$
\begin{array}{lrcl}
\text{(i)} & P^{(0)} & = & \bot \\
\text{(ii)} & \mathrm{STOP}^{(n+1)} & = & \mathrm{STOP} \\
\text{(iii)} & (a \rightarrow P)^{(n+1)} & = & (a \rightarrow P^{(n+1)}) \\
\text{(iv)} & (P \,\Box\, Q)^{(n+1)} & = & P^{(n+1)} \,\Box\, Q^{(n+1)} \\
\text{(v)} & (P \sqcap Q)^{(n+1)} & = & P^{(n+1)} \sqcap Q^{(n+1)} \\
\text{(vi)} & x^{(n+1)} & = & x \\
\text{(vii)} & (\mu x.P)^{(n+1)} & = & P[(\mu x.P)^{(n)} \setminus x].
\end{array}
$$

Every finite approximation to a term P is also a finite approximation to some unrolling of that term:

Lemma 2.4: If $Q \in \mathrm{FIN}(P)$ then there is an n such that $Q \prec P^{(n)}$.

Proof. See [Gu]. ∎

Corollary: For all P, $\mathrm{FIN}(P) = \bigcup_{n=0}^{\infty} \mathrm{FIN}(P^{(n)})$.

Lemma 2.5:

$$
\begin{array}{ll}
\text{(i)} & \mathrm{FIN}(\bot) = \{\bot\} \\
\text{(ii)} & \mathrm{FIN}(\mathrm{STOP}) = \{\bot, \mathrm{STOP}\} \\
\text{(iii)} & \mathrm{FIN}(P \,\Box\, Q) = \{\bot\} \cup \{P' \,\Box\, Q' \mid P' \in \mathrm{FIN}(P) \ \&\ Q' \in \mathrm{FIN}(Q)\} \\
\text{(iv)} & \mathrm{FIN}(P \sqcap Q) = \{\bot\} \cup \{P' \sqcap Q' \mid P' \in \mathrm{FIN}(P) \ \&\ Q' \in \mathrm{FIN}(Q)\} \\
\text{(v)} & \mathrm{FIN}(a \rightarrow P) = \{\bot\} \cup \{(a \rightarrow P') \mid P' \in \mathrm{FIN}(P)\} \\
\text{(vi)} & \mathrm{FIN}(x) = \{\bot, x\}.
\end{array}
$$

Proof. Elementary. ∎

In a sense, a term P is the "syntactic limit" of its finite approximation set FIN(P). Recall that this set is directed with respect to the syntactic relation $\prec$, and therefore the semantic images of the finite approximations to P form a directed set with respect to the semantic order $\sqsubseteq$. The following results show that the semantics of a term is uniquely determined by the semantics of its finite approximations, and allow us to deduce that the semantics of a term P is in fact the limit of the semantics of its finite approximations. We omit proofs, as they follow standard lines. More details can be found in [B1].

Lemma 2.6: If P is finite and $P \sqsubseteq Q$, then there is a finite approximation R of Q such that $P \sqsubseteq R$.

Theorem 2.7: For all P and u,

$$\mathcal{D}[\![P]\!]u = \bigcap \{\, \mathcal{D}[\![Q]\!]u \mid Q \in \mathrm{FIN}(P) \,\}.$$

Proof. By structural induction on P. ∎

Theorem 2.8: For all P and u,

$$\mathcal{F}[\![P]\!]u = \bigcap \{\, \mathcal{F}[\![Q]\!]u \mid Q \in \mathrm{FIN}(P) \,\}.$$

Proof. By structural induction. ∎

Proof system.

All of the axioms and inference rules of Table 1 are still valid. Let $\mathcal{L}$ be the proof system containing all axioms and rules of the earlier system together with the following additions:

$$\begin{array}{ll} \text{(B1)} & P \Box \bot = \bot \\ \text{(B2)} & P \sqcap \bot = \bot \\ \text{(B3)} & \bot \sqsubseteq P \\ \text{(B4)} & P[(\mu x.P) \setminus x] \sqsubseteq \mu x.P \end{array}$$

$$\text{(R)} \quad \frac{\forall Q \in \mathrm{FIN}(P).\, Q \sqsubseteq R}{P \sqsubseteq R}$$

The new axioms state that the two conditional combinators are *strict*, and that $\bot$ is the bottom element with respect to $\sqsubseteq$. The new inference rule essentially says that any property of a term is deducible from the properties of its finite approximations. This is an *infinitary rule,* because a term may have an infinite set of syntactic approximants; in such a case one would need an infinite number of premises in order to use rule (R). It seems unlikely that a finitary proof system could be found which was still complete, although some interesting sublanguages (in which use of recursion is constrained) will presumably have decidable proof systems. This remains a topic for future work. Now we are concerned with the soundness and completeness of our enlarged proof system.

Soundness.

Under the interpretation that for closed terms P and Q, $P \sqsubseteq Q$ means

$$\mathcal{F}[\![P]\!]u \supseteq \mathcal{F}[\![Q]\!]u \;\&\; \mathcal{D}[\![P]\!]u \supseteq \mathcal{D}[\![Q]\!]u$$

for all environments u, the proof system $\mathcal{L}$ is sound. We need merely to check that the axioms are valid and the proof rules sound. Since the semantics was defined to make the conditional operators strict, the new axioms are clearly valid. Soundness of rule (R) follows from Theorems 2.7 and 2.8. It is easy to check validity of the old axioms and rules. Thus we have:

Theorem 2.9: For all closed terms P and Q, and all u,

$$\vdash_{\mathcal{L}} P \sqsubseteq Q \Rightarrow P \sqsubseteq Q.$$

Completeness.

In order to establish that the new proof system is complete, we must first modify the definition of normal form. Essentially, we just allow $\bot$ as well as STOP in building up normal forms.

Definition 2.10: A term P in RCSP is in normal form iff it has the structure:

$$\begin{array}{ll} \text{either} & P = \text{STOP}, \\ \text{or} & P = \bot, \\ \text{or} & P = \sqcap_{B \in \mathcal{B}} \Box_{b \in B} (b \to P_b) \end{array}$$

where $\mathcal{B}$ is convex and each P_b is in normal form.

It is easy to modify the proof of Lemmas 1.5 and 1.6 to show that any *finite* term can be reduced to normal form using the axioms and rules, and that whenever P and Q are normal forms

$$P \sqsubseteq Q \Rightarrow \vdash_{\mathcal{L}} P \sqsubseteq Q.$$

The completeness theorem relies on Lemma 2.6, which states that whenever P is finite and $P \sqsubseteq Q$ there is a finite term $R \in \mathrm{FIN}(Q)$ such that $P \sqsubseteq R$.

Theorem 2.11: For all terms P and Q,

$$P \sqsubseteq Q \Rightarrow \vdash_L P \sqsubseteq Q.$$

Proof. Let P' be a finite approximation to P and suppose $P \sqsubseteq Q$. Then

$$P' \sqsubseteq P \sqsubseteq Q.$$

By Lemma 2.6 there is a finite approximation Q' to Q such that $P' \sqsubseteq Q'$. But then

$$\vdash P' \sqsubseteq Q'.$$

Since for every $Q' \in \mathrm{FIN}(Q)$ the formula $Q' \sqsubseteq Q$ is provable, we have

$$\vdash P' \sqsubseteq Q.$$

The result follows by an application of rule (R). ∎

3. Adding more CSP operations.

We may extend the proof system to encompass other CSP operations provided we add enough axioms and rules to allow normal form reductions. We must introduce failure sets and divergence sets for the new forms of processes, by extending the definition of $\mathcal{D}$ and $\mathcal{F}$ accordingly. We must also add axioms and inference rules corresponding to these definitions, in such a way that Theorems 2.7 and 2.8 still hold. This will keep the proof system complete and consistent.

In keeping with the notion that a divergent process is totally unpredictable, and that divergence of a component process should also give rise to divergence of the compound process (so that a process built from divergent components diverges) we stipulate that all operations should be *strict*, in that they map $\perp$ to $\perp$. Now we consider extending the proof system and the semantic defnitions to include parallel composition, interleaving, and hiding. It should be clear how to include the other operations of [HBR], with these examples as illustration of the general method. Essentially, we make each operation strict, and include axioms for strictness and for distribution over $\sqcap$ and guarded terms.

Parallel composition.

For the parallel composition $P \| Q$, for example, we require divergence when either P or Q diverges. This combination performs an event only if both component processes perform it, and can refuse an event if either component can refuse it; and thus we specify:

(i) $\mathcal{D}[\![P\|Q]\!]u = \{\, st \mid s \in (\mathcal{D}[\![P]\!]u \cup \mathcal{D}[\![Q]\!]u) \cap (\mathrm{traces}(P) \cap \mathrm{traces}(Q))\,\}$

(ii) $\mathcal{F}[\![P\|Q]\!]u = \{\, (s, X \cup Y) \mid (s,X) \in \mathcal{F}[\![P]\!]u \;\&\; (s,Y) \in \mathcal{F}[\![Q]\!]u \,\}$
$\{\, (st, X) \mid s \in \mathcal{D}[\![P\|Q]\!]u \,\}.$

It should be evident that the semantic definition captures the intuition stated above. Again we should check that our definition does yield a divergence set and failure set satisfying the conditions (1)–(5) of page 12. The details are left as an exercise.

Extending the syntactic approximation relation in the obvious way, we add the clause

$$P_1 \prec P_2,\; Q_1 \prec Q_2 \Rightarrow P_1 \| Q_1 \prec P_2 \| Q_2$$

to Definition 2.3. Then the finite approximations of $P \| Q$ are built up as parallel compositions of finite approximations of P and Q:

$$\mathrm{FIN}(P\|Q) = \{\perp\} \cup \{\, P'\|Q' \mid P' \in \mathrm{FIN}(P) \;\&\; Q' \in \mathrm{FIN}(Q) \,\}.$$

It is clear from this that Theorems 2.7 and 2.8 still hold.

We add axioms for strictness and manipulation of normal forms. In each case the axiom is either a restatement of an earlier result which clearly still holds in the extended model, or is self-evident. In the axioms we adopt the convention that a term P_B stands for

$$\Box_{b\in B}(b \rightarrow P_b).$$

$$\text{(PAR 0)} \qquad P \| \bot \equiv \bot$$

$$\text{(PAR 1)} \qquad P \| (Q \sqcap R) \equiv (P \| Q) \sqcap (P \| R)$$

$$\text{(PAR 2)} \qquad P_B \| Q_C \equiv \Box_{a\in B\cap C}(a \rightarrow P_a \| Q_a).$$

It is easy to check that these axioms enable any parallel composition of normal forms to be reduced to normal form. Note also the special case of (PAR 2) when $C = \emptyset$: the axiom reduces in this case to the identity $P_B \| \text{STOP} = \text{STOP}$.

Interleaving.

For the interleaving operation $P|||Q$ we want divergence when either component process can diverge. And at any stage a trace of $P|||Q$ is to be an interleaving of a trace of P with a trace of Q, and the process can refuse an event only if both components refuse it.

(i) $\mathcal{D}[\![P|||Q]\!]u = \text{merge}(\mathcal{D}[\![P]\!]u, \text{traces}(Q)) \cup \text{merge}(\text{traces}(P), \mathcal{D}[\![Q]\!]u)$

(ii) $\mathcal{F}[\![P|||Q]\!]u = \{ (u, X) \mid \exists s, t. (s, X) \in \mathcal{F}[\![P]\!]u \ \&\ (t, X) \in \mathcal{F}[\![Q]\!]u \ \&\ u \in \text{merge}(s, t) \}$
$\cup \{ (st, X) \mid s \in \mathcal{D}[\![P|||Q]\!]u \}.$

Here we have used the merge function on traces and its natural extension to sets of traces. It can be defined inductively as follows:

$$\text{merge}(\langle\rangle, t) = \text{merge}(t, \langle\rangle) = \{ t \}$$
$$\text{merge}(as, bt) = \text{merge}(bt, as) = \{ au, bv \mid u \in \text{merge}(s, bt),\ v \in \text{merge}(as, t) \}.$$

For syntactic approximation we add to Definition 2.3:

$$P_1 \prec P_2,\ Q_1 \prec Q_2 \Rightarrow P_1|||Q_1 \prec P_2|||Q_2.$$

Again the finite approximations of an interleaved process are formed by interleaving finite approximations to the components:

$$\text{FIN}(P|||Q) = \{ \bot \} \cup \{ P'|||Q' \mid P' \in \text{FIN}(P) \ \&\ Q' \in \text{FIN}(Q) \}.$$

Again Theorems 2.4 and 2.5 are still true.

Our definition yields a strict operation, since $\mathcal{D}[\![\bot|||Q]\!]u = \Sigma^*$. Otherwise it has similar properties to the interleaving operation of [HBR]. We add axioms:

$$\text{(INT 0)} \qquad P|||\bot \equiv \bot$$

$$\text{(INT 1)} \qquad P|||(Q \sqcap R) \equiv (P \sqcap Q)|||(P \sqcap R)$$

$$\text{(INT 2)} \qquad P_B|||Q_C \equiv (\Box_{b\in B}(b \rightarrow (P_b|||Q_C))) \Box (\Box_{c\in C}(c \rightarrow (P_B|||Q_c))).$$

Again it is easy to check the validity of these axioms, and to verify that an interleaving of two normal forms can be reduced to normal form. In particular, the special case of (INT 2) when C is empty is to be interpreted as the identity: $P_B|||\text{STOP} \equiv P_B$.

Hiding.

For the hiding operator, we have to model the fact that hiding a potentially infinite sequence of actions produces divergence: we are identifying the phenomenon of infinite internal chatter with divergence. This version of hiding is closely related to the second form of hiding introduced in [B] and in [HBR], where infinite chatter was identified with CHAOS; here a process which is chattering has the same failure set as CHAOS, but (unlike CHAOS) can also diverge. It is simple to alter the proofs given in [HBR] for the chaotic version of hiding, to show that this form enjoys similar properties, such as continuity.

(i) $\mathcal{D}[\![P/b]\!]u = \{ (s\backslash b)t \mid s \in \mathcal{D}[\![P]\!]u \} \cup \{ (s\backslash b)t \mid \forall n.\ sb^n \in \text{traces}(P) \}.$

(ii) $\mathcal{F}[\![P/b]\!]u = \{ (s\backslash b, X) \mid (s, X \cup \{b\}) \in \mathcal{F}[\![P]\!]u \} \cup \{ (st, X) \mid s \in \mathcal{D}[\![P/b]\!]u \}.$

For finite approximations, we again add to Definition 2.3:

$$P' \prec P \Rightarrow P'/b \prec P/b.$$

The finite approximations to a process formed by hiding are again formed by hiding:

$$\text{FIN}(P/b) = \{ \bot \} \cup \{ P'/b \mid P' \in \text{FIN}(P) \}.$$

Our new hiding operator is strict. We add axioms:

(HIDE 0) $\quad \bot/b \equiv \bot$

(HIDE 1) $\quad (P \sqcap Q)/b \equiv (P/b) \sqcap (Q/b)$

(HIDE 2) $\quad (b \to P)/c \equiv (b \to P/c) \quad$ if $b \neq c$,
$\qquad\qquad \equiv P/c \quad$ if $b = c$.

(HIDE 3) $\quad P_B/c \equiv \Box_{b\in B}((b \to P_b)/c), \quad$ if $c \notin B$,
$\qquad\qquad \equiv (P_c/c) \sqcap \Box_{b\in B}((b \to P_b)/c) \quad$ if $b \in C$.

Again the validity of these axioms is easy to check, and one can use the axioms to produce normal forms.

Examples.

Example 11. The term $P = \mu x.(a \to x)$ has finite approximations

$$P_n = (a^n \to \bot), \qquad \text{for all } n,$$

using the obvious abbreviations. Thus, the term P/a has finite approximations

$$\bot, \text{ and } P_n/a = (a^n \to \bot)/a,$$

for all n. Using (HIDE 2) we see that, for each n,

$$\vdash (a^n \to \bot)/a \equiv \bot/a,$$

and so, by (HIDE 1) every finite approximation to P/a is provably equivalent to $\bot$. By rule (R), it follows that P/a is equivalent to $\bot$, as expected because P/a diverges.

Example 12. A slightly more complicated argument shows that for the term

$$Q = \mu x.((a \to x) \Box (b \to \text{STOP}))$$

Q/a is also equivalent to $\bot$. One can also show that Q/b is equivalent to $\mu x.(a \to x)$.

4. Conclusions.

We have introduced a semantics for processes based on the concepts of failures and divergence. The semantic mapping from terms to meanings has been described in the denotational style, in which the denotation of a complex term is built up from the meanings of its parts. In addition, we gave a set of axioms and proof rules characterising this semantics in the sense that two terms in the language of processes denote identical values (have the same meaning) if and only if this fact is provable within the formal system. The proof system contained an infinitary axiom to the effect that the semantics of an arbitrary term is determined uniquely by its syntactically finite approximations. It does not appear true that a finitary (and decidable) proof system exists for the language including recursion, although we do not investigate this issue here. Our axiomatic presentation demonstrates that the denotational semantics can be characterised by means of algebraic relations between processes, a fact of interest in itself. An attempt to treat the failures model (without divergence) in a similar way is reported in [N].

We have not tried in this paper to apply this proof system to problems involving large processes. It is certainly possible to represent some interesting behavioural properties of processes within our framework. For instance, the potential for deadlocking after performing a sequence of actions s in an environment represented by Q would correspond to an assertion of the form

$$P \| (s \rightarrow Q) \sqsubseteq (s \rightarrow \mathrm{STOP}),$$

and the inability to refuse any event in the sequence s would be represented by

$$P \| (s \rightarrow \mathrm{STOP}) \equiv (s \rightarrow \mathrm{STOP}).$$

The possibility of divergence after performing s is captured by the assertion

$$P \| (s \rightarrow Q) \equiv (s \rightarrow \bot).$$

It remains to be seen how useful our proof system is in helping to formalise proofs for complex processes. Nevertheless, it is clear that the semantics given here both denotationally and axiomatically can serve as the foundation of a theory of processes, and can be used to justify reasoning about the behaviour of processes as in [R,B1,HBR].

It would be very interesting to extend our work to cover a language more directly derived from Hoare's original CSP, for which there are existing Hoare-style axiom systems. In its original formulation, CSP processes were able to perform essentially two different kinds of event: communication with another process, and assignment to a local variable. We have not specified the nature of events in our model, but one can certainly specialize the model to cases where the events are of particular forms. It is to be hoped that such an approach would help to bridge the gap between abstract languages (such as FCSP and RCSP) and their more concrete counterparts (CSP). In doing so, we would hope to shed some light on the existing proof systems for CSP [AFR,LG], and on the relationships between them.

5. Acknowledgements.

I am grateful to many people for advice and encouragement during the development of this work, which is based on part of my Ph.D. thesis. Particular thanks are due to Prof. C.A.R. Hoare, the author's thesis advisor; and to Bill Roscoe, who commented in detail and suggested some improvements and corrections. I have also been influenced by the work of Robin Milner, Matthew Hennessy and Rocco de Nicola.

6. References.

[AFR] Apt, K.R., Francez, N., and de Roever, W.P., *A Proof System for Communicating Sequential Processes,* ACM Transactions on Programming Languages and Systems, Vol 2. No. 3 (July 1980).

[B1] Brookes, S.D., *A Model for Communicating Sequential Processes,* Ph.D thesis, Oxford University (submitted 1983).

[B2] Brookes, S.D., *On the Relationship of CCS and CSP,* CMU Technical Report CMU-CS-83-111, also to appear in Proceedings of ICALP 1983 (pub. Springer).

[Gu] Guessarian, I., *Algebraic Semantics,* Springer-Verlag Lecture Notes in Computer Science Vol. 99 (1981).

[H1] Hoare, C.A.R., *Communicating Sequential Processes,* Communications of the ACM (August 1978).

[H2] Hoare, C.A.R., *A Model for Communicating Sequential Processes,* Technical Report PRG-22, Oxford University Computing Laboratory, Programming Research Group (1981).

[HBR] Hoare, C.A.R., Brookes, S.D., and Roscoe, A.W., *A Theory of Communicating Sequential Processes,* Technical Report PRG-16, Oxford University Computing Laboratory, Programming Research Group (May 1981). (an extended version will appear in JACM)

[HN] Hennessy, M.C.B., and de Nicola, R., *Testing Equivalences for Processes,* to appear in Proceedings of ICALP 1983.

[LG] Levin, G.M., and Gries, D., *A Proof Technique for Communicating Sequential Processes,* Acta Informatica 15 (1981).

[LNS] Lassez, J.-L., Nguyen, V.L., and Sonenberg, E.A., *Fixed Point Theorems and Semantics: A Folk Tale,* Information Processing Letters, Vol. 14 No. 3, May 1982.

[M] Milner, R., *A Calculus of Communicating Systems,* Springer-Verlag Lecture Notes in Computer Science Vol. 92 (1980).

[N] de Nicola, R., *A Complete Set of Axioms for a Theory of Communicating Sequential Processes,* Department of Computer Science Technical Monograph, University of Edinburgh (1983).

[R] Roscoe, A.W., *A Mathematical Theory of Communicating Processes,* Ph. D. thesis, Oxford University (1982).

Non-standard Fixed Points in First Order Logic

Robert Cartwright†

Computer Science Program
Department of Mathematical Sciences
Rice University
Houston, TX 77251

and

Computer Science Department
Stanford University
Stanford, CA 94305

1. Introduction

In first order programming logic, recursive programs are interpreted as definitions extending a finitely generated, continuous structure D that is the least model of a first order theory T_D similar to Peano arithmetic. The core of the theory is an axiom scheme Ind_D asserting that the familiar principle of structural induction holds for arbitrary formulas including those involving function symbols introduced in recursive programs. In the structure D, Kleene's Recursion Theorem guarantees that the function symbols F defined in a recursive program P have a natural interpretation: the least fixed-point F the functional Π corresponding to P. If F is total (convergent when all inputs are convergent), then F is the unique interpretation of F over D consistent with P. On the other hand, if F includes partial functions, then Π may have extraneous fixed-points which are possible interpretations for F. In this case, to obtain a unique interpretation for F we must strengthen the definition P. The most elegant solution (first proposed by McCarthy [9]) is to augment P by a first order scheme Min_P asserting that interpretation of the function symbols F is the least possible one satisfying the equations P.

In non-standard models, the preceding approach to interpreting recursive programs breaks down. The crux of the problem is that the least fixed-point of the functional Π corresponding to a program does not necessarily obey the principle of structural induction. Although the practical significance of this observation is questionable (since real computations are performed within standard models), many computer scientists have interpreted it as strong evidence that first order logic is too weak a formal system for reasoning about recursive programs.

In response to this criticism, this paper shows that under modest assumptions about the underlying theory T_D, a recursive program has a natural, intuitively plausible interpretation as a definition in *every* model of the theory T_D. Moreover, first order programming logic is complete with respect to this interpretation; a statement about a recursive program is provable iff it is true in all models of T_D. Instead of the least fixed-point, the correct interpretation for a recursive program P extending an arbitrary model of the theory T_D is the *least definable-fixed-point* of the functional Π corresponding to P. This interpretation of the program function symbols F is the unique meaning of the definition $P \cup Min_P$ since it is the *only* interpretation of F over D consistent with the $P \cup Min_P \cup Ind_D$. In the standard model, the least definable-fixed-point reduces to the conventional least fixed-point.

The most interesting technical result underlying the correct interpretation of recursive programs in non-standard models is a generalization of Kleene's Recursion Theorem which asserts that every continuous functional over an arithmetic structure has a least definable fixed-point.

2. Mathematical Preliminaries

As a foundation for the remainder of the paper, we briefly summarize the important definitions and notational conventions of our treatment of first order logic. Readers who are unfamiliar with the formulation of first order logic presented in this paper are encouraged to consult Enderton's text [10].

---

†This research has been partially supported by the National Science Foundation under grant MCS81-04209 and by DARPA under contract N00039-82-C-0250.

In first order programming logic, recursive programs are expressed within a conventional *first order logical language* L *with equality*. A *first order signature* is a triple <G, R, #> consisting of a set of function symbols G, a set of relation symbols R, and an associated "arity" function $\#: G \cup R \rightarrow Nat$ (where Nat denotes the natural numbers) specifying the *arity* #p for each function and relation symbol p. Nullary function symbols serve as constants. The *first order language (with equality)* L_σ determined by the signature $\sigma = \langle G,R,\# \rangle$ contains two classes of strings: a set of *terms* constructed from variables and function symbols G, and a set of *formulas* constructed from relation symbols $\{=\} \cup R$ applied to terms (forming *atomic formulas*) and from logical connectives $\{\forall, \exists, \wedge, \vee, \supset, \neg\}$ applied to simpler formulas. Each function and relation symbol p is constrained to take exactly #p arguments. A complete definition of the syntax of first order languages appears in Enderton [10].

An occurrence of a variable v in a formula α is *bound* if the occurrence is contained within a subformula of the form $\forall v \beta$ or $\exists v \beta$. An occurrence of a variable is *free* iff it is not bound. Terms and formulas containing no occurrences of free variables are called *variable-free terms* and *sentences*, respectively. Let $\alpha(x)$ denote a formula possibly containing the variable x and let t denote an arbitrary term. Then $\alpha(t)$ denotes the formula obtained from $\alpha(x)$ by replacing every free occurrence of x by t.

The additional logical connectives $\{\equiv, \exists!\}$ are defined as abbreviations for combinations of primitive connectives by the following syntactic rules

$(\alpha \equiv \beta)$ abbreviates $((\alpha \supset \beta) \wedge (\beta \supset \alpha))$
$\exists! v\ \alpha(v)$ abbreviates $\exists v\ (\alpha(v) \wedge \forall u(\alpha(u) \supset u=v))$

where α and β denote arbitrary formulas and u and v denote arbitrary distinct variables.

In formulas with elided parentheses, unary connectives take precedence over binary ones and binary connectives associate according to the preceding ranking $\{\wedge\} > \{\vee,\oplus\} > \{\supset\} > \{\equiv\}$, and the convention that adjacent connectives of equal precedence associate to the right. For the sake of clarity, we will occasionally substitute square brackets for the parentheses enclosing formulas. In place of a sentence, a formula α abbreviates the sentence $\forall \overline{v}\ \alpha$ where $\overline{v}$ is a list of the free variables of α. Similarly, the forms $\forall x{:}p\ \alpha$ and t:p, where p is a unary relation symbol, abbreviate the formulas $\forall x [p(x) \supset \alpha]$ and p(t), respectively.

Let S denote a (possibly empty) set of function and relation symbols (with associated arities) not in the language L_σ. Then $\sigma \cup S$ denotes the signature consisting of σ augmented by the symbols S. Similarly, $L_\sigma \cup S$ denotes the first order language $L_{\sigma \cup S}$; $L_\sigma \cup S$ is called an *expansion* of L_σ.

The meaning of a first order language L_σ with signature $\sigma = \langle G,R,\# \rangle$ is formalized as follows. A (*first order*) *structure* M (*with signature* σ) is a triple $\langle |M|, M_G, M_R \rangle$ where |M| (called the *universe*) is a set of (data) values; M_G is a function mapping each function symbol $g \in G$ into a #g-ary function on |M|; and M_R is a function mapping each relation symbol $r \in R$ into a #r-ary *relation* on |M|. Given a structure M with signature σ and a *state* s mapping the variables of L_σ into |M|, every term in L_σ denotes an object in |M| and every formula denotes a truth value TRUE or FALSE. The meaning of terms and formulas of L_σ is defined by structural induction in the obvious way; a rigorous definition appears in Enderton [10]. To simplify notation, we will often denote the first order language corresponding to a particular structure A as L_A.

Let H be a subset of the function symbols of the first order language L_σ. A structure M with signature σ is called an *H-term structure* iff the universe |M| consists of equivalence classes of variable-free terms constructed solely from the function symbols in H. A structure with signature σ is *finitely generated* iff there exists a finite subset H of the function symbols (called *generators*) of L_σ such that M is isomorphic to an H-term structure.

Let M be a structure with signature σ, let S denote a set of function predicate symbols (with associated arities) not in L_σ, and let **S** denote a set of functions and relations over |M| interpreting S. Then $M \cup$ **S** denotes the structure consisting of M augmented by the functions and predicates **S**; $M \cup$ **S** is called an *expansion* of M. Let M' be an arbitrary structure with signature $\sigma \cup S$. We say that M' is an *extension* of M (or alternatively that M is a *substructure* of M') iff $|M'| \supseteq |M|$ and every operation (function or predicate) of M is the restriction of the corresponding operation of M' to |M|. If |M'| properly contains |M|, then M' is called a *proper extension of* M (or alternatively M is called a *proper substructure* of M').

To distinguish symbols, formulas, and terms in a first order language L_σ from their interpretations, we will use the following notation. Function and relation symbols, terms, and formulas appear in ordinary type and stand for themselves. In contexts involving a single structure M, a function or relation symbol p written in boldface (**p**) denotes the interpretation of p in M. In more general contexts, M[p] denotes the interpretation of the symbol p in the structure

M. Similarly, $M[\alpha][s]$ denotes the meaning of the formula or term α in M under the state s.

Let T be a set of sentences in the first order language L_σ. A *model* of T is a structure M with signature σ such that every sentence of T is **TRUE** in M. We say that a structure M *satisfies* T or alternatively, that T is an *axiomatization* of M, iff M is a model of T. An set of sentences T is *effective* iff it is recursive. A sentence $\alpha \in L$ is *logically implied* by T iff α is **TRUE** in every model of T. The set of sentences T forms a *theory* iff it satisfies the following two properties:

(i) *Semantic consistency*: there exists a model for T.

(ii) *Closure under logical implication*: every sentence that is logically implied by T is a member of T.

The set of sentences logically implied by T is called the *theory generated by* T.

A set of sentences T typically has an intended model called the *standard model* of T. Any model that is not isomorphic to the standard model is called a *non-standard model*. Two structures with the same signature σ are *elementarily distinct* iff there exists a sentence S in L_σ such that S is true in one structure but not in the other. A set of sentences T is *incomplete* iff it has elementarily distinct models; otherwise, it is *complete*. A set of sentences T is *term-complete* iff the following two conditions hold. First, for every relation symbol r and vector of variable-free terms $\bar{u}$, either $r(\bar{u})$ or $\neg r(\bar{u})$ is logically implied by T. Second, for every pair of variable-free terms u and v in L_σ, either the sentence $u=v$ or the sentence $u \neq v$ is logically implied by T. In this paper, we will confine our attention to axiomatizations that are term-complete.

Given a recursively enumerable set of axioms A, it is possible to enumerate all of the sentences that are logically implied by A. A *first order deductive system* Γ is a finite set of syntactic rules that generates a set of sentences from A. A *proof* of a sentence α from A in the deductive system Γ is simply its derivation in Γ from A. A deductive system Γ is *sound* iff every sentence derivable from an axiom set A is logically implied by A. A deductive system Γ is *complete* iff every sentence in the theory generated by A is derivable (provable) in Γ from A. A remarkable property of first order logic is the existence of sound, complete deductive systems for arbitrary-axiom sets A.

There are many different ways to formulate a sound, complete deductive system for first order logic. Two approaches that are well known to computer scientists are resolution and Gentzen natural deduction [17]. Of course, every first order deductive system that is sound and complete derives exactly the same set of sentences. In this paper, we will leave the choice of deductive system unspecified, since we are not interested in the syntactic details of formal proofs.

Let A be a structure and $S = \{s_1,...,s_n\}$ be a finite set of function and relation symbols not associated with A. A *definition for* S *over* A is a collection of sentences Δ in the language $L_A \cup S$ such that A can be expanded—by adding interpretations for the new function and relation symbols in S—to a model for Δ. An *unambiguous definition for* S *over* A is a definition that determines a *unique* expansion of A. A formula $\alpha(x_1,...,x_k)$ in L_A *defines the k-ary relation* r *in* A iff α contains no free variables other than x_1, ..., x_k and for all states s over $|A|$, $A[\alpha(x_1,...,x_k)][s]$ is **TRUE** iff $(s(x_1),...,s(x_k)) \in r$. Similarly, a formula $\alpha(x_1,...,x_k, y)$ in L_A *defines the k-ary function* g in A iff α contains no free variables other than x_1, ..., x_k and for all states s over $|A|$, $A[\alpha(x_1,...,x_k, y)][s] = \mathbf{TRUE}$ iff $g(s(x_1),...,s(x_k)) = s(y)$. A set S $= \{s_1,...,s_n\}$ of relations and functions interpreting the symbols S is *definable in* A iff there exist formulas α_1, ..., α_n defining s_1, ..., s_n, respectively.

3. Synopsis of First Order Programming Logic

In first order programming logic, data domains are formalized as finitely generated structures specified by first order axiomatizations similar to Peano's axioms for the natural numbers. In this context, a recursive program is simply a definition, consisting of a set of recursion equations, that adds new functions to the data domain. A unique property of the logic is that it manages to specify the meaning of recursive programs programs without explicit reference either to a least fixed-point operator or to a program interpreter. As a result, it is possible to prove properties of recursive programs within first order programming logic by using simple induction arguments analogous to those used in Peano arithmetic to prove properties of the addition and multiplication functions. Several successful verification systems for recursive programs (most notably the Boyer-Moore theorem prover [2,3]) are based on the logic.

3.1. Domain Restrictions

To accommodate recursive programs as definitions, first order programming logic stipulates that the data domain must be *continuous*. Otherwise, recursive programs may be inconsistent with the data domain. For example, the program

$f(x) = f(x) + 1$

is inconsistent with the data domain N consisting of the natural numbers (without $\perp$) and the primitive operations 0, 1, and +. The interpretation of f must be a (total) function on the natural numbers, yet no such function exists. The following series of definitions specifies a restriction on structures—continuity—that guarantees recursive programs are meaningful. Expository discussions to the concept of continuity appear in Manna [12] and Stoy [13].

Definition A *complete partial ordering* $\sqsubseteq$ on a set S is a binary relation on S such that:

(i) $\sqsubseteq$ is a partial ordering (reflexive, antisymmetric, and transitive relation) on S.

(ii) The set S contains a least element $\perp$ under the partial ordering $\sqsubseteq$.

(iii) Every chain (denumerable sequence ordered by $\sqsubseteq$) $x_0 \sqsubseteq x_1 \sqsubseteq x_2 \sqsubseteq \ldots$ in S has a least upper bound.

A set S with a corresponding complete partial ordering $\sqsubseteq$ is called a *complete partial order* (abbreviated *cpo*); the partial ordering $\sqsubseteq$ is called the *approximation ordering* for S. A member $s \in S$ is said to be *divergent* iff $s = \perp$; it is *convergent* iff $s \neq \perp$.

Definition Given cpo's A and B, a function f: A → B is *continuous* iff the image of an arbitrary chain $X = x_0 \sqsubseteq x_1 \sqsubseteq x_2 \sqsubseteq \ldots$ in A is a chain in B and the image of the least upper bound of X is the least upper bound of the chain image.

There are two standard methods for building composite cpo's from simpler ones. First, given the cpo's $A_1, \ldots, A_m$ under the approximation orderings $\sqsubseteq_1, \ldots, \sqsubseteq_m$, respectively, the Cartesian product $A_1 \times \ldots \times A_m$ forms a cpo under the ordering $\sqsubseteq$ defined by

$$\bar{x} \sqsubseteq \bar{y} \equiv \bigwedge_{1 \le i \le n} [x_i \sqsubseteq_i y_i].$$

Second, given the cpo A under $\sqsubseteq_A$ and the cpo B under $\sqsubseteq_B$, the set of continuous functions mapping A into B forms a cpo under the ordering $\sqsubseteq$ defined by

$$g \sqsubseteq h \equiv \forall \bar{x} \in A\ [g(\bar{x}) \sqsubseteq_B h(\bar{x})].$$

Definition A structure D including the constant $\perp$ is *continuous* under the binary relation $\sqsubseteq$ on |D| iff |D| forms a complete partial order under $\sqsubseteq$ and every function f: $|D|^{\#f} \to |D|$ in D is continuous.

Definition Given a continuous data domain D with signature $\sigma = \langle G,R,\# \rangle$, a recursive program P over D is a set of recursion equations: $\{ f_1(\bar{x}_1)=t_1, f_2(\bar{x}_2)=t_2, \ldots, f_n(\bar{x}_n)=t_n \}$ where $n>0$; the set F of function symbols $\{f_1,f_2,\ldots,f_n\}$ is disjoint from $G \cup R$; $\bar{x}_1, \bar{x}_2, \ldots, \bar{x}_n$ are lists of variables; and $t_1, t_2, \ldots, t_n$ are terms in the language $L_\sigma \cup F$ such that each term t_i contains no variables other than those in $\bar{x}_i$. The intended *meaning* of the n-tuple of function symbols $[f_1,\ldots,f_n]$ introduced in the program P is the least fixed-point of the functional

$$\Pi = \lambda f_1,\ldots,f_n . [\lambda \bar{x}_1 . t_1, \ldots, \lambda \bar{x}_n . t_n]$$

corresponding to P.

Remark By Kleene's Recursion Theorem ([14]), Π must have a least fixed-point $[f_1,\ldots,f_n]$, because it is a continuous mapping from the cpo $(|D|^{\#f_1} \to |D|) \times \ldots \times (|D|^{\#f_n} \to |D|)$ into itself. A proof that Π is continuous can be found in Vuillemin [15].

Although continuity ensures that recursive programs are well-defined, it does not guarantee that they have effective implementations. For this reason, first order programming logic stipulates that program data domains must satisfy several additional constraints which are summarized in the term *arithmeticity*. The most important difference between an arithmetic domain and a continuous domain is that the former must be finitely generated. First order programming logic critically depends on this property, because it presumes that the domain obeys the principle of structural induction. The remaining properties that distinguish arithmetic domains from continuous ones (items (i) and (iii) in the definition of arithmeticity below) are not essential.

Definition A structure D is *flat* iff it is continuous under the binary relation $\sqsubseteq$ defined by the identity $a \sqsubseteq b \equiv [a = b \vee a = \perp]$.

Definition A continuous function f: $A_1 \times \ldots \times A_m \to B$ is *strict* iff $f(x_1,\ldots,x_m)$ diverges ($= \perp$) when any argument x_i diverges.

Definition Let D be a data domain (structure) with signature $\sigma = \langle G,R,\# \rangle$. D is an *arithmetic domain* iff it satisfies the following properties:

(i) D is flat.

(ii) D is finitely generated by the set of generators $Gen_D = \{g_1,...,g_k\}$.

(iii) The set of functions **G** includes the constants {**true**, **false**} and the special function **if-then-else** which partitions |D| into three non-empty disjoint subsets D_{true}, D_{false}, $D_{\perp}$ such that

$$\begin{aligned}
&\mathbf{true} \in D_{true}\\
&\mathbf{false} \in D_{false}\\
&\perp \in D_{\perp}\\
&\mathbf{if}\ p\ \mathbf{then}\ \alpha\ \mathbf{else}\ \beta = \alpha \ \text{ if } p \in D_{true}\\
&\mathbf{if}\ p\ \mathbf{then}\ \alpha\ \mathbf{else}\ \beta = \beta \ \text{ if } p \in D_{false}\\
&\mathbf{if}\ p\ \mathbf{then}\ \alpha\ \mathbf{else}\ \beta = \perp \ \text{ if } p \in D_{\perp}.
\end{aligned}$$

All functions in **G** other than **if-then-else** must be strict.

Remark With the exception of the finite generation property (ii), the preceding list of conditions on **D** can be formally expressed by a finite set of sentences in the language L_σ. The finite generation property cannot be expressed in L_σ, because it is equivalent to asserting that induction holds for all unary relations—an uncountable set with many members that cannot be defined within L_σ.

3.2. Status of Induction

Before we complete our synopsis of basic first order programming logic by stating the soundness theorem, we must clarify the status of induction in arithmetic domains that are augmented by definitions. Formalizing induction in first order logic requires an axiom scheme: a template with a free formula parameter. The scheme represents the infinite recursive set of sentences consisting of all possible instantiations of the template. Let **D** be a structure that is finitely generated by the function symbols $Gen_D = \{g_1,...,g_k\}$. Obviously, the following structural induction principle $\mathbf{Ind_D}$ holds for every unary relation $\rho(x)$ over **D**,

$$[\bigwedge_{1\le i\le k} \forall x_1,...,x_{\#g_i} (\rho(x_1) \wedge ... \wedge \rho(x_{\#g_i}) \supset \rho(g_i(x_1,...,x_{\#g_i})))] \supset \forall x\, \rho(x).$$

A first order axiomatization A_D for **D** typically includes the following axiom scheme Ind_D formalizing the induction principle $\mathbf{Ind_D}$

$$[\bigwedge_{1\le i\le k} \forall x_1,...,x_{\#g_i} (\rho(x_1) \wedge ... \wedge \rho(x_{\#g_i}) \supset \rho(g_i(x_1,...,x_{\#g_i})))] \supset \forall x\, \rho(x)$$

where $\rho(x)$ is an arbitrary formula in L_σ defining a unary relation. The scheme asserts that structural induction holds for every *definable* unary relation in the domain, a denumerable subset of the set of all unary relations on |D|.

When we augment a finitely generated domain D by a definition Δ introducing new function and relation symbols P, how should we interpret the induction scheme Ind_D? Does the formula parameter ρ range over all formulas of the expanded language or only formulas of the original language? On the assumption that we are interested in formulating the strongest possible theory, the answer is clear. Since the universe of the expanded structure is identical to the finitely generated universe of the original domain, the induction principle holds for all new relations that are definable in the expanded structure (using the augmented language). Consequently, first order programming logic stipulates that the induction scheme ranges over all formulas in the expanded language. This convention is consistent with the treatment of "logical" axiom schemes[1] in first order deductive systems (e.g., the scheme defining the equality relation [10]).

To accommodate this interpretation of the induction scheme Ind_D without introducing more notation, we will follow the convention that unless we specifically state otherwise, a definition Δ over a finitely generated domain **D** implicitly includes all of the new instances of the structural induction scheme Ind_D for D. In this context, $A_D \cup \Delta$ denotes the set of axioms consisting of the union of A_D, Δ, and the set *all new instances* of the induction scheme Ind_D. For reasons that will become clear when we discuss non-standard models, we will follow exactly the same convention for definitions over non-standard models corresponding to finitely generated domains (see Section 5). To distinguish the two possible interpretations of the induction scheme Ind_D for a finitely generated domain, we will use the term *arithmetic definition* to identify a definition that implicitly includes the new instances of Ind_D and the term *non-arithmetic*

[1]Many first order deductive systems (such as the Hilbert-style system described by Enderton [10]) include "logical" axiom schemes: templates that generate sentences that are true regardless of the structure in which they are interpreted. In this context, the sentences forming the axiomatization of a particular theory are called "non-logical" axioms.

definition to identify one that does not.

The following theorem is the foundation of first order programming logic; it firmly establishes that we can interpret recursive programs as definitions in first order logic.

Theorem (Soundness Theorem) Let P be a recursive program $\{ f_1(\bar{x}_1)=t_1, f_2(\bar{x}_2)=t_2, \ldots, f_n(\bar{x}_n)=t_n \}$ over an arithmetic domain D, and let F denote the least fixed-point of the functional for P. Then P is an arithmetic definition over D satisfying the model $D \cup F$.

Proof A simple application of Kleene's Recursion Theorem [14]. See reference [8]. □

To reason about a recursive program P over an arithmetic domain D, we apply conventional first order deduction to a suitable[2] first order axiomatization including a structural induction axiom scheme Ind_D for D. The following example demonstrates the simplicity of the approach.

Let the function zero over the natural numbers N augmented by $\{\bot\}$ be defined by the recursive program:

(1) zero(n) = if n equal 0 then 0 else zero(n−1).

We will prove that the function zero equals 0 for all natural numbers.

Theorem $\forall n\, [n \neq \bot \supset zero(n) = 0]$.

Proof The proof proceeds by induction on n.

Basis: n = 0.

This case is a trivial simplification using axioms of the data domain and the equation (1): zero(n) = if 0 equal 0 then 0 else zero(n−1) = 0.

Induction step: n>0.

We assume by hypothesis that the theorem holds for all n'<n. Since n>0

zero(n) = if n equal 0 then 0 else zero (n−1) = zero(n−1)

which is 0 by hypothesis.

4. Ambiguity in First Order Programming Logic

Although the soundness theorem of first order programming logic shows that recursive programs are arithmetic definitions over an arithmetic domain D, it does not rule out the possibility of ambiguity in the definitions. In fact, recursive programs can be ambiguous. As a result, unless we add extra machinery to first order programming logic, it is not complete relative to the underlying data domain theory. In other words, given a program P over an arithmetic data domain with signature σ, there are true sentences (using the standard least fixed-point interpretation for the program) in the expanded language $L_\sigma \cup P$ that are not derivable from the definition P even if we have access to an oracle for sentences in the language L_D.

The source of the incompleteness is the fact that the functional corresponding to a recursive program can have multiple fixed-points. Interpreting a recursive program P over an arithmetic data domain D as definition expanding D forces the defined functions F to be a fixed-point of the corresponding functional Π, but not the *least* fixed-point. If we augment D by any fixed-point F of the functional Π for P, the expanded structure $D \cup F$ is a model for P.

In practice, recursive programs are rarely ambiguous because practical programs typically do not include divergent functions. If every function in a recursive program P is total, the program is unambiguous (and hence the logic is complete relative to an oracle for the data domain) because the least fixed-point is the *only* fixed-point. On the other hand, if some function in the least fixed-point is partial, the program may or may not be ambiguous. In the latter case, there is a serious incompleteness problem, because the only provable properties of the program are those that hold for all fixed-points.

As an illustration, consider the following two examples. Given the program

(2) f(x) = f(x) ,

we cannot prove anything interesting about the function f since any interpretation for f over the domain satisfies equation (2), not just the everywhere undefined function. In contrast, the program

(3) f(x) = f(x) + 1 ,

[2]We will make this notion precise (as the property of *arithmetical completeness*) in Section 5.

which determines exactly the same function f, is unambiguous. Consequently, given equation (3), we can easily prove in first order programming logic that

$\forall x\, f(x) = \bot$.

Fortunately, there are two elegant solutions to the ambiguity problem. First, there is a simple construction[3] that converts recursive programs into equivalent recursive programs (called *complete* programs) with unique fixed-points, yet preserves the intuitive content of the original programs. This approach is discussed in reference [10]. Second, it is possible to augment a recursive program P by a *minimization* scheme Min_P asserting that set of functions F defined in P approximates every definable set of functions F' satisfying the same set of equations P. In this paper, we will focus on the latter approach, which is conceptually simpler, although less constructive.

Definition Let P be the recursive program $\{ f_1(\bar{x}_1)=t_1,\ f_2(\bar{x}_2)=t_2,\ \ldots,\ f_n(\bar{x}_n)=t_n \}$ over the arithmetic domain D with signature σ. The *minimization scheme* Min_P corresponding to P is the set of all sentences of the form

$$\bigwedge_{1\le i\le n} [\forall \bar{x}_i\ [\mathit{f}_i(\bar{x}_i) \supseteq t_{i[F\leftarrow \mathcal{F}]}] \supset \bigwedge_{1\le i\le n} [f_i(\bar{x}_i) \subseteq \mathit{f}_i(\bar{x}_i)]$$

where the function symbols f_i, i=1,...,n denote functions *definable in* D with arities $\# f_i$, i=1,...,n; $t_{[F\leftarrow \mathcal{F}]}$ denotes the term t with every occurrence of a program function symbol f_i replaced by the corresponding function symbol f_i; and the formula $\alpha \subseteq \beta$ (alternately $\beta \supseteq \alpha$) abbreviates the formula $\alpha = \beta \vee \alpha = \bot$.

Remark The function parameters $\mathit{f}_1,\ldots,\mathit{f}_n$ may be instantiated by any n-tuple of functions defined by formulas $\varphi_1(\bar{x}_1,y),\ldots,\varphi_n(\bar{x}_n,y)$.

In order to formulate and prove the theorem asserting that a recursive program P (over a non-trivial data domain) augmented by the minimization scheme Min_P is an unambiguous definition over D, we must introduce some new definitions. In particular, we need to introduce what John McCarthy calls *elementary syntax*. Elementary syntax is a unambiguous definition over the data domain D that introduces functions for encoding finite sequences of domain elements as individual elements. We formalize the notion as follows.

Definition A data domain D *supports elementary syntax*[4] iff there exists an unambiguous definition Elem over D introducing a set of functions and relations **Code** including the constant **empty**; unary functions **mkatom** (denoted by the prefix operator ' (quote)), **extract**, **head**, **tail**; the binary function **cons**; the unary relations **code**, **seq**, **atom**; and the binary relation **occur** (denoted by the infix operator $\in$) satisfying the following set A_{Code} sentences:

(a) $\forall x\, [x{:}atom \equiv x \neq \bot \wedge \exists y\ x = 'y]$
(b) $\forall x\, [x{:}seq \equiv x \neq \bot \wedge (x = empty \vee \exists u{:}code, v{:}seq\ cons(u,v) = x)]$
(c) $\forall x,y\, [x{:}atom \wedge y{:}seq \supset x \neq y]$
(d) $\forall x\, [x{:}code \equiv x{:}atom \vee x{:}seq]$
(e) $'\bot = \bot \wedge \forall x\, [x \neq \bot \supset extract('x) = x]$
(f) $head(empty) = \bot \wedge tail(empty) = \bot$
(g) $\forall x\, [cons(x,\bot) = \bot \wedge cons(\bot,x) = \bot]$
(h) $\forall x{:}code, y{:}seq\, [head(cons(x,y)) = x \wedge tail(cons(x,y)) = y]$
(i) $\forall x,y\, [x \in y \equiv x{:}code \wedge y{:}seq \wedge (x = head(y) \vee x \in head(y) \vee x = tail(y) \vee x \in tail(y))]$
(j) $\forall z{:}seq[\forall y{:}seq\, (y \in z \supset \rho(y)) \supset \rho(z)] \supset \forall x{:}seq\ \rho(x)$ for every formula $\rho(x)$ in $L_\sigma \cup Code$.

Remark Any effective arithmetic domain in which the the four integer operations 0, 1, +, and × are definable (up to isomorphism) supports elementary syntax since arbitrary sequences and atoms can be coded as Godel numbers.

Theorem (Completeness Theorem) Let P be a recursive program $\{ f_1(\bar{x}_1)=t_1,\ f_2(\bar{x}_2)=t_2,\ f_n(\bar{x}_n)=t_n \}$ over an arithmetic domain D supporting elementary syntax, and let F denote the least fixed-point of the functional for P. Then P augmented by the minimization scheme Min_P is an unambiguous definition over D. In fact, there exists a set Φ of *program* formulas $\varphi_i(\bar{x}_i,y)$, i=1,...,n, constructible[5] from P such that $\varphi_i(\bar{x}_i,y)$ defines f_i.

Proof For the sake of simplicity, we will assume that P consists of a single recursion equation $\{ f(\bar{x})=t \}$ where $\bar{x}$ is a $\#$f-tuple of variables. The generalization to arbitrary recursive programs straightforward, but requires more complex notation.

---

[3]There are many syntactically different ways to formulate the construction that are all logically equivalent.

[4]There are many different ways to formalize this notion that are logically equivalent, just as there are many different but equivalent formulations of the notion of computable function.

The critical step in the proof is constructing the program formula $\varphi(\bar{x},y)$ in $L_\sigma \cup$ Code defining the least fixed-point of the functional Π corresponding to P. The key idea underlying the construction is that for each pair (a,b) in f where b is convergent, there exists a witness: the least finite function[6] $f^* \subseteq f$ such that:

(i) The pair $(a,b) \in f^*$ (i.e, $f^*(a)=b$).

(ii) The function f^* is *closed under* P: $f^* \subseteq \Pi(f^*)$.

Using elementary syntax we can build simple finite representations in |D| for witnesses on D.

Notation Let the form $\langle e_1,\ldots,e_{n-1},e_n\rangle$ (where $n>0$) abbreviate the term $cons(e_1,cons(\ldots,cons(e_{n-1},cons(e_n,empty))\ldots))$ denoting the sequence of elements $e_1,\ldots,e_n$ in |D|.

As a concrete representation for witnesses, we define a special form of sequence called a hereditary tree. Within a hereditary tree, a data object $d \in |D|$ other than $\bot$ is represented by the atom 'd (mkatom(d)) to distinguish it from codes for sequences. The representation of the data object $\bot$ poses a special problem because it cannot be quoted or embedded inside a sequence. For this reason, we use the object **empty** to represent $\bot$ inside a hereditary tree.

Definition Given an element $d \in |D|$, let $R[d]$ denote the object in |D| representing d: **empty** if $d=\bot$ and 'd otherwise. R[d] is called the *internal name* for d. Similarly, given an #f-tuple $\bar{a}$ over |D|, let $R[\bar{a}]$ denote the *internal name* for $\bar{a}$: $\langle R[a_1],\ldots,R[a_{\#f}]\rangle$. Given an internal name α for a #f-tuple $\bar{a}$, let $A[\alpha]$ denote $\bar{a}$; A is the inverse of R. The relation $\{(\bar{d}, R[\bar{d}]) \mid \bar{d} \in |D|^{\#f}\}$ is clearly definable over D by a formula $\Theta(\bar{x},x')$ in L_D. The details are left to the reader.

Definition Let P be a recursive program $\{ f(\bar{x})=t \}$ over an arithmetic domain D supporting elementary syntax and let the infix operator $\sqcup$ denote the least upper bound operation[7] on functions mapping $|D|^{\#f} \to |D|$. The corresponding set of the *hereditary trees*, set of *hereditary graphs*, and the abstraction function **Fun** mapping hereditary trees and graphs into corresponding witnesses (finite functions on |D|) are inductively defined as follows:

(i) The object **empty** is a hereditary graph. $\mathbf{Fun}(\mathbf{empty}) = \{(d,\bot) \mid d \in |D|\}$.

(ii) The object $\langle g_1,\ldots,g_n\rangle$ in |D| is a hereditary graph iff $g_1,\ldots,g_n$ are hereditary trees. $\mathbf{Fun}(\langle g_1,\ldots,g_n\rangle) = (\bigsqcup_{1\le i\le n}(\mathbf{Fun}(g_i))$.

(iii) The object $\langle\langle R[\bar{a}],'b\rangle,G\rangle$ is a hereditary tree iff $\bar{a}$ is an #f-tuple over |D|, b is a data object other than $\bot$, G is a hereditary graph, and $(\bar{a},b) \in \Pi(\mathbf{Fun}(G))$. $\mathbf{Fun}(\langle\langle R[\bar{a}],'b\rangle,G\rangle = \{(a,b)\} \sqcup \mathbf{Fun}(G)$.

A hereditary tree of the form $\langle\langle R[\bar{a}],'b\rangle,G\rangle$ is called a *witness tree* for the pair $(\bar{a},b)$.

Definition The *program formula* $\varphi(\bar{x},y)$ corresponding to P has the form

$$\exists g{:}seq\,(Witness(\bar{x},y,g)) \lor (\forall g{:}seq\,[\neg Witness(\bar{x},y,g)] \land y=\bot)$$

where $Witness(\bar{x},y,g)$ is a formula asserting that g is a hereditary tree of P, y is convergent, and $(\bar{x},y) \in \mathbf{Fun}(g)$. $Witness(\bar{x},y,g)$ has the form

$$\exists x',G{:}seq\,[\Theta(\bar{x},x') \land \langle\langle x','y\rangle,G\rangle=g] \land$$
$$\forall H,u'{:}seq\,\forall \bar{u},v\,[(\Theta(\bar{u},u') \land \langle\langle u','v\rangle, H\rangle \Subset g) \supset \pi(\bar{u},v,H)]$$

where the infix relation symbol $\Subset$ is defined by

$$u \Subset v \equiv u=v \lor u \in v$$

and $\pi(\bar{u},v,H)$ is the *functional formula* generated from the program text P asserting that v is convergent and the pair $(\bar{u},v) \in \Pi(\mathbf{Fun}(H))$.

The formula $Witness(\bar{x},y,g)$ asserts that:

(i) g has the form [[x','y],G] where x' is the internal name of $\bar{x}$.

(ii) For every subsequence of g of the form $\langle\langle u','v\rangle,H\rangle$ (including $H=G$), the formula $\pi(\bar{u},v,H)$ holds.

Condition (i) implicitly asserts that y is convergent, because the functions **mkatom** (') and cons ($\langle\rangle$) are strict.

Definition Let P be a recursive program $\{ f(\bar{x})=t \}$ over an arithmetic domain D supporting elementary syntax, and let y and G be variables distinct from $\bar{x}$. The *functional formula* $\pi(\bar{x},y,G)$ corresponding to P is defined by

---

[5]The function mapping P to Φ is recursive.

[6]A function that converges at only a finite number of points in its domain.

[7]If we eliminate pairs of the form $(d,\bot)$ from graphs, the two operations—lub and set union are identical.

$\pi(\bar{x},y,G) \equiv Fm[t](\bar{x},y,G)$

where *Fm* is a syntactic function[8] mapping terms containing no free variables other than $\bar{x}$ into formulas with no free variables other than G, $\bar{x}$, and y. Given a term u (with no free variables other than $\bar{x}$), *Fm*[u] is a formula defining the function $\lambda\bar{x}.u$ where the function symbol f is interpreted as Fun(G). *Fm* is determined by the following inductive definition:

(i) For every term u not containing the program function symbol f

$$Fm[u] \equiv y=u\,.$$

(ii) For every term u that is a conditional expression if γ then α else β containing an occurrence of f,

$$Fm[u] \equiv (Fm[\gamma](\bar{x},\text{true},G) \wedge Fm[\alpha](\bar{x},y,G)) \vee (Fm[\gamma](\bar{x},\text{false},G) \wedge Fm[\beta](\bar{x},y,G))\,.$$

(iii) For every term u of the form $h(\alpha_1,\ldots,\alpha_{\#h})$ containing an occurrence of f where h is a function symbol in $L_\sigma \cup$Code other than if-then-else

$$Fm[u] \equiv \exists z_1,\ldots,z_{\#h}\,(\textstyle\bigwedge_{1\le i\le\#h}[Fm[\alpha_i](\bar{x},z_i,G)] \wedge y=h(z_1,\ldots,z_{\#h}))\,.$$

(iv) For every term u of the form $f(\alpha_1,\ldots,\alpha_{\#f})$

$$Fm[u] \equiv \exists z_1,\ldots,z_{\#h}\,(\textstyle\bigwedge_{1\le i\le\#f}[Fm[\alpha_i](\bar{x},z_i,G)] \wedge \exists x'{:}\text{code}\,\exists H{:}\text{seq}\,[\Theta(\bar{x},x) \wedge \langle\langle x','y\rangle,H\rangle \in G])\,.$$

Given these constructions, the proof of the theorem reduces to the proof of two lemmas.

Lemma 1 Let P be a recursive program { $f(\bar{x})=t$ } over an arithmetic domain D supporting elementary syntax and let f denote the least fixed-point of the corresponding functional Π. For every pair $(\bar{a},b)$ in $|D|^{\#f}\times|D|$ where b is convergent, there exists a witness tree g for $(\bar{a},b)$ iff $(\bar{a},b)\in f$.

Proof One direction ($\rightarrow$) is a straightforward induction on the structure of g. The converse ($\leftarrow$) is an induction on the smallest integer k such that $(\bar{a},b)\in\Pi^k(\lambda\bar{x}.\bot)$. □

Lemma 2 Let P be a recursive program { $f(\bar{x})=t$ } over an arithmetic domain D supporting elementary syntax and let $(\bar{a},b)\in f$ where b is convergent. A sequence $g \in |D|$ is a witness tree for $(\bar{a},b)$ iff the formula Witness($\bar{a}$,b,g) is TRUE in D.

Proof. For any particular program P, the proof is a tedious induction on the structure of g. □

Given the preceding two lemmas, $\varphi(\bar{x},y)$ obviously defines f in D. As a result, the arithmetic definition $P\cup Min_P$ must be unambiguous because any other interpretation $\tilde{f}$ for f would contradict the sentence in Min_P where the formula parameter *f* is instantiated by f (the function defined by $\varphi(\bar{x},y)$). □ (Completeness Theorem).

5. Recursive Programs in Non-standard Models

In first order logic, there is no way to avoid the issue of non-standard models. First, by the Lowenheim-Skolem Theorem [10], every structure with an infinite universe has non-isomorphic models (although they may be elementarily equivalent to the standard one). Second, and more importantly, Godel's Incompleteness Theorem asserts that every recursively enumerable axiomatization of a structure supporting elementary syntax must be incomplete. Hence, by the Completeness Theorem for first order logic (also due to Godel), there must be non-standard models in which the unprovable true statements are refuted.

Before we can make precise statements about non-standard models, we need to introduce some additional terminology.

Definition Let D be a finitely generated domain with generator set Gen_D. An axiomatization A_D for D is inductive iff A_D logically implies the structural induction axiom scheme Ind_D for D.

Definition Assume that we are given an arithmetic domain D and generator set Gen_D. A set A_D sentences in the language L_D is an *arithmetically complete* axiomatization of D iff

(i) D is a model of A_D.

(ii) A_D logically implies all the sentences expressing the arithmetic properties of D (listed in the definition of arithmetic domain in Section 4) except the structural induction principle Ind_D (which cannot be expressed within a

---

[8] *Fm* is analogous to a macro-instruction in an assembly language program..

first order theory).

(iii) A_D is inductive.

(iv) A_D is term-complete.[9]

Given an arithmetic domain D, it is a straightforward but tedious (and error-prone) exercise to devise an effective, arithmetically complete axiomatization for D (see [8]). An arithmetically complete axiomatization A_D for an arithmetic domain D has many distinct (non-isomorphic) models. The non-standard models (models other than D) are not necessarily arithmetic, since induction may fail for unary relations that are not definable. On the other hand, they do satisfy the structural induction scheme Ind_D for D.

Definition A structure D' is *weakly arithmetic* iff it is a model of an arithmetically complete set of sentences T.

The only difference between an arithmetic and a weakly arithmetic model of T is that induction may fail in a weakly arithmetic model for relations that are not definable in T. If we confine out attention to arithmetically complete axiomatizations, then non-standard models are weakly arithmetic structures. Given a recursive program P over the arithmetic domain D, we can interpret P as a definition over an arbitrary non-standard model D' if we can find an interpretation F' for the function symbols F (introduced in P) such that $D' \cup F'$ is a model for $P \cup Ind_D$.

As formulated in Sections 3 and 4, the soundness and the completeness theorems for first order programming logic say nothing about what recursive programs over D mean in weakly arithmetic domains. Do they necessarily mean anything at all? Can we generalize the soundness and completeness theorems so that they apply to non-standard models? The remainder of this paper focuses on answering these questions.

5.1. Three Examples

To gain insight into the behavior of recursive programs over non-standard models, we will examine a series of three examples. First, let N denote the structure consisting of the natural numbers, the constant 0, and the strict unary function suc. The following axioms form a complete axiomatization A_N for N (for a proof of completeness, see reference [10]).

(i) $\forall x\ suc(x) \neq 0$

(ii) $\forall x\ (x \neq 0 \supset \exists y\ x = suc(y))$

(iii) $\forall x,y\ [suc(x) = suc(y) \supset x = y]$

(iv) $\rho(0) \wedge \forall y\ [\rho(y) \supset \rho(suc(y))] \supset \forall x\ \rho(x)$ for every formula ρ in the language of N.

Obviously, the two operations 0 and suc generate the domain.

The smallest non-standard model for A_N is the structure N' consisting of a universe containing the natural numbers augmented by a single *Z-chain* $\{\omega_i \mid i \in \{...,-1,0,1,2,...\}\}$ the constant 0, and the function suc' extending suc determined by $suc'(\omega_i = \omega_{i+1}$. The following sentence

(4) $\forall x\ [0 + x = x] \wedge \forall x,y\ [suc(x) + y = suc(x + y)]$

is an unambiguous arithmetic definition over N of the addition function +. However, it is easy to prove by contradiction that equation (4) is inconsistent with N'. Assume that +' is an interpretation for + over |N'| satisfying (4). What is the value of the term $\omega_0 + \omega_0$? It must be some element of |N'|, but all possible choices contradict the two following two facts:

(i) For all integers i and j, $\omega_i = \omega_j$ iff $i = j$.

(ii) For all integers i and natural numbers j, $\omega_i \neq j$.

Although this example demonstrates that an unambiguous definition over the standard (least) model of a complete inductive theory does not necessarily have any interpretation in a non-standard (elementarily equivalent) model, its relevance to first order programming logic is not immediately obvious, because N is not an arithmetic domain and (4) is technically not a recursive program (although it closely resembles one). In fact, interpreting definitions over non-standard models of first order programming logic is a more tractable problem than it is in a more general setting since all the models of an arithmetically complete axiomatization A_D of an arithmetic domain D are continuous, implying

[9]Although none of the theorems that we prove in this paper depend on this property, it ensures that an arithmetically complete axiomatization has a unique (up to isomorphism) arithmetic model. In addition, it guarantees that arithmetically complete axiomatizations for non-trivial arithmetic domains support elementary syntax (see below).

that every recursive program over D has a least fixed-point in every model of A_D.

Let us examine a variation on the previous example involving a recursive program over an arithmetic domain. Let N^+ be the arithmetic data domain consisting of a universe containing of the natural numbers augmented by $\perp$, the constants $\perp$ and 0 (false); the strict unary functions **suc** and **pred**; the strict binary function **equal**; and the ternary conditional function **if-then-else**. A complete axiomatization A_{N^+} for N^+ appears in Appendix I. The three operations $\perp$, 0, and **suc** generate the domain.

The smallest non-standard model for A_{N^+} is the structure $N^{+\prime}$ consisting of universe containing the natural numbers augmented by $\perp$ and a *Z-chain* $\{\omega_i, i \in \{...,-1,0,1,2,...\}\}$, and the set of functions containing the obvious extensions of the operations of N. The recursive program

(5) $x + y = \text{if } x \text{ equal } 0 \text{ then } y \text{ else suc(pred}(x) + y)$

is an unambiguous arithmetic definition over N of the addition function +. In the non-standard model $N^{+\prime}$, however, we encounter a surprisingly anomaly. Since $N^{+\prime}$ is continuous, the functional for P over $N^{+\prime}$ has a least fixed-point $+'$ defined by

$$x +' y = \begin{cases} x + y & \text{if } x,y \in |N^+| \\ \perp & \text{otherwise} \end{cases}$$

where + denotes the interpretation of + in N^+. In addition, $+'$ is the only function over $|N^{+\prime}|$ satisfying equation (5). Nevertheless, in first order programming logic, it is trivial to prove by structural induction that the function denoted by the symbol + is total (converges for convergent arguments), yielding an apparent contradiction. What is going on?

The answer is that the function $+'$ violates the induction principle $\mathbf{Ind}_{N^+}$ corresponding to the generator set $\{\perp, 0, \text{suc}\}$. $N^{+\prime}$ is a model for the axiomatization A_{N^+} only because the functions and relations on $|N^{+\prime}|$ that violate the induction principle $\mathbf{Ind}_{N^+}$ are not definable in $N^{+\prime}$. Since the axiom scheme Ind_{N^+} formalizing $\mathbf{Ind}_{N^+}$ asserts that induction holds only for definable relations $A_N{}^+$ does not exclude $N^{+\prime}$ as a model. Augmenting $A_N{}^+$ by equation (5) and the corresponding extra instances of the induction scheme Ind_{N^+} eliminates $N^{+}+$ as a model. The program (5) makes sense as a *non-arithmetic* definition over $N^{+\prime}$ but not as an *arithmetic* one.

As a final example, consider the following program (taken from Hitchcock and Park [16]) over N^+

(6) $\text{zero}(n) = \text{if } n \text{ equal } 0 \text{ then } 0 \text{ else zero}(n-1)$,

defining the strict function **zero** that is 0 everywhere except at $\perp$. Over the standard model N^+, it is an unambiguous arithmetic definition. On the other hand, as a non-arithmetic definition over the non-standard model $N^{+\prime}$, (6) is ambiguous! The functional Π' on $N^{+\prime}$ corresponding to P has two fixed-points: the least fixed-point $\mathbf{zero}^+$ defined by:

$$\mathbf{zero}^+(x) = 0 \quad \text{if } x \text{ is a standard natural number}$$
$$= \perp \quad \text{otherwise } (x \text{ is } \perp \text{ or non-standard}) .$$

and the strict function **zero'** that is 0 everywhere except at $\perp$. In first order programming logic we can prove (the example at the end of Section 3) that the function defined in equation (6) is identically 0 except at $\perp$. Although the least fixed-point $\mathbf{zero}^+$ over the non-standard model $N^{+\prime}$ violates the induction principle $\mathbf{Ind}_{N^+}$, the other fixed-point **zero'** does not. As an arithmetic definition over the non-standard model $N^{+\prime}$, equation (6) is unambiguous because **zero'** is the only interpretation consistent with both P and the induction principle $\mathbf{Ind}_D$.

5.2. Generalizing Least Fixed-Point Semantics

The preceding examples demonstrate is that the least fixed-point interpretation for recursive programs does not work in non-standard models. Moreover, not every recursive program over an arithmetic domain (such as the definition of addition over N^+) is meaningful in every non-standard model of a corresponding arithmetically complete theory. For this reason, some computer scientists—believing that program proofs should address the behavior of recursive programs in all models—have rejected first order logic as a formal system for reasoning about recursive programs.

Our interpretation of the significance of the of this phenomenon is quite different. First, the meaning of recursive programs in non-standard models is not very important in practice. To programmers interested in proving properties of recursive programs over standard arithmetic domains, the behavior of those programs in non-standard models is irrelevant. Regardless of the meaning (or lack of it) of recursive programs in non-standard models, first order programming logic provides a sound, yet intuitively appealing formal system for deducing the properties of recursive programs. Second, the final example above suggests that under modest assumptions about either the program or the underlying data domain, recursive programs may be meaningful as arithmetic definitions in all models (including non-standard ones) of a corresponding arithmetically complete theory. However, in seeking to generalize first order programming logic to non-standard models, we cannot rely on the familiar least fixed-point interpretation for programs; instead, we must confine our attention to interpretations that are definable.

Let **D'** be a weakly arithmetic domain and let $\mathbf{Fun}_D$' denote the set of all continuous functions that are definable over **D'**. Given a recursive program P over D', under what circumstances does the corresponding functional Π' have a solution in $\mathbf{Fun}_{D'}$? The following definition identifies the critical extra property that guarantees the existence of a least definable-fixed-point, the least fixed-point that lies within $\mathbf{Fun}_{D'}$.

Definition An arithmetically complete theory (axiomatization) T_D *supports elementary syntax* iff there is an unambiguous definition Elem introducing a set of functions and relations **Code** in every model of T_D such that the set of sentences A_{Code} (defined in Section 4) is derivable from $T_D \cup$Elem.

Fortunately, all models of non-trivial, arithmetically complete theories possess this property. In the second example above, the axiomatization A_{N+} does not support elementary syntax because it excludes the functions the + and $\times$. With the addition of a set of axioms Arith (possibly in the form of a recursive program) specifying these functions, A_{N+} would support elementary syntax. Many models of A_{N+} (inlcuding N+') have no expansion that satisfies the expanded axiomatization $A_{N+} \cup$Arith. Enriching a domain to support elementary syntax eliminates the pathological non-standard models.

Given the preceding definition, we can now formulate and prove the critical theorem underlying the generalization of first order programming logic to non-standard models.

Theorem (Generalized Recursion Theorem) For every recursive program P over a weakly arithmetic domain **D'** supporting elementary syntax, the corresponding functional **P'** has a least *definable* fixed-point.

Proof Let **D** and A_D be the arithmetic domain and arithmetically complete axiomatization corresponding to **D'**. Let Elem be the definition of elementary syntax extending A_D. From the completeness theorem for first order programming logic, we know that there exists a set of formulas that defines the least fixed-point of the functional Π for the program P over **D**. What does it mean in the weakly arithmetic model **D'**? The following lemma provides the answer—proving the theorem.

Lemma Let P be a recursive program over a weakly arithmetic domain **D'** supporting elementary syntax. The *program* formulas $\varphi_i(\bar{x}_i,y)$, $i=1,\ldots,n$, corresponding to P define a set of functions F' in D' such that $\Pi(F')=F'$ and F' approximates all other definable fixed-points of Π.

Proof For the sake of simplicity, we will assume that P consists of a single recursion equation $\{ f(\bar{x})=t \}$. First, we must establish that the formula $\varphi(\bar{x},y)$ defines a function $\tilde{f}$ in **D'**. It is easy to prove by induction on the structure of hereditary trees[10] that hereditary trees are mutually consistent: if $\langle\langle x,y\rangle,G\rangle$ appears in hereditary tree g and $\langle\langle x,z\rangle,H\rangle$ appears in hereditary tree h, then $y=z$. Similarly, we can prove by induction on g that the formula Witness($\bar{x}$,y,g) is TRUE for convergent y iff there is a witness tree g for ($\bar{x}$,y). Hence $\varphi(\bar{x},y)$ defines a function $\tilde{f}$.

For a particular program P, we can prove by induction on the structure of hereditary trees that $\tilde{f}$ (as defined by $\varphi(\bar{x},y)$) is a fixed-point of Π. Similarly, given that f' is some other fixed point defined by a formula $\varphi'(\bar{x},y)$, we can prove that $\tilde{f} \subseteq f'$ by induction on hereditary trees. □ (Lemma and Theorem).

5.3. Generalized Soundness and Completeness Theorem

Given the Generalized Recursion Theorem, the following generalization of the soundness and completeness theorems is a simple consequence.

Theorem (Generalized Soundness and Completeness Theorem) Let P be a recursive program

$$\{ f_1(\bar{x}_1)=t_1,\ f_2(\bar{x}_2)=t_2,\ \ldots,\ f_n(\bar{x}_n)=t_n \}$$

[10] In non-standard models, there are non-standard hereditary trees that are not denoted by any variable-free term in the language L_D.

over any model D' of an arithmetically complete axiomatization supporting elementary syntax, and let F' denote the least definable-fixed-point of the functional for P over D'. The program P augmented by the minimization scheme Min_P is an unambiguous arithmetic definition over D' determining the model $D' \cup F'$. In fact, there exists a set Φ of *program* formulas $\varphi_i(\bar{x}_i,y)$, $i=1,...,n$, constructible from P such that $\varphi_i(\bar{x}_i,y)$ defines f_i'.

Proof The soundness portion of the proof is identical to the proof of the soundness theorem in Section 3, except that the Generalized Recursion Theorem (requiring the elementary syntax hypothesis) is invoked instead of Kleene's Recursion Theorem.

The remainder of the proof proceeds as follows. The lemma embedded in the proof of Generalized Recursion Theorem establishes that the *program* formulas $\varphi_i(\bar{x}_i,y)$, $i=1,...,n$, define the least definable fixed-point F'. Let F denote an arbitrary interpretation for F over D' satisfying $A_D \cup P \cup Min_P$. From $A_D \cup P$, it is provable by induction on hereditary trees that $F' \subseteq F$. By the minimization scheme Min_P, $F=F'$, establishing that $P \cup Min_P$ is an unambiguous definition. □

The practical significance of the completeness theorem is demonstrated by the following corollary which asserts that can we can uniformly reduce the proof of properties of recursive programs to properties of the underlying theory.

Corollary (Elimination Property) Let A_D be an arithmetically complete axiomatization supporting elementary syntax. Given an arbitrary recursive program P and an arbitrary sentence ρ in $L_D \cup F$, there is an effective procedure for constructing a sentence ρ' such that $\rho \equiv \rho'$ is provable from A_D.

Proof The formula ρ' is $i=1,...,n$ generated by the following iterative process. Let ρ_0 be the formula ρ. For $i=1,2,...$ the formula ρ_i, is defined as follows:

(i) If ρ_{i-1} does not contain an occurrence of of a function symbol in F, then the process terminates with $\rho' \equiv \rho_{i-1}$.

(ii) Otherwise, let $f_k(\bar{u})$ be the leftmost occurrence of an application of function symbol in F and define ρ_i as

$$\exists z_i\ \varphi_k(\bar{u},z_i) \wedge \rho_{i-1}'$$

where ρ_{i-1}' denotes ρ_i with the leftmost occurrence $f_k(\bar{u})$ replaced by z_i.

Since the number of occurrences of function symbols F in is finite, the process obviously terminates. Furthermore, since φ_i defines f_i, each step in the process obviously preserves the meaning of the original formula ρ. For any particular program P and formula ρ, this argument is provable from $A_D \cup P \cup Min_P$. □

6. Related and Future Research

A group of Hungarian logicians—Andreka, Nemeti, and Sain—have independently developed a programming logic [1] with metamathematical properties similar to first order programming logic, although the pragmatic details are completely different. Their logic formalizes flowchart programs as relation definitions within a first order theory of the data domain excluding $\perp$. Given a flowchart program P, they generate a formula $\pi_P(x,y)$ that is true (in the standard model of the data domain) iff y is the output produced by applying program P to input x. The most attractive property of their logic is that it is complete with respect to the corresponding definition of computation—just as first order programming logic is complete with respect to least definable-fixed-point semantics. In order words, if a property holds for a computation in all models then it is provable in their logic. The intuitive explanation for this completeness property is that in non-standard models, a program generates non-standard computations.

The same idea can be exploited in the context of first order programming logic. It is possible to formulate a computational semantics for first order programming logic, based on term rewriting systems, with same completeness property. The trick is to formalize the notion of computation within the data domain theory itself by using elementary syntax to represent computation sequences. In a non-standard model, applying a function to a non-standard input produces a non-standard computation sequence.

As a formal system for reasoning about recursive programs, the major limitation of first order programming logic (as formulated in this paper) is that it does not accommodate "higher order" data domains—structures that are not flat. In practice, this restriction may not be very important since higher order objects can always be modeled by intensional descriptions (e.g., computable functions as program text). Nevertheless, we believe that an important direction for future research is to extend first order programming logic to "higher-order" domains. With this objective in mind, we are exploring the implications of allowing lazy (non-strict) constructors (e.g., lazy cons in LISP) in the data domain.

References

[1] H. Andreka, I. Nemeti and I. Sain. A complete logic for reasoning about programs via nonstandard model theory. Theoretical Computer Science 17 (1982), pp. 193-212, 259-278.

[2] R. Boyer and J Moore. Proving Theorems about LISP Functions, JACM 22, 1 (January 1975), pp. 129-144.

[3] R. Boyer and J Moore. A Computational Logic, Academic Press, New York, 1979.

[4] R. Cartwright. User-Defined Data Types as an Aid to Verifying LISP Programs. Proceedings of the Third International Colloquium on Automata, Languages, and Programming, S. Michaelson and R. Milner, eds. Edinburgh Press, Edinburgh, 1976, pp. 228-256.

[5] R. Cartwright. A Practical Formal Semantic Definition and Verification System for Typed LISP, Stanford A. I. Memo AIM-296, Stanford University, Stanford, California, 1976 (also published as a monograph in the Outstanding Dissertations in Computer Science series, Garland Publishing Company, New York, 1979).

[6] R. Cartwright. First Order Semantics: A Natural Programming Logic for Recursively Defined Functions, Technical Report TR 78-339, Computer Science Department, Cornell University, Ithaca, New York, 1978.

[7] R. Cartwright. Computational Models for Programming Logics, Technical Report, Computer Science Program, Mathematical Sciences Department, Rice University, 1983.

[8] R. Cartwright. Recursive Programs as Definitions in First Order Logic, SIAM Journal on Computing (to appear in 1983).

[9] R. Cartwright and J. McCarthy, Representation of Recursive Programs in First Order Logic, Stanford Artificial Intelligence Memo AIM-324, Stanford University, Stanford, California, 1979.

[10] H. Enderton, A Mathematical Introduction to Logic, Academic Press, New York, 1972.

[11] P. Hitchcock and D.M.R. Park. Induction Rules and Proofs of Program Termination. Proceedings of the First International Colloquium on Automata, Languages, and Programming, M. Nivat, ed. North-Holland, Amsterdam, 1973, pp. 225-251.

[12] Z. Manna. Introduction to the Mathematical Theory of Computation, MccGraw-Hill, New York, 1974.

[13] J. Stoy. Denotational Semantics: the Scott-Strachey Approach to Programming Language Theory, MIT Press, 1977.

[14] A. Tarski. A Lattice-Theoretical Fixpoint Theorem and its Applications, Pacific J. Math. 5 (1955), pp. 285-309.

[15] J. Vuillemin. Proof Techniques for Recursive Programs, Stanford A.I. Memo AIM-218, Stanford University, 1973.

Appendix I

Axiomatization of N^+

(1) $\forall x\ suc(x) \neq 0$

(2) $\forall x\ (x \neq 0 \supset \exists y\ x = suc(y))$

(3) $\forall x,y\ [suc(x) = suc(y) \supset x = y]$

(4) $\forall x\ [x{:}N \equiv x \neq \bot]$

(5) $\rho(0) \wedge \forall x{:}N[\rho(x) \supset \rho(suc(x))] \supset \forall x{:}N\ \rho(x)$ for every formula $\rho(x)$.

(6) $0{:}N \wedge \forall x{:}N\ [suc(x){:}N]$.

(7) $suc(\bot) = \bot$.

(8) $true = suc(0) \wedge false = 0$.

(9) $\forall x,y{:}N\ [(x = y \supset x\ equal\ y = true) \wedge (x \neq y \supset x\ equal\ y = false)]$

(10) $\forall x\ [\bot\ equal\ x = \bot \wedge x\ equal\ \bot = \bot]$

(11) $\forall y,z\ [if\ false\ then\ y\ else\ z = z]$.

(12) $\forall x{:}N\ \forall y,z\ [if\ suc(x)\ then\ y\ else\ z = y]$.

(13) $\forall y,z\ [if\ \bot\ then\ y\ else\ z = \bot]$.

Automatic Verification of Asynchronous Circuits†

by
E. Clarke and B. Mishra
Department of Computer Science
Carnegie-Mellon University
Pittsburgh, Pennsylvania 15213

Abstract.

Establishing the correctness of complicated asynchronous circuit is in general quite difficult because of the high degree of nondeterminism that is inherent in such devices. Nevertheless, it is also very important in view of the cost involved in design and testing of circuits. We show how to give specifications for circuits in a branching time temporal logic and how to mechanically verify them using a simple and efficient model checker. We also show how to tackle a large and complex circuit by verifying it hierarchically.

0. Introduction.

Verification of the correctness of asynchronous circuits has been considered an important problem for a long time. But, a lack of any formal and efficient method of verification has prevented the creation of practical design aids for this purpose. Since all the known techniques of simulation and prototype testing are time-consuming and not very reliable, there is an acute need for such tools. Moreover, as we build larger and more complex circuits, the cost of a single design error is likely to become even higher. In this paper, we describe an automatic verification system for asynchronous circuits, in which the specifications are expressed in a propositional temporal logic. We illustrate the use of our system by verifying a version of the self-timed queue element given in [MC80].

Bochmann [BO82] was probably the first to recognize the usefulness of temporal logic to describe circuits; he verified an implementation of a self-timed arbiter using linear temporal logic and what he called "reachability analysis". The work of Malchi and Owicki [MO82] identified additional temporal operators required to express interesting properties of a circuit and also gave specifications of a large class of modules used in self-timed systems.

Although these researchers have contributed significantly toward developing an adequate notation for expressing the correctness of asynchronous circuits, the problem of mechanically verifying a circuit using efficient algorithms still remains unsolved. In this paper we show how a simple and efficient algorithm, called a ***model checker***, can be used to verify various temporal properties of an asynchronous circuit. Roughly speaking, our method works by first building a labelled state-transition graph for an asynchronous circuit. This graph can be viewed as a finite ***Kripke Structure***. Then by using the model checker we determine the truth of various temporal formulæ in this Kripke Structure. As a result, it is possible to avoid the complexity associated with proof construction.

Most complex circuits are built out of relatively less complex modules in a hierarchical manner. Hence it should be possible to verify these circuits in a hierarchical manner, *i.e.* to verify the correctness of a larger module, given the premises that the smaller modules are correct. A hierarchical approach to verification is important in practice, because it enables us to verify circuits incrementally, to localize faults to small submodules and most importantly, to handle large circuits without a large growth in complexity. We show how the hierarchical method can be incorporated in a mechanical approach to circuit verification.

---

†.This research was partially supported by NSF Grant Number MCS-8216706.

The paper is organized as follows: Section 1 contains a brief description of the syntax and semantics of CTL, the temporal logic used in this paper, and also explains the algorithms used in the model checker. In Section 2, we give a simple step-by-step method used to verify circuits. In Section 3, we illustrate these methods by establishing some interesting properties of a Self-Timed Queue (FIFO) Element. In Section 4, we introduce a Hierarchical method to be used in verifying large and complex circuit and study some of the model-theoretic properties of the operation of "restriction" on a Kripke Structure. The paper concludes by pointing out the shortcomings of our approach and with a discussion of some remaining open problems.

1. CTL and Model Checker.

The logic that we use to give the specifications of a circuit is a propositional temporal logic of branching time, called CTL (Computation Tree Logic). This logic is essentially the same as that described in [CES83], [EC80] and [BMP81].

The syntax for CTL is given below:

Let $\mathcal{P}$ be the set of all the atomic propositions in the language, $\mathcal{L}$. Then

1. Every atomic proposition P in $\mathcal{P}$ is a formula in CTL.

2. If f_1 and f_2 are CTL formulæ, then so are $\neg f_1$, $f_1 \wedge f_2$, $\forall \mathbf{X} f_1$, $\exists \mathbf{X} f_1$, $\forall[f_1 \mathbf{U} f_2]$ and $\exists[f_1 \mathbf{U} f_2]$.

In this logic the propositional connectives $\neg$ and $\wedge$ have their usual meanings of negation and conjunction. The temporal operator $\mathbf{X}$ is the nexttime operator. Hence the intuitive meaning of $\forall \mathbf{X} f_1$ ($\exists \mathbf{X} f_1$) is that f_1 holds in every (in some) immediate successor state of the current state. The temporal operator $\mathbf{U}$ is the until operator. The intuitive meaning of $\forall[f_1 \mathbf{U} f_2]$ ($\exists[f_1 \mathbf{U} f_2]$) is that for every computation path (for some computation path), there exists an initial prefix of the path such that f_2 holds at the last state of the prefix and f_1 holds at all other states along the prefix.

We also use the following syntactic abbreviations:

$f_1 \vee f_2 \equiv \neg(\neg f_1 \wedge \neg f_2)$, $f_1 \rightarrow f_2 \equiv \neg f_1 \vee f_2$, and $f_1 \leftrightarrow f_2 \equiv (f_1 \rightarrow f_2) \wedge (f_2 \rightarrow f_1)$

$\forall \mathbf{F} f_1 \equiv \forall[\mathbf{true}\ \mathbf{U} f_1]$ which means for every path, there exists a state on the path at which f_1 holds.

$\exists \mathbf{F} f_1 \equiv \exists[\mathbf{true}\ \mathbf{U} f_1]$ which means for some path, there exists a state on the path at which f_1 holds.

$\forall \mathbf{G} f_1 \equiv \neg \exists \mathbf{F} \neg f_1$ which means for every path, at every node on the path f_1 holds.

$\exists \mathbf{G} f_1 \equiv \neg \forall \mathbf{F} \neg f_1$ which means for some path, at every node on the path f_1 holds.

$\forall[f_1 \mathbf{W} f_2] \equiv \neg \exists[(f_1 \wedge f_2) \mathbf{U} (\neg f_1 \wedge f_2)]$ which means that for every computation path, and for every initial prefix of the path, if f_2 holds at all the states along the prefix then f_1 holds at all the states along the same prefix.

$\exists[f_1 \mathbf{W} f_2] \equiv \neg \forall[(f_1 \wedge f_2) \mathbf{U} (\neg f_1 \wedge f_2)]$ which means that for some computation path, and for every initial prefix of the path, if f_2 holds at all the states along the prefix then f_1 holds at all the states along the same prefix.

In the last two formulæ $\mathbf{W}$ is the *while* operator. The formula $\forall[f_1 \mathbf{W} f_2]$ ($\exists[f_1 \mathbf{W} f_2]$) is read as "for every (some) path f_1 *while* f_2".

The semantics of a CTL formula is defined with respect to a labelled state-transition graph. A CTL structure is a triple $\mathcal{M} = (S, R, \Pi)$ where

1. S is a finite set of states.

2. R is a total binary relation on S ($R \subseteq S \times S$) and denotes the possible transitions between states.

3. Π is an assignment of atomic proposition to states, i.e. $\Pi : S \mapsto 2^P$.

A *path* is an infinite sequence of states $(s_0, s_1, s_2, \ldots)$ such that $\forall_i[(s_i, s_{i+1}) \in R]$. For any structure $\mathcal{M} = (S, R, \Pi)$ and state $s_0 \in S$, there is an *infinite computation tree* with root labelled s_0 such that $s \to t$ is an arc in the tree *iff* $\langle s, t\rangle \in R$.

The truth in a structure is expressed by $\mathcal{M}, s_0 \models f$, meaning that the temporal formula f is satisfied in the structure $\mathcal{M}$ at state s_0. The semantics of temporal formulæ is defined inductively as follows:

$s_0 \models P$ *iff* $P \in \Pi(s_0)$.

$s_0 \models \neg f$ *iff* $s_0 \not\models f$.

$s_0 \models f_1 \wedge f_2$ *iff* $s_0 \models f_1$ and $s_0 \models f_2$.

$s_0 \models \forall \mathbf{X} f_1$ *iff* for all states t such that $\langle s_0, t\rangle \in R, t \models f_1$.

$s_0 \models \exists \mathbf{X} f_1$ *iff* for some state t such that $\langle s_0, t\rangle \in R, t \models f_1$.

$s_0 \models \forall[f_1 \mathbf{U} f_2]$ *iff* for all paths $(s_0, s_1, s_2, \ldots)$, $\exists_{i \geq 0}[s_i \models f_2 \wedge \forall_{0 \leq j < i}[s_j \models f_1]]$.

$s_0 \models \exists[f_1 \mathbf{U} f_2]$ *iff* for some path $(s_0, s_1, s_2, \ldots)$, $\exists_{i \geq 0}[s_i \models f_2 \wedge \forall_{0 \leq j < i}[s_j \models f_1]]$.

From these it is quite easy to see that the semantics of $\mathbf{U}$, the until operator can be easily given in terms of a *least fixed-point* characterization:

$\forall[f_1 \mathbf{U} f_2] \equiv \mu \mathcal{F}. f_2 \vee (f_1 \wedge \forall \mathbf{X} \mathcal{F})$.

$\exists[f_1 \mathbf{U} f_2] \equiv \mu \mathcal{F}. f_2 \vee (f_1 \wedge \exists \mathbf{X} \mathcal{F})$.

The Model Checker for CTL can now be thought of as an algorithm that determines the satisfiability of a given temporal formula f_1 in a model $\mathcal{M}$, by computing these fixed points. A full description of the algorithm is given in [CES83].

In order to determine if a CTL formula f is true in a structure $\mathcal{M} = (S, R, \Pi)$, the algorithm labels each state of S so that when the algorithm terminates, the label of each state $s \in S$, *label*(s), will be equal to $\{f' \in sub(f) \mid \mathcal{M}, s \models f'\}$, where each element of $sub(f)$ is either a subformula of f or the negation of the subformula. Hence $\mathcal{M}, s \models f$ *iff* $f \in label(s)$ at the termination of the algorithm.

The labelling algorithm works in several stages. In the ith stage the algorithm labels the states by the subformulæ of length i. The labels assigned in the earlier stages, corresponding to the subformulæ of length less than i are used to perform the labelling in this stage. It can be shown that the algorithm makes at most $n = |f|$ stages of computation and that the total amount of the work involved in each stage is $O(\|S\| + \|R\|)$. Hence the time complexity of the Model Checker is $O(|f| \cdot (\|S\| + \|R\|))$. The algorithm is also fairly simple, since it involves only a few straightforward graph theoretic algorithms.

2. Verification of Circuits.

Given a circuit to be verified, the steps involved in using the Model Checker to assert the correctness of the temporal specifications are as follows:

Step 1. Building the Model.

The structure associated with the circuit is essentially a finite state-transition graph, with its vertices corresponding to the distinct states and the edges corresponding to the (possibly nondeterministic) transition between the states. The initial label associated with each state is the set of propositions true in that state. This labelled state-transition graph can be built using the following simple algorithm:

```
begin
    L := {initial state};
    while L ≠ ∅ do
    choose a state, say s from L and delete it from L;
        for all sets of inputs, possible in s do
            simulate s with this set of inputs;
            let L' be the set of new states;
            for each s' ∈ L' do
                s' is a successor of s;
                if s' has not been visited then
                    add s' to L;
            end;
        end;
    end;
end.
```

Algorithm 2.1

The Algorithm to build the Kripke Structure for an Asynchronous Circuit.

Step 2. Giving the Specifications of the Circuit in CTL.

This corresponds to the specifications of the temporal behaviour of the circuit. It usually involves *structural properties* (*i.e.* the specifications for different components of the circuit, specifications of the signalling scheme used for communication with various other modules, etc.), *safeness properties* and *liveness properties*. It should probably be pointed out that one need not give the complete specification of the circuit in order to verify some selected properties of the circuit using the model checker.

Step 3. Verifying the Circuit using the Model Checker.

This step involves the model checker which checks the truth of the specification (a formula in CTL) in the structure constructed in the *step 1.* The working of the Model Checker is described in the previous section.

3. Extended Example.

We illustrate the ideas presented so far by verifying some interesting properties of an asynchronous circuit. The example chosen for this purpose is one element of a Self-timed (FIFO) Queue , which originally appeared in an article by C. Seitz on self-timed system [MC80].

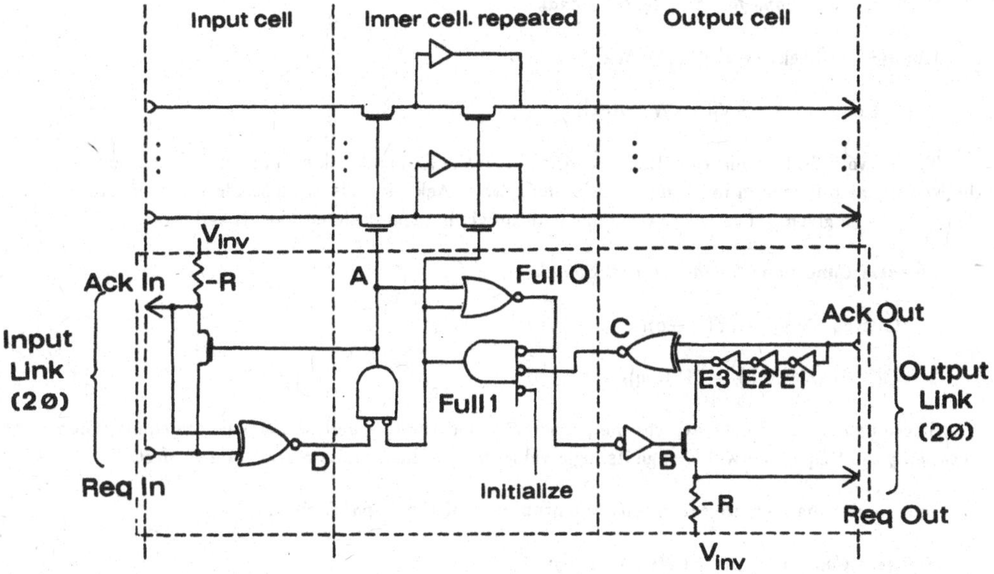

Figure. 3.1.
Queue (FIFO) element

a. Self-Timed FIFO Queue Element: The electrical circuit shown in *figure.* 3.1 is an implementation of a single FIFO queue element combined with some input and output logic. This circuit is of very practical importance; in pipeline processes in which operation times are variable, increased throughput can be achieved by interconnecting the processing elements through queues. The implementation uses simple asynchronous control and hence, can be used to build very fast and area-efficient queues.

The *inner cell* is intended to be replicated as many times as the number of words the queue is to be able to store, and the same control will operate a queue of any word length. The *input cell* and the *output cell* can be thought of as logic circuits converting the *two-cycle* signalling scheme at the input link to a *four-cycle* signalling scheme at the internal link and *vice versa*. The *inner cell* can be thought of as a latch that stores the state of the cell (*i.e.* whether the cell is *full* or *empty*), together with logic to generate a *load* signal and a set of *static registers* to store the *bits*. However, the design shown is *not* speed-independent, and uses the 3/2-rules. That is one may expect misoperation if particular sets of 3 gates have a smaller cumulative propagation delay time than other sets of 2 gates.

In the following subsections we specify and verify some interesting properties of the Queue element with a single inner cell.

b. Temporal Specifications for the Self-Timed Queue Element: We give examples of the ways in which various properties of a circuit can be given in CTL. In case of the Queue Element some of the *structural properties* that we might like to specify, are that the two-cycle signalling used at the *input links* and the *output links* is safe and live. Recall that the structural properties are specifications for various components and signalling schemes and thus, may be considered as premises that must be true in any CTL structure modelling the circuit. Hence the *request* signal must satisfy the following *safeness* and *liveness* conditions. (In the following CTL specifications we will use symbols Req and Ack for the *request* and the *acknowledgement* signals respectively.)

Safeness Conditions for the Request Signal.

1. $\forall\mathbf{G}((\neg Req \wedge Ack) \rightarrow \forall[\neg Req\ \mathbf{W}\ Ack])$

2. $\forall\mathbf{G}((Req \wedge \neg Ack) \rightarrow \forall[Req\ \mathbf{W}\ \neg Ack])$

These two CTL formulæ essentially express that if the Req and Ack signals are non-equipotential then the Req signal will remain in its stable logic value while Ack signal is in its stable value. In other words, Req will not be given unless acknowledgement to previous request signal has arrived.

Liveness Conditions for the Request Signal.

1. $\forall\mathbf{G}((Req \wedge Ack) \rightarrow \forall\mathbf{F}(\neg Req))$

2. $\forall\mathbf{G}((\neg Req \wedge \neg Ack) \rightarrow \forall\mathbf{F}(Req))$

These two CTL formulæ express the property that if the Req and Ack signals are equipotential then *eventually* the Req signal will change its logic value, thus indicating an arrival of a request.

In a similar manner, we can specify the properties of the *response* signal.

Safeness Conditions for the Response Signal.

1. $\forall\mathbf{G}((Req \wedge Ack) \rightarrow \forall[Ack\ \mathbf{W}\ Req])$

2. $\forall\mathbf{G}((\neg Req \wedge \neg Ack) \rightarrow \forall[\neg Ack\ \mathbf{W}\ \neg Req])$

Informally, they express the fact that Ack will not be given unless there has been a Req signal to cause it.

Liveness Conditions for the Response Signal.

1. $\forall\mathbf{G}((Req \wedge \neg Ack) \rightarrow \forall\mathbf{F}(Ack))$

2. $\forall\mathbf{G}((\neg Req \wedge Ack) \rightarrow \forall\mathbf{F}(\neg Ack))$

That is, if there had been a Req signal then *eventually* there will be an Ack signal in response to the request.

We can also give the *safeness* and the *liveness properties* of the FIFO Queue element in CTL. The following is a representative list of some of the properties, and by no means, exhaustive and complete. In the CTL formulæ given below, ReqIn stands for *request* at the *input links*, AckIn, for *acknowledgement* at the *input links*, ReqOut, for *request* at the *output links*, AckOut, for *acknowledgement* at the *output links* and Full1, for the state of the queue element when it holds some data.

Some Safeness Properties of the Queue Element.

$1. \forall\mathbf{G}(\neg(\text{ReqIn}=\text{AckIn}) \wedge \neg(\text{ReqOut}=\text{AckOut}) \rightarrow \forall[\neg(\text{ReqIn}=\text{AckIn})\,\mathbf{U}\,(\text{ReqOut}=\text{AckOut})])$

This formula states that if there have been a ReqIn and a ReqOut, then AckIn will not be given until AckOut has arrived.

Some Liveness Properties of the Queue Element.

$1. \forall\mathbf{G}(\neg(\text{ReqIn}=\text{AckIn}) \wedge \neg\text{Full1} \rightarrow \forall\mathbf{F}(\text{A}))$

This formula states that if there has been a ReqIn, and the memory element was empty, then ***eventually*** it will be loaded with the input data.

$2. \forall\mathbf{G}(\text{Full1} \rightarrow \forall\mathbf{F}(\neg(\text{ReqOut}=\text{AckOut})))$

That is the Queue Element is full then ***eventually*** a request at the ***output links*** will be generated in order to move the data to the next element in the queue.

$3. \forall\mathbf{G}((\text{ReqOut}=\text{AckOut}) \rightarrow \forall\mathbf{F}(\neg\text{Full1}))$

That is if the acknowledgement arrives at the ***output links*** thus indicating that the data stored in the current Queue Element has been moved to the next element, then ***eventually*** the Queue Element will mark its state as empty.

In the next subsection we show how these specifications can be verified automatically by using a Model Checker.

c. Verification of the Circuit: As a first step for the verification of the circuit, we build a labelled finite state-transition graph corresponding to the circuit given in ***figure.*** 3.1, using the algorithm given in section 2. For this model, we assume that each gate of the circuit has ***one unit delay.*** This is done in order to take care of the speed-dependent properties of the circuit. This is equivalent to assuming that for any state in the graph, any of the successor states is arrived at after one unit gate-delay. The label associated with each state is the set of nodes in the circuit which assume the logical value 1 in that state. The nodes of the circuit are — AckIn, ReqIn, D, A, Full0, Full1, C, B, E1, E2, E3, ReqOut and AckOut. The initial state corresponds to the situation when ReqIn and AckIn as well as ReqOut and AckOut are equipotential.

Now, the model checker can take a description of the model and a temporal formula specifying some property of the circuit, and determine truth of the formula in that model. However the circuit shown does ***not*** obey the 3/2 rule as advertised, and the model checker determines that the safeness property of the queue element, given in the previous subsection is ***not true.***

Informally, the problem can be described as follows: When an AckOut is received in response to the ReqOut signal, the AckOut signal travels via two different electrical paths — one involving three inverters and the other involving four gates. This creates a race condition and produces a glitch of about one gate delay on the ReqOut bus. Though this glitch may not always be able to drive the bus to create a spurious ReqOut, it has the potential to do so. However, this problem can be easily rectified by making the inverters slow or by putting five inverters on that path instead of three. The labelled state-transition graph for the corrected circuit is shown in ***figure.*** 3.2.

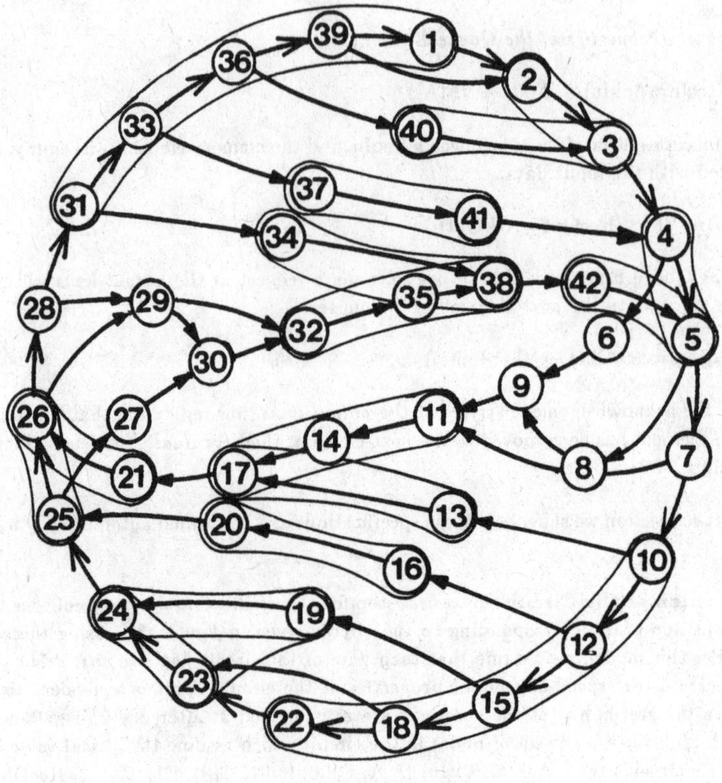

Figure. 3.2.
The State-Transition Graph for the Self-Timed Queue Element

The state-transition graph shown in *figure.* 3.2. is only one portion of the complete state-transition graph for the FIFO Queue Element and corresponds to the initial state where both ReqIn and AckIn are both at logical-zero value and both ReqOut and AckOut are at logical-zero value. But the state in which both ReqIn and AckIn are at logical-zero and both ReqOut and AckOut are at logical-one can not be reached from this state-transition graph. In fact the state-graph with this situation as the initial condition is symmetric to the one shown and the complete state-transition graph consists of both of these components.

A sample run using the model checker is shown in *figure.* 3.3. In the formula shown `A` stands for $\forall$, `E` for $\exists$, `|` for $\vee$, `&` for $\wedge$, `~` for $\neg$ and `->` for $\rightarrow$. Similarly, `G`, `F`, `U` and `W` will stand for **G**, **F**, **U** and **W**, respectively. The first component of "**time:**" is the cumulative time in 60th of a second; the second component is the portion of the cumulative time allocated to 'garbage collection'. The number to the right of each formula gives the time taken to determine the truth of the formula.

```
time:  (1453 168)
|= AG(((~ ReqIn & AckIn) | (ReqIn & ~ AckIn)) &
((~ ReqOut & AckOUt) | (ReqOut & ~ AckOut)) ->                    [ <  7 secs.]
A[((~ ReqIn & AckIn) | (ReqIn & ~ AckIn)) U
((ReqOut & AckOut) | (~ ReqOut & ~ AckOut))])

t

time:  (2263 300)
|= AG( ((~ ReqIn & AckIn) | (ReqIn & ~ AckIn)) & (~ Full1) -> AF(A))
                                                                  [ < 8 secs.]
t

time:  (2694 300)
|= AG(Full1 -> AF( ((~ ReqOut & AckOut) | (ReqOut & ~ AckOut))))
                                                                  [ < 8 secs.]
t

time:  (3150 300)
|= AG(((ReqOut & AckOut) | (~ ReqOut & ~ AckOut)) -> AF(~ Full1))
                                                                  [ < 7 secs.]
t
```

Figure. 3.3
A sample run using the Model Checker.

4. Hierarchical Verification of Circuits.

The scheme given so far can be practical only for very small circuits. This is because it suffers from the problem that the state transition graph may have number of states, exponential in number of gates. However, this problem can be avoided, if circuits are verified in a hierarchical manner. That is, first small modules are verified and then bigger module is verified assuming that the smaller modules it is composed of are correct. Since at any hierarchical level, the number of small modules that a big module is composed of is relatively small, this method is amenable to proving correctness of large circuits without a large growth of the time complexity. Moreover, hierarchical verification permits the localization of faults to small submodules, thus allowing the designer to rectify the fault by redesigning the appropriate submodule.

In a hierarchical approach, the state transition graph for a circuit is built out of the descriptions of the constituent submodules. We obtain short a description of a module by using an operation called 'restriction'. If $\mathcal{L}$ is the language for the module with a set of atomic propositions $\mathcal{P}$, corresponding to the input, output and internal nodes, then the operation restriction on $\mathcal{L}$, obtains a $\mathcal{L}'$ with atomic propositions $\mathcal{P}'$, corresponding to the input and the output nodes only.

Roughly speaking, the effect of restriction is to make the internal nodes invisible, since in building the state transition graph for the bigger module, we only require input-output behaviour of the constituent submodules. But when the internal nodes are made invisible, certain portions of the state graph will have same labelling of the atomic (input and output) propositions. The restriction operation defines exactly when such states can be collapsed into a single state.

Unfortunately, when we restrict a CTL structure to obtain a smaller structure, some formulæ that are true in the former structure may not be true in the restricted structure. However, by appropriately constraining CTL, we can show that the formulæ in the constrained logic have the desirable property that the truth properties of such formulæ are preserved with respect to the restriction operation. All of the formulæ used in ***section 3.*** have the desired syntax.

Let the CTL structure for $\mathcal{L}$ be $\mathcal{M} = (S, R, \Pi)$. Let $\mathcal{P}$ be the set of all atomic propositions in the language $\mathcal{L}$, consisting of $\mathcal{I}$, the set of atomic propositions corresponding to the ***inputs***; $\mathcal{O}$, the set of atomic propositions corresponding to the ***outputs*** and ***Int***, the set of atomic propositions corresponding to the ***internal nodes*** of the circuit. That is $\mathcal{P} = \mathcal{I} \cup \mathcal{O} \cup Int$. Let $\mathcal{L}'$ be the language with the atomic propositions, $\mathcal{P}' = \mathcal{I} \cup \mathcal{O}$. Define $\Pi_{\mathcal{P}'} : S \mapsto 2^{\mathcal{P}'}$ to be the restriction of Π to $\mathcal{P}'$, *i.e.* $\forall_{s \in S}[\Pi_{\mathcal{P}'}(s) = \Pi(s) \cap \mathcal{P}']$. Now we can define a relation $\mathcal{E}$ ($\mathcal{E} \subseteq S \times S$) over the set of states of $\mathcal{M}$ such that

$s\mathcal{E}s'$ ***iff*** for some path $(s_0, s_1, \ldots, s_n)$ of $\mathcal{M}$, $n \geq 0$, $s = s_0$ and $s_n = s'$ and for each predecessor of s_i, s'_i $(1 \leq i \leq n)$, $\Pi_{\mathcal{P}'}(s'_i) = \Pi_{\mathcal{P}'}(s_i)$

It is quite easy to see that $\mathcal{E}$ is a ***reflexive, asymmetric*** and ***transitive*** relation over S. The transitive closure of $\mathcal{E}$ can be defined as

$$\mathcal{E}^* = \mathcal{E} \cup \mathcal{E}^2 \cup \mathcal{E}^3 \cup \ldots \cup \mathcal{E}^n \cup \ldots$$

The ***$\mathcal{E}$-closure*** of a state s is defined by $\mathcal{E}^*(s) = \{s' \mid s\mathcal{E}^*s'\} = \{s' \mid s\mathcal{E}s'\}$, since $\mathcal{E}$ is a transitive relation, *i.e.* $\mathcal{E}^* = \mathcal{E}$.

For a set of sets $\{u_j\}$, $\max(\{u_j\})$ will denote the set of all distinct sets in $\{u_j\}$ maximal under inclusion. We define a mapping $\varphi : S \mapsto 2^S$ such that for each $s \in S$,

$$\varphi(s) = \max(\{H_i \mid s \in H_i \wedge \exists_{s_i \in S}\mathcal{E}^*(s_i) = H_i\}),$$

i.e. $\varphi(s)$ is the set of maximal $\mathcal{E}$-closures containing s. We consider the following subsets of S,

$$\Delta = \varphi(S) = \bigcup_{s \in S} \varphi(s).$$

Since every element $s \in S$ belongs to at least one subset H_i of Δ, Δ is called a ***decomposition*** of S and the H_i's are called the ***blocks*** of the decomposition. In a block H_i, the relation $\mathcal{E}$ defines a partial order over the set of states of H_i. We will say s ***dominates*** s', if $s\mathcal{E}s'$. We define the ***dominant states*** of H_i, $\mathrm{dom}(H_i)$ as the set of states that dominate every other states in H_i.

The decomposition Δ naturally leads to a ***substructure*** of a model $\mathcal{M}$ (notation $\mathcal{M}' = (S', R', \Pi') = \mathcal{M}/\Delta$). The states of $\mathcal{M}'$ will be the blocks of Δ. A block H_i of Δ, when considered as an element of S', will be denoted by $\overline{H}_i$. Let R' ($R' \subseteq S' \times S'$) be the total binary relation on S', corresponding to R and induced by the decomposition Δ *i.e.*

$$\langle \overline{H}_i, \overline{H}_j \rangle \in R' \text{ iff for some } s_i \in H_i, s_j \in H_j, \langle s_i, s_j \rangle \in R.$$

Similarly, let $\Pi' : S' \mapsto 2^{\mathcal{P}'}$ be the mapping corresponding to Π and induced by the decomposition Δ, *i.e.*

$$\Pi'(\overline{H}_i) = \mathcal{P}' \cap \bigcap_{s \in H_i} \Pi(s).$$

The model $\mathcal{M}' = (S', R', \Pi')$ is called a *restriction* of $\mathcal{M} = (S, R, \Pi)$ with respect to $\mathcal{P}' \subseteq \mathcal{P}$. From the definition it is easy to prove that

LEMMA 4.1. *If $\mathcal{M}' = (S', R', \Pi')$, is a restriction of $\mathcal{M} = (S, R, \Pi)$, with respect to $\mathcal{P}'$, then*

(i) For all $\overline{\Pi}_i, \overline{\Pi}_j \in S'$, $\langle \overline{\Pi}_i, \overline{\Pi}_j \rangle \in R'$ iff there is a path from s'_i to s'_j ($s'_i \in dom(\Pi_i)$, $s'_j \in \Pi_j$) such that $(s'_i = s_0, \ldots, s_k, s_{k+1}, \ldots, s_m = s'_j)$ in $\mathcal{M}$ and for some $0 < k < m$, $s_0, \ldots, s_k \in \Pi_i$ and $s_{k+1}, \ldots, s_m \in \Pi_j$.

(ii) For all s such that $s \in \Pi$, $\Pi'(\overline{\Pi}) = \Pi(s) \cap \mathcal{P}'$.

Proof. Trivial. Directly follows from the definitions. ∎

We extend the operation of restriction to a path in a CTL structure. Let $p = (s_0, \ldots, s_n, s_{n+1}, \ldots)$ be a path in $\mathcal{M}$. Then define

$$\mathcal{R}_{\mathcal{P}'}(p) = \begin{cases} \overline{\Pi}_0 \mathcal{R}_{\mathcal{P}'}(s_{n+1}, \ldots), & \text{if } (s_0, \ldots, s_n) \text{ is a finite prefix of } p \text{ such that} \\ & \quad s_0, \ldots s_n \in \Pi_0 \text{and } s_{n+1} \not\in \Pi_0; \\ \overline{\Pi}_0, \overline{\Pi}_0, \ldots, & \text{Otherwise,} \\ & \quad \text{and } s_0, \ldots \in \Pi_0. \end{cases}$$

LEMMA 4.2. *Let $(s_0, \ldots, s_n, s_{n+1}, \ldots)$ be a path in $\mathcal{M}$. Then $\mathcal{R}_{\mathcal{P}'}(s_0, \ldots, s_n, s_{n+1}, \ldots)$ is a path in $\mathcal{M}'$. Conversely, if $(\overline{\Pi}_0, \overline{\Pi}_1, \ldots)$ is a path in $\mathcal{M}'$ and $s_0 \in dom(\Pi_0)$, then there is a path $(s_0, s_1, \ldots)$ in $\mathcal{M}$ and $\mathcal{R}_{\mathcal{P}'}(s_0, s_1, \ldots) = (\overline{\Pi}_0, \overline{\Pi}_1, \ldots)$.*

Proof. From definition and lemma 4.1.(i). ∎

In the following theorem, we show that there are CTL formulae whose truth-properties are not preserved with respect to restriction.

THEOREM 4.1. *There exists a CTL structure $\mathcal{M} = (S, R, \Pi)$ and a formula $\mathcal{F}$ where $\mathcal{F}$ is a CTL formula such that*

$$\mathcal{M}, s_0 \models \mathcal{F} \quad \textit{but} \quad \mathcal{M}', \overline{\Pi}_0 \not\models \mathcal{F}, \quad \textit{and } s_0 \in dom(\Pi_0).$$

Proof. The counter-examples involving formulæ of the form $\forall \mathbf{X} P$, $\exists \mathbf{X} P$ and $\forall[\exists \mathbf{F} P_1 \mathbf{U} P_2]$, are given in [MC83]. ∎

However, there exists a large subclass of CTL formulæ with the desirable property that if a formula in this subclass is satisfiable in the unrestricted CTL structure, $\mathcal{M}$, then it is satisfiable in the CTL structure, $\mathcal{M}'$ obtained by restriction. We call this subclass CTL$^-$. Given a set of atomic propositions $\mathcal{P}$:

1. Every atomic proposition $P \in \mathcal{P}$ is a propositional formula in CTL$^-$.

2. If f_1 and f_2 are propositional formulæ in CTL$^-$, then so are $\neg f_1$, $f_1 \wedge f_2$.

3. If f_1 is a propositional formula and f_2 is a CTL$^-$formula, then $\forall[f_1 \mathbf{U} f_2]$ and $\exists[f_1 \mathbf{U} f_2]$ are CTL$^-$formulæ.

THEOREM 4.2. *Let $\mathcal{F}$ be a CTL$^-$formula in $\mathcal{L}'$. Then*

$$\mathcal{M}, s_i \models \mathcal{F} \quad \textit{iff} \quad \mathcal{M}', \overline{\Pi}_i \models \mathcal{F}, \quad \textit{where } s_i \in dom(H_i).$$

Proof. By induction on the structure the CTL formula $\mathcal{F}$ and the Computation Tree rooted at s_i. See [MC83] for a full proof. ∎

COROLLARY 4.1. *Let $\mathcal{F}$ be a CTL formula in $\mathcal{L}'$. Then*

$$\mathcal{M}, s_0 \models \mathcal{F} \quad \textit{iff} \quad \mathcal{M}', \overline{\Pi}_0 \models \mathcal{F}, \qquad \textit{where } s_0 \in dom(\Pi_0).$$

Proof. Corollary to theorem 4.2. ∎

With each model $\mathcal{M}$, one can associate an automaton such that its states and transitions are same as that of $\mathcal{M}$, but the transitions are additionally labelled with the set of input signals that cause the transition and the set of output signals associated with the transition. let A and A' be the automata associated with the models $\mathcal{M}$ and $\mathcal{M}'$, respectively. It can be easily shown that the relation φ is a *weak homomorphism* of A onto A' and hence A' is a *covering* of A [Gl68].The above result can be strengthened, if we notice that‡

$$\begin{aligned} \varphi^{-1} M^A_{\epsilon^\cdot \sigma \epsilon^\cdot} &= M^{A'}_{\epsilon^\cdot \sigma \epsilon^\cdot} \varphi^{-1}, \quad \text{and} \\ \varphi^{-1} N^A_{\epsilon^\cdot \sigma \epsilon^\cdot} &= N^{A'}_{\epsilon^\cdot \sigma \epsilon^\cdot}, \quad \text{and} \\ \varphi\varphi^{-1} &\supseteq I_{S^A}, \end{aligned}$$

where M^A and $M^{A'}$ are the transition functions and where N^A and $N^{A'}$ are the output functions of the automata A and A', respectively.

THEOREM 4.3. *Let A and A' be the automata associated with the models $\mathcal{M}$ and $\mathcal{M}'$, respectively. Then the models $\mathcal{M}$ and $\mathcal{M}'$ are input-output equivalent in the sense that for a sequence of input signals, x,*

$$\begin{aligned} N^A_x &\subseteq \varphi N^{A'}_x, \quad \textit{and} \\ \varphi^{-1} N^A_x &= N^{A'}_x, \end{aligned}$$

where N^A and $N^{A'}$ are the output functions of the automata A and A', respectively.

Proof. Let x be $\sigma_1\sigma_2\ldots\sigma_k$. Then

$$\begin{aligned} \varphi^{-1} M^A_x &= \varphi^{-1} M^A_{\epsilon^\cdot \sigma_1 \epsilon^\cdot} M^A_{\sigma_2} \ldots M^A_{\sigma_k} \\ &= M^{A'}_{\epsilon^\cdot \sigma_1 \epsilon^\cdot} \varphi^{-1} M^A_{\sigma_2} \ldots M^A_{\sigma_k} \\ &= M^{A'}_{\sigma_1} M^{A'}_{\sigma_2} \ldots M^{A'}_{\sigma_k} \varphi^{-1} = M^{A'}_x \varphi^{-1} \end{aligned}$$

Similarly,

$$\begin{aligned} \varphi^{-1} N^A_x &= \varphi^{-1} M^A_{\sigma_1} M^A_{\sigma_2} \ldots M^A_{\sigma_{k-1}} N^A_{\sigma_k} \\ &= M^{A'}_{\sigma_1} M^{A'}_{\sigma_2} \ldots M^{A'}_{\sigma_{k-1}} \varphi^{-1} N^A_{\epsilon^\cdot \sigma_k \epsilon^\cdot} \\ &= M^{A'}_{\sigma_1} M^{A'}_{\sigma_2} \ldots M^{A'}_{\sigma_{k-1}} N^{A'}_{\epsilon^\cdot \sigma_k \epsilon^\cdot} = N^{A'}_x \end{aligned}$$

But since $\varphi\varphi^{-1} \supseteq I_{S^A}$ we have

$$\begin{aligned} \varphi^{-1} N^A_x = N^{A'}_x \quad &\Rightarrow \varphi\varphi^{-1} N^A_x = \varphi N^{A'}_x \\ &\Rightarrow I_{S^A} N^A_x \subseteq \varphi N^{A'}_x \\ &\Rightarrow N^A_x \subseteq \varphi N^{A'}_x. \end{aligned}$$ ∎

Hence we see that even if the operation of restriction does not preserve all the CTL formulæ, the restricted model is equivalent to the original model in terms of its behaviour.

---

‡.We represent the composition of functions $\varphi_1 : D_1 \mapsto D_2$ and $\varphi_2 : D_2 \mapsto D_3$ by $\varphi_1\varphi_2 : D_1 \mapsto D_3$. The transition function is $M : \Sigma \mapsto (S \mapsto S)$ and the output function is $N : \Sigma \mapsto (S \mapsto \Theta)$.

We show how to build $\mathcal{M}'$ from $\mathcal{M}$ in the following three steps. $\mathcal{M}'$ is essentially a restriction of $\mathcal{M}$ with additional optimizations and labelling of the transitions of the state-transition graph.

step 1. Relabel the vertices and the edges of the CTL structure $\mathcal{M}$. (*a*) Label each state by the subset of the propositions involving only the inputs and the outputs of the module. (*b*) Label the edges between two states with the same set of atomic propositions, by ϵ.

step 2. Construct the blocks of $\mathcal{M}$, by first determining the dominant states using a depth first search over the underlying graph. Build $\mathcal{M}'$ by replacing each block by a single state. The graph can be optimized further by collapsing the "indistinguishable nodes" (*i.e.* nodes with the same label and successor states) into single node.

step 3. Label the edges of the graph by the set of input signals that causes the transition and the set of output signals associated with the transition.

This construction is illustrated by taking the restriction of the state-transition graph for the FIFO Queue Element shown in *figure.* 3.2. The states shown in groups are the blocks constructed in *step 2.* The resulting labelled state-transition graph is shown in *figure.* 4.1.

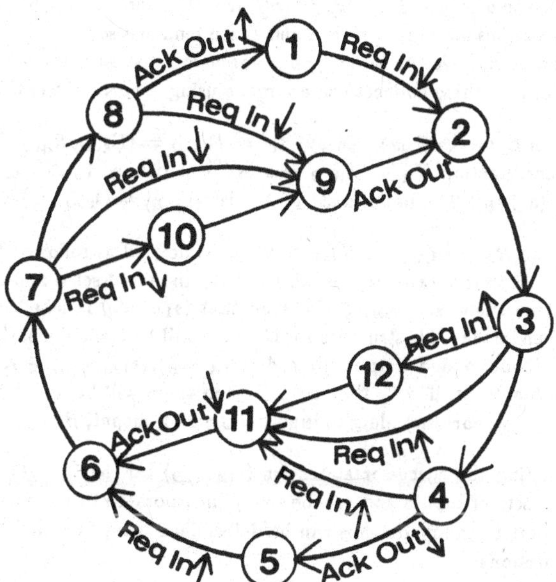

figure. 4.1.
The Restricted State Transition Graph.

It should be mentioned that since we combine successive states in the operation of *step 2*, the restricted model may not be a unit-delay model even if the original unrestricted model was so. This notion is essentially captured in Theorems 4.1. and 4.2. However, this does not pose a probelm, since good design methodology forces the designer not to make the modules at higher level in the hierarchy speed-dependent. Moreover, since a speed-dependent circuits must be small enough to fit in an ***equipotential region*** and equipotential regions must be small enough that the potential on any wire in this area will equalize in a "short" time for any large circuit, the modules at higher level have to be speed-independent [MC80].

As the first step for verifying the correctness of a circuit using a hierarchical approach, we construct a CTL structure for a module at some hierarchical level, using the CTL structures for the submodules at the immediately lower level. In order to avoid building large-sized CTL structures, we use the restriction operation on the CTL structures of the submodules and obtain smaller descriptions of these. Moreover, the transitions of the state-transition graph are additionally labelled with the associated set of input signals and set of output signals, as explained earlier in this section.

Given two submodules A and B which are used to build a module C at a higher level by connecting the inputs and outputs of A and B, we show how to build a CTL structure for the module C using an operation called "composition". It can be shown that the composition operation is ***commutative*** and ***associative*** and hence can be generalized easily to the case where a module consists of more than two submodules. The reader may note a close analogy between the operations we define and the operations defined in [MI80].

Let the restricted models of A and B be $\mathcal{M}'_A = (S'_A, R'_A, \Pi'_A)$ and $\mathcal{M}'_B = (S'_B, R'_B, \Pi'_B)$, respectively. We assume that the propositions associated with A and B are renamed so that the input and output nodes of A and B that are connected, have the same proposition associated with them. Furthermore, we make the important assumption that these connections are made using ***"short" bilateral*** wires.

The CTL structure of $C = A \circ B$ is given by $\mathcal{M}_C = \mathcal{M}_{A\circ B} = (S_{A\circ B}, R_{A\circ B}, \Pi_{A\circ B})$, where $S_{A\circ B} = S_A \times S_B$. The assignment function $\Pi_{A\circ B} : S_{A\circ B} \mapsto 2^{P'_A \cup P'_B}$ is defined by $\Pi(s_{A\circ B}) = \Pi'(s_A) \cup \Pi'(s_B)$ where the state $s_{A\circ B} = \langle s_A, s_B\rangle$. The initial state of $\mathcal{M}_C$ is $s_{0(A\circ B)} = \langle s_{0A}, s_{0B}\rangle$.

The transition relation $R_{A\circ B}$ ($R_{A\circ B} \subseteq S_{A\circ B} \times S_{A\circ B}$) is defined as follows. Assume that there is a transition $\langle s_{1A}, s_{2A}\rangle \in R'_A$ such that $\langle s_{1A}, s_{2A}\rangle$ is labelled with the input set α and output set β. Similarly assume that there is a transition $\langle s_{1B}, s_{2B}\rangle \in R'_B$ such that $\langle s_{1B}, s_{2B}\rangle$ is labelled with the input set γ and the output set δ. Then in the CTL structure for C, there will be transitions, $\langle\langle s_{1A}, s_{1B}\rangle, \langle s_{2A}, s_{1B}\rangle\rangle \in R_{A\circ B}$, corresponding to input, α and output, β; and $\langle\langle s_{1A}, s_{1B}\rangle, \langle s_{1A}, s_{2B}\rangle\rangle \in R_{A\circ B}$, corresponding to input, δ and output, γ. Moreover, if $\gamma \subseteq \beta$ or $\alpha \subseteq \delta$, then there will be an additional transition from $\langle\langle s_{1A}, s_{1B}\rangle, \langle s_{2A}, s_{2B}\rangle\rangle \in R_{A\circ B}$, corresponding to input, $\alpha \cup \gamma$ and output, $\beta \cup \delta$.

The step of constructing the successor states for $\langle s_{1A}, s_{1B}\rangle$ can be thought of as simulating C at $\langle s_{1A}, s_{1B}\rangle$ for all possible sets of inputs and can be easily incorporated into algorithm 2.1. Now various properties of C with respect to the model $\mathcal{M}_C$ can be determined using the model checker algorithm, as explained in the earlier sections.

5. Conclusion.

We have shown that it is possible to do automatic verification of asynchronous circuit efficiently. We have also indicated how this method can be extended to do hierarchical verification of large and complex circuits. We believe that this approach may eventually turn out to be quite practical.

However, there are many problems that need to be addressed before this approach is made feasible in practice. In this paper we have used a unit-delay model for the circuit. Similarly, it is quite easy to use a steady-state model, in which each state in the state-transition graph corresponds to a stable state and only in response to an input change does a state change occur. While the steady-state model is useful for speed-independent self-timed circuits, the unit-delay model is needed to model properties of a speed-dependent circuit. Unfortunately, even for the speed-dependent circuits the assumption that each gate has one unit gate-delay is rather unrealistic, because two similar gates may have different delays depending on process variations, fan-outs of a gate etc. Moreover, because of various capacitive effects, the delay associated with a 0-to-1 transition is not equal to the one associated with a 1-to-0 transition. It is felt that it is necessary to find models that capture these properties better. Also, we do not know how to handle the effect of large fan-out, charge sharing etc. In addition, we felt that CTL is rather weak for succinctly expressing many properties of circuits. A notation based on temporal intervals [HMM83] may be more suitable for this purpose.

An interesting area for future research is the usefulness of restriction operation in the context of hierarchical verification. We have defined a "restriction" operation and shown that the truth-properties of the CTL^- formulæ are preserved with respect to the operation of restriction. It appears that any weaker version of "restriction" will not result in any substantial reduction of the size of the CTL structures and hence will make hierarchical verification rather expensive. On the other hand, it seems any stronger version of "restriction", will severely limit the class of CTL formulæ that will be preserved with respect to restriction.

6. Acknowledgement.

Thanks to Larry Rudolph of C-M. U. and Chuck Seitz of Caltech for helpful discussions.

7. References.

[BO82] G. V. Bochmann, "Hardware Specification with Temporal Logic: An Example", *IEEE Transactions on Computers*, Vol C-31,No. 3, March 1982.

[BMP81] M. Ben-Ari, Z. Manna and A. Pnueli, "The Logic of Nexttime", *Eighth ACM Symposium on Principle of Programming Languages*, Williamsburg, VA, January 1981.

[CES83] E. M. Clarke, E. A. Emerson and A. P. Sistla, "Automatic Verification of Finite-State Concurrent Systems using Temporal Logic Specifications: A Practical Approach", *Tenth ACM Symposium on Principles of Programming Languages*, Austin, Texas, January 1983.

[EC80] E. A. Emerson, E. M. Clarke, "Characterizing Properties of Parallel Programs as Fixpoints", *Proceedings of the Seventh International Colloquium on Automata, Languages and Programming*, Lecture Notes in Computer Science No. 85, Springer Verlag, 1981.

[GI68] A. Ginzburg, *Algebraic Theory of Automata*, Academic Press, New York . London, 1968.

[HMM83] J. Halpern, Z. Manna and B. Moszkowski, "A Hardware Semantics based on Temporal Intervals", Report No. STAN-CS-83-963, Department of Computer Science, Stanford University, Stanford University, Stanford, CA 94305, March 1983.

[MC80] C. A. Mead and L. A. Conway, *Introduction to VLSI Systems*, Reading, MA, Addison-Wesley, 1980, Ch. 7.

[MC83] B. Mishra and E. Clarke, "Automatic Verification of Asynchronous Circuits", C.-M. U. Tech Report, 1983. (To Appear)

[MI80] R. Milner, *A Calculus of Communicating Systems*, University of Edinburgh, June 1980.

[MO81] Y. Malchi and S. S. Owicki, "Temporal Specifications of Self-Timed Systems", in *VLSI Systems and Computations* (Ed. H. T. Kung, Bob Sproull, and G. Steele), Computer Science Press, 1981.

MATHEMATICS AS PROGRAMMING

R. L. Constable
Cornell University

In a sufficiently rich programming language it is possible to express a very substantial amount of mathematics in a natural way. I don't mean only that one can write down functions or solve equations, I mean that one can write theorems and proofs. Moreover, expressing mathematics in this way reveals its computational content and makes it available for use with digital computers.

This point is illustrated with reference to a programming language which is sufficiently rich in the above sense. I develop parts of Basic Recursive Function Theory and logic to illustrate the way in which doing some rather abstract mathematics is like programming. I chose BRFT in order to make certain points about the programming language by reflecting part of it inside itself. For example, while Church's Thesis can be false inside the language, it is true outside, reflecting in some sense the fact that while we may believe it, we do not expect to prove it. I chose a bit of logic to illustrate that the virtues of model theory (a certain abstractness and notation independence) are sometimes possible without sacrificing computational meaning.

I. Introduction

For some time now my colleagues and I have been concerned, as have several research groups, with making "programming more mathematical". This is in fact a common theme of this conference. We indeed advocate the practical use of "programming logics", and our latest effort at Cornell is concerned with treating constructive proofs as programs (see [2,7,10]). So the title of this talk might seem rather curious, "Mathematics as Programming". It is the converse of the business at hand.

In this paper then, I will emphasize another goal of our work which is not shared by many other groups. I will argue that this goal is at least as interesting as the common goal. To this end I want to make a point that is not widely understood, that mathematics is programming in a very real sense. Though I have believed this and written about it for a long time [7], it has only been in the last few years that I have seen a really simple and obvious road to this vantage point. I will try to take you on a rapid journey down that road, pointing out some of the interesting landscape as we go by - at a disorienting speed. One of the landmarks is a way of defining the partial recursive functions in a programming logic with only total functions, another is a way to do logic abstractly using constructive abstract data types. The journey begins over some rather dry territory, but if you stay with me I think you'll find these two highlights worth seeing.

II. A Theory of Types and Sets

We consider an informal programming logic with a rich type structure from which we define a notion of set. The theory we use here can be formalized in a number of ways (see for instance [3,11,20,21,23]; the reader unfamiliar with a careful theory of types should consult one of these sources for details). The critical notions in this account are the propositions-as-types principle, a notion of universe, and the concepts of set and subset. The notion of a quotient type also plays a role.

Starting from the programming language point of view, with Algol 68 [22,27] or ML [14] as examples, we have these type constructors present.

	ML-like	Algol-like
products (structures or records)	A×B,	prod(x:A,y:B)
unions	A+B	union(A,B)
functions	A→B	proc(x:A)B

There are primitive types such as <u>int</u>, <u>bool</u>, <u>char</u>, and we can consider also <u>nat</u>, for the natural numbers and <u>rat</u>, for the rationals. We might also use some notion of enumeration type, $\{e_1,\ldots,e_n\}$.

In order to treat types as objects, we add as well the type of types, <u>type</u>. We will consider as well a hierarchy, <u>large type</u>, <u>very large type</u>, etc. This will be a cumulative hierarchy, with <u>type</u> in <u>large type</u>, etc. Such a hierarchy in one form or another is the essence of a type theory in the sense of Bertrand Russell [25]. The practical need for such a hierarchy arises from attempts to treat parameterized types and to abstract with respect to type. These notions provide a version of polymorphism by allowing types as parameters to procedures and definitions.

This type theory departs from ML and Algol in another critical way. The concepts of product and union are generalized. The product or record is generalized in the direction of the Pascal variant record [16]. We might call this construct a <u>dependent product</u> (see [11]).

	ML-like	Algol-like
dependent product	Σx:A.B	prod(x:A,y:B)
	where occurrences of x in B are <u>bound</u> by x:A.	

The function space constructor is generalized in the direction of the AUTOMATH dependent function space.

	ML-like	Algol-like
dependent functions	Πx:A.B	proc(x:A)B
	where occurrences of x in B are <u>bound</u> by x:A.	

Now in the context of this very rich type structure it is possible to define a higher order predicate calculus using the propositions-as-types principle [15]. This is a fundamental organizing principle of AUTOMATH [13] and of Martin-Löf's type theories ([20,21], which we denote M-L75 and M-L82 respectively). We call theories based on this organization "AUTOMATH/Martin-Löf-like type theories."

Among the AUTOMATH/M-L-like theories are those designed at Cornell as programming logics [3,11]. These theories introduce additional concepts to facilitate information hiding and reasoning about programs as objects. First, we allow subsets on a type A, denoted {x:A|B} for B a proposition on A (type on A), as the type $\Sigma x{:}A.B$ with the proof component, b:B(a/x), hidden. Let Pow(A) = $\Sigma x{:}type. \exists P{:}A\to type.(x=\{y{:}A|P(y)\})/E$ where E is the equivalence relation defined by the condition

$$E(X,Y) \text{ iff } \forall x{:}A.(pred(X)(x) \Leftrightarrow pred(Y)(x))$$
$$\text{where } pred(\{x{:}A|B\}) = \lambda x.B$$

The rule for introducing elements into subsets is simply

$$\frac{a{:}A,\ b{:}B(a/x)}{a \in \{x{:}A|B\}}$$

The rule for using the information $y \in \{x{:}A|B\}$ is that if exp is defined over $\Sigma x{:}A.B$ and does not "use" the proof component, then exp is defined over {x:A|B} (see [3] for details).

III. Basic Concepts

In this paper we are principally concerned with results about the nonnegative integers N. The finite intervals, [n,m], are defined as subsets: [n,m] = $\{i{:}N|n\le i\le m\}$. We say that a type T is <u>finite</u> iff there is a bijection between T and some [1,n].

There are subsets of $N\to N$ say {f,g} for which we can not tell whether f=g and hence for which we cannot say that {f,g} is finite, but we can say it has no more than two elements. We call such types <u>subfinite</u>, they are subsets of finite sets.

One might expect a type to be <u>countable</u> precisely when there is a mapping $f{:}N\to T$ which is onto T, i.e. such that for all t:T, there is some n:N, f(n)=t. Such a notion is a bit too strong for subsets {x:A|B} because perhaps by discarding the information B we can no longer find an n such that f(n)=a. So we say that a subset of A {x:A|B} is <u>countable</u> iff the type $\Sigma x{:}A.B$ is countable. We call a subset of a countable set <u>subcountable</u>. It is easy to show:

Theorem: If I is countable and if for each $i{:}I$, $\{x{:}A \mid B(i)\}$ is countable, then $\{x{:}A \mid \exists i{:}I.B(i)\}$ is countable, i.e. a countable union of countable sets is countable.

We also have Cantor's fundamental theorem, stated here for N.

Theorem: $N \to N$ is uncountable.

IV. Function Classes

The type $N \to N$ includes all the functions from N to N definable in this theory. The definitions of such functions may involve arbitrary types, say $A \to B$, arbitrarily high in the hierarchy of types, say $A \to B$ a very large type. We are interested in defining various subsets over $N \to N$. We also want to consider a generalization of it to the type of partial functions and its subtype of partial recursive functions. Since all the functions in $N \to N$ and all the partial functions are computable, it is interesting to compare these types to the partial recursive functions. We can even state a mathematical version of Church's thesis (CT).

First as a prelude to defining the partial recursive functions, let us define the primitive recursive functions. We want to consider functions of arbitrary finite arity, to this end define a parameterized cartesian product as

$$A^{(0)} = N_1 \quad \text{where } N_1 = \{0_1\}$$
$$A^{(1)} = A$$
$$A^{(n+2)} = A \times A^{(n+1)}$$

Officially $A^{(n)}$ is defined by recursion. In M-L82 for example it would be written

$$ind(u,v)(n,N_1,ind(z,w)(u,A,A\times w))$$

(where $ind(u,v)$ is written $R(u,v)$ in M-L82).

The functions of arbitrary arity over N are $\Sigma i{:}N.(N^{(i)} \to N)$. Call this $\mathbf{F}$. Given f in this type we write arity(f) for the first component, and fn(f) for the second, so arity(f):N and $fn(f){:}N^{(arity(f))} \to N$. We will define the primitive recursive functions as a subtype of $\mathbf{F}$ of the form $R = \{f{:}\mathbf{F} \mid \exists g{:}R^1.f = fn(g)\}$ where R^1 describes the structure of f.

Informally R^1 is obtained from the base functions successor, $\lambda x.s(x)$, constant $\lambda x.i$, projection $\lambda x_1,\ldots,x_u.x_i$ using the operations of composition and primitive recursion. The projection functions will be written as P(n,i) meaning select the i-th of n arguments. The composition operation, C, satisfies this condition: $C(n)(m)(h,g)(x) = h(g(x))$ where $x{:}N^{(n)}$ and g maps from $N^{(n)}$ to an m-vector. The primitive recursion operator, R, satisfies this condition:

$$R(n)(g,h)(0,x)=g(x),\ R(n)(g,h)(m+1,x)=h(m,R(n)(g,h)(m,x),x).$$

In formalizing all this we use the type $N_2 = \{0_2, 1_2\}$, essentially the booleans, and its associated case analysis operation.

$$case_2(0_2, a, b) = a, \; case_2(1_2, a, b) = b.$$

For eq: $N \times N \to N_2$ we let x eq y = 0_2 iff $x =_N y$. Also for $a, b \in A \times B$ we let lof(a,b) = a, 2of(a,b) = b. With these definitions P belongs to $\Pi n{:}N^+ . \Pi i{:}[1,n] . N^{(n)} \to N$ where $N^+ = \{x{:}N \mid x>0\}$ and satisfies

$$P(1,i) = \lambda x.x$$
$$P(n+1,i) = \lambda x.case_2(i \text{ eq } 1, \, lof(x), \, P(n,i-1)(2of(x)))$$

Using the induction form, the complete definition is

$$P = \lambda n.ind(u,v)(n-1, \lambda i.\lambda x.x, case_2(i \text{ eq } 1, \, lof(x), v(i-1)(2of(x)))).$$

To define composition $C(n)(m)(h,g)(x) = h(g(x))$ we need these auxillary notions:

Let $T(n,m) = (N^{(n)} \to N)^{(m)}$ define $ap(0) = \lambda g.\lambda x.0_1$
$ap(1) = \lambda g.\lambda x.g(x)$
and $ap(m+2) = \lambda g.\lambda x.(lof(g)(x), \, ap(m+1)(2of(g)(x)))$

So ap(m)(g)(x) applies g in T(n,m) componentwise to $x{:}N^n$, e.g. if $g = (f_1, f_2)$ then $ap(2)(g)(x) = (f_1(x), f_2(x))$.

Officially we add n as a parameter to ap as follows

$$\begin{aligned} ap = \lambda n.\lambda m.case_2(&m \text{ eq } 0, \, \lambda g.\lambda x.0_1, \\ &ind(u,v)(m-1, \lambda g.\lambda x.g(x), \\ &\quad \lambda g.\lambda x.(lof(g)(x), v(2of(g))(x)))) \end{aligned}$$

Now we can define composition

$$C{:} \;\; \Pi n{:}N.\Pi m{:}N.\Pi h{:}(N^{(m)} \to N).\Pi g{:}(N^{(n)} \to N)^{(m)}.(N^{(n)} \to N)$$

by

$$C = \lambda n.\lambda m.\lambda h.\lambda g.\lambda x.h(ap(n)(m)(g)(x)).$$

So C(n)(m) composes h and the vector of functions g even for m=0.

We also need this vector operation

For $g{:}A \to B$ and $x{:}A^{(m)}$, $vect(m)(g){:}A^{(m)} \to B^{(m)}$, $vect(0)(g)(x) = 0_1$
$vect(1)(g)(x) = g(x)$, $vect(m+2)(g)(x) = (g(lof(x)), \, vect(m+1)(g)(2of(x)))$

Define the primitive recursion operator

$$R(n)(g,h)(0,x) = g(x)$$
$$R(n)(g,h)(m+1,x) = h(m, R(n)(g,h)(m,x), x)$$

We need $R{:}\Pi n{:}N^+.\Pi g{:}N^{(n-1)} \to N.\Pi h{:}N^{(n+2)} \to N.(N^{(n)} \to N)$
$R = \lambda n.\lambda g.\lambda h.\lambda m.\lambda x.ind(u,v)(m, g(x), h(u,v,x))$

Now we can define the base case of the inductive definition of the primitive recursive functions over N. Write $z{:}Ux{:}A.B$ in place of $z{:}\Sigma x{:}A.B$ when we intend z to denote 2of(z).

$$\text{Base} = \{f{:}N\to N \mid f=\lambda x.s(x)\} + (\text{U}i{:}N.\{f{:}N^0\to N \mid f=\lambda x.i\} + \text{U}n{:}N^+.\text{U}i{:}[1,n].\{f{:}N^{(n)}\to N \mid f=P(n,i)\})$$

Use 1,2of(x) for 1of(2of(x)), generally take $n_1,n_2,\ldots,n_k$ of(x) for $n_1$of($n_2$of(...$n_k$of(x)...)).

$$\mathbf{R}'_{(0)}(N) = \Sigma i{:}N.\{f{:}N^{(i)}\to N \mid \exists g{:}\text{Base}. (g=\text{inl}(f) \vee g=\text{inr}(\text{inr}(f)) \vee g=\text{inl}(\text{inr}(f)))\}$$

$$\begin{aligned}\mathbf{R}'_{(n+1)}(N) = \Sigma i{:}N.\Sigma f{:}N^{(i)}\to N.\ & [\exists g{:}\mathbf{R}'_{(n)}(N).(f=1,2\text{of}(g)). \\ & \vee \\ & \quad \exists n{:}N.\exists m{:}N.\exists h{:}\mathbf{R}'_{(n)}(N).\exists g{:}(\mathbf{R}'_{(n)}(N))^{(m)}. \\ & \quad (\forall i{:}[1,m].(\text{arity}(P(m,i)(g)) = n)\ \& \\ & \quad 1\text{of}(h)=m\ \&\ f=C(n)(m)(1,2\text{of}(h),\text{vect}(m)(\lambda z.1,2\text{of}(z),g) \\ & \vee \\ & \quad (i>0)\ \&\ \exists g{:}\mathbf{R}'_{(n)}(N).\exists h{:}\mathbf{R}'_{(n)}(N). \\ & \quad (1\text{of}(g) = i-1\ \&\ 1\text{of}(h) = i+2\ \& \\ & \quad f = R(i)(1,2\text{of}(g),\ 1,2\text{of}(h)))]\end{aligned}$$

where arity(f) = 1of(f).

Define the primitive recursive _schemes_ as $\mathbf{R}^1(N) = \Sigma j{:}N.\mathbf{R}'_{(j)}(N)$. With each element of $\mathbf{R}^1(N)$ there is a _level_, level(f) = 1of(f), an arity, arity(f) = 1of(2of(f)), a function, fn(f) = 1,2of(2of(f)), and a complete description of its construction, 2,2,2of(f). For example, (0,(0,λx.2)) represents $\lambda x.2{:}N^{(0)}\to N$ but (1,1,λx.2, inl(0,(0,0,λx.2), (0,1,λx.x))) represents λx.2:N→N.

Partial Functions and μ-Recursive Functions

Define $\mathbf{P}(N) = \Sigma i{:}N.\Sigma P{:}N^{(i)}\to\text{Type}.((\Sigma x{:}N^{(i)}.P(x))\to N)$. Call these the partial functions over N. In this case i represents the arity, P represents the dom and f the op.

We will define the μ-recursive functions as an inductive class in the style of $\mathbf{R}^1(N)$. We take $\mathbf{PR} = \Sigma j{:}N.\mathbf{PR}_{(j)}$. To accomplish this we must define C(n)(m), R(n) on partial functions and define min on partial functions. The interesting part is computing the domain component, dom. Here is how it is done for C and R.

$$C:\Pi n:N.\Pi m:N.\Pi h:\{f:P(N)\,|\,arity(f) = m\}.\ \Pi g:\{f:P(N)^{(m)}\,|\,\forall i:[1,m].arity(P(m,i)(f) = n)\}.\ P(N)$$

$$\begin{aligned}C = \lambda n.\lambda m.\lambda h.\lambda g.\ &(n,\\ &\lambda x.\exists p:(\forall i:[1,m].dom(P(m,i)(g))(x)).\\ &\quad dom(h)(pop(n)(m)(op(g))(tuple(m)(x,p))),\\ &\lambda x.h(pop(n)(m)(op(g))(x))\\ &)\end{aligned}$$

where op is defined as fn except on partial functions and pop applies a vector of partial functions to the vector of arguments formed by applying tuple to $x:N^n$ and $p:\forall i:[1,m].dom(P(m,i)(g))(x)$.

Recall $P(N) = \Sigma i:N.\Sigma P:N^{(i)}\rightarrow Type.((\Sigma x:N^{(i)}.P(x))\rightarrow N)$ and for $f \in P(N)$, $arity(f) = i$, $dom(f) = P$ and $op(f):(\Sigma x:N^{(i)}.P(x))\rightarrow N$.

As in APL there are numerous kinds of vector operation, e.g.

$$prop:\Pi m:N.\Pi g:P(N)^{(m)}.\ \Pi\ A:\{F:\Pi j:[1,m].N^{(n)}\rightarrow Type\,|\ \forall i:[1,m].dom(P(m)(i)(g)) = F(i)\}.$$

$$\Pi p:(\Pi i:[1,m].(N^{(n)} \times A(i)))\ \text{where}\ n = arity(g)$$

$$\begin{aligned}prop(1)(g,A,p) &= g(p(1))\\ prop(m)(g,A,p) &= (1of(g)(p(1)),\ prop(m)(2of(g),\ \lambda i.p(i+1)))\end{aligned}$$

To define the μ-recursive functions, **PR**, we need C, R, min on P(N). C has been defined. Consider now R.

$$\begin{aligned}&R:\Pi n:N^{+}.\Pi g:\{f:P(N)\,|\,arity(f) = n-1\}.\Pi h:\{f:P(N)\,|\,arity(f) = n+1\}.P(N)\\ &R = \lambda n.\lambda g.\lambda h.(n,\lambda m.\lambda x.\exists y:N.GD(m,x)(y),\ \lambda z.1,2of(z))\end{aligned}$$

where GD is

$$\begin{aligned}\lambda m.\lambda x.ind(u,v)(m,&\lambda y.\exists d:dom(g)(x).(y=g(x,d)),\\ &\lambda y.\exists z:N.(v(z)\ \&\ \exists d:dom(h)(u,z,x).\\ &\qquad (y=h((u,z,x),d))))\end{aligned}$$

$$\begin{aligned}&min:\Pi n:N.\Pi g:\{f:P(N)\,|\,arity(f) = n+1\}.P(N)\\ &min = \lambda n.\lambda g.\\ &\quad (n,\\ &\quad \lambda x.\exists y:N.(\forall z:[0,y].dom(g)(z,x)\ \&\\ &\qquad \exists p:(\forall z:[0,y].dom(g)(z,x).(op(g)(z,pz) =_N 0)),\\ &\quad \lambda z.least(n)(g,1of(z),1,2of(z),\ 1,2,2of(z),\ 0)\end{aligned}$$

where $least:\Pi k:N.\Pi g:\{f:P(N)\,|\,arity(f) = k+1\}.\Pi x:N^{(k)}.\Pi n:N.$
$\Pi d:(\Pi j:[0,n].dom(g)(j,x)).\Pi m:[0,n].N$

$$\begin{aligned}least_{(k)}(g,x,n,d,m) = &\text{ if } m \geq n \text{ then } n\\ &\text{ else if } g(((m,x),d(m))) = 0 \text{ then } m\\ &\qquad \text{else } least_{(k)}(g,x,n,d,m+1)\end{aligned}$$

(Actually least is defined by recursion on (n-m).)

$$PR = \Sigma j{:}N.PR_{(j)}$$

$$PR_{(0)} = \Sigma i{:}N.\Sigma P{:}N^{(i)}\to Type.\Sigma f{:}((\Sigma x{:}N^{(i)}.P(x))\to N).$$
$$\exists g{:}Base.(\forall x{:}\{y{:}N^{i} \mid P(y)\}.\ "f(x) = g(x)")$$

$$PR_{(n+1)} = \Sigma i{:}N.\Sigma P{:}N^{(i)}\to Type.\Sigma f{:}((\Sigma x{:}N^{(i)}.P(x))\to N)).$$
$$[\exists g{:}PR_{(n)}.(op(f) = op(g)) \vee$$
$$\exists k{:}N.\exists m{:}N.\exists h{:}PR_{(n)}.\exists g{:}PR^{(m)}_{(n)}.$$
$$(arity(h)=m\ \&\ \forall i{:}[1,m].arity(P(m,i)(g)) = k\ \&$$
$$dom(f) = dom(C(k)(m)(h,g))\ \&\ f = C(k)(m)(h,g)) \vee$$
$$\exists k{:}N^{+}.\exists g{:}PR_{(n)}.\exists h{:}PR_{(n)}.(arity(g) = k-1\ \&\ arity(h) = k\ \&$$
$$dom(f) = dom(R_{(n)}(g,h))\ \&\ op(f) = op(R_{(n)}(g,h))) \vee$$
$$\exists k{:}N^{+}.\exists g{:}PR_{(n)}.(arity(g) = k+1\ \&\ dom(f) = dom(min(g))\ \&$$
$$op(f) = op(min(g)))]$$

V. Formal Logic

Let SA stand for Simple Arithmetic, the theory defined in [19] Chapter 4. We can carry out inside our programming language the study of SA presented in [19]. To do so we define SA as a type and define inductively the type of theorems of SA.

Let $AX{:}\Pi D{:}Type.\Pi zero{:}D.\Pi one{:}D.\Pi plus{:}D\times D\to D.\Pi times{:}D\times D\to D.$

$$(plus(zero,one) = one\ \&\ \forall x{:}D.(\neg plus(x,one)=0)\ \&$$

$$\forall x{:}D.(\neg(x=0) \Rightarrow \exists z{:}D.(plus(z,one) = x))\ \&\ \ldots\ )$$

Let SA be the abstract type†

$$\exists D{:}Type.\exists zero{:}D.\exists one{:}D.\exists plus{:}D\times D\to D.\exists times{:}D\times D\to D.$$
$$(AX(D,zero,one,plus,times)).$$

Given SA we define the terms over SA, Term(SA), and the <u>propositional functions over SA</u>, Prop(SA), inductively as follows:

---

†We have been calling such structures <u>abstract types</u>, indeed Gordon Plotkin pointed out to me that the proof rules for this type are in fact congruent to those for abstract types in such languages as CLU.

$$
\begin{aligned}
&\mathrm{Terms(SA)} \subseteq \Sigma i{:}N.(D^{(i)}\to D)\\
&\quad \mathrm{Terms(SA)}(0) = \{f{:}\Sigma i{:}N.(D^{(i)}\to D) \mid\\
&\qquad (\mathrm{arity}(f) = 0 \;\&\; \mathrm{op}(f) = \lambda x.\mathrm{one} \vee \mathrm{op}(f) = \lambda x.\mathrm{zero})\\
&\qquad \vee\\
&\qquad (\mathrm{arity}(f) = 2 \;\&\; \mathrm{op}(f) = \mathrm{plus} \vee \mathrm{op}(f) = \mathrm{times})\\
&\qquad \vee\\
&\qquad \exists n{:}N.(f = P(n))\} \quad \text{where P is similar to the P of IV.}
\end{aligned}
$$

$$
\begin{aligned}
\mathrm{Terms(SA)}(n+1) = \{f{:}\Sigma i{:}N.(D^{(i)}\to D) \mid\ & \exists g{:}\mathrm{Terms(SA)}(n).(f=g) \vee\\
& \exists m{:}N.\exists h{:}\mathrm{Terms(SA)}(n).\exists g{:}(\mathrm{Terms(SA)}(n))^{m}.\\
& (f = C(h,g)).\}
\end{aligned}
$$

$$\mathrm{Terms(SA)} = \Sigma j{:}N.\mathrm{Terms(SA}(j))$$

Before we can define the propositions over SA we must describe how to treat quantification as a propositional operator. (It is already clear how to treat &, $\vee$, $\Rightarrow$ as operators on propositions, namely and$(p,q) = \lambda x.(p(x) \;\&\; q(x))$.)

Let the __propositional functions__ over D be defined as

$$\mathrm{PF}(D) = \Sigma i{:}N.(D^{(i)}\to \mathrm{Type}).$$

Then define $\exists$: PF(D) $\to$ PF(D) by

$$\exists(f) = \lambda x.\exists z{:}D.(f(z,x)) \quad \text{for arity}(f) > 0 \quad \text{and}$$

$$\exists(f) = f \quad \text{for arity}(f) = 0.$$

Likewise define $\pi(f) = \lambda x.\forall z{:}D.(f(z,x))$ and $\pi(f) = f$ for arity$(f) = 0$.

Now define the propositional functions Prop(SA) = $\Sigma j{:}N.\mathrm{Prop(SA)}(j)$ where:

$$
\begin{aligned}
\mathrm{Prop(SA)}(0) = \{f{:}\Sigma i{:}N.(D^{(i)}\to \mathrm{Type}) \mid\ & \exists(g_1,g_2){:}\mathrm{Terms(SA)}.(\mathrm{arity}(g_1) = \mathrm{arity}(g_2) = \mathrm{arity}(f) \;\&\\
& \qquad f = \lambda x.(g_1(x) = g_2(x))) \vee\\
& \exists p{:}\text{Atomic prop(SA)}.(f=p)\}
\end{aligned}
$$

$$
\begin{aligned}
\mathrm{Prop(SA)}(n+1) = \{f{:}\Sigma i{:}N.(D^{(i)}\to \mathrm{Type}) \mid\ & \exists g{:}\mathrm{Prop(SA)}(n).(f=g) \vee\\
& \exists(p_1,p_2){:}\mathrm{Prop(SA)}(n).\\
& \quad (f = \mathrm{and}(p_1,p_2) \vee\\
& \quad\ f = \mathrm{or}(p_1,p_2) \vee\\
& \quad\ f = \mathrm{imp}(p_1,p_2) \vee\\
& \quad\ f = \exists(p_1) \vee\\
& \quad\ f = \pi(p_1)) \vee\\
& \exists m{:}N.\exists p{:}\mathrm{Prop(SA)}(n).\exists g{:}(\mathrm{Term(SA)})^{m}.(f = C(p,g)))
\end{aligned}
$$

where C is the composition operator defined previously.

We can now consider an inductive definition of the class of theorems of SA, say Thm(SA). If we use a Hilbert-style system, then it will be easy to write an inductive definition of classes Thm(SA)(n) of those theorems provable from the axioms in n steps. Implication and universal quantification are defined in terms of an axiom scheme over propositions. We write a function $K:Prop(SA) \to Prop(SA) \to Prop(SA)$ such that $K(p)(q) = p \Rightarrow (q \Rightarrow p)$ and a function $S:Prop(SA) \to Prop(SA) \to Prop(SA) \to Prop(SA)$ such that $S(p)(q)(r) = (p \Rightarrow (q \Rightarrow r)) \Rightarrow (p \Rightarrow q) \Rightarrow (p \Rightarrow r)$. We assert that $K(p)(q)$ and $S(p)(q)(r)$ are theorems for any p,q,r. Here is a sketch of the definition. Now we can define the theorems of SA inductively as follows:

$Thms(SA)(0) = \{f:Prop(SA) \mid SAaxiom(f) \vee equalityaxiom(f)\}$

$Thms(SA)(n+1) = \{f:Prop(SA) \mid$

	$\exists g:Thms(SA)(n).(f=g) \vee$
andin	$\exists a_1,a_2:Thms(SA)(n).(f = and(a_1,a_2)) \vee$
andel	$\exists(a,b):Thms(SA)(n).(b = and(a,f) \vee b = and(f,a)) \vee$
orin	$\exists d:Thms(SA)(n).\exists g:Prop(SA).(f = or(d,g) \vee f = or(g,d)) \vee$
orel	$\exists d:Thms(SA)(n).\exists(g_1,g_2):Thms(SA)(n).\exists d_1,d_2:Prop(SA).$ $(d = or(d_1,d_2) \,\&\, g_1 = imp(d_1,f) \,\&\, g_2 = imp(d_2,f)) \vee$
impin	$\exists(p,q,r):Prop(SA).(f = K(p)(q) \vee f = S(p)(q)(r)) \vee$
allin	$\exists g:Thm(SA)(n).(f = \Pi(g)) \vee$
$\exists$-in	$\exists p:Prop(SA).\exists d:Terms(SA).(arity(p) \geq 1 \,\&\, \exists t:Thm(SA)(n).$ $(t = C(p,d))) \,\&\, f = \exists(p)) \vee$
allel	$\exists g:Thms(SA)(n).\exists t:Terms(SA).\exists p:Prop(SA).(g = \Pi(p) \,\&$ $f = C(p,t)) \vee$
$\exists$-el	$\exists g_1,g_2:Thms(SA)(n).\exists p:Prop(SA).(g_1 = \exists(p) \,\&\, g_2 = imp(p,f))\}$

Put $Thms(SA) = \Sigma j:N.Thms(SA)(j)$. We know from "cardinality" results that Prop(SA) and Thms(SA) are countable types. That is

Thm $\exists e_p:N \xrightarrow{onto} Prop(SA) \;\&\; \exists e_t:N \xrightarrow{onto} Thms(SA)$.

The logically true theorems of SA are those which hold independently of the axioms, AX, that is propositions P such that

$*\ \forall D:Type:\forall zero:D.\forall one:D.\forall plus:D \times D \to D.\forall times:D \times D \to D.P.$

P is logically false iff * holds with $\neg P$ for P. Notice that we are not speaking of "provability in SA" here but we are speaking of truth in the programming language. Also, if P is logically true, then $\neg P$ is logically false.

Theorem 4.3.1 (of [19]) General Undecidability Theorem.

For any minimally adequate theory, say SA, there is no recursive function to separate its theorems, say Thms(SA), from logically false sentences, say False(SA).

Pf: Here is a version of the proof in [19] which is correct for the programming logic.

If $\phi_i(i) = 0$, then AX & S(i) is a theorem because $\phi_i(i) = 0$ is representable and AX is provable. So $\neg$(AX $\Rightarrow$ $\neg$S(i)) is also a theorem.

If $\phi_i(i) = 1$, then AX $\Rightarrow$ $\neg$S(i) is logically true since $\phi_i(i) = 1$ is representable (so F(i,i,1) is provable from AX and $0 \neq 1$ is provable, so $\neg$F(i,i,0) is provable from AX), and thus AX $\Rightarrow$ $\neg$S(i) is provable in any D. By definition $\neg$(AX $\Rightarrow$ $\neg$S(i)) is logically false.

Let $S_0 = \{i{:}N \mid \phi_i(i) = 0\}$, $S_1 = \{i{:}N \mid \phi_i(i) = 1\}$.

Let $E_0 = \{j{:}N \mid j = e_t(\neg(AX \Rightarrow \neg S(i)))$ for $i \in S_0\}$

$E_1 = \{j{:}N \mid j = e_t(AX \Rightarrow \neg S(i))$ for $i \in S_1\}$

Notice that $E_0 \subseteq$ Thms(SA) and

$E_1 \subseteq$ False(SA).

So any recursive function to separate Thms(SA) and False(SA) would separate E_0, E_1 and hence also S_0, S_1.

QED.

Acknowledgements

I would like to thank Stuart F. Allen for his numerous helpful comments about this paper and for many stimulating discussions about doing mathematics in type theory. In response to this paper, Stuart has developed a very elegant alternative definition of partial functions which I hope will appear elsewhere.

I also want to thank Donette Isenbarger for her excellent preparation of the manuscript.

References

[1] Aczel, P., "The Type Theoretic Interpretation of Constructive Set Theory", Logic Colloquium '77, A. MacIntyre, L. Pacholaki and J. Paris (eds.), North-Holland, Amsterdam, 1978, 55-66.

[2] Bates, J.L. and R.L. Constable, "Proofs as Programs", Dept. of Computer Science Technical Report, TR 82-530, Cornell University, Ithaca, NY, 1982.

[3] Bates, J.L. and R.L. Constable, "The Nearly Ultimate PRL", Department of Computer Science Technical Report TR 83-551, Cornell University, April 1983.

[4] Bishop, E., Foundations of Constructive Analysis, McGraw Hill, NY, 1967, 370 pp.

[5] Beeson, M., "Formalizing Constructive Mathematics: Why and How?", Constructive Mathematics (ed., F. Richman), Lecture Notes in Computer Science, Springer-Verlag, NY, 1981, 146-190.

[6] Bourbaki, N., Elements of Mathematics, Vol I, Theory of Sets, Addison-Wesley, Reading, 1968.

[7] Constable, Robert L., "Constructive Mathematics and Automatic Program Writers", Proc. of IFIP Congress, Ljubljana, 1971, pp 229-233.

[8] Constable, Robert L. and M.J. O'Donnell, A Programming Logic, Winthrop, Cambridge, 1978.

[9] Constable, Robert L., S.D. Johnson and C.D. Eichenlaub, Introduction to the PL/CV2 Programming Logic, Lecture notes in Computer Science, Vol. 135, Springer-Verlag, NY, 1982.

[10] Constable, Robert L., "Programs As Proofs", Department of Computer Science, Technical Report TR 82-532, Cornell University, 1982. (To appear in Information Processing Letters, 1983.)

[11] Constable, Robert L. and D.R. Zlatin, "The Type Theory of PL/CV3", IBM Logic of Programs Conference, Lecture Notes in Computer Science, Vol. 131, Springer-Verlag, NY, 1982, 72-93.

[12] Curry, H.B. and R. Feys, Combinatory Logic, North-Holland, Amsterdam, 1968.

[13] deBruijn, N.G., "A Survey of the Project AUTOMATH", Essays on Combinatory Logic, Lambda Calculus and Formalism, (eds. J.P. Seldin and J.R. Hindley), Academic Press, NY, 1980, 589-606.

[14] Gordon, M., R. Milner and C. Wadsworth, Edinburgh LCF: A Mechanized Logic of Computation, Lecture Notes in Computer Science, Vol. 78, Springer-Verlag, 1979.

[15] Howard, W.A., "The Formulas-As-Types Notion of Construction" in Essays on Combinatory Logic, Lambda Calculus and Formalism, (eds., J.P. Seldin and J.R. Hindley), Academic Press, NY, 1980.

[16] Jensen, K. and N. Wirth, Pascal User Manual and Report, (2nd ed.), Springer-Verlag, New York, 1975.

[17] Jutting, L.S., "Checking Landau's 'Grundlagen' in the AUTOMATH System" (Doctoral Thesis, Eindhoven University), Math. Centre Tracts No. 83, Math. Centre, Amsterdam, 1979.

[18] Kleene, S.C., Introduction to Metamathematics, D. Van Nostrand, Princeton, 1952, 550 pp.

[19] Machtey, Michael and P. Young, An Introduction to the General Theory of Algorithms, North-Holland, NY, 1978.

[20] Martin-Löf, Per, "An Intuitionistic Theory of Types: Predicative Part", Logic Colloquium, 1973, (eds. H.E. Rose and J.C. Shepherdson), North-Holland, Amsterdam, 1975, 73-118.

[21] Martin-Löf, Per, "Constructive Mathematics and Computer Programming", 6th International Congress for Logic, Method and Phil. of Science, North-Holland, Amsterdam, 1982.

[22] McGettrick, A.D., Algol 68, A First and Second Course, Cambridge University Press, Cambridge, 1978.

[23] Nordstrom, B., "Programming in Constructive Set Theory: Some Examples", Proc. 1981 Conf. on Functional Prog. Lang. and Computer Archi, Portsmouth, 1981, 141-153.

[24] Reynolds, John C, "Towards a Theory of Type Structure", Proc. Colloque su, la Programmation, Lecture Notes in Computer Science, 19, Springer-Verlag, pp. 408-425, 1974.

[25] Russell, B., "Mathematical Logic as Based on a Theory of Types", Am. J. of Math., 30, 1908, pp. 222-262.

[26] Stenlund, S., Combinators, Lambda-terms, and Proof-Theory, D. Reidel, Dordrecht, 1972, 183 pp.

[27] van Wijngaarden, A.B.J. et al. Revised Report on the Algorithmic Language ALGO 68, Supplement to ALGO BULLETIN, University of Alberta, 1974.

CHARACTERIZATION OF ACCEPTABLE BY ALGOL-LIKE PROGRAMMING LANGUAGES

Ch. Crasemann
H. Langmaack
Institut für Informatik und Praktische Mathematik
Christian-Albrechts-Universität Kiel
Olshausenstr. 40, D-2300 Kiel

Abstract
It is proved that the procedure concept of ALGOL60-like programming languages with the standard call-by-name static scope semantics without arithmetic and without array allows any effective computation over arbitrary signatures.

I. Introduction

In order to cope with effective enumeration of partially correct Hoare assertions Lipton [Li77] introduces the term of "acceptable" programming languages. In his rather vague definition he wants to capture all languages of programs executable by an interpreter. More precisely, Clarke, German and Halpern [CGH81/82] demand that such programs describe functions which w.r.t. an algebraic structure are effectively computable by means of deterministic algorithms. The class of these functions may be defined in several ways constituting the base for an appropriately generalized Church-Turing thesis.

To recall some approaches we mention H. Friedman's "effective definitional schemes"[Fr69, Ti79] as well as his generalized Turing algorithms [Fr69] and while-programs with arithmetic and an infinite (ω-indexed) array [CG72, Gr75].

Starting with the latter characterization we prove that an ALGOL-like programming language (even ALGOL60-like) with procedures but without array and without arithmetic, i.e. with simple variables only, computes the same general class of functions. This means that ALGOL-like programming languages are universal subject to a generalized Church-Turing thesis. The power of arithmetic and an infinite array in a while program is certainly sufficient to simulate an ALGOL-like program and its run-time system. To prove the other way we proceed as follows: In [La74] it is shown that the pure procedure mechanism of ALGOL60 can simulate any Turing machine. Here we give a direct simulation of partial μ-recursive functions through appropriate procedures. Unlike Clarke in [Cl77/79] we do not make use of global "read-write" variables of procedures (his procedures have non-simple sideeffects). We exploit the power of declaration nestings and self-application instead. For elimination of subscripted variables we need simple variables global to some newly defined parameterless procedures which, statically linked at run-time, simulate a (potentially infinite) array. These simple variables are global "read-only" variables. Thus our procedures have simple sideeffects only.

All given program transformations preserve functional equivalence w.r.t. all interpretations (schematological equivalence). We do not give full proofs for which the formal copy or rewrite rule semantics as described in [La73] (a kind of algebraic semantics [Ni75]) seems to be an adequate tool. For a better readability of the transformations, we introduce the concept of higher determinate functionals. In this framework, ALGOL60-procedures are simple functionals with a certain basic result type. Higher functionals do not increase the power of an ALGOL60-like language, they can be effectively eliminated [Cr 83].

Applying our result to the area of comparative schematology [CG72] we get the equivalence of the concepts of an infinite array plus arithmetic on the one hand and a procedure concept with call-by-name parameter passing on the other. This answers an open question stated in [Cri 82].

As a second implication it is constituted that without restriction of generality we may use ALGOL-like programming languages as a basis for research work on the existence of Hoare logics in the sense of Lipton. The constructs available in languages of ALGOL-type seem to be of interest as an explicit measure for the limits of what can be achieved.

II. Basic definitions

Let Σ denote an effectively presented (one-sorted) <u>signature</u> of sets C of <u>constants</u> ($\perp \in C$), R of <u>relator</u> and F of <u>function symbols</u>. Σ_ω is the signature of the language of arithmetic. VI_Σ, FVI_Σ, FI, FFI are mutually disjoint enumerable sets of <u>simple Σ-variable identifiers</u> (simple Σ-variables), <u>formal Σ-variables</u>, <u>function identifiers</u> and <u>formal function identifiers</u>.
$EXPR_\Sigma$, LF_Σ, BE_Σ are the usual sets of <u>expressions</u>, (<u>first order</u>) <u>logical</u> and <u>quantifier free logical formulas</u> (Boolean expressions) over Σ and $VI_\Sigma \cup FVI_\Sigma$.
Let α be the distinguished name for a family of $EXPR_\Sigma$ -indexed <u>subscripted Σ-variables</u>, each written as $\alpha[\tilde{e}]$ for $\tilde{e} \in^{\omega} EXPR_{\Sigma_\omega}$. This explains the sets $EXPR_{\Sigma,\alpha}$, $LF_{\Sigma,\alpha}$ and $BE_{\Sigma,\alpha}$.

The set AT of <u>applicative terms</u> is defined inductively: $\mathfrak{t} \in VI_\Sigma \cup FVI_\Sigma \cup FI \cup FFI \subseteq AT$ is a simple applicative term, $\mathfrak{f}(\vec{\mathfrak{t}}) \in AT$ is a compound one, $\mathfrak{f} \in AT \setminus (VI_\Sigma \cup FVI_\Sigma)$, $\mathfrak{t} \in AT$, $\vec{\ }$ indicates a list of length $|\vec{\ }| \geq 0$.[1)] For given Σ and Σ_ω, we are going to consider ALGOL-like programming languages with array and arithmetic. For convenience we introduce so-called higher determinate functionals. Programs π, statements σ and declarations δ are given by the following <u>context-free-like grammar</u> G:

$$P ::= \underline{\text{begin}}\ \{\underline{\text{var}}\ \alpha\text{: }\underline{\text{array}}[0:\infty]\ \underline{\text{of}}\ \Sigma,\}\ \overrightarrow{\underline{\text{var}}\ \tilde{v}:\Sigma_\omega,}\ D,\ S\ \underline{\text{end}}$$

$$\begin{aligned} S ::= {} & v := e \mid \tilde{v} := \tilde{e} \mid \underline{\text{push}}\ e \mid \underline{\text{skip}} \mid \underline{\text{error}} \\ & \mid \underline{\text{if}}\ b\ \underline{\text{then}}\ S_1\ \underline{\text{else}}\ S_2\ \underline{\text{fi}} \mid \underline{\text{while}}\ b\ \underline{\text{do}}\ S_1\ \underline{\text{od}} \\ & \mid \underline{\text{begin}}\ D,\ S_1\ \underline{\text{end}} \mid \mathfrak{f}(\vec{\alpha}) \mid (S_1;\ S_2) \end{aligned}$$

$$D ::= \overrightarrow{\text{var } v\text{: } \Sigma \mid \underline{\text{funct}}\ f \Leftarrow \lambda\vec{x}^1.\ \ldots\ .\lambda\vec{x}^m.\ S_f}$$

where $v \in VI_\Sigma \cup FVI_\Sigma$, $\tilde{v} \in VI_{\Sigma_\omega}$, $e \in EXPR_{\Sigma,\alpha}$, $\tilde{e} \in EXPR_{\Sigma_\omega}$, $b \in BE_{\Sigma_\omega} \cup BE_{\Sigma_\omega}$, $f \in FI$, $x \in FFI \cup FVI_\Sigma$,

---

1) $\mathfrak{f}(\vec{\mathfrak{t}})$ with an empty $\vec{\mathfrak{t}}$ is $\mathfrak{f}(\ )$ and not $\mathfrak{f}$.

$\mathfrak{f}(\vec{\alpha}) \in AT$, $m \geq 1$. { } indicates an option.

Applied occurrences of identifiers in π are either free or have unique associated defining occurrences according to the rules of lexical (static) scoping. A range ρ in a program π is the program itself, a block begin $\vec{\delta}$, σ end, a function body σ_f or an abstraction $\lambda \vec{x}^1. \ldots .\lambda \vec{x}^m. \sigma_f$. Identifiers in a range ρ are either locally defined or global to ρ. In case $\rho = \sigma_f$ these latter ones are either formal parameters of f or global parameters. The main part $\mathfrak{M}_\rho$ of a range ρ in π is that part outside all abstractions.

We define the set ICT of incomplete types[2] inductively: The two symbols v and c are basic types (for Σ-variables and the results of function calls, continuations in our case); $(\vec{t} \to c) \in ICT$ with basic types t is a simple functional type; $(\vec{t} \to t') \in ICT$ with basic types t and $t' \in ICT \setminus \{c,v\}$ is a type of higher functionality.

With every program π generated by G we (implicitly or explicitly) associate a type function $type^\pi$ associating a type in ICT with defining occurrences idf of identifiers $\neq \alpha$:

$$type^\pi(idf) =_{df} \begin{cases} v & \text{if } idf \in VI_\Sigma \cup FVI_\Sigma, \\ c & \text{if } idf \in FFI \\ (type^\pi(\vec{x}^1) \to (\ldots \to (type^\pi(\vec{x}^m) \to c) \ \ldots))^{3)} & \\ & \text{if } \underline{funct}\ idf \Leftarrow \lambda \vec{x}^1. \ldots .\lambda \vec{x}^m. \sigma_{idf} \end{cases}$$

For applied occurrences idf of identifiers we define $type^\pi(idf)$ to be the type of the associated defining occurrence if there is one; free Σ-variables have type v; $type^\pi$ is undefined for other identifier occurrences.

For occurrences $\mathfrak{f}$ of applicative terms in π the identifiers of which are all non-formal we define

---

2) We only differentiate between variables and functions as parameters. The latter ones are not further specified.

3) $type^\pi(\vec{x}^i)$ stands for $\overrightarrow{type^\pi(x)}^i$. The type is $(\to c)$ if funct idf $\Leftarrow \lambda.\sigma_{idf}$ is declared.

$$\mathrm{type}^{\pi}(\mathfrak{f}) =_{df} \begin{cases} v & \text{if } \mathfrak{f} \in VI_{\Sigma} \\ (\vec{t}^{k+1} \to (\ldots \to (\vec{t}^{m} \to c)\ldots))^{4)} & \\ \quad \text{if } \mathfrak{f} = f(\vec{\mathfrak{a}}^{1}) \ldots (\vec{\mathfrak{a}}^{k}),\ f \in FI, & \\ \quad 0 \leq k \leq m,\ \mathrm{type}^{\pi}(f) = (\vec{t}^{1} \to (\ldots \to (\vec{t}^{m} \to c)\ldots)), & \\ \quad |\vec{\mathfrak{a}}^{i}| = |\vec{t}^{i}| \text{ for } 1 \leq i \leq k \text{ with} & \\ \quad t = v \text{ iff } \mathfrak{a} \in VI_{\Sigma} \text{ and } t = c \text{ iff } \mathfrak{a} \notin VI_{\Sigma} & \\ \text{undefined otherwise} & \end{cases}$$

A program π generated by G is called <u>proper</u> iff the only free identifiers in π are non-formal Σ-variables $\in VI_{\Sigma}$.

We remark that Σ_{ω}-variables are global to all functions (totally global). Functions of simple functional type are <u>procedures</u> in the sense of ALGOL60. Functions of higher functionality are called <u>higher functionals</u>.

Let $\mathcal{L}^{\omega,\alpha}$ be the class of all proper <u>ALGOL-like programs with arithmetic and array</u> generated by G. We define subclasses of $\mathcal{L}^{\omega,\alpha}$ by imposing restrictions: We have in

$\mathcal{L}^{\omega}$ — no subscripted variables, but arithmetic,

$\mathcal{L}$ — neither arithmetic nor an array, the class of <u>ALGOL-like programs</u>,

$\mathcal{L}_{60}^{\omega,\alpha}$ — no higher functionals,

$\mathcal{L}_{W}^{\omega,\alpha}$ — no function declarations, the class of <u>while-programs with arithmetic and array</u>,

$\mathcal{L}_{60}^{\omega} = \mathcal{L}^{\omega} \cap \mathcal{L}_{60}^{\omega,\alpha}$,

$\mathcal{L}_{60} = \mathcal{L} \cap \mathcal{L}_{60}^{\omega}$, the class of <u>ALGOL60-like programs</u>

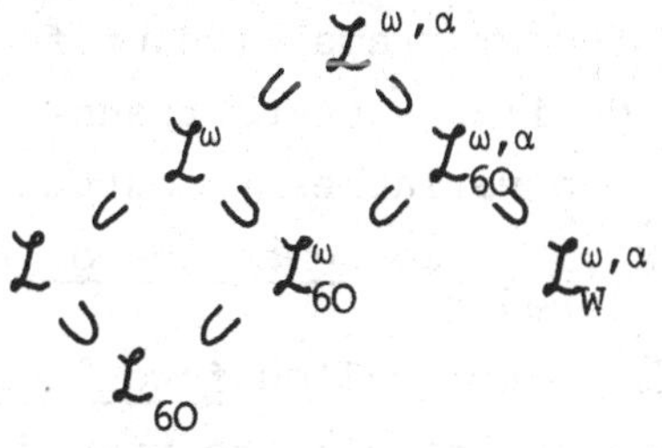

4) In case k=m this is understood to be c

We now define a semantics for $\mathcal{L}^{\omega,\alpha}$ as far as we shall need it. Let $\mathcal{R}_\Sigma$ be a <u>relational structure</u> $\langle dom(\mathcal{R}_\Sigma), F_\Sigma, R_\Sigma\rangle$ realizing the symbols in Σ in the well-known way, Let $\mathcal{N}$ be the standard structure for the language of arithmetic. A <u>state</u> s is a total mapping associating elements of dom ($\mathcal{N}$) resp. dom ($\mathcal{R}_\Sigma$) with elements of VI_{Σ_ω} resp. $VI_\Sigma \cup \{ \alpha[i] \mid i \in \omega\}$. Given the concept of a state, we know how to define the standard semantics for $EXPR_{\Sigma_\omega}$, LF_{Σ_ω}, $EXPR_{\Sigma,\alpha}$ and $LF_{\Sigma,\alpha}$.

It is important for our proceeding that we choose function calls to be treated with <u>call-by-name</u> parameter evaluation. The semantics of function calls is explained by an ALGOL-like <u>copy- or rewrite rule</u>. <u>Algebraic semantics</u> proceeds similarly [Ni75] and facilitates proofs of certain program equivalences.

A proper program π generates another program π' ($\pi \vdash \pi'$) iff the following holds:
Let a statement $f(\vec{\mathfrak{a}}^1) \ldots (\vec{\mathfrak{a}}^k)$ with $f \in FI$ and associated declaration <u>funct</u> f $\Leftarrow \lambda\vec{x}^1. \ldots .\lambda\vec{x}^m.\sigma_f$ occur in $\mathfrak{M}_\pi$ such that $type^\pi(f(\vec{\mathfrak{a}}^1) \ldots (\vec{\mathfrak{a}}^k))$ is defined and equal c. π' is obtained from π by inserting σ_f' for the calling statement where σ_f' results by substitution $\sigma_f[\vec{\mathfrak{a}}^1, \ldots, \vec{\mathfrak{a}}^m / \vec{x}^1, \ldots, \vec{x}^m]$ of actual parameters $\mathfrak{a} \in AT$ for the formal ones $x \in FVI \cup FFI$. It is clear that bound renamings of identifiers have to take place in order to avoid <u>binding conflicts w.r.t. static scoping rules</u>.

$\vdash^*$ denotes the reflexive, transitive closure of $\vdash$. For any $\pi \in \mathcal{L}^{\omega,\alpha}$ we define the <u>formal execution lattice</u> $E_\pi =_{df} \{\pi' \mid \pi \vdash^* \pi'\}$. A <u>reduced program</u> π_{red} is one in which all function delarations are erased and all calls are substituted by <u>error</u> ($\perp$ in [Ni75]). We assume that we know how to define a (denotational) <u>semantics</u> for programs without functions, i.e. for $\mathcal{L}_W^{\omega,\alpha}$. Thus, any π_{red} defines a state transformation $M_{\pi_{red}}$ mapping input values of free variables to output values.
We may define $M_\pi =_{df} \bigcup_{\pi' \in E_\pi} M_{\pi'_{red}}$ as <u>semantics of $\pi \in \mathcal{L}^{\omega,\alpha}$</u>.

Two programs π, $\tilde{\pi} \in \mathcal{L}^{\omega,\alpha}$ are called <u>functionally equivalent</u> w.r.t. $\mathcal{R}_\Sigma$ iff they denote the same state transformation. π and $\tilde{\pi}$ are said to be <u>schematologically equivalent</u> iff they are functionally equivalent for all structures $\mathcal{R}_\Sigma$. We mention the following

Lemma 1 [Cr83]: Any $\pi \in \mathcal{L}^{\omega,\alpha}$ can be effectively transformed into a schematologically equivalent $\tilde{\pi} \in \mathcal{L}_{60}^{\omega,\alpha}$. The analogous statement holds for $\mathcal{L}^{\omega}$ and for $\mathcal{L}$.

Using $\approx$ to indicate schematological equivalence we may now depict the relationship between the defined classes of programs w.r.t. $\approx$:

$$\begin{array}{ccccc}
 & & \mathcal{L}^{\omega,\alpha} \approx \mathcal{L}_{60}^{\omega,\alpha} & & \\
 & & \subsetneq \qquad\qquad \supsetneq & & \\
 & \mathcal{L}^{\omega} \approx \mathcal{L}_{60}^{\omega} & & & \mathcal{L}_{W}^{\omega,\alpha} \\
 & \subsetneq & & & \\
\mathcal{L} \approx \mathcal{L}_{60} & & & &
\end{array}$$

So we are free to use higher functionals to make transformations of especially ALGOL60-like programs more transparent.

III. Normal forms

We say that a program π is in tail recursive [BaW81] normal form (or simply in normal form) iff any statement $\sigma = (\sigma_1;\sigma_2)$ is such that σ_1 is an assignment, push, skip or error statement and no while-statements occur in π. Being in normal form means that the program terminates iff all function calls and block entrances made in the program are terminated successively in reversed order without any other statement being executed in between. In other words: Any function ever called during the execution of the program is still active in the dynamic chain of a run-time system as long as no call is terminated, and actual parameters once passed are still potentially accessible.

We shall now give an algorithm which transforms any $\pi \in \mathcal{L}^{\omega,\alpha}$ into a schematologically equivalent $\nu(\pi) \in \mathcal{L}^{\omega,\alpha}$ in normal form.

Algorithm 1: Transformation into normal form.

W.r.o.g. we may assume that any successively compounded statement is parenthesized to the right: $(\sigma_1; (\sigma_2;\sigma_3))$. This simplifies the algorithmic process, but the algorithm works without this assumption. With the help of two mappings

$\nu_\sigma | \{\sigma\} \times (\mathrm{FIUFFI}) \to \{\sigma\}$,

$\nu_\delta | \ \{\delta\} \rightarrow \{\delta\}$

of statements and declarations we can define the mapping

$\nu | \ \mathcal{L}^{\omega,\alpha} \rightarrow \ \mathcal{L}^{\omega,\alpha}$

we are interested in.

Let $\pi \in \mathcal{L}^{\omega,\alpha}$ be

$\underline{\text{begin}}\ \{\underline{\text{var}}\ \alpha\text{: } \underline{\text{array}}\ [0{:}\infty]\ \underline{\text{of}}\ \Sigma,\}\ \ \overrightarrow{\underline{\text{var}}\ \tilde{v}{:}\Sigma_\omega}, \vec{\delta},\ \sigma\ \underline{\text{end}}$

Then

$$\nu(\pi) =_{df} \underline{\text{begin}}\ \{\underline{\text{var}}\ \alpha{:}\underline{\text{array}}[0{:}\infty]\ \underline{\text{of}}\ \Sigma,\}\ \overrightarrow{\underline{\text{var}}\ \tilde{v}{:}\Sigma_\omega},$$
$$\underline{\text{funct}}\ \text{stop} \Leftarrow \lambda.\underline{\text{skip}},$$
$$\nu_\delta(\vec{\delta}),\ \nu_\sigma(\sigma,\ \text{stop})\ \underline{\text{end}}$$

where stop $\in$ FI and not in π.

ν_δ and ν_σ are defined by structural induction:

$$\nu_\delta(\delta) =_{df} \begin{cases} \delta & \text{if } \delta = \underline{\text{var}}\ v{:}\Sigma \\ \underline{\text{funct}}\ f \Leftarrow \ \lambda\vec{x}^1.\ \ldots\ \lambda\vec{x}^m,\ c.\nu_\sigma(\sigma_f, c) & \text{where } c \in \text{FFI is not in } \delta \\ & \text{if } \delta = \underline{\text{funct}}\ f \Leftarrow \lambda\vec{x}^1.\ \ldots\ .\lambda\vec{x}^m.\sigma_f \end{cases}$$

$$\nu_\sigma(\sigma,\kappa) =_{df}$$

$$\begin{cases} (\sigma;\ \kappa()\ ) & \text{if } \sigma = v{:}=e\,|\,\tilde{v}{:}=\tilde{e}\,|\,\underline{\text{push}}\ e\,|\,\underline{\text{skip}}\,|\,\underline{\text{error}} \\ (\sigma_1;\ \nu_\sigma(\sigma_2,\kappa)) & \text{if } \sigma = (\sigma_1;\sigma_2) \text{ and} \\ & \sigma_1 = v{:}=e\,|\,\tilde{v}{:}=\tilde{e}\,|\,\underline{\text{push}}\ e\,|\,\underline{\text{skip}}\,|\,\underline{\text{error}} \\ \underline{\text{begin}}\ \underline{\text{funct}}\ c \Leftarrow \lambda.\nu_\sigma(\sigma_2,\kappa)\ ,\ \nu_\sigma(\sigma_1,c)\ \underline{\text{end}} & \\ & \text{where } c \in \text{FI is not in } \sigma \text{ and } \neq \kappa \\ & \text{if } \sigma = (\sigma_1;\sigma_2) \text{ and } \sigma_1 \text{ is not of the form above} \\ \underline{\text{if}}\ b\ \underline{\text{then}}\ \nu_\sigma(\sigma_1,\kappa)\ \ \underline{\text{else}}\ \nu_\sigma(\sigma_2,\kappa)\ \ \underline{\text{fi}} & \\ & \text{if } \sigma = \underline{\text{if}}\ b\ \underline{\text{then}}\ \sigma_1\ \underline{\text{else}}\ \sigma_2\ \underline{\text{fi}} \\ \nu_\sigma(\underline{\text{begin}}\ \underline{\text{funct}}\ \text{while} \Leftarrow \lambda.\underline{\text{if}}\ b\ \underline{\text{then}}\ \sigma_1;\ \text{while}\ ()\underline{\text{else}}\ \underline{\text{skip}}\ \underline{\text{fi}}, & \\ \qquad \text{while}\ ()\ \underline{\text{end}},\kappa) & \\ & \text{where while} \in \text{FI is not in } \sigma \text{ and } \neq \kappa \\ & \text{if } \sigma = \underline{\text{while}}\ b\ \underline{\text{do}}\ \sigma_1\ \underline{\text{od}} \\ \underline{\text{begin}}\ \nu_\delta(\vec{\delta}),\ \nu_\sigma(\sigma_1,\kappa)\ \underline{\text{end}} & \\ & \text{if } \sigma = \underline{\text{begin}}\ \vec{\delta},\ \sigma_1\ \underline{\text{end}} \\ \mathfrak{f}(\vec{\mathfrak{a}},\kappa) & \text{if } \sigma = \mathfrak{f}(\vec{\mathfrak{a}}) \end{cases}$$

◇

Theorem 1: For any $\pi \in \mathcal{L}^{\omega,\alpha}$, π and $\nu(\pi)$ are schematologically equivalent and $\nu(\pi)$ is in normal form.

◇

Remark 1: In order to define transformation ν we must be able to declare and call parameterless functions and to extend parameter lists by one parameter standing for parameterless functions. So no more tools are necessary than available in PASCAL which we consider as an ALGOL60-sublanguage whose formal functions have no functions as parameters (special case of "no selfapplication") [JW75].

Example 1:

```
π = begin funct p ⇐ λx.(r(); x:= x+1; x:= x+2),
          funct r  ⇐ λ. skip
          (p(y)  ; y:= y+1 ) end
```

where $\Sigma = \Sigma_\omega$ and y is free.

$\nu(\pi)$ =

```
begin funct stop ⇐  λ.skip ,
      funct p  ⇐ λ.x,c1. begin
                              funct c2 ⇐ λ.(x:= x+1  ; x:=x+2;
                                                 c1()),
                              r(c2)  end,
      funct r ⇐ λc3.(skip ; c3() ),
      begin funct c4⇐ λ.(y:= y+1 ; stop () ),
            p(y,c4) end end
```

◇

IV. Elimination of subscripted variables

We are going to show that $\mathcal{L}^{\omega}$ and $\mathcal{L}^{\omega,\alpha}$ have the same computational power by presenting an algorithm eliminating subscripted variables.

Algorithm 2: Elimination of subscripted variables.

We start with programs in normal form. W.r.o.g. we may assume that subscripted variables only occur in assignments of the form $v{:=}\alpha[\tilde{e}]$.

We define

$\psi \mid \nu(\mathcal{L}^{\omega,\alpha}) \to \mathcal{L}^{\omega}$:

Let π be begin var α:array[0:∞] of Σ, $\overrightarrow{\text{var } \tilde{v}:\Sigma_\omega}$,
funct stop $\Leftarrow \lambda$.skip, $\vec{\delta}$, σ end

Then

$\psi(\pi) =_{df}$ begin $\overrightarrow{\text{var } \tilde{v}:\Sigma_\omega}$,
var $\widetilde{top}:\Sigma_\omega$, var $\widetilde{goal}:\Sigma_\omega$, var $\widetilde{count}:\Sigma_\omega$,
var $\widetilde{v_{glob}}:\Sigma$, funct stop $\Leftarrow \lambda c$.skip,
$\psi_\delta(\vec{\delta})$, ($\widetilde{top}$:= 0; $\psi_\sigma(\sigma$,stop)) end

where $\widetilde{top}$, $\widetilde{goal}$, $\widetilde{count}$, v_{glob} are distinct identifiers not in π. In case π has no array π is left unchanged by ψ. The auxiliary mapping ψ_δ is defined like ν_δ with ψ_σ replacing ν_σ.
$\psi_\sigma \mid \{\sigma\} \times (\text{FI} \cup \text{FFI}) \to \{\sigma\}$ is defined by
$\psi_\sigma(\sigma, \mathcal{K}) =_{df}$

- begin var cont:Σ,
  funct arr $\Leftarrow \lambda$.
  if $\widetilde{goal}$=$\widetilde{count}$ then $\widetilde{v_{glob}}$:= cont
  else $\widetilde{count}$:= $\widetilde{count}\dot{-}1$; $\mathcal{K}$() fi,
  cont:= e; $\widetilde{top}$:= $\widetilde{top}$ +1; $\psi_\sigma(\sigma_2$, arr) end
  where arr, cont are identifiers not in σ and $\neq \mathcal{K}$
  if σ= (push e; σ_2)
- if $\tilde{e}$>$\widetilde{top}$ then error
  else $\widetilde{goal}$:= $\tilde{e}$; $\widetilde{count}$:= $\widetilde{top}$; $\mathcal{K}$() ; v:= v_{glob}; $\psi_\sigma(\sigma_2, \mathcal{K})$ fi
  if σ= (v:= α[e]$\cdot\sigma_2$)
- (σ_1; $\psi_\sigma(\sigma_2, \mathcal{K})$)
  if σ= (σ_1;σ_2) and not of the forms above
- if b then $\psi_\sigma(\sigma_1, \mathcal{K})$ else $\psi_\sigma(\sigma_2, \mathcal{K})$ fi
  if σ= if b then σ_1 else σ_2 fi
- begin $\psi_\delta(\vec{\delta})$, $\psi_\sigma(\sigma_1, \mathcal{K})$ end
  if σ= begin $\vec{\delta}$, σ_1 end
- $f(\vec{a}, \mathcal{K})$ if σ= $f(\vec{a})$

Every push-operation is replaced by an assignment to a local variable cont. Series of cont-s represent a stack. Everv function gets an additional parameter c passing parameterless functions arr linking together the stack. Every $v := \alpha[\tilde{e}]$ -operation initiates a search down the stack.

<u>Theorem 2:</u> $\pi \in \mathcal{L}^{\omega,\alpha}$ and $\psi(\nu(\pi)) \in \mathcal{L}^{\omega}$ are schematologically equivalent.

<u>Remark 2:</u> In order to perform transformation ψ we need the same tools as for ν and we have to allow simple sideeffects (assignments v_{glob}:= to a totally global variable) and global "read-only" variables (:=cont).[5)]

<u>Example 2:</u>

```
π= begin var α:array [0:∞] of Σ, var i:Σ_ω,
        funct stop ⇐ λc.skip,
        funct r ⇐  λc.begin
                          funct c̄ ⇐λ.( z:= α[i]; c() ),
                          (i:= 1; c̄() ) end,
        push x; r(stop) end
```

where x, z are free Σ-variables and π is in normal form.

```
ψ(π)= begin var i:Σ_ω, var to͠p:Σ_ω, var go͠al:Σ_ω, var cou͠nt:Σ_ω,
            var v_glob:Σ, funct stop  = λ.skip
            funct r ⇐ λc, c_1.
                  begin funct c̄ <= λc_1.
                             if i>to͠p then error
                             else go͠al:= ẽ; cou͠nt:= to͠p;
                                c_1(); z:= v_glob; c(c_1) fi,
                  (i:= 1; c̄(c_1) ) end,
            top:= 0; begin var cont:Σ,
                  funct arr <=λ.
                  if go͠al=cou͠nt then v_glob:= cont
                             else cou͠nt:= cou͠nt ∸1 ; stop() fi,
            cont:= x; to͠p:= to͠p+1; r(stop,arr) end end
```

5) Making strong use of arithmetic and Gödelizations it is even possible to do without global "read only" variables.

V. Elimination of recursive functions

In [La74] it has been shown that the procedure mechanism in ALGOL60-like programming languages has the power of Turing machines. Thus, we just have to find the adequate means for a direct simulation of recursive functions in order to effectively transform programs in $\mathcal{L}^{\omega}$ into schematologically equivalent programs in $\mathcal{L}$. We start with an observation.

Lemma 2 [BrLa74]: Every partial μ-recursive function can be programmed using the following constructs:

$\tilde{v}$:= 0 | $\tilde{v}$:= $\tilde{w}$ | $\tilde{v}$:= $\tilde{v}\dot{-}1$ | begin var $\tilde{v}:\Sigma_{\omega}$, ... end | $\tilde{v}$:= $\tilde{v}$+1
| while $\tilde{v}$>0 do ... od.

◊

We assume that only these arithmetic constructs are used in programs $\pi \in \mathcal{L}^{\omega}$. It is no restriction that Σ_{ω}-variables are defined in the outermost block.

Algorithm 3: Elimination of arithmetic

We start with programs π in $\mathcal{L}^{\omega}$ in normal form. Note that $\tilde{v}$>0-tests only occur in conditional statements because while-constructs have been eliminated (by ν).

We define

$\rho | \nu(\mathcal{L}^{\omega}) \rightarrow \mathcal{L}$:

Let π be begin var $\tilde{v}_1:\Sigma_{\omega}$, ..., $\tilde{v}_n:\Sigma_{\omega}$,
funct stop <= λ.skip, $\vec{\delta}$, σ end

Then

$\rho(\pi) =_{df}$
begin
funct $N_o \Leftarrow \lambda D,C,V_1,\ldots,V_n.C(V_1,\ldots,V_n)$,
funct $N_1 \Leftarrow \lambda N.\lambda TM,C,V_1,\ldots,V_n.TM(N,C,V_1,\ldots,V_n)$ 6)
funct $MON_1 \Leftarrow \lambda N,C,V_1,\ldots,V_n.C(N,V_2,\ldots,V_n)$,
⋮

6) ρ may as well be defined without use of higher functionals (continued next page)

$\vdots$

$\underline{\text{funct}}$ $MON_i \Leftarrow \lambda N, C, V_1, \ldots, V_n . C(V_1, \ldots, \underbrace{N}_{\text{i-th position}}, \ldots, V_n)$,

$\vdots$

$\underline{\text{funct}}$ $MON_n \Leftarrow \lambda N, C, V_1, \ldots, V_n . C(V_1, \ldots, V_{n-1}, N)$,

$\underline{\text{funct}}$ $stop \Leftarrow \lambda V_1, \ldots, V_n . \underline{\text{skip}}$,

$\rho_\delta(\vec{\delta})$, $\rho_\delta(\sigma, \underbrace{N_o, \ldots, N_o}_{\text{n-times}})$ $\underline{\text{end}}$

where N_o, N_1, $MON_1, \ldots, MON_n \in FI$ and $N, C, D, TM, V_1, \ldots V_n \in FFI$ are distinct and not in π.

We define

$\rho_\delta | \{\delta\} \rightarrow \{\delta\}$ with

$$\rho_\delta(\delta) =_{df} \begin{cases} \underline{\text{var}}\ z : \Sigma & \text{if } \delta = \underline{\text{var}}\ z : \Sigma \\ \underline{\text{funct}}\ f \Leftarrow \lambda \vec{x}^1 . \ldots . \lambda \vec{x}^m, V_1, \ldots, V_n . \rho_\sigma(\sigma_f, V_1 \ldots, V_n) & \\ \quad \text{where } V_1, \ldots, V_n \text{ are distinct and} & \\ \quad \text{do not occur in } \delta & \\ \quad \text{if } \delta = \underline{\text{funct}}\ f = \lambda \vec{x}^1 . \ldots . \lambda \vec{x}^m . \sigma_f & \end{cases}$$

We define

$\rho_\sigma | \{\sigma\} \times AT \rightarrow \{\sigma\}$ with

$\rho_\sigma(\sigma, \kappa_1, \ldots, \kappa_n) = \rho_\sigma(\sigma, \vec{\kappa}) =_{df}$

$$\begin{cases} (\sigma_1 ; \rho_\sigma(\sigma_2, \vec{\kappa})) & \text{if } \sigma = (\sigma_1 ; \sigma_2) \text{ and } \sigma_1 = v := e | \underline{\text{skip}} | \underline{\text{error}} \\ \rho_\sigma(\sigma_2, \kappa_1, \ldots, \underbrace{N_o}_{\text{i-th position}}, \ldots, \kappa_n) & \text{if } \sigma = (\tilde{v}_i := 0 ; \sigma_2) \\ \rho_\sigma(\sigma_2, \kappa_1, \ldots, \underbrace{N_1(\kappa_i)}_{\text{i-th position}}, \ldots, \kappa_n) & \text{if } \sigma = (\tilde{v}_i := \tilde{v}_i + 1 ; \sigma_2)^{6)} \\ \rho_\sigma(\sigma_2, \kappa_1, \ldots, \underbrace{\kappa_j}_{\text{i-th position}}, \ldots, \kappa_n) & \text{if } \sigma = (\tilde{v}_1 := \tilde{v}_j ; \sigma_2) \end{cases}$$

---

according to Lemma 1. Then $\underline{\text{funct}}$ $N_1 \Leftarrow \ldots$ must be dropped and the definition of ρ_σ has to be changed in case $\sigma = (\tilde{v}_i := \tilde{v}_i + 1, \sigma_2)$: $\rho_\sigma(\sigma, \vec{\kappa}) =_{df}$ $\underline{\text{begin}}$ $\underline{\text{funct}}$ $\tilde{N}_1 \Leftarrow \lambda TM, C, V_1, \ldots, V_n . TM(\kappa_i, C, V_1, \ldots, V_n)$, $\rho_\sigma(\sigma_2, \kappa_1, \ldots, \underbrace{\tilde{N}_1}_{\text{i-th position}}, \ldots, \kappa_n)$ $\underline{\text{end}}$.

This is a simplified version of the general transformation [LS77].

$$\left\{\begin{array}{ll}
\underline{\text{begin}}\ \underline{\text{funct}}\ \tilde{c} \Leftarrow \lambda V_1,\ldots,V_n.\rho_\sigma(\sigma_2,V_1,\ldots,V_n), & \\
\quad \mathcal{t}_i(\underline{\text{MON}}_i,\ \tilde{c},\mathcal{t}_1,\ldots,\mathcal{t}_n)\ \underline{\text{end}} & \\
\quad \text{where } \tilde{c},\ V_1,\ldots,\ V_n \text{ are distinct and do not oc-} & \\
\quad \text{cur in } \sigma \text{ and are } \neq N_o, N_1, MON_i & \\
\quad \text{if } \sigma = (\tilde{v}_i := \tilde{v}_i \dot{-} 1;\sigma_2) & \\
\underline{\text{if}}\ b\ \underline{\text{then}}\ \rho_\sigma(\sigma_1,\vec{\mathcal{t}})\ \underline{\text{else}}\ \rho_\sigma(\sigma_2,\vec{\mathcal{t}})\ \underline{\text{fi}} & \\
\quad \text{if } \sigma = \underline{\text{if}}\ b\ \underline{\text{then}}\ \sigma_1\ \underline{\text{else}}\ \sigma_2 \text{ fi and } b\in BE_\Sigma & \\
\underline{\text{begin}}\ \underline{\text{funct}}\ \text{if} \Leftarrow \lambda N,C,V_1,\ldots,V_n.c_1(V_1,\ldots,V_n), & \\
\quad \underline{\text{funct}}\ c_1 \Leftarrow \lambda V_1,\ldots,V_n.\ \rho_\sigma(\sigma_1,V_1,\ldots,V_n), & \\
\quad \underline{\text{funct}}\ c_2 \Leftarrow \lambda V_1,\ldots,V_n.\ \rho_\sigma(\sigma_2,\ V_1,\ \ldots,V_n), & \\
\quad \mathcal{t}_i(\text{if},\ c_2,\mathcal{t}_1,\ldots,\mathcal{t}_n)\ \underline{\text{end}} & \\
\quad \text{where if, } c_1,c_2,N,V_1,\ldots,V_n \text{ are distinct} & \\
\quad \text{and not in } \sigma \text{ and } \neq N_o,N_1 & \\
\quad \text{if } \sigma = \underline{\text{if}}\ \tilde{v}_i > 0\ \underline{\text{then}}\ \sigma_1\ \underline{\text{else}}\ \sigma_2\ \underline{\text{fi}} & \diamond \\
\mathfrak{f}(\vec{\mathfrak{a}},\vec{\mathcal{t}}) \qquad \text{if } \sigma = \mathfrak{f}(\vec{\mathfrak{a}}) &
\end{array}\right.$$

Theorem 3: $\pi\in\mathcal{L}^\omega$ and $\rho(\nu(\pi))\in\mathcal{L}$ are schematologically equivalent.

If we use the power of recursive functions to model a run-time system, we may easily "compile" $\pi\in\mathcal{L}$ or $\in\mathcal{L}^{\omega,\alpha}$ into a schematologically equivalent $\pi\in\mathcal{L}_W^{\omega,\alpha}$. Thus we have

Theorem 4: $\mathcal{L}^{\omega,\alpha} \approx \mathcal{L}_{60}^{\omega,\alpha} \approx \mathcal{L}^\omega \approx \mathcal{L}_{60}^\omega \approx \mathcal{L} \approx \mathcal{L}_{60} \approx \mathcal{L}_W^{\omega,\alpha}$.

This means that ALGOL-like, even ALGOL60-like programming languages without arithmetic and without array are universal in the sense of an appropriately generalized Church-Turing thesis for effective computations over signatures.

Remark 3: In order to define ρ we need selfapplication of functions (procedures) and either higher functionalities (available in ALGOL68) or procedure nesting, available in ALGOL60.

Example 3:

We indicate how 1.) a test $\underline{\text{if}}\ \tilde{v}_i>0\ \underline{\text{then}}\ \sigma_1\ \underline{\text{else}}\ \sigma_2\ \underline{\text{fi}}$ resp. 2.) a monus $\tilde{v}_i := \tilde{v}_i \dot{-} 1\ ;\ \sigma_2$ in $\pi\in\nu(\mathcal{L}^\omega)$ is simulated in $\rho(\pi)\in\mathcal{L}$. Let a computation of π have reached the considered statement in state s with $s_{\tilde{v}_i} = k\in\omega$, the content of variable $\tilde{v}_i\in VI_{\Sigma_\omega}$. The corresponding computation of $\rho(\pi)$ has then reached

1.) $\varkappa_i(\text{if}, c_2, \varkappa_1, \ldots, \varkappa_n)$ resp. 2.) $\varkappa_i(\text{MON}_i, \tilde{c}, \varkappa_1, \ldots, \varkappa_n)$ where $\varkappa_i$ represents $\underbrace{N_1(\ldots(N_1}_{k\text{-times}}(N_o))\ldots)$

1.) If k=0 then $c_2(\varkappa_1, \ldots, \varkappa_n)$, $\rho_\sigma(\sigma_2, \varkappa_1, \ldots, \varkappa_n)$ are executed where the latter statement corresponds to σ_2.
If k>0 then $\text{if}(\underbrace{N_1(\ldots(N_1}_{k-1 \text{ times}}(N_o))\ldots), c_1, \varkappa_1, \ldots, \varkappa_n)$

and $c_1(\varkappa_1, \ldots, \varkappa_n)$ and $\rho_\sigma(\sigma_1, \varkappa_1, \ldots, \varkappa_n)$ are executed. Again we have obtained the right correspondence (to σ_1).

2.) If k=0 then $\tilde{c}(\varkappa_1, \ldots, \varkappa_n)$ and $\rho_\sigma(\sigma_2, \varkappa_1, \ldots, \varkappa_n)$ are executed.
If k>0 then $\text{MON}_i(\underbrace{N_1(\ldots(N_1}_{k-1 \text{ times}}(N_o))\ldots)\ \tilde{c}, \varkappa_1, \ldots, \varkappa_n)$

and $\tilde{c}\ (\varkappa_1, \ldots, \underbrace{N_1(\ldots(N_1(N_o))\ldots)}_{k-1 \text{ times, } i\text{-th position}}, \ldots, \varkappa_n)$ and

$\rho_\sigma(\sigma_2, \varkappa_1, \ldots, \underbrace{N_1(\ldots(N_1}_{k-1 \text{ times}}(N_o))\ldots), \ldots, \varkappa_n)$ are executed.

Both computations yield the right correspondences.

◊

VI. Conclusions

The authors of [CGH81/82] have defined the notion of an acceptable programming language $\mathcal{A}$ in the sense of [Li77] in the following way: $\mathcal{A}$ is a decidable set of programs with state transformations as their semantics such that every $\mathcal{A}$-program is effectively associated with a schematologically equivalent $\mathcal{L}_W^{\omega,\alpha}$-program and such that $\mathcal{A}$ fulfills certain closure properties. Due to our investigations $\mathcal{L}_W^{\omega,\alpha}$-programs can be nicely replaced by $\mathcal{L}$- or even $\mathcal{L}_{60}$ programs, i.e. programs without arithmetic and without array. The essential advantage is that $\mathcal{L}$ and $\mathcal{L}_{60}$ allow to define many natural subclasses by varying restrictions of concepts connected with the function (or procedure) mechanism, e.g. the class of programs with finite mode functions (without self-application) [DJ82], or with regular formal call trees [Ol1 81], or without side-effects [La82], or with PASCAL-like procedures [Ol3 81]. The variety of available language constructs gives a fairly good insight in the limits of existence of Hoare logics for sequential imperative programming languages [Cl77/79, LO80, Ol2 81, La82].

Nondeterminism generated by Dijstra's □ -operator can easily be included in our transformations. This promises a base for tackling the problem of extending the results in [Li77, CGH81/82] to the nondeterministic case.

As a further result we have answered an up-to-date open question in the area of comparative schematology [CG72] . Recently Critcher stated in [Cri82]:"It is not clear even with passing parameters by name (in function calls), whether recursion has the same power as infinite arrays (plus arithmetic)". We have shown that both concepts are equivalent in the presence of function declaration nestings or higher functionals. Programs without both these concepts can be transformed into schematologically equivalent RPS-like programs (recursive program schemes) [Ni75], even in the case of self-applicative function calls [Cr83].

References

[BaW81] Bauer, F., Wössner, H.: Algorithmische Sprache und Programmentwicklung. Springer-Verlag 1981

[BrLa74] Brainerd, W.S., Landweber, L.H.: Theory of computation. John Wiley, New York 1974

[Cl77/79] Clarke, E.M., Jr.: Programming language constructs for which it is impossible to obtain good Hoare axiom systems. J. ACM 26, 1, 129-147 (1979)

[Cr83] Crasemann, Ch.: On the power of higher functionalities and function declaration nestings in ALGOL-like programming languages. Bericht des Inst.f.Inform. u. Prakt.Math., Christian-Albrechts-Universität Kiel, Juni 1983

[Cri82] Critcher, A.: On the ability of structures to store and access information. In: Proceedings of the 9th annual ACM symposium on principles of programming languages, pp. 366-378 (1982)

[CG72] Constable, R.L., Gries, D.: On classes of program schemata. SIAM J. Comp. 1, pp. 66-118 (1972)

[CGH81/82] Clarke, E.M., German, S.M., Halpern, J.Y.: On effective axiomatizations of Hoare logics. In: Proceedings of the 9th annual ACM symposium on principles of programming languages, pp. 309-321 (1982)

[DJ82] Damm, W., Josko, B.: A sound and relatively* complete Hoare logic for a language with higher type procedures. Schriften Informatik Angew. Math. 77 (1982)

[Fr69] Friedman, H.: Algorithmic procedures, generalized Turing algorithms, and elementary recursion theory. In: R.O. Gandy, C.M.E. Yates (eds.): Logic colloquium '69. North Holland Publishing Company, studies in logic and the foundations of mathematics, vol. 61, pp. 361-389 (1971)

[Gr75] Greibach, S.A.: Theory of program structures: schemes, semantics, verification. LNCS 36, Springer-Verlag 1975

[JW75] Jensen, K., Wirth, N.: PASCAL user manual and report. Springer, Berlin, Heidelberg, New York 1975

[La73] Langmaack, H.: On correct procedure parameter transmission in higher programming languages. Acta Informatica 2, 110-142 (1973)

[La74] Langmaack, H.: On procedures as open subroutines I, II. Acta Informatica 2, pp. 311-333 (1973) and Acta Informatica 3, pp. 227-241 (1974)

[La79/82] Langmaack, H.: On termination problems for finitely interpreted ALGOL-like programs. Acta Informatica 18, 79-108 (1982)

[Li77] Lipton, R.J.: A necessary and sufficient condition for the existence of Hoare logics. In: 18th IEEE symposium on foundations of computer science, Providence, Rhode Island, pp. 1-6, New York, IEEE 1977

[LO80] Langmaack, H., Olderog, E.R.: Present-day Hoare-like systems for programming languages with procedures: power, limits, and most likely extensions. In: J.W. de Bakker, J. van Leeuwen: Proceed. Autom. Lang. Progr., 7th Coll., Noordwijkerhout, July 1980. LNCS 85, pp. 363-373 (1980)

[LS77] Lippe, W.M., Simon, F.: Untersuchungen zur Beziehung zwischen ALGOL60 und ALGOL60-P-G. Bericht des Inst.f.Inform.u.Prakt.Math., Christian-Albtechts-Universität Kiel, Dez. 1977.

[Ni75] Nivat, M.: On the interpretation of recursive polyadic program schemes. Symposia Mathematica, Vol 15, 1975

[Ol1 81] Olderog, E.R.: Sound and complete Hoare-like calculi based on copy rules. Acta Informatica 16, 161-197 (1981)

[Ol2 81] Olderog, E.R.: Charakterisierung Hoarescher Systeme für ALGOL-ähnliche Programmiersprachen. Dissertation Kiel 1981

[Ol3 81] Olderog, E.R.: Correctness of PASCAL-like programs without global variables. Bericht des Inst.f.Inform. u. Prakt.Math., Christian-Albrechts-Universität Kiel, Nov. 1981, will appear in TCS

[Ti79] Tiuryn, J.: Logic of effective definitions. Bericht Nr. 55 der RWTH Aachen, Juli 1979

A RIGOROUS APPROACH TO FAULT-TOLERANT SYSTEM DEVELOPMENT

(extended abstract*)

Flaviu Cristian
IBM Research Laboratory
San Jose, California 95193

ABSTRACT: This paper investigates the issue of what it means for a system to behave correctly despite of hardware fault occurrences. Using a stable storage system as a running example, a framework is presented for specifying, understanding, and verifying the correctness of fault-tolerant systems.

A clear separation is made between the notions of software correctness and system reliability in the face of hardware malfunction. Correctness is established by using a programming logic augmented with fault axioms and rules. Stochastic modelling is employed to investigate reliability/availability system properties.

Index Terms: Correctness, Fault-Tolerance, Reliability.

1. INTRODUCTION

Computer systems are unreliable because of hardware, software, and user faults. Good programming and design verification methods can prevent software faults. Hardware and user faults *are* unavoidable. Most of the current work in programming methodology and verification relies nevertheless on the (often implicit) assumption that the hardware and the users are fault-free. One may consider this as being a reasonable first approximation to reality. Indeed, for short time intervals, the probability of hardware and user fault manifestations is relatively low. This probability increases to one when longer time intervals are considered. Thus, long term correct system behaviour can *only* be achieved by incorporating fault-tolerance into a system.

In [BC,C1,C2] we have investigated the design and verification of programs which are tolerant of faulty user inputs. This paper presents a framework for specifying, designing, and verifying the correctness of, systems which are tolerant of *hardware faults*.

Rather than giving an abstract general presentation of our ideas, we prefer to introduce them through an example. The example, inspired by [LS], is that of designing a stable storage management system. The system has to maintain the integrity of stored information in spite of random decays of the physical storage medium and processor crashes. The atomic update operations provided by the system can be used to implement higher level atomic transactions in distributed, as well as non-distributed, systems [LS].

In designing the system, we will make use of: a standard Pascal-like programming language $\mathscr{L}$ (defined in Appendix A), a standard axiomatic deductive system $\mathscr{F}$ for proving the total correctness of programs written in $\mathscr{L}$ (given in Appendix B), some observations and statistics about likely faults that may affect existing long term storage devices, and some elementary stochastic process theory [GM].

The paper is organized as follows. A precise description of the classes of faults that the stable storage system is intended to tolerate is given in §2. §3 presents the correctness and availability requirements that the system should satisfy. A design of the system is presented in §4. §5 states the correctness properties that the

---

* The full version of this paper is available as IBM Report RJ 3754 (January 1983)

system can be proved to have, provided enough underlying hardware is operational. The reliability analysis of §6 allows a system parameter to be tuned so as to ensure that the probability of enough hardware remaining operational in the presence of periodic maintenance is higher than a specified threshold. A similar separation between correctness and reliability validation aspects was also considered in [WA]. Some of the advantages and limitations associated with the presented approach are summarized in §7. We do not assume familiarity with [LS], but the reader may find comparison fruitful.

2. FAULT HYPOTHESES

The hardware of the stable storage management system includes a processor, main store and magnetic disks [LS]. These components may be affected by faults caused by adverse mechanical, chemical or electromagnetic phenomena. In contrast to the hardware, the software of the system is a mathematical abstraction which is not subject to physical wear out. One of its roles will be to mask to system users occasional hardware malfunctions.

We assume that programs written in the language $\mathscr{L}$ are executed in a manner which is *consistent* with their specified semantics $\mathscr{T}$. That is, we assume that programs are *correctly compiled* and are interpreted by a *fault-secure* (or fail-stop) processor/main store. By fault-secure it is meant that transient faults in the processor or main store are masked (e.g., by using error correcting codes and instruction retry mechanisms) and that permanent fault occurrences cause an immediate halt of computation. It is not the purpose of this paper to investigate the design of such interpreters. One possible implementation, among many others, is the use of two synchronized processors with independent stores, which continuously compare their results and stop at the first disagreement. When processing stops, either because of a solid fault detection or because the system operator pushes the 'halt' button, a *processor crash* is said to occur.

Under the above consistent interpretation hypothesis, the logical deductive system $\mathscr{T}$ can be used to derive *valid* statements about the behavior of programs written in $\mathscr{L}$ *when no crashes occur*. The effect of crashes on program executions will be discussed later. The language $\mathscr{L}$ has assignments, conditionals, loops, and procedures, but does not provide any input/output (I/O) facilities. As the stable storage system will use disks for long term storage, we need to extend $\mathscr{L}$ with disk I/O commands.

The state d of a disk can be understood as being a function from a set AD={0,1,...,max} of block addresses to a set BL of possible block contents: $d \in AD \rightarrow BL$. For an ideal disk, reading at address $a \in AD$ should return the block d(a) stored at a. Writing a block $b \in BL$ at an address $a \in AD$ should yield a new state function d;a:b which is the same as d, except that when applied to a it yields b: (d;a:b)(x) $\equiv$ *if* x=a *then* b *else* d(x) .

In practice things are more complicated. Adverse electromagnetic phenomena or processor crashes during disk updates may render some of the blocks of a disk *unreadable* [LS]. Thus, the state d of a disk is in reality a *partial* function: the state of the blocks with addresses outside the domain of d is undefined. We use the symbol d (possibly primed or subscripted) to stand for a typical element of the set of partial functions $AD \rightarrow BL$. The domain of a function d (i.e. the set of readable addresses) is denoted dom(d).

In order to model the influence of adverse physical phenomena on physical disks, we postulate the existence of *a special kind of operation*: DECAY, which is performed by the Adverse Environment on *any* physical disk system at *random time intervals*.

Many advantages follow from modelling faults as being a (special) kind of operation, performed on any system by a special user: the Adverse Environment. Indeed, if faults are just another type of operation (i.e. state transition) then all the known axiomatic methods for reasoning about (ordinary user invocable) operations become applicable to reasoning about fault-tolerant systems. Such methods make it possible to express with great accuracy one's assumptions about the most likely adverse phenomena which will affect a physical system. The fault-tolerance properties that a system should possess can also be naturally described as being properties that should hold over certain sequences of user, Adverse Environment and recovery operation invocations. Correctness of a design with respect to a given specification and a set of assumed fault hypotheses can then be proven in a rigorous way. It is also possible to rigorously infer the limits of the fault-tolerance capabilities of systems.

2.1 Decay Hypothesis

We consider the effect of a DECAY operation on a disk as being to render some blocks with addresses in a *decay set* unreadable [LS]. We denote DS a typical non-empty decay set $DS \subseteq AD$. Giving an axiomatic semantics for this operation will amount to stating formally what our decay hypothesis is:

$$P\ \{DECAY(d)\}\ \exists\, d',DS:\ DS \neq \{\ \}\ \&\ P[d'/d]\ \&\ d = d' \setminus DS \qquad \text{(D)}$$

The above *decay axiom* gives, for any precondition P, the strongest postcondition [dB,Fl] which holds after a DECAY invocation. P[d'/d] denotes the result of substituting d' (the previous disk state) for all free occurrences of d (the new, or 'current' state) in P. It is assumed that DS is not free in P (i.e. it is a *new* decay set). The new disk state $d' \setminus DS$ is less defined that the previous state: $dom(d' \setminus DS) \equiv dom(d') - DS$. Only the blocks in the decays set DS are affected: the blocks with addresses outside the set DS preserve their prior values: $\forall x \in dom(d' \setminus DS)$: $(d' \setminus DS)(x) = d'(x)$. Note that there are many *decay models* which satisfy this decay axiom, e.g., decays which affect only some blocks of a disk track, or all blocks of a track, or a set of adjacent tracks, etc. The intention is to tolerate all such kinds of decay.

The axiom (D) captures only one half of the meaning of DECAY: its effect on the state of a disk. The other important characteristic of this 'operation' is that it occurs *at random time intervals*. We assume that available *reliability statistics* indicate that the *average* time interval between successive decay occurrences is α days (say α=20).

2.2 Input/Output Operations

Fortunately, a disk system does not provide operations only to its Adverse Environment; the users can also invoke read (R) and write (W) operations. We assume that these operations are implemented as procedures with parameters passed 'by reference':

proc R(d:Disk,a:AD,b:BL,u:Bool)
proc W(d:Disk,a:AD,b:BL)

If the block $a \in AD$ to be read has suffered a decay, the final value of the 'return code' u (meaning: *u*ndefined buffer) is true. In such a case nothing can be said about the final value of the buffer b:

$$a \notin dom(d)\ \&\ P\ \{R(d,a,b,u)\}\ \exists u':\ P[u'/u]\ \&\ u = true \quad (\text{provided } b \notin Free(P)) \qquad \text{(IO1)}$$

Free(P) denotes the set of free variables of P. If the block at address $a \in AD$ is readable, the procedure R sets the return code u to false and returns in b the value of the block:

$$a \in dom(d)\ \&\ P\ \{R(d,a,b,u)\}\ \exists b',u':\ P[b'/b,u'/u]\ \&\ b = d(a)\ \&\ u = false \qquad \text{(IO2)}$$

A write operation always succeeds in writing a buffer b at any address $a \in AD$:

$$P\ \{W(d,a,b)\}\ \exists d':\ P[d'/d]\ \&\ d = d';a:b \qquad \text{(IO3)}$$

The above (IO) formulae define the semantics of the I/O commands by which the language $\mathscr{L}$ will be extended to form a richer language $\mathscr{L}_1$. If one adds to the axioms of $\mathscr{T}$ some new axioms defining the meaning of the d(a), d;a:b, $d \setminus DS$, d=d' algebraic operators over the set of partial functions $AD \rightarrow BL$, together with the aforementioned formulae, one constructs a new theory $\mathcal{T}_1$ for this extended language. Within $\mathcal{T}_1$ one can prove correctness statements about programs with disk I/O operations.

2.3 Crash Hypotheses

The other kind of adversity that the stable storage manager should be able to tolerate are processor crashes. A crash can occur during the interpretation of any program C. If the execution of a program C is interrupted by a crash, we will say that the (Adverse Environment) operation "¤" has been applied to C. Thus, "¤C" denotes a program C whose execution is interrupted by a crash.

A *volatile* main store is assumed: a crash causes the contents of the main store to be lost [LS]. On the other hand, disks provide *non-volatile* storage: if a crash does not occur while a disk d is being written, d retains its state prior to the crash. We assume that program variables which are not of type disk are located in main store. From this it follows that in reasoning about the effect of programs which crash, one has to use a *restricted class of postconditions*, in which the only free *program* variables which are allowed to occur are of type Disk.

The effect of applying the ¤ operator to programs can be defined by induction on their syntactic structure.

If a processor crash occurs during the execution of an assignment or a read command, the state of disks is not affected:

$$P\ \{¤\, i := i+1\}\ P \qquad \text{(C1)}$$

$$P\ \{¤\, R(d,a,b,u)\}\ P \qquad \text{(C2)}$$

For a crashed write on d at block $a \in AD$, one of the following alternatives is possible: either the crash occurred before the write was started, or it occurred after the write was completed, or it occurred somewhere in between. In the latter case we assume that the half-written block at a is left in an *unreadable* state:

$$P\ \{¤\, W(d,a,b)\}\ \exists d',a',b': P[d'/d,a'/a,b'/b]\ \&\ (d = d' \vee d = d';a':b' \vee d = d' \smallsetminus \{a'\}) \qquad \text{(C3)}$$

When a sequential composition of two syntactic constructs C_1, C_2 is interrupted by a crash, then either the execution of C_1 is crashed, or the crash occurs after the completion of C_1, but before the start of C_2, or, the execution of C_2 is crashed after the termination of C_1:

$$\frac{P\ \{¤C_1\}\ Q, \quad P\ \{C_1\}\ R, \quad R\ \{¤C_2\}\ S}{P\ \{¤(C_1;C_2)\}\ Q \vee R \vee S} \qquad \text{(C4)}$$

The effect of crashes on other compound syntactic constructs like loops, conditionals, procedures, and so on, can be formalized in a similar manner. For simplicity we mention only the case of loops. The rules for conditionals and procedures may be found in Appendix B.

$$\frac{P\&b\ \{C\}\ P, \quad P\&b\ \{¤C\}\ Q}{P\ \{¤\, \textit{while}\ b\ \textit{do}\ C\}\ P \vee Q} \qquad \text{(C5)}$$

Crashes, like decays, occur at random time intervals. We assume that available statistics indicate that, on the average, a crash occurs every γ days (say γ=4) and that one out of θ crashes (say θ=10) occurs while some disk of the stable storage manager is being written.

The above D, IO and C groups of formulae reflect our understanding of decays, disk I/O operations and processor crashes. Together, these formulae characterize the classes of hardware faults that the stable storage manager must cope with. These fault hypotheses are stronger than (the more realistic) fault hypotheses considered in [C3]. The simpler fault model was adopted in this paper for readability reasons.

3. CORRECTNESS AND AVAILABILITY REQUIREMENTS

The concrete read (R) and write (W) operations provided by physical disks are fairly rough approximations of the ideal read and write operations one would like to use. The objective will be to construct a more reliable (abstract) disk system which will provide its users with better approximations of these ideal read and write operations. The state $s \in AD \rightarrow BL$ of the abstract storage system should be a *total* function, unaffected by decays or crashes. (We use s, possibly primed, to denote a typical total function of type $AD \rightarrow BL$.) Moreover, the abstract write operation provided by the system should be *atomic with respect to crashes*. That is, a crashed write execution should either leave the state of the storage system unchanged or should yield a new correct state.

The adjective 'atomic' is also used in multiprocessing contexts [BR] to qualify interference-free operation executions. Clearly, atomicity with respect to exceptions [C1] or crashes [LS] and atomicity with respect to synchronization [BR] are inter-related concepts [LS]. However, to simplify this presentation, we abstract from synchronization aspects by assuming that the externally visible system operations are executed in some serial order.

Let r and w be the abstract read and write operations that the users should be able to invoke in full confidence

proc r(s:Disk,a:AD,b:BL)

proc w(s:Disk,a:AD,b:BL)

and let decay be the operation that the Adverse Environment will *still* occasionally perform. A decay can cause the state of the physical hardware configuration which hosts the stable storage abstraction to degrade from an error-free *All Perfect* status to a *Gracefully Degraded* status. A decay should nevertheless not alter the *visible* abstract state s of the storage system. We assume that initially all hardware is working properly, that is, the initial system status is All Perfect. A repair operation will be invoked periodically by an operator to repair the damage caused by decays and crashes and bring the system back to All Perfect status.

The (user) operations "r" and "w", (Adverse Environment) operation "decay", and (maintenance) operation "repair" are the only operations that are invoked on the stable storage system by its various kinds of 'users'.

Let $\mathcal{P}$ and $\mathcal{D}$ be two predicates, true when the system status is All Perfect and Gracefully Degraded, respectively. The following *correctness requirements* specify the behaviour that the stable storage system is expected to have, *provided* it is in All-Perfect or Gracefully-Degraded status.

Users should be able to read and write blocks at any address:

$$(\mathcal{P} \vee \mathcal{D})\ \&\ P\ \{r(s,a,b)\}\ (\mathcal{P} \vee \mathcal{D})\ \&\ \exists b'{:}\ P[b'/b]\ \&\ b = s(a) \quad \text{(A1)}$$

$$(\mathcal{P} \vee \mathcal{D})\ \&\ P\ \{w(s,a,b)\}\ (\mathcal{P} \vee \mathcal{D})\ \&\ \exists s'{:}\ P[s'/s]\ \&\ s = s';a{:}b \quad \text{(A2)}$$

Decay operations should not alter the state s seen by users:

$$\mathcal{P}\ \&\ P\ \{decay(s)\}\ \mathcal{D}\ \&\ P \quad \text{(A3)}$$

Storage update operations should be atomic with respect to crashes:

$$\mathcal{P}\ \&\ P\ \{\sharp w(s,a,b)\}\ \exists s',a',b'{:}\ (\mathcal{P} \vee \mathcal{D})\ \&\ P[s'/s,a'/a,b'/b]\ \&\ (s = s' \vee s = s';a'{:}b') \quad \text{(A4)}$$

The repair operation should periodically bring the system into All-Perfect status without altering its abstract state:

$$(\mathcal{P} \vee \mathcal{D})\ \&\ P\ \{repair(s)\}\ \mathcal{P}\ \&\ P \quad \text{(A5)}$$

Crashed repair attempts should be tolerable:

$$(\mathcal{P} \vee \mathcal{D})\ \&\ P\ \{\unlhd \mathrm{repair(s)}\}\ (\mathcal{P} \vee \mathcal{D})\ \&\ P \tag{A6}$$

That is, any finite sequence of crashed repair executions followed by a successful repair termination should bring the system into All-Perfect status (this follows from (A5,A6) by induction on the number of crashed repair attempts).

The above correctness requirements, describing the behaviour the stable storage manager is expected to have, are conditioned by the truth of the *system status predicates* $\mathcal{P}$ and $\mathcal{D}$. As will be seen later, these predicates are true when there is enough underlying hardware operational to interpret the user invocable operations. Reliability (or availability) specifications can be used to constrain these predicates to be true with probabilities greater than certain acceptable risk levels.

The *availability specification* for the storage manager is: the probability of the system being in All-Perfect or Gracefully-Degraded modes should be greater than λ (say λ=0.997):

$$Prob(\mathcal{P} \vee \mathcal{D}) \geq \lambda\ . \tag{A7}$$

4. DESIGN

Two independent physical disks d_1,d_2 will be used *redundantly* to construct a better abstract disk. The objective will be to implement three out of the four operations mentioned in §3, namely the read, write and repair operations. The 'implementation' of the decay operation is the responsibility of the Adverse Environment. Because of the *independence* hypothesis about the disks d_1,d_2, we take the meaning of a Decay operation on the pair of disks (d_1,d_2) to be:

$$P\ \{\mathrm{Decay}(d_1,d_2)\}\ \exists d_1',d_2',DS:\ DS \neq \{\ \}\ \&\ P[d_1'/d_1,d_2'/d_2]\ \& \tag{DD}$$

$$(d_1 = d_1' \setminus DS\ \&\ d_2 = d_2' \vee d_1 = d_1'\ \&\ d_2 = d_2' \setminus DS)$$

That is, we will assume that a Decay operation on a pair of physically independent disks affects only one of them. It will be the goal of the reliability analysis of §6 to show that the probability of a second decay occurrence on a disk while the other disk is decayed is smaller than the specified threshold 1-λ.

The read (RR) operation will be implemented as follows. First an attempt to read the first disk is made. If it is successful, the buffer read is passed to the user. Otherwise, an attempt to read the other disk is made.

```
proc RR(d1,d2:Disk,a:AD,b:BL)
var u: Bool;
R(d1,a,b,u);
if u then R(d2,a,b,u) else fi;
```

The write operation (WW) writes on both disks.

```
proc WW(d1,d2:Disk,a:AD,b:BL)
W(d1,a,b); W(d2,a,b);
```

Let $\mathcal{T}_2$ be the theory obtained by joining to $\mathcal{T}_1$ the decay and crash axioms and rules. The following theorem of $\mathcal{T}_2$ expresses an important property of the WW operation: if d_1,d_2 are not decayed when an execution of WW is interrupted by a crash, then no more than one of the pair of blocks at address $a \in AD$ on d_1 and d_2 can be damaged:

$$P\ \{\unlhd \mathrm{WW}(d_1,d_2,a,b)\}\ \exists d_1',d_2',a',b':\ P[d_1'/d_1,d_2'/d_2,a'/a,b'/b]\ \&\ (OK \vee LAG \vee DEC) \tag{1}$$

The 'OK' disjunct in the postcondition of (1) corresponds to the case when a crash interrupts the execution of WW before the initiation of the first write on d_1 or after the completion of the second write on d_2:

$$OK \equiv d_1 = d_1' \,\&\, d_2 = d_2' \vee d_1 = d_1';a':b' \,\&\, d_2 = d_2';a':b'$$

The 'LAG' disjunct reflects the possible phase lag between disks which can be generated when a crash occurs after the completion of the first write, but before the initiation of the second write:

$$LAG \equiv d_1 = d_1';a':b' \,\&\, d_2 = d_2'$$

The 'DEC' disjunct corresponds to the case when a write on one of the disks is interrupted in the middle by a crash and results in a decay on that disk:

$$DEC \equiv d_1 = d_1' \setminus \{a'\} \,\&\, d_2 = d_2' \vee d_1 = d_1';a':b' \,\&\, d_2 = d_2' \setminus \{a'\}$$

The third operation to be implemented is the RECovery procedure. This will scan all pairs of blocks with equal addresses $a \in AD$ on d_1 and d_2. If $a \notin dom(d_1)$, the value of $d_2(a)$ will be written on d_1 at a. Similarly, if $a \notin dom(d_2)$, the value of $d_1(a)$ should be written on d_2 at a. If both blocks at address a are readable, but different, then there exists a phase lag of d_2 with respect to d_1 caused by some crashed WW execution. In that case the block $d_1(a)$ is the most recently written one, so its value will be written on d_2 at a.

```
proc REC(d1,d2)
var a: 0..max+1; x,y: BL;
u1,u2: Bool;
a:=0;
while a≤max
do R(d1,a,x,u1);
   R(d2,a,y,u2);
   if u1 then W(d1,a,y) else fi;
   if u2 V (x≠y) then W(d2,a,x) else fi;
   a:=a+1;
od;
```

We assume that available statistics indicate that the average time necessary for the termination of the REC procedure is ρ hours (say ρ=0.2, that is, 12 minutes).

5. CORRECTNESS

The following theorems of $\mathcal{T}_2$ (together with theorem (1) of §4) describe the behaviour of the operations RR, WW, and REC in the presence of decays and crashes. No proofs are displayed for reasons of brevity.

If at least one of the disks is ok, it is possible to read at any address:

$$(dom(d_1) = AD \vee dom(d_2) = AD) \,\&\, P\, \{RR(d_1,d_2,a,b)\}\, \exists b': P[b'/b] \,\& \quad (2)$$

$$b = \mathit{if}\ a \in dom(d_1)\ \mathit{then}\ d_1(a)\ \mathit{else}\ d_2(a)$$

It is always possible to write a buffer b on both disks:

$$P\, \{WW(d_1,d_2,a,b)\}\, \exists d_1',d_2': P[d_1'/d_1,d_2'/d_2] \,\&\, d_1 = d_1';a:b \,\&\, d_2 = d_2';a:b \quad (3)$$

If at least one of the disks is ok, the RECovery procedure repairs the damage caused by Decay and processor crashes:

$$(\mathrm{dom}(d_1) = AD \vee \mathrm{dom}(d_2) = AD)\ \&\ P\ \{REC(d_1,d_2)\}\ \exists d_1',d_2'\colon P[d_1'/d_1,d_2'/d_2]\ \& \tag{4}$$
$$d_1 = d_2\ \&\ \forall a \in AD\colon d_1(a) = \textit{if } a \in \mathrm{dom}(d_1') \textit{ then } d_1'(a) \textit{ else } d_2'(a)$$

A crashed execution of the RECovery procedure does not cause any irreparable damage:

$$(\mathrm{dom}(d_1) = AD \vee \mathrm{dom}(d_2) = AD)\ \&\ P\ \{\text{¤}REC(d_1,d_2)\}\ \exists d_1',d_2'\colon P[d_1'/d_1,d_2'/d_2]\ \& \tag{5}$$
$$\forall a \in AD\colon \textit{if } a \in \mathrm{dom}(d_1') \textit{ then } d_1(a) = d_1'(a) \textit{ else } d_2(a) = d_2'(a)$$

Other interesting facts about the fault-tolerance capabilities, as well as limits, of the design can be inferred. For example, it is possible to show that a RECovery execution (or a sequence of ¤REC executions followed by a successful REC termination) can repair the situation when *both* disks d_1 and d_2 have suffered decays, provided their decay sets are disjoint:

$$\mathrm{dom}(d_1) \cup \mathrm{dom}(d_2) = AD\ \&\ P\ \{REC(d_1,d_2)\}\ \exists d_1',d_2'\colon P[d_1'/d_1,d_2'/d_2]\ \& \tag{6}$$
$$d_1 = d_2\ \&\ \forall a \in AD\colon d_1(a) = \textit{if } a \in \mathrm{dom}(d_1') \textit{ then } d_1'(a) \textit{ else } d_2'(a)$$

It is also possible to prove that certain sequences of fault occurrences *cannot* be tolerated by the proposed design. For example, when two successive Decay operations affect both d_1 and d_2 in such a way that their decay sets have a nonempty intersection, it is impossible for the RECovery procedure to recover the values of some of the blocks that have been written previously:

$$a \in AD - \mathrm{dom}(d_1) \cup \mathrm{dom}(d_2)\ \&\ \{REC(d_1,d_2)\}\ a \in AD - \mathrm{dom}(d_1) \cup \mathrm{dom}(d_2) \tag{7}$$

In order to cope with such possibilities (which should have an occurrence probability lower than the specified threshold $1\text{-}\lambda$) periodic check pointing on magnetic tapes might be used. The investigation of these back-up facilities is not required by the specification of §3, so we will not discuss them further.

There are other interesting observations (c.f. [C3]) about the limitations of the system. At this point of our presentation it is, however, opportune to notice that the design presented seems to satisfy all the correctness requirements of §3. Indeed, the properties proven so far about the design closely resemble the correctness axioms (A1)-(A6). The apparent differences stem only from the fact that the abstract symbols used when writing the requirements were different from the concrete symbols used in the implementation. What is needed is to define a translation function Υ from abstract to concrete symbols and to show that the translations (through Υ) of the axioms (A1)-(A6) are theorems of the implementation theory $\mathcal{T}_2$.

The All-Perfect status predicate is interpreted as being true when both disks are ok and 'in step':

$$\Upsilon(\mathcal{P}) \equiv \mathrm{dom}(d_1)=AD\ \&\ d_1=d_2$$

The $\mathcal{D}$ predicate is interpreted as being true when one of the disks is decayed and the other is ok, or when both are ok, but out of phase because of some previous crash occurrence:

$$\Upsilon(\mathcal{D}) \equiv\ \exists DS\colon DS \neq \{\ \}\ \&\ (\ \mathrm{dom}(d_1)=AD\ \&\ d_2=d_1 \setminus DS \vee \mathrm{dom}(d_2)=AD\ \&\ d_1=d_2 \setminus DS\ )$$
$$\vee\ \exists a,b\colon \mathrm{dom}(d_1)=AD\ \&\ d_2=d_1;a{:}b\ \&\ d_1(a) \neq b$$

The state s of the stable storage is defined to be equal to d_1 if the first disk is ok and otherwise equal to d_2:

$$\Upsilon(s) \equiv \textit{if } \mathrm{dom}(d_1)=AD \textit{ then } d_1 \textit{ else } d_2\ .$$

The abstract operation symbols r, w, repair and decay are translated as :

$\Upsilon(r(s,a,b)) \equiv RR(d_1,d_2,a,b), \quad \Upsilon(w(s,a,b)) \equiv WW(d_1,d_2,a,b),$

$\Upsilon(repair(s)) \equiv REC(d_1,d_2), \quad \Upsilon(decay(s)) \equiv Decay(d_1,d_2).$

Other remaining symbols used in writing the correctness requirements, like "{", "V", "¤", "∃", etc., go through Υ unchanged. The final theorem of this section (stated without proof for reasons of brevity) is:

The translation through Υ of the correctness specifications (A1)-(A6) are theorems of the implementation theory T_2, provable from the previously stated correctness lemmas (1)-(5).

Thus, the presented design is correct with respect to the functional specification (A1)-(A6). What remains to be seen is whether the reliability specification can also be satisfied.

6. RELIABILITY ANALYSIS

The objective of this section is the determination of a lower bound on the frequency with which the RECovery procedure has to be invoked, in order to ensure that, in *steady state operation*, the system will satisfy the availability specification (A7) . For this purpose, we will use some classical stochastic process theory [GM].

The two physically independent disk systems d_1 and d_2 will be regarded as being two *random variables*. Each d_i may be in one of the following states: ok (state 1) or decayed (state 2). Thus, there will be 4 different states for the *stochastic process* $\{d_1,d_2\}$. If d_1 is in state $i \in \{1,2\}$ and d_2 is in state $j \in \{1,2\}$, the state of the process is denoted by (i,j).

State transitions of type $(1,j) \rightarrow (2,j)$ or $(i,1) \rightarrow (i,2)$ occur when Decay and ¤ operations are performed by the Adverse Environment on the system. (Note: actually, not every crash which occurs during a write causes a decay; in what follows some worst case assumptions are made in order to simplify the reliability calculations.) According to the reliability hypotheses of §2, the aforementioned state transitions occur at a constant rate:

$$s = \frac{1}{24\alpha} + \frac{1}{24\gamma \cdot 2\theta}$$

where 24α and $48\gamma\theta$ are the mean times (in hours) between successive Decay operations and crashes, respectively, on each disk. The transitions $(1,2) \rightarrow (1,1)$ and $(2,1) \rightarrow (1,1)$ occur when a decay on the first and second disk, respectively, is repaired (c.f. theorem (4) of §5) by the RECovery procedure. If we denote by δ the time between successive RECovery invocations (in hours), then the decay repair rate is

$$r = \frac{1}{\delta + \rho}$$

where ρ (taken in §4 to be 0.2 hours) is the average time necessary for the RECovery procedure to terminate. Finally, we assume that if the system reaches the state (2,2) because of two close Decay or ¤ operations, the repair action carried out either automatically (c.f. theorem (5)) or manually as discussed in §5, takes on the average σ hours (say $\sigma = 1$). Thus, the rate associated with the transition $(2,2) \rightarrow (1,1)$ is

$$R = \frac{1}{\delta + \sigma} .$$

This information about the stochastic process $\{d_1,d_2\}$ can be summarized pictorially by the *balance diagram* [GM] given below. In this diagram a node (i,j) represents the process state (i,j). There is an arc from a node (i_1,j_1) to some other node (i_2,j_2) if the transition rate from state (i_1,j_1) to state (i_2,j_2) is non-zero. Each arc of the diagram is labelled by the corresponding transition rate.

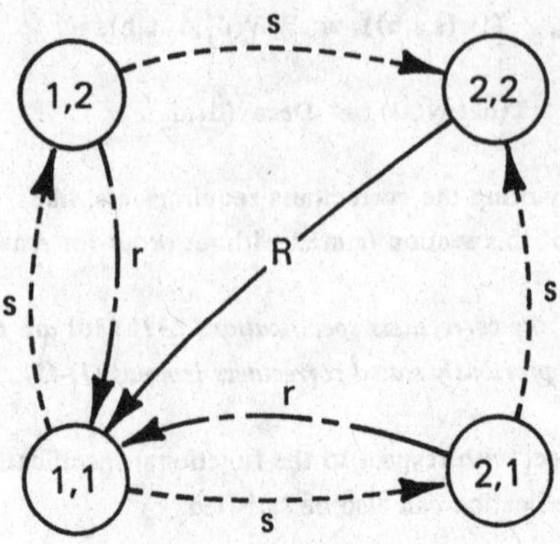

If we associate with each node (i,j) the steady state probability p_{ij} of the process $\{d_1,d_2\}$ being at that node, from the above graphical description one can obtain easily the set of *balance equations* [GM] which are satisfied by these probabilities:

$$2s \cdot p_{11} = 2r \cdot p_{12} + R \cdot p_{22} \tag{0}$$
$$s \cdot p_{12} + r \cdot p_{12} = s \cdot p_{11} \tag{1}$$
$$R \cdot p_{22} = 2s \cdot p_{12} \tag{2}$$

When writing the above equations, we have taken into account the fact that the symmetry of the balance diagram implies $p_{ij}=p_{ji}$. The p_{ij} should also satisfy the normalizing equation

$$p_{11} + 2p_{12} + p_{22} = 1\,. \tag{3}$$

The above system of equations defines, in fact, a set of possible steady state probability distributions, depending on the set of values that the decay detection time parameter δ can take. We are interested only in those distributions which are *consistent* with the availability specification (A7). The translation of this requirement into our stochastic model is:

$$p_{11} + 2p_{12} \geq \lambda \tag{4}$$

What is needed is to solve the above system of equations and inequations in δ. If a solution exists, the availability requirements can be satisfied. If there are several solutions the most interesting is the greatest one, since that minimizes the frequency with which the RECovery procedure has to be invoked. The conclusion of this section (stated, again, without proof) is:

For $\lambda = 0.997$ there exists a (maximal) integer $\delta=12$ hours, which constrains the $\{d_1,d_2\}$ stochastic process to have a steady-state probability distribution consistent with the availability specification (A7).

Thus, if the RECovery procedure is invoked (at least) twice a day, a decay of a disk is detected and repaired rapidly enough to ensure that the probability of the other disk remaining operational in the mean time is greater than the specified threshold of 0.997.

7. CONCLUSION

The question addressed in this paper is: what does design correctness mean for programs which have to work in the presence of hardware faults ? An answer to this question was suggested with the help of a little example: a stable storage management system which maintains the integrity of stored information despite random decays of the storage medium and system crashes. This system was specified, designed, and proven correct with respect to its specification. It is believed that the approach presented embodies a number of ideas whose usefulness extends beyond the particular application described.

The view was adopted that a fault-tolerant system specification consists of two parts: the correctness requirements and the reliability (or availability) requirements. A proof that a design satisfies these specifications is accordingly factored into two parts. The correctness verification relies on a number of fault hypotheses about those classes of faults which are most likely to occur (in our example decays and crashes). It is carried out under the assumption that certain 'system status' predicates (which express the fact that enough operational hardware is available for interpreting system operations) are true. The reliability proof, relying on statistics about fault occurrence rates, consists of showing that these 'status' predicates will be true during the system operation with a probability greater than certain specified thresholds. Together, the correctness and reliability proofs show that, under the given fault and reliability hypotheses, the system will behave as specified by the correctness requirements, with a probability greater than that specified by the reliability requirements. This notion of system correctness generalizes the classical notion of software correctness, which assumes that the underlying hardware works properly at any time with probability one.

Functional correctness was verified by using an extension of a classical programming logic. The fault hypotheses were encoded as axioms and inference rules of this extended system. Adverse Environment invocable operations were introduced to model random electromagnetic interferences and physical wear-out phenomena. An attempt was made to elucidate the axioms and inference rules underlying our reasoning abut the effects of crashed program executions. In the correctness specification and verification some 'off the shelf' partial function theory was used and assumed to be well known. A higher degree of formality could be achieved (at the expense of making the presentation longer) by defining the meaning of all non-logical symbols used 'from scratch', by suitable sets of axioms. This may be necessary when machine checked verification is the objective. Our goal was mainly to show how the entire verification process can be decomposed into small and separately analyzable pieces.

One of the main difficulties in fault-tolerant system design and validation is to make sure that all fault cases and combinations of fault cases to be tolerated are taken into account. The obligation to formalize the assumptions, goals and deductions made at each design step leaves little room for 'forgotten' cases and helps to increase one's confidence in a design. It enables one to establish with precision not only what classes of faults can indeed be tolerated, but also what classes of faults cannot be tolerated. The use of a precise descriptive formalism also makes possible a clear analysis and discussion (among the members of a design team) of the partial reliability and correctness objectives to be achieved at each level of abstraction (e.g., hardware, software) in order to make sure that the global system requirements can be met. Another practical benefit which follows from a carefully conducted reliability analysis is the ability to estimate what average maintenance costs will be associated with long term system operation.

Some reservations about the approach presented should also be made For example, one may question the probability of mistakes being made in the correctness or reliability verifications, or even in writing the system specifications themselves. The example presented was simple enough so that no major difficulties were encountered in specifying and verifying it. For more complex systems the problem can become serious. Mechanical assistance in carrying out the correctness [MS,WA] and reliability [CA,NA] verifications can greatly reduce the probability of mistakes, but what uncertainty levels remain? Moreover, such proofs are only as good as the fault and reliability hypotheses on which they are based. Good fault and reliability models can be elaborated with accuracy only for well-known hardware technologies, for which substantial amounts of observations and statistics exist. The high frequency with which technology changes occur does not make the elaboration of such models an easy task.

In view of the increasing costs associated with computer system failures, it is reasonable to expect that formal specification and verification methods will play an increasing role in the development of fault-tolerant systems, in spite of the difficulties mentioned above. Such methods have already been used in an experimental system design [MS,WA]. Their use is also advocated in [SS], where 'fault-tolerant actions' are proposed for the design of verifiable fault-tolerant distributed systems. The work reported in this paper provides a basis on which such higher level verifiable fault-tolerant actions can be built. It is nevertheless only a first step along what threatens to be a long road.

REFERENCES

[BC] Best E. and F. Cristian "Systematic Detection of Exception Occurrneces", *Science of Computer Programming*, Vol 1, No 1, (1981).

[BR] Best E. and B. Randell "A Formal Model of Atomicity in Asynchronous Systems", *Acta Informatica*, Vol 16, pp. 93-124, (1981).

[CA] Costes, A. et al., "SURF: A Program for Dependability Evaluation of Complex Fault-Tolerant Systems," *IEEE 11th Int. Conf. on Fault-Tolerant Computing*, pp. 72-78 (1981).

[C1] Cristian, F., "Robust Data Types" *Acta Informatica* Vol. 17, pp 365-397, (1982).

[C2] Cristian, F., "Correct and Robust Programs" IBM Research Report RJ3753 (1983). To appear in *IEEE Transactions on Software Engineering*.

[C3] Cristian, F., "A Rigorous Approach to Fault-Tolerant System Development" IBM Research Report RJ3754 (January 1983)

[dB] de Bakker, J, *Mathematical Theory of Program Correctness* Prentice Hall, (1980).

[Fl] Floyd, R.W., "Assigning Meanings to Programs", in *Mathematical Aspects of Computer Science*, XIX American Mathematical Society, pp 19-32, (1967).

[GM] Gelenbe, E. and I. Mitrani, *Analysis and Synthesis of Computer Systems*, Academic Press (1980).

[LS] Lampson, B. W. and H. E. Sturgis, "Crash Recovery in a Distributed Data Storage System," Xerox PARC Report, Palo Alto, Calif. (April 1979).

[MS] Melliar-Smith, P. M. and R. L. Schwartz, "Formal Specificatoin and Mechanical Verification of SIFT: A Fault-Tolerant Flight Control System," *IEEE Trans. on Computers*, Vol. *C-31*(7) (1982).

[NA] Ng, Y. W. and A. Avizienis, "ARIES: An Automated Reliability Evaluation System," *Proc. 1977 Annual Reliability and Maintainability Symposium*, pp. 182-188 (1977).

[SS] Schlichting, R. D. and F. B. Schneider, "Verification of Fault-Tolerant Software," TR 80-446, Cornell University (1980).

[WA] Wensley, J. H. et al., "SIFT: Design and Analysis of a Fault-Tolerant Computer for Aircraft Control," *Proceedings of the IEEE* Vol. *66*(10), pp. 1240-1255 (October 1978).

APPENDIX A : SYNTAX OF $\mathcal{L}$

Capital letters will be used to denote non-terminal symbols. The vertical bar " | " separates syntactic alternatives.

A program consists of a sequence of variable declarations VDECL followed by a sequence of procedure declarations PDECL and a command C:

$\mathcal{L}$ ::= VDECL; PDECL; C .
VDECL ::= | *var* ID : TYPE ; VDECL .
PDECL ::= | *proc* ID(PARMS); VDECL; C ; PDECL .

TYPE specifies the set of values that a variable with name ID may take. PARMS denotes the list of parameters of a procedure. For simplicity in this paper only procedures with parameters passed 'by reference' are considered. We assume that each variable which occurs free in a procedure body is either locally declared or is a parameter (no global variables), that local variable identifiers are distinct from parameter identifiers, and that procedures are not recursive.

Commands C may be empty, or may be sequences of other commands like assignments, conditionals, loops, and procedure calls (with actual argument lists ARGS):

C ::= | C;C | ID:= E | *if* B *then* C *else* C *fi* | *while* B *do* C *od* | ID(ARGS) .

We do not give any detailed syntax for expressions E and Boolean expressions B. We assume that a generic predicate def (which may be defined by induction on the syntactic structure of E, see [5]) yields true when the evaluation of an expression E terminates properly. For simplicity, we assume that the evaluation of Boolean expressions always terminates properly.

APPENDIX B : AXIOMATIC SEMANTICS $\mathcal{T}$

The goal in defining a total correctness theory $\mathcal{T}$ for a language $\mathcal{L}$ is to allow one to infer theorems of the form P {C} Q about the behavior of programs C written in $\mathcal{L}$. The interpretation of "P {C} Q" is "If P is true then C terminates in a state in which Q is true".

Let $\mathcal{A}$ denote the assertion language used in defining the semantics of $\mathcal{L}$. The set of all valid assertions of $\mathcal{A}$ forms the *axioms* of $\mathcal{T}$. The proof rules of $\mathcal{T}$ are:

1. Empty command:

$$\frac{P \Rightarrow Q}{P\ \{\ \}\ Q}$$

2. Assignment

$$\frac{P \Rightarrow def(e)}{P\ \{v:=e\}\ \exists v'\colon P[v'/v]\ \&\ v=e[v'/v]}$$

3. Conditional rule:

$$\frac{P\&b\ \{C_1\}\ Q,\ \ P\&\neg b\ \{C_2\}\ Q}{P\ \{\textit{if}\ b\ \textit{then}\ C_1\ \textit{else}\ C_2\ \textit{fi}\}\ Q}$$

4. Loop rule (U denotes a monotonically decreasing integer *variant* function, which, for given values of the program variables yields an upper bound on the number of iterations still to be performed):

$$\frac{P\&(U\leq 0)\Rightarrow\neg b\ ,\ \ P\&b\&(U=t)\ \{C\}\ P\&(U<t)}{P\ \{\textit{while}\ b\ \textit{do}\ C\ \textit{od}\}\ P\&\neg b}$$

5. Sequencing rule:

$$\frac{P\ \{C_1\}\ R,\ \ R\ \{C_2\}\ Q}{P\ \{C_1;C_2\}\ Q}$$

6. Let *proc* Pr ($\bar{x}$); VDECL; body; be a procedure with a list of parameters $\bar{x}$ passed 'by reference', and let P and Q be two assertions which do not contain free any of the (local) variables declared in VDECL. The proof rule for an invocation of Pr with a list of arguments $\bar{a}$ is:

$$\frac{P\ \{body\}\ Q}{P[\bar{a}/\bar{x}]\ \{Pr(\bar{a})\}\ Q[\bar{a}/\bar{x}]}$$

The expression $P[\bar{a}/\bar{x}]$ denotes the result of substituting the arguments $\bar{a}$ for the free occurrences of the corresponding formal parameters $\bar{x}$ in P.

7. Consequence rule:

$$\frac{P \Rightarrow S,\ S\ \{C\}\ R,\ \ R \Rightarrow Q}{P\ \{C\}\ Q}$$

8. Conjunction rule:

$$\frac{P\ \{C\}\ Q,\ \ P\ \{C\}\ R}{P\ \{C\}\ (Q\&R)}$$

9. Disjunction rule:

$$\frac{P\ \{C\}\ R,\ \ Q\ \{C\}\ R}{(P \vee Q)\ \{C\}\ R}$$

10. Invariant rule:

$$P\ \{C\}\ P \qquad \text{(provided } Free(P) \cap Free(C) = \{\ \})$$

11. ∃-Rule

$$\frac{P\ \{C\}\ Q}{\exists x{:}P\ \{C\}\ \exists x{:}P} \qquad \text{(provided } x \notin Free(C))$$

12. ∀-rule

$$\frac{P\ \{C\}\ Q}{\forall x{:}P\ \{C\}\ \forall x{:}P} \qquad \text{(provided } x \notin Free(C))$$

Besides the rules given above, we also used in this paper the following crash rules:

Conditional interrupted by a crash:

$$\frac{P\&b\ \{\text{¤}C_1\}\ Q,\ \ P\&\neg b\ \ \{\text{¤}C_2\}\ Q}{P\ \{\text{¤}\,\textit{if}\ b\ \textit{then}\ C_1\ \textit{else}\ C_2\ \textit{fi}\}\ Q} \qquad \text{(C6)}$$

Crashed procedure with parameters 'by reference':

$$\frac{P\ \{\text{¤}\,body\}\ Q}{P[\bar{a}/\bar{x}]\ \{\text{¤}\,Pr(\bar{a})\}\ Q[\bar{a}/\bar{x}]} \qquad \text{(C7}$$

A Sound and Relatively* Complete Axiomatization of Clarke's Language L_4

(Extended Abstract)

Werner Damm   Bernhard Josko

Lehrstuhl für Informatik II, RWTH Aachen

Büchel 29-31, D-5100 Aachen

1. INTRODUCTION

In his 1979 paper [Cla] Clarke put a borderline to the growing extensions of programming languages with complete Hoare-calculi (in the sense of Cook [Coo]). He proved, that there exists no sound and relatively complete Hoare-logic for a programming language which simultaneously uses the features

(1) procedures are allowed in parameter positions (without self-application)
(2) recursion
(3) static scope
(4) global variables in procedure bodies
(5) nested procedure declarations.

In the same paper he claimed, that the languages L_i obtained by disallowing feature (i) do have a sound and relatively complete Hoare-logic. While for $i \neq 4$ these claims were either already proved in [Cla] or established subsequently by Olderog [Old 1] , the claim regarding the language L_4 turned out to be "a challenge to develop new tools and methods in the field of Hoare-like systems" [Lan Old] . This paper provides such a proof-system for a language restricted to the critical features of L_4 .

To explain the difficulties arising in the treatment of L_4 , consider the following program Γ (essentially taken from [Old 1]).

```
begin
    int  x,w,z;
    proc P(x,w,z:q);
       begin  proc S  (x,w:); begin  x:=x+1;q(x,w:)  end;
              x:=x+1;  if x≤z  then P(x,w,z:S)  else  q(x,w:) fi
       end;
    proc Q(x,w:); begin  w:=x  end;
    P(x,w,z:Q)
end
```

Note that P takes a procedure q as parameter and that each call of S leads to a call of the actual procedure parameter of P . Hence the calling behaviour of Γ is represented by the *formal execution tree* of Γ [Lan 1] in figure 1 (in which for clarity we omitted the unchanged integer parameters and indicated the binding to the currently valid local declaration of S).

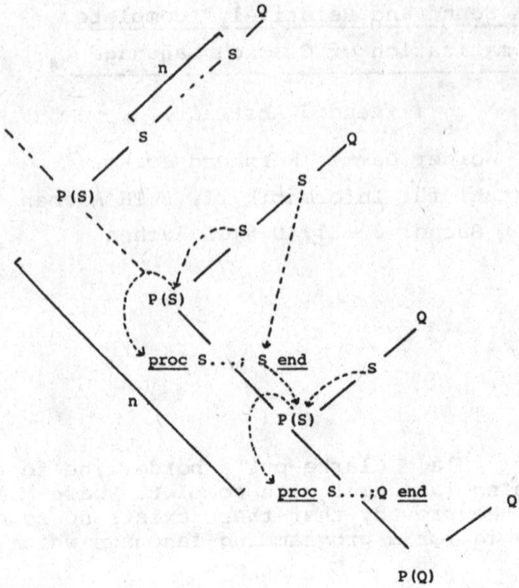

- fig 1 -

Note that this tree has an infinite number of different subtrees and is thus *not regular*. On the other hand, as was lucidly demonstrated by Olderog, the construction of proof-trees by present-day Hoare-like systems depends essentially on regularity of execution trees of the considered programming language (up to injective renamings of the nodes). In fact, the proof-tree can be obtained by "blowing-up" the generating part of the regular tree, where "blowing-up" results from either inserting proof-lines for conditionals, composition, and assignments, or from proving a particular correctness formula (for a procedure call) out of the corresponding *most general formula* [Gor] using some tricky substitutions. Note that *cutting* the tree after the generating part is formalized by the *recursion-rule*.

From an ALGOL-point of view it is natural to deal with the correctness of a procedure call with actual (procedure-) parameters as *one* entity: proving a partial-correctness assertion for a call $P(\bar{x} : \bar{q})$ amounted to proving a partial correctness assertion for the body of P after replacing actuals by formals (using the appropriate renaming for static scope). However, keeping the called procedure together with its actual parameters also lead to the complexity of the execution tree (as seen in Figure 1), hence to incompleteness. The crucial idea, then, was to prove the correctness of a call $P(\bar{x} : q_1, \ldots, q_n)$ by *separately* proving a partial correctness assertion for P and its actual procedure parameters $q_1, \ldots, q_n$. From a λ-calculus point of view, this rule almost comes automatically, since it just follows the syntactic pattern of *application*.

While separating the called procedure from its actuals decreases the complexity of the tree, the price to be paid is an increase in complexity of the correctness formulas : proving P now means proving a partial correctness assertion no longer of a program transforming *states into states* but rather *state -transformations into state-transformations*.

Hence, in order to allow the proof to proceed inductively on applications, all concepts for Hoare-style proof-systems have to be lifted to higher levels : the assertion language, partial correctness assertions, the notion of strongest postconditions, etc. These ideas are incorporated into a Hoare-style proof system, which is proved to be complete relative to oracle calls in the extended assertion language.

This paper is intended to be an introduction into the extension of Hoare logics to higher types, hence we stress motivations and omit all proofs. For a detailed exposition of this subject we refer the reader to [Da Jo]. Similarly, to free the exposition of the main ideas from too many technical details, we restrict overselves to a programming language containing only the critical aspects of L_4 . A full treatment of this language will be given in [Jo 2].

The starting point of this paper was the survey on "Present-day Hoare-systems" by Langmaack and Olderog [LanOld]. Olderog independently obtained a relatively complete proof system for the restriction of L_4 to the PASCAL-case of mode-depth ≤ 2, i.e. where a procedure occurring as parameter may not have procedure parameters itself [Old].

This result and the results of this paper were presented at the 1982-Workshop on "Formale Methoden und Mathematische Hilfsmittel für die Softwarekonstruktion". Recently Langmaack [Lan4] has obtained a similar completeness result for a language with both higher type functions and procedures using oracle calls in weak n-th order predicate calculus transforming any such program into a program with type n procedure variables which has a regular call structure. This also extends results in [Ba Kl Me] on axiomatizing higher order functions. Finally Clarke et al [Ge Cl Ha] have announced a solution for the PASCAL-case, which uses only first-order oracle calls.

2. DESCRIPTION OF THE PROGRAMMING LANGUAGE

For the purposes of this paper we will restrict ourselves to a language *without variables*. In this case, the integer-parameters of procedures can be eliminated by assuming implicitly that all integer identifiers are declared at top-level. As can be seen from Γ this restriction does not factor out the problems with completeness, since the complexity of the execution tree remains unchanged.

While Clarke suggested to prove the completeness-result for L_4 by transforming any such program into an equivalent one without nested procedure declarations, such an approach seems hardly feasible, since the execution trees of L_4 become increasingly complex with increasing mode-depth (in fact form a strict hierarchy of infinite trees [Da]) while the denested programs have regular execution-trees [Old 2]. However, programs in L_4 *can be* denested, if one allows *complex calls* in parameter positions, by passing the global procedure parameters *explicitly* to inner declared procedures, for the sample program leading to (where <u>mode</u> M = <u>proc</u> <u>void</u>) :

<u>proc</u> $P(y_M)$ ⇐ x:=x+1; <u>if</u> $x \leq z$ <u>then</u> $P(S(y_M))$ <u>else</u> y_M <u>fi</u> <u>corp</u>;
<u>proc</u> $S(y_M)$ ⇐ x:=x+1; y_M <u>corp</u>;
<u>proc</u> Q ⇐ w:=x <u>corp</u>;
P(Q)

Note the slight change in notation : procedure parameters (from now on denoted y) carry their *mode* explicitly with them ; in particular it can be checked that all calls (as in $P(S(y_M))$) are well-typed (in the sense of λ-calculus ; note that our language is just an imperative variant of a typed λ-calculus with fixed point operators written as equations ; the restriction *no self-application* by Clarke is intended to mean *finitely typed*). It is for this language that we prove the completeness result. Let us point out that this equivalence-preserving (see [Da Jo]) transformation preserves the "complexity" of the execution tree ; in particular, the execution-tree of the unnested version of Γ shown in figure 2 is still context-free.

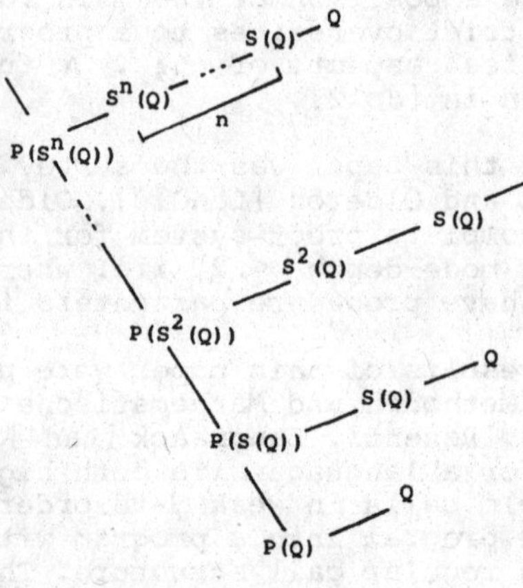

- fig. 2 -

Let us now define the type structure we want to consider.

Rather than starting with a single base type (e.g. void for continuations), we will need more detailed information about what variables (out of a fixed countable set *Var*) will be effected by executing a base type statement and thus make this information availabe through its type.

Thus - at base level - we start out with

$$Gtype := \{X \subseteq Var \mid X \text{ is finite}\} \quad .$$

Semantically, a type X will denote the cpo $Cont^X$ of state-relations θ which *operate* on X , i.e. which satisfy

(1) $(\sigma,\sigma') \in \theta \rightsquigarrow \forall x \in Var \setminus X : \sigma(x) = \sigma'(x)$

(2) $(\sigma,\sigma') \in \theta$, $\tilde{\sigma}_{|X} = \sigma_{|X}$, $\tilde{\sigma}'_{|X} = \sigma'_{|X}$ and [1]

$\tilde{\sigma}_{|Var \setminus X} = \tilde{\sigma}'_{|Var \setminus X} \rightsquigarrow (\tilde{\sigma},\tilde{\sigma}') \in \theta$,

---

1 - for a function f and $A \subseteq dom(f)$ we denote by $f_{|A}$ the *restriction* of f to A .
- as usual a *state* $\sigma \in \Sigma$ maps *Var* into the carrier of an interpretation of the operation and predicate symbols which we will assume to be fixed throughout this paper.

ordered under set inclusion.

Given types $\tau_j \in Type$,

$$\tau \equiv \tau_1 \times \ldots \times \tau_m \rightarrow \tau_0 \in Type$$

will be associated to a procedure expecting (procedure) parameters satisfying the "change of variables constraints" expressed by $\tau_1, \ldots, \tau_m$ and delivering a procedure of type τ_0 as value. Semantically, τ denotes the cpo $Cont^{\tau}$ of all continuous functions from $Cont^{\tau_1} \times \ldots \times Cont^{\tau_m}$ to $Cont^{\tau_0}$. Note that there is a natural ordering on types inherited from set inclusion at the base-level: if P promises to change only variables in X_{result} when obtaining a parameter which changes only variables in X_{par} , then it will make the same promise for $X'_{par} \subseteq X_{par}$; this can be weakened to $X'_{result} \supseteq X_{result}$. We denote this ordering on types by $\leqslant$.

As indicated above, parameters y_τ will indicate their type as subscript. A list of parameters $(y_{\tau_1}, \ldots, y_{\tau_n})$ will be abbreviated y_α , where $\alpha \equiv \tau_1 \times \ldots \times \tau_n$. We assume that the set Par^τ of parameters of type τ is well ordered. For each type τ , procedure identifiers of type τ are taken from the set $Pvar^\tau$. With these notations we can now define the syntax of statements in our language.

2.1 Definition

For each $\tau \in Type$, the set $Stat^\tau$ of *statements of type* τ $(S_\tau \in Stat^\tau)$, is the smallest set St^τ with

- $x := e \in St^{\{x\} \cup var(e)}$ *(assignment)*
- $\underline{id} \in St^{\emptyset}$ *(identity)*
- $Pvar^\tau \subseteq St^\tau$ *(procedure call)*
- $Par^\tau \subseteq St^\tau$ *(formal procedure call)*
- $S_1 \in St^{X_1}$, $S_2 \in St^{X_2}$ $\rightsquigarrow$ $S_1;S_2 \in St^{X_1 \cup X_2}$ *(composition)*
- $S_1 \in St^{X_1}$, $S_2 \in St^{X_2}$ $\rightsquigarrow$ $\underline{if}$ b $\underline{then}$ S_1 $\underline{else}$ S_2 $\underline{fi}$ $\in St^{X_1 \cup X_2 \cup free(b)}$ *(conditional)*
- $S \in St^X \rightsquigarrow$ $\underline{while}$ b $\underline{do}$ S $\underline{od}$ $\in St^{X \cup free(b)}$ *(while-statement)*
- $S \in St^{\tau_1 \times \ldots \times \tau_m \rightarrow \tau}$, $S_i \in St^{\tau'_i}$ with $\tau'_i \leqslant \tau_i$, $1 \leqslant i \leqslant m$ $\rightsquigarrow$ $S(S_1, \ldots, S_m) \in St^\tau$ *(application)*
- $S \in St^\tau \rightsquigarrow$ $\underline{abs}$ $y_\alpha \cdot S$ $\underline{sba}$ $\in St^{\alpha \rightarrow \tau}$ *(abstraction)*

□

Note that actual parameters with type less than the expected type are implicitly coerced.

We will assume standard λ-calculus terminology (cf.e.g. [Bar]) when talking about statements and e.g. refer to the set of parameters occurring free in S by $frpar(S)$. The set of variables affected by applying S to all its parameters down to base type can be recovered from its type τ : if $\tau \equiv (\alpha_m \rightarrow (\ldots(\alpha_0 \rightarrow X)\ldots))$, then $var(S) := X_\tau := X$.

A *unit* consists of a statement S of some type τ and a set of mutually recursive procedure declarations D , which bind to each procedure identifier P occurring in S a closed statement over *pvar*(S) of type *type*(P) . We will refer to this statement as the *body* of P and denot it by D(P) . Since procedures can be denested using complex calls (cf. [Lan 1], [Da Fe], [Tr Me Ha]) we will w.l.o.g. restrict ourselves to *programs* which are simply units $\langle D|S\rangle$ with *closed* statement S .

We could assume a standard (i.e. fixed-point) denotational semantics for our language relative to a set of *environments Env* which map parameters to state-transformations of matching type. However, as is by now well known (cf. e.g. [Apt, Old 1]), an *approximating* semantics allows a much easier (though somewhat debatable [Mey]) justification of the proof rule dealing with recursive procedures. In this approach, the semantics of a program $\langle D|S\rangle$ is obtained as the join over the semantics of all approximations $\langle D^{(n)}|S\rangle$, where $D^{(n)}$ is derived from D by expanding all calls in parallel up to calling depth n and replacing the remaining calls by some diverging program of appropriate type (for a more formal definition see [Da] or [Da Jo]). We denote the meaning of a unit $\langle D|S\rangle$ in an environment ρ by $C[\![\langle D|S\rangle]\!]\rho$. Note that the type of this *higher type state-transformation* equals the type of S .

3. THE ASSERTION LANGUAGE

The definition of the assertion language can hardly be appreciated without an intuitive understanding of the kind of correctness formulae used in our proof-system. Indeed, "designing" the proper notion of correctnes formulae was the key to solving the completeness problem for higher type procedures.

Let us now explain the basic idea underlying the definition of higher type correctness formulae.

To this end, consider a procedure P which takes a parameter of base type {x} , say, and delivers a base type procedure as vaule. Intuitivel a partial correctness formula for P can be pictured as

{ —— *pre* —— *post* ——} P {—— *post* —— *pre* —— *post* ——}

where *pre* and *post* are *predicatevariables* corresponding to the formal procedure parameter of P . Such a correctness formula is valid, intuitively, if for all acutals parameters S which are partially correct with respect to a precondition p and postcondition q , the (classical) partial correctness formula

{ —— p —— q ——} P {—— q —— p —— q ——}

is valid; note that the semantics of P(S) is a state transformation.

In the formal treatment, we deviate from this intuitive picture in two ways (which make formalization easier):

- we eliminate *pre* and just associate *one* predicate variable whth each formal procedure parameter by considering only postconditions with respect to the canonical precondition of the Gorelick formula (in our example: x = z) ;
- rather than substituting directly the postcondition q of the actual parameter into the pre- and postconditions f_{pre} , f_{post}

of P , we formally *apply* f_{pre} and f_{post} to q (and thus view them as *predicate transformers*) ; if f_{pre} and f_{post} are an *abstraction* with respect to the predicate variable *post* , then these applications *reduce* to the pre/postconditions for P(S) obtained by substitution.

As a concrete example, consider the situation where $f_{post} \equiv$ abs post-$y_{\{x\}}$ .x > 0 ∧ post-$y_{\{x\}}$ sba and S satisfies $\{x=z\}$ S $\{x=z^2\}$. Then in the postcondition of P(S) the relation variable post-$y_{\{x\}}$ (related to the formal procedure parameter $y_{\{x\}}$ of P) is bound to the actual postcondition $x = z^2$ (for the "actual parameter" S) . Note that this postcondition $f_{post}(x = z^2)$ is equivalent to $x > 0 \wedge x = z^2$ (via β-reduction).

Thus our assertion language is essentially a typed λ-calculus which allows abstraction with respect to predicate variables out of a set *Predvar* := {post-y_τ | $y_\tau \in$ *Pvar*} . We use again $post_\alpha$ to abbreviate a list (post-y_{τ_1},...,post-y_{τ_n}) where $\alpha = \tau_1 \times \ldots \times \tau_n$. Moreover we have to delay substitution of expressions into a predicate until the actual postconditions are substituted (consider e.g. an instance of the assignment axiom for the postcondition post-y). To this end we introduce an unevaluated substitution subst(p,x,e) . Intuitively subst(post-y,x,e) means to substitute e for x in the predicate assigned to post-y by an appropriate environment.

In an expression e occurring in a formula f , auxiliary variables, $\tilde{x}$, are allowed. Syntactically they are used in the same manner as variables, e.g. $e_0 \equiv g(x_1,h(x_2,\tilde{x}))$ would be a well-defined expression. *var*(e) denotes the set of variables and *aux*(e) denotes the set of auxiliary variables in an expression e , e.g. *var*$(e_0) = \{x_1,x_2\}$ and *aux*$(e_0) = \{\tilde{x}\}$. Semantically auxiliary variables will be evaluated in the environment. Let us motivate the introduction of auxiliary variables. Assume that f_0 is a formula of type (X,X') and f_1 a formula of type $X \cup \{z\}$, where z is not in X . If we fix the value of the variable z , f_1 becomes a formula of type X and we can apply the formula f_0 to it. This can be described by auxiliary variables. subst$(f_1,z,\tilde{x})$ is a formula of type X and thus f_0(subst$(f_1,z,\tilde{x})$) or $\exists\tilde{x}.f_0$(subst$(f_1,z,\tilde{x})$) are well-defined formulae. Observe that $f_0(\exists z.f_1)$ expresses a predicate which is in general different form $\exists\tilde{x}.f_0$(subst$(f_1,z,\tilde{x})$). The need for including this feature of freezing variables of formulae in applied positions arises from investigation of expressiveness with respect to modified assertion language, see [Jo 1]. Roughly, computable functionals can be described by defining their value on finite approximations of their input through a formula in the assertion language. This formula will involve existential quantification over the indices representing the finite approximations of the argument, which can only be expressed through auxiliary variables.

Finally recall, that a predicate variable post-$y_{\{x\}}$ will be interpreted as a postcondition for $y_{\{x\}}$ with respect to the canonical precondition x = z and thus will depend on both x and z . In general, the postcondition for y_τ will operate on *ptype*(τ) , where *ptype* : *Type* → *Type* is defined inductively by

- *ptype*(X) := $X \cup \{z_1,\ldots,z_n\}$ where $X = \{x_1,\ldots,x_n\}$ and
  $z_j := min(Var \setminus (\{x_1,\ldots,x_n\} \cup \{z_i \mid 1 \le i < j\}))$ $1 \le j \le n$
- *ptype*$(\tau_1 \times \ldots \times \tau_n \to \tau)$:= *ptype*$(\tau_1) \times \ldots \times$ *ptype*$(\tau_n) \to$ *ptype*(τ_0) .

We use $ptype(\alpha)$ to abbreviate $ptype(\tau_1)\times\ldots\times ptype(\tau_n)$.

We are now prepared to give the formal definition of the syntax of our assertion language.

3.1 Definition

The set $Form^{\tau}$ of formulae of type τ ($f_{\tau} \in Form^{\tau}$) is the smallest set F^{τ} with

- $\{\underline{true},\underline{false}\} \subseteq F^{\emptyset}$
- $e_1 = e_2 \in F^{var(e_1)\,\cup\, var(e_2)}$
- $r(e_1,\ldots,e_n) \in F^X$ where $X = var(e_1) \cup \ldots \cup var(e_n)$ and r is a relation symbol in the underlying signature
- $y \in Par^{\tau} \leadsto$ post-$y \in F^{ptype(\tau)}$
- $f \in F^X$ and $frpred(f) = \emptyset \leadsto \neg f \in F^X$
- $f_1 \in F^{X_1}$, $f_2 \in F^{X_2} \leadsto (f_1 \vee f_2)$, $(f_1 \wedge f_2) \in F^{X_1 \cup X_2}$
- $f \in F^X \leadsto (\exists x.f)$, $(\forall x.f) \in F^{X \setminus \{x\}}$ for $x \in Var$
- $f \in F^X \leadsto (\exists \tilde{x}.f)$, $(\forall \tilde{x}.f) \in F^X$ for $\tilde{x} \in Aux$
- $f \in F^X$ and $x_1,\ldots,x_n$ are distinct variables $\leadsto$

  $\underline{subst}(f,(x_1,\ldots,x_n),(e_1,\ldots,e_n)) \in F^{X'}$ where

  $X' = (X \setminus \{x_1,\ldots,x_n\}) \cup \bigcup \{var(e_j) \mid 1 \leq j \leq n \text{ and } x_j \in X\}$
- $f \in F^{\tau_1\times\ldots\times\tau_n \to \tau}$, $f_i \in F^{\tau'_i}$ with $\tau'_i \leq \tau_i$ for all $1 \leq i \leq n$

  $\leadsto f(f_1,\ldots,f_n) \in F^{\tau}$
- $f \in F^{\tau} \leadsto \underline{abs}\ \text{post}_{\alpha}.\ f\ \underline{sba} \in F^{ptype(\alpha)\to\tau}$

where $frpred(f)$ is the set of free predicate variables of a formula f which is defined as in the classical setting of λ-calculus

□

We will use $f_1 \to f_2$, $\exists\overline{x}.f$, $\forall\overline{x}.f$, $\overline{x} = \overline{z}$ as abbreviations for the obvious formulae, and use $free(f)$, $fraux(f)$, $frpred(f)$ etc. to denote the set of free variables (resp. auxiliary variables,...) of f . Note that we allow negation only for *closed* formulae, since we want the semantics of a formula to be continuous in its free predicate variables.

As indicated before, a level-1 assertion will denote a predicate transformer, hence in this context

- a basetype X denotes the cpo $Pred^X$ of predicates $\pi : \Sigma \to \{tt,ff\}$ which *operate on* X , i.e. which satisfy

  $\forall\sigma \in \Sigma\ \forall x \in Var \setminus X \quad \pi\sigma = \pi(\sigma[x/a])$

  for an arbitrary a in the domain of the interpretation; the ordering $\sqsubseteq$ is given by $\pi\sigma = tt \Rightarrow \pi'\sigma = tt$, i.e. by implication;

- a type $\tau \equiv \tau_1 \times \ldots \tau_n \to \tau_0$ denotes the cpo $Pred^{\tau}$ of all continuous functions $Pred^{\tau_1} \times \ldots \times Pred^{\tau_n} \to Pred^{\tau_0}$.

We will only give the nonobvious clauses in the definition of the semantics of formulae. Clearly formulae will have to be evaluated in an environment, which binds predicate variables to higher-type predicate-transformations of a matching type while associating domain-values to auxiliary variables. The set of such environments is called *Predenv*.

3.2 Definition

The semantics of formulae $F : Form \to Predenv \to Pred$ is given by

$F[\![\forall \tilde{x}.f]\!]\rho\sigma = tt$ iff for all a in the domain it is the case that $F[\![f]\!]\rho[\tilde{x}/a]\sigma = tt$

$F[\![\underline{subst}(f,(x_1,\ldots,x_n),(e_1,\ldots,e_n))]\!]\rho\sigma :=$
$F[\![f]\!]\rho\sigma[(x_1,\ldots,x_n)/E[\![e_1]\!]\rho\sigma,\ldots,E[\![e_n]\!]\rho\sigma)]$

$F[\![post\text{-}y]\!]\rho := \rho(post\text{-}y)$

$F[\![f(f_1,\ldots,f_n)]\!]\rho := F[\![f]\!]\rho(F[\![f_1]\!]\rho,\ldots,F[\![f_n]\!]\rho)$

$F[\![\underline{abs}\ post_\alpha.f\ \underline{sba}]\!]\rho := (\pi_{ptype(\alpha)} \mapsto F[\![f]\!]\rho[post_\alpha/\pi_{ptype(\alpha)}])$

□

Note that the semantics of a formula of type τ is a predicate of type τ .

4. SYNTAX AND SEMANTICS OF CORRECTNESS FORMULAE

With the careful introduction of the assertion language we have paved an easy way to the formal treatment of higher type correctness formulae: a type τ partial correctness formula is a tripel $\{f_1\}\langle D|S\rangle\{f_2\}$, where the statement-part of the unit $\langle D|S\rangle$ is of type τ and the formulae f_1,f_2 have type $ptype(\tau)$ (possibly weakened in $X_{ptype(\tau)}$, i.e. the variables f_j operates on when applied to all arguments down to base-type). An informal definition for validity of higher type partial correctness assertions was already given in section 3. Here we continue by formalizing these ideas; we do so first for the corresponding semantical objects by induction on the functional level.

Consider higher type predicates π,π' , and a higher-type store transformation θ , all of matching type. We want to define relations $\pi \models_\theta \pi'$ (read: θ transforms π into π') , and we want this to define the semantics of a partial correctness formula.

Thus, if π,π' , and θ are of base type, then $\pi \models_\theta \pi'$ simply means, that π' is a valid postcondition with respect to θ and the precondition π , i.e. if must be the case that

$$\forall\sigma,\sigma' \in \Sigma[\pi\sigma = tt \wedge (\sigma,\sigma') \in \theta \Rightarrow \pi\sigma' = tt] .$$

Now assume that π,π' , and θ have types matching $\tau_1\times\ldots\times\tau_n\to\tau_0$. Then $\pi \models_\theta \pi'$ iff for all arguments $\pi_\alpha = (\pi_{\tau_1},\ldots,\pi_{\tau_m})$, $\theta_\alpha = (\theta_{\tau_1},\ldots,\theta_{\tau_n})$, whenever the canonical preconditions for θ_j are transformed into π_j (for all $j \in \{1,\ldots,n\}$) , then $\pi(\pi_\alpha)$ must be transformed by $\theta(\theta_\alpha)$ into $\pi'(\pi_\alpha)$. Thus this concept is perfectly defined, once we show the canonical preconditions.

4.1 Definition

The formula pre_τ is defined inductively by

$pre_X := x_1 = z_1 \wedge \ldots \wedge x_n = z_n$ where

$\{x_1,\ldots,x_n\} = X$ with $x_1 < \ldots < x_n$ and

$ptype(X) = X \cup \{z_1,\ldots,z_n\}$ with $z_1 < \ldots < z_n$.

$pre_{\alpha\to\tau} := \underline{abs}\ post_\alpha . pre_\tau\ \underline{sba}$ where $post_\alpha = (post\text{-}y_1,\ldots,post\text{-}y_{lg(\alpha)})$

with $y_i = min(Par^{\alpha(i)} \setminus \{y_j \mid 1 \leq j < i\})$ for $1 \leq i \leq lg(\alpha)$ □

Now note that the syntactic objects in a partial correctness formula depend on both a predicate environment and an environment which associates a higher-type store transformation to each parameter. To overcome this seeming difficulty we will have to formalize what we were suggesting by notation: that these environments are not independent but rather have to be such that the predicate bound to post-y really is a postcondition for the higher-type store-transformation bound to y_τ . Rather than formalizing such a relation between the environments we will in this paper take a shortcut and *construct* such a continuation environment for a given predicate environment ρ , in fact it will be the *maximal* such environment compatible with ρ .

4.2 Definition

Given $\rho \in Predenv$ define $predrel(\rho) \in Env$ by

$$predrel(\rho)(y_\tau) = \bigsqcup \{\theta \in Cont^\tau \mid pre_\tau \models_\theta \rho(post\text{-}y_\tau)\}$$

□

Note that $Cont^\tau$ is in fact a complete lattice, hence the above join is well defined. pre_τ is shorthand for the semantics of pre_τ (in any environment).

For proof-theory this means that formal procedure parameters are dealt with as if the maximal compatible storetransformation were plugged in for it (which is not expressible as a statement in our language, since the language itself is deterministic; in fact the semantics was made nondeterministic to overcome this difficulty). Thus the assertions proved e.g. for the sample program in the introduction are so strong, that they subsume all particular actual parameters $S^n(Q)$ of P.. In practice this has the disadvantage of making it hard to find general enough pre/post-specifications for procedures of higher type.

The name *predrel* in definition 4.2 hints, that this environment can be defined inductively using isomorphisms $predrel^\tau$ and $relpred^\tau$ between predicate and storetransformations of type (matching) τ . This finer analysis is used heavily in proofs, in particular to establish the various properties of strongest postconditions listed in section 6, but will not be given here due to space considerations.

The formal definition of validity of higher type correctness formula is now straightforward.

4.3 Definition

A unit $\langle D|S\rangle$ is partially correct with respect to precondition f and postcondition f' (of matching type; notation: $\models \{f\} \langle D|S\rangle \{f'\}$) iff for all predicate environments ρ

$C[\![\langle D|S\rangle]\!] predrel(\rho)$ transforms $F[\![f]\!]\rho$ into $F[\![f']\!]\rho$

□

5. THE HOARE CALCULUS H

In this section we integrate the ideas developed before into a proof system H. For clarity of exposition, we will assume that abstractions are only used to declare formal parameters of procedures (any of the denesting techniques mentioned in section 2 establishes this assumption). Thus the declaration D can be written in the form

$$\underline{\text{proc}} \quad P_1(y_{\alpha_{m_1}})\ldots(y_{\alpha_{k_1}}) \Leftarrow S_1 \quad \underline{\text{corp}} \;;$$
$$\vdots$$
$$\underline{\text{proc}} \quad P_n(y_{\alpha_{m_n}})\ldots(y_{\alpha_{k_n}}) \Leftarrow S_n \quad \underline{\text{corp}} \;;$$

where the S_j are abstraction-free statements. For the rest of this paper we will slightly revise our terminology and refer to S_j as *body*-P_j.

Most rules and axioms are just slight modifications of the standard proof system for parameterless recursive procedures (see eg. [Apt]) and will be given without further comment.

AXIOMS OF H

Assignment axiom

Ax_1 : $\{\underline{subst}(f,x,e)\}<D|x := e>\{f\}$

Parameter axiom

Ax_2 : $\{pre_\tau\}<D|y_\tau>\{post\text{-}y_\tau\}$

Invariance axiom

Ax_3 : $\{f\}<D|S>\{f\}$ where $type(f) \in Gtype$ and $free(f) \cap var(S) = \emptyset$

Recall that unevaluated substitutions were introduced to delay the substitution until the actual postconditions are known.
Clearly the parameter axiom is valid by definition: the environment *predrel*(ρ) was constructed so as to make Ax_2 true.
The invariance axiom is needed for arbitrary units. It also demonstrates the need for having exact information about what variables S depends on and thus motivated the more refined type structure. Note that without this refinement we could not instantiate the invariance axiom for statements which contain free predicate variables.

Out of the rules of H listed below, only rules 7 to 10 deserve some further comment.

PROOF-RULES OF H

Composition rule

$$R_1: \quad \frac{\{f_1\}<D|S_1>\{f_2\},\{f_2\}<D|S_2>\{f_3\}}{\{f_1\}<D|S_1;S_2>\{f_3\}}$$

<u>Conditional rule</u>

$$R_2: \frac{\{f_1 \wedge b\}\langle D|S_1\rangle\{f_2\}, \{f_1 \wedge \neg b\}\langle D|S_2\rangle\{f_2\}}{\{f_1\}\langle D|\ \underline{if}\ b\ \underline{then}\ S_1\ \underline{else}\ S_2\ \underline{fi}\rangle\{f_2\}}$$

<u>While rule</u>

$$R_3: \frac{\{f \wedge b\}\langle D|S\rangle\{f\}}{\{f\}\langle D|\underline{while}\ b\ \underline{do}\ S\ \underline{od}\rangle\{f \wedge \neg b\}}$$

<u>Conjunction rule</u>

$$R_4: \frac{\{f\}\langle D|S\rangle\{f_1\}, \{f\}\langle D|S\rangle\{f_2\}}{\{f\}\langle D|S\rangle\{f_1 \wedge f_2\}}$$

<u>Substitution rule I</u>

$$R_5: \frac{\{f\}\langle D|S\rangle\{f'\}}{\{\underline{subst}(f,\bar{z},\bar{e})\}\langle D|S\rangle\{\underline{subst}(f',\bar{z},\bar{e})\}}, \text{ where } \bar{z} = (z_1,\ldots,z_n),$$

$$\bar{e} = (e_1,\ldots,e_n) \text{ and } (\{z_1,\ldots,z_n\} \cup \bigcup_{1 \leq i \leq n} var(e_i)) \cap var(S) = \emptyset$$

<u>Substitution rule II</u>

$$R_6: \frac{\{f\}\langle D|S\rangle\{f'\}}{\{\underline{subst}(f,\bar{z},\bar{w})\}\langle D|S\rangle\{f'\}}, \text{ where } \bar{z} = (z_1,\ldots,z_n),$$

$$\bar{w} = (w_1,\ldots,w_n) \text{ and } \{z_1,\ldots,z_n\} \cap (free(f') \cup var(S)) = \emptyset$$

<u>Consequence rule</u>

$$R_7: \frac{f_1 \Rightarrow f_1', \{f_1'\}\langle D|S\rangle\{f_2'\}, f_2' \Rightarrow f_2}{\{f_1\}\langle D|S\rangle\{f_2\}}$$

<u>Application rule</u>

$$R_8: \frac{\{f\}\langle D|S\rangle\{f'\}, \{pre_{\tau_1}\}\langle D|S_1\rangle\{f_1\},\ldots,\{pre_{\tau_n}\}\langle D|S_n\rangle\{f_n\}}{\{f(f_1,\ldots,f_n)\}\langle D|S(S_1,\ldots,S_n)\rangle\{f'(f_1,\ldots,f_n)\}},$$

where $\tau_i = type(S_i)$ $(1 \leq i \leq n)$

<u>Abstraction rule</u>

$$R_9: \frac{\{f(post_\alpha)\}\langle D|S(y_\alpha)\rangle\{f'(post_\alpha)\}}{\{f\}\langle D|S\rangle\{f'\}}, \text{ where}$$

$$y_\alpha \cap frpar(S) = \emptyset \text{ and } post_\alpha \cap (frpred(f) \cup frpred(f')) = \emptyset$$

Recursion rule

$$R_{10}:\ \frac{\begin{array}{l}(\{f\}\langle D|P(y_{\alpha_m})\ldots(y_{\alpha_k})\rangle\{f'\})\\ \{f\}\langle D|\text{body-}P\rangle\{f'\}\end{array}}{\{f\}\langle D|P(y_{\alpha_m})\ldots(y_{\alpha_k})\rangle\{f'\}}$$

Note that the consequence-rule introduces a new kind of syntactic object in its premises: the proof system allows oracle calls of the form $f_1 \Rightarrow f_2$, where f_1 and f_2 are formulas of matching type. Such a formula is valid iff for all predicate environments ρ $\mathcal{F}[\![f_1]\!]\rho \sqsubseteq \mathcal{F}[\![f_2]\!]\rho$, hence $\Rightarrow$ generalizes implication.

The application rule is sound again almost by definition, since the whole logic and its semantics was build to make it sound. Note that the fact that this breaks up the execution tree into a regular structure is a direct consequence of leaving application *uninterpreted* . This idea was already exploited in [Da] to show that the semantics of finite mode ALGOL 68 programs can be obtained as homomorphic image of *regular* infinite trees. We use the abstraction rule R_9 instead of the obvious rule

$$\frac{\{f\}\langle D|S\rangle\{f'\}}{\{\underline{\text{abs}}\ post_\alpha.f\ \underline{\text{sba}}\}\langle D|\ \underline{\text{abs}}\ y_\alpha.S\ \underline{\text{sba}}\rangle\{\underline{\text{abs}}\ post_\alpha.f'\underline{\text{sba}}\}}$$

since we consider programs with no explicit abstraction.
The recursion rule R_{10} eliminates the *assumption* about the call of P with the formal parameter lists y_{α_m} to y_{α_k} once the correctness of the body with respect to the pre/postconditions of the call is established. Since also higher-order partial correctness formulae are valid iff all their approximations are valid, soundness of this rule can be proved exactly as in the case of (basetype) parameterless procedures (cf. e.g. [Apt]).

Once the logic is set up correctly (and assuming familiarity with higher types), proving *correctness* of the proof system is standard.

5.1 Theorem

Any correctness formula provable in *H* is valid

□

6. STRONGEST POSTCONDITIONS, EXPRESSIVITY, AND COMPLETENESS

To construct the proof tree bottom-up for a valid correctness formula, we have to extend the strongest-postcondition-calculus to higher types. In particular we have to show how to break up a valid correctness formula of a call $P(S_1,\ldots,S_n)$ so as to obtain correctness formulae for the actual parameters and the calling procedure. It turns out that it is sufficient to demand the existence of strongest postconditions for base type objects, since the appropriate formula of higher type can be derived using abstractions.

In the sequel we assume that the underlying interpretation is expressive for the assertion language *Form* in the following sense:

6.1 Assumption

$\forall$ f $\in$ *Form* of basetype, $\forall$ basetype units <D|S> $\exists$ sp(f,<D|S>) $\in$ *Form* of basetype s.t. $F[\![sp(f,<D|S>)]\!]\rho\sigma = tt$ iff

$$\exists \sigma' \in \Sigma \quad F[\![f]\!]\rho\sigma' = tt \wedge (\sigma',\sigma) \in C[\![<D|S>]\!]predrel(\rho)$$

for all $\rho \in$ *Predenv* .

□

In [Jo 1] it is shown, that essentially all finitely generated finite and weakly arithmetical [Cl Ge Ha] structures are expressive in the above extended meaning. Together with a recent result in [Ge Cl Ha] this implies that a finitely generated structure is expressive in the extended meaning iff it is expressive under the classical definition (i.e. using first-order-predicate calculus formula and e.g. WHILE-programs).

Given the existence of strongest postconditions at base type, we define a formula sp(f,<D|S>) for S of type $\alpha \to \tau$ and f of matching type inductively by

$$sp(f,<D|S>) \equiv \underline{abs}\ post_\alpha . sp(f(post_\alpha)|<D|S(y_\alpha)>)\ \underline{sba} \quad ,$$

where the parameters have to be chosen carefully so as not to interfere with the free parameters of S and the free predicate variables in f. The following lemma lists the properties of strongest postconditions needed in the completeness proof. Let us mention that showing such "obvious" properties as that sp(f,<D|S>) is indeed a valid postcondition is tedious and requires the deeper analysis of *predrel* mentioned in section

6.2 Lemma

a) $\models$ {f}<D|S>{sp(f,<D|S>)}

b) $\models$ {f}<D|S>{f'} iff $\models$ sp(f,<D|S>) $\Rightarrow$ f'

c) $\models sp(f,<D|x:=e>) \Leftrightarrow \exists u[\underline{subst}(f,x,u) \wedge x = e[x/u]]$
where $u \notin (var(S) \cup free(f) \cup \{x\})$

d) $\models sp(pre_\tau,<D|y_\tau>) \Leftrightarrow post\text{-}y_\tau$

e) $\models sp(f,<D|S_1;S_2>) \Leftrightarrow sp(sp(f,<D|S_1>),<D|S_2>)$

f) $\models sp(f,<D|\underline{if}\ b\ \underline{then}\ S_1\ \underline{else}\ S_2\ \underline{fi}>)$
$\Leftrightarrow sp(f \wedge b,<D|S_1>) \vee sp(f \wedge \neg b,<D|S_2>)$

g) $\models sp(pre_\tau,<D|S_0(S_1,\dots,S_n)>)$
$\Leftrightarrow sp(pre_{(\alpha,\tau)},<D|S_0>)(sp(pre_{\alpha(1)},<D|S_1>),\dots,sp(pre_{\alpha(n)},<D|S_n>))$

h) If {f}<D|S>{f'} is valid, then it is provable in *H* from the assumption $\{pre_\tau\}<D|S>\{sp(pre_\tau,<D|S>)\}$

□

h) shows, that most general formulae (or: Gorelick formulae [Gor]) exist at higher types, thus completeness result can be proved by using the Gorelick formula for the procedure calls $P(y_{\alpha_m})\dots(y_{\alpha_k})$ - for each P declared in D - as initial assumption set $Assm_D$. To obtain the completeness result, we prove for an arbitrary subset M of the initial assumption set, that any valid correctness assertion on higher types is provable in *H* from M.

6.3 Theorem

Let $M \subseteq Assm_D$.

If {f}<D|S>{f'} is valid, then it is provable in *H* using only assumptions in M .

□

REFERENCES

[ADJ] Goguen, J.A./Thatcher, J.W./Wagner, E.G./Wright, J.B.: *Initial algebra semantics and continuous algebras.* J.ACM 24, 68-95 (1977)

[Apt] Apt, K.R.: *Ten years of Hoare's logic : a survey-part I.* ACM TOPLAS 3, 431-483 (1981)

[BaKlMe] de Bakker, J.W./Klop, J.W./Meyer J.-J.Ch. : *Correctness of programs with function procedures.* Report IW 170/81, Mathematisch Centrum, Amsterdam (1981)

[Bar] Barendregt, H.P. : *The type free lambda calculus.* Handbook of Mathematical Logic, North-Holland (1977)

[Cla] Clarke, E.M. : *Programming language constructs for which it is impossible to obtain good Hoare-like axioms.* JACM 26, 129-147 (1979)

[ClGeHa] Clarke, E.M,/German, S.M./Halpern, J.Y. : *On effective axiomatizations of Hoare-logics.* 9th Anual ACM Symposium on Principles of Programming Languages, 309-321 (1982)

[Coo] Cook, S. A. : *Soundness and completeness of an axiom system for program verification.* SIAM J. Comput. 7, 70-90 (1978)

[Da] Damm, W. : *The IO - and OI - hierarchies.* TCS 20, 95-207 (1982)

[DaFe] Damm, W./Fehr, E. : *A schematological approach to the analysis of the procedure concept in ALGOL-languages.* Proc. 5ème Colloque sur les Arbres en Algèbre et en Programmation, Lille, 130-134 (1980)

[DaJo] Damm, W./Josko, B. : *A sound and relatively* complete Hoare logic for a language with higher type procedures* Schriften zur Informatik und Angewandten Mathematik Nr. 77 TH Aachen (1982) (to appear in Acta Informatica)

[GeClHa] German, S.M./Clarke, E.M./Halpern, J.Y. : *A stronger axiom system for reasoning about procedures as parameters.* Proc. Workshop on Logics of Programs, Pittsburgh (1983)

[Gor] Gorelick, G.A. : *A complete axiomatic system for proving assertions about recursive and non-recursive programs.* Techn. Rep. 75, Dept. of Computer Sci., Univ. Of Toronto (1975)

[Hoa] Hoare, C.A. R. : *An axiomatic basis for computer programming.* Comm. ACM 12 576-583 (1969)

[Jo1] Josko, B. : *On expressive interpretations of a Hoare-logic for a language with higher type procedures,* Schriften zur Informatik und Angewandten Mathematik, Nr. 88,TH Aachen (1983)

[Jo2] Josko, B. : *A Hoare-calculus for ALGOL-like programs with finite mode procedures without global variables,* Aachen (1983)

[Lan1] Langmaack, H. : *On procedures as open subroutines I, II* Acta Informatica 2, 311-333 (1973) and 3, 227-241 (1974)

[Lan2] Langmaack, H. : *On a theory of decision problems in programing languages.* Proc. Int. Conf. on Mathematical Studies of Information Processing, LNCS 75, 538-558 (1979)

[Lan3] Langmaack, H. : *On termination problem for finitely interpreted ALGOL-like programs.* Acta Informatica 18, 79-108 (1982)

[Lan4] Langmaack, H. : *Aspects of Programs with Finite Modes,* Proc. of the International Conference on Foundations of Computation Theory 1983

[LanOld] Langmaack, H./Olderog, E.-R. : *Present-day Hoare-like systems for programming languages with procedures : power limits and most likely extensions.* Proc. 7th Coll. Automata, Languages and Programming, LNCS 85, 363-373 (1980)

[Lip] Lipton, R.J. : *A nexessary and sufficient condition for the existence of Hoare logics.* 18th IEEE Symp. on Foundations of Computer Science, 1-6 (1977)

[Old1] Olderog, E.-R. : *Sound and complete Hoare-like calculi based on copy rules.* Acta Informatica 16, 161-197 (1981)

[Old2] Olderog, E.R. : *Hoare-style proof and formal computations.* GI-11. Jahrestagung, IFB 50, 65-71 (1981)

[Old3] Olderog, E.-R. : *Correctness of programs with PASCAL-like procedures without global variables.* (to appear in TCS)

[TrHaMe] Trakthenbrot, B.A./Halpern, J.Y./Meyer, A.R. : *From denotational to copy-rule to axiomatic semantics* Proc. Workshop on Logics of Programs, Pittsburgh (1983).

DECIDING BRANCHING TIME LOGIC: A TRIPLE EXPONENTIAL DECISION PROCEDURE FOR CTL*

E. Allen EMERSON[1] and A. Prasad SISTLA[2]

1. Computer Sciences Department, University of Texas, Austin, TX 78712
2. Aiken Computation Lab, Harvard University, Cambridge, MA 02138

1. Introduction

In this paper we study the full branching time logic CTL* defined in [EH83]. It subsumes a number of logics described in the literature including the systems of [LA80], [GPSS80], [BMP81], [EH82], [CES83], as well as the *Computation Tree Logic* of [CE81]. In CTL* we allow a path quantifier, either A ("for all paths") or E ("for some paths"), to prefix an assertion composed of arbitrary combinations of the usual linear time operators G ("always"), F ("sometime"), X ("nexttime"), and U ("until"). In particular, we consider the problem of deciding if a given CTL* formula f_0 is satisfiable in a structure generated by a binary relation (cf. [EM81]). For some time no such decision procedure for CTL* of elementary complexity was known (cf. [EH83]) although recently several other researchers ([PS83], [VW83], [Wo82]) have announced four or five exponential decision procedures. We show that CTL* is decidable in triple exponential time.

We can give the following overview of our approach:

1. We place the CTL* formula f_0 in a *normal form*. This is essentially conjunctions and disjunctions of formulae of the form Ap_0, $AGEp_0$, Ep_0 where p_0 is a pure linear time formulae (i.e. p_0 contains no nested path quantifiers).

2. For each such formula Ap_0, $AGEp_0$, or Ep_0, we build a *complemented pairs tree automaton* of size ($\exp^2(|p_0|)$ states, $\exp(|p_0|$ pairs). (Note: $\exp^2(n)$ denotes $\exp(\exp(n))$, etc.) These tree automata are then combined using a cross product construction to get a complemented pairs tree automaton for f_0 of size ($\exp^2(|f_0|)$ states, $\exp(|f_0|)$ pairs. This automaton accepts an infinite tree iff it defines a model of f_0. By the results of Streett [ST81] the emptiness problem of this automaton is decidable in $\exp^3(|f_0|)$ time.

3. It turns out that construction of the tree automata for $AGEp_0$, Ep_0 is straightforward. However, construction of the tree automaton for Ap_0 is much more subtle. To get such a

[1]The first author was partially supported by NSF Grant MCS-8302878.

[2]The second author was partially supported by NSF Grant MCS-8105553.

tree automaton, one needs a deterministic automaton on infinite strings for the linear time formula p_0. The tableau construction, applied to p_0, yields a nondeterministic (Buchi) string automaton accepting {strings x: $x \models p_0$} with $N = \exp(|p_0|)$ states. The "classical" method for determinizing such a string automaton involves application of McNaughton's construction [McN66] and yields an equivalent deterministic automaton with $\exp^2(N)$ states. We show that the automaton for p_0 has a special structure which allows construction of an equivalent deterministic automaton of size ($\exp(N^2)$ states, N^2 pairs). This allows us to construct the desired tree automaton for Ap_0.

In the full paper we describe the normal form and the design of the tree automata in detail. We also show that even without any special structure we can determinize an arbitrary Buchi automaton with N states to get a deterministic pairs automaton of size ($\exp(N^3)$ states, N^2) pairs using a somewhat more complicated but straightforward extension of the construction presented here. However, in this abridged version, we focus on the problem of determinizing the Buchi automaton for a linear time formula p_0. The remainder of the report is organized as follows: In Section 2 we give some preliminary definitions and terminology. Then in Section 3 we describe how the tableau for a linear time formula p_0 may be viewed as defining a Buchi automaton and discuss its structure. Finally, in Section 4 we describe how to determinize this Buchi automaton.

2. Preliminaries: Definitions and Terminology

2.1 Syntax. We inductively define a class of state formulae (true of false of states) and a class of path formulae (true or false of paths):

S1. Any atomic proposition P is a state formula.
S2. If p,q are state formulae then so are $p \wedge q$, $\neg p$.
S3. If p is a path formula then Ep is a state formula.
P1. Any state formula p is a path formula.
P2. If p,q are path formulae then so are $p \wedge q$, $\neg p$.
P3. If p,q are path formulae then so are Xp, (p U q).

The set of state formulae generated by the above rules forms the language CTL*. The other connectives are introduced as abbreviations in the usual way: $p \vee q$ abbreviates $\neg(\neg p \wedge \neg q)$, $p \Rightarrow q$ abbreviates $\neg p \vee q$, Ap abbreviates $\neg E \neg p$, Fp abbreviates *true* U p, Gp abbreviates $\neg F \neg p$, etc.

2.2 Semantics. We define the semantics of a CTL* formula with respect to a structure M = (S, R, L) where

S is a nonempty *set of states*,
R is a nonempty, total *binary relation* on S, and
L is a *labelling* which assigns to each state a set of atomic propositions true in the state

A *fullpath* $(a_1, a_2, a_3, \ldots)$ is an infinite sequence of states such that $(a_i, a_{i+1}) \in R$ for all i. We write M,a $\models$ p (M,x $\models$ p) to mean that state formula p (path formula p) is true in structure M at state a (of path x, respectively). When M is understood, we write simply a $\models$ p (x $\models$ p). We define $\models$ inductively using the convention that $x = (a_1,a_2,a_3,...)$ denotes a path and x^i denotes the suffix path $(a_i,a_{i+1},a_{i+2},...)$:

S1. a $\models$ p iff p $\in$ L(s) for any atomic proposition p
S2. a $\models$ p $\wedge$ q iff a $\models$ p and a $\models$ q
  a $\models$ $\neg$p iff not (a $\models$ p)
S3. a $\models$ Ep iff for some fullpath x starting at a, x $\models$ p
P1. x $\models$ p iff $a_1 \models$ p for any state formula p
P2. x $\models$ p $\wedge$ q iff x $\models$ p and x $\models$ p
  x $\models$ $\neg$p iff not (x $\models$ p)
P3. x $\models$ Xp iff $x^2 \models$ p
  x $\models$ (p U q) iff for some $i \geq 1$, $x^i \models$ q and for all $j \geq 1$
    [$j \leq i$ implies $x^j \models$ p]

We say that state formula p is *valid*, and write $\models$ p, if for every structure M and every state a in M, M,a $\models$ p. We say that state formula p is *satisfiable* if for some structure M and some state s in M, M,a $\models$ p. In this case we also say that M defines a *model* of p. We define validity and satisfiability similarly for path (i.e., linear time) formulae.

Note that in determining whether x $\models$ p_0 only the truth values of the atomic propositions actually appearing in p_0 matter. In the subsequent sections, we thus assume that a fullpath x = $a_1a_2a_3...$ is an infinite string of sets of atomic propositions of p_0, i.e., each $a_i \in$ PowerSet(AtomicPropositions(p_0)) where AtomicPropositions(p_0) denotes the set of atomic propositions appearing in p_0.

2.3 Definition. The *Fischer-Ladner Closure of p_0, FL(p_0)*, is the least set of formulae such that

(1) $p_0 \in$ FL(p_0)

(2) if p $\wedge$ q $\in$ FL(p_0) then p,q $\in$ FL(p_0)

(3) if $\neg$p $\in$ FL(p_0) then p $\in$ FL(p_0)

(4) if (p U q) $\in$ FL(p_0) then p,q, X(p U q) $\in$ FL(p_0)

(5) if Xp $\in$ FL(p_0) then p $\in$ FL(p_0)

Note: $|FL(p_0)| = O(|p_0|)$

The *Extended Fischer-Ladner closure of p_0, EFL(p_0)*, is the set FL(p_0) $\cup$ {$\neg$p: p $\in$ FL(p_0)}

2.4 Definition. A set $s \subseteq EFL(p_0)$ is *maximal* provided that $\forall p = \neg q \in EFL(p_0)$, at least one of $q, \neg q \in s$.

A set $s \subseteq EFL(p_0)$ is *consistent* provided that

(1) $\forall p = \neg q \in s$ at most one of q, $\neg q \in s$

(2) $(p \wedge q) \in s$ iff $p \in s$ and $q \in s$
$\neg(p \wedge q) \in s$ iff $\neg p \in s$ or $\neg q \in s$

(3) $(p\ U\ q) \in s$ iff $q \in s$ or $p, X(p\ U\ q) \in s$
$\neg(p\ U\ q) \in s$ iff $\neg q, \neg p \in s$ or $\neg q, \neg X(p\ U\ q) \in s$

2.5 Definition. The *tableau* for p_0 is a labelled, directed graph $\mathcal{T} = (V,R)$ where the set of nodes $V = \{s \subseteq EFL(p_0)$: s is maximal and consistent$\}$ and $R = \{$arcs $s \rightarrow t$: $s,t \in V$ and for each formula $Xp \in EFL(p_0)$ $[Xp \in s$ iff $p \in t]\}$.

2.6 Terminology. We use the symbols $\overset{\infty}{\exists}$ and $\overset{\infty}{\forall}$ which are read "there exist infinitely many" and "for all but a finite number", respectively. We also write *i.o.* to abbreviate "infinitely often", *f.o.* to abbreviate "only finitely often", and *a.e.* to abbreviate "almost everywhere" (meaning "at all but a finite number of instances"). We also extend the *AtomicPropositions(c)* notation to indicate the set of all atomic propositions appearing in formula c or elements of node c or input symbol c.

3. The Tableau as a Nondeterministic Finite Automaton

We may view the tableau for a linear time formula p_0 as defining the transition diagram of a nondeterministic finite automaton $\mathcal{A}$ on infinite strings which accepts $\{x : x \models p_0\}$ by letting the arc $u \rightarrow v$ be labelled with AtomicPropositions(v). A run r of $\mathcal{A}$ on input $x = a_1a_2a_3...$ is an infinite sequence $r = s_0s_1s_2s_3...$ of tableau nodes such that $\forall i \geq 0\ \delta(s_i, a_{i+1}) \supseteq \{s_{i+1}\}$ where δ is the transition function of $\mathcal{A}$. (Actually, s_0 is not a tableau node but the unique *start state* defined so that $\delta(s_0, a) = \{$tableau nodes u: $p_0 \in u$ and AtomicPropositions(u) $=$ AtomicPropositions(a)$\}$.). Note that $\forall i \geq 1$ AtomicPropositions(s_i) $=$ AtomicPropositions(a_i). Any run of $\mathcal{A}$ would correspond to a model of p_0 (in that, $\forall i \geq 1$, $x^i \models \{$formulas p: $p \in s_i\}$) except that eventualities might not be fulfilled. To check fulfillment, we can define acceptance via complemented pairs: if $EFL(p_0)$ has m eventualities, we let $\mathcal{A}$ have m pairs (RED_i, $GREEN_i$) of lights. Each time a state containing $(p_i\ U\ q_i)$ is entered, flash RED_i; each time a state containing q_i is entered, flash $GREEN_i$. A run r is *accepted* iff $\forall i \in [1:m]$ $[[\overset{\infty}{\exists}$ RED_i flashes $\Rightarrow \overset{\infty}{\exists}$ $GREEN_i$ flashes$]$ iff every eventuality is fulfilled iff $x \models p_0$.

However, we find it more convenient to convert $\mathcal{A}$ into an equivalent nondeterministic Buchi automaton, $\mathcal{A}_1$, where acceptance is defined in terms of a single GREEN light flashing i.o. . We need some terminology. We say that the eventuality $(p\ U\ q)$ is *pending* at state s of run r provided that $(p\ U\ q) \in s$ and $q \notin s$. Observe that run r of $\mathcal{A}$ on input x corresponds to a model of p_0 iff not($\exists$ eventuality $(p\ U\ q)$, $(p\ U\ q)$ is pending a.e. along r) iff ($\forall$ eventuality (p U q), (p U q) is *not* pending i.o. along r). The Buchi automaton $\mathcal{A}_1$ is then obtained from $\mathcal{A}$ by augmenting the state with an m+1 valued counter. The counter is incremented from i to i+1 (mod(m+1)) when the ith eventuality, $(p_i \text{ U } q_i)$, is next seen to be not pending along the run r. When the counter is reset to 0, flash GREEN and set the counter to 1. (If m=0, flash GREEN in every state). Now observe that $\overset{\infty}{\exists}$ GREEN flashes iff $\forall i \in [1{:}m]$ ((p_i U q_i) is not pending i.o.) iff every pending eventuality is sometime fulfilled iff $x \models p_0$.

Moreover, $\mathcal{A}_1$ still has $N = \exp(|p_0|) \bullet O(|p_0|) = \exp(|p_0|)$ states.

The automaton $\mathcal{A}_1$ has a special structure so that runs cannot merge:

3.1 Theorem. If $r_1=(s_0,s_1,s_2,...)$ and $r_2=(t_0,t_1,t_2,...)$ are two runs of $\mathcal{A}_1$ on input $x = a_1a_2a_3...$,
and r_1,r_2 "intersect" after having read the same finite prefix of x (technically, $\exists k\ s_k = t_k$),
Then r_1,r_2 coincide up to the point of intersection (technically, $\forall j \leq k\ s_j = t_j$).

This theorem follows from the structure of the tableau:

3.2 Lemma. If s_1,s_2,t are nodes of $\mathcal{T}$ such that s_1,s_2 are both immediate predecessors of t, and AtomicPropositions(s_1) = AtomicPropositions(s_2),
Then $s_1 = s_2$.

Proof. We argue by induction on the structure of formulas in s_1,s_2 that $p' \in s_1$ iff $p' \in s_2$, for all $p' \in EFL(p_0)$. The basis case of atomic propositions follows directly by assumption.
Suppose $p' \in s_1$. If $p' = \neg p$ then $p \notin s_1$. By induction hypothesis, $p \notin s_2$. So $\neg p \in s_2$ by maximality.
If $p' = p \wedge q \in s_1$ then consistency of s_1 implies $p,q \in s_1$. By induction hypothesis, $p,q \in s_2$ so, again, by consistency $p \wedge q \in s_2$.
If $p' = Xp \in s_1$ then, by definition of the tableau, $p \in t$ and so $Xp \in s_2$.
Finally suppose $p' = (p \text{ U } q) \in s_1$. By consistency, either $q \in s_1$ or $p, X(p \text{ U } q) \in s_1$. If $q \in s_1$ then, by induction hypothesis, $q \in s_2$, so consistency implies $p \text{ U } q \in s_2$ also. If $p, X(p \text{ U } q) \in s_1$ then by induction hypothesis, $p \in s_2$. By definition of the tableau, $(p \text{ U } q) \in t$ and also $X(p \text{ U } q) \in s_2$. By consistency then, $(p \text{ U } q) \in s_2$.

We just showed that $p' \in s_1$ implies $p' \in s_2$. By symmetry, $p' \in s_1$ iff $p' \in s_2$. □

Given a Buchi nfa $\mathcal{A}_1$ for linear time formula $p_0' = \neg p_0$ with $N = \exp(|p_0'|) = \exp(|p_0|)$ states, we will show in the next section how to construct an equivalent deterministic pairs automaton $\mathcal{A}^*$ of size ($\exp(N^2)$ states, N^2 pairs). Since $\mathcal{A}^*$ is deterministic and $\mathcal{A}^*$ accepts x iff $x \models \neg p_0$, we may view $\mathcal{A}^*$ as a deterministic *complemented* pairs automaton which accepts x iff $x \models p_0$. This, in turn, allows us to construct the desired tree automaton for Ap_0.

4. How to Determinize the Buchi Automaton

4.1 The Run Tree. The set of all runs of the nondeterministic Buchi automaton $\mathcal{A}_1$ on input x may be viewed as an infinite Directed Acyclic Graph (DAG) of width $\leq N = \exp(|p_0|)$ where the nodes on level i of the DAG represent the possible states $\mathcal{A}_1$ could be in after having read the first i symbols of x. Since by Theorem 3.1 no two runs on x can merge, it is actually a tree. However, a run can *dead end*, (e.g. if $\neg Fp \in$ a node on level i and p appears in $i+1^{st}$ input symbol). Observe that, while there may be an infinite number of runs in this tree, there are at most N distinct runs of infinite length; the rest are finite.

In the sequel, we will say that a *P-node* of the run tree is one corresponding to a state of $\mathcal{A}_1$ where $\mathcal{A}_1$'s GREEN light flashes.

4.2 Intuition. The dfa $\mathcal{A}^*$ is based on the *subset construction* - it builds the tree of all runs on input x, a level at a time - plus some machinery to do, roughly, a *depth first search* of the run tree looking for an infinite run along which there are infinitely many P-nodes. The problem is complicated by the possibility that there may be infinitely many P-nodes in the run tree but only a finite number of them on any one path. Up to N markers are used in order to follow each active run. Associated with each marker i are N pairs of lights: $<i,0>,\ldots<i,N-1>$. There are thus a total of N^2 pairs of lights. The need for multiple pairs of lights per marker is explained subsequently.

Intuitively, $\mathcal{A}^*$ operates as follows. As each symbol of x is read, the next level of the run tree is built from the current level which will shortly become the new current level. (Only two levels are kept in memory at one time.) Each state of the current level is the tip of an active run which is associated with some marker i. Note that some runs split apart and others die out. Whenever (the) run (associated with marker) i splits, one alternative is followed by marker i and the other alternatives are assigned "free" (i.e., currently unused) markers $j_1 \ldots j_k$. We then say that the runs just started up, $j_1,\ldots,j_k$, spawn off run i. When and if run i dies, its marker becomes free for use with another run that may later start up. Since there are at most N active runs at any level, the N markers can be re-cycled indefinitely so that each active run is always assigned a marker.

We want each marker i to follow an infinite run if possible. However, run i may split apart many (even infinitely many) times. Some branches may be infinite and others finite. How does $\mathcal{A}^*$ know which of the alternatives is infinite and should be followed? If there were a way for $\mathcal{A}^*$ to know this, one pair of lights per run would suffice. For we could then simply have, for each run i, the pair of lights $<i,0>$ flash GREEN whenever marker i encountered a P-node and flash RED whenever run i encountered a dead end. See Figure 4.1. (The RED flashes are needed to ensure that an infinite number of "non-collinear" P-nodes do not cause erroneous acceptance.)

However, there is in general no way for $\mathcal{A}^*$ to know which alternatives to follow because

Note: In these figures, ● denotes a P-node.

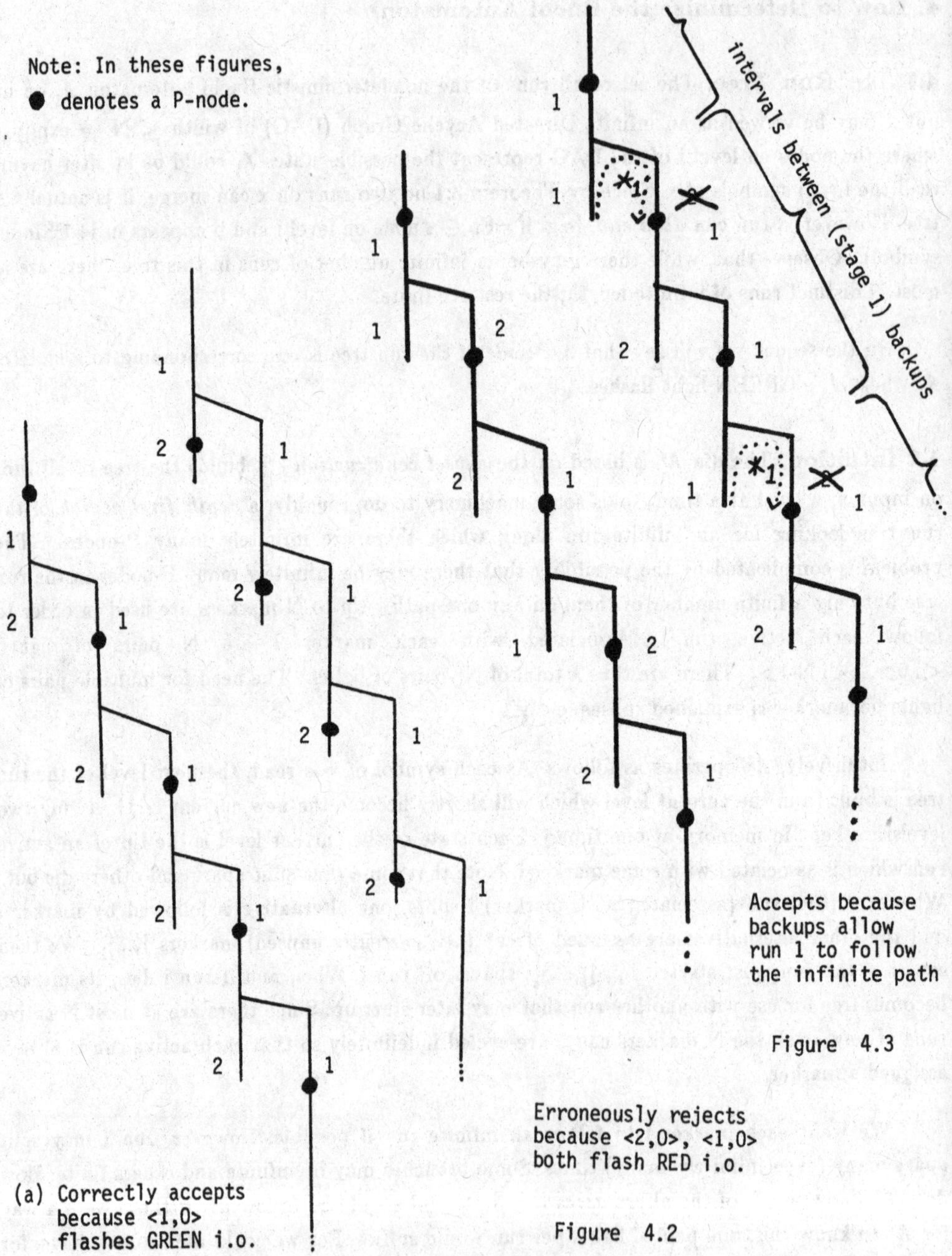

Accepts because backups allow run 1 to follow the infinite path

Figure 4.3

Erroneously rejects because <2,0>, <1,0> both flash RED i.o.

Figure 4.2

(a) Correctly accepts because <1,0> flashes GREEN i.o.

(b) Correctly rejects because <2,0> flashes RED i.o.

Figure 4.1

this depends on the suffix of the input yet to be read: one suffix might make alternative A infinite and alternative B finite while another suffix might do the opposite. Since $\mathcal{A}^*$ is deterministic, on some inputs it may repeatedly make poor decisions in which case the above rules can lead to false results. For example, in Figure 4.2, $\mathcal{A}^*$ erroneously rejects because both $\langle 1,0 \rangle$ and $\langle 2,0 \rangle$ flash RED as well as GREEN i.o. .

The problem is that the single infinite path in the run tree has been parsed into infinitely many finite pieces rather than a single infinite piece. The solution is to have any run i which dead ends *backup* - but as little as possible - by taking over the "youngest" surviving run j which previously spawned off i. For example, in Figure 4.3 because "father" run 1 is older than its "son" run 2 (it was "born" earlier), when run 1 dead ends it takes over its youngest son, run 2. The rules for the backup (which are described in detail subsequently) require that $\mathcal{A}^*$ flash RED on pair $\langle 2,0 \rangle$, $\langle 2,1 \rangle$ since run 2 is totally obliterated when run 1 takes it over. $\mathcal{A}^*$ also flashes RED on the pair $\langle 1,0 \rangle$. This ensures that $\mathcal{A}^*$ will not falsely accept due to GREEN flashes on $\langle 1,0 \rangle$ caused by non-collinear P-nodes detected by run 1 prior to backups. Then, $\mathcal{A}^*$ flashes GREEN on the pair $\langle 1,1 \rangle$ iff a P-node has been seen on the finite path from the site of the previous backup of run 1 to the site of the current backup (indicated by *'s).

For simplicity, assume that the width, N, of the run tree is at most 2. Then for any input x, one of two situations obtains:

(1) After a certain depth, $\mathcal{A}^*$ always makes "good" decisions and run 1 never again has to backup. Then pair $\langle 1,0 \rangle$ will never again flash RED. It will flash GREEN i.o. iff $\overset{\infty}{\exists}$ P-nodes along the run 1.

(2) $\mathcal{A}^*$ makes infinitely many "poor" decisions so that run 1 backs up i.o. in which case $\langle 1,0 \rangle$ flashes RED i.o. Then $\overset{\infty}{\exists}$ P-nodes along run 1 iff $\overset{\infty}{\exists}$ GREEN flashes of $\langle 1,1 \rangle$.

In general, we may have N pairs of lights and associated *stages* of backups for each marker i. By convention, when marker i is pushed from a node to a successor node without any actual backup we have a stage 0 backup of run i. P-nodes detected in this way are "recorded" via GREEN flashes of $\langle i,0 \rangle$. In general, a backup of run i is of stage m when the highest stage of previous backups of run i which must be "undone" is m-1. See Figure 4.4. P-nodes detected by run i on the path between consecutive stage m backups are recorded via GREEN flashes of $\langle i,m \rangle$.

To perform these backups, $\mathcal{A}^*$ does not have to re-read portions of the input. Instead, $\mathcal{A}^*$ is able to remember enough information in various "flag bits" to "simulate" re-reading of input as needed. As it turns out, $0(N^2)$ bits of information suffice for the implementation of $\mathcal{A}^*$.

4.3 The Spawning Tree. The main "data structure" used in implementing $\mathcal{A}^*$ is the *spawning tree*. It is defined as follows:

1. There is one node, labelled i, for each active run i. Thus, there are at most N nodes.
2. If run i has spawned, in order, runs $j_1,\dots,j_k$ then node i has sons, in order from left to right, $j_k,\dots,j_1$. (Note: if two or more sons are spawned simultaneously, order them using some fixed convention.)

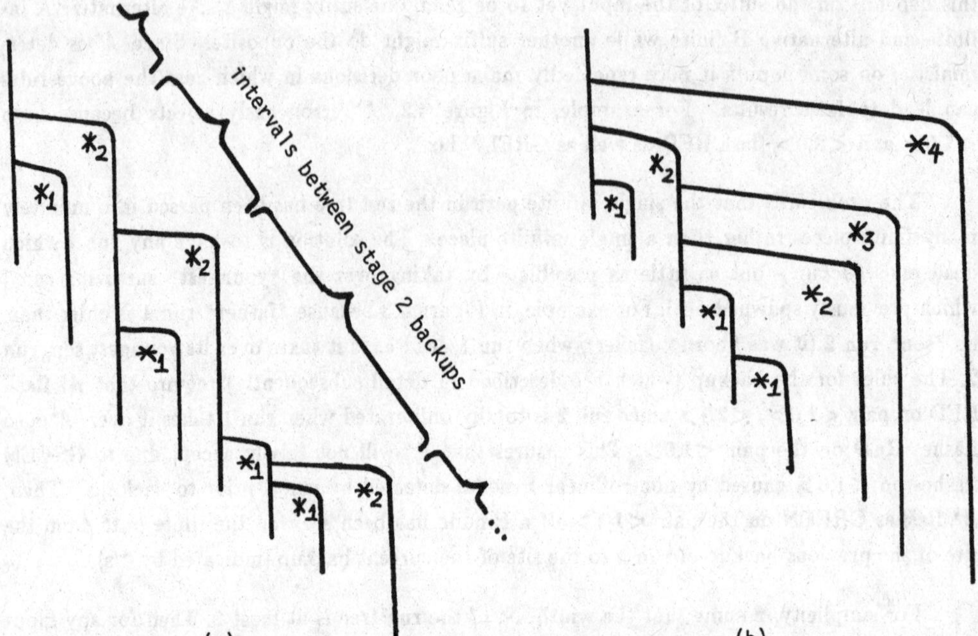

(a)

A path parsed by stage 2 backups

(b)

A stage 4 backup. Note nested stage 1, 2, 3 backups.

Figure 4.4

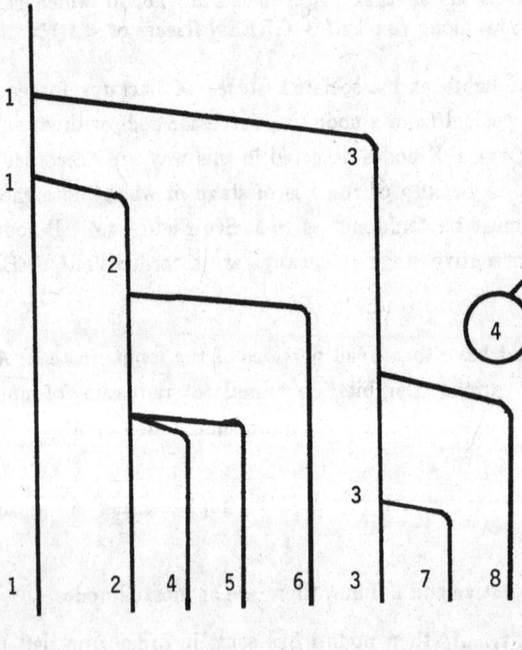

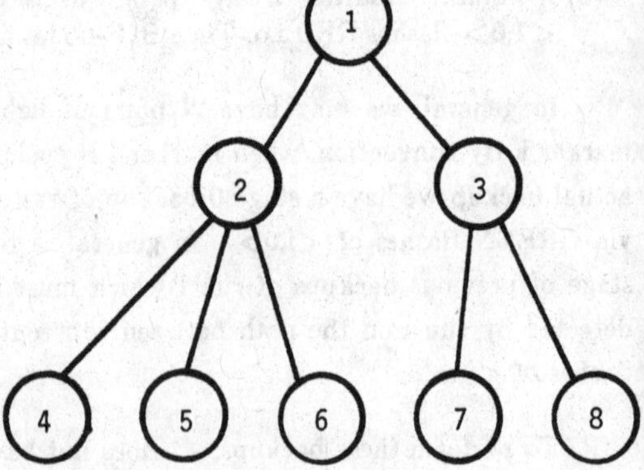

A run tree (at left) and its corresponding spawning tree (above).

Figure 4.5

3. Each node i is labelled with its *name* as well as

   a. birth[i] - a ***single bit*** = 1 iff a P-node has ever been seen along i since its birth

   b. bstage[i] - a ***O(log N bit)*** counter = m, the maximum of the stage numbers of the backups of h, the father run of i, which have occurred at descendents of the point where i spawned off from h.

   c. backup[i] - an ***array of N bits***: backup[i][k]=1 iff a P-node had been seen along i since its last stage k backup.

   d. fbirth[i] - a ***single bit*** = 1 iff, at the time i spawns off from its father h, h has seen a P-node since its birth.

   e. fbackup[i] - an ***array of N bits***: fbackup[i][k] = 1 iff, at the time i spawns off from its father h, h had seen a P-node since its last stage k backup.

   f. state[i] - a ***O(log N bit)*** counter = k iff the current state associated with run i is state k.

See Figure 4.5 for an example of the spawning tree and how it represents active runs. Note also that the spawning tree can be represented using $O(N^2)$ bits.

4.4 Implementation of the Deterministic Automaton.

```
Flash GREEN on <-,0> pairs with P-nodes:

for each active marker i
  if state[i] ⊨ P then flash GREEN on <i,0>
                  birth[i] := 1
                  backup[i] := (1,...,1)
end

Read input symbol
Pre-compute successor states of each current state associated with a node of
   the spawning tree.
In the spawning tree, cross-out all nodes corresponding to markers with no successor.

Backup as needed:

 Repeat the following until all crossed-out nodes are deleted.

  Find a topmost crossed-out node: i

  Pre-order walk the subtree rooted at i to try to find the first non-crossed-out node: j

  if j exists then
     Run j is the "youngest" surviving descendant run of i
     Let i backup and take over run j as described below

  if j does not exist then
     delete the entire subtree rooted at i from the spawning tree
     flash RED on <k,0>,...,<k,N-1> for all k in the subtree
```

```
    return all such k to the pool of available markers

End of repeat

(At this point, all remaining runs have ≥ 1 successors)

for each active run i
  if i has a single descendant, advance marker i to it

  if i has several descendants s_1,...,s_k then
    assign i to s_1
    assign "free" markers i_2,...,i_k to s_2,...,s_k, respectively
    for each i' ∈ {i_2,...,i_k}
      add i' as a leftmost son of i in the spawning tree
      let bstage[i'] := 0
      let fbackup[i'] := backup[i]
      let fbirth[i'] := birth[i]
    end
end
```

We now describe how to do a backup of run i. Refer to Figure 4.6 as needed. Suppose the current node, A, associated with marker i has no successors, there is a descendant run of i which survives beyond depth(A), and i is not taken over at this depth by a backup of an ancestor run. Let run j be the "youngest" (as determined above) descendant run of run i which survives beyond depth(A). Let the sequence of descendant runs of i that are ancestors of j be $i = k_0,k_1,...,k_l = j$. (Possibly, $l = 1$ so that $k_1 = j$; if $l > 1$ then runs $k_1,...,k_{l-1}$ dead end at depth(A) just as does run i). Run i will *take over* run j (as well as runs $k_1,...,k_{l-1}$) in a *backup of stage* $bs = 1 + \text{bstage}[k_1]$ by performing the actions numbered below.

Note that node B is the current node of run j, node C is the first node of run j, and node D is the deepest node of run i which has a descendent node (namely, some immediate successor of B) at a depth greater than depth(A). We say that, for this backup of run i, node A is the *dead point*, node B is the *advance point*, node C is the *backup point*, and node D is the *branch point*. We also say that the backup *occurs* at location node C at time depth(A).

(1) Flash RED on $\langle i,bs\text{-}1\rangle$, $\langle i,bs\text{-}2\rangle$,...,$\langle i,0\rangle$ since for each $m < bs$, the most recent previous stage m backup of run i has failed in that its backup point does not live on any infinite path.

(2) Flash RED on $\langle k,N\text{-}1\rangle$,...,$\langle k,0\rangle$ for each run k whose node is encountered in performing the preorder *walk* from (but not including) i to (and including) j in the spawning tree because each such run dies at depth(A). (Each of $k_1,...,k_l = j$ is such a k but there may be more.)

(3) Flash GREEN on $\langle i,bs\rangle$ iff fbackup[k_1][bs] (iff between the time of the previous stage bs backup of i and this new stage bs backup point, run i has seen a P-node; note that the new stage bs backup point is the first node of run k_1).

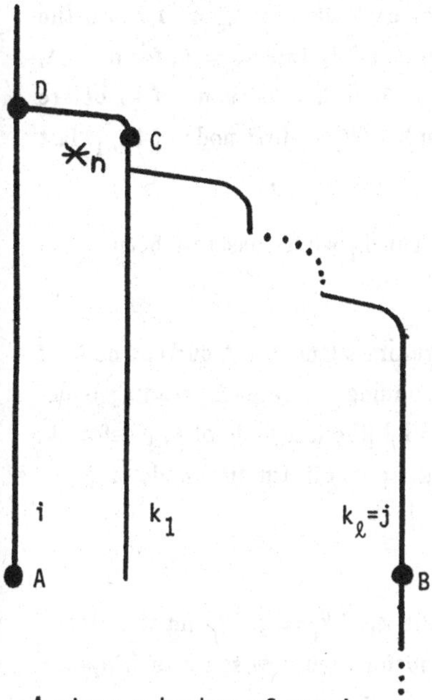

A stage n backup of run i

Figure 4.6

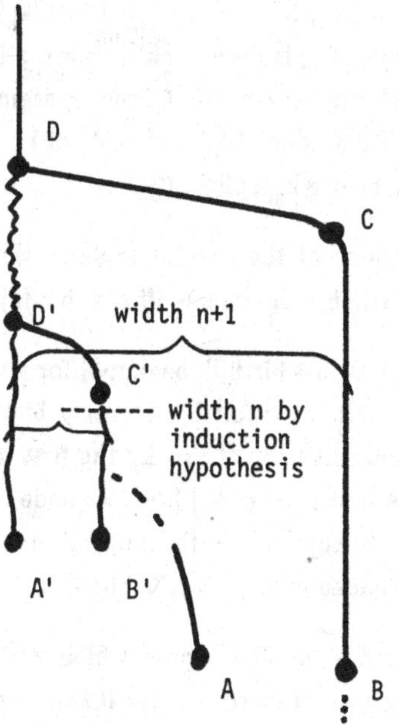

Figure 4.7

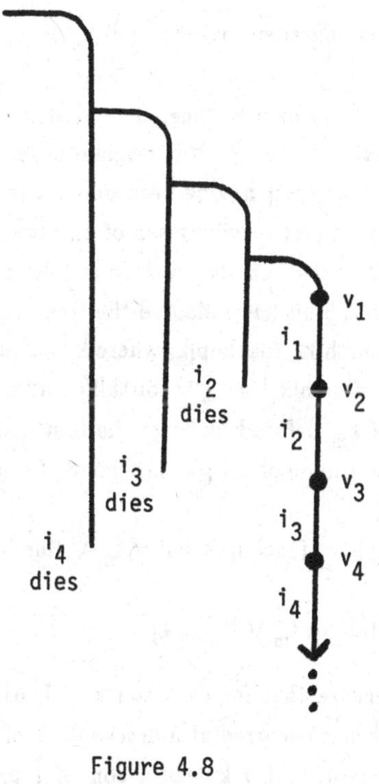

Figure 4.8

(4) For each $m \in [1:l]$, let $t_m := \bigvee_{n \in [2:m]} fbirth[k_n]$ so that for each such m, $t_m = 1$ iff on the path from where k_m is born back to run i, a P-node occurs. (Note that $t_1 = 0$; for $m > 1$, this path includes exactly the following segments [first node of k_1: last node of k_1 before k_2 splits off] [first node of k_2: last node of k_2 before k_3 splits off]... [first node of k_{m-1}: last node of k_{m-1} before k_m splits off]).

(5) Let run i resume at the current node of the run j = run k_l which has just been taken over: Flash GREEN on <i,0> iff $t_l \vee birth[j]$.

(6) We must now adjust birth[i], backup[i] for where run i resumes (the "old" current node of j, node B): $birth[i] := fbirth[k_1] \vee t_l \vee birth[j]$ corresponding to the path, reading backwards, [the current node of $j = k_l$: the first node of $j = k_l$] [the last node of k_{l-1} before k_l splits off: the first node of k_1] [the last node of i before k_1 splits off: the first node of i]
For $n \neq bs$, $backup[i][n] := fbackup[k_1][n] \vee t_l \vee birth[j]$
For $n = bs$, $backup[i][bs] := t_l \vee birth[j]$.

(7) Now i may get some new sons k which were sons of the $k_1,...,k_l = j$. We must collapse the spawning tree properly to install these new sons, and for each new son k of i, update fbirth[k], fbackup[k]:

for n := 1 to l
    add the oldest surviving son of k_n as a son of i
    ...
    add the youngest surviving son of k_n as a son of i
end

(When the above loop is done, the oldest group of sons of i will be those that were there originally, still present in their original order. The next oldest group of sons will be those of k_1, with the oldest having been added first, the youngest last. So the youngest son of i will be the youngest surviving son of k_l, provided it exists.)
Delete all the nodes on the *walk* from (but not including) i to (and including) j from the spawning tree. This has collapsed the tree and installed i's new sons k.
To adjust fbirth[k], fbackup[k] where k is a surviving son of k_m, $1 \leq m \leq l$:
$fbirth[k] := fbirth[k_1] \vee t_m \vee fbirth[k]$ corresponding to the path, reading backwards, [the last node of k_m before k is born: the first node of k_m] [the last node of k_{m-1} before k_m is born: the first node of k_1] [the last node of i before k_1 is born: the first node of i]
for $n \neq bs$,
$fbackup[k][n] := fbackup[k_1][n] \vee t_m \vee fbirth[k]$
for $n = bs$,
$fbackup[k][bs] := t_m \vee fbirth[k]$

(8) We must ensure that for each son k of i, bstage[k] = the maximum stage of backup of run i, which has occurred at a descendents of the point where k split off from i. If k is an older sibling of k_1 (so k was a son of i present before this backup), let bstage[k] =

max{bs, bstage[k]} to reflect the fact that i took over k_1 at a descendant of k via a stage bs backup. If k is a son just added to i, let bstage[k] = 0 to reflect that no backups of i have yet occurred below where k splits off from the "new, backup" i.

4.5 Correctness.

4.5.1 Proposition. If a stage n backup of run i occurs then (using the notation of Figure 4.5) we have the following:

(a) For each m < n, a stage m backup of i has previously occurred whose branch point is a descendant node of D.

(b) Each backup of run i that has previously occurred whose branch point is a descendant node of D is of stage m < n.

(c) Moreover, each such branch point lies on no infinite path.

(d) For some d, depth(C) ≤ d ≤ depth(A), the width of the run tree at depth d is at least n+1.

Proof. We can argue by induction on n. Recall that, by convention, a stage 0 backup means no actual backup at all. So for n = 0 parts (a)-(c) hold vacuously and (d) holds trivially.

Now, suppose a stage n>0 backup occurs. This means run i takes over $k_1,...,k_l=j$ and that bstage[k_1] = n - 1. By the way the algorithm maintains bstage[-], there has been a stage n-1 backup of i whose branch point is a descendant of D. By induction hypothesis, we see that for each m < n, there is a stage m backup's branch point at a descendant of D. This establishes (a). The truth of (b) also follows from the way bstage[-] is maintained: if there were previously a stage n or higher backup of i at a descendant of D, then bstage[k_1] > n - 1, a contradiction. To see that (c) is true, note that the algorithm is designed so that, for any backup, its branch point D" is the deepest ancestor node of its dead point A" which has any descendant node at depth greater than depth(A"). Finally, to establish (d) note that, by part (a), there is a stage n-1 backup whose branchpoint D' is a descendent of D. By induction hypothesis, there is a d' such that depth(C') ≤ d' ≤ depth(A') (where C' is the backup point, A' is the dead point of this stage n-1 backup) and the width at depth d' is at least n. Since the path from B up to C does not include any descendent nodes of D' accessed by the time of the stage n-1 backup, depth(C) = depth(D)+1 ≤ depth(D')+1 = depth(C'), and depth(A') ≤ depth(A), we have that depth(C) ≤ d' depth(A) and the width at depth d' is at least n+1. See Figure 4.7. □

4.5.2 Proposition. Every infinite run r is eventually assigned a marker i that follows it (allowing for backups) forever. This marker never has to make more than a stage N-1 backup to follow r.

Proof. Suppose r is an infinite run. After a certain depth, every node on r of greater depth lies on only 1 infinite run, namely r. (If this were not true, the width of the run tree would increase without bound.) Let v_1 be such a node. Now v_1 is assigned a marker, i_1. Since v_1 has a unique infinite path (the suffix of r starting at v_1) coming out of it, the only way i_1 will not follow r forever (allowing for backups) is if i_1 is taken over by an ancestor marker i_2. So either i_1 follows r forever after v_1, or i_1 is taken over by an ancestor i_2 at some node v_2. In the latter case, either i_2 follows r forever, or i_2 is taken over by an ancestor i_3 at some node v_3. Etc. This process must stop with some ancestor run i_j for $j \leq N$ because, otherwise, the width of the tree would exceed N. To see this, note that run i_2 started prior to run i_1 and continued down to depth(v_2) ($>$ depth(v_1)) where it takes over i_1. Similarly, i_3 started prior to i_2 and continues down to depth(v_3) ($>$ depth(v_2)) where it takes over i_2. Etc. When i_j takes over i_{j-1} the width at depth(v_1) must be at least j. So the process must stop by i_N. See Figure 4.8.

To see that a backup of stage $>$ N-1 is not required, observe that by part (a) of the previous Proposition, a backup of stage $>$ N-1 would imply that the width of the run tree was $>$ N. □

4.5.3 Proposition. Suppose that, for run i,

(1) At time t there is a stage n backup with backup point C,

(2) At time t' $>$ t there is a stage m backup with backup point C',

(3) For every backup occurring at time $t^* \in (t{:}t')$, the backup point C^* is a descendent of C, and

(4) $m \leq n$

Then C' is a descendent of C.

Proof. Suppose (1),(2),(3) hold. Immediately prior to the time t' backup, run i is a line segment of the form (first node of i):C:A' where A' is the dead point of the t' backup. Thus branch point D' is either an ancestor of C or a descendent of C. If D' is an ancestor of C then $m > n$ by the way backup stages are computed. Now if (4) holds so that $m \leq n$, then D' (and C') must be a descendent of C. □

4.5.4 Theorem. For any input x,

$\exists$ a run r of $\mathcal{A}_1$ along which $\overset{\infty}{\exists}$ P-nodes iff
$\exists$ a pair $<i,j>$ of $\mathcal{A}^*$ which flashes GREEN i.o. and RED f.o. .

Proof. ($\Rightarrow$:) By proposition 4.5.2, any infinite run r in the run tree of $\mathcal{A}_1$ on an input x, will eventually be assigned, by $\mathcal{A}^*$, a marker i, which it keeps forever allowing for backups of i. After that point, we consider run r parsed by the backups of marker i. We have the following cases:

$\overset{\infty}{\exists}$ stage N-1 backups of i along r or

$\neg\overset{\infty}{\exists}$ stage N-1 backups of i along r and $\overset{\infty}{\exists}$ stage N-2 backups of i along r or ...

$\neg\overset{\infty}{\exists}$ stage N-1 backups, $\neg\overset{\infty}{\exists}$ stage N-2 backups,..., and $\neg\overset{\infty}{\exists}$ stage 1 backups of i along r.

If the last case obtains, then there are only finitely many backups of any stage of marker i as it follows the path r. After the last backup, marker i is always pushed forward directly to the next node of r, and <i,0> flashes GREEN every time a new P-node is encountered on r. If there are infinitely many such P-nodes, then plainly <i,0> flashes GREEN i.o.; furthermore, after the last backup, <i,0> will never again flash RED so it flashes RED f.o. .

For the other cases, let j be the maximal j' such that $\overset{\infty}{\exists}$ stage j' backups of run i. Then for all j" ∈ (j:N), there are only finitely many stage j" backups of run i. So after some time, there will never again be a RED flash of the <i,j> pair. Consider the suffix of r after that time. It is parsed by the infinitely many stage j backups of i into infinitely many contiguous segments. Infinitely many of these segments will contain P-nodes iff $\overset{\infty}{\exists}$ P-nodes along r. Hence, at infinitely many of the stage j backups, a P-node will be detected in the segment from the previous to the current backup point. Accordingly, the pair <i,j> will flash GREEN each such time and hence i.o. .

(⇐:) When j=0 we note that if <i,0> flashes GREEN i.o., RED f.o., then (by construction of $\mathcal{A}^*$) the marker i never backs up after the last RED flash. So at a certain node, say v, in the run tree, marker i is assigned and is thereafter always pushed forward without backing up. Since there are infinitely many GREEN flashes, (by construction of the $\mathcal{A}^*$) there is an infinite path r' starting at v followed by marker i with no backups which has infinitely many P-nodes along it. Since there is a finite path r from the root to v, r ∘ r' is the desired infinite run with infinitely many P-nodes along it.

Otherwise assume j > 0 and <i,j> flashes GREEN i.o., RED f.o. That there is a last RED flash of <i,j> means that there are no more backups taken by marker i of stage j' > j. Consider the GREEN flashes occurring after the last RED flash of <i,j>. For each n, at the nth such GREEN flash of <i,j>, marker i backs up (via a stage j backup) with a backup point that is some node v_n. After being assigned to node v_n, marker i is never taken over by an ancestor marker i' (because if it were, <i,j> would again flash RED). For each n, v_{n+1} is a descendant of v_n (because it is reached from v_n without any backups of stage j' > j and repeatedly applying Proposition 4.5.3) and there is a P-node on the finite path from v_n to v_{n+1}. Let r be the finite path from the root to v_1. Then r ∘ $(v_1,v_2,v_3,...)$ is the desired infinite run along which there are infinitely many P-nodes. □

5. Bibliography

[AB80] Abrahamson, K., Decidability and Expressiveness of Logics of Processes, PhD Thesis, Univ. of Washington, 1980.

[BMP81] Ben-Ari, M., Manna, Z., and Pnueli, A., The Temporal Logic of Branching Time. 8th Annual ACM Symp. on Principles of Programming Languages, 1981.

[CE81] Clarke, E. M., and Emerson, E. A., Design and Synthesis of Synchronization

Skeletons using Branching Time Temporal Logic, Proceedings of the IBM Workshop on Logics of Programs, Springer-Verlag Lecture Notes in Computer Science #131, 1981.

[CES83] Clarke, E. M., Emerson, E. A., and Sistla, A. P., Automatic Verification of Finite State Concurrent Programs: A Practical Approach, POPL83.

[EC82] Emerson, E. A., and Clarke, E. M., Using Branching Time Logic to Synthesize Synchronization Skeletons, Tech. Report TR-208, Univ. of Texas, 1982. (to appear in SCP)

[EH82] Emerson, E. A., and Halpern, J. Y., Decision Procedures and Expressiveness in the Temporal Logic of Branching Time. 14th Annual ACM Symp. on Theory of Computing, 1982.

[EH83] Emerson, E. A., and Halpern, J. Y., 'Sometimes' and 'Not Never' Revisited: On Branching versus Linear Time. POPL83.

[EM81] Emerson, E. A., Alternative Semantics for Temporal Logics, Tech. Report TR-182, Univ. of Texas, 1981. (To appear in TCS)

[FL79] Fischer, M. J., and Ladner, R. E, Propositional Dynamic Logic of Regular Programs, JCSS vol. 18, pp. 194-211, 1979.

[GPSS8O] Gabbay, D., Pnueli, A., *et al.*, The Temporal Analysis of Fairness. 7th Annual ACM Symp. on Principles of Programming Languages, 1980.

[LA8O] Lamport, L., "Sometimes" is Sometimes "Not Never." 7th Annual ACM Symp. on Principles of Programming Languages, 1980.

[MC66] McNaughton, R., Testing and Generating Infinite Sequences by a Finite Automaton, Information and Control, vol. 9, 1966.

[PN77] Pnueli, A., The Temporal Logic of Programs, 19th Annual Symp. on Foundations of Computer Science, 1977.

[PN81] Pnueli, A., The Temporal Logic of Concurrent Programs, Theoretical Computer Science, V13, pp. 45-60, 1981.

[PS83] Pnueli, A. and Sherman, R., Personal Communication, 1983.

[RA69] Rabin, M., Decidability of Second order Theories and Automata on Infinite Trees, Trans. Amer. Math. Society, vol. 141, pp. 1-35, 1969.

[RA70] Rabin, M., Automata on Infinite Trees and the Synthesis Problem, Hebrew Univ., Tech. Report no. 37, 1970.

[ST81] Streett, R., Propositional Dynamic Logic of Looping and Converse (PhD Thesis), MIT Lab for Computer Science, TR-263, 1981. (a short version appears in STOC81)

[Wo82] Wolper, P., A Translation from Full Branching Time Temporal Logic to One Letter Propositional Dynamic Logic with Looping, unpublished manuscript, 1982.

[VW82] Vardi, M., and Wolper, P., Yet Another Process Logic, this workshop, 1983.

EQUATIONS IN COMBINATORY ALGEBRAS

Erwin Engeler
ETH Zurich

1. The reduction of algorithmic problems to combinatorial equations

The algorithmic problems we have in mind are not decision problems such as: does x have property F ? Rather, we think of problems of the form: Find x such that $F(x)$. The latter is one of the archetypes of mathematical activities and, to obtain a realistic analysis, it is perhaps best to orient ourselves on classical examples of problems and solutions to visualize the spectrum of notions involved.

To fix ideas, consider the similarity type of relational structures $\underline{A} = \langle A,R,f,c\rangle$ with relation R, operation f, constant c, and let Γ be an axiom system specifying the actual class of models we have in mind.

Algebraic problems in Γ would be posed by equations of the form $t_1(x) = t_2(x)$, $t_1(x) = x$, $t_1(x) = c$, where t_1,t_2 are terms in the language of Γ. To solve the problem in $\underline{A}$ means to exhibit an element $a \in A$ which satisfies the equation in $\underline{A}$, to solve it explicitly means to describe a as a constant term in the language of Γ. Note that this term may be considered as a straight-line program using only assignments of the form $x_i := f(x_j,x_k)$. Some algebraic problems are only solved in extensions of the original structure, e.g. $x^2 = 2$ is not solvable in $\mathbb{Q}$ but only in $\mathbb{Q}(\sqrt{2})$. In this case, to solve the problem means to generate information about $\sqrt{2}$, e.g. $1 < \sqrt{2} < 2$, but also to be able to manipulate $\sqrt{2}$, at the least be able to perform the field operations involving $\sqrt{2}$. Thus, the solution $\sqrt{2}$ in a sense consists of a set X of formulas, and to manipulate $\sqrt{2}$ would mean to manipulate X . Before we make this any more definite, consider another type of problems.

Basic problems in Γ would be posed by basic, i.e. quantifier-free first-order, formulas $F(x)$ of the language of Γ . Classical examples are provided by elementary geometry. Take a geometry with two sorts, lines and points, and ask for the foci of a conic section given by five points. The theory of geometrical constructions with ruler and compass illustrate the notion of an algorithmic solution: it consists of exhibiting a program which constructs (using instructions corresponding to the construction tools) the required points. This can in the present case be done by a loop-free program, i.e. we are close to the case of explicit solution. But let us imagine a geometry of points and circles as sorts and ask for the angular bisector of two given lines. It can be shown, that all solution programs must contain a loop. Thus, if we identify "solution" with "solution program", the concept of algorithmic solution should incorporate a sufficiently large class of programs. As in the case of $\sqrt{2}$, there are classical examples of basic problems in geometry which have no solution in some given model (trisection of angles). Again, the solution would be a set X (of properties of the solution line), and would be algorithmic, if the solution program generated X and if it allowed to manipulate X in some manner associated to the relations and operations of the theory.

Algorithmic problems arise also in elementary geometry, the most celebrated one is the quadrature of the circle: We ask for a line segment, whose length is equal to the circumference of a given circle. This is not a basic problem (nor is it elementary, i.e. posed by a first-order formula of elementary geometry). But it can very easily be posed by a program (ruler and compass), which tests, whether the proposed line segment is indeed a solution: it does not terminate iff the line segment is a solution. Again, there is no explicit, but only an algorithmic solution to the problem.

The first purpose is now to create a framework, in which the common denominator of the above examples can be precisely formulated. The main new idea is that algorithms and algorithmic properties of structures should be included in the consideration of problems and solutions. We propose to do this by suitably enlarging the set of objects of the theory, concretely: to show that graph models of combinatory logic can serve as the basic structure in which the envisioned class of problems can be reformulated as equations.

Let A be any non-empty set. Consider the set $G(A)$ defined recursively by

$$G_0(A) = A$$

$$G_{n+1}(A) = G_n(A) \cup \left\{(\alpha \to b) : \alpha \subseteq G_n(A),\ \alpha \text{ finite},\ b \in G_n(A)\right\}$$

$$G(A) = \bigcup_n G_n(A)$$

Graph algebras over A are constructed as sets of subsets of $G(A)$ closed under the following binary operation

$$M \cdot N = \left\{b : \exists \alpha \subseteq N \cdot (\alpha \to b) \in M\right\} .$$

We now illustrate how graph algebras arise as formal counterparts to relational structures by associating to the field $\underline{\mathbb{Q}}$ its <u>state field</u> $\underline{\mathbb{Q}}^s$. For this purpose, let A be the set of all quantifier-free formulas of the first-order language of the field $\underline{\mathbb{Q}} = \langle \mathbb{Q},+,\cdot,-,^{-1},0,1,\leq \rangle$.

(a) The state objects of $\underline{\mathbb{Q}}^s$ are exactly the subsets M of A for which there is an assignment of rational numbers to the variables occurring in M which satisfies all formulas in M.

(b) The state transformation objects of $\underline{\mathbb{Q}}^s$ are defined as follows $[x_i := x_j + x_k]$ consists of all $(\alpha \to b)$, where $\alpha \subseteq A$, $b \in A$ with the following properties: α is consistent with the theory Γ of $\underline{\mathbb{Q}}$; if $i \neq j,k$ and x,y,z do not occur in α or b and b' results from substituting x for x_i, y for x_j and z for x_k then b' is a consequence of Γ, α and the equations $x = x_j + x_k$, $y = x_j$, $z = x_k$; if $i = j$, say, then the equation $y = x_j$ is to be suppressed, similarly for $i = k$ and $i = j = k$.
The state transformers corresponding to the other instructions, $[x_i := x_j \cdot x_k]$, $[x_i := -x_j]$, $[x_i := x_j^{-1}]$ are defined in like manner.
The truth value objects are defined using the important auxilliary constructs

$$K = \left\{ \{\alpha\} \to (\phi \to a) \ : \ a \in G(A) \right\},$$

$$I = \left\{ \{\alpha\} \to a \ : \ a \in G(A) \right\},$$

$$\text{true} = K,$$

$$\text{false} = K \cdot I.$$

Then $[x_i \leq x_j]$ consists first of all $(\alpha \to b)$ where $\alpha \subseteq A$, $x_i \leq x_j$ is a consequence of Γ and α and

$b \in K$ = true and second of all $(\alpha \to c)$ where $x_j > x_i$ is a consequence of α and Γ and $c \in K \cdot I$ = false.

(c) Finally $\underline{\mathbb{Q}}^s$ is the graph algebra generated by the objects introduced in (a) and (b) above.

We observe that all the objects of $\underline{\mathbb{Q}}^s$ are recursively enumerable subsets of $G(A)$. Indeed the generators are, and if M and N are recursively enumerable then so is $M \cdot N$. Thus $\underline{\mathbb{Q}}^s$ forms what we would like to call a <u>computable graph algebra.</u>

A first extension of $\underline{\mathbb{Q}}^s$ is suggested by algebraic problems. It consists in the adjunction of the composition object B whose defining property is $BMNL = M(NL)$ for all $M,N,L \subseteq G(A)$. Such an object can easily be constructed for graph algebras, e.g.

$$B = \left\{(\alpha \to (\beta \to (\gamma \to a))) \ : \ a \in \alpha(\beta\gamma), \alpha, \beta, \gamma \subseteq G(A), \text{ finite}\right\} .$$

Indeed, as shown in [4], every object F given by a defining relation $F \cdot x_1 \cdot \ldots \cdot x_n = t(x_1, \ldots, x_n)$ where t is any combination of the x_i by means of $\cdot$ can be realized by a (recursively enumerable) set of elements of $G(A)$. Observe now, that any algebraic problem $p(x) = 0$ over $\underline{\mathbb{Q}}$ can be reformulated as an equation

$$P \cdot X = \text{true} ,$$

where P is composed of state transformers and B. In general, solutions X are not among the state objects of $\underline{\mathbb{Q}}^s$ since as state objects they should include the equation $x^2 = 0$ which is impossible in $\underline{\mathbb{Q}}$. However, algorithms such as Newton's method generate a set of nested intervals.

This generating process can be reformulated as one that generates the set $\left\{q_i < x < p_i \ : \ q_i, p_i \text{ the endpoints of the Newton intervals}\right\}$ which is a solution. Now, the algorithm underlying Newton's method employs program connectives other than composition, essentially a while loop. To mirror this construction algorithm by an object in a graph algebra we need to have an object $[\underline{\text{while}}] \subseteq G(A)$ with the appropriate properties. Newton's method then is realized in the graph algebra by a composite object [newton] with the property $P \cdot \left([\text{newton}] \cdot \{x^2 = 2\}\right) = \text{true}$ and $[\text{newton}] \cdot \{x^2 = 2\}$ contains a set of convergent nested intervals (as formulas $p_i < x < q_i$).

Observe, that we have created a sequence of adjunctions to $\mathbb{Q}^s$, viz. $\mathbb{Q}^s \subseteq \mathbb{Q}^s(B) \subseteq \mathbb{Q}^s\left(B, \{x^2 = 2\}, [\underline{\text{while}}]\right)$ which not only let us encompass new solutions but also new problems, in fact algorithmic problems of the kind envisioned above.

There are a number of obvious questions that arise here. First, clearly, the state field approach to computing is one that has the promise of actual realization on the computer. This has in part been accomplished by Fehlmann [5], [6] who has written a system CONCAT which takes a large sublanguage of PASCAL, translates its programs into graph-algebra objects and performs the PASCAL computations with such objects. The effect of this method is to obtain (from PASCAL algorithms that are correct only for infinitely exact reals) a corresponding graph-algebra computation which is correct to any desired accuracy.

Second, our approach gives a new point of view in the logic of programs. Indeed, it is of considerable interest to investigate the definitional power of program connectives.

This translates here into the algebraic question of comparing extensions of $\underline{\mathfrak{Q}}^s$ by B, [<u>while</u>] and other objects corresponding to program connectives; e.g. whether [<u>recursion</u>] would give a proper extension of $\underline{\mathfrak{Q}}^s$(B, [<u>while</u>]), and whether such answers depend, and how, on the original state structure, (here $\underline{\mathfrak{Q}}^s$). Some such effects are well known.

Third, there now arise quite general questions of the following nature: Let $\underline{B}$ be any graph algebra and let $t_1(x) = t_2(x)$ be an equation. Can this equation be solved (in some extension of) $\underline{B}$ and if so, by what means can the graph-algebra object x be obtained? The remainder of this paper addresses itself to some aspects of this question in a more abstract setting.

2. Algebraic extensions of graph algebras

It is well-known (see e.g. [4]) that the graph algebra consisting of all subsets of G(A) constitutes a <u>combinatory algebra,</u> i.e. there are subsets $S,K \subseteq G(A)$ such that $Kxy = x$, $Sxyz = xy(xz)$ for all $x,y,z \subseteq G(A)$. Indeed, one can also find $L \subseteq G(A)$ such that $(L\cdot x)\cdot y = x\cdot y$ and $\forall z(x\cdot z = y\cdot z). \supset L\cdot x = L\cdot y$, which makes it a <u>combinatory model,</u> (even a <u>stable</u> one, by managing $L\cdot L = L$). As we have seen in the first section of this paper, some mathematically and computationally interesting structures can be realized as subalgebras of such combinatory models. Indeed, as has also been shown in [4], every algebraic structure can be isomorphically embedded in an appropriate combinatory model.

Taking into account this embeddability, we now consider the question of solving algebraic equations in the richer context of combinatory algebras, specifically the above so-called graph models. Let therefore $X_1,\ldots,X_m$ be variables, $A_1,\ldots,A_k$ be constants denoting elements of $\underline{G(A)}$, i.e. subsets of $G(A)$. The problem to be solved is presented by one or more equations in the "unknowns" X_i and "parameters" A_i , written in the form $t_j(X_1,\ldots,X_m) = t'_j(X_1,\ldots,X_m)$, where the t_j, t'_j are composed by the binary operation of our structure $\underline{G(A)}$. A is assumed countable.

For convenience, and without loss of generality, we consider instead of $G(A)$ the following set L of "lists". The set L is obtained as a set of syntactical terms constructed by means of a binary syntactical operation c and unary operations $f_1,\ldots,f_n$ as follows: The empty list O is a list. If u and v are lists, then $c(u,v)$ and $f_1(u),\ldots,f_n(u)$ are lists.

If M is any set of lists and u is a list, we define $u \leqq M$ recursively by:

(a) $O \leqq M$.

(b) $c(u,v) \leqq M$ iff $u \in M$ and $v \leqq M$.

With this notation we introduce the application of the combinatory algebra $\underline{L}$ (which consists of subsets of L) by:

$$M \cdot N = \left\{u : \exists v.\ c(u,v) \in M \wedge v \leqq N\right\} .$$

We are now ready to state the main result of this paper. Let $A_1,\dots,A_k$ be recursively enumerable subsets of L, let E be a set of equations with parameters A_i and unknowns $X_1,\dots,X_m$, where length(E) $\leqq n$, the number of unary syntactical operations f_i. A solution of E consists of sets $A'_1,\dots,A'_k$, $X'_1,\dots,X'_m$ with $A'_i \supseteq A_i$ such that E is satisfied.

THEOREM. If E is solvable, then E has a recursively enumerable solution.

The proof of the above theorem is an application of logic programming, (see e.g. [2],[3],[7]). This framework allows us to state the recursive enumeration of the parameter sets A_i and the solution conditions of E conveniently as a set of (universal) first-order formulas. Our use of logic programming may be formulated as the following lemma.

LEMMA. Let $W \subseteqq L$ be recursively enumerable. Then there exist predicate symbols $P_1,\dots,P_m$, W, and a quantifier-free conjunction of positive Horn formulas, ϕ_W, such that for all $w \in L$: $\forall\vec{x}\ \phi_W(x) \wedge \neg W(w)$ is inconsistent iff $w \in W$. □

(Recall that for atomic formulas α_i, β we call $\neg\alpha$ a negative, and $\alpha_1 \wedge \dots \wedge \alpha \supset \beta$ and α_i positive Horn formulas). By Herbrand's theorem, we have:

COROLLARY. $w \in W$ iff there exists n and $\vec{u}_1,\dots,\vec{u}_n$ in L such that $\bigwedge_{i=1}^{n} \phi_W(\vec{u}_i) \wedge \neg W(w)$ is inconsistent, i.e. iff $W(w)$ is provable from $\phi_W(\vec{u}_1),\dots,\phi_W(\vec{u}_n)$ in propositional logic.

Logic programming consists in essence of a systematic way of generating terms (here "lists") and substituting them in sets of copies of the set of clauses ϕ_W that constitutes the "logic program" for W. This is usually done by some refined methods of unification and resolution on which rest the practicability of the approach. We refer the reader to the literature cited above. We now sketch the proof of the theorem using the equation

$$A \cdot X = B \cdot (X \cdot C) \quad .$$

Let A, B, C be recursively enumerable sets of lists and let the corresponding formulas ("logic programs") be given as ϕ_A, ϕ_B and ϕ_C. To the conjunction of these formulas we add the following formulas, corresponding roughly to $D = A \cdot X$, $E = X \cdot C$, $F = B \cdot E$:

$$\begin{cases} A(c(x,y)) \wedge \overline{X}(y) . \supset D(x) , & D(x) \supset . \overline{X}(f_1(x)) \wedge A(c(x,f_1(x)) \\ \overline{X}(c(x,y)) . \equiv X(x) \wedge \overline{X}(y) , & \overline{X}(0) \end{cases}$$

$$\begin{cases} B(c(x,y)) \wedge \overline{E}(y) . \supset F(x) , & F(x) . \supset \overline{E}(f_2(x)) \wedge B(c(x,f_2(x)) \\ \overline{E}(c(x,y)) . \equiv E(x) \wedge \overline{E}(y) , & \overline{E}(0) \end{cases}$$

$$\begin{cases} X(c(x,y)) \wedge \overline{C}(y) . \supset E(x) , & E(x) \supset . \overline{C}(f_3(x)) \wedge X(c(x,f_3(x)) \\ \overline{C}(c(x,y)) . \equiv C(x) \wedge \overline{C}(y) , & \overline{C}(0) \end{cases}$$

The equation itself induces us to add conjunctively

$$\{ D(x) \equiv F(x) \quad .$$

Let $\psi(x,y)$ be the resulting formula.

The initial step of the algorithm that produces $X \subseteq L$ consists of refuting

$$\forall z\ \forall xy\Big(\psi(x,y) \wedge \neg X(z)\Big)$$

by a counterexample $X(w_1)$ (which is possible because we assume of course that the equation has a nontrivial solution).

In the k-th iteration step we first make sure that all of A,B,C are eventually taken in consideration. This is done by adding to ψ formulas $A(u_i')$, $B(u_i'')$, $C(u_i''')$ for the first k elements of A,B,C resepectively. We also add $X(w_1),\ldots,X(w_{k-1})$ for the w_i obtained at earlier steps. The resulting formula

$$\forall z\ \forall xy\Big(\psi(x,y) \wedge z \neq w_1 \wedge \ldots \wedge z \neq w_{k-1} \wedge \neg X(z)\Big)$$

is again provided with a counterexample (if one exists) otherwise, i.e. if the search for a counterexample does not succeed, we have already finished constructing our solution set X , because the set X of lists w_i for which the formula $X(w_i)$ is ever added to ψ solves the equation. Namely: let $A',B',\ldots$ be the sets of $v \in L$ for which $A(v)$, $B(v)$, ... can be proved from ψ at some stage of the algorithm. Then, by construction, $A' \cdot X = D'$, etc., hence $A' \cdot X = B' \cdot (X' \cdot C')$ as claimed.

<u>Remarks</u>

1. For some parameter values A_i it is possible to restrict A_i' to equal A_i , e.g. for the combinators K , L and S . At the time of this writing we are not yet able to determine a general criterion for this behaviour.

2. In $\underline{L}$ it is possible to reduce finite sets of equations to a normal form as follows:

LEMMA. Let E be a finite set of equations of the form

$$y_1 \ldots y_n.\ t_i(A_1,\ldots,A_k,X_1,\ldots,X_m,y_1,\ldots,y_n) = t_i'(A_1,\ldots,y_n)$$

with parameters $A_i \subseteq L$, recursively enumerable, unknowns X_i and variables y_i. Then there are recursively enumerable sets $A,B \subseteq L$ such that solving E is equivalent to solving the single equation $A \cdot Z = B \cdot Z$ for Z. □

3. The present approach to models of combinatory logic owes much to the pioneering work of Plotkin [10], Scott (e.g. [11]), Meyer [9], Longo [8] and Barendregt (e.g. [1]) and to conversations with these authors.

References

[1] Barendregt, H., Lambda Calculus and its Models. To appear in the proceedings of the Logic Colloquium'82, Florence, Italy.

[2] Clark, K.L. and Tärnlund, S.-A. (editors), Logic Programming. Academic Press, 1982.

[3] Clocksin, W.F. and Mellish, C.S., Programming in Prolog. Springer-Verlag, 1981.

[4] Engeler, E., Algebras and Combinators. Algebra Universalis 13 (1981), 389-392.

[5] Fehlmann, T., Theorie und Anwendung des Graphmodells der kombinatorischen Logik. Berichte des Instituts für Informatik, ETH Zürich, Nr. 41, 1981.

[6] Fehlmann, T., Concat Reference Manual and Implementation Notes. ETH Zürich, 1981, 48 pp.

[7] Kowalski, R.A., Logic for Problem Solving. North-Holland Publ. Co., 1979.

[8] Longo, G., Set-theoretical Models for the λ-calculus: Theories, Expansions, Isomorphisms. To appear in the Annals of Mathematical Logic.

[9] Meyer, A.R., What is a Model of the Lambda Calculus? Preprint MIT/LCS/TM-201, 1981.

[10] Plotkin, G.D., A Set-theoretical Definition of Application. Memorandum MIP-R-95, University of Edinburgh, 1972.

[11] Scott, D.S., Relating Theories of the λ-calculus. In: Essays on Combinatory Logic, Lambda Calculus and Formalism (to H.B. Curry), Seldin & Hindley, eds. Academic Press, New York, 1980, pp. 403-450.

Reasoning About Procedures as Parameters

S. M. German*
Harvard University

E. M. Clarke, Jr.
Carnegie-Mellon University

J. Y. Halpern
IBM Research, San Jose

1. Introduction

In [2] it was shown that for sufficiently complex Algol-like languages there cannot be a Hoare axiom system which is sound and relatively complete in the sense of Cook [4]. The incompleteness exists whenever a programming language contains (or can simulate) the following combination of features: (i) procedures with procedures passed as parameters, (ii) recursion, (iii) use of non-local variables, (iv) static scoping, and (v) local procedure declarations. Moreover, if any one of the features (i), (ii), (iv), or (v) is dropped from Algol, a sound and relatively complete axiomatization can be obtained for the resulting languages (called L2, L3, L5, and L6 in [2]). It has long been conjectured that the same is true for the language L4 which results when feature (iii), use of non-local variables, is dropped.

The languages L2, L3, L5, and L6 are relatively easy to axiomatize, since they all have the *finite range* property. Informally, this property is that for each program, there is a bound on the number of distinct procedure environments, or associations between procedure names and bodies, that can be reached. However, L4 does not have the finite range property. Intuition suggests that some new reasoning methods are needed for such programs. This intuition is supported by [9], where a precise characterization is given for the class of Hoare axiom systems based on copy rules, and it is shown that none of these axiom systems can deal adequately with infinite range.

The main new results in this paper are an axiom system for reasoning about programs with infinite range and a new technique for constructing relative completeness proofs for languages with procedure parameters. We also present a new way of formalizing the semantics of programs with free procedure names. Many of the techniques introduced in this paper are of general use beyond the immediate problem of the language L4. In the course of the relative completeness proof, we develop results of independent interest concerning the existence in general programming languages of *interpreter programs*; i.e., fixed programs capable of simulating any program in the language.

---

*Current Address: GTE Laboratories, Inc., 40 Sylvan Road, Waltham, Ma 02254

This research was supported by NSF Grant MCS-82-16706.

For a brief preview of our approach to reasoning about programs with infinite range, let us consider a small example of a formula in our logic. We retain the idea of using partial correctness assertions {U}S{V}, where U and V are first order, for specifying and reasoning about statements. To specify a procedure p with a procedure parameter r, we construct more complicated formulas containing partial correctness assertions, to describe how the semantics of r affects the semantics of p(r). For instance, let p be the procedure

proc p(x:r); **begin** r(x); r(x) **end**

which calls the formal procedure r twice on the variable parameter x. For an arithmetic domain, p satisfies the formula

$$\forall r,v(\{y=y_0\}\ r(y)\{y=y_0\cdot v\}\ \rightarrow\ \{x=x_0\}\ p(x:r)\ \{x=x_0\cdot v^2\})$$

Intuitively, this formula says that for all procedures r and domain values v, if the call r(y) multiplies y by v, then for the same procedure r and value v, the call p(x:r) multiplies x by v^2.

At this point, one might wonder whether this approach is sufficient to specify all procedures. Indeed, the essence of the relative completeness proof for our axiom system is that in L4, the necessary facts about procedures can always be expressed by an appropriate formula of our logic.

A different approach to axiomatizing procedures as parameters, based on the use of higher order logic in the assertion language, has been developed in [10, 5]. In both of these papers, the axiom system is assumed to include as axioms all of the formulae valid in a certain higher order theory related to the interpretation. In contrast, our axiom system includes as axioms only the first order theory of the interpretation. Also, in [10, 5], the notion of expressiveness used in establishing relative completeness takes a more general form, involving higher order formulas, while we use the familiar notion of expressiveness as in [4]. It has been conjectured that the two notions of expressiveness are equivalent; this problem is under study [6].

2. Programming Language

A statement has one of the forms:

<statement> ::= x := e | S_1; S_2 | **if** b **then** S_1 **else** S_2 | S_1 **or** S_2

| **begin var** x; S **end** | **begin** E; S **end** | $p(\bar{x}:\bar{r})$

The statement S_1 **or** S_2 makes a nondeterministic choice and executes one of the statements. In **begin** E; S **end**, E is a *procedure environment*; i.e., a set of *procedure declarations*. We sometimes abbreviate this as E | S. In $p(\bar{x}:\bar{r})$, $\bar{x}$ is a list of variable identifiers and $\bar{r}$ is a list of procedure identifiers. We often abbreviate **begin** E; S **end** to E | S.

A set of procedure declarations has the form

$$\text{proc } p_1(\bar{x}_1:\bar{r}_1);\ B_1$$
$$\vdots$$
$$\text{proc } p_m(\bar{x}_m:\bar{r}_m);\ B_m$$

and introduces possibly mutually recursive declarations of $p_1 \ldots p_m$. The p_i are called *declared procedure names*; the r_i are *formal procedure names*. B_i is the body of procedure p_i.

An occurrence of an identifier in a statement may be either *free* or *bound* in the usual sense. Note that we allow free procedure identifiers to appear in statements. A *program* A is a statement with no free procedures.

A declaration proc $p(\bar{x}:\bar{r})$; B is said to *have no global variables* if all the free variables of B are in $\bar{x}$. An environment (statement, program) has no global variables if all its declarations have no free variables. Note that such an environment (statement, program) *may* have free procedures.

We are primarily concerned with programs which have no global variables. For historical reasons [2] this language is often called L4. In L4, the only variables that can be accessed or changed by a procedure call are the actual variable parameters in the call. This property will help us to get a sound and relatively complete axiom system for L4.

3. Semantics of statements

Let I be a given first order interpretation. A program *state* is a mapping from the set of program variables to dom(I). The meaning of a statement is a binary relation on states. Given procedure environment E, we associate with each statement A its meaning in I and E via the function $\mathcal{M}_{I,E}$. We define $\mathcal{M}_{I,E}$ first for statements without procedure calls or procedure declarations by induction on structure of the statement:

$$\mathcal{M}_{I,E}(\text{error}) = \emptyset$$

$$\mathcal{M}_{I,E}(x:=e) = \{(s,s[I(e)/x]) \mid s \text{ is a state}\}$$

$$\mathcal{M}_{I,E}(A_1;A_2) = \{(s,s') \mid \exists\, t\,((s,t) \in \mathcal{M}_{I,E}(A_1) \text{ and } (t,s') \in \mathcal{M}_{I,E}(A_2))\}$$

$$\mathcal{M}_{I,E}(A_1 \text{ or } A_2) = \mathcal{M}_{I,E}(A_1) \cup \mathcal{M}_{I,E}(A_2)$$

$$\mathcal{M}_{I,E}(\text{if } b \text{ then } A_1 \text{ else } A_2) = \{(s,s') \in \mathcal{M}_{I,E}(A_1) \mid I,s \models b\} \cup \{(s,s') \in \mathcal{M}_{I,E}(A_2) \mid I,s \models \neg b\}$$

$$\mathcal{M}_{I,E}(\text{begin var } x;\ A \text{ end}) = \{(s,s') \mid \exists\, (u,u') \in \mathcal{M}_{I,E}(A),\ u = s[I(\underline{a}/x)],\ s' = u'[s(x)/x]\}$$

(where $\underline{a}$ is a fixed constant)

We give meaning to statements with procedure declarations and procedure calls by first converting them to statements without procedure declarations and calls, by using an auxiliary function Approx_E^k. Informally, Approx_E^k

gives the kth approximation to the fixed-point meaning of a recursively defined procedure in procedure environment E. We define $Approx_E^k$ by induction on k and the structure of statements:

1. $Approx_E^k$ (**error**) = **error**

2. $Approx_E^k$ (x:=e) = x:=e

3. $Approx_E^k$ $(A_1;A_2)$ = $Approx_E^k(A_1)$;$Approx_E^k(A_2)$

4. $Approx_E^k$ $(A_1$ **or** $A_2)$ = $Approx_E^k(A_1)$ **or** $Approx_E^k(A_2)$

5. $Approx_E^k$ (if b then A_1 else A_2) = if b then $Approx_E^k$ (A_1) else $Approx_E^k(A_2)$

6. $Approx_E^k$ (**begin var** x; A **end**) = **begin var** x; $Approx_E^k$(A) **end**

   renaming the bound variable x if it appears free in E (see below).

7. $Approx_E^k$ (E' | A) = $Approx_{E \cup E'}^k$ (A)

   renaming bound variables in E' if necessary (see below).

8. $Approx_E^k$ $(p(\bar{x}:\bar{q}))$ =

   error if k=0 and p is declared in E

   $Approx_E^{k-1}$ $([\bar{x}/\bar{x}', \bar{q}/\bar{q}']B)$if k > 0 and the declaration **proc** $p(\bar{x}':\bar{q}')$; B ∈ E

   E_k | $p(\bar{x}:\bar{q})$ otherwise, where E_k is defined below.

If E consists of the declarations **proc** $p_i(\bar{x}_i:\bar{r}_i)$; B_i, i=1, ..., n, then E_K consists of the declarations **proc** $p_i(\bar{x}_i:\bar{r}_i)$; $Approx_E^k(p_i(\bar{x}_i:\bar{r}_i))$. Note $Approx_E^k(p_i(\bar{x}_i:\bar{r}_i))$ = $Approx_E^{k-1}(B_i)$ if k > 0, so this inductive definition is indeed well defined.

In clause 6 if the bound variable x appears free in E, then we have to rename the x to some fresh variable x' to avoid capturing the free variable in E. Thus we would get

begin var x'; $Approx_E^{k-1}$([x'/x]A) **end**

Similarly, in clause 7, if some procedure identifier declared in E' already appears in E, we have to rename the identifiers in E' (and all their bound occurrences in A) to avoid naming conflicts.

Note that if A is a program, then $Approx_E^k(A)$ = $Approx_\emptyset^k$(A) (i.e., $Approx_E^k$(A) is independent of E), and $Approx_\emptyset^k$(A) does not contain any procedure declarations or procedure calls.

Given a procedure environment E and statement A, let E^A = E ∪ {$p(\bar{x}:\bar{r})$; **error** | p appears free in (E | A)}. Note $E^A|A$ is a program, since it has no free procedure identifiers. To complete our semantics, we define, for any statement A,

$$\mathcal{M}_{I,E}(A) = \cup_k \mathrm{Approx}^k_{\emptyset}(E^A|A)$$

We next define two statements A_1 and A_2 to be equivalent, written $A_1 \equiv A_2$, if $\mathcal{M}_{I,E}(A_1) = \mathcal{M}_{I,E}(A_2)$ for all interpretations I and procedure environments E. Similarly, we write $A_1 \leq A_2$ if $\mathcal{M}_{I,E}(A_1) \subseteq \mathcal{M}_{I,E}(A_2)$ for all interpretations I and procedure environments E.

The following lemma will be used throughout the paper.

Lemma 1:

(a) If $p(\bar{x}:\bar{r}); B \in E$, then

$$E \mid p(\bar{y}:\bar{s}) \equiv E \mid [\bar{x}/\bar{y}, \bar{r}/\bar{s}]B$$

(b) $E|A_1;A_2 \equiv (E|A_1);(E|A_2)$

(c) $E|A_1$ or $A_2 \equiv E|A_1$ or $E|A_2$

(d) E | **if** b **then** A_1 **else** $A_2 \equiv$ **if** b **then** $E|A_1$ **else** $E|A_2$

(e) If x does not appear free in A, then

E| **begin var** x; A **end** $\equiv$ **begin var** x; E|A **end**

(f) If E_1,E_2 do not contain distinct declarations for the same procedure identifier, then

$E_1|(E_2|A) \equiv (E_1 \cup E_2)|A$

(g) If none of the procedures declared in E appear free in A, then

$E|A \equiv A$

(h) If A and A' are identical up to renaming of bound varaibles,

$A \equiv A'$

From Lemma 1, we immediately get the following:

Corollary: Every statement is equivalent to one in a normal form, where E|A occurs only if A is a procedure call.

4. Syntax and Semantics of Formulas

To define the set of formulas used in our axiom system, we begin by fixing a first order type Σ which determines the finite set of constant, predicate, and function symbols that can appear in programs and first-order formulas. We permit three distinct kinds of variables: <u>ordinary</u> variables (x), <u>environment</u> variables (v), and <u>procedure</u> variables (r). The syntactic distinction between ordinary and environment variables is that ordinary variables, like the variables in most Hoare axiom systems, may appear in both programs and first-order formulas; environment variables are a new class of variables which may appear only in first-order formulas. Procedure variables may appear only in programs, subject to these restrictions on the use of variables, a formula has the form

<formula> $::= \; U \mid \{U\}\; S\; \{V\} \mid \{H_1, \ldots, H_n\} \mid (H_1 \rightarrow H_2) \mid \forall v H \mid \forall r H$

where U and V are first order, S is any statement, H and $H_1, \ldots, H_n$ are formulas, v is an environment variable and r is a procedure variable. Arbitrary nesting of $(H_1 \rightarrow H_2)$, $\forall vH$, and $\forall rH$, is permitted.

In order to give meaning to formulas we need an interpretation I, which gives meaning to the symbols in Σ in the usual way, an environment valuation σ which assigns an element of dom(I) to each environment variable, and a procedure environment E.

$I, E, \sigma \models U$ iff for all s, $I, s \models U$ (where $I, s \models U$ is defined in the usual way)

$I, E, \sigma \models \{U\}\, A\, \{V\}$ iff for all s,s': $I, s \models U$ and $(s,s') \in \mathcal{M}_{I,E}(A)$ implies $I, s' \models V$.

$I, E, \sigma \models \{H_1, \ldots, H_n\}$ iff $I, E, \sigma \models H_i$, $i = 1, \ldots, n$.

$I, E, \sigma \models H_1 \rightarrow H_2$ iff $I, E, \sigma \models H_1$ implies $I, E, \sigma \models H_2$.

$I, E, \sigma \models \forall v\, H$ iff for all $d \in$ dom(I): $I, E, \sigma[d/v] \models H$.

$I, E, \sigma \models \forall r\, H$ iff for all procedure declarations **proc** $r'(\bar{x};\bar{q})$; B $\;I, E \cup \{$**proc** $r'(\bar{x};\bar{q})$; B$\} \models H[r'/r]$.

where r' is a fresh variable which does not appear in E and has the same type as r.

Finally, we define $I \models H$ iff for all E, σ: $I, E, \sigma \models H$.

Note that the meaning of a free environment variable in a formula is the same wherever it appears. In contrast, the meaning of a program variable is "local" to each partial correctness assertion in which it appears, since it is effectively universally quantified. For example, consider the following two formulas

(1) $\{True\}\; y := y\; \{x = 3\} \rightarrow \{True\}\; y := y\; \{False\}$

(2) $\{True\}\; y := y\; \{v = 3\} \rightarrow \{True\}\; y := y\; \{False\}$

where x and y are ordinary variables and v is an environment variable. Formula 1 is valid, because the antecedent $\{True\}\; y := y\; \{x = 3\}$ is false: it is not the case that for all initial values of x and y, $y := y$ sets x to 3. Formula 2 is *not* valid (in any interpretations with more than one domain element), because v is quantified over the whole formula. For $\sigma(v) = 3$, the antecedent is true but the consequent is false, giving a counterexample to (2).

5. Axiom System

Consider the following collection of axiom schemes and rules of inference.

Axiom schemes

AX 1. {True} error {False}

AX 2. {U [c / x]} x : = c {U}

AX 3. $\{\{U\}\ A_1\ \{V\}, \{V\}\ A_2\ \{W\}\} \rightarrow \{U\}\ A_1;A_2\ \{W\}$

AX 4. $\{\{U \wedge b\}\ A_1\ \{V\}, \{U \wedge \neg b\}\ A_2\ \{V\}\} \rightarrow \{U\}$ **if** b **then** A_1 **else** $A_2\ \{V\}$

AX 5. $\{\{U\}\ A_1\ \{V\}, \{U\}\ A_2\ \{V\}\} \rightarrow \{U\}\ A_1$ **or** $A_2\ \{V\}$

AX 6. {U} A[x' / x] {V} → {U} **begin var** x; A **end** {V}, where x' does not appear in U,V, or A.

AX 7. $\{U_1 \supset U, \{U\}\ A\ \{V\}, V \supset V_1\} \rightarrow \{U_1\}\ A\ \{V_1\}$

AX 8. $\{U\}\ A\ \{V\} \rightarrow \{\exists\, y\, U\}\ A\ \{\exists\, yV\}$ if y is an ordinary variable not free in A.

AX 9. $\{U\}\ A\ \{V\} \rightarrow \{U \wedge Q\}\ A\ \{V \wedge Q\}$ if no variable free in Q is also free in A.

AX 10. $\{U\}\ A\ \{V\} \rightarrow \{U\}\ A'\ \{V\}$ provided $A \equiv A'$ via the rules of Lemma 1.

AX 11a. $\forall vH \rightarrow H[v' / v]$

AX 11b. $\forall rH \rightarrow H[r' / r]$ where v is an environment variable, and r is a procedure variable.

AX 12. $\{U\}\ A\ \{V\} \rightarrow \{U\,\pi\}\ A\,\pi\ \{V\,\pi\}$ where π is an injective mapping on the set of ordinary variables.

AX 13. H → H & C

provided C is a first order formula whose only free variables are environment variables and H & C is defined. We define H & C by induction. For cases 3-6 below, H & C is defined on the left side of the equivalence if all of the formulas on the right side are defined.

1. H & C is not defined if H is a first order formula.

2. $\{U\}\ A\ \{V\}\ \&\ C \equiv \{U \wedge C\}\ A\ \{V \wedge C\}$.

3. $\{H_1, \ldots, H_n\}\ \&\ C \equiv \{H_1\ \&C, \ldots, H_n\ \&\ C\}$.

4. $(H_1 \rightarrow H_2)\ \&\ C \equiv H_1\ \&\ C \rightarrow H_2\ \&\ C$.

5. $(\forall v H)\ \&\ C \equiv \forall v' (H[v'/v]\ \&\ C)$ where v' is not free in H, C.

6. $(\forall r H)\ \&\ C \equiv \forall r (H\ \&\ C)$.

AX 14. $\{H_1, \ldots, H_n\} \rightarrow H_i \quad 1 \leq i \leq n$

AX 15a. $(H_1 \rightarrow (H_2 \rightarrow H_3)) \rightarrow (H_1 \cup H_2 \rightarrow H_3)$

AX 15b. $((H_1 \cup H_2) \rightarrow H_3) \rightarrow (H_1 \rightarrow (H_2 \rightarrow H_3))$

AX 16a. $H \rightarrow (\emptyset \rightarrow H)$

AX 16b. $(\emptyset \rightarrow H) \rightarrow H$

AX 17. $\{H_1 \rightarrow H_2, H_3 \rightarrow H_4\} \rightarrow \{H_1 \cup H_3 \rightarrow H_2 \cup H_4\}$

AX 18. $\{H_1 \rightarrow H_2, H_2 \rightarrow H_3\} \rightarrow \{H_1 \rightarrow H_3\}$

Rules of Inference

R1. $$\frac{H_1, (H_1 \rightarrow H_2)}{H_2}$$

R2. $$\frac{H_1 \rightarrow H_2}{E \mid H_1 \rightarrow E \mid H_2}$$

where $E \mid H$ is the result of replacing every p.c.a. $\{U\} A \{V\}$ in H by $\{U\} E \mid A \{V\}$, subject to the usual conditions about renaming bound variables to avoid capture of free variables in E.

R3. $$\frac{H \rightarrow \{U\} A \{V\}}{H \rightarrow \{\exists v\, U\} A \{\exists v\, V\}}$$

R4. $$\frac{H \rightarrow H_1, \ldots, H \rightarrow H_n}{H \rightarrow \{H_1, \ldots, H_n\}}$$

R5. $$\frac{H \rightarrow H'}{\{H \rightarrow \forall v\, H', H \rightarrow \forall r\, H'\}}$$

provided v and r are not free in H.

R6. Suppose E consists of the declarations proc $p_i(\bar{x}_i : \bar{r}_i)$; B_i, $i = 1, \ldots, n$,

and $p_1, \ldots, p_n$ do not appear free in $H, H_1, \ldots, H_n$.

$$\frac{H \rightarrow (\{\forall \bar{r}_i, \bar{v}_i (H_i \rightarrow \{U_i\}\, p_i(\bar{x}_i:\bar{r}_i)\, \{V_i\}), i = 1, \ldots, n\} \rightarrow \{\forall \bar{r}_i, \bar{v}_i (H_i \rightarrow \{U_i\}\, B_i\, \{V_i\}), i = 1, \ldots, n\})}{H \rightarrow \{\forall \bar{r}_i, \bar{v}_i (H_i \rightarrow \{U_i\}\, E \mid p_i(\bar{x}_i : \bar{r}_i) \{V_i\}), i = 1, \ldots, n\}}$$

Roughly speaking R6, the recursion rule, says that whenever we can infer something about a call $p_i(\bar{x}_i:\bar{r}_i)$ from some hypotheses H_i, we can infer the same thing about the associated body B_i (again from the hypothesis H_i) then from the hypothesis H_i we can draw the same conclusion about the declared call $E \mid p_i(\bar{x}_i:\bar{r}_i)$.

Several of the rules, such as R3, R4, R5, and R6, involve a formula H which appears in both the antecedent and consequent of the rule. In all of these rules, the role of H is to allow the rule to be applied relative to some chosen set of assumptions. Rule R4, for instance, could have been stated in a less general form as

R4'

$$\frac{H_1, \ldots, H_n}{\{H_1, \ldots, H_n\}}$$

which says that if all of the H_i are valid formulas, then $\{H_1, \ldots, H_n\}$ is valid. However, it is sometimes necessary to make more general deductions of the form: if each of the H_i is a valid consequence of H, then so is $\{H_1, \ldots, H_n\}$.

6. Soundness of R3

In this section we show that the axiom schemes and rules of inference presented in the previous section are sound; i.e., if $Th(I) \vdash H$ then $I \models H$ for any interpretation I and formula H (where $Th(I)$ is the set of all first-order formulas valid in I). We will concentrate on proving the soundness of the recursion rule R6 here, leaving the soundness of the rest of the system to the full paper. We must show that whenever the antecedent of R6 is valid, then the conclusion is also valid. So suppose that

(0) $I \models H \rightarrow (\{\forall \bar{r}_i, \bar{v}_i (H_i \rightarrow \{U_i\}\, p_i(\bar{x}_i:\bar{r}_i)\, \{V_i\}), i=1, \ldots, n\} \rightarrow \{\forall \bar{r}_i, \bar{v}_i (H_i \rightarrow \{U_i\} B_i \{V_i\}), i=1, \ldots, n\})$

We want to show that for all environments F and valuations σ that

(1) $I, F, \sigma \models H \rightarrow (\{\forall \bar{r}_i, \bar{v}_i (H_i \rightarrow \{U_i\} p_i(\bar{x}_i:\bar{r}_i)\{V_i\}), i=1, \ldots, n\}$

So suppose

(2) $I, F, \sigma \models H$

(otherwise the result is immediate). Thus we must show

(3) $I,F,\sigma \models \{\forall \bar{r}_i,\bar{v}_i(H_i \rightarrow \{U_i\}\ p_i\ (\bar{x}_i:\bar{r}_i)\ \{V_i\}), i=1, \ldots, n\}$

We can suppose without loss of generality that $p_1, \ldots, p_n$, do not appear in F (otherwise we could just rename these bound variables). Let $F_m = F \cup \{\mathbf{proc}\ p_i(\bar{x}_i:\bar{r}_i);\ \mathrm{Approx}^m_\varnothing(E|p_i\ (\bar{x}_i:\bar{r}_i)), i=1, \ldots ,n\}$. We will show by induction on m that for all m

(4) $I,F_m,\sigma \models \{\forall \bar{r}_i,\bar{v}_i(H_i \rightarrow \{U_i\}\ p_i(\bar{x}_i:\bar{r}_i)\ \{V_i\}), i=1, \ldots, n\}$

By a straightforward argument we can show that no matter how the procedures in $\bar{r}_i$ are declared in F we have

$$\mathcal{M}_{I,F}(E|p_i(\bar{x}_i,\bar{r}_i)) = \cup_m \mathcal{M}_{I,F_m}(p_i(\bar{x}_i:\bar{r}_i))$$

Thus (4) suffices to prove (3). Proving (4) for $m = 0$ is trivial, since in F_0, we have $\mathbf{proc}\ p_i(\bar{x}_i:\bar{r}_i)$; **error**. Assume (4) holds for $m = N - 1$. We now show it holds for $m = N$. It clearly suffices to show, for all choices of F and σ that

(5) $I,F_N,\sigma \models \{H_i \rightarrow \{U_i\}\ p_i(\bar{x}_i:\bar{r}_i)\{V_i\}, i=1, \ldots ,n\}$

Without loss of generality, we can assume

(6) $I,F_N,\sigma \models \{H_1, \ldots, H_n\}$

Under this assumption, we must show

(7) $I,F_N,\sigma \models U_i\{p_i(x_i:r_i)\}V_i$

Using our inductive hypothesis (4) for $m = N\text{-}1$, the validity of (0), assumption (2), and the fact that free $(H) \cap \{p_1, \ldots, p_n\} = \varnothing$, we get

(8) $I,F_{N-1}, \sigma \models \{\forall\ \bar{r}_i,\bar{v}_i\ (H_i \rightarrow \{U_i\}\ B_i\ \{V_i\}), i = 1, \ldots, n\}$

From (6) and the fact that free $(H_1, \ldots, H_n) \cap \{p_1, \ldots, p_n\} = \varnothing$, we get

(9) $I,F_{N-1}, \sigma \models \{H_1, \ldots, H_n\}$

Using (8) and (9), we can conclude

(10) $I,F_{N-1}, \sigma \models \{U_i\}\ B_i\ \{V_i\}$

We will now show

(11) $\mathcal{M}_{I,F_{N-1}}(B_i) \supseteq \mathcal{M}_{I,F_N}(p_i(x_i:r_i))$

(7) follows immediately from (10) and (11), so the proof of (11) will complete the inductive step of our proof. The

proof of (11) follows from the following chain of containments:

$$\mathcal{M}_{I,F_N}(p_i(\bar{x}_i:\bar{r}_i))$$
$$= \mathcal{M}_{I,F_N}(\text{Approx}_{\emptyset}^{N}(E \mid p_i(\bar{x}_i:\bar{r}_i)))$$
$$= \mathcal{M}_{I,F_{N-1}}(\text{Approx}_{\emptyset}^{N}(E \mid p_i(\bar{x}_i:\bar{r}_i))) \text{ (since } F_{N-1}, F_N \text{ only differ on procedures declared in } E)$$
$$= \mathcal{M}_{I,F_{N-1}}(\text{Approx}_{\emptyset}^{N-1}(E \mid B_i)) \text{ (by definition of Approx)}$$
$$\subseteq \mathcal{M}_{I,F_{N-1}}(B_i)$$

The last containment follows by induction on N followed by a subinduction on the structure of B_i. The only difficulty occurs if B_i is of the form $p_k(\bar{y}:\bar{q})$ where p_k is declared in E. Note that

$$\mathcal{M}_{I,F_{N-1}}(p_k(\bar{y}:\bar{q})) = \mathcal{M}_{I,F_{N-1}}([\bar{y}/\bar{x}_k,\bar{q}/\bar{r}_k])(\text{Approx}_{\emptyset}^{N-1}(E \mid p_k(\bar{x}_k:\bar{r}_k)))$$

(since in F_{N-1}, we have the declaration proc $p_k(\bar{x}_i:\bar{r}_i)$, $(\text{Approx}_{\emptyset}^{N-1}(E \mid p_k(\bar{x}_k:\bar{r}_k)))$

Thus we must show

$$\mathcal{M}_{I,F_{N-1}}(\text{Approx}_{\emptyset}^{N-1}(E \mid p_k(\bar{y},\bar{q}))) \subseteq \mathcal{M}_{I,F_{N-1}}([\bar{y}/\bar{x}_k,\bar{q}/\bar{r}_k])(\text{Approx}_{\emptyset}^{N-1}(E \mid p_k(\bar{x}_k:\bar{r}_k)))$$

This last inequality follows from the more general

(12) $\mathcal{M}_{I,F_{N-1}}(\text{Approx}_{\emptyset}^{N-1}(E \mid S(\bar{q},\bar{y}))) \subseteq \mathcal{M}_{I,F_{N-1}}([\bar{y}/\bar{x}_k,\bar{q}/\bar{r}_k])(\text{Approx}_{\emptyset}^{N-1}(E \mid S(\bar{x}_k:\bar{r}_k)))$

(12) is proved by induction on N and a subinduction on the structure of S. We leave details to the reader. □

7. Relative Completeness

In this section, we outline a proof of the relative completeness of the axiom system. The proof uses some interesting new ideas to deal with statements having free procedure names. The following discussion, however, is intended only to give an informal overview of the completeness proof. A more precise account appears in the final version of the paper and in [7].

First we need the following definitions. An interpretation I is *Herbrand definable* if every element of dom(I) is represented by a term involving only the constant and function symbols of I. In a fixed interpretation I, the *strongest postcondition* of a program A with respect to a (first order) precondition U, SP(A,U), is the set of all final states A can reach when started in a state satisfying U:

$$SP(A,U) = \{s' \mid \exists s\,(I,s \models U \wedge (s,s') \in \mathcal{M}_I(A))\}.$$

An interpretation I is *expressive* for a programming language L if for every program A ∈ L and precondition U, SP(A,U) can be expressed by a first order formula using only the symbols of I.

Our main result is

Relative Completeness: Let I be Herbrand definable and expressive for L4, and let $A \in$ L4. Then $I \models \{U\}\ A\ \{V\}$ implies $Th(I) \vdash \{U\}\ A\ \{V\}$; i.e., if a partial correctness assertion is true in an interpretation I, then it can be proved in our system using the first order theory of I as axioms.

In contrast, the relative completeness results obtained in [10, 5] depend on a more general notion of expressiveness with respect to preconditions in a higher order logic and require that a certain higher order theory of the interpretation be added as axioms.

The completeness proof uses the fact that in a language which does not permit non-local use of variables, a procedure call $p(\bar{x}:\bar{r})$ does not depend on any variables other than the ones in $\bar{x}$. Without this restriction, $p(\bar{x}:\bar{r})$ could depend on variables global to the body of p, global to procedures free in the body of p, or global to any of the procedures in $\bar{r}$.

One of the central ideas of the proof is that the act of passing a procedure parameter may be regarded as passing an input-output relation on a set of variables: in the call $p(:r)$, where r has type $r(\bar{x})$, r is a relation on $\bar{x}$. When r has higher type $r(\bar{x}:\bar{q})$, r is still an input-output relation on $\bar{x}$, but one which depends on the relations corresponding to its procedure parameters in $\bar{q}$. We wish to show that these relations can be represented by formulas in our logic. Returning to the example formula mentioned in the introduction,

$$\forall r,v\,(\{y=y_0\}\ r(y)\ \{y=y_0\cdot v\} \ \rightarrow\ \{x=x_0\}\ p(x:r)\ \{x=x_0\cdot v^2\})$$

observe how the environment variable v, appearing in the postconditions of the calls $r(y)$ and $p(x:r)$, is used to express the relationship between the semantics of $r(y)$ and $p(x:r)$. The formula states that if $r(y)$ multiplies y by v, then $p(x:r)$ multiplies x by v^2. In order to prove relative completeness, we must show that the logic can express all of the necessary relations of this sort. We will return to this problem and make it more precise later.

Another problem related to expressiveness is the question of when we can assume that the strongest postcondition of a statement is expressible in the first order assertion language. Roughly speaking, most relative completeness proofs proceed by showing the following is provable in the axiom system:

(2) $\vdash \{U\}\ A\ \{SP(A,U)\}$

for any statement A and precondition U. From $\vdash \{U\}\ A\ \{SP(A,U)\}$ and rule of consequence one can prove that if $I \models \{U\}\ A\ \{V\}$, then $Th(I) \vdash \{U\}\ A\ \{V\}$ for it must be the case that if $\models U\ A\ V$, then $I \models SP(A,U) \supset V$. This chain of reasoning depends on the assumption of expressiveness, which was used implicitly in writing (2).

However, the usual notion of expressiveness is that $SP(A,U)$ can be expressed for *any program A*. By definition, a program does not have free procedure names; hence expressiveness does not immediately guarantee that one can express $SP(A,U)$ for an arbitrary statement A which may have free procedure names. Thus, our relative completeness proof cannot proceed directly by proving a lemma of the same form as (2). Roughly, if A is a statement with free procedures, we will be able to show $\vdash H \rightarrow \{U\}\ A\ \{SP(A,U)\}$, where H is a suitably chosen set of hypothesis about the free procedures in A, and $\hat{A}$ is a program (with no free procedures), which in some sense simulates A. We proceed by using some of the properties of the Herbrand definable interpretations.

Lemma 2 [8]. If I is an interpretation which is Herbrand definable and the programming language is L4 (or more generally, any "acceptable programming language with recursion" in the sense of [3]) then either

1. I is finite or
2. there are programs in the language which simulate arithmetic in dom (I).

One can use this fact about Herbrand definable domains to prove the existence of *interpreter programs.* Roughly speaking, an interpreter program receives as inputs a number of ordinary variables containing an encoding of an arbitrary relation to be computed, and a number of other variables to which the relation is to be applied. The interpreter then modifies the second set of variables according to the relation. Using interpreter programs, we can transform any L4 program into a program without procedures passed as parameters by adding additional ordinary variables to pass values which encode the procedures. Specifically, one can show that for any statement A in L4, there is another statement A^* having the following properties. In place of each formal procedure name r free in A, A^* has a new group of free ordinary variables, r^*. The r^* variables are distinct from all other variables. If A is a statement whose only free procedure names are the formals $r_1, \ldots, r_n$, then the relational semantics of A in an environment where r_i is bound to B_i is the same as the semantics of A^* provided r_i^* is initially set to the encoding of the relation corresponding to procedure r_i. For a program A, $\mathcal{M}(A) \equiv \mathcal{M}(A^*)$.

As it happens, there is a way to construct A^* so that if A has no non-local use of variables, then neither does A^*. This means that if A is in L4 and the only procedures free in A are formals, then A^* is a program of L4. Consequently, if I is expressive then $SP(A^*,U)$ is expressible in I for such A.

Using A^*, we can carry out the relative completeness proof without the expressiveness problems of formula (2). For each statement A whose free procedures are the formals $r_1, \ldots, r_n$ and declared procedures $p_1, \ldots, p_k$, we can show that the following is provable in the axiom system

(3) $\vdash \{R_1, \ldots, R_n, P_1, \ldots, P_k\} \rightarrow \{U\}\ A\ \{SP(E \mid A)^*\}$

where E is any environment such that $(E \mid A)^*$ is a program, and $R_1, \ldots, R_n$ and $P_1, \ldots, P_k$ are formulas of the logic which describe $r_1, \ldots, r_n$ and $p_1, \ldots, p_k$, respectively. Intuitively, R_i has the form $R_i(r_i, r_i^*)$, and says that the semantics of r_i is a subset of the relation encoded by r_i^*. For r_i of type $r_i(\bar{x})$, R_i is just $\{\bar{x} = \overline{x0}\} r_i(\bar{x})\ \{SP(r_i(\bar{x})^*, \bar{x} = \overline{x0}\}$. For higher types, a more complex formula is defined by induction; e. g., for $r_j(\bar{x} : r_i)$ where r_i has type $r_i(\bar{x})$, R_j is

$$\forall r_i\ r_i^*(R_i(r_i, r_i^*) \rightarrow \{\bar{x} = \overline{x0}\}\ r_j(\bar{x} : r_i)\ \{SP(r_j(\bar{x} : r_i)^*, \bar{x} = \overline{x0})\})$$

Similarly, P_i is a formula which says that the semantics of p_i is a subset of the semantics determined by the environment E and the relations for $r_1, \ldots, r_n$ encoded by $r_1^*, \ldots, r_n^*$. The formulas R_i and P_i give the general representation in our logic of the meaning of procedures, as alluded to earlier.

In the full paper, we show that (3) is provable, by induction on the structure of statements. For a program A, (3) gives

$$\vdash \{U\} \wedge \{SP(A^*,U)\}$$

from which the desired result follows because

$$I \models SP(A^*,U) \equiv SP(A,U).$$

Hence, if $I \models \{U\} \wedge \{V\}$, then $Th(I) \vdash \{U\} \wedge \{V\}$.

8. Conclusion

We have presented a sound and relatively complete axiom system for the language L4. Such an axiom system has been sought by a number of other researchers since the appearance of [CL79]. But because of the infinite range problem, no completely satisfactory axiomatization has been previously given.

In order to deal with infinite range, we introduce a class of generalized partial correctness assertions, which permit implication between partial correctness assertions, universal quantification over procedure names, and universal quantification over environment variables. These assertions enable us to relate the semantics of a procedure with the semantics of procedures passed to it as parameters. By using these assertions we are able to provide a new principle for reasoning about procedures with procedure parameters; this principle is incorporated in our recursion rule.

Many of the techniques introduced in this paper appear to have application beyond L4. We believe that the ideas used in our recursion rule may be helpful with other languages which have infinite range [1]. Moreover, the way that we have structured the inductive argument in the relative completeness proof is new and may also be useful in this respect. Finally, in the course of the relative completeness proof we have derived some new results of independent interest about the power of acceptable programming languages and the existence of expressive interpretations.

9. Acknowledgment

We want to thank Magdalena Muller for her infinite patience in typing this document.

10. References

1. de Bakker, J. W., Klop, J. W., Meyer, J.-J. Ch. Correctness of programs with function procedures. Tech. Rept. IW 170/81, Mathematisch Centrum, Amsterdam, 1981.

2. Clarke, E. M. "Programming language constructs for which it is impossible to obtain good Hoare-like axioms." *JACM 26* (1979), 129-147.

3. Clarke, E. M., Jr., German, S., and Halpern, J. Y. "Effective axiomatization of Hoare logics." *JACM 30* (1983), 612-636.

4. Cook, S. A. "Soundness and completeness of an axiom system for program verification." *SIAM J. Comput. 7* (1978), 70-90.

5. Damm, W. and Josko, B. A sound and relatively complete Hoare-logic for a language with higher type procedures. Tech. Rept. Bericht No. 77, Lehrstuhl fur Informatik II, RWTH Aachen, April, 1982.

6. Damm, W. and Josko, B. personal communication. .

7. German, S. Relative completeness proofs for languages with infinite range.

8. German, S. and Halpern, J. On the power of acceptable programming languages with recursion.

9. Olderog, E.-R. "Sound and complete Hoare-like calculi based on copy rules." *Acta Informatica 16* (1981), 161-197.

10. Olderog, E.-R. "Hoare-style proof and formal computations." *Jahrestagugn, IFB 50 GI-11* (1981), 65-71.

Introducing Institutions

J. A. Goguen[1] and R. M. Burstall
SRI International and the University of Edinburgh

Abstract

There is a population explosion among the logical systems being used in computer science. Examples include first order logic (with and without equality), equational logic, Horn clause logic, second order logic, higher order logic, infinitary logic, dynamic logic, process logic, temporal logic, and modal logic; moreover, there is a tendency for each theorem prover to have its own idiosyncratic logical system. Yet it is usual to give many of the same results and applications for each logical system; of course, this is natural in so far as there are basic results in computer science that are independent of the logical system in which they happen to be expressed. But we should not have to do the same things over and over again; instead, we should generalize, and do the essential things once and for all! Also, we should ask what are the relationships among all these different logical systems. This paper shows how some parts of computer science can be done in any suitable logical system, by introducing the notion of an **institution** as a precise generalization of the informal notion of a "logical system." A first main result shows that if an institution is such that interface declarations expressed in it can be glued together, then **theories** (which are just sets of sentences) in that institution can also be glued together. A second main result gives conditions under which a theorem prover for one institution can be validly used on theories from another; this uses the notion of an institution morphism. A third main result shows that institutions admiting free models can be extended to institutions whose theories may include, in addition to the original sentences, various kinds of constraints upon interpretations; such constraints are useful for defining abstract data types, and include so-called "data," "hierarchy," and "generating" constraints. Further results show how to define insitutions that mix sentences from one institution with constraints from another, and even mix sentences and (various kinds of) constraints from several different institutions. It is noted that general results about institutions apply to such "multiplex" institutions, including the result mentioned above about gluing together theories. Finally, this paper discusses some applications of these results to specification languages, showing that much of that subject is in fact independent of the institution used.

1 Introduction

Recent work in programming methodology has been based upon numerous different logical systems. Perhaps most popular are the many variants of first order logic found, for example, in the theorem provers used in various program verification projects. But also popular are equational logic, as used in the study of abstract data types, and first order Horn clause logic, as used in "logic programming." More exotic logical systems, such as temporal logic, infinitary logic, and continuous algebra have also been proposed to handle features such as concurrency and non-termination, and most systems exist in both one-sorted and many-sorted forms. However, it seems apparent that much of programming methodology is actually *completely*

---

[1]Research supported in part by Office of Naval Research contracts N00014-80-0296 and N00014-82-C-0333, and National Science Foundation Grant MCS8201380.

independent of what underlying logic is chosen. In particular, if [Burstall & Goguen 77] are correct that the essential purpose of a specification language is to say how to put (small and hopefully standard) theories together to make new (and possibly very large) specifications, then much of the syntax and semantics of specification does not depend upon the logical system in which the theories are expressed; the same holds for implementing a specification, and for verifying correctness. Because of the proliferation of logics of programming and the expense of theorem provers, it is useful to know when sentences in one logic can be translated into sentences in another logic in such a way that it is sound to apply a theorem prover for the second logic to the translated sentences.

This paper approaches these problems through the theory of institutions, where an **institution** is a logical system suitable for programming methodology; the paper also carries out some basic methodological work in an arbitrary institution. Informally, an institution consists of

- a collection of signatures (which are vocabularies for use in constructing sentences in a logical system) and signature morphisms, together with for each signature Σ
- a set of Σ-sentences,
- a set of Σ-models, and
- a Σ-satisfaction relation, of Σ-sentences by Σ-models,

such that when you change signatures (with a signature morphism), the satisfaction relation between sentences and models changes consistently. One main result in this paper is that any institution whose syntax is nice enough to support gluing together interface declarations (as given by signatures) will also support gluing together **theories** (which are collections of sentences) to form larger specifications. A second main result shows how a suitable **institution morphism** permits a theorem prover for one institution to be used on theories from another. A third main result is that any institution supporting free constructions extends to another institution whose sentences may be either the old sentences, or else any of several kinds of constraint on interpretations. Such constraints are useful, for example, in data type declarations, and we believe that they are valuable as a general formulations of the kinds of induction used in computer science. Again using the notion of institution morphism, it is shown how sentences from one institution can be combined with constraints from another in a "duplex" institution; more generally, sentences and constraints from several institutions can be mixed together in a "multiplex" institution. This gives a very rich and flexible framework for program specification and other areas of theoretical computer science.

The notion of institution was first introduced as part of our research on Clear, in [Burstall & Goguen 80] under the name "language." The present paper adds many new concepts and results, as well as an improved notation. The "abstract model theory" of [Barwise 74] resembles our work in its intention to generalize basic results in model theory and in its use of elementary category theory; it differs in being more concrete (for example, its syntactic structures are limited to the usual function, relation and logical symbols) and in the results that are generalized (these are results of classical logic, such as those of Lowenheim-Skolem and Hanf).

The first two subsections below try to explain the first two paragraphs of this introduction a little more gradually. The third indicates what we will assume the reader knows about category theory. Section 2 is a brief review of general algebra, emphasizing results used to show that equational logic is indeed an institution. Section 3 introduces the basic definitions and results for institutions and theories, and considers the equational, first order, first order with equality, Horn clause, and conditional equational institutions. Section 4 discusses the use of constraints to specify abstract data types. Section 5 considers the use of two or more institutions together. Section 6 discusses applications to programming methodology and shows how certain general specification concepts can be expressed in any suitable institution. All of the more difficult proofs and many of the more difficult definitions are omitted in this condensed version of the paper; these details will appear elsewhere at a later time.

1.1 Specifications and Logical Systems

Systematic program design requires careful specification of the problem to be solved. But recent experience in software engineering shows that there are major difficulties in producing consistent and rigorous specifications to reflect users' requirements for complex systems. We suggest that these difficulties can be ameliorated by making specifications as modular as possible, so that they are built from small, understandable and re-usable pieces. We suggest that this modularity may be useful not only for understanding and writing specifications, but also for proving theorems about them, and in particular, for proving that a given program actually satisfies its specification. Modern work in programming methodology supports the view that abstractions, and in particular data abstractions, are a useful way to obtain such modularity, and that parameterized (sometimes called "generic") specifications dramatically enhance this utility. One way to achieve these advantages is to use a specification language that puts together parameterized abstractions.

It is important to distinguish between specifications that are written directly in some logical system, such as first order logic or the logic of some particular mechanical theorem prover, and specifications that are written in a genuine specification language, such as Special [Levitt, Robinson & Silverberg 79], Clear [Burstall & Goguen 77], OBJ [Goguen & Tardo 79], or Affirm [Gerhard, Musser et al. 79]. The essential purpose of a logical system is to provide a relationship of "satisfaction" between its *syntax* (i.e., its theories) and its *semantics* or models; this relationship is sometimes called a "model theory" and may appear in the form of a "Galois connection" (as in Section 3.2 below). A specification written directly in such a logical system is simply an unstructured, and possibly very large, set of sentences. On the other hand, the essential purpose of a specification language is to make it easy to write and to read specifications of particular systems, and especially of large systems. To this end, it should provide mechanisms for putting old and well-understood specifications together to form new specifications. In particular, it should provide for parameterized specifications and for constructions (like blocks) that define local environments in which specification variables may take on local values.

In order for a specification written in a given specification language to have a precise meaning, it is necessary for that language to have a precise semantics! Part of that semantics will be an underlying logic which must have certain properties in order to be useful for this task. These properties include a suitable notion of model; a satisfaction relationship between sentences and models; and a complete and reasonably simple proof theory. Examples include first order logic, equational logic, temporal logic, and higher order logic. In general, any mechanical theorem prover will have its own particular logical system (e.g., [Boyer & Moore 80], [Aubin 76], [Shostak, Schwartz & Melliar-Smith 81]) and the utility of the theorem prover will depend in part upon the appropriateness of that logical system to various application areas.

There is also the interesting possibility of using two (or even more) institutions together, as discussed in Section 5 below: then one can specify data structures in one institution and at the same time use the more powerful axioms available in other institutions; this has been used to advantage in some specifications in Clear [Burstall & Goguen 81] and also in the language

Ordinary [Goguen 82a, Goguen 82b]. This permits utilizing induction in institutions where it makes sense, and also writing sentences in other more expressive institutions where induction does not always make sense.

We wish to emphasize that a specification language is not a programming language. For example, the denotation of an Algol text is a function, but the denotation of a specification text is a **theory**, that is, a set of sentences *about* programs.

1.2 Parameterization over the Underlying Logic

Since a specification language is intended to provide mechanisms for structuring specifications, its definition and meaning should be as *independent* as possible of what underlying logical system is used. In fact, dependence on the logical system can be relegated to the level of the syntax of the sentences that occur in theories. This also serves to simplify the task of giving a semantics for a specification language.

In order to achieve the benefits listed above, we introduce the notion of an institution, which is an abstraction of the notion of a logical system [Burstall & Goguen 80]. We have designed our specification languages Clear and Ordinary in such a way that they can be used with *any* institution. This means, in particular, that they could be used in connection with any theorem prover whose underlying logic is actually an institution. Roughly speaking, an **institution** is a collection of signatures (which are vocabularies for constructing sentences) together with for each signature Σ: the set of all Σ-sentences; the category of all Σ-models; and a Σ-satisfaction relationship between sentences and models, such that when signatures are changed (with a signature morphism), satisfaction is preserved.

1.3 Prerequisites

Although relatively little category theory is required for most of this paper, we have not resisted the temptation to add some more arcane remarks for those who may be interested. We must assume that the reader is acquainted with the notions of category, functor and natural transformation. Occasional non-essential remarks use adjoint functors. There are several introductions to these ideas which the unfamiliar reader may consult, including [Arbib & Manes 75], [Goguen, Thatcher, Wagner & Wright 75a] and [Burstall & Goguen 82], and for the mathematically more sophisticated [MacLane 71] and [Goldblatt 79]. Familiarity with the initial algebra approach to abstract data types is helpful, but probably not necessary. Colimits are briefly explained in Section 3.4.

1.4 Acknowledgements

Thanks go to the Science Research Council of Great Britain for financial support and a Visiting Fellowship for JAG, to the National Science Foundation for travel money, to the Office of Naval Research and the National Science Foundation for research support, to Eleanor Kerse for typing some early drafts, and to Jose Meseguer for his extensive comments. We are grateful to many people for helpful conversations and suggestions, notably to our ADJ collaborators Jim Thatcher, Eric Wagner, and Jesse Wright, also to Peter Dybjer, Gordon Plotkin, David Rydeheard, Don Sanella, John Reynolds and Steve Zilles. Special thanks to Kathleen Goguen and Seija-Leena Burstall for extreme patience.

2 General Algebra

This section is quick review of many-sorted general algebra. This will provide our first example of the institution concept, and will also aid in working out the details of several other institutions. If you know all about general algebra, you can skip to Section 3, which defines the abstract notion of institution and gives some further examples. We will use the notational approach of [Goguen 74] (see also [Goguen, Thatcher & Wagner 78]) based on "indexed sets," in contrast to the more complex notations of [Higgins 63], [Benabou 68] and [Birkhoff & Lipson 70]. If I is a set (of "indices"), then an **I-indexed set** (or a family of sets indexed by I) A is just an assignment of a set A_i to each **index** i in I. If A and B are I-indexed sets, then a **mapping, map**, or **morphism** of I-indexed sets, f: A→B, is just an I-indexed family of functions f_i: A_i→ B_i one for each i in I. There is an obvious composition[2] of I-indexed mappings, $(f;g)_i=f_i;g_i$ where f;g denotes composition of the functions f and g in the order given by (f;g)(x)=g(f(x)). This gives a category $\mathbf{Set}_I$ of I-indexed sets. We may use the notations $A=\langle A_i \mid i \text{ in } I\rangle$ for an I-indexed set with components A_i and $f=\langle f_i \mid i \text{ in } I\rangle$ for an I-indexed mapping A→B of I-indexed sets where f_i: $A_i \to B_i$. Notice that the basic concepts of set theory immediately extend component-wise to I-indexed sets. Thus, $A \subseteq B$ means that $A_i \subseteq B_i$ for each i in I, $A \cap B = \langle A_i \cap B_i \mid i \text{ in } I\rangle$, etc.

2.1 Equational Signatures

Intuitively speaking, an equational signature declares some sort symbols (to serve as names for the different kinds of data around) and some operator symbols (to serve as names for functions on these various kinds of data), where each operator declaration gives a tuple of input sorts, and one output sort. A morphism between signatures should map sorts to sorts, and operators to operators, so as to preserve their input and output sorts.

Definition 1: An **equational signature** is a pair $\langle S,\Sigma\rangle$, where S is a set (of **sort** names), and Σ is a family of sets (of **operator** names), indexed by S^*xS; we will often write just Σ instead of $\langle S,\Sigma\rangle$. σ in Σ_{us} is said to have **arity** u, **sort** s, and **rank** u,s; we may write σ: u→s to indicate this. []

In the language of programming methodology, a signature declares the interface for a package, capsule, module, object, abstract machine, or abstract data type (unfortunately, there is no standard terminology for these concepts).

Definition 2: An **equational signature morphism** ϕ from a signature $\langle S,\Sigma\rangle$ to a signature $\langle S',\Sigma'\rangle$ is a pair $\langle f,g\rangle$ consisting of a map f: S→S′ of sorts and an SxS*-indexed family of maps g_{us}: $\Sigma_{us} \to \Sigma'_{f^*(u)f(s)}$ of operator symbols, where f^*: $S^* \to S'^*$ is the extension of f to strings[3]. We will sometimes write $\phi(s)$ for f(s), $\phi(u)$ for $f^*(u)$, and $\phi(\sigma)$ or $\phi\sigma$ for $g_{us}(\sigma)$ when $\sigma \in \Sigma_{us}$. []

The signature morphism concept is useful for expressing the *binding* of an actual parameter to the formal parameter of a parameterized software module (see Section 6.2). As is standard in category theory, we can put the concepts of Definitions 1 and 2 together to get

Definition 3: The **category of equational signatures**, denoted **Sig**, has equational

---

[2] This paper uses ; for composition in any category.

[3] This extension is defined by: $f^*(\lambda)=\lambda$, where λ denotes the empty string; and $f^*(us)=f^*(u)f(s)$, for u in S^* and s in S.

signatures as its objects, and has equational signature morphisms as its morphisms. The identity morphism on $\langle S,\Sigma\rangle$ is the corresponding pair of identity maps, and the composition of morphisms is the composition of their corresponding components as maps. (This clearly forms a category.) []

2.2 Algebras

Intuitively, given a signature Σ, a Σ-algebra interprets each sort symbol as a set, and each operator symbol as a function. Algebras, in the intuition of programming methodology, correspond to concrete data types, i.e., to data representations in the sense of [Hoare 72].

Definition 4: Let $\langle S,\Sigma\rangle$ be a signature. Then a **Σ-algebra** A is an S-indexed family of sets $|A|=\langle A_s \mid s \text{ in } S\rangle$ called the **carriers** of A, together with an S*xS-indexed family α of maps α_{us}: $\Sigma_{us}\to[A_u\to A_s]$ for u in S* and s in S, where $A_{s1...sn}=A_{s1}\mathbf{x}...\mathbf{x}A_{sn}$ and $[A\to B]$ denotes the set of all functions from A to B. (We may sometimes write for A for |A| and A_s for $|A|_s$.) For $u=s1...sn$, for σ in Σ_{us} and for $\langle a1,...,an\rangle$ in A_u we will write $\sigma(a1,...,an)$ for $\alpha_{us}(\sigma)(a1,...,an)$ if there is no ambiguity. []

Definition 5: Given a signature $\langle S,\Sigma\rangle$ a **Σ-homomorphism** from a Σ-algebra $\langle A,\alpha\rangle$ to another $\langle A',\alpha'\rangle$, is an S-indexed map f: $A\to A'$ such that for all σ in Σ_{us} and all $a=\langle a1,...,an\rangle$ in A_u the **homomorphism condition**

$$f_s(\alpha(\sigma)(a1,...,an))=\alpha'(\sigma)(f_{s1}(a1),...,f_{sn}(an))$$

holds. []

Definition 6: The **category $\mathbf{Alg}_\Sigma$** of **Σ-algebras** has Σ-algebras as objects and Σ-homomorphism as morphisms; composition and identity are composition and identity as maps. (This clearly forms a category). []

We can extend **Alg** to a functor on the category **Sig** of signatures: it associates with each signature Σ the category of all Σ-algebras, and it also defines the effect of signature morphisms on algebras. In the definition below, $\mathbf{Cat}^{op}$ denotes the opposite of the category **Cat** of all categories, i.e., $\mathbf{Cat}^{op}$ is **Cat** with its morphisms reversed.

Definition 7: The functor **Alg**: $\mathbf{Sig}\to\mathbf{Cat}^{op}$ takes each signature Σ to the category of all Σ-algebras, and takes each signature morphism $\phi=\langle f: S\to S', g\rangle: \Sigma\to\Sigma'$ to the functor $\mathbf{Alg}(\phi)$: $\mathbf{Alg}_{\Sigma'}\to\mathbf{Alg}_\Sigma$ sending

1. a Σ'-algebra $\langle A',\alpha'\rangle$ to the Σ-algebra $\langle A,\alpha\rangle$ with $A_s=A'_{f(s)}$ and $\alpha=g;\alpha'$, and
2. sending a Σ'-homomorphism h': $A'\to B'$ to the Σ-homomorphism $\mathbf{Alg}(\phi)(h')=h$: $\mathbf{Alg}(\phi)(A')\to\mathbf{Alg}(\phi)(B')$ defined by $h_s=h'_{f(s)}$.

It is often convenient to write $\phi(A')$ or $\phi A'$ for $\mathbf{Alg}(\phi)(A')$ and to write $\phi(h')$ for $\mathbf{Alg}(\phi)(h')$. []

If S is the sort set of Σ, then there is a **forgetful functor** U: $\mathbf{Alg}_\Sigma\to\mathbf{Set}_S$ sending each algebra to its S-indexed family of carriers, and sending each Σ-homomorphism to its underlying S-indexed map.

For each S-indexed set X, there is a **free algebra** (also called a "term" or "word" algebra), denoted $T_\Sigma(X)$, with $|T_\Sigma(X)|_s$ consisting of all the Σ-terms of sort s using "variable" symbols from X; i.e., $(T_\Sigma(X))_s$ contains all the s-sorted terms with variables from X that can be constructed using operator symbols from Σ; moreover, the S-indexed set T_Σ forms a Σ-algebra in a natural way.

We begin our more precise discussion with a special case, defining $(T_\Sigma)_s$ to be the least set of strings of symbols such that

1. $\Sigma_{\lambda,s} \subseteq T_{\Sigma,s}$, and
2. σ in $\Sigma_{s1...sn,s}$ and ti in $T_{\Sigma,si}$ implies the string σ(t1,...,tn) is in $T_{\Sigma,s}$.

Then the Σ-structure of T_Σ is given by α defined by:

1. for σ in $\Sigma_{\lambda,s}$ we let $\alpha(\sigma)$ be the string σ of length one in $T_{\Sigma,s}$; and
2. for σ in $\Sigma_{s1...sn,s}$ and ti in $T_{\Sigma,si}$ we let $\alpha(\sigma)$(t1,...,tn) be the string σ(t1,...,tn) in $T_{\Sigma,s}$.

Next, we define $\Sigma(X)$ to be the S-sorted signature with $(\Sigma(X))_{us}=\Sigma_{us} \cup X_s$ if $u=\lambda$ and $(\Sigma(X))_{us}=\Sigma_{us}$ if $u \neq \lambda$. Then $T_\Sigma(X)$ is just $T_{\Sigma(X)}$ regarded as a Σ-algebra rather than as a $\Sigma(X)$-algebra.

The freeness of $T_\Sigma(X)$ is expressed precisely by the following.

Theorem 8: Let i_X: $X \to U(T_\Sigma(X))$ denote the inclusion described above. Then the following "universal" property holds: for any Σ-algebra B, every (S-indexed) map f: $X \to B$, called an **assignment**, extends uniquely to a Σ-homomorphism $f^\#$: $T_\Sigma(X) \to B$ such that $i_X;U(f^\#)=U(f)$.
[]

We will often omit the U's in such equations, as in the following traditional diagram of S-indexed sets and mappings for the above equation:

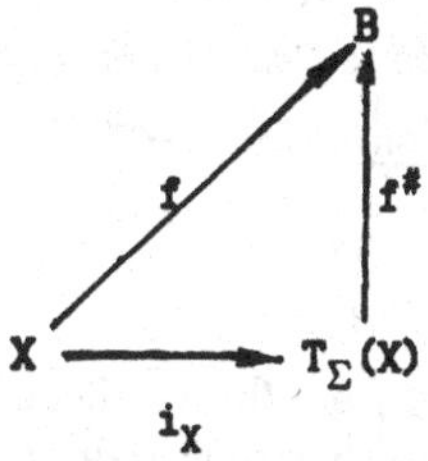

In particular, taking $X=\emptyset$, we see that there is a unique Σ-homomorphism from T_Σ to any other Σ-algebra; for this reason T_Σ is called the **initial** Σ-algebra.

2.3 Equations and Satisfaction

We now define the equations over a given signature, and what it means for an algebra to satisfy an equation.

Definition 9: A **Σ-equation** e is a triple $\langle X,\tau1,\tau2\rangle$ where X is an S-indexed set (of variable symbols) and $\tau1$ and $\tau2$ in $|T_\Sigma(X)|_s$ are terms over X of the same sort s in S. Such an equation might be written

for all X, $\tau1=\tau2$

or

$(\forall X)\ \tau1=\tau2$.

[]

The necessity for explicitly including declarations for variables in equations (as in [Burstall & Goguen 77]) is shown in [Goguen & Meseguer 81]: without this one gets an unsound deductive system for many-sorted equational logic.

Definition 10: A Σ-algebra A **satisfies** a Σ-equation $\langle X,\tau 1,\tau 2\rangle$ iff for all assignments f: $X \to |A|$ we have $f^{\#}(\tau 1)=f^{\#}(\tau 2)$. We will write $A \models e$ for "A satisfies e." []

We now define another functor, Eqn, on the category of signatures. In order to do so, we first define for each signature morphism ϕ: $\Sigma \to \Sigma'$ a function $\phi^{\sim}$ from Σ-terms to Σ'-terms. To this end, we first give a simpler definition for sort maps.

Definition 11: If X is an S-sorted set of variables and if f: $S \to S'$, then we define $f^{\sim}(X)$ to be the S'-indexed set X' such that

$$X'_{s'}=\cup\{X_s \mid f(s)=s'\} .$$

(Notice that without loss of generality, we can assume disjointness of the sets X_s for s in S: if the X_s were not disjoint, we could just take a disjoint union in the above formula.)

Now let ϕ: $\Sigma \to \Sigma'$ be the signature morphism $\langle f: S \to S', g\rangle$. Let X be an S-indexed set (of variables) and let X' be $f^{\sim}(X)$. We will define an S-indexed map $\phi^{\sim}$: $|T_{\Sigma}(X)| \to |\phi(T_{\Sigma'}(X'))|$. First, note that[4] $X \subseteq |\phi(T_{\Sigma'}(X'))|$ since if x is in X_s then x is in $X'_{f(s)}$ and $X'_{f(s)} \subseteq |T_{\Sigma'}(X')|_{f(s)} = |\phi(T_{\Sigma'}(X'))|_s$; let j: $X \to |\phi(T_{\Sigma'}(X'))|$ denote this inclusion. Then j has a unique extension as a Σ-homomorphism $j^{\#}$: $T_{\Sigma}(X) \to \phi(T_{\Sigma'}(X'))$ by Theorem 8, and we simply define $\phi^{\sim}=|j^{\#}|$. []

Definition 12: The functor Eqn: **Sig**$\to$**Set** takes each signature Σ to the set Eqn(Σ) of all Σ-equations, and takes each $\phi=\langle f,g\rangle$: $\Sigma \to \Sigma'$ to the function Eqn(ϕ): Eqn(Σ)$\to$Eqn(Σ') defined by

$$\mathrm{Eqn}(\phi)(\langle X,\tau 1,\tau 2\rangle)=\langle f^{\sim}(X),\phi^{\sim}(\tau 1),\phi^{\sim}(\tau 2)\rangle .$$

It is often convenient to write ϕ(e) or ϕe instead of Eqn(ϕ)(e). []

Proposition 13: Satisfaction Condition. If ϕ: $\Sigma \to \Sigma'$, if e is an Σ-equation, and if A' is a Σ'-algebra, then

$$A' \models \phi(e) \text{ iff } \phi(A') \models e . \ []$$

The not entirely trivial proof is omitted from this version of the paper. This concludes our review of general algebra. We now turn to our generalization.

3 Institutions

An institution consists of a category of signatures such that associated with each signature are sentences (e.g., equations), models (e.g., algebras), and a relationship of satisfaction that is, in a certain sense, invariant under change of signature. This is an abstraction of first order model theory. A different approach, axiomatizing the category of theories as well as that of signatures, is given in [Goguen & Burstall 78]; another uses the notion of monadic theory [Burstall & Rydeheard 80]. The generality of these approaches is useful in dealing with aspects of programming, such as errors and infinite data structures, that seem to require theories and models that are in some way more complicated than those of ordinary logic. Another motivation is the elegant way that data definitions can be handled (see Section 5).

[4] This means that $X_s \subseteq |\phi(T_{\Sigma'}(X'))|_s$ for each s in S.

3.1 Definition and Examples

The essence of the notion of institution is that when signatures are changed (with a signature morphism) then sentences and models change consistently. This consistency is expressed by the "Satisfaction Condition," which goes a step beyond the classical conception of "semantic truth" in [Tarski 44]. The wide range of consequences and the fact that Proposition 13 is not entirely trivial, suggest that this is not a trivial step. A philosophical argument can also be given: it is a familiar and basic fact that the truth of a sentence (in logic) is independent of the vocabulary chosen to represent the basic relationships that occur in it. It is also fundamental that sentences translate in the same direction as a change of symbols, while models translate in the opposite direction; the Satisfaction Condition is an elegant expression of the invariance of truth under the renaming of basic symbols taking account of the variance of sentences and the covariance of models. (It also generalizes a condition called the "Translation Axiom" in [Barwise 74].)

Definition 14: An **institution** I consists of

1. a category **Sign** of "signatures,"
2. a functor Sen: **Sign**→**Set** giving the set of **sentences** over a given signature,
3. a functor **Mod**: **Sign**→**Cat**^{op} giving the category (sometimes called the **variety**) of **models** of a given signature (the arrows in **Mod**(Σ) are called **model morphisms**), and
4. a **satisfaction** relation $\models \subseteq$ |**Mod**(Σ)| **x** Sen(Σ) for each Σ in **Sign**, sometimes denoted $\models_\Sigma$

such that for each morphism ϕ: $\Sigma \rightarrow \Sigma'$ in **Sign**, the **Satisfaction Condition**

$$m' \models \phi(e) \text{ iff } \phi(m') \models e$$

holds for each m′ in |**Mod**(Σ')| and each e in Sen(Σ). []

For some purposes this definition can be simplified by replacing **Mod**: **Sign**→**Cat**^{op} by Mod: **Sign**→**Set**^{op}. Then Mod(Σ) is the *set* of all Σ-models; the two versions of the definition are thus related by the equation Mod(Σ)=|**Mod**(Σ)|. Indeed, our original version [Burstall & Goguen 80] was the second. Some reasons for changing it are: first, it is more consistent with the categiorical point of view to consider morphisms of models along with models; and secondly, we would like every liberal institution to be an institution, rather than just to determine one (liberal institutions will play an important role later in this paper).

There is a more categorical definition of the institution concept, replacing the rather ad hoc looking family of satisfaction relations by a functor into a category of "twisted relations." This will be given in the full version of this paper.

Example 1: Equational Logic. The work of Section 2 shows that (many sorted) equational logic is an institution, with **Sign** the category **Sig** of equational signatures (Definition 3), with **Mod**(Σ)=**Alg**(Σ) (Definition 6; see Definition 7 for the functor **Alg** which instantiates the functor **Mod**), with Sen(Σ) the set of all Σ-equations (Definition 8; see Definition 12 for the functor Eqn, which instantiates the functor Sen), and with satisfaction given in the usual way (Definition 10). The Satisfaction Condition holds by Proposition 13. Let us denote this institution $\mathcal{EQ}$. **End of Example 1.**

Example 2: First Order Logic. We follow the path of Section 2 again, but now showing that a more complicated logical system is an institution. Our work on equational logic will greatly aid with this task. Many details are omitted.

Definition 15: A **first order signature** Ω is a triple $\langle S,\Sigma,\Pi \rangle$, where

1. S is a set (of **sorts**),
2. Σ is an S*xS-indexed family of sets (of **operator** symbols, also called **function** symbols), and
3. Π is an S*-indexed family of sets (of **predicate symbols**).

A **morphism of first order signatures**, from Ω to Ω′, is a triple $\langle\phi_1,\phi_2,\phi_3\rangle$, where
1. ϕ_1: S→S′ is a function,
2. ϕ_2: Σ→Σ′ is an S*xS-indexed family of functions $(\phi_2)_{us}$: $\Sigma_{us}\to\Sigma'_{\phi_1{*}(u)\phi_1(s)}$ and
3. ϕ_3: Π→Π′ is an S*-indexed family of functions $(\phi_3)_u$: $\Pi_u\to\Pi'_{\phi_1{*}(u)}$.

Let **FoSig** denote the category with first order signatures as its objects and with first order signature morphisms as its morphisms. []

Definition 16: For Ω a first order signature, an **Ω-model** (or **Ω-structure**) A consists of
1. an S-indexed family |A| of non-empty sets $\langle A_s \mid s \text{ in } S\rangle$, where A_s is called the **carrier** of sort s,
2. an S*xS-indexed family α of functions α_{us}: $\Sigma_{us}\to[A_u\to A_s]$ assigning a function to each function symbol, and
3. an S*-indexed family β of functions β_u: $\Pi_u\to\mathrm{Pow}(A_u)$ assigning a relation to each predicate symbol, where Pow(X) denotes the set of all subsets of a set X.

For π in Π_u with u=s1...sn and ai in A_{si} for i=1,...,n, we say that "π(a1,...,an) holds" iff (a1,...,an) is in β(π); and as usual, we may abbreviate this assertion by simply writing "π(a1,...,an)."

Next, we define a **first order Ω-homomorphism** f: A→A′ of Ω-models A and A′ to be an S-indexed family of functions f_s: $A_s\to A'_s$ such that the homomorphism condition holds for Σ (as in Definition 5) and such that for π in Π_u with u=s1...sn, and with ai in A_{si} for i=1,...,n,

$$\pi(a1,...,an) \text{ implies } \pi'(f_{s1}(a1),...,f_{sn}(an)) ,$$

where π denotes β(π) and π′ denotes β′(π).

Let **FoMod** denote the category with first order models as its objects and with first order morphisms as its morphisms. We now extend **FoMod** to a functor **FoSig→Cat**^{op}. Given a first order signature morphism φ: Ω→Ω′, define the functor **FoMod**(Ω′)→**FoMod**(Ω) to send: first of all, A′ in **FoMod**(Ω′) to A=φA′ defined by
1. $A_s=A'_{s'}$ for s in S with $s'=\phi_1(s)$,
2. $\alpha_{us}(\sigma)=\alpha'_{u's'}((\phi_2)_{us}(\sigma))$ for u in S*, s in S and σ in Σ_{us} where $u'=\phi_1{*}(u)$ and $s'=\phi_1(s)$, and
3. $\beta_{us}(\pi)=\beta'_{u'}((\phi_3)_u(\pi))$ for u in S* and π in Π_u with u′ as above;

and secondly, to send f′: A′→B′ in **FoMod**(Ω′) to f=φf′: A→B in **FoMod**(Ω), where A=φA′ and B=φB′, defined by $f_s=f'_{s'}$ where $s'=\phi_1(s)$. This construction extends that of Definition 7, and it is easy to see that it does indeed give a functor. []

The next step is to define the sentences over a first order signature Ω. We do this in the usual way, by first defining terms and formulas. Let X be an S-indexed set of variable symbols, with each X_s the infinite set $\{x^s_1, x^s_2, ...\}$; we may omit the superscript s if the sort is clear from context. Now define the S-indexed family TERM(Ω) of **Ω-terms** to be the carriers of $T_\Sigma(X)$, the free Σ-algebra with generators X, and define a(n S-indexed) function Free on TERM(Ω) inductively by

1. $Free_s(x)=\{x\}$ for x in X_s, and
2. $Free_s(\sigma(t1,...,tn))=\cup_{i=1}^{n} Free_{si}(ti)$.

Definition 17: A (well formed) **Ω-formula** is an element of the carrier of the (one sorted) free algebra WWF(Ω) having the **atomic formulae** $\{ \pi(t1,...,tn) \mid \pi \in \Pi_u$ with u=s1...sn and ti $\in$ $TERM(\Omega)_{si}$ $\}$ as generators, and having its (one sorted) signature composed of

1. a constant true,
2. a unary prefix operator $\neg$,
3. a binary infix operator &, and
4. a unary prefix operator $(\forall x)$ for each x in X.

The functions Var and Free, giving the sets of **variables** and of **free variables** that are used, respectively, in Ω-formulae, can be defined in the usual way, inductively over the above logical connectives. We then define Bound(P)=Var(P)-Free(P), the set of **bound variables** of P.

We can now define the remaining logical connectives in terms of the basic ones given above in the usual way.

Finally, define an **Ω-sentence** to be a **closed** Ω-formula, that is, an Ω-formula P with Free(P)=$\emptyset$. Finally, let FoSen(Ω) denote the set of all Ω-sentences. []

We now define the effect of FoSen on first order signature morphisms, so that it becomes a functor **FoSig→Set**. Given ϕ: $\Omega \to \Omega'$, we will define FoSen(ϕ): FoSen(Ω)→FoSen(Ω') using the initiality of TERM(Ω) and WFF(Ω). Since (ϕ_1,ϕ_2): $\Sigma \to \Sigma'$ is a signature morphism, there is an induced morphism ψ: $T_\Sigma(X) \to T_{\Sigma'}(X)$ which then gives ψ: TERM(Ω)→TERM(Ω'). We can now define WFF(ϕ): WFF(Ω)→WFF(Ω') by its effect on the generators of WFF(Ω), which are the atomic formulae, namely

$$WFF(\phi)(\pi(t1,...,tn))=\phi_3(\pi)(\psi(t1),...,\psi(tn)) .$$

Finally, we define FoSen(ϕ) to be the restriction of WFF(ϕ) to FoSen(Ω) $\subseteq$ WFF(Ω). For this to work, it must be checked that WFF(ϕ) carries closed Ω-formulae to closed Ω'-formulae; but this is easy.

It remains to define satisfaction. This corresponds to the usual "semantic definition of truth" (originally due to [Tarski 44]) and is again defined inductively. If A is a first order model, let Asgn(A) denote the set of all **assignments** of values in A to variables in X, i.e, [X→A], the set of all S-indexed functions f: X→A.

Definition 18: Given a sentence P, define Asgn(A,P), the set of assignments in A for which P is true, inductively by

1. if P=π(t1,...,tn) then f$\in$Asgn(A,P) iff $(f^{\#}(t1),...,f^{\#}(tn)) \in \beta(\pi)$, where $f^{\#}(t)$ denotes the evaluation of the Σ-term t in the Σ-algebra part of A, using the values of variables given by the assignment f,

2. Asgn(A,true)=Asgn(A),
3. Asgn(A,¬P)=Asgn(A)-Asgn(A,P),
4. Asgn(A,P&Q)=Asgn(A,P)∩Asgn(A,Q), and
5. Asgn(A,(∀x)P)={f | Asgn(A,f,x)⊆Asgn(A,P)}, where Asgn(A,f,x) is the set of all assignments f′ that agree with f except possibly on the variable x.

Then a model A **satisfies** a sentence P, written A |= P, iff Asgn(A,P)=Asgn(A). []

Finally, we must verify the satisfaction condition. This follows from an argument much like that used for the equational case, and is omitted here. Thus, first order logic is an institution; let us denote it $\mathcal{FO}$. **End of Example 2.**

Example 3: First Order Logic with Equality. This institution is closely related to that of Example 2. A signature for first order logic with equality is a first order signature $\Omega=\langle S,\Sigma,\Pi\rangle$ that has a particular predicate symbol $\equiv_s$ in Π_{ss} for each s in S. A morphism of signatures for first order logic with equality must preserve these predicate symbols, i.e., $\phi_3(\equiv_s)=\equiv_{\phi_1(s)}$. This gives a category **FoSigEq** of signatures for first order logic with equality.

If Ω is a signature for first order logic with equality, then a model for it is just an Ω-model A in the usual first order sense satisfying the additional condition that for all s in S, and for all a,a′ in A_s, $a\equiv_s a'$ iff a=a′.

A homomorphism of first order Ω-models with equality is just a first order Ω-homomorphism (in the sense of Definition 16), and we get a category **FoModEq**(Ω) of Ω-models for each signature Ω in |**FoSigEq**|, and **FoModEq** is a functor on **FoSigEq**. Ω-sentences are defined just as in Example 2, and so is satisfaction. We thus get a functor FoSenEq: **FoSigEq→Set**. The Satisfaction Condition follows immediately from that of first order logic without equality. Let us denote this institution by $\mathcal{FOEQ}$. **End of Example 3.**

Example 4: Horn Clause Logic with Equality. We now specialize the previous example by limiting the form that sentences can take, but without resticting either the predicate or operator symbols that may enter into them. In particular, we maintain the equality symbol with its fixed interpretation from Example 3; but we require that all sentences be of the form

$$(\forall \underline{x})\ A_1 \& A_2 \& \ldots A_n \Rightarrow A\ ,$$

where each A_i is an atomic formula $\pi(t_1,\ldots,t_m)$. In particular, we do not allow disjunction, negation or existential quantifiers. That this is an institution follows from the fact that first order logic with equality is an institution. Let us denote this institution $\mathcal{HORN}$. **End of Example 4.**

Example 5: Conditional Equational Logic. As a specialization of the first order Horn clause logic with equality, we can consider the case where equality is the only predicate symbol. This gives the institution often called conditional equational logic. **End of Example 5.**

Example 6: Horn Clause Logic without Equality. We can also restrict Example 4 by dropping equality with its fixed interpretation. This too is obviously an institution because it is just a restriction of ordinary first order logic. **End of Example 6.**

It seems clear that we can do many-sorted temporal or modal logic in much the same way, by adding the appropriate modal operators to the signature and defining their correct interpretation in all models; the models may be "Kripke" or "alternative world" structures. Higher order equational logic is also presumably an institution; the development should again follow that of equational logic, but using higher order sorts and operator symbols.[5] Quite possibly, the "inequational logic" of [Bloom 76], the order-sorted equational logic of [Goguen 78], and various kinds of infinitary equational logic, such as the logic of continuous algebras in [Goguen, Thatcher, Wagner & Wright 75b] and [Wright, Thatcher, Wagner & Goguen 76] are also institutions. We further conjecture that in general, mechanical theorem provers, such as those of [Boyer & Moore 80], [Aubin 76] and [Shostak, Schwartz & Melliar-Smith 81], are based on logical systems that are institutions (or if they are not, should be modified so that they are!). Clearly, it would be helpful to have some general results to help in establishing whether or not various logical systems are institutions.

There is a way of generating many other examples due to [Mahr & Makowsky 82a]: take as the sentences over a signature Σ all specifications using Σ written in some specification language (such as Special or Affirm); we might think of such a specification as a convenient abbreviation for a (possibly very large) conjunction of simpler sentences. However, this seems an inappropriate viewpoint in the light of Section 6 which argues that the real purpose of a specification language is to define the meanings of the basic symbols (in Σ), so that the signature should be constructed (in a highly structured manner) right along with the sentences, rather than being given in advance.

This and the next section assume that a fixed but arbitrary institution has been given; Section 5 discusses what can be done with more than one institution.

3.2 Theories and Theory Morphisms

A Σ-theory, often called just a "theory" in the following, consists of a signature Σ and a closed set of Σ-sentences. Thus, this notion differs from the [Lawvere 63] notion of "algebraic theory," which is independent of any choice of signature; the notion also simplifies the "signed theories" of [Burstall & Goguen 77]. The simpler notion is more appropriate for the purposes of this paper, as well as easier to deal with. In general, our theories contain an infinite number of sentences, but are defined by a finite presentation.

Definition 19:

1. A Σ-**theory presentation** is a pair $\langle\Sigma,E\rangle$, where Σ is a signature and E is a set of Σ-sentences.
2. A Σ-model A **satisfies** a theory presentation $\langle\Sigma,E\rangle$ if A satisfies each sentence in E; let us write $A \models E$.
3. If E is a set of Σ-sentences, let E^* be the set[6] of all Σ-models that satisfy each sentence in E.
4. If M is a set of Σ-models, let M^* be the set of all Σ-sentences that are satisfied by each model in M; we will hereafter also let M^* denote $\langle\Sigma,M^*\rangle$, **the theory of** M.
5. By the **closure** of a set E of Σ-sentences we mean the set E^{**}, written $E^\bullet$.
6. A set E of Σ-sentences is **closed** iff $E=E^\bullet$. Then a Σ-**theory** is a theory presentation $\langle\Sigma,E\rangle$ such that E is closed.

---

[5] The sorts involved will be the objects of the free Cartesian closed category on the basic sort set [Parsaye-Ghomi 82].

[6] In the terminology of axiomatic set theory, this will often turn out to be a class rather than a set of models, but this distinction will be ignored in this paper.

7. The Σ-theory **presented by** the presentation $\langle\Sigma,E\rangle$ is $\langle\Sigma,E^{\bullet}\rangle$.

[]

Notice that we have given a model-theoretic definition of closure. For some institutions, a corresponding proof-theoretic notion can be given, because there is a complete set of inference rules. For the equational institution, these rules embody the equivalence properties of equality, including the substitution of equal terms into equal terms [Goguen & Meseguer 81].

We can also consider closed sets of models (in the equational institution these are usually called varieties). The **closure** of a set M of models is M^{**}, denoted $M^{\bullet}$, and a full subcategory of models is called **closed** iff its objects are all the models of some set of sentences.

Definition 20: If T and T' are theories, say $\langle\Sigma,E\rangle$ and $\langle\Sigma',E'\rangle$, then a **theory morphism** from T to T' is a signature morphism $F\colon \Sigma\rightarrow\Sigma'$ such that $\phi(e)$ is in E' for each e in E; we will write $F\colon T\rightarrow T'$. The **category of theories** has theories as objects and theory morphisms as morphisms, with their composition and identities defined as for signature morphisms; let us denote it **Th**. (It is easy to see that this is a category.) []

Notice that there is a forgetful functor Sign: **Th→Sign** sending $\langle\Sigma,E\rangle$ to Σ, and sending ϕ as a theory morphism to ϕ as a signature morphism.

Proposition 21: The two functions, *: sets of Σ-sentences → sets of Σ-models, and *: sets of Σ-models → sets of Σ-sentences, given in Definition 19, form what is known as a **Galois connection** [Cohn 65], in that they satisfy the following properties, for any sets E,E' of Σ-sentences and sets M,M' of Σ-models:

1. $E \subseteq E'$ implies $E'^{*} \subseteq E^{*}$.
2. $M \subseteq M'$ implies $M'^{*} \subseteq M^{*}$.
3. $E \subseteq E^{**}$.
4. $M \subseteq M^{**}$.

These imply the following properties:

5. $E^{*}=E^{***}$.
6. $M^{*}=M^{***}$.
7. There is a dual (i.e., inclusion reversing) isomorphism between the closed sets of sentences and the closed sets of models.
8. $(\cup_n E_n)^{*}=\cap E_n{}^{*}$.
9. $\phi(E^{*})=(\phi E)^{*}$, for $\phi\colon \Sigma\rightarrow\Sigma'$ a signature morphism.

[]

For a theory T with signature Σ, let **Mod**(T) and also T^{*} denote the **full subcategory** of **Mod**(Σ) of all Σ-models that satisfy all the sentences in T. This is used in the following.

Definition 22: Given a theory morphism $F\colon T\rightarrow T'$, the **forgetful functor** $F^{*}\colon T'^{*}\rightarrow T^{*}$ sends a T'-model m' to the T-model F(m'), and sends a T'-model morphism $f\colon m'\rightarrow n'$ to $F^{*}(f)=$**Mod**$(F)(f)\colon F(m')\rightarrow F(n')$. This functor may also be denoted **Mod**(F). []

For this definition to make sense, we must show that if a given Σ'-model m' satisfies T', then $\phi^{*}(m')$ satisfies T. Let e be any sentence in T. Because ϕ is a theory morphism, $\phi(e)$ is a sentence of T', and therefore $m' \models \phi(e)$. The Satisfaction Condition now gives us that $\phi(m')$

$\models$ e, as desired. We also need that the morphism $\phi^*(f)$ lies in T^*, but this follows because T^* is a full subcategory of **Mod**(Σ), and the source and target objects of $\phi^*(f)$ lie in T^*.

3.3 The Closure and Presentation Lemmas

Let us write $\phi(E)$ for $\{\phi(e) \mid e \text{ is in } E\}$ and $\phi(M)$ for $\{\phi(m) \mid m \text{ is in } M\}$. Let us also write $\phi^{-1}(M)$ for $\{m \mid \phi(m) \text{ is in } M\}$. Using this notation, we can more compactly write the Satisfaction Condition as

$$\phi^{-1}(E^*)=\phi(E)^* ,$$

and using this notation, we can derive

Lemma 23: <u>Closure</u>. $\phi(E^\bullet) \subseteq \phi(E)^\bullet$.

Proof: $\phi(E^{**})^*=\phi^{-1}(E^{***})=\phi^{-1}(E^*)=\phi(E)^*$, using the Satisfaction Condition and 5. of Proposition 21. Therefore $\phi(E^\bullet)=\phi(E^{**}) \subseteq \phi(E^{**})^{**}=\phi(E)^{**}=\phi(E)^\bullet$, using 3. of Proposition 21 and the just proved equation. []

The following gives a necessary and sufficient condition for a signature morphism to be a theory morphism.

Lemma 24: <u>Presentation</u>. Let ϕ: $\Sigma \rightarrow \Sigma'$ and suppose that $\langle\Sigma,E\rangle$ and $\langle\Sigma',E'\rangle$ are presentations. Then ϕ: $\langle\Sigma,E^\bullet\rangle \rightarrow \langle\Sigma',E'^\bullet\rangle$ is a theory morphism iff $\phi(E) \subseteq E'^\bullet$.

Proof: By the Closure Lemma, $\phi(E^\bullet) \subseteq \phi(E)^\bullet$. By hypothesis, $\phi(E) \subseteq E'^\bullet$. Therefore, $\phi(E^\bullet) \subseteq \phi(E)^\bullet \subseteq E'^{\bullet\bullet}=E'^\bullet$, so ϕ is a theory morphism. Conversely, if ϕ is a theory morphism, then $\phi(E^\bullet) \subseteq E'^\bullet$. Therefore $\phi(E) \subseteq E'^\bullet$, since $E \subseteq E^\bullet$. []

If an institution has a complete set of rules of deduction, then the Presentation Lemma tells us that to check if ϕ is a theory morphism, we can apply ϕ to each sentence e of the source presentation E and see whether ϕ(e) can be proved from E'. There is no need to check all the sentences in $E^\bullet$.

3.4 Putting Theories Together

A useful general principle is to describe a large widget as the interconnection of a system of small widgets, using widget-morphisms to indicate the interfaces over which the interconnection is to be done. [Goguen 71] (see also [Goguen & Ginali 78]) gives a very general formulation in which such interconnections are calculated as colimits. One application is to construct large theories as colimits of small theories and theory morphisms [Burstall & Goguen 77]. In particular, the pushout construction for applying parameterized specifications that was implicit in [Burstall & Goguen 77] has been given explicitly by [Burstall & Goguen 78] and [Ehrich 78]. For this to make sense, the category of theories should have finite colimits. For the equational institution, [Goguen & Burstall 78] have proved that the intuitively correct syntactic pasting together of theory presentations exactly corresponds to theory colimits. Colimits have also been used for many other things in computer science, for example, pasting together graphs in the theory of graph grammars [Ehrig, Kreowski, Rosen & Winkowski 78]. Let us now review the necessary categorical concepts.

Definition 25: A **diagram** D in a category **C** consists of a graph G together with a labelling of each node n of G by an object D_n of **C**, and a labelling of each edge e (from node n to node n' in G) by a morphism D(e) in **C** from D_n to $D_{n'}$; let us write D: G→**C**. Then a **cone** α in **C** over the diagram D consists of an object A of **C** and a family of morphisms α_n: $D_n \rightarrow A$, one for each node n in G, such that for each edge e: n→n' in G, the diagram

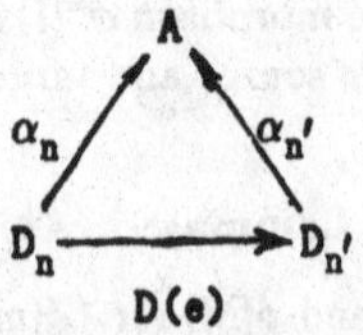

commutes in **C**. We call D the **base** of the cone α, A its **apex**, G its **shape**, and we write α: D$\Rightarrow$A. If α and β are cones with base D and apexes A,B (respectively), then a **morphism of cones** $\alpha \rightarrow \beta$ is a morphism f: A$\rightarrow$B in **C** such that for each node n in G the diagram

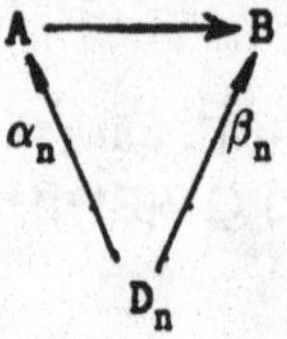

commutes in **C**. Now let **Cone**(D,**C**) denote the resulting category of all cones over D in **C**. Then a **colimit** of D in **C** is an initial object in **Cone**(D,**C**). []

The uniqueness of initial objects up to isomorphism implies the uniqueness of colimits up to cone isomorphism. The apex of a colimit cone α is called the **colimit object**, and the morphisms α(n) to the apex are called the **injections** of D(n) into the colimit. The colimit object is also unique up to isomorphism.

Definition 26: A category **C** is **finitely cocomplete** iff it has colimits of all finite diagrams, and is **cocomplete** iff it has colimits of all diagrams (whose base graphs are not proper classes). A functor F: **C**$\rightarrow$**C'** **reflects colimits** iff whenever D is a diagram in **C** such that the diagram D;F in **C'** has a colimit cone α': D$\Rightarrow$A' in **C'**, then there is a colimit cone α: D$\Rightarrow$A in **C** with $\alpha' = \alpha$;F (i.e., $\alpha'_n = F(\alpha_n)$ for all nodes n in the base of D). []

Here is the general result about putting together theories in any institution with a suitable category of signatures. The proof is omitted.

Theorem 27: The forgetful functor Sign: **Th**$\rightarrow$**Sign** reflects colimits. []

It now follows, for example, that the category **Th** of theories in an institution is [finitely] cocomplete if its category **Sign** of signatures is [finitely] cocomplete.

The category of equational signatures is finitely cocomplete (see [Goguen & Burstall 78] for a simple proof using comma categories), so we conclude that the category of signed equational theories is cocomplete. Using similar techniques, we can show that the category of first order signatures is cocomplete, and thus without effort conclude that the category of first order theories is cocomplete (this might even be a new result).

4 Constraints

To avoid overspecifying problems, we often want *loose* specifications, i.e., specifications that have many acceptable models. On the other hand, there are also many specifications where one wants to use the natural numbers, truth values, or some other fixed data type. In such cases, one wants the subtheories that correspond to these data types to be given *standard* interpretations. Moreover, we sometimes want to consider parameterized standard data types, such as **Set**[X] and **List**[X]. Here, one wants sets and lists to be given standard interpretations, once a suitable interpretation has been given for **X**.

So far we have considered the category T*=**Mod**(T) of *all* interpretations of a theory T; this section considers how to impose constraints on these interpretations. One kind of constraint requires that some parts of T have a "standard" interpretation relative to other parts; these constraints are the "data constraints" of [Burstall & Goguen 80], generalizing and relativizing the "initial algebra" approach to abstract data types introduced by [Goguen, Thatcher, Wagner & Wright 75b, Goguen, Thatcher & Wagner 78]. However, the first work in this direction seems to be that of [Kaphengst & Reichel 71], later generalized to "initially restricting algebraic theories" [Reichel 80]. Data constraints make sense for any "liberal" institution, and are more expressive even in the equational institution. Actually, our general results apply to many different notions of what it means for a model to satisfy a constraint. In particular, we will see that "generating constraints" and "hierarchy constraints" are special cases; these correspond to the conditions of "no junk" and "no confusion" that together give the more powerful notion of "data constraint." Section 5 generalizes this to consider "duplex constraints" that involve a different insititution than the one in which models are taken.

4.1 Free Interpretations

For example, suppose that we want to define the natural numbers in the equational institution. To this end, consider a theory **N** with one sort **nat**, and with a signature Σ containing one constant 0 and one unary operator inc; there are no equations in the presentation of this theory. Now this theory has many algebras, including some where inc(0)=0. But the natural numbers, no matter how represented, give an **initial** algebra in the category $\mathbf{Alg}_\Sigma$ of all algebras for this theory, in the sense that there is *exactly* one Σ-homomorphism from it to any other Σ-algebra. It is easy to prove that any two initial Σ-algebras are Σ-isomorphic; this means that the property "being initial" determines the natural numbers uniquely up to isomorphism. This characterization of the natural numbers is due to [Lawvere 64], and a proof that it is equivalent to Peano's axioms can be found in [MacLane & Birkhoff 67], pages 67-70.

The initial algebra approach to abstract data types [Goguen, Thatcher, Wagner & Wright 75b, Goguen, Thatcher & Wagner 78] has taken this "Lawvere-Peano" characterization of the natural numbers as a paradigm for defining other abstract data types; the method has been used for sets, lists, stacks, and many many other data types, and has even been used to specify database systems [Goguen & Tardo 79] and programming languages [Goguen & Parsaye-Ghomi 81]. The essential ideas here are that concrete data types are algebras, and that "abstract" in "abstract data type" means *exactly* the same thing as "abstract" in "abstract algebra," namely defined uniquely up to isomorphism. A number of less abstract equivalents of initiality for the equational institution, including a generalized Peano axiom system, are given in [Goguen & Meseguer 83].

Let us now consider the case of the parameterized abstract data type of sets of elements of a sort **s**. We add to **s** a new sort **set**, and operators[7]

∅: **set**

{_}: **s** → **set**

_U_: **set**,**set** → **set** ,

subject to the following equations, where S, S′ and S″ are variables of sort **set**,

∅US=S=SU∅

SU(S′US″)=(SUS′)US″

SUS′=S′US

[7] We use "mixfix" declarations in this signature, in the style of OBJ [Goguen 77, Goguen & Tardo 79]: the underbars are placeholders for elements of a corresponding sort from the sort list following the colon.

SUS=S .

Although we want these operators to be interpreted "initially" in some sense, we do *not* want the initial algebra of the theory having sorts **s** and **set** and the operators above. Indeed, the initial algebra of this theory has the *empty* carrier for the sort **s** (since there are no operators to generate elements of **s**) and has only the element ∅ of sort **set**. What we want is to permit *any* interpretation for the parameter sort **s**, and then to require that the new sort **set** and its new operators are interpreted freely *relative* to the given interpretation of **s**.

Let us make this precise. Suppose that F: T→T' is a theory morphism. Then there is a forgetful functor from the category of T'-models to the category of T-models, F^*: $T'^* \to T^*$ as in Definition 22. In the equational case T^*=**Alg**(T) and a very general result of [Lawvere 63] says that there is a functor that we will denote by $F^{\$}$: $T^* \to T'^*$ called the **free functor** determined by F, characterized by the following "universal" property: given a T-model A, there is a T'-model $F^{\$}(A)$ and a T-morphism η_A: A→$F^*(F^{\$}(A))$, called the **universal** morphism, such that for any T'-model B' and any T-morphism f: A→F^*(B'), there is a unique T'-morphism $f^\#$: $F^{\$}$(A)→B' such that the diagram

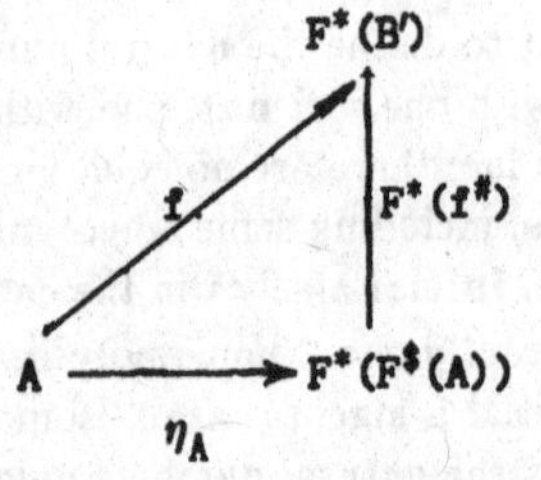

commutes in **Mod**(T). It can be shown [MacLane 71] that if for each A there is an object $F^{\$}$(A) with this universal property, then there is a unique way to define $F^{\$}$ on morphisms so as to get a functor.

For this to make sense in an arbitrary institution, we need the existence of free constructions over arbitrary theory morphisms, as expressed in the following.

Definition 28: An institution is **liberal** iff for every theory morphism F: T→T' and every T-model A, there is a T'-model $F^{\$}$(A) with a **universal** T-morphism η_A: A→$F^*(F^{\$}(A))$ having the property that for each T'-model B' and T-morphism f: A→F^*(B'), there is a unique T'-morphism $f^\#$: $F^{\$}$(A)→B' such that the above diagram commutes (in the category **Mod**(T)). []

As in the equational case, the existence of a universal morphism for each T-model A guarantees the existence of a unique functor $F^{\$}$ having the value $F^{\$}$(A) on the object A [MacLane 71]; this functor $F^{\$}$ is called a **free** functor, just as F^* is called a **forgetful** functor. ($T^{\$}$ is left adjoint to F^*, and is unique up to isomorphism of its value objects if it exists. Thus an institution is liberal iff the forgetful functors induced by theory morphisms always have left adjoints.) The equational institution is liberal, but the first order logic instituion is not. The Horn clause first order logic with equality discussed in Example 4 is another liberal institution, by deep results of [Gabriel & Ulmer 71]; so is the conditional equational institution of Example 5.

Returning to our set example, consider the theory morphism, Set, that is the inclusion of the trivial theory, **Triv** having just the sort **s**, into the theory of sets of **s**, let's call it **Set-of-Triv**, obtained by adding the sort **set** and the operators and equations given above. Then Set^* takes a **Set-of-Triv**-algebra (which is just a set) and forgets the new sort **set** and the three new operators, giving an algebra that has just the set of **s**-sorted elements. The free functor $Set^{\$}$

takes a **Triv**-algebra A and extends it freely to a **Set-of-Triv**-algebra, the new operators giving distinct results except where the equations of **Set-of-Triv** force equality.

Given a **Set-of-Triv**-algebra B, there is a natural way to check whether or not its **set** sort and operators are free over its parameter sort **s**: in the above diagram, let A=Set*(B) and let $f=id_{Set^*(B)}$; then $f^{\#}$: Set$(Set*(B))→B restricted to the parameter sort is the identity (because Set*($f^{\#}$)=f), and $f^{\#}$ itself should be an isomorophism if the **set** part of B is to be free over its parameter part. In the general case, the morphism $(id_{F^*(B)})^{\#}$: F$(F*(B))→B is called the **counit** (of the adjunction) and denoted ϵ_B. The discussion of this example motivates the following.

Definition 29: Let F: T→T' be a theory morphism. Then a T'-model B is **F-free** iff the counit morphism $\epsilon_B=(id_{F^*(B)})^{\#}$: F$(F*(B))→B is an isomorphism. []

The notion of F-free for the equational case is due to [Thatcher, Wagner & Wright 79][8] .

Results of [Mahr & Makowsky 82b] and [Mahr & Makowsky 82a] show that, in a sense, the most general sublanguage of first order logic that admits initial models is Horn clause logic with infinitary clauses; further, the most general finitary language uses finitary Horn clauses; the most general equational language uses (infinitary) conditional equations; and the most general finitary equational sublanguage consists of finitary conditional equations. These results apply to the existence of initial models, rather than to left adjoints of forgetful functors; it would be interesting to know whether or not they extend in this way. It is also interesting to note that they have made use of abstractions of the notion of "logical system" similar to that of an "institution."

4.2 Constraining Theories

It is very convenient in program specification to let theories include not just the sentences provided by an institution, but also declarations that certain subtheories should be interpreted freely relative others in the sense of Section 4.1. We call such sentences **data constraints** and we call theories that can include them **constraining theories**. Such a theory could require that subtheories defining data types such as natural numbers, sets, and strings be given their standard interpretations (uniquely up to isomorphism), while permiting a sort with a partial ordering to have any interpretation (that satisfies the partial order theory), and thus to be "loose," or to be parametric as are the "meta-sort" or "requirement" theories of Clear [Burstall & Goguen 77].

Returning to the Set example of the previous subsection, let us further enrich **Set-of-Triv** with some new sorts and operators to get a theory **Set-of-Triv-Etc**. For example, we might add an operator

choice: **set** → **s**

that chooses an arbitrary element of any non-empty set; this is a good example of a loose specification. For example, the enriched theory might include the conditional equation

choose(s) in s if $s \neq \emptyset$.

Let Etc: **Set-of-Triv**→**Set-of-Triv-Etc** be the theory inclusion and let

etc: Sign(**Set-of-Triv**)→Sign(**Set-of-Triv-Etc**)

---

8 [Burstall & Goguen 80] defined B to be F-free if B≈F$(F*(B)); however, there are examples in which these two objects are isomorphic, but not naturally so by the counit morphism η. Our thanks to Eric Wagner for this comment.

be the corresponding signature morphism. Then a **Set-of-Triv-Etc**-algebra A interprets sets as intended if etc*(A) satisfies **Set-of-Triv** and is Set-free. This motivates the following.

Definition 30: Let Σ be a signature. Then a **Σ-constraint** is a pair

$\langle F: T'' \rightarrow T', \theta: \mathrm{Sign}(T') \rightarrow \Sigma \rangle$

consisting of a theory morphism and a signature morphism. (We may call a Σ-constraint a **Σ-data constraint** if it is used to define a data type.) A Σ-model A **satisfies** the Σ-constraint $c = \langle F: T'' \rightarrow T', \theta: \mathrm{Sign}(T') \rightarrow \Sigma \rangle$ iff $\theta(A)$ satisfies T' and is F-free; we write $A \models_{\Sigma} c$ in this case. []

A picture of the general situation in this definition may help:

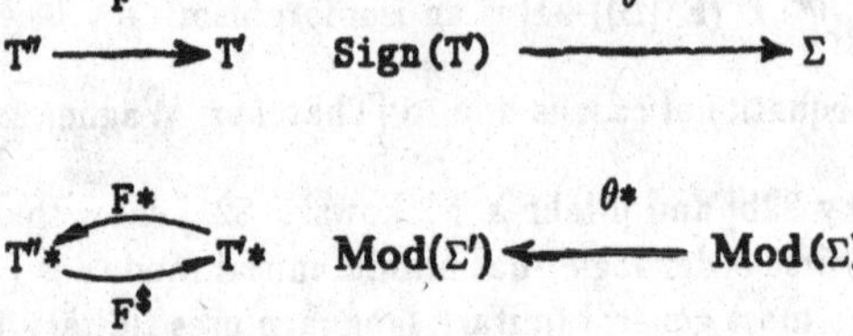

In the Set-etc example, $F: T'' \rightarrow T'$ is the theory inclusion Etc: **Triv→Set-of-Triv**, and θ: $\mathrm{Sign}(T') \rightarrow \Sigma$ is the signature morphism underlying the theory inclusion Etc: **Set-of-Triv→Set-of-Triv-Etc**. For any Σ-algebra A, it makes sense to ask whether θA satisfies T'* and is F-free, as indeed Definition 30 does ask.

Our work on constraints dates from the Spring of 1979, and was influenced by a lecture of Reichel in Poland in 1978 and by the use of functors to handle parametric data types in [Thatcher, Wagner & Wright 79]. There are three main differences between our approach and the "initial restrictions" of [Reichel 80]: first, an initial restriction on an algebraic theory consists of a pair of subtheories, whereas we use a pair of theories with an arbitrary theory morphism between them, and a signature morphism from the target theory. The use of subtheories seems very natural, but we have been unable to prove that it gives rise to an institution, and conjecture that it does not do so; we also believe that the added generality may permit some interesting additional examples. The second difference is simply that we are doing our work over an arbitrary liberal institution. The third difference lies in the manner of adding constraints: whereas [Reichel 80] defines a "canon" to be an algebraic theory together with a set of initial restrictions on it, we will define a new institution whose sentences on a signature Σ include both the old Σ-sentences, and also Σ-constraints. This route has the technical advantage that both kinds of new sentence refer to the same signature. Historically the first work in this field seems to have been the largely unknown paper of [Kaphengst & Reichel 71], which apparently considered the case of a single chain of theory inclusions.

We now show that constraints behave like sentences even though they have a very different internal structure. Like sentences, they impose restrictions on the allowable models. Moreover, a signature morphism from Σ to Σ' determines a translation from Σ-constraints to Σ'-constraints just as it determines a translation from of Σ-sentences to Σ'-sentences.

Definition 31: Let $\phi: \Sigma \rightarrow \Sigma'$ be a signature morphism and let $c = \langle F, \theta \rangle$ be a Σ-constraint. Then the **translation** of c by ϕ is the Σ'-constraint $\langle F, \theta;\phi \rangle$; we write this as $\phi(c)$. []

It is the need for the translation of a constraint to be a constraint that leads to constraints in which θ is not an inclusion. We now state the Satisfaction Condition for constraints.

Lemma 32: Constraint Satisfaction. If ϕ: $\Sigma \rightarrow \Sigma'$ is a signature morphism, if c is a Σ-constraint, and if B is a Σ'-model then

$$B \models \phi(c) \text{ iff } \phi(B) \models c\ .$$ []

Given a liberal institution $\mathcal{I}$, we can construct another institution having as its sentences both the sentences of $\mathcal{I}$ and also constraints.

Definition 33: Let $\mathcal{I}$ be an arbitrary liberal institution. Now construct the institution $C(\mathcal{I})$ whose theories contain both constraints and $\mathcal{I}$-sentences as follows: the category of signatures of $C(\mathcal{I})$ is the category **Sign** of signatures of $\mathcal{I}$; if Σ is an $\mathcal{I}$-signature, then $\mathrm{Sen}_{C(\mathcal{I})}(\Sigma)$ is the union of the set $\mathrm{Sen}_{\mathcal{I}}(\Sigma)$ of all Σ-sentences from $\mathcal{I}$ with the set of all Σ-constraints[9]; also **Mod**(Σ) is the same for $C(\mathcal{I})$ as for $\mathcal{I}$; we use the concept of constraint translation in Definition 31 to define Sen(ϕ) on constraints; finally, satisfaction for $C(\mathcal{I})$ is as in $\mathcal{I}$ for Σ-sentences from $\mathcal{I}$, and is as in Definition 30 for Σ-constraints. []

We now have the following.

Proposition 34: If $\mathcal{I}$ is a liberal institution, then $C(\mathcal{I})$ is an institution. []

This means that all the concepts and results of Section 3 can be applied to $C(\mathcal{I})$-theories that include constraints as well as sentences. Let us call such theories **constraining theories**. Thus, we get notions of presentation and of closure, as well as of theory. In particular, the Presentation and Closure Lemmas hold and we therefore get the following important result:

Theorem 35: Given a liberal institution with a [finitely] cocomplete category of signatures, its category of constraining theories is also [finitely] cocomplete.

Proof: Immediate from Theorems 27 and 34. []

Let us consider what this means for the equational institution. While the proof theory for inferring that an equation is in the closure of a set of equations is familiar, we have no such proof theory for constraints. However, this should be obtainable because a constraint corresponds to an induction principle plus some inequalities [Burstall & Goguen 81, Goguen & Meseguer 83]; in particular, the constraint that sets are to be interpreted freely will give us all the consequences of the induction principle for sets. In more detail, this constraint for sets demands that all elements of sort **set** be generated by the operators $\emptyset$, {_} and _∪_, and this can be expressed by a principle of structural induction over these generators (notice that this is not a first order axiom). The constraint also demands that two elements of sort **set** are *unequal* unless they can be proved equal using the given equations. We cannot express this distinctness with equations; one way to express it is by adding a new boolean-valued binary operator on the new sort, say $\equiv$, with some new equations such that $t \equiv t' = \text{false}$ iff $t \neq t'$, and also such that $\text{true} \neq \text{false}$ [Goguen 80].

Let now us consider an easier example, involving equational theories with the following three (unconstrained) presentations:

1. **E** -- the empty theory: no sorts, no operators, no equations.
2. **N** -- the theory with one sort **nat**, one constant 0, one unary operator inc, and no equations.

[9] There are some foundational difficulties with the size of the closure of a constraint theory that we will ignore here; they can be solved by limiting the size of the category of signatures used in the original liberal institution.

3. **NP** -- the theory with one sort **nat**, two constants 0 and 1, one unary operator inc, one binary infix operator +, and equations 0+n=n, inc(m)+n=inc(m+n), 1=inc(0).

Let Σ^N and Σ^{NP} be the signatures of **N** and **NP** respectively, and let F^N: **E**→**N** and F^{NP}: **N**→**NP** denote the inclusion morphisms. Now **NP** as it stands has many different interpretations, for example the integers modulo 10, or the truth values with 0=false, 1=true, inc(false)=false, inc(true)=true, false+n=false, true+n=true. In the latter model, + is not commutative. In order to get the *standard* model suggested by the notation, we need to impose the constraint $\langle F^N, F^{NP}\rangle$ on the theory **NP**. Then the only model (up to isomorphism) is the natural numbers with the usual addition. Note that the equation m+n=n+m is satisfied by this model and therefore appears in the equational closure of the presentation; it is a property of + provable by induction. There are also extra constraints in the closure, for example $\langle f', \phi\rangle$, where f' is the inclusion of the empty theory **E** in the theory with 0, 1 and + with identity, associativity and commutativity equations, and ϕ is its inclusion in **NP**. This constraint is satisfied in all models that satisfy the constraint $\langle F^N, F^{NP}\rangle$. In this sense, the constraint on 0, 1 and + gives a derived induction principle. Further examples can be found in [Burstall & Goguen 81].

In general, the closure of a constraining presentation to a "constraining theory" adds new equations derivable by induction principles corresponding to the constraints; and it also adds some new constraints that correspond to derived induction principles. The new equations are important in giving a precise semantics for programming methodology. For example, we may want to supply **NP** as an actual parameter theory to a parameterized theory whose meta-sort demands a commutative binary operator. The new constraints seem less essential. [Clark 78] and [McCarthy 80] discuss what may be a promising approach to the proof-theoretic aspect of constraining theories. Clark calls his scheme "predicate completion" and thinks of it as a method for infering new sentences under a "closed world" assumption (the common sense assumption that the information actually given about a predicate is all and only the relevant information about that predicate; McCarthy identifies this with Occam's famous razor). We, of course, identify that "closed world" with the initial model of the given theory. Clark's scheme is simply to infer the converse of any Horn clause. This is *sound* for the institutions of conditional equations and first order Horn clauses (in the sense that all the sentences thus obtained are true of the initial model); it is not clear that it is complete. McCarthy calls his scheme "circumscription" and is interested in its application in the context of full first order logic; he has shown that it is sound when there exist minimal models. It can be unsound when such models do not exist.

It is worth considering what happens if we add extra silly equations to **NP** constrained by $\langle F^N, \Sigma N^P\rangle$. For example, 1+n=n contradicts the constraint; in fact, if we add it, we simply get an inconsistent constraining theory (it has no algebras).

4.3 Other Kinds of Constraint

Because a number of variations on the notion of data constraint have recently been proposed, it seems worthwhile to examine their relationship to the very general machinery developed in this paper. In fact, very little of Section 4.2 or Section 5 depends upon "F-freeness" in the definition of constraint satisfaction. This suggests weakening that notion. Recall that a Σ-algebra A satisfies a data constraint $c=\langle F\colon T\to T', \theta\colon \mathrm{Sign}(T')\to\Sigma\rangle$ iff θA satisfies T' and is F-free, which means that $\epsilon_{\theta A}\colon F^{\$}(F^*(\theta A))\to A$ is an isomorphism. For the equational institution, the most obvious ways of weakening the F-free concept are to require that $\epsilon_{\theta A}$ is only injective or only surjective, rather than bijective as for F-free. For $\epsilon_{\theta A}$ to be injective corresponds to what has been called a "hierarchy constraint" [Broy, Dosch, Partsch, Pepper & Wirsing 79]; it means that no elements of θA are identified by the natural mapping from $F^\$(F^*(\theta A))$; this condition generalizes the "no confusion" condition of [Burstall & Goguen 82]. For $\epsilon_{\theta A}$ to be surjective corresponds to what has been called a "generating constraint" [Ehrig, Wagner & Thatcher 82]; it means that all elements of θA are generated by elements of $F^*(\theta A)$; this condition generalizes the "no junk" condition of [Burstall & Goguen 82]. Notice that these two together give that θA is F-free. Now here is the general notion:

Definition 36: Let $\mathcal{I}$ be an institution, let $\mathcal{M}$ be a class of model morphisms from $\mathcal{I}$, let $c=\langle F\colon T\to T',\ \theta\colon Sign(T')\to\Sigma\rangle$ be a constraint from $\mathcal{I}$, and let A be a Σ-model from $\mathcal{I}$. Then A **$\mathcal{M}$-satisfies** c iff θA satisfies T' and $\epsilon_{\theta A}$ lies in $\mathcal{M}$. []

In particular, for a liberal institution $\mathcal{I}$, modifying the construction of $\mathcal{C}(\mathcal{I})$ to use the notion of $\mathcal{M}$-satisfaction, gives an institution (generalizing Proposition 34), and theories in this institution will be as cocomplete as $\mathcal{I}$ is (generalizing Theorem 35). This means, for example, that we can glue together theories that use hierarchy constraints with the usual colimit constructions, and in particular, we can do the specification language constructions of Section 6.

5 Using More than One Institution

After the work of Section 4.2, we know how to express constraints in any liberal institution; in particular, we can use constraints in the equational institution to specify parameterized abstract data types. We can also give loose specifications in any institution. Liberality is a fairly serious restriction since non-liberal institutions can often be more expressive than liberal institutions. For example, if one adds negation to the equational institution, it ceases to be liberal. Thus, the ambitious specifier might want both the rich expressive power of first order logic and also the data structure definition power of the equational institution. This section shows how he can eat his cake and have it too. The basic idea is to precisely describe a relationship between two institutions, the second of which is liberal, in the form of an institution morphism, and then to permit constraints that use theories from the second institution as an additional kind of sentence in this "duplex" institution. There are also other uses for institution morphisms; in particular, we will use this concept in showing when a theorem prover for one institution is sound for theories from another institution.

5.1 Institution Morphisms

Let us consider the relationship between the institution of first order logic with equality, $\mathcal{FOEQ}$, and the equational institution, $\mathcal{EQ}$. First of all, any first order signature can be reduced to an equational signature just by forgetting all its predicate symbols. Secondly, any equation can be regarded as a first order sentence just by regarding the equal sign in the equation as the distinguished binary predicate symbol (the equal sign in the equations of the equational institution is *not* a predicate symbol, but just a punctuation symbol that separates the left and right sides). Thirdly, any first order model can be viewed as an algebra just by forgetting all its predicates. These three functions are the substance of an institution morphism $\mathcal{FOEQ}\to\mathcal{EQ}$; there are also some conditions that must be satisfied.

Definition 37: Let $\mathcal{I}$ and $\mathcal{I}'$ be institutions. Then an **institution morphism** $\Phi\colon \mathcal{I}\to\mathcal{I}'$ consists of

1. a functor Φ: **Sign**$\to$**Sign**',

2. a natural transformation α: Φ;Sen′⇒Sen, that is, a natural family of functions
   α_Σ: Sen′($\Phi(\Sigma)$)→Sen(Σ), and
3. a natural transformation β: **Mod**⇒Φ;**Mod′**, that is, a natural family of functors
   β_Σ: **Mod**(Σ)→**Mod′**($\Phi(\Sigma)$),

such that the following **satisfaction condition** holds

$$A \models_\Sigma \alpha_\Sigma(e') \text{ iff } \beta_\Sigma(A) \models'_{\Phi(\Sigma)} e'$$

for A a Σ-model from $\mathcal{I}$ and e′ a $\Phi(\Sigma)$-sentence from $\mathcal{I}'$. []

The reader may wish to verify that Φ: $\mathcal{FOEQ}\to\mathcal{EQ}$ as sketched in the first paragraph of this subsection really is an institution morphism.

Notice that an institution morphism Φ: $\mathcal{I}\to\mathcal{I}'$ induces a functor Φ: $\mathbf{Th}_{\mathcal{I}}\to\mathbf{Th}_{\mathcal{I}'}$ on the corresponding categories of theories by sending a Σ-theory T to the $\Phi(\Sigma)$-theory $\beta_\Sigma(T^*)^*$. We now have the following useful result, whose proof is omitted in this version of this paper:

Theorem 38: If Φ: $\mathcal{I}\to\mathcal{I}'$ is an institution morphism such that Φ: **Sign**→**Sign′** is [finitely] cocontinuous, then Φ: $\mathbf{Th}_{\mathcal{I}}\to\mathbf{Th}_{\mathcal{I}'}$ is also [finitely] cocontinuous. []

Actually, a stronger result is true: Φ on theories preserves whatever colimits Φ preserves on signatures. By Theorem 38, if a large theory in the source institution is expressed as a colimit of smaller theories, the corresponding theory in the target institution can also be so expressed. Another reason for being interested in this result has to do with using theorem provers for one institution on theories in another (see below).

Definition 39: An institution morphism Φ: $\mathcal{I}\to\mathcal{I}'$ is **sound** iff for every signature Σ' and every Σ'-model A′ from $\mathcal{I}'$, there are a signature Σ and a Σ-model A from $\mathcal{I}'$ such that $A'=\beta_\Sigma(A)$. []

This condition is clearly satisfied by the institution morphism from $\mathcal{FOEQ}$ to $\mathcal{EQ}$ discussed above.

Proposition 40: If Φ: $\mathcal{I}\to\mathcal{I}'$ is a sound institution morphism and if P is a set of Σ'-sentences from $\mathcal{I}'$, then a Σ'-sentence e′ is in $P^\bullet$ iff αe is in $\alpha_\Sigma(P)^\bullet$, where Σ is a signature from I such that $\Sigma'=\Phi(\Sigma)$. []

We now know, for example, that the institution morphism from $\mathcal{FOEQ}$ to $\mathcal{EQ}$ permits using a theorem prover for first order logic with equality on equational theories.

5.2 Duplex Institutions

This subsection gives a construction for an institution whose theories can contain both sentences from a nonliberal institution $\mathcal{I}$ and constraints from a liberal institution $\mathcal{I}'$. What is needed to make the construction work is an institution morphism Φ: $\mathcal{I}\to\mathcal{I}'$ expressing the relationship between the two institutions. This idea was introduced informally in [Goguen 82a] and [Burstall & Goguen 81]. Note that all the results of this section generalize to the notion of $\mathcal{M}$-satisfaction given in Definition 36, although they are stated for the case of data constraints, i.e., the case where $\mathcal{M}$ is the class of isomorphisms.

Definition 41: Let $\mathcal{I}'$ be a liberal institution, let Φ: $\mathcal{I}\to\mathcal{I}'$ be an institution morphism, and let Σ be a signature from $\mathcal{I}$. Then a Σ-**duplex constraint** is a pair

$$c=\langle F: T''\to T',\ \theta: \mathrm{Sign}(T')\to\Phi(\Sigma)\rangle\ ,$$

where F is a theory morphism from $\mathcal{I}'$ and θ is signature morphism from $\mathcal{I}$. Furthermore, a Σ-model A from $\mathcal{I}$ **satisfies** the duplex constraint c iff $\theta(\beta_\Sigma(A))$ satisfies T' and is F-free; as usual, write $A \models_\Sigma c$. []

A picture of the general situation in this definition may help:

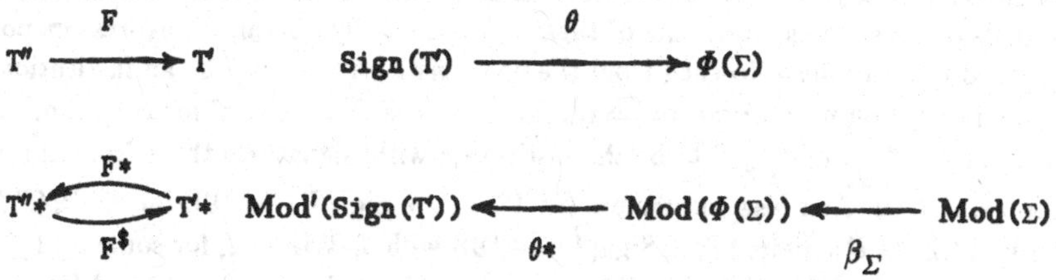

It is worth remarking that in practice T" and T' could be just presentations, as long as F is a theory morphism in $\mathcal{I}$.

Definition 42: Let Φ: $\mathcal{I} \rightarrow \mathcal{I}'$ be an institution with $\mathcal{I}'$ liberal, let Σ be a signature from $\mathcal{I}$, let $c = \langle F, \theta \rangle$ be a Σ-duplex constraint, and let ϕ: $\Sigma \rightarrow \Sigma'$ be a signature morphism from $\mathcal{I}$. Then the **translation** of c by ϕ is the Σ'-duplex constraint $\phi c = \langle F, \theta;\Phi(\phi) \rangle$. []

Lemma 43: Satisfaction. Let Φ: $\mathcal{I} \rightarrow \mathcal{I}'$ be an institution morphism with $\mathcal{I}'$ liberal, let Σ be a signature from $\mathcal{I}$, let $c = \langle F, \theta \rangle$ be a Σ-duplex constraint, let ϕ: $\Sigma \rightarrow \Sigma'$ be a signature morphism from $\mathcal{I}$, and let B be a Σ'-model from $\mathcal{I}$. Then

$B \models_{\Sigma'} \phi c$ iff $\phi B \models_\Sigma c$. []

Definition 44: Let Φ: $\mathcal{I} \rightarrow \mathcal{I}'$ be an institution morphism with $\mathcal{I}'$ liberal and let Σ be a signature from $\mathcal{I}$. Then the **duplex institution** over Φ, denoted $\mathcal{D}(\Phi)$ has: its signatures those from $\mathcal{I}$; its Σ-sentences the Σ-sentences from $\mathcal{I}$ plus the Σ-duplex constraints; its Σ-models the Σ-models from $\mathcal{I}$; and satisfaction is as defined separately for the sentences from $\mathcal{I}$ and the duplex constraints. []

Theorem 45: If $\mathcal{I}'$ is a liberal institution and Φ: $\mathcal{I} \rightarrow \mathcal{I}'$ is an institution morphism, then $\mathcal{D}(\Phi)$ is an institution. []

This result implies (by Theorem 27) that if the category of signatures of $\mathcal{I}$ is [finitely] cocomplete then so is the category of constraining theories that use as sentences both the sentences from $\mathcal{I}$ and the duplex constraints constructed using $\mathcal{I}'$, since this is the category $\mathbf{Th}_{\mathcal{D}(\Phi)}$ of theories of the duplex institution $\mathcal{D}(\Phi)$. Examples using this idea have been given in the specification languages Clear [Burstall & Goguen 81] and Ordinary [Goguen 82a, Goguen 82b].

There is another much simpler way to use an institution morphism Φ: $\mathcal{I} \rightarrow \mathcal{I}'$ to construct a new institution in which one simply permits sentences from either $\mathcal{I}$ or $\mathcal{I}'$.

Definition 46: Let Φ: $\mathcal{I} \rightarrow \mathcal{I}'$ be an institution morphism. Then $\mathcal{T}(\Phi)$ is the institution with: its signatures Σ those from $\mathcal{I}$; its Σ-sentences either Σ-sentences from $\mathcal{I}$, or else pairs of the form $c = \langle T, \theta\colon \mathrm{Sign}(T) \rightarrow \Phi(\Sigma) \rangle$, where T is a theory from $\mathcal{I}'$ and θ is a signature morphism; the Σ-models of $\mathcal{T}(\Phi)$ are those of $\mathcal{I}$; and c is **satisfied** by a Σ-model A means that $\theta(\beta_\Sigma(A))$ satisfies T. []

Proposition 47: $\mathcal{T}(\Phi)$ is an institution. []

For example, it may be convenient to use already existing equational theories when construcing new first order theories.

5.3 Multiplex Institutions

Actually, we can use many different institutions all at once, some of them liberal institutions for various kinds of constraints, and some of them not necessarily liberal, for expressive power; all that is needed is a morphism to each from the basic institution. Let $\mathcal{I}$ be an institution and let Φ_i: $\mathcal{I} \to \mathcal{I}_i$ be institution morphisms for i=1,...,m+n, where $\mathcal{I}_i$ are liberal for i=1,...,n. Then we define $\mathcal{A}(\Phi_1,...,\Phi_n; \Phi_{n+1},...,\Phi_{n+m})$ to be the institution with: signatures those from $\mathcal{I}$; sentences either sentences from $\mathcal{I}$, or else constraints $\langle F: T'' \to T', \theta: Sign(T') \to \Phi_i(\Sigma)\rangle$ for θ, T'', T' from $\mathcal{I}_i$ for some $1 \leq i \leq n$, or else pairs $\langle T, \theta: Sign(T) \to \Phi_i(\Sigma)\rangle$ with θ, T from $\mathcal{I}_i$ for some $n+1 \leq i \leq n+m$; with its models those of $\mathcal{I}$; and with satisfaction as usual for the $\mathcal{I}$-sentences and for the constraints, and as in Definition 46 for the others. Notice that the liberal insititutions can each use a different collection $\mathcal{M}$ of morphisms to define constraint satisfaction. One can even use the same liberal institution with different classes $\mathcal{M}$. In particular, this means that one can glue together (with colimits) first order theories that use combinations of generating constraints, hierarchy constraints, and data constraints in the equational institution, as well as loose first order axioms.

6 Specification

There is now enough technical machinery so that we can consider some operations on theories that are useful in constructing specifications. For more detailed explanations and examples, see the Clear language and its semantics [Burstall & Goguen 80, Burstall & Goguen 81]; similar ideas appear in several other specification languages.

A specification can be given directly by a presentation in the appropriate institution, taken to denote the theory which is the closure of the presentation. More complex theories can be built up from smaller ones by applying combination operations. A specification language, such as Clear, gives a notation for these operators on theories. An alternative approach is to consider operations on categories of models instead of operations on theories. This has been pursued by [Thatcher, Wagner & Wright 79] and should also fit into the institutional framework. Another approach favoured by some is to consider operations on the presentations; however, we prefer a more "semantic" approach.

6.1 Combining Theories

Suppose that we have separately specified a theory **Bool** of truth values and a theory **Nat** of natural numbers, each with appropriate operators. We would have to combine these to get, say, **Bool + Nat**, before defining an extra operator such as $\leq$: **nat x nat→bool**, whose definition involves sorts and operators taken from each theory. (We call adding such extra operators or sorts **enriching** a theory).

There are some issues about the most convenient definition of the combine operation. Suppose that we combine theories T and T' in the equational institution. Should we take the union of their sorts, operators and equations? This would handle correctly cases where they both use sorts like **bool** which should be the same in each (such cases are quite common). Or should we take the disjoint union? This would correctly handle cases where there is an operator appearing in each with the same name, but inadvertently so; for example, the writers of the two specifications may have used the same name by chance (this is not unlikely with large specifications).

Clear allowed shared subtheories, while still attempting to avoid the problems associated with a chance reuse of the same name. Each theory keeps track of the theories from which it is constructed, so that, for example, it is known that T + T' and T' + T'' both contain T. If these two theories are themselves combined, then the sorts and operators in T will not be duplicated. But if the same name is used by chance in T' and in T'', then separate copies will be kept, disjoint union style. The mechanism is to use not simple theories but rather "based theories," which are cones in the category of theories. The tip of the cone is the current theory, and the diagram forming the base of the cone shows which theories were used to build it up (see [Burstall & Goguen 80] for details). The coproduct of two such cones gives the required combine operation, written T + T'.

This works, but it is rather sophisticated. Another approach is to ensure that each sort or operator gets a unique name when it is declared; then we can take a simple union of the theories. But union is a set theoretic notion, while the institutional framework uses an arbitrary category of signatures. The solution seems to be to use a subcategory of signature **inclusions**, that is, a full subcategory that is a poset and whose morphisms are called inclusions, and should all be monics. We then no longer need to use cones, and can simply take as T + T' their coproduct in the subcategory of inclusions. Enrichments will give rise to inclusions. (This proposed simpler semantics needs further study.)

6.2 Parameterised Specifications

We often want to write a specification using some "unknown" sorts and operators, that can later be instantiated (as with generic packages in Ada). Then we can develop a library of such parameterised specifications. Thinking of them as specification-building operations, or as specification-valued procedures, we can design a specification language as a functional language whose data elements are theories. An attractive mathematical framework for this uses the pushout construction to apply a parameterised specification to an argument, as we shall explain.

A parameterised specification may be taken to denote a theory, P, having a distinguished subtheory, R; that is, there is an inclusion morphism p: R→P. The subtheory R shows which part of P is the parameter part to be instantiated. For example, P might be a theory about ordered sequences of elements, and R might be the subtheory of the elements and their ordering. By choosing different instances of R, for example natural numbers with their usual ≤ ordering, or sets with the inclusion ordering, we get different instances of P, namely ordered sequences of numbers, or ordered sequences of sets.

What do we mean by saying that a theory A is an instance of a theory R? For equational theories we need to map the sorts and operators of R to sorts and operators of A, in such a way that equations of R are preserved. In general we need a theory morphism f: R→A. We may call R the **requirement**, f the **fitting morphism**, and A the **actual parameter**. Thus we have the diagram

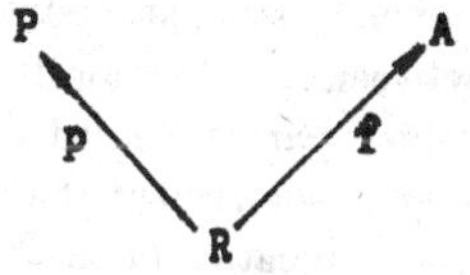

The fitting morphism serves to *bind* the material in the actual parameter to the "required" material in the requirement theory. Since the fitting morphism must be a theory morphism, just its existence implies that the actual parameter satisfies the axioms given in the requirement theory, once its syntax has been changed in accord with the bindings given by the fitting morphism.

What do we mean by applying the parameterised theory P to the argument theory A (or more accurately, by applying p to f)? We want a theory that includes what is in P, as well as the new material from A, suitably instantiated by identifying the R part of P with the corresponding elements in A (this correspondence being given by f). It turns out that the pushout of the above diagram is the required categorical construction; we can think of it as yielding the sum of P and A, amalgamating their R parts. (For the equational institution, it has been *proven* that theory really do behave this way [Goguen & Burstall 78].) Writing p[f] for the result of the application, we have the pushout diagram

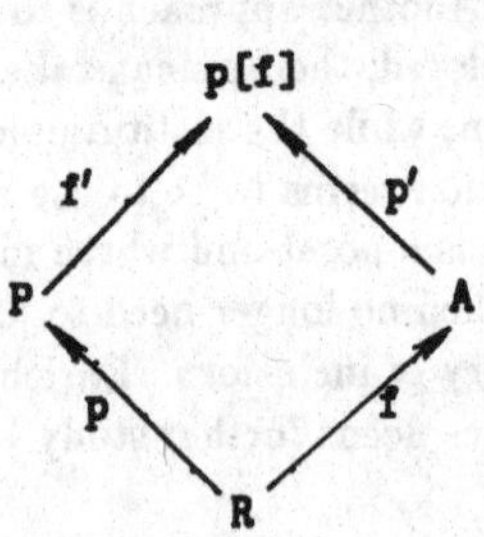

We would expect p and p' to both be inclusions in this diagram.

6.3 Enrichments

We can enrich a specification to get a larger specification. In the case of equational theories, this is done by adding new sorts, operators and equations; for example, adding to **Bool + Nat** the new operator $\leq$: **nat x nat→bool** with its defining equations, such as $0 \leq n$=true. Note that the new material does not itself constitute a theory, so we cannot use combine here.

However, enrichment is really just a special case of applying a parameterised specification. Suppose that we wish to enrich a theory T. The new operator declarations may refer to sorts in T, and the new equations to operators in T. So there is a minimal subtheory of T needed to support this new material, say T', with $T' \subseteq T$, that is, with an inclusion i: $T' \to T$. T' together with the new material forms a theory T", with $T' \subseteq T''$. We may think of the enrichment as an abbreviation for an inclusion j: $T' \to T''$. The result of the enrichment is just the pushout of i and j, or considering j as a parameterised specification and i as the fitting morphism, it is j[i].

6.4 An Analogy

This section has applied ideas of the preceding sections to problems of program specification, including theory combination, theory environments, and parameterized theories. The discussion follows an analogy [Burstall & Goguen 77] between specification languages and programming languages, in which theories are treated as values, parameterized theories correspond to procedures, based theories are environments, and requirement theories correspond to types. This last part of the analogy can be seen as an application of the "correspondence principle" of [Landin 66].

Just as declarations for variables and procedures create environments containing local values for identifiers in a programming language, so do declarations in a specification language create environments having local values. Whereas an environment in a programming language is just an assignment of values (and possibly types) to identifiers, environments in a specification language must also keep track of relationships between theories, so that there is not only an assignment of theories to identifiers, but also a collection of theory inclusions among the given theories, indicating that some theories are contained in others. The basic semantic insight is that to put theories together, whether for combining, enriching, or for applying a parameterized theory to an actual theory, one can simply take colimits of appropriate diagrams.

7 Summary

We have formalized the intuitive notion of a "logical system" or "abstract model theory" with the abstract notion of an institution, and have shown that institutions whose signatures have finite colimits are suitable for use in programming methodology. In a liberal institution, the forgetful functors induced by theory morphisms, have corresponding free functors, and data types can be defined by "constraints," which are abstract induction principles. Allowable kinds of constraint include data, generating, and hierarchy. We have introduced the notion of an institution morphism and shown how to use it in determining when a theorem prover for one institution can be soundly used on (translations of) theories from another institution. Institution morphisms were also used in defining duplex and multiplex institutions, which formalize the simultaneous use of more than one institution; this permits combining the greater expressive power of nonliberal institutions with the data type definition capability of liberal institutions. Finally, we showed how to formulate a number of basic specification language constructions in an arbitrary institution having finite colimits.

References

[Arbib & Manes 75]
Arbib, M. A. and Manes, E.
Arrows, Structures and Functors.
Academic Press, 1975.

[Aubin 76] Aubin, R.
Mechanizing Structural Induction.
PhD thesis, University of Edinburgh, 1976.

[Barwise 74] Barwise, J.
Axioms for Abstract Model Theory.
Annals of Mathematical Logic 7:221-265, 1974.

[Benabou 68] Benabou, J.
Structures Algebriques dans les Categories.
Cahiers de Topologie et Geometrie Differentiel 10:1-126, 1968.

[Birkhoff & Lipson 70]
Birkhoff, G. and Lipson, J.
Heterogeneous Algebras.
Journal of Combinatorial Theory 8:115-133, 1970.

[Bloom 76] Bloom, S. L.
Varieties of Ordered Algebras.
Journal of Computer and System Sciences 13:200-212, 1976.

[Boyer & Moore 80]
Boyer, R. and Moore, J. S.
A Computational Logic.
Academic Press, 1980.

[Broy, Dosch, Partsch, Pepper & Wirsing 79]
Broy, M., Dosch, N., Partsch, H., Pepper, P. and Wirsing, M.
Existential Quantifiers in Abstract Data Types.
In *Proceedings, 6th ICALP*, pages 73-87. Springer-Verlag, 1979.
Lecture Notes in Computer Science, volume 71.

[Burstall & Goguen 77]
Burstall, R. M. and Goguen, J. A.
Putting Theories together to Make Specifications.
Proceedings, Fifth International Joint Conference on Artificial Intelligence 5:1045-1058, 1977.

[Burstall & Goguen 78]
Burstall, R. M. and Goguen, J. A.
Semantics of Clear.
1978.
Unpublished notes handed out at the Symposium on Algebra and Applications, Stefan Banach Center, Warszawa, Poland.

[Burstall & Goguen 80]
Burstall, R. M., and Goguen, J. A.
The Semantics of Clear, a Specification Language.
In *Proceedings of the 1979 Copenhagen Winter School on Abstract Software Specification*, pages 292-332. Springer-Verlag, 1980.
Lecture Notes in Computer Science, Volume 86.

[Burstall & Goguen 81]
Burstall, R. M. and Goguen, J. A.
An Informal Introduction to Specifications using Clear.
In Boyer, R. and Moore, J (editor), *The Correctness Problem in Computer Science*, pages 185-213. Academic Press, 1981.

[Burstall & Goguen 82]
Burstall, R. M. and Goguen, J. A.
Algebras, Theories and Freeness: An Introduction for Computer Scientists.
In *Proceedings, 1981 Marktoberdorf NATO Summer School*, . Reidel, 1982.

[Burstall & Rydeheard 80]
Burstall, R. M. and Rydeheard, D. E.
Signatures, Presentations and Theories: a Monad Approach.
Technical Report, Computer Science Department, University of Edinburgh, 1980.

[Clark 78] Clark, K. L.
Negation as Failure.
In H. Gallaire and J. Minker (editor), *Logic in Data Bases*, pages 293-322. Plenum Press, 1978.

[Cohn 65] Cohn, P. M.
Universal Algebra.
Harper and Row, 1965.
Revised edition 1980.

[Ehrich 78] Ehrich, H.-D.
On the Theory of Specification, Implementation and Parameterization of Abstract Data Types.
Technical Report, Forschungsbericht, Dortmund, 1978.

[Ehrig, Kreowski, Rosen & Winkowski 78]
Ehrig, E., Kreowski, H.-J., Rosen, B. K. and Winkowski, J.
Deriving Structures from Structures.
In *Proceedings, Mathematical Foundations of Computer Science*, . Springer-Verlag, Zakopane, Poland, 1978.
Also appeared as technical report RC7046 from IBM Watson Research Center, Computer Sciences Dept.

[Ehrig, Wagner & Thatcher 82]
Ehrig, H., Wagner, E. and Thatcher, J.
Algebraic Specifications with Generating Constraints.
Technical Report, IBM Research Center, Yorktown Heights, New York, 1982.
Draft report.

[Gabriel & Ulmer 71]
Gabriel, P. and Ulmer, F.
Lokal Prasentierbare Kategorien.
Springer-Verlag, 1971.
Springer Lecture Notes in Mathematics, vol. 221.

[Gerhard, Musser et al. 79]
Gerhard, S. L., Musser, D. R., Thompson, D. H., Baker, D. A., Bates, R. W., Erickson, R. W., London, R. L., Taylor, D. G., and Wile, D. S.
An Overview of AFFIRM: A Specification and Verification System.
Technical Report, USC Information Sciences Institute, Marina del Rey, CA, 1979.

[Goguen 71] Goguen, J.
Mathematical Foundations of Hierarchically Organized Systems.
In E. Attinger (editor), *Global Systems Dynamics*, pages 112-128. S. Karger, 1971.

[Goguen 74] Goguen, J. A.
Semantics of Computation.
In *Proceedings, First International Symposium on Category Theory Applied to Computation and Control*, pages 234-249. University of Massachusetts at Amherst, 1974.
Also published in Lecture Notes in Computer Science, Vol. 25., Springer-Verlag, 1975, pp. 151-163.

[Goguen 77] Goguen, J. A.
Abstract Errors for Abstract Data Types.
In *IFIP Working Conference on Formal Description of Programming Concepts*, . MIT, 1977.
Also published by North-Holland, 1979, edited by P. Neuhold.

[Goguen 78] Goguen, J. A.
Order Sorted Algebra.
Technical Report, UCLA Computer Science Department, 1978.
Semantics and Theory of Computation Report No. 14; to appear in *Journal of Computer and System Science.*

[Goguen 80] Goguen, J. A.
How to Prove Algebraic Inductive Hypotheses without Induction: with applications to the correctness of data type representations.
In W. Bibel and R. Kowalski (editor), *Proceedings, 5th Conference on Automated Deduction*, pages 356-373. Springer-Verlag, Lecture Notes in Computer Science, Volume 87, 1980.

[Goguen 82a] Goguen, J. A.
Ordinary Specification of Some Construction in Plane Geometry.
In Staunstrup, J. (editor), *Proceedings, Workshop on Program Specification*, pages 31-46. Springer-Verlag, 1982.
Lecture Notes in Computer Science, Volume 134.

[Goguen 82b] Goguen, J. A.
Ordinary Specification of KWIC Index Generation.
In Staunstrup, J. (editor), *Proceedings, Aarhus Workshop on Specification*, pages 114-117. Springer-Verlag, 1982.
Lecture Notes in Computer Science, Volume 134.

[Goguen & Burstall 78]
Goguen, J. A. and Burstall, R. M.
Some Fundamental Properties of Algebraic Theories: a Tool for Semantics of Computation.
Technical Report, Dept. of Artificial Intelligence, University of Edinburgh, 1978.
DAI Research Report No. 5; to appear in *Theoretical Computer Science.*

[Goguen & Ginali 78]
Goguen, J. A. and Ginali, S.
A Categorical Approach to General Systems Theory.
In Klir, G. (editor), *Applied General Systems Research*, pages 257-270. Plenum, 1978.

[Goguen & Meseguer 81]
Goguen, J. A. and Meseguer, J.
Completeness of Many-sorted Equational Logic.
SIGPLAN Notices 16(7):24-32, July, 1981.
Also appeared in *SIGPLAN Notices*, January 1982, vol. 17, no. 1, pages 9-17; extended version as SRI Technical Report, 1982, and to be published in *Houston Journal of Mathematics.*

[Goguen & Meseguer 83]
Goguen, J. A. and Meseguer, J.
An Initiality Primer.
In Nivat, M. and Reynolds, J. (editor), *Application of Algebra to Language Definition and Compilation*, . North-Holland, 1983.
To appear.

[Goguen & Parsaye-Ghomi 81]
Goguen, J. A. and Parsaye-Ghomi, K.
Algebraic Denotational Semantics using Parameterized Abstract Modules.
In J. Diaz and I. Ramos (editor), *Formalizing Programming Concepts*, pages 292-309. Springer-Verlag, Peniscola, Spain, 1981.
Lecture Notes in Computer Science, volume 107.

[Goguen & Tardo 79]
Goguen, J. A. and Tardo, J.
An Introduction to OBJ: A Language for Writing and Testing Software Specifications.
In *Specification of Reliable Software*, pages 170-189. IEEE, 1979.

[Goguen, Thatcher & Wagner 78]
Goguen, J. A., Thatcher, J. W. and Wagner, E.
An Initial Algebra Approach to the Specification, Correctness and Implementation of Abstract Data Types.
In R. Yeh (editor), *Current Trends in Programming Methodology*, pages 80-149. Prentice-Hall, 1978.
Original version, IBM T. J. Watson Research Center Technical Report RC 6487, October 1976.

[Goguen, Thatcher, Wagner & Wright 75a]
Goguen, J. A., Thatcher, J. W., Wagner, E. G., and Wright, J. B.
An Introduction to Categories, Algebraic Theories and Algebras.
Technical Report, IBM T. J. Watson Research Center, Yorktown Heights, N. Y., 1975.
Research Report RC 5369.

[Goguen, Thatcher, Wagner & Wright 75b]
Goguen, J. A., Thatcher, J. W., Wagner, E. and Wright, J. B.
Abstract Data Types as Initial Algebras and the Correctness of Data Representations.
In *Computer Graphics, Pattern Recognition and Data Structure*, pages 89-93. IEEE, 1975.

[Goldblatt 79] Goldblatt, R.
Topoi, The Categorial Analysis of Logic.
North-Holland, 1979.

[Higgins 63] Higgins, P. J.
Algebras with a Scheme of Operators.
Mathematische Nachrichten 27:115-132, 1963.

[Hoare 72] Hoare, C. A. R.
Proof of Correctness of Data Representation.
Acta Informatica 1:271-281, 1972.

[Kaphengst & Reichel 71]
Kaphengst, H. and Reichel, H.
Algebraische Algorithemtheorie.
Technical Report WIB Nr. 1, VEB Robotron, Zentrum fur Forschung und Technik, Dresden, 1971.
In German.

[Landin 66] Landin, P. J.
The Next 700 Programming Languages.
Communications of the Association for Computing Machinery 9, 1966.

[Lawvere 63] Lawvere, F. W.
Functorial Semantics of Algebraic Theories.
Proceedings, National Academy of Sciences 50, 1963.
Summary of Ph.D. Thesis, Columbia University.

[Lawvere 64] Lawvere, F. W.
An Elementary Theory of the Category of Sets.
Proceedings, National Academy of Sciences, U.S.A. 52:1506-1511, 1964.

[Levitt, Robinson & Silverberg 79]
Levitt, K., Robinson, L. and Silverberg, B.
The HDM Handbook.
Technical Report, SRI, International, Computer Science Lab, 1979.
Volumes I, II, III.

[MacLane 71] MacLane, S.
Categories for the Working Mathematician.
Springer-Verlag, 1971.

[MacLane & Birkhoff 67]
MacLane, S. and Birkhoff, G.
Algebra.
Macmillan, 1967.

[Mahr & Makowsky 82a]
Mahr, B. and Makowsky, J. A.
An Axiomatic Approach to Semantics of Specification Languages.
Technical Report, Technion, Israel Institute of Technology, 1982.
Extended Abstract.

[Mahr & Makowsky 82b]
Mahr, B. and Makowsky, J. A.
Characterizing Specification Languages which Admit Initial Semantics.
Technical Report, Technion, Israel Institute of Technology, February, 1982.
Technical Report #232.

[McCarthy 80] McCarthy, J.
Circumscription - A Form of Non-Monotonic Reasoning.
Artificial Intelligence 13(1,2):27-39, 1980.

[Parsaye-Ghomi 82]
Parsaye-Ghomi, K.
Higher Order Data Types.
PhD thesis, UCLA, Computer Science Department, January, 1982.

[Reichel 80] Reichel, H.
Initially Restricting Algebraic Theories.
Springer Lecture Notes in Computer Science 88:504-514, 1980.
Mathematical Foundations of Computer Science.

[Shostak, Schwartz & Melliar-Smith 81]
Shostak, R., Schwartz, R. & Melliar-Smith, M.
STP: A Mechanized Logic for Specification and Verification.
Technical Report, Computer Science Lab, SRI International, 1981.

[Tarski 44] Tarski, A.
The Semantic Conception of Truth.
Philos. Phenomenological Research 4:13-47, 1944.

[Thatcher, Wagner & Wright 79]
Thatcher, J. W., Wagner, E. G. and Wright, J. B.
Data Type Specification: Paramerization and the Power of Specification Techniques.
In *Proceedings of 1979 POPL*, . ACM, 1979.

[Wright, Thatcher, Wagner & Goguen 76]
Wright, J. B., Thatcher, J. W., Wagner, E. G. and Goguen, J. A.
Rational Algebraic Theories and Fixed-Point Solutions.
Proceedings, 17th Foundations of Computing Symposium :147-158, 1976.
IEEE.

Table of Contents

A COMPLETE PROOF RULE FOR STRONG EQUIFAIR TERMINATION

Orna Grümberg
Dept. of Computer Science
Technion - Israel Institute of Technology
Haifa, Israel

Nissim Francez[1]
IBM T. J. Watson Research Center
Mathematical Sciences Dept.
Yorktown Heights, N. Y.

Shmuel Katz
Dept. of Computer Science
Technion - Israel Institute of Technology
Haifa, Israel

Typed by: Barbara J. White

ABSTRACT: The notion of *equifairness*, strengthening the familiar notion of *fairness*, is introduced as a scheduling policy of non-determinism and concurrency. Under this notion, it is infinitely often the case that the number of selections of each of a family of infinitely-often jointly-enabled processes is equal. A proof rule for proving *strong equifair-termination* is introduced, applied to examples and shown to be (semantically) complete.

C.R. Categories and subject description:

[F 3.1] Logics and meanings of programs: specifying and verifying and reasoning about programs.

Other keywords and phrases: non-determinism, fairness, equifairness, termination, ordinals, invariant.

---

[1]World-trade Visiting Scientist on a sabbatical leave from the Technion, Haifa, Israel. (Work of the 2nd author was partially supported by the Fund for Aiding Research, The Technion)

1. INTRODUCTION

In this paper we introduce the new concept of *equifairness*, a strengthening of the familiar fairness property, one of the central notions in the theory of nondeterminism and concurrency. It is a companion paper to [GF], where *weak equifairness* was treated.

We study the property of *strongly-equifair termination*, the corresponding strengthening of *fair termination* [GFMR, LPS, AO, APS]. In particular, we present a proof-rule for equifair termination for the language GC of guarded commands [D], and prove its soundness and (semantic) completeness with respect to the natural semantics, assigning each nondeterministic GC program a tree of computation states. Thus, the paper is a contribution towards the understanding of properties of programs executed under a variety of restrictions on its infinite behavior.

As is well known, a fair execution of an iterative statement with n guarded commands means, that every guard which is infinitely often enabled (true for the state at the corresponding time instant) is also infinitely often passed, and the corresponding command executed. However, there is no further commitment (by the fair scheduler) as to the relative scheduling of the enabled guards, e.g. as far as the number of times they are chosen for execution.

Here we are interested in a more committed scheduler - one that tries to give *an equally fair chance to each guard in a group of jointly enabled guards*. We assume that if such a group of guards is infinitely-often, jointly-enabled, then there exist infinitely many time instants where all these guards are *equalized*, namely have been (*all*) chosen the *same* number of times. We shall call such an execution a *strongly-equifair execution*, and the corresponding scheduler a *strongly-equifair scheduler*.

One possible interpretation of this concept is in terms of a situation in which n processors, roughly of the same speed, execute a program. They overtake each other locally, but in the long run are equal. Another interpretation is an abstraction of a specific kind of a probabilistic execution, allowing probabilistic details to be disregarded in reasoning about the program.

To give the flavor of the concept, we note that in an equifair behavior of an unbounded buffer, the buffer becomes empty infinitely often, whenever the 'read' and 'write' operations have been equalized.

As noted above, we concentrate on termination under an execution by a strongly-equifair scheduler, called *strong-equifair-termination*. A typical simple program to exemplify the concept is the following (where x, y and z are integer valued):

$$
\begin{aligned}
P:: *[\ & 1{:}z>0 && \rightarrow x:=x+1 \\
& \square && \\
& 2{:}z>0 && \rightarrow y:=y+1 \\
& \square && \\
& 3{:}z>0 \wedge x=y && \rightarrow z:=z-1 \\
].
\end{aligned}
$$

This program is not fairly terminating in an initial state $x = y \wedge z \geq 0$, as the infinite fair sequence $1(12)^{\omega}$ shows. However, it is equifairly terminating; whenever the first two guards (clearly jointly enabled, being the same Boolean expression) were equalized and have been executed $k > 0$ times since the previous equalization, the new values of x and y are $x_0 + k$, $y_0 + k$ (where x_0 and y_0 are the old value at the previous equalization state). In such a state, the third guard is enabled, and eventually executed. Thus, an infinite sequence containing infinitely many equalized states would cause an eventual dropping of z below 0 - a contradiction. This phenomenon will be the basis of our intended proof-rule.

A simple "implementation" of a scheduler, which guarantees strong equifairness, uses a random (natural) number generator. It keeps a table T(A, i), $\phi \neq A \subseteq \{1,\ldots, n\}$, $i \in A$, initially with all entries equal to zero. Whenever it discovers that all the entries corresponding to some A are equal to zero, it draws a random natural number, say k, and reinitializes all these entries to k. Whenever the guard b_i, $1 \leq i \leq n$ is selected for execution, the entries corresponding to all sets containing i which are jointly-enabled at that stage are decremented by 1. A guard will not be selected for execution if there is an entry corresponding to a set of jointly-enabled guards containing it and equal to 0, even though it is enabled at that stage.

Actually, for technical reasons, we consider a slight variation, where the table has some arbitrary initial values (this becomes clear when the recursive application of the intended rule is discussed).

The ability to use arbitrary random natural numbers implies that equifair execution can generate unbounded (countable) nondeterminism. This is not surprising, being the case for (simple) fairness also.

We would like to mention that the studied property of equifairness needs an augmentation of the state for its expressibility, to keep track of the number of times each guard (direction in our terminology) has been passed. In general, this information need not be retrievable from the (proper) state. Thus, we augment all our example programs with *direction counters* – auxiliary variables counting the number of times each direction is passed, with respects to other directions with which it is jointly enabled. Another use of auxiliary variables in a related context appears in [AO]. The explicit inclusion of the scheduler in the program might lead to a proof-rule along the lines of [AO] and [APS].

2. A PROOF RULE FOR STRONG EQUIFAIR TERMINATION

We consider the language GC of *guarded commands* [D], using the following notation for an iteration statement:

$$C:: \; *[\mathop{\Box}_{i=1}^{n} i:\; b_i \rightarrow C_i] \,.$$

The b_i's are Boolean (quantifier free) expressions called *guards*. We call

$i:\; b_i \rightarrow C_i$ the i'th *direction*

A state σ for C is a mapping from the program variables to their corresponding value domains. A direction *i* is *enabled* in some state σ (in which control is located in front of the iteration statement) if b_i is true for that state.

A set of directions $A \subseteq \{1,..., n\}$ is *jointly-enabled* in a state σ if $B_A = \bigwedge_{i \in A} b_i$ is true in σ. According to the standard semantics of GC, there is no restriction on the direction selected for execution in consecutive iterations of C; whenever a direction is enabled, it may be executed. Thus, we can assign to each GC program C and (initial) state ξ_0 a labeled tree $T_C(\xi_0)$. The root of $T_C(\xi_0)$ is labeled with ξ_0. A node labeled with ξ is a leaf if $\bigvee_{i=1}^{n} b_i$ is false in ξ. Otherwise, that node has a subtree for each enabled direction *i*, corresponding to the execution of C_i, inductively defined in the usual way. Note that $T_C(\xi)$ is a finitely branching tree for every C and ξ, though it may contain infinite paths in case C diverges on ξ (in the standard semantics). A path in a tree $T_C(\xi)$ is called an *execution-sequence* (of C on ξ).

In order to be able to express the property in which we are interested, we augment each n-directional GC program with $n \cdot 2^{n-1}$ *direction-counters,* which are auxiliary variables, needed only for the sake of the proof.

For each $i \in \{1,..., n\}$, let A_i^j, $1 \leq j \leq 2^{n-1}$, be some fixed enumeration of the subsets of $\{1,..., n\}$ containing i. The counter c_i^j will count the number of times the direction *i* was executed when the set of directions A_i^j was jointly-enabled. Thus, the form of an augmented iteration statement becomes the following:

$$
\begin{aligned}
C'::*[\ \mathop{\square}_{i=1}^{n}\ i\colon b_i \rightarrow [\quad & B_{A_i^1} \rightarrow c_i^1 := c_i^1 + 1 \\
\square \quad & \\
& \neg B_{A_i^1} \rightarrow \text{skip} \\
]; \quad & \\
\vdots \quad & \\
[\quad & B_{A_i^{2^{n-1}}} \rightarrow c_i^{2^{n-1}} := c_i^{2^{n-1}} + 1 \\
\square \quad & \\
& \neg B_{A_i^{2^{n-1}}} \rightarrow \text{skip} \\
]; \quad & \\
& C_i \\
].
\end{aligned}
$$

We abbreviate the auxiliary section increasing the counters of direction i as INC(i). Its effect is to increase c_i^j by one–before C_i is executed–for every jointly-enabled set of directions A_i^j (containing i). Also, C_i' denotes the augmented body of direction i in C'.

Note that the counters were not initialized to zero, but may have any initial values satisfying a precondition. At the top-level of a proof of termination we shall assume initial values equal to 0.

In the examples, we shall augment the programs only with those counters that participate in the proof, and omit reference to all others. Obviously, C and C' have the same computations modulo the original states, since the added counters do not have any effect on the flow of the computation.

The introduction of the c_i^j's can be avoided in case their value can be determined from the state. We shall not bother with this issue here. We shall use the abbreviation $E_A(\xi)$, for an augmented state ξ, to mean that ξ is an *A-equalized* state, i.e., $c_{i_1} = \ldots = c_{i_k}$ holds in ξ, for $A = \{i_1, \ldots, i_k\}$, $k \geq 1$. Thus, the initial values of the counters are taken into account also. Note that for $|A| = 1$, *every* state is A-equalized. Two A-equalized states are *distinct* if the values of the counters in the two states are different.

Definition :

1. A computation sequence π of C' is *strongly equifair* iff it is finite, or infinite and contains infinitely many distinct A-equalized states for any $A \subseteq \{1,..., n\}$ that is infinitely-often jointly enabled along π.

2. A program C' is *strongly-equifair terminating* iff all its strongly equifair execution sequences are finite.

□

Thus, in a strongly-equifair terminating program C', every infinite execution sequence contains only finitely many A-equalized states for some infinitely-often jointly-enabled set of directions $A \subseteq \{1,..., n\}$. In other words, from some point onwards, all states are non-A-equalized.

Hence, if a strongly-equifair terminating program is executed by a strongly-equifair scheduler, it will always terminate, since infinite strongly equifair sequences are not generated by such a scheduler, by its definition. For the rest of the paper, we shall use 'equifair' to mean strongly-equifair.

We use the notation $[r]\ C'\ [q]$ to denote the fact that, given a precondition r, C' is equifairly terminating with a post-condition q holding upon termination. Since the establishment of q is a partial-correctness property that is independent of fairness, we restrict attention to termination only, taking $q \equiv$ true.

Obviously, every fairly terminating GC program [GFMR] is also equifairly terminating, since an equifair computation sequence is also fair.

Following is another (less obvious) example of an equifairly terminating program.

Q::{x = y∧a = b∧z≥0}

```
* [ 1:z>0          → x: = x + 1
  □
  2:z>0            → [x = y → a: = a + 1
                      □
                      x≠y → skip
                      ] ; y: = y + 1
  □
  3:z>0 ∧ x = y →  b: = b + 1
  □
  4:z>0 ∧ a = b →  z: = z − 1
]
```

By {1,2}-equalization, x=y will infinitely-often be the case. Then, by {2,3}-equalization, a=b will infinitely-often be the case, and hence direction 4 is infinitely-often enabled, and z decremented, and hence P_2 equifairly terminates. A formal equifair termination proof follows the introduction of the proof-rule.

We next proceed to introduce our proof-rule for equifair-termination. The basic intuition behind the suggested rule is to find a well founded partially ordered set, and a variant function of the state, *which decreases whenever the state becomes A-equalized (for some "helpful" set of directions A)* and does not increase between consecutive *A*-equalized states. The "helpful" sets A vary with the computation. Thus, an infinite decreasing sequence would occur in the presence of infinitely many *A*-equalized states, in contradiction to well-foundedness. As the completeness proof will show, we can always consider an initial sequence of the countable ordinals as the required well-founded partially-ordered set. Without loss of generality, we assume that the well-founded set has a unique minimal element, denoted by 0. Let Σ denote the domain of states of an (augmented) GC iteration command C′.

To prove $[r]\ C'\ [true]$:

find: a) a well-founded, partially-ordered, set $(W, \leq)$, a predicate $p(\xi,w)$, $\xi \in \Sigma$, $w \in W$,

(*parametrized invariant*),

b) for each $0<w \in W$, a set $\phi \neq D_w \subseteq \{1,\dots, n\}$ (*decreasing set*) satisfying:

1)(BOUNDARY) $r(\xi) \supset \exists w.p(\xi,w)$, $p(\xi,0) \supset \neg \bigvee_{i=1,n} b_i(\xi)$, $p(\xi,w) \wedge w>0 \supset \bigvee_{i=1,n} b_i(\xi)$

2)(DEC) $[p(\xi,w) \wedge w>0 \wedge b_i]\ C_i'\ [E_{D_w}(\xi) \supset \exists v.v<w \wedge p(\xi,v)]$, $i \in D_w$

3)(NOINC) $[p(\xi,w) \wedge w>0 \wedge b_i]\ C_i'\ [\exists v.v \leq w \wedge p(\xi,v)]$, $i \in \{1,\dots, n\}$

4)(DER) $[p(\xi,w) \wedge w>0]\ C_w{::}^*\ [\ \square_{i=1}^{n}\ i{:}b_i \wedge \neg B_{D_w} \rightarrow C_i']\ [true]$

Rule SEFT (Strongly-Equifair termination)

The meaning of the proof rule is as follows (omitting state arguments for brevity):

Find a well-founded ordering $(W, \leq)$, an invariant $p(w)$, and a decreasing set D_w for each $w > 0$. Show that the invariant is initially established, and implies a possible continuation until 0 is reached (BOUNDARY). Show that the invariant is preserved with a non-increasing parameter v after the execution of any enabled direction (NOINC), and is preserved with a strictly smaller parameter v whenever the result of following an enabled direction in the decreasing set is an equalized state for that set D_w (DEC).

Finally, show that each decreasing-set is infinitely-often jointly-enabled, by proving the equifair termination of the *derived-program* (DER). The derived program conjoins to each guard the negation of joint-enableness of the direction in the decreasing set, and terminates once they do become jointly enabled (or the whole original program terminates). Note, that the precondition $p(\xi,w)$ may imply initial values of the counters of the derived program.

<u>Example 1</u>. We consider again the program P (over natural numbers), mentioned in the introduction, augmented with appropriate counters. Since the first two guards are identical, we omit the test of joint-enabledness before incrementing the counters.

$$P'::[x = y \wedge c_1^{1,2} = c_2^{1,2} = 0]$$

$$\begin{aligned}
* [\ & 1{:}z>0 && \rightarrow x:=x+1;\ c_1^{1,2}:=c_1^{1,2}+1 \\
\square \\
& 2{:}z>0 && \rightarrow y:=y+1;\ c_2^{1,2}:=c_2^{1,2}+1 \\
\square \\
& 3{:}z>0 \wedge x=y && \rightarrow z:=z-1 \\
]\ & [\mathrm{true}].
\end{aligned}$$

For convenience we specified sets of directions by members instead of by index.

As our well-founded set we choose the natural numbers N, under the usual ordering. The parametrized invariant is

$$p(x, y, z, c_1^{1,2}, c_2^{1,2}, n) \overset{df}{\equiv} (z = n \geq 0 \wedge c_1^{1,2} - c_2^{1,2} = x - y)$$

to be abbreviated as p(n). The decreasing set is taken as $D_n = \{3\}$, $n>0$. We now show that the clauses of the proof rule are satisfied

(1) <u>BOUNDARY</u>: To initialize p(n), take n=z, the initial value of z. Also, $p(n) \wedge n > 0$ implies $z > 0$, and hence the first two guards are enabled, while p(0) implies z=0, and hence, no guard is enabled.

(2) <u>DEC</u>: Since $|D_n| = 1$ for all $n \geq 1$, every state satisfies E_{D_n}, and we have to show

$$[p(n) \wedge n>0 \wedge z>0 \wedge x = y]\ z: = z - 1\ [\exists m \bullet m<n \wedge p(m)]$$

which holds for $m = n-1$.

(3) <u>NOINC</u>: Immediate with same n, since the first two directions do not modify z.

(4) DER: After some trivial simplification, the derived program, for every $n>0$, is the following.

$$P_n'::\{z = n>0 \wedge c_1^{1,2}-c_2^{1,2} = x-y\}$$

$$* [\ 1{:}z>0 \wedge x\neq y \rightarrow x:=x+1;\ c_1^{1,2}:=c_1^{1,2}+1$$

$$\square$$

$$2{:}z>0 \wedge x\neq y \rightarrow y:=y+1;\ c_2^{1,2}:=c_2^{1,2}+1$$

$$]\ \{true\}.$$

The initial values of the counters are implied by the precondition p(n).

In order to prove equifair-termination of P_n', we choose $W = \{0,1\}$, with $0<1$. The invariant is

$$p'(x, y, z, c_1^{1,2}, c_2^{1,2}, w) \overset{df}{\equiv} (z>0 \wedge c_1^{1,2}-c_2^{1,2} = x-y \wedge (w = 1 \supset x\neq y) \wedge (w = 0 \supset x = y)).$$

The decreasing set is $D_1 = \{1,2\}$. We now check that all the clauses of the rule are satisfied.

(1) BOUNDARY: To establish p', take $w = \begin{cases} 1 & x\neq y \\ 0 & x=y \end{cases}$.

$p'(w) \wedge w>0$ implies $w=1$ and hence $x\neq y$, so both guards are enabled.

$p'(0)$ implies $x=y$, so both guards are disabled and P_n terminates.

(2) DEC: the condition $E_{\{1,2\}}$, i.e. $c_1^{1,2} = c_2^{1,2}$, implies $x=y$, hence $p'(0)$, which means decrease.

(3) NOINC: trivial; take same $w=1$.

(4) DER: The derived program has all guards false and hence terminates.

This completes the proof of termination of P_n', and hence of the original program.

Example 2: Consider again the program Q from the beginning of this section, augmented with the appropriate counters. We insert the counter-incrementation to locations in the program where the implied test for joint-enabledness would succeed.

Q':: $[x = y \wedge a = b \wedge c_1^{1,2} = c_2^{1,2} = c_2^{2,3} = c_3^{2,3} = 0]$

```
* [ 1:z>0            → x:=x+1; c1^{1,2}:=c1^{1,2}+1
  □
    2:z>0            → [x=y→a:=a+1; c2^{2,3}:=c2^{2,3}+1
                        □
                        x≠y→skip
                        ]; y:=y+1; c2^{1,2}:=c2^{1,2}+1
  □
    3:z>0 ∧ x=y→ b:=b+1
  □
    4:z>0 ∧ a=b→ z:=z−1; c3^{2,3}:=c3^{2,3}+1
  ] [true].
```

This program generates a more complicated equifair termination proof, by having more levels of application of the rule, with non-disjoint decreasing sets.

We start by choosing $W \underset{df}{=} N$ again, with the parametrized invariant $p(x, y, z, a, b, c_1^{1,2}, c_2^{1,2}, c_2^{2,3}, c_3^{2,3}, n) \equiv (z = n \geq 0 \wedge c_1^{1,2} - c_2^{1,2} = x - y \wedge c_2^{2,3} - c_3^{2,3} = a - b)$. We also take $D_n = \{4\}$, $n>0$.

The proof of the first three clauses is along the line of example 1. For (DER), we obtain after some simplification of guards the following derived program, augmented with the appropriate counters, whose initial values is again implied by the precondition.

Q_n':: $[z>0 \wedge c_1^{1,2} - c_2^{1,2} = x-y \wedge c_2^{2,3} - c_3^{2,3} = a-b]$

```
* [ 1:z>0 ∧ a≠b        → x:=x+1; c1^{1,2}:=c1^{1,2}+1
  □
    2:z>0 ∧ a≠b        → [x=y→a:=a+1; c2^{2,3}:=c2^{2,3}+1
                          □
                          x≠y→skip
                          ]; y:=y+1; c2^{1,2}:=c2^{1,2}+1

  □
    3:z>0 ∧ a≠b∧ x=y→ b:=b+1; c3^{2,3}:=c3^{2,3}+1
  ] [true].
```

To prove equifair-termination of Q_n', we take $W = \{0,1\}$ and $D_1 = \{2,3\}$. The invariant is $p'(x, y, z, a, b, c_1^{1,2}, c_2^{1,2}, c_2^{2,3}, c_3^{2,3}, w) \overset{df}{\equiv} (p(z) \wedge (w = 1 \supset a \neq b) \wedge (w = 0 \supset a = b))$.

We leave it for the reader to verify the first three clauses. As for (DER), we obtain the following derived program.

$Q_{n,1}'$:: $\{p'(w) \wedge w = 1\}$

$*[\ 1{:}z>0 \wedge x \neq y \wedge a \neq b \rightarrow x := x+1;\ c_1^{1,2} := c_1^{1,2} + 1$

$\square$

$2{:}z>0 \wedge x \neq y \wedge a \neq b \rightarrow y := y+1;\ c_2^{1,2} := c_2^{1,2} + 1;\ [...]$.

$]\ \{true\}$.

We again may choose $V = \{0,1\}$, $D_1 = \{1,2\}$ and the invariant $p''(\ldots, v) \overset{df}{\equiv} (p'(v) \wedge (v = 1 \supset x \neq y) \wedge (v = 0 \supset x = y))$, and the verification is now routine.

This completes example 2.

3. SOUNDNESS AND COMPLETENESS

Theorem 1 (Soundness):

For any (augmented) GC program C′, if clauses (1), (2), (3) and (4) of the proof-rule were successfully applied w.r.t. assertions r,q, then $[r]\ C'\ [q]$ holds, i.e., C′ (strongly) equifairly terminates w.r.t r,q.

Proof of Theorem 1: Assume that all the clauses apply, but the program does not (strongly) equifairly terminate. Thus, there exists an initial state ξ satisfying r, for which an infinite (strongly) equifair computation exists.

By clause (1), the invariant p(w) is established, for some w>0. By clause (3), there exist an infinite sequence $w = v_1 \geq v_2 \geq \ldots \geq v_i \ldots$, such that $p(v_i)$ holds for the corresponding sequence of states. By the well-foundedness of W, there is an $i_0 \geq 1$, such that in the above sequence, $v_k = v_{i_0}$ for all $k \geq i_0$ (otherwise, an infinite decreasing sequence would be obtained). By (2), $\neg E_{D_{i_0}}$ holds from that point onwards (otherwise, $v_{i_0} > v_{i_0+1}$ would be the case). By clause (4), which asserts that under the assumption $p(v_{i_0})$ $C_{v_{i_0}}$ terminates, we obtain that $D_{v_{i_0}}$ was infinitely often jointly enabled (i.e., $B_{D_{v_{i_0}}}$ holds infinitely-often), which contradicts the definition of (strongly) equifairness assumed initially.

□

<u>Theorem 2</u> (Semantic Completeness):

For any (augmented) GC program C', pre- and post-conditions r,q, if $[r]\ C'\ [q]$, then we can find a well-founded, partially-ordered set $(W, \leq)$, an invariant $p(\xi, w)$ and decreasing sets D_w, $w>0$, which satisfy clauses (1), (2), (3) and (4) of the proof-rule.

Note that we are interested here only in *semantic* completeness, i.e., in the set-theoretical existence of the invariant; we shall not explore here the syntactic completeness of an assertion language to express the invariant.

The proof is along similar lines to these in [GFMR], the idea being to take an infinite, not well-founded tree $T_{C'}(\xi_0)$ which is (strongly) equifair and contract it to another infinite tree $T^*_{C'}(\xi_0)$ which is well-founded (but, of course, *not* necessarily finitely branching as $T_{C'}(\xi_0)$ is).

<u>Proof of Theorem 2</u>: Consider any initial state ξ_0 satisfying r, and the tree $T_{C'}(\xi_0)$. By our assumption, every path in this tree represents some (strongly) equifair computation. If $T_{C'}(\xi_0)$ (which is finitely branching) is a finite tree, we use the usual construction of a parametrized invariant, since C' terminates without any fairness assumptions. Thus, assume $T_{C'}(\xi_0)$ is infinite, and hence has at least one infinite path with only finitely many A-equalized states residing along it, for some $A \subseteq \{1,..., n\}$ infinitely-often jointly-enabled.

<u>Definition.</u> For any $A \subseteq \{1,..., n\}$ and a state occurrence $\xi \in T_{C'}(\xi_0)$, we let $CONE_A(\xi)$ be $\{\xi\}$ union the set of all state occurrences residing on infinite paths of $T_{C'}(\xi_0)$

starting at ξ and containing *no* A-equalized states (other than possibly ξ) with A infinitely-often jointly-enabled. Such a path will be called A-equalization avoiding.

□

Such a cone will be contracted to a single node in $T^*_{C'}(\xi_0)$. Note that $CONE_A(\xi)$ is never empty, since it contains a least ξ, its *root*. The set A is call the cone's *directive*.

Lemma 1: If an infinite computation path along which A is infinitely-often jointly-enabled leaves a cone $CONE_A(\xi)$, it contains an A-equalized state (see Figure 1).

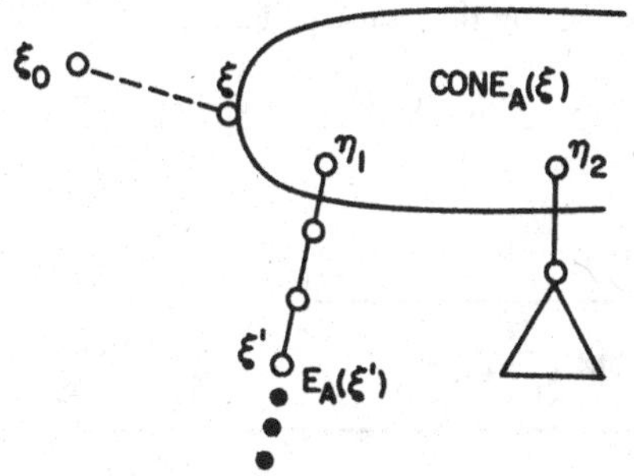

Figure 1 Cone exits

Proof of Lemma 1: Assume the contrary, i.e. that such an infinite path leaves $CONE_A(\xi)$, say at a node labeled η, and has no occurrences of A-equalized states along it except of, possibly, ξ itself. Then, by the definition of the cone, all the occurrences of states along this infinite path belong to $CONE_A(\xi)$, and the path should not leave the cone at all, contradicting the assumption.

□

We now proceed with an inductive definition of a family of cones, covering all the states occurring on infinite paths of $T_{C'}(\xi_0)$.

Induction basis: Construct $CONE_{A_0}(\xi_0)$, where A_0 is any set of directions.

Induction step: Assume that $CONE_{A_{i-1}}(\xi_{i-1})$ was constructed at level i−1 at an equalized root. If no infinite path leaves $CONE_{A_{i-1}}(\xi_{i-1})$, it has no descendent cones. Otherwise, consider such an infinite path leaving the cone. By Lemma 1, it contains an occurrence of an A_{i-1}-equalized state. For any such path construct $CONE_{A_i}(\xi_i)$ at level i, for ξ_i the nearest A_{i-1}-equalized state along the path (see Figure 2). The set of directions A_i is determined as follows. Consider all sets A for which an A-unequifair infinite computation leaves ξ_i (at least one exists, since the computation is infinite, and hence unequifair by assumption). Among these sets, choose A_i to be the one appearing least recently (possibly never) as a cone-directive on the initial sequence of cones up to ξ_i. Note that a node at some level may have infinitely many descendant cones by this construction.

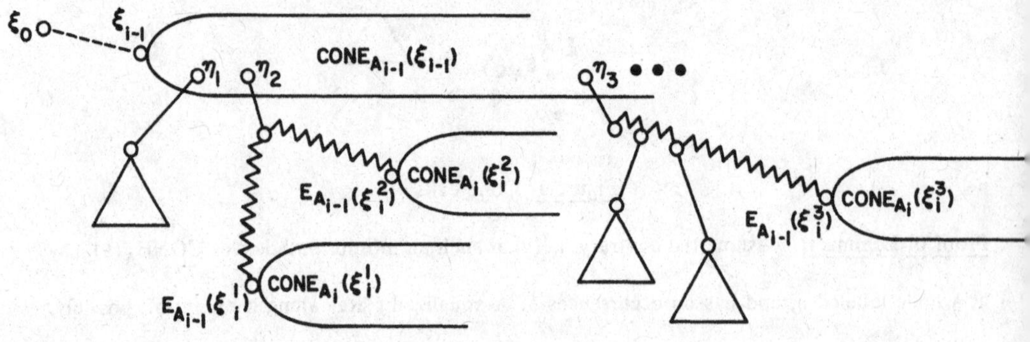

Figure 2: descendant cones

Lemma 2: There does not exist an infinite chain of descendant cones $CONE_{A_i}(\xi_i)$, whose roots reside on a computation sequence of $T_{C'}(\xi_0)$.

Proof of Lemma 2: Assume the contrary, i.e., the existence of an infinite chain of descendant cones whose roots reside on a computation sequence (a path) of $T_{C'}(\xi_0)$, (as shown in Figure 3).

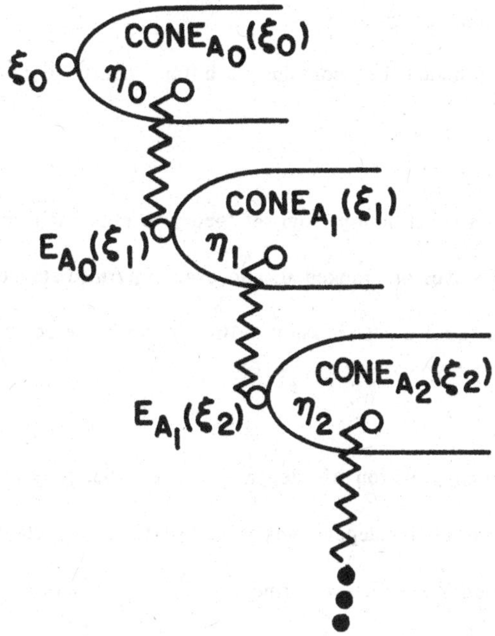

Figure 3: An infinite chain of descendant cones

Consider the infinite path π^* passing through $\xi_0, \xi_1, \xi_2, \ldots$. It must be unequifair by assumption. Suppose it is A*-unequifair, for some $A^* \subseteq \{1, \ldots, n\}$. Thus, there exist some i_0, such that from ξ_{i_0} onwards (along π^*), no A*-equalized state exists. Hence, there is also some $i^* \geq i_0$, for which A* is as above, and is also the set of direction which appeared less recently as a cone-directive (up to that point). By definition, we would have $\text{CONE}_{A^*} = \text{CONE}_{A_i^*}$, and π^* should not leave $\text{CONE}_{A_i^*}$, contrary to the assumption that it has (infinitely many) descendant cones. Hence, such an infinite chain cannot exist.

□

Now we have all we need for the construction of $T^*_{C'}(\xi_0)$. The nodes are all the cones in the above inductive construction as well as all the nodes of $T_{C'}(\xi_0)$ not residing within any cone (remember that such nodes always have a subtree which is finite, or have a descendant which is a root of another cone). The edges are all the edges of $T_{C'}(\xi_0)$ leaving or entering cones, or not residing within cones.

Claim: $T^*_{C'}(\xi_0)$ is well founded, i.e., contains no infinite paths. Follows immediately from Lemma 2.

We now use a known construction from set theory to rank each node on $T^*_{C'}(\xi_0)$ with countable ordinals. All leaves are ranked 0, and every intermediate node is ranked by the least upper bound of the ranks of its (possibly infinitely many) descendants. We denote this ranking function by ρ^*.

Note that the whole construction still depends on the initial state ξ_0, whose tree $T_{C'}(\xi_0)$ was considered. To get rid of this dependency on initial states, we actually rank a larger tree, obtained by creating a fictitious root and turning all the $T^*_{C'}(\xi_0^\alpha)$ to be its subtrees. Denote the resulting tree by $T^*_{C'}$ (see Figure 4).

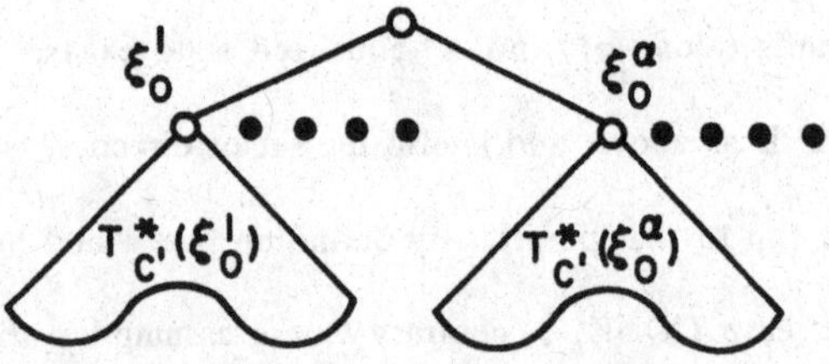

Figure 4: The tree $T^*_{C'}$

We still have one final step before defining the invariant and decreasing sets needed for the proof-rule. Recall that the decreasing set D_w depends on w only. It is our intention to choose as D_w a directive of a cone ranked w. However, it may be the case that several cones, with different directives, all receive the same rank by ρ^*. To avoid this situation, we perform a *rank-shift* (compare with [GFMR]), modifying the ranks appropriately (this may cause a larger ordinal to be used). Denote the new rank by ρ. Using the ranking ρ we are now able to construct the required parametrized invariant and decreasing sets. We define:

$$p(\xi,w) \overset{df}{\equiv} \exists\, \xi',A' \bullet [\xi \in CONE_{A'}(\xi') \wedge \rho(CONE_{A'}(\xi')) = w]$$

$$\vee$$

$$\neg \exists\, \xi', A' \bullet [\xi \in CONE_{A'}(\xi')] \wedge \rho(\xi) = w.$$

Thus, p(w) is satisfied in state ξ in case ξ resides in a cone ranked w, or ξ does not reside in any cone, and is itself ranked w. As for the choice of a decreasing set D_w, w>0, we have again the two possibilities, depending whether w is a rank of cone or of a "simple" node.

$$D_w = \begin{cases} A & \text{there is a cone } CONE_A \text{ whose rank is } w \\ \{1,\ldots,n\} & \text{there is no cone ranked } w \text{ (i.e. only "simple nodes" are ranked } w). \end{cases}$$

By the rank-shift mentioned above, D_w is well-defined.

We now have to show that the invariant p and the descending sets as defined above satisfy all the clauses of the proof rule.

<u>Clause 1</u>: (Boundary)

Trivial, since $\xi_0 \in CONE_{A_0}(\xi_0)$. Thus $\rho(CONE(\xi_0))$ can be chosen as the initial w establishing the invariant. The other boundary conditions are also clear, since it only leaves are ranked 0, and hence $\neg \bigvee_{i=1,n} b_i$ is satisfied.

<u>Clause 2</u>: (Decrease).

Suppose $p(w) \wedge w>0 \wedge b_i$ hold for some ξ, where $i \in D_w$. We distinguish between two cases:

a. $\xi \in \mathrm{CONE}_A(\xi')$ and $\rho(\mathrm{CONE}_A(\xi')) = w$. In this case, applying direction i in a way that causes E_A to hold in the resulting state means, that the move left the cone (lemma 1), and hence the resulting state has a lower rank.

b. ξ is ranked w and does not reside within a cone. By the construction, it either has a finite subtree, or another cone-descendent, and all its descendants have a lower rank.

Clause 3: (Non-increase).

Similar. A move either stays within a cone, resulting in state with the same rank, or leaves a cone, resulting in a state with a smaller rank.

Clause 4: (Equifair termination of the derived program).

First, we note that any execution-path of C_w is also (a tail of) an execution-path of the original program C. We want to show that for a path π of C having an infinite tail π' of C_w which is strongly fair w.r.t. C_w, π itself is strongly fair w.r.t. to C. This yields a contradiction, since C is given not to have such paths. The only problem is that the same direction has different guards in C and C_w. Let $A \subseteq I$, and suppose that B_A is infinitely often enabled in C along such a path π. Since π has an infinite tail π' in C_w, it means that B_{D_w} does not hold along π' (otherwise C_w would terminate). Hence, $\bigwedge_{j \in A} (B_j \wedge \neg B_{D_w})$ is infinitely often enabled in C_w, and hence A is infinitely often equalized and π is indeed strongly fair w.r.t. to C, showing the required contradiction.

This shows that semantically the derived program strongly-equifair terminates. We now apply an inductive hypothesis to derive provability by SEFT. The induction is on the number of directions. As we apply the recursion again and again, the guards have the form

$$b_i \wedge \neg \bigwedge_{j \in D_{w_1}} b_j \wedge \neg \bigwedge_{j \in D_{w_2}} b_j \ldots .$$

This can go on at most until all subsets of I are exhausted. Thus, at some stage a level of proof is reached where in the cone construction $T^*_S = T_S$, and the original tree is finite, at which stage we appeal to the proof rule for ordinary termination, without a further recursive call.

4. CONCLUSION

In this paper, we presented a concept generalizing the infinite behavior of nondeterministic programs beyond the well known concept of fairness. According to this scheduling strategy coined here as "equifairness", infinitely often along an infinite execution, it is the case that the number of times that all the directions in an infinitely-often jointly-enabled set of directions have been scheduled for execution (up to that point) is the same. We presented a sound and (semantically) complete proof rule for (strong) equifair termination -- termination under execution by a scheduler guaranteeing the above described property.

We believe that investigating termination under a large variety of infinite behaviors is an important issue, and should be pursued. One way of avoiding discussing explicitly probabilistic assumptions about the underlying guard scheduling (or process scheduling in the context of concurrency) is to find an appropriate abstraction which characterizes the required probabilistic scheduling policy. Thus, the usual fairness is an abstraction of selecting each direction with some positive probability. Also, a variety of infinite behaviors may arise by abstracting from implementation details with elaborate queueing disciplines.

REFERENCES

[AO] K.R. Apt and E.R. Olderog, Proof Rules and Transformations Dealing with Fairness, TR 82-47, LITP, University of Paris 7, October 1982. To appear in Science of Computer Programming.

[APS] K.R. Apt, A. Pnueli and J. Stavi, Fair Termination Revisited with Delay, Proceedings of 2nd conference on foundations of software technology and theoretical computer science (FST-TCS), Bangalore, India, December 1982. Also: TR 82-51, LITP, Univ. of Paris 7, October 1982.

[D] E.W. Dijkstra, A Discipline of Programming, Prentice Hall, Englewood Cliffs, N.J., 1976.

[GF] O. Grümberg, N. Francez, A complete proof-rule for (weak) equifairness. IBM T.J. Watson Research Center RC-9634, October 1982 (submitted for publication).

[GFMR] O. Grümberg, N. Francez, J.A. Makowsky and W.P. de Roever, A Proof Rule for Fair Termination of Guarded Commands, Proc. of the Int. Symp. on Algorithmic Languages, Amsterdam, October 1981, North-Holland, 1981.

[LPS] D. Lehmann, A. Pnueli and J. Stavi, Impartiality, Justice and Fairness: the Ethics of Concurrent Termination, Proc. ICALP 81, in: Lecture notes in computer science 115 (S. Even, O. Kariv - eds.), Springer 1981.

[P] D. Park, A Predicate Transformer for Weak Fair Iteration, Proc. 6 IBM Symp. on Math. Foundation of Computer Science, Hakone, Japan, 1981.

NECESSARY AND SUFFICIENT CONDITIONS FOR THE UNIVERSALITY OF PROGRAMMING FORMALISMS

(Partial Report)

A.J. Kfoury
Computer Science Department
Boston University

P. Urzyczyn
Institute of Mathematics
University of Warsaw

INTRODUCTION

It is well known that over the natural numbers, the notion of "computable" coincides with the notion of "flowchartable". That is, any partial recursive function is defined by a flowchart program over the datatype

$$(\mathbb{N};=;\underline{succ},0) \quad \text{or} \quad (\mathbb{N};=;\underline{succ},\underline{pred},0)$$

where $\mathbb{N}$ is the set of natural numbers, and succ and pred are the successor and predecessor operations on $\mathbb{N}$, respectively.

It is also known that there are datatypes over which the notion of "computable" is strictly more general than the notion of "flowchartable".

In this paper we formulate and prove several necessary and sufficient conditions in order that the notion of "computable" over the domain of an arbitrary datatype $\mathfrak{A}$ coincides, respectively, with the notions of:

"definable by a flowchart program over $\mathfrak{A}$",

"definable by a flowchart program with counters over $\mathfrak{A}$",

"definable by a recursive program over $\mathfrak{A}$",

"definable by a recursive program with counters over $\mathfrak{A}$".

The necessary and sufficient conditions are expressed algebraically, putting restrictions on the primitive operations of the datatype $\mathfrak{A}$. These are Theorems 2.2, 2.3, and 2.4 below. Contrary to first impressions, these results are not simply based on standard (number-theoretic) coding and decoding methods. They also involve a variation of the "pebble game" and various techniques closely related to term-rewriting.

A later extended version of this report is due to appear in Acta Informatica. The later version includes all proofs omitted in this report, as well as applications to various commonly encountered datatypes.

§1. PRELIMINARY DEFINITIONS AND RESULTS

The general setting of this paper is defined by the following concepts.

1.1 DATA TYPES: We take a data type $\mathfrak{A}$ to be an object of the form

$$\mathfrak{A} = (\mathbb{A}; \doteq , r_1^A ,\dots,r_m^A; f_1^A ,\dots,f_n^A)$$

where $\mathbb{A}$ is a set of individual elements, $\doteq$ is the equality relation on $\mathbb{A}$ (different from the metatheoretic =)*, and $r_1^A ,\dots, r_m^A; f_1^A ,\dots, f_n^A$ are primitive relations and functions on $\mathbb{A}$, each with a fixed arity ≥ 0. A data type $\mathfrak{A}$ as just defined may be viewed as a one-sorted (first-order) structure. The sequence τ of primitive relation and function symbols, namely $\tau = (r_1 ,\dots, r_m; f_1,\dots,f_n)$, is the signature of $\mathfrak{A}$.

1.2 PROGRAMS AND PROGRAM SCHEMES: Given a signature τ, associated with some structure $\mathfrak{A}$, we consider two basic classes of program schemes: flowchart program schemes and recursive program schemes. A "flowchart program scheme" can be drawn as a flowchart which only mentions relation and function names from τ ; whereas a "recursive program scheme" can be drawn as a flowchart which may also mention in its instructions names of program schemes (including itself).

Program schemes can be with or without counters. We shall refer to the four classes of program schemes thus defined by:

Fc = {flowchart program schemes},

FcC = {flowchart program schemes with counters},

Rec = {recursive program schemes},

RecC = {recursive program schemes with counters}.

We formally define a flowchart program scheme S (possibly with counters) -- with input locations $\{x_1,x_2,\dots,x_k\}$, $k \geq 0$ and over signature $\tau = (r_1,\dots,r_m ; f_1,\dots,f_n)$ -- to be a finite flow-diagram built up from two kinds of instructions: assignments and tests. In the following definitions we assume we have an infinite supply of work locations $\{y_i \mid i \in \omega\}$ and counters $\{c_i \mid i \in \omega\}$. Input and work locations (together called memory locations) are assigned values from the universe $\mathbb{A}$ of a structure $\mathfrak{A}$, whereas counters are assigned values from $\mathbb{N}$ (the set of natural numbers).

(1) An assignment instruction can take one of the following forms:

---

* We shall use = not only as the metatheoretic equality but also to denote equality between syntactic objects (for example, if t_1 and t_2 are terms then "$t_1 = t_2$" means that t_1 and t_2 are identical expressions). The symbol $\doteq$ will be only used to denote equality between algebraic objects, i.e. elements in the universe $\mathbb{A}$. This explicit distinction between = and $\doteq$ is helpful in avoiding several confusions later.

(1.1) $y_i := x_j$ where $i \in \omega$ and $j \in \{1,\dots,k\}$.

(1.2) $y_i := y_j$ where $i, j \in \omega$.

(1.3) $y_i := f(y_{j_1},\dots,y_{j_p})$ where $i, j_1,\dots,j_p \in \omega$ $f \in \{f_1,\dots,f_n\}$ and $p \geq 0$ is the arity of f.

(1.4) $c_i := c_j$ where $i, j \in \omega$.

(1.5) $c_i := 0$, $c_i := c_i + 1$, $c_i := c_i \dot{-} 1$ where $i \in \omega$

Note that counters do not "communicate" with input and work locations. Also assignment instructions do not change the values of input locations, only the values of work locations and counters.

(2) A test instruction can take one of the following forms:

(2.1) $y_i \,\hat{=}\, y_j$? (yes / no) where $i, j \in \omega$

(2.2) $r(y_{j_1},\dots,y_{j_p})$? (yes / no) where $j_1,\dots,j_p \in \omega$ $r \in \{r_1,\dots,r_m\}$ and $p \geq 0$ is the arity of r.

(2.3) $c_i = c_j$? where $i, j \in \omega$.

To complete the specification of program scheme S we require that it (as a flow-diagram) have exactly one entry point labelled with input locations $x_1,\dots,x_k$; and each of the exit points of S be labelled either with a work location from which an output value is to be read off, or with a special instruction DIVERGE which stands for any self-loop :

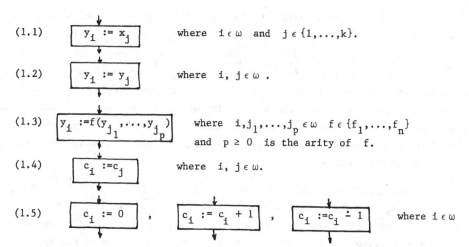

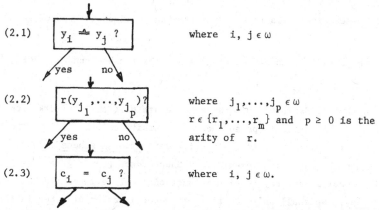

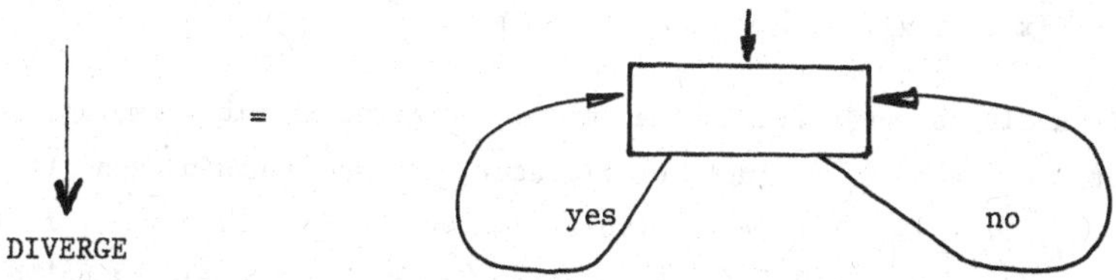

A flowchart program scheme S is said to be without counters if S does not use instructions of the forms (1.4), (1.5), and (2.3).

If we give to each relation and function symbol appearing in S its proper meaning in structure $\mathfrak{A}$, we obtain a flowchart program over $\mathfrak{A}$ denoted by $S^{\mathfrak{A}}$. Clearly $S^{\mathfrak{A}}$ defines a k-ary (partial) function on $\mathbb{A}$. We denote the computation of $S^{\mathfrak{A}}$ on input $(a_1,\ldots,a_k) \in \mathbb{A}^k$ by $S^{\mathfrak{A}}(a_1,\ldots,a_k)$. The computation $S^{\mathfrak{A}}(a_1,\ldots,a_k)$ corresponds to a unique path, possibly infinite, through the flow-diagram of S; and a step in the computation is any instruction along the path thus determined. (The results of this paper apply only to deterministic programs.) Note that the presence of the DIVERGE instruction in our programming formalism allows loop-free programs to compute non-total functions.

A recursive program scheme S (possibly with counters) -- with input variables $\{x_1,x_2,\ldots,x_k\}$ and over signature $\tau = (r_1,\ldots,r_m; f_1,\ldots,f_n)$ -- is more general than a flowchart program scheme in that it allows in an assignment instruction of the form (1.3) the function symbol f to be also the name of a program scheme (possibly S itself). An apparently more general notion of "recursive program scheme" also allows in a test instruction of the form (2.2) the relation symbol r to be the name of a program scheme (possibly S itself) with each of its exit points having a label from {yes, no}; however, in the presence of the equality relation $\doteq$ and two distinguished elements (identified with "yes" and "no" respectively), there is no loss of generality in restricting recursive calls to appear in assignment instructions of the form (1.3) only.

More on the classical theory of program schemes can be found in [BGS], [CG],[GL] and [LPP].

1.3 FED'S and RED'S: Sometimes program schemes are difficult to work with, especially in the presence of nested loops and nested recursive calls. It is often simpler to work with their translations into effective definitional schemes, which were defined by Friedman [F], and later examined by Shepherdson [S] in great detail. An effective definitional scheme can be either functional (abbreviated fed) or relational (abbreviated red). We shall only use the more general notion of a fed in this paper, the notion of a red being only used to define two-valued functions.

Formally, a fed F over signature $\tau = (r_1,\ldots,r_m; f_1,\ldots,f_n)$ and with input variables $\{x_1,\ldots,x_k\}$, is a recursively enumerable sequence of ordered pairs. Assuming F infinite, we can write it as follows:

$$F(x_1,\ldots,x_k) = (\langle \alpha_i,t_i \rangle \mid i \in \omega),$$

where α_i is a finite conjunction of atomic and negated atomic formulas, and t_i is a term -- both α_i and t_i being over signature τ and containing no free variable other than $\{x_1,\ldots,x_k\}$. When F is finite, we write $F = (\langle \alpha_i,t_i \rangle \mid i \in I)$ for some initial finite segment $I \subset \omega$. Each pair $\langle \alpha_i,t_i \rangle$ in a fed is called a clause.

If we interpret fed F in a structure $\mathfrak{A}$ we obtain a function $F^{\mathfrak{A}} : \mathbb{A}^k \to \mathbb{A}$

whose value at $(a_1,\ldots,a_k) \in \mathbb{A}^k$ is:

$$F^{\mathfrak{A}}(a_1,\ldots,a_k) = \begin{cases} t_i^A(a_1,\ldots,a_k), & \text{where } i \in \omega \text{ is the smallest index for which } \mathfrak{A} \models \alpha_i[a_1,\ldots,a_k]; \\ \text{undefined}, & \text{otherwise;} \end{cases}$$

where t_i^A is the interpretation of term t_i in $\mathfrak{A}$.

We say that program scheme $S(x_1,\ldots,x_k)$ and fed $F(x_1,\ldots,x_k)$ are $\mathfrak{A}$-equivalent if program $S^{\mathfrak{A}}$ computes function $F^{\mathfrak{A}}$ on $\mathbb{A}$. And we say that S and F are equivalent if they are $\mathfrak{A}$-equivalent for every structure $\mathfrak{A}$. [We assume that S, F, and $\mathfrak{A}$ all have the same signature.]

The important fact linking program schemes and fed's is the following one.

1.4 THEOREM:

(a) Given an arbitrary program scheme S, we can effectively find a fed F equivalent to S;

(b) Given an arbitrary fed F, we can effectively find a recursive program scheme S with counters which is equivalent to F. □

In view of this basic result, if we are given a program scheme S, we shall write fed(S) for the corresponding (effectively defined) fed.

In part (a) above, an "arbitrary program scheme" refers not only to an arbitrary recursive or flowchart program scheme with or without counters but also to any other kind of program scheme defined in the literature. We may thus think of the language of fed's as a "universal programming language". Hence, part (b) above shows that the language of recursive program schemes with counters is also "universal".

For a precise statement of the next theorem, which relates fed's to flowchart program schemes with counters, we need the following definitions.

Let τ be a fixed signature. We denote the sequence of variables $(x_1,\ldots,x_k)$ for some fixed $k \geq 0$, by $\vec{x}$. The set of $\vec{x}$-terms is the set of all terms in the signature τ which do not mention variables other than $\{x_1,\ldots,x_k\}$.

With every $\vec{x}$-term t we can associate a finite dag (directed acyclic graph) G_t, with as many input nodes as there are variables and o-ary function symbols in t, and with exactly one output node labelled with the full expression for t. For example, if c and g are 0-ary and 2-ary function symbols, respectively, then we can represent the (x_1,x_2)-term $g(c,g(g(c,x_1),x_1))$ by the following dag:

(see figure at top of next page)

Strictly speaking if nodes u_1 and u_2 are incident to node v in this dag -- and

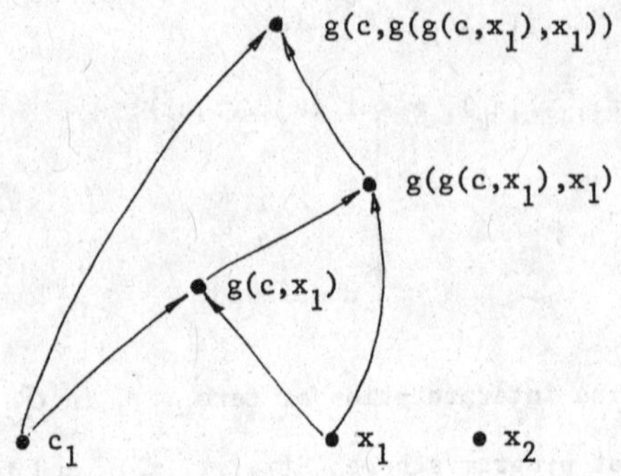

u_1,u_2,v are associated with terms $t_1,t_2,\ g(t_1,t_2)$ respectively -- we should label the edges (u_1,v) and (u_2,v) with 1 and 2, respectively, corresponding to the order of the two arguments in $g(t_1,t_2)$. For our present purposes however, we may ignore the ordering of edges incident to the same node in G_t.

We define the <u>pebble complexity</u> of t as follows:

<u>pebble</u>(t) = minimum number of pebbles required to pebble G_t, i.e. to reach the putput node of G_t.

We assume known the rules of the pebble game on a finite dag, as well as the proper correspondence between pebbles and work locations. (A good reference on the pebble game is [Pi].) Note that the pebble complexity of a term is always ≥ 1.

Any $\vec{x}$-term t can be "decomposed" into a finite sequence of assignment instructions. For example, for the (x_1,x_2)-term above we may write:

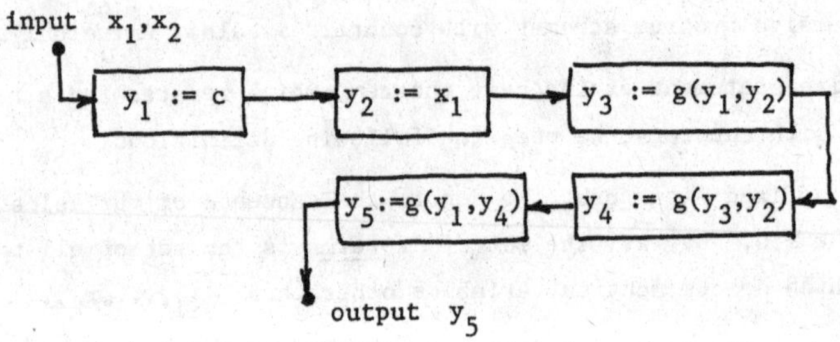

This is a "straight-line" program scheme which uses five work locations $\{y_1,\ldots,y_5\}$, and therefore the corresponding pebbling of G_t uses five pebbles. Another decomposition of the same (x_1,x_2)-term, which now uses only two work locations $\{y_1,y_2\}$, follows:

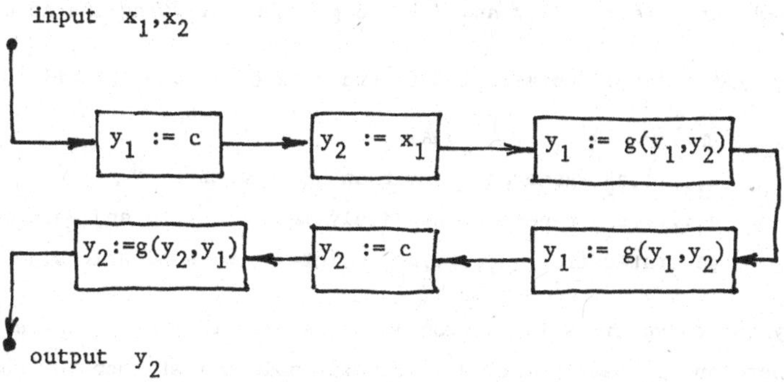

This sequence of assignments corresponds to a pebbling of G_t using only two pebbles.

For each $\ell \geq 1$ we define the set of all ℓ-$\vec{x}$-terms as follows:

$$\{t \mid t \text{ is a } \vec{x}\text{-term and } \underline{\text{pebble}}(t) \leq \ell\},$$

An ℓ-$\vec{x}$-term is therefore an $\vec{x}$-term which can be decomposed into a sequence of assignment instructions using at most ℓ work locations.

1.5 THEOREM: Let F be a fed with input variables $\vec{x} = (x_1,\ldots,x_k)$. Then $F = \underline{\text{fed}}(S)$ for some flowchart program scheme S with counters $\Longleftrightarrow$ there is a positive integer ℓ such that every term appearing in F is a ℓ-$\vec{x}$-term.

§2. NECESSARY AND SUFFICIENT CONDITIONS

We start by defining what it means for a programming formalism to be universal for a structure $\mathfrak{A}$.

2.1 DEFINITION: Let $\mathfrak{A}$ be an arbitrary structure, and $\mathcal{P}$ a class of program schemes. We say that $\mathcal{P}$ is universal for $\mathfrak{A}$ if for every fed F there is a program scheme $S \in \mathcal{P}$ which is $\mathfrak{A}$-equivalent to F. Put differently, every function computed by a fed over $\mathfrak{A}$ is also computed by a program scheme $S \in \mathcal{P}$ over $\mathfrak{A}$.

(We assume that fed's, program schemes, and the structure $\mathfrak{A}$ in which they are interpreted, all have the same signature.)

2.2 THEOREM: *FcC* is universal for structure $\mathfrak{A}$ if and only if

$(\forall k)(\exists \ell)(\forall a_1,\ldots,a_k,b \in \mathbb{A})$
[element b is generated by $a_1,\ldots,a_k \Rightarrow$
b can be generated from $a_1,\ldots,a_k$ using ℓ work locations.]

2.3 THEOREM: *Rec* is universal for structure $\mathfrak{A}$ if and only if

$(\forall k)(\exists \ell)(\forall a_1,\ldots,a_k \in \mathbb{A})$
$[a_1,\ldots,a_k$ generate more than ℓ elements $\Rightarrow$
$a_1,\ldots,a_k$ generate infinitely many elements.]

Combining Theorems 2.2 and 2.3, we get the following characterization.

2.4 THEOREM: *Fc* is universal for structure $\mathfrak{A}$ if and only if

$(\forall k)(\exists \ell)(\forall a_1,\ldots,a_k \in \mathbb{A})$
[$a_1,\ldots,a_k$ generate more than ℓ elements $\Rightarrow$
$a_1,\ldots,a_k$ generate infinitely many elements and each such element can be generated from $a_1,\ldots,a_k$ using ℓ work locations.]

By our conventions in Section 1, it is easy to see that if a program mentions no work location (in particular, all its exit points must then be labelled with the special instruction DIVERGE), then the program computes the empty function. For $m \geq 1$, let *Fc*[m] denote the class of flowchart program schemes which use each m work locations. Clearly, *Fc* as defined earlier is $\cup\{Fc[m] \mid m \in \omega\}$.

We define similarly the class *FcC*[m] of all flowchart programs schemes with counters which use each m work locations. Here, $FcC = \cup\{FcC[m] \mid m \in \omega\}$.

2.5 THEOREM: *FcC* [m] is universal for structure $\mathfrak{A}$ for some m if and only if
$(\exists \ell)(\forall k)(\forall a_1,\ldots,a_k,b \in \mathbb{A})$
[element b is generated by $a_1,\ldots,a_k$ $\Rightarrow$
b can be generated from $a_1,\ldots,a_k$ using ℓ work locations.]

2.6 THEOREM: *Fc* [m] is universal for structure $\mathfrak{A}$ for some m if and only if
$(\exists \ell)(\forall k)(\forall a_1,\ldots,a_k \in \mathbb{A})$
[$a_1,\ldots,a_k$ generate more than ℓ elements $\Rightarrow$
$a_1,\ldots,a_k$ generate infinitely many elements and each such element can be generated from $a_1,\ldots,a_k$ using ℓ work locations.]

2.7 EXAMPLE: There are examples of structures in the literature for which *Fc* or *FcC* is not universal. By going back to the papers in which they are defined ([F], [K1] and [LB1]), the reader will find that these structures are rather intricate. We now give a very simple example of a structure for which *FcC* is not universal. $\mathfrak{N}$ is the structure $(\mathbb{N}; \doteq; g, 0)$ where the primitive function $g: \mathbb{N} \times \mathbb{N} \to \mathbb{N}$ is defined by

$$g(m,n) = \begin{cases} n+1, & \text{if } m = \lfloor n/2 \rfloor; \\ 0, & \text{otherwise.} \end{cases}$$

$\mathfrak{N}$ does not satisfy the condition of Theorem 2.2, so that *FcC* is not universal for $\mathfrak{N}$. On the other hand, every effectively computable function on $\mathbb{N}$ (i.e. every "partial recursive" function) is programmable by a recursive program over with at most one recursive call, so that *Rec* is universal for $\mathfrak{N}$.

2.8 EXAMPLE: Ann Yasuhara and her co-workers have considered the following structure: $\mathfrak{L} = (\mathbb{B}; \doteq; \underline{cons}, \underline{car}, \underline{cdr}, \Lambda)$ where $\mathbb{B}$ is the collection of all finite binary trees built up from the "atom" Λ (the empty binary tree) using the "construction" function $\underline{cons}: \mathbb{B} \times \mathbb{B} \to \mathbb{B}$. The unary functions car and cdr return the left-subtree and the right-subtree, respectively, of a binary tree. $\mathfrak{L}$ is none other than the list structure of pure LISP. (The reader is referred to [Y], [V], [H], and [HVY].)

The class of functions computed by flowchart programs (without counters) over $\mathfrak{L}$ satisfy a "universal function theorem", a "s-m-n theorem", and a "recursion theorem" [Y]. This gives support to the view that the functions flowchartable over $\mathfrak{L}$ are to the universe $\mathbb{B}$ of binary trees what the "partial recursive" functions are to the universe $\mathbb{N}$ of natural numbers.

This view is now further supported by the fact that *Fc* is universal for $\mathfrak{L}$. Indeed, an immediate consequence of the "enumeration of $\mathbb{B}$ theorem" (Section 3 in [Y]) is that structure $\mathfrak{L}$ satisfies the condition of Theorem 2.4 above.

2.9 EXAMPLE: The structure $\mathfrak{Z}$ is $(\mathbb{Z}; ==; g, 0)$ where $\mathbb{Z}$ is the set of all integers, and g is a binary function defined by

$$g(m,n) = \begin{cases} m+1, & \text{if } m \geq 0; \\ (m+1)/2, & \text{if } m < 0,\ m \text{ odd, and } m = n+1; \\ m, & \text{if } m < 0,\ m \text{ even or } m \neq n+1; \end{cases}$$

for all $m,n \in \mathbb{Z}$. $\mathfrak{Z}$ satisfies the condition of Theorem 2.4, but not that of Theorem 2.6, so that *Fc* is universal for $\mathfrak{Z}$ but not *FcC*[m] or *Fc*[m] for any $m \in \omega$.

2.10 EXAMPLES: A group $\mathcal{G}$ is a structure of the form $(G; \circ, (\ )^{-1}, e)$ where $\circ$ is the binary group operation, $(\ )^{-1}$ is the unary inverse operation, and e is the group identity. Using Theorem 2.5, we show *FcC*[3] is universal for $\mathcal{G}$.

A ring $\mathcal{R}$ is a structure of the form $(\mathbb{R}; +, \times, -(\ ), 0, 1)$ where $+$ and $\times$ are binary, and $-(\ )$ is unary. Using Theorem 2.5, *FcC*[4] is universal for $\mathcal{R}$.

A field $\mathcal{F}$ is a structure of the form $(\mathbb{F}; +, \times, -(\ ), (\ )^{-1}, 0, 1)$ where $+$ and $\times$ are binary, and $-(\ )$ and $(\ )^{-1}$ are unary. Using Theorem 2.5, we show that *FcC*[5] is universal for $\mathcal{F}$.

REFERENCES

[A] Abramson, F., "Interpolation theorems for program schemata", Information & Control, 36, February 1978.

[BGS] Brown, Gries, and Szymanski, "Program schemes with pushdown stores", SIAM on Computing, 1, 242-268, 1972.

[CG] Constable, R.C. and Gries, D., "On classes of program schemata", SIAM. J. On Computing, 1, 66-118, 1972.

[E1] Engeler, E., "Algorithmic properties of structures", Math. Systems Theory, 1, 183-195, 1967.

[E2] Engeler, E., "Algorithmic logic" in Foundations of Computer Science, ed. J.W. de Bakker, Mathematical Centre Trace, 63, 57-85, Amsterdam 1975.

[E3] Engeler, E., "Generalized Galois Theory and its application to complexity", Theoretical Computer Science, 13, 271-293, March 1981.

[F] Friedman, H., "Algorithmic procedures, generalized Turing algorithms and elementary recursion theory" in Logic Colloquium '69 edited by R.O. Gaudy & C.M.E. Yates, 361-389, North-Holland, Amsterdam, 1971.

[GL] Garland and Luckham, "Program schemes, recursion schemes, and formal languages", J. of Comp. & System Sciences, 7, 1973.

[H] Hawrusik, F., Ph.D. Thesis, Dept. of Computer Science, Rutgers University, 1983.

[HVY] Hawrusik, F., Venkataraman, K.N., and Yasuhara, A., "Classes of functions for computing on binary trees", STOC 1981.

[K1] Kfoury, A.J., "Translatability of schemas over restricted interpretations", J. of Comp. & System Sciences, 8, 387-408, June 1974.

[K2] Kfoury, A.J., "Definability by programs in first-order structures", to appear in Theoretical Computer Science, January 1983.

[KMA] Kfoury, A.J., R.N. Moll and M.A. Arbib, A Programming Approach to Computability, Springer-Verlag, 1982.

[LPP] Luckham, D., Park, D.M.R., and Paterson, M.S., "On formalized computer programs", J. of Comp. & System Sciences, 4, 220-249, 1970.

[L] Lynch, N.A., "Straight-line program length as a parameter for complexity analysis", J. of Comp. & System Sciences, 21, 251-280, December 1980.

[LB1] Lynch, N.A. and Blum, E.K., "A difference in expressive power between flowcharts and recursion schemes", Mathematical System Theory , 12 205-211, 1979.

[LB2] Lynch, N.A. and Blum, E.K., "Relative complexity of operations on numeric and bit-string algebras", Mathematical Systems Theory, 13, 187-207, 1980.

[LB3] Lynch, N.A. and Blum, E.K., "Relative complexity of algebras", Mathematical Systems Theory, 14, 193-214, 1981.

[PH] Paterson, M. and Hewitt, C., "Comparative schematology", MIT AI Lab. Memo No. 201., November 1970.

[Pi] Pippenger, N., "Pebbling", in Proc. of Fifth IBM Symposium on Math. Foundations of Comp. Size, IBM Japan, May 1980.

[S] Shepherdson, J.C., "Computation over abstract structures: serial and parallel procedures and Friedman's effective definitional schemes", in Logic Colloquium '73 ed. by J.C. Shepherdson and J. Rose, 445-513, North-Holland, Amsterdam, 1975.

[U] Urzyczyn, P., "The unwind property in certain algebras", Information & Control, 50, 91-109, 1981.

[V] Venkataraman, K.N., "Decidability of the purely existential fragment of the theory of term algebras", CTA-TR-4, Dept. of Computer Science, Rutgers University, Oct. 1981.

[W] Winkler, P., "Classification of algebraic structures by work space", to appear in Algebra Universalis, 1982.

[Y] Yasuhara, A., "Computability on term algebras: Part 1," DCS-TR-79, Dept. of Computer Science, Rutgers University, 1979.

THERE EXIST DECIDABLE CONTEXT FREE PROPOSITONAL DYNAMIC LOGICS

Tmima Koren
Department of Mathematics, Tel-Aviv University
Ramat-Aviv, Israel

Amir Pnueli
Department of Applied Mathematics
The Weizmann Institute of Science
Rehovot, Israel

Abstract:

It is shown that PDL remains decidable when we allow as programs regular expressions over a finite alphabet as well as over the single context free program $A^{\Delta}B^{\Delta} = \{A^iB^i \mid i \geq 0\}$. The decision algorithm constructs a finite push-down model for all satisfiable $PDL_{RG(A^{\Delta}B^{\Delta})}$ formulas. Generalization to additional context free programs whose addition does not destroy decidability is discussed.

1. Introduction:

The interesting question of what happens to propositional dynamic logic if we also allow non-regular programs was raised first in [HPS1], [HPS2]. Our intuition, based on language theory, says that all properties of regular languages are decidable but there is an elementary stratum of some restricted context free languages for which most of these properties are still decidable. For example, the equivalence problem is decidable for LL(k) languages and some other deterministic languages. Once we insist on decidable inclusion we must be satisfied with much more restricted classes of languages. Based on this experience one would naturally expect that there would be some simple restricted context free languages that their addition as possible programs (modelling recursive procedures) to PDL would still leave the system decidable.

The results of [HPS1,2] seemed to indicate otherwise. If one adds just the simple languages $\{A^iB^i, B^iA^i \mid i \geq 0\}$ or even the single language $\{A^iBA^i \mid i \geq 0\}$, the validity problem of such augmented PDL system becomes Π^1_1 undecidable. This seemed to imply that any non-regular addition would immediately turn the whole system undecidable.

In this paper we show that the formal languages intuition is in fact justified. There are in fact simple languages whose addition to the set of programs preserves decidability. In this paper we study in detail the effects of augmentation by a single context free language $\{A^iB^i \mid i \geq 0\}$. At the end we present some immediate generalizations and also a characterization which we believe to be sufficient for the preservation of decidability.

The contribution of the paper is not only in clarifying the situation with respect to context free augmentation, but also in that it gives a significant example of a PDL system which is decidable but does not have the finite model property. Indeed our decision procedure hinges on the construction of a push-down model which is finite

---

This research was supported in part by a grant from the Israeli Academy of Science - the Basic Research Foundation. The work is part of the first author's Ph.D. thesis.

representation of an infinite model in much the same way that a push-down automaton is a finite representation of a special type of an infinite state automaton. We believe that this idea of exploring different types of automatons as finite representation of infinite models would prove quite fruitful.

Preliminaries:

Let Σ_0 be a set of atomic programs including the programs A, B, and let Φ_0 be a set of atomic propositions.

Let $C = Rg(\Sigma_0, A^{\Delta}B^{\Delta})$ be the set of regular expressions over the finite alphabet Σ_0 and the special string $A^{\Delta}B^{\Delta}$. We call C the set of programs. Example of a program is $A^*(B \cup A^{\Delta}B^{\Delta})^*A^{\Delta}B^{\Delta}$. Some times we use ";" to denote concatenation or language product.

With each expression in C, $a \in C$ we associate a language over Σ_0, $L(a) \subseteq \Sigma_0^*$ by the obvious rules:

$L(D) = \{D\}$ for each $D \in \Sigma_0$

$L(A^{\Delta}B^{\Delta}) = \{A^iB^i \mid i \geq 0\}$

$L(a;b) = L(a) \cdot L(b)$

$L(a \cup b) = L(a) \cup L(b)$

$L(a^*) = \{\Lambda\} \cup L(a) \cup L^2(a) \cup L^3(a) \cup \ldots$

The formulas of the propositional dynamic logic of C, Φ_C, are defined as follows:

1) For each $P \in \Phi_0$, $P \in \Phi_C$ and $\sim P \in \Phi_C$

2) If $p,q \in \Phi_C$ then so do $p \vee q \in \Phi_C$, $p \wedge q \in \Phi_C$

3) If $p \in \Phi_C$ and $a \in C$ then $\langle a \rangle p$, $[a]p \in \Phi_C$.

As seen from this definition we allow negation to be applied only to atomic propositions.

A model is a labelled directed graph consisting of the following elements.

N - Set of nodes.

E - Set of directed edges. Each edge $e \in E$ connects two nodes from n, and we denote $n_1 \xrightarrow{e} n_2$

ν - Node labelling. This is a mapping $\nu: N \to 2^{\Phi_0}$ assigning to each node $n \in N$, a set of atomic propositions which are precisely the propositions that are true on n.

λ - Edge labelling. The mapping $\lambda: E \to \Sigma_0$ assigns to each edge an atomic program. If $e \in E$ connects n_1 to n_2 and $\lambda(e) = D \in \Sigma_0$ we denote $n_1 \xrightarrow{D} n_2$.

Given a model $M = (N,E,\nu,\lambda)$, we define a path in the model to be a sequence:

$$n_0 \xrightarrow{e_1} n_1 \xrightarrow{e_2} n_2 \cdots \longrightarrow n_k$$

A path π is uniquely identified by the sequence of edges $e_1,\ldots,e_k$ leading from n_0 to n_k. The empty path ε is considered to lead from each node n to itself.

Given a path π we define the label of π as follows: $\lambda(\varepsilon) = \Lambda$ the empty word

$$\lambda(e_1,\ldots,e_k) = \lambda(e_1)\ldots\lambda(e_k).$$

Thus for every path π $\lambda(\pi) \in \Sigma_0^*$.

We define now the notion of satisfaction of a formula φ in a node n in the model, which is denoted by $M,n \models \varphi$.

For simplicity we assume a fixed model and omit the M prefix.

1) For a proposition $P \in \Phi_0$,

$$n \models P \text{ iff } P \in \nu(n)$$
$$n \models {\sim}P \text{ iff } P \notin \nu(n).$$

2) For a disjunction $p \vee q$,

$$n \models p\vee q \text{ iff either } n \models p \text{ or } n \models q$$

3) For a conjunction $p \wedge q$,

$$n \models p\wedge q \text{ iff both } n \models q \text{ and } n \models q$$

4) For a diamond formula $\langle a\rangle p$,

$n \models \langle a\rangle p$ iff there exists a path π leading from n to some n' such that $\lambda(\pi) \in L(a)$ and $n' \models p$.

5) For a box formula $[a]p$,

$n \models [a]p$ iff for all paths π leading from n to some n' such that $\lambda(\pi) \in L(a)$ it follows that $n' \models p$.

A model M is said to be a model for a formula φ if there exists a node $n \in N^M$ such that $M,n \models \varphi$. The formula φ is said to be satisfiable if there exists a model for it.

Push Down Model:

Next, we consider the notion of a pushdown model. A pushdown model is again a labelled directed graph with the following components:

N - Set of nodes.

R - Set of roots, $R \subseteq N$.

E - Set of edges.

Γ - A stack alphabet, a finite set of symbols that appear on the pushdown stack.

ν - Node labelling, $\nu\colon N \to 2^{\Phi_0}$.

λ - Edge labelling. For each edge $e \in E$, λ assigns a label $\lambda(e)$ which may assume one of the following forms:

λ_1 : D/c, $D \in \Sigma_0$ - On passing this edge clear the stack.

λ_2 : A/c, +X, X ∈ Γ - On passing this edge clear the stack and then push X. The resulting stack is X.

λ_3 : A/+X, X ∈ Γ - On passing this edge push X to the top of the stack.

λ_4 :B/-Y,c, Y ∈ Γ - This edge is passable only if the stack's top is Y, and then the stack is cleared.

λ_5 :B/-Y, Y ∈ Γ - This edge is passable only if the stack's top is Y. On passing the edge, the Y symbol is removed (popped) from the stack.

In Fig. 1 we have an example of a pushdown model.

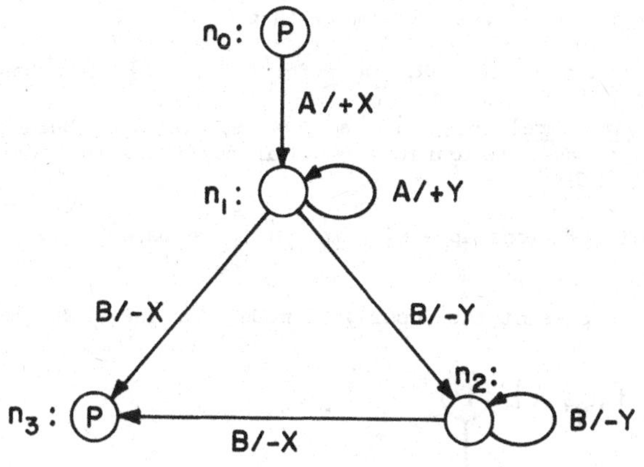

Fig. 1

Here the root set consists of $R = \{n_0\}$ and the stack alphabet given by $\Gamma = \{X,Y\}$.

Given a PDM (pushdown model) M, we define a configuration of M to be a pair $\{n,\sigma\}$ with $n \in N$ and $\sigma \in \Gamma^*$ a possible stack.

We define the configuration graph $C(M)$ corresponding to a PDM M, as follows:

Nodes in the configuration graph are all the possible configurations of M. Their labelling is determined by the M's node component, i.e.

$$\nu(\{n,\sigma\}) = \nu(n).$$

Edges in the configuration graph are induced by edges in the PDM. Let an edge e with label λ connect n to n' in M:

$$n \xrightarrow[e]{\lambda} n'$$

According to the form of λ we obtain the following families of edges in $C(M)$ induced by e.

For $\lambda = D/c$ we have

$$(n,\sigma) \xrightarrow{D} (n',\Lambda) \quad \text{for every } \sigma \in \Gamma^*.$$

For $X = A/c, +X$ we have

$$(n,\sigma) \xrightarrow{A} (n',X) \quad \text{for every} \quad \sigma \in \Gamma^*$$

For $X = A/+X$ we have

$$(n,\sigma) \xrightarrow{A} (n',X\cdot\sigma) \quad \text{for every} \quad \sigma \in \Gamma^*.$$

For $X = B/-Y,c$ we have

$$(n,Y\sigma) \xrightarrow{B} (n',\Lambda) \quad \text{for every} \quad \sigma \in \Gamma^*.$$

For $X = B/-Y$ we have

$$(n,Y\sigma) \xrightarrow{B} (n',\sigma) \quad \text{for every} \quad \sigma \in \Gamma^*.$$

For every root node $n_0 \in R$, we refer to $\{n_0,\Lambda\}$ as a <u>base configuration</u>.

The <u>underlying model</u> $U(M)$ for a PDM m, is the subgraph of $C(M)$ obtained by taking all the base configurations and all configurations which are reachable from them by paths in $C(M)$.

To the configurations appearing in $U(M)$ we refer as the <u>attainable configurations</u> of M.

In Fig. 2 we present the underlying model for the PDM presented in Fig. 1.

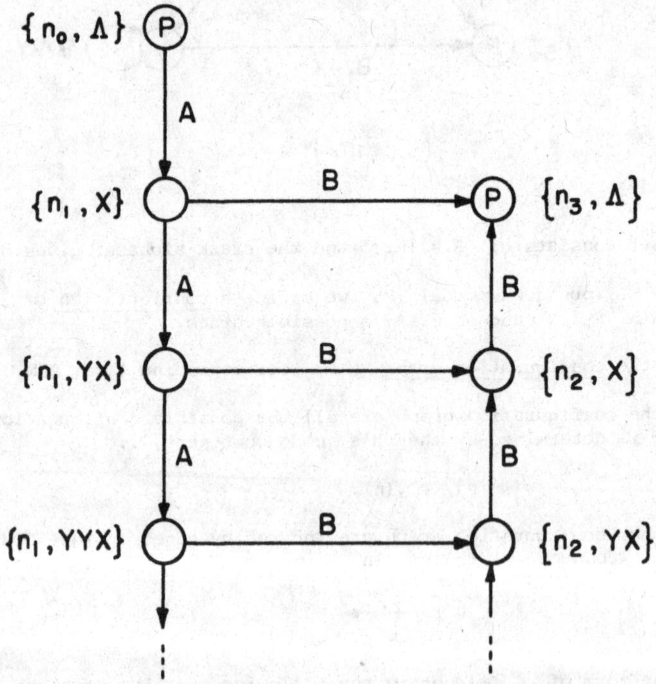

Fig. 2

This is a model for:

φ: $P \wedge [A^*]\langle AA^*B^*B\rangle P \wedge [AA^*B^*BA]$ false $\wedge [A^\Delta B^\Delta B]$ false $\wedge [AA^*A^\Delta B^\Delta]\sim P$

in the sense that $U(M),\{n_0,\Lambda\} \models \varphi$. No finite model for the formula φ exists.

We may consider therefore a pushdown model M as a succinct representation for the underlying model U(M). In particular, the useful cases are these in which M is finite while U(M) is infinite.

Motivated by this we say that a PDM M is a PDM for a formula φ if for some root node $n_0 \in R^M$, $U(M),\{n_0,\Lambda\} \models \varphi$.

The main result of this paper is that a $PDL_{RG(A^\Delta B^\Delta)}$ formula φ is satisfiable iff it has a finite PDM. Decidability will follow from that.

Closures:

We classify formulas according to their main operator into α-formulas and β-formulas. For each type of formula we define two subformulas. For an α formula, the two suformulas α_1 and α_2 are such that α holds iff both α_1 and α_2 hold. For a β formula, the subformulas β_1 and β_2 are such that β holds iff either β_1 or β_2 hold.

α-formulas	α_1	α_2
$p \wedge q$	p	q
$[a \cup b]p$	$[a]p$	$[b]p$
$[a,b]p$	$[a][b]p$	-
$\langle a;b\rangle p$	$\langle a\rangle\langle b\rangle p$	-
$[a^*]p$	p	$[a][a^*]p$
$[A^\Delta B^\Delta]p$	p	$[A][A^\Delta B^\Delta][B]p$

β-formulas	β_1	β_2
$p \vee q$	p	q
$\langle a\cup b\rangle p$	$\langle a\rangle p$	$\langle b\rangle p$
$\langle a^*\rangle p$	p	$\langle a\rangle\langle a^*\rangle p$
$\langle A^\Delta B^\Delta\rangle p$	p	$\langle A\rangle\langle A^\Delta B^\Delta\rangle\langle B\rangle p$

Given a formula φ over $PDL_{A^\Delta B^\Delta}$ we define its Fischer-Ladner closure, $FL(\varphi)$ as the smallest set of formulas S, satisfying

$\varphi \in S$.

If $\sim p \in S$ then $p \in S$.

For each α-formula $\alpha \in S \Rightarrow \alpha_1, \alpha_2 \in S$.
For each β-formula $\beta \in S \Rightarrow \beta_1, \beta_2 \in S$.
For each $[D]p \in S$, $p \in S$.
For each $\langle D\rangle p \in S$, $p \in S$.

Obviously for a formula φ containing a subexpression $A^\Delta B^\Delta$, the set $FL(\varphi)$ is infinite. This is because with each $[A^\Delta B^\Delta]p$ we also have $[A^\Delta B^\Delta][B^n]p$ and $[B^n]p$ for every $n = 1,2,\ldots$. A similar case occurs for $\langle A^\Delta B^\Delta\rangle p$.

Let S be a set of formulas. The set S is said to be booleanly closed if it satisfies the following requirements:

1. For each atomic proposition P, $\sim P \in S \Rightarrow P \notin S$
2. For each α-formula $\alpha \in S$, both $\alpha_1 \in S$ and $\alpha_2 \in S$.
3. For each β-formula $\beta \in S$, either $\beta_1 \in S$ or $\beta_2 \in S$.

Let S_0 be some set of formulas. A set S_1 is said to be a boolean closure of S_0 if S_1 is booleanly closed, it contains S_0, and no strict subset of S_1, $S_1' \subset S_1$ satisfies all these conditions. For a given S_0 we denote by $BC(S_0)$ all the sets S_1 which are a boolean closure of S_0.

For example

$$BC(\{P \vee Q\}) = \{P \vee Q, P\},\quad \{P \vee Q, Q\}$$

While the FL closure is in general infinite, we proceed to define the small closure $SC(\varphi)$ for a formula φ, as the smallest set of formulas S, satisfying

$\varphi \in S$.

If $\sim P \in S$ then $P \in S$.

For every α-formula α, both $\alpha_1 \in S$ and $\alpha_2 \in S$

For every β-formula β, both $\beta_1 \in S$ and $\beta_2 \in S$.

For each $[D]p \in S$ such that $[D]p \neq [A][A^{\Delta}B^{\Delta}][B]q$ for some q, $p \in S$. Here D is any letter in Σ_0.

For each $\langle D\rangle p \in S$ such that $\langle D\rangle p \neq \langle A\rangle\langle A^{\Delta}B^{\Delta}\rangle\langle B\rangle q$ for some q, $p \in S$.

For each $[A][A^{\Delta}B^{\Delta}][B]p \in S$, $[B]p \in S$.

For each $\langle A\rangle\langle A^{\Delta}B^{\Delta}\rangle\langle B\rangle p \in S$, $\langle B\rangle p \in S$.

The restrictions on the expansion of $[D]p$, $\langle D\rangle p$ formulas guarantee that $SC(\varphi)$ is always finite. In fact its size is linear in the length of φ.

Formulas which are in $FL(\varphi) - SC(\varphi)$ are called long formulas. They all have one of the following forms:

$$\langle A^{\Delta}B^{\Delta}\rangle\langle B^n\rangle p,\quad \langle B^n\rangle p,\quad [A^{\Delta}B^{\Delta}][B^n]p,\quad [B^n]p$$

for some $n \geq 0$ and $p \in SC(\varphi)$. Formulas of the two first forms are referred to as long diamond formulas, while the last two forms are called long box formulas.

A Tableaux Construction

We describe a tableaux construction for checking whether a $PDL_{A^{\Delta}B^{\Delta}}$ formula φ is satisfiable and constructing a model for it in case φ is satisfiable. The construction is not effective since it deals with infinite objects.

We define a graph M_0 as follows:

The nodes in M_0 are all the finite booleanly closed subsets of $FL(\varphi)$ containing at most one long diamond formula.

Edges in M_0 are defined as follows.

For each $D \in \Sigma_0$, node $n \in M_0$ such that $\langle D\rangle p \in n$ and $[D]q_1, \ldots, [D]q_n$ are all the $[D]q$ formulas in n, and each $n' \in M_0$ such that $n' \in BC(\{p, q_1, \ldots, q_n\})$ connect $n \xrightarrow{D} n'$.

We now define a deletion process intended to omit all the nodes containing an unsatisfiable diamond formula. For $i = 0,1,...$ we define M_{i+1} to be the subgraph of M_i consisting of all nodes $n \in M_i$ such that each formula $\langle a\rangle p \in n$ has a satisfying a-path in M_i.

We define now the limit of the chain of these subgraphs, $M_\omega = \bigcap_{i<\omega} M_i$.

Consider the limit graph M_ω. If M_ω contains some node $n_0 \in M_\omega$ such that $n_0 \in BC(\{\varphi\})$ we call n_0 the <u>root</u> and define $M = M_\omega$. We call M the cannonical model (structure) for φ.

Otherwise we say that the construction failed to yield a cannonical model for φ.

<u>Theorem 1</u>:

A formula φ is satisfiable iff it has a cannonical model M constructed as above. This model has the following properties:

a) Nodes in the model are finite booleanly closed subsets of $FL(\varphi)$.

b) There exists a root $n_0 \in M$ such that $\varphi \in n_0$.

c) Edges in the graph are of the form

$$n = \{\langle D\rangle p, [D]q_1, ..., [D]q_n ...\} \xrightarrow{D} n'.$$

where $n' \in BC(\{p, q_1, ..., q_n\})$.

For each $\langle D\rangle p \in n$ there exists at least one such edge.

d) Each node contains at most one long diamond formula. It may appear in two different contexts such as:

$\langle A^\Delta B^\Delta\rangle\langle B^n\rangle p$ and $\langle B^n\rangle p$, or

$\langle A^\Delta B^\Delta\rangle\langle B^n\rangle p$ and $\langle A\rangle\langle A^\Delta B^\Delta\rangle\langle B\rangle\langle B^n\rangle p$.

The nontrivial part in the proof of this theorem is to show that if a formula is satisfiable then the limit graph M_ω contains at least one root $n_0 \in BC(\{\varphi\})$. This is done be assuming some model M' for φ. We then establish correspondence between states in M' and some of the nodes in M_0, such that if $s \in M'$ corresponds to $n \in M_0$ then each $p \in n$ holds at s, i.e. $M', s \models p$. Then we show that nodes in M_0 corresponding to states in M' could never be deleted, i.e. they must belong also to $M_1, M_2, ..., M_\omega$. To argue that it is sufficient to consider nodes containing at most one long diamond formula, we observe that long diamond formulas are expanded in order to satisfy some diamond formula in $SC(\varphi)$. Since in PDL each diamond formula may be satisfied by a separate path, each node in the model is dedicated to the satisfaction of at most one diamond formula.

The theorem established a model of a certain form for all satisfiable formulas. Unfortunately the resulting model is usually infinite.

In the rest of the paper we will concentrate on "folding" this infinite model into a finite push down model.

<u>Encoding of Long Formulas</u>:

We begin by introducing a convention by which the long formulas in a node of M can be encoded in a <u>stack</u>. The stack consists of two tracks to which we refer as the <u>box</u> and <u>diamond</u> tracks respectively. We employ two special symbols $\hat{b}$ and $\hat{d}$

that serve as pointers to the previous square of the stack in the box and diamond tracks respectively. When they appear outside the stack they refer to the top square of the stack. When they appear inside the stack in some square they refer to the square immediately below.

A <u>well formed</u> box track has the form:

Top →	$[B](C_1 \wedge \hat{b})$	$[B](C_2 \wedge \hat{b})$	...	$[B](C_k \wedge \hat{b})$	$[B]C_{k+1}$

Here each C_i, $i = 1,\dots,k+1$ is a conjunction $C_i = \bigwedge_j p^i_j$ of formulas $p^i_j \in SC(\varphi)$. All of $C_1,\dots,C_k$ but not C_{k+1} may be empty conjunctions. The formula that this track encodes is

$$[B](C_1 \wedge [B](C_2 \wedge \dots [B](C_k \wedge [B]C_{k+1})\dots)).$$

Note that this is equivalent to the conjunction of the formulas:

$$[B]C_1, [B^2]C_2, \dots, [B^k]C_k, [B^k]C_{k+1}.$$

A <u>well formed</u> diamond track has the form:

Top →	$\langle B\rangle\hat{d}$	......	$\langle B\rangle\hat{d}$	$\langle B\rangle p$

for some $p \in SC(\varphi)$.

It encodes the formula $\langle B^m\rangle p$, where $m \geq 1$ is the length of the track.

When two well formed tracks are combined they form a well formed stack whose depth is the maximum of the lengths of the two tracks.

Thus the following stack:

Top →	$[B]\hat{b}$	$[B]\hat{b}$	$[B](r\wedge\hat{b})$	$[B]\hat{b}$	$[B]s$
	$\langle B\rangle\hat{d}$	$\langle B\rangle\hat{d}$	$\langle B\rangle\hat{d}$	$\langle B\rangle t$	-

Encodes the set of long formulas:

$$[B^3]r, \quad [B^5]s, \quad \langle B^4\rangle t.$$

We define the <u>extended small closure</u> of a formula φ, $ESC(\varphi)$ by:

$$ESC(\varphi) = SC(\varphi) \cup \{\hat{b}, \hat{d}, [A^\Delta B^\Delta]\hat{b}, \langle A^\Delta B^\Delta\rangle\hat{d}, [A][A^\Delta B^\Delta][B]\hat{b}, \langle A\rangle\langle A^\Delta B^\Delta\rangle\langle B\rangle\hat{d}\}.$$

<u>Claim</u>: every node $n \in M$, can be represented by a pair $\langle m,\sigma\rangle$, where

m is a booleanly closed set of formulas, $m \subseteq ESC(\varphi)$,
σ is a stack over an alphabet Γ.

The stack alphabet Γ is defined so as to encode all the possible combinations of long formulas, restrictied to a single long diamond formula. Formally

$$\Gamma = 3 \times 2^{SC(\varphi)} \times 3 \times SC(\varphi).$$

Thus each letter of Γ is a quadruple $\langle a,S,b,p\rangle$ where:

$a \in \{0,1,2\}$ is an indicator of the location of the square in the box track. The value $a = 2$ indicates that the square is not empty and also that this is not the bottom square in the box track. The value $a = 1$ indicates that this is the bottom square in the box track. Value of $a = 0$ indicates that the square is empty.

$b \in \{0,1,2\}$ plays a similar role for the diamond track.

$S \subseteq SC(\varphi)$ is the set of formulas whose conjunction appears in the box square.

$p \in SC(\varphi)$ is meaningful only when $b = 1$, and then it is the formula at the end of the $\langle B^k \rangle p$ long diamond formula.

Any of the tracks could be completely empty which is signified by the corresponding indicator being continuously 0. We exclude from Γ any letters such that both $a = b = 0$.

In the sequel we use the more intuitively appealing representation of the symbols of Γ. Thus $[2,\{p,q\},1,s]$ will be represented as $[[B](p \wedge q \wedge \hat{b}), \langle B \rangle s]$ and $[1,\{p\},0,-]$ as $[[B]p,-]$.

We denote by $W(\Gamma)$ the set of all well formed stacks over a stack alphabet Γ.

The representation of an M node n by the pair $\langle m,\sigma \rangle$ is obtained as follows:

First we put into m all the formulas $p \in n \cap SC(\varphi)$. Then we collect all the long formulas of the form $[B^n]p$ appearing in the contexts: $[B^n]p$, $[A^\Delta B^\Delta][B^n]p$ or $[A][A^\Delta B^\Delta][B][B^n]p$; as well as long formulas of the form $\langle B^k \rangle p$ appearing in the contexts: $\langle B^k \rangle p$, $\langle A^\Delta B^\Delta \rangle \langle B^k \rangle p$ or $\langle A \rangle \langle A^\Delta B^\Delta \rangle \langle B \rangle \langle B^k \rangle p$. All these long formulas are encoded in the stack σ.

Lastly for each long formula of one of the forms:

$$[B^n]p,\ [A^\Delta B^\Delta][B^n]p,\ [A][A^\Delta B^\Delta][B][B^n]p,\ \langle B^k \rangle p,\ \langle A^\Delta B^\Delta \rangle \langle B^k \rangle p,\ \langle A \rangle \langle A^\Delta B^\Delta \rangle \langle B \rangle \langle B^k \rangle p,$$

we add to m the formula $\hat{b}$, $[A^\Delta B^\Delta]\hat{b}$, $[A][A^\Delta B^\Delta][B]\hat{b}$, $\hat{d}$, $\langle A^\Delta B^\Delta \rangle \hat{d}$, $\langle A \rangle \langle A^\Delta B^\Delta \rangle \langle B \rangle \hat{d}$ respectively.

Let $m \subseteq ESC(\varphi)$. For brevity we write $f(\hat{b}) \in m$ to denote the fact that

$$m \cap \{\hat{b},\ [A^\Delta B^\Delta]\hat{b},\ [A][A^\Delta B^\Delta][B]\hat{b}\} \neq \emptyset$$

i.e. $\hat{b}$ apears in some formula in m. Similarly for $f(\hat{d}) \in m$.

A pair $\langle m,\sigma \rangle$ such that $m \subseteq ESC(\varphi)$ is booleanly closed and $\sigma \in W(\Gamma)$ is said to be <u>proper</u> if:

$f(\hat{b}) \notin m \iff$ the box track in σ is empty

$f(\hat{d}) \notin m \iff$ the diamond track in σ is empty.

Of course if both tracks in σ are empty $\sigma = \Lambda$ (the empty stack).

Obviously the pair $\langle m,\sigma \rangle$ encoding a node $n \in M$ is always proper.

In the other direction, given a proper pair $\langle m,\sigma \rangle$, there always exists a booleanly closed $n \in FL(\varphi)$ such that $\langle m,\sigma \rangle$ encodes n. We only have to evaluate the long formulas ecoded by the stack and substitute them for each appearance of $\hat{b}$ and $\hat{d}$ in m.

We denote by $n = n(m,\sigma)$ the booleanly closed set that $\langle m,\sigma \rangle$ encodes.

With this encoding we can conclude the following.

Theorem 2:

A formula φ over $PDL_{A^{\Delta}B^{\Delta}}$ is satisfiable iff it has a push down model M that has the following properties:

a) Nodes

The nodes in the model are proper pairs of the form $\langle m,\sigma\rangle$ where $m \subseteq ESC(\varphi)$ is booleanly closed and $\sigma \in W(\Gamma)$. The nodes in M fall into one of three categories

1. $\langle m,\Lambda\rangle$ where $m \subseteq SC(\varphi)$. These are called stackless nodes.

2. $\langle m,\sigma\rangle$ where $|\sigma| > 0$ and $m \cap \{[A^{\Delta}B^{\Delta}]\hat{b}, \langle A^{\Delta}B^{\Delta}\rangle\hat{d}\} \neq \emptyset$.

Nodes falling into these two categories are called push nodes.

3. $\langle m,\sigma\rangle$ where $|\sigma| > 0$ and $m \cap \{[A^{\Delta}B^{\Delta}]\hat{b}, \langle A^{\Delta}B^{\Delta}\rangle\hat{d}\} = \emptyset$

but $m \cap \{\hat{b},\hat{d}\} \neq \emptyset$

These nodes are called pop nodes.

Push nodes $\langle m,\sigma\rangle$ with $|\sigma| \leq 1$ are referred to as shallow nodes.

b) Roots

There exists at least one node $\langle m_0,\Lambda\rangle$ such that $\varphi \in m_0$. All the nodes of the form $\langle m,\Lambda\rangle \in M$ are taken to be the roots of M.

c) Edges

For each node $\langle m,\sigma\rangle \in M$ there are the following edges.

A - edges

Let

$$m = \{\langle A\rangle p_1,\ldots,\langle A\rangle p_{\ell}, [A]q_1,\ldots,[A]q_t,$$
$$\langle A\rangle\langle A^{\Delta}B^{\Delta}\rangle\langle B\rangle r_1,\ldots,\langle A\rangle\langle A^{\Delta}B^{\Delta}\rangle\langle B\rangle r_k,$$
$$[A][A^{\Delta}B^{\Delta}][B]s_1,\ldots,[A][A^{\Delta}B^{\Delta}][B]s_n,\ldots\}$$

where the explicitly shown formulas are all the formulas of the forms $\langle A\rangle p$ or $[A]q$ in m. One of the r_i may be $\hat{d}$ and one of the s_j may be $\hat{b}$.

$\langle A\rangle p$ - edges:

For each $i = 1,\ldots,\ell$ define $X_i = [[B] \bigwedge_{i=1}^{n} s_i, -] \in \Gamma$.

Then there must be an edge

$$\langle m,\sigma\rangle \xrightarrow{\lambda} \langle m',\sigma'\rangle$$

according to one of the cases:

- If $n = 0$ then $\lambda = A/c$, $m' \in BC(\{p_i,q_1,\ldots,q_t\})$ and $\sigma' = \Lambda$. We refer to this edge as type A.1.

- If $n > 0$ but $\hat{b} \notin \{s_1,\ldots,s_n\}$ then $\lambda = A/c,+X_i$

$$m' \in BC(\{p_i,q_1,\ldots q_t, [A^{\Delta}B^{\Delta}]\hat{b}\}) \text{ and } \sigma' = X_i.$$

We refer to this edge as type A.2.

• If $n > 0$ and $\hat{b} \in \{s_1,\ldots,s_n\}$ then $\lambda = A/{+}X_i$ $m' \in BC(\{p_i,q_1,\ldots,q_t,[A^{\Delta}B^{\Delta}]\hat{b})$ and $\sigma' = X_i \cdot \sigma$.

We refer to this edge as type A.3.

$\langle A\rangle\langle A^{\Delta}B^{\Delta}\rangle\langle B\rangle r$ - edges

For each $i = 1,\ldots,k$ define $Y_i = [[B] \bigwedge_{i=1}^{n} s_i, \langle B\rangle r_i]$. If $n = 0$ then $Y_i = [-,\langle B\rangle r_i]$.

There must be an edge

$$\langle m,\sigma\rangle \overset{\lambda}{\rightarrow} \langle m',\sigma'\rangle$$

where $m' \in BC(\{\langle A^{\Delta}B^{\Delta}\rangle\hat{d},\ q_1,\ldots,q_t\})$ if $n = 0$ and $m' \in BC(\{\langle A^{\Delta}B^{\Delta}\rangle\hat{d},\ q_1,\ldots,q_t, [A^{\Delta}B^{\Delta}]\hat{b}\})$ if $n > 0$. The form of λ, σ' is determined by:

If $r_i \neq \hat{d}$ and $\hat{b} \notin \{s_1,\ldots,s_n\}$ then:

$$\lambda = A/c,{+}Y_i, \quad \sigma' = Y_i.$$

This again is an edge of type A.2.

Otherwise:

$\lambda = A/{+}Y_i$, $\sigma' = Y_i \cdot \sigma$

This again is an edge of type A.3.

B - Edges

Let

$$m = \{\langle B\rangle p_1,\ldots,\langle B\rangle p_\ell,\quad [B]q_1,\ldots,[B]q_t,\ldots\}$$

where the explicitly shown formulas are all the formulas of the form $\langle B\rangle p$ or $[B]q$ in m.

Let $Y = [[B]r,\langle B\rangle u] \in \Gamma$ where each of the components could be empty.

$\langle B\rangle p$ - Edges

For each $i = 1,\ldots,\ell$, there must be an edge:

$$\langle m,\sigma\rangle \overset{\lambda}{\rightarrow} \langle m',\sigma'\rangle$$

according to one of the cases:

• If $\hat{b} \notin m$ then $\lambda = B/c$, $m' \in BC(p_i,q_1,\ldots,q_t)$ and $\sigma' = \Lambda$.

We refer to this edge as type B.1.
For the next two cases $\hat{b} \in m$ and let $\sigma = Y \cdot \tilde{\sigma}$ for some $Y = [[B]r,\langle B\rangle u] \in \Gamma$

• If $\hat{b} \in m$ but $\hat{b} \notin r$ (that is, $[B]r \in Y$ is the bottom of the box track in σ) then

$$\lambda = B/{-}Y,c,\quad m' \in BC(p_i,q_1,\ldots,q_t,r) \text{ and } \sigma' = \Lambda.$$

We refer to this edge as type B.2.

• If $\hat{b} \in m$ and $\hat{b} \in r$ then

$\lambda = B/{-}Y$, $m' \in BC(p_i,q_1,\ldots,q_t,r)$ and $\sigma' = \tilde{\sigma}$.

We refer to this edge as type B.3.

Note that in this case $|\sigma'| > 0$.

$\hat{d}$ - Edges

If $\hat{d} \in m$ then $\sigma = Y\cdot\tilde{\sigma}$ for some $Y = [[B]r, \langle B\rangle u] \in \Gamma$. There must be an edge

$$\langle m,\sigma\rangle \xrightarrow{\lambda} \langle m',\sigma'\rangle$$

where λ, m', σ' are determined as follows:

If $\hat{b} \notin m$ then $m' \in BC(\{u,q_1,\ldots,q_t\})$.

If $\hat{b} \in m$ then $m' \in BC(\{u,q_1,\ldots,q_t,r\})$.

- If $\hat{d} \notin u$ (i.e. $\langle B\rangle u$ is the bottom of the diamond track) and either $\hat{b} \notin m$ or $\hat{b} \notin r$, then

$$\lambda = B/\text{-}Y,c, \quad \sigma' = \Lambda.$$

This is again a B.2 edge.

- Otherwise (i.e. $\hat{d} \in u$ or $\hat{b} \in m$ and $\hat{b} \in r$)

$$\lambda = B/\text{-}Y, \quad \sigma' = \tilde{\sigma}$$

This is again a B.3 edge and $\sigma' = \tilde{\sigma} \neq \Lambda$.

C - Edges

Let $C \in \Sigma_0 - \{A,B\}$, i.e. any atomic program different from A and B, and let

$$m = \{\langle C\rangle p_1,\ldots,\langle C\rangle p_\ell, [C]q_1,\ldots,[C]q_t,\ldots,\}$$

where the explicitly indicated formulas are all the formulas of the forms $\langle C\rangle p$ or $[C]q$ in m.

Then for each $i = 1,\ldots,\ell$ there must be an edge

$$\langle m,\sigma\rangle \xrightarrow{C/c} \langle m',\Lambda\rangle$$

where

$$m' \in BC(\{p_i,q_1,\ldots,q_t\}).$$

This concludes the enumeration of types of edges in M.

d) Attainable Configurations

For each node $\langle m,\sigma\rangle \in M$, the configuration $\{\langle m,\sigma\rangle,\sigma\}$ is attainable. That is, there exists a traversable path leading from a base configuration $\{\langle m_0,\Lambda\rangle,\Lambda\}$ to $\{\langle m\ \sigma\rangle,\sigma\}$. Vice versa, any attainable configuration $\{\langle m,\sigma\rangle,\sigma'\}$ necessarily satisfies $\sigma = \sigma'$. That is, the stack with which a node is reachable is uniquely determined by the node.

e) Satisfaction of Formulas

Recollect that we denote by $n(m,\sigma)$ the set of formulas encoded by the pair $\langle m,\sigma\rangle$. Then for each formula $p \in n(m,\sigma)$, $M,\langle m,\sigma\rangle \models p$. Actually, we should have specified a configuration $\{\langle m,\sigma\rangle,\sigma'\}$ at which p is satisfied. But from the above we know that the only attainable configurations are of the form $\{\langle m,\sigma\rangle, \sigma\}$.

This concludes the statement of theorem 2. The proof is a direct consequence of encoding the model M assured by theorem 1. Each node n of M is encoded by a pair $\langle m,\sigma\rangle$ such that $n = \tilde{n}(m,\sigma)$. Then, the edges of M are translated into edges in $\mathcal{M}$ according to the different cases enumerated in c) above. The other properties of $\mathcal{M}$ follow from the corresponding properties of M. In particular it follows that $\mathcal{M}$ is a pushdown model for φ.

□

Theorem 2 established the existence of a pushdown model for each satisfiable formula. Unfortunately it is still an infinite model. It can also be considered a degenerate pushdown model, since the whole idea in a pushdown model is to have one node representing many configurations, while in $\mathcal{M}$, each node corresponds to a single configuration.

We proceed to correct these deficiencies by defining a homomorphism on $\mathcal{M}$ that will fold it into a finite pushdown model.

We summarize some of the observations made above about the structure $\mathcal{M}$.

For a node $\langle m,\sigma\rangle \in \mathcal{M}$ we refer to m as a <u>type</u>. Let T denote the set of all types in $\mathcal{M}$. Since each $m \in T$ is a subset $m \subseteq ESC(\varphi)$, the set of types T is necessarily finite. We partition the set T into <u>push</u> types S and pop types P, $T = S \cup P$.

A type $m \in T$ is a push type if it satisfies the following two requirements:

$$\hat{b} \in m \Rightarrow [A^{\Delta}B^{\Delta}]\hat{b} \in m$$

$$\hat{d} \in m \Rightarrow \langle A^{\Delta}B^{\Delta}\rangle\hat{d} \in m$$

A type $m \in T$ is a pop type if it either contains $\hat{b}$ but not $[A^{\Delta}B^{\Delta}]\hat{b}$, or contains $\hat{d}$ but not $\langle A^{\Delta}B^{\Delta}\rangle\hat{d}$.

Out of a push node $\langle m,\sigma\rangle \in \mathcal{M}$, $m \in S$ we may have the following edges:

A

A.1: $\langle m,\sigma\rangle \xrightarrow{A/c} \langle m',\Lambda\rangle \qquad m' \in S$

A.2: $\langle m,\sigma\rangle \xrightarrow{A/c,+X} \langle m',X\rangle \qquad m' \in S$

A.3: $\langle m,\sigma\rangle \xrightarrow{A/+X} \langle m',X\cdot\sigma\rangle \qquad m' \in S$

B

B.1: $\langle m,\sigma\rangle \xrightarrow{B/c} \langle m',\Lambda\rangle \qquad m' \in S$

B.2: $\langle m,X\sigma\rangle \xrightarrow{B/-X,c} \langle m',\Lambda\rangle \qquad m' \in S$

B.3: $\langle m,X\sigma\rangle \xrightarrow{B/-X} \langle m',\sigma\rangle \qquad \sigma \neq \Lambda,\ m' \in P$

C

C: $\langle m,\sigma\rangle \xrightarrow{C/c} \langle m',\Lambda\rangle \qquad m' \in S$

Out of a pop node $\langle m,\sigma\rangle \in \mathcal{M}$, $m \in P$ we may have only the following edges:

A

A.1: $\langle m,\sigma\rangle \xrightarrow{A/c} \langle m',\Lambda\rangle \qquad m' \in S$

A.2: $\langle m,\sigma\rangle \xrightarrow{A/c,+X} \langle m',X\rangle \qquad m' \in S$

B

B.1: $\langle m,\sigma\rangle \xrightarrow{B/c} \langle m',\Lambda\rangle \qquad m' \in S$

$$\text{B.2:}\quad \langle m, X\sigma\rangle \xrightarrow{B/-X,c} \langle m',\Lambda\rangle \qquad m' \in S$$

$$\text{B.3:}\quad \langle m, X\sigma\rangle \xrightarrow{B/-X} \langle m',\sigma\rangle \qquad \sigma \neq \Lambda,\; m' \in P$$

C

$$\text{C:}\quad \langle m,\sigma\rangle \xrightarrow{C/c} \langle m',\Lambda\rangle \qquad m' \in S.$$

Note that all edges save A.3 and B.3 always lead to shallow nodes.

Thus we cannot perform from a pop node a push operation that maintains the old stack, because no A.3 edge may depart from a pop node.

In the same way that we represented M by encoding it into the pushdown model $\mathcal{M}$, we can encode the whole tableaux construction as follows:

Construct an initial pushdown structure $\mathcal{M}_0$ by having:

Nodes: All the proper pairs $\langle m,\sigma\rangle$ over $FL(\varphi)$.

Edges: Edges of types A.1-A.3, B.1-B.3 and C wherever applicable.

Next we construct the deletion sequence $\mathcal{M}_1,\mathcal{M}_2,\ldots$ as follows. Let $\varphi \in m$ and $\langle m,\sigma\rangle \in \mathcal{M}_i$. We denote by $n(\varphi,\sigma)$ the interpretation of φ under σ (in case that φ contains $\hat{b}$ or $\hat{d}$). We retain in $\mathcal{M}_{i+1}$ all the nodes $\langle m,\sigma\rangle$ of $\mathcal{M}_i$ such that for each $\varphi \in m$ the formula $n(\varphi,\sigma)$ is fulfilled in $\mathcal{M}_i$, that is, there exists a fulfilling path for $n(\varphi,\sigma)$ traversing $\mathcal{M}_i$ nodes.

We then define $\mathcal{M} = \bigcap_{i<\omega} \mathcal{M}_i$. $\mathcal{M}$ contain a root $\langle n_0,\Lambda\rangle \in \mathcal{M}$ such that $n_0 \in BC(\{\varphi\})$ iff φ is satisfiable.

For a possible stack $\sigma \in \Gamma^*$ we define

$$\tau(\sigma) = \{m \mid \langle m,\sigma\rangle \in \mathcal{M}\}$$

i.e. the set of all types that appear together with σ in $\mathcal{M}$. We denote by $\tau_p(\sigma)$ the set of all pop types that appear jointly with σ, i.e. $\tau_p(\sigma) = \tau(\sigma) \cap P$.

Define an equivalence relation on stacks by

$$\sigma_1 \approx \sigma_2 \quad \text{if} \quad \sigma_1 = X\tilde{\sigma}, \text{ and } \sigma_2 = X\tilde{\sigma}_2 \quad \text{such that} \quad \tau_p(\tilde{\sigma}_1) = \tau_p(\tilde{\sigma}_2)$$

for some $X \in \Gamma$.

Thus we require that σ_1 and σ_2 have the same first symbol and their suffices share the same set of pop types in $\mathcal{M}$.

Obviously this is an equivalence relation. It also follows that Λ is not equivalent to any other stack.

Lemma E1 $\quad \sigma_1 \approx \sigma_2 \Rightarrow \tau_p(\sigma_1) = \tau_p(\sigma_2)$

Proof: Let $\sigma_1 = X\tilde{\sigma}$, $\sigma_2 = X\tilde{\sigma}_2$, such that $\tau_p(\tilde{\sigma}_1) = \tau_p(\tilde{\sigma}_2)$. Let m be a pop type such that $\langle m, X\sigma_1\rangle \in \mathcal{M}$.

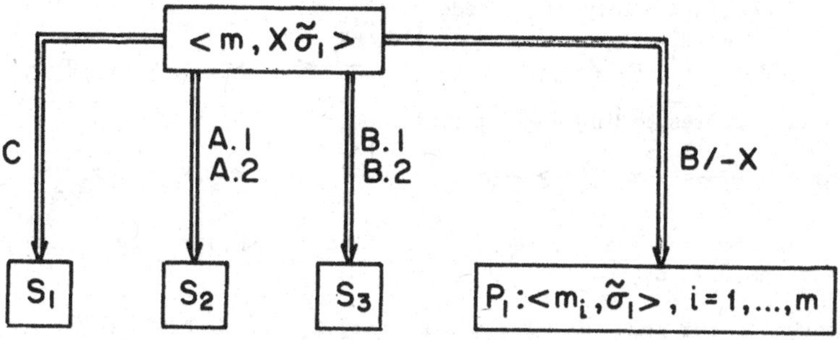

Fig. 3

The sets S_1, S_2 and S_3 are sets of shallow nodes obtained via edges of types A.1, A.2, B.1, B.2 and C. They are completely independent of $\tilde{\sigma}_1$. The set P_1: $<m_i,\tilde{\sigma}_1>$, $i = 1,\ldots,m$ is a set of pop nodes obtained via B.3 edges.

Consider now possible edges out of the node $<m,X\tilde{\sigma}_2>$ as constructed in M_0. Under the same A.1, A.2, B.1, B.2 and C edges, it has at least the same sets of shallow successors S_1, S_2 and S_3. Under the same B.3 edges, B/-X, it connects to a similar set $<m_i,\tilde{\sigma}_2>$, $i = 1,\ldots,m$ of pop successors. Since $\sigma_1 \approx \sigma_2$ and $<m_i,\tilde{\sigma}_1> \in M$ it follows also that $<m_i,\tilde{\sigma}_2> \in M$. Consequently $<m,X\tilde{\sigma}_2>$ has in M at least an equivalent set of successors to that of $<m,X\tilde{\sigma}_1>$ which are not deleted. Therefore, since $<m,X\sigma_1>$ was not deleted from M, there is no reason to delete $<m,X\tilde{\sigma}_2>$. We concluded that $<m,X\tilde{\sigma}_2> \in M$. The lemma follows immediately.

□

Lemma E2 $\quad \sigma_1 \approx \sigma_2 \Rightarrow Y\sigma_1 \approx Y\sigma_2$.

Obvious from the previous lemma and the definition of $\approx$.

Lemma E3 $\quad \sigma_1 \approx \sigma_2 \Rightarrow \tau(\sigma_1) = \tau(\sigma_2)$.

Let $\sigma_1 \approx \sigma_2$ and $m \in T$ be any type. If m is a pop type then it follows from lemma E1 that

$$<m,\sigma_1> \in M \iff <m,\sigma_2> \in M.$$

Let now m be a push type. Assume that $<m,\sigma_1> \in M$, and $<m,\sigma_2> \notin M$. Then $<m,\sigma_2>$ was deleted at some stage. This must have happended at the i-th iteration, for some $i \geq 0$, as a result of some diamond formula $\varphi \in m$ not being fulfilled at $<m,\sigma_2>$ by paths within M_i. Consider such a pair, i.e. $<m,\sigma_1> \in M$ and $<m,\sigma_2> \notin M_{i+1}$, $\sigma_1 \approx \sigma_2$ for which the index i is minimal.

Thus there must exist a diamond formula $\varphi \in m$ such that φ is not fulfilled at $<m,\sigma_2>$ in M_{i+1}. On the other hand, since $<m,\sigma_1>$ was not deleted, there must exist a path π proceeding through, M - nodes fulfilling φ at $<m,\sigma_1>$. Note, by the way, that $n(\varphi,\sigma_1)$ and $n(\varphi,\sigma_2)$ may be different due to differences between σ_1 and σ_2.

In general the path π may contain several A.3 edges and then may traverse an edge of a different type.

Case π consists solely of A.3 edges:

$$\pi: \langle m,\sigma_1\rangle \xrightarrow{A/+X_1} \langle m_1, X_1\sigma_1\rangle \quad \cdots \quad \xrightarrow{A/+X_k} \langle m_k, X_k \cdots X_1\sigma_1\rangle.$$

There is a corresponding M_0 path

$$\pi: \langle m,\sigma_2\rangle \xrightarrow{A/+X_1} \langle m_1, X_1\sigma_2\rangle \longrightarrow \cdots \xrightarrow{A/+X_k} \langle m_k, X_k \cdots X_1\sigma_2\rangle.$$

It is easy to show that if φ is fulfilled at $\langle m,\sigma_1\rangle$ by π then φ is fulfilled at $\langle m,\sigma_2\rangle$ by $\tilde{\pi}$.

Consequently for some j, $1 \leq j \leq k$ $\langle m_j, X_j \cdots X_1\ \sigma_2\rangle \notin M_i$. But this contradicts the minimality of i since $\langle m_j, X_j \cdots X_1, \sigma_1\rangle \in M$ and by lemma E2, $X_j \cdots X_1\sigma_1 \approx X_j \cdots X_1\sigma_2$. We conclude that this case is impossible.

Case π contains additional types of edges.

Consider the segment containing the first non A.3 edge:

$$\pi: \langle m,\sigma_1\rangle \to \cdots \to \langle m_k, X_k \cdots X_1\sigma_1\rangle \to \langle m',\sigma_1'\rangle.$$

By the argument of minimality the segment

$$\tilde{\pi}: \langle m,\sigma_2\rangle \to \cdots \to \langle m_k, Y_k \cdots X_1\sigma_2\rangle$$

must be fully contained in M_i. The first non A.3 edge can lead either to a shallow node or be a B/-Y edge. In the first case the shallow node $\langle m',\sigma_1'\rangle \in M$ and is also directly connected to $\langle m_k, X_k \cdots X_1\ \sigma_2\rangle$.

In the second case m' is a pop node and $\sigma_1' = X_k \cdots X_1\sigma_1/Y$. Define $\sigma_2' = X_k \cdots X_1\sigma_2/Y$. Since $\sigma_1 \approx \sigma_2$ it follows that $\tau_p(\sigma_1') = \tau_p(\sigma_2')$. Consequently $\langle m',\sigma_2'\rangle \in M$. Thus, in any of the cases π leads to a node $\langle m',\sigma_2'\rangle$ that is in M and fulfills any diamond formula not already fulfilled in $\tilde{\pi}$. It is not difficult to conclude that in this case also $\langle m,\sigma_2\rangle$ should not have been deleted from M_i.

We are ready now to construct the finite pushdown model corresponding to a satisfiable φ. We denote this structure by $\tilde{M}$.

Nodes The nodes in $\tilde{M}$ are given by the set

$$N: \{\langle m,\tau(\sigma)\rangle \mid \langle m,\sigma\rangle \in M\}.$$

Thus node in $\tilde{M}$ have the structure $\langle m,t\rangle$ with $m \in T$ and $t \subseteq T$.

Roots

As roots in $\tilde{M}$ we designate all nodes of the form $\langle m,\tau(\Lambda)\rangle$.

Stack The stack alphabet $\tilde{\Gamma} = \Gamma \times 2^T$. Thus, elements of $\tilde{\Gamma}$ have the form (X,t) with $X \in \Gamma$ and $t \subseteq T$ a set of types of M. The intended meaning of any segment of the stack:

$$\tilde{\sigma} = (X_1,t_1)(X_2,t_2) \cdots (X_k,t_k)$$

is that for every $i = 1,\ldots,k$, $t_i = \tau(X_{i+1},\ldots,X_k)$, i.e. t_i is the set of all types m such that $\langle m, X_{i+1},\ldots,X_k\rangle \in M$. For a stack $\tilde{\sigma}$ as above we define the projection $p(\tilde{\sigma}) = X_1X_2 \cdots X_k$.

Edges Each edge in M induces an edge in $\tilde{M}$.

- Each M-edge of type A.1, B.1 or C, of the form:

$$\langle m,\sigma\rangle \xrightarrow{D/c} \langle m',\Lambda\rangle$$

induces in $\tilde{M}$ the edge:

$$\langle m,\tau(\sigma)\rangle \xrightarrow{D/c} \langle m',\tau(\Lambda)\rangle$$

- Each M-edge of type A.2, having the form:

$$\langle m,\sigma\rangle \xrightarrow{A/c,+X} \langle m',X\rangle$$

induces in $\tilde{M}$ the edge:

$$\langle m,\tau(\sigma)\rangle \xrightarrow{A/c,+[X,\tau(\Lambda)]} \langle m',\tau(X)\rangle$$

- Each M-edge of type A.3, having the form:

$$\langle m,\sigma\rangle \xrightarrow{A/+X} \langle m',X\cdot\sigma\rangle$$

induces in $\tilde{M}$ the edge:

$$\langle m,\tau(\sigma)\rangle \xrightarrow{A/+[X,\tau(\sigma)]} \langle m',\tau(X\cdot\sigma)\rangle$$

- Each M-edge of type B.2, having the form:

$$\langle m,X\cdot\sigma\rangle \xrightarrow{B/-X,c} \langle m',\Lambda\rangle$$

induces in $\tilde{M}$ the edge:

$$\langle m,\tau(X\cdot\sigma)\rangle \xrightarrow{B/-[X,\tau(\sigma)],c} \langle m',\tau(\Lambda)\rangle$$

- Each M-edge of type B.3, having the form:

$$\langle m,X\cdot\sigma\rangle \xrightarrow{B/-X} \langle m',\sigma\rangle$$

induces in $\tilde{M}$ the edge:

$$\langle m,\tau(X\cdot\sigma)\rangle \xrightarrow{B/-[X,\tau(\sigma)]} \langle m',\tau(\sigma)\rangle.$$

End of Definition.

The main argument justifying that $\tilde{M}$ is a PDM for φ iff M is, is based on establishing correspondence between the attainable configurations in M and those of $\tilde{M}$.

Attainable configurations in M have all the form $\{\langle m,\sigma\rangle,\sigma\}$. For conciseness we refer to them simply as $\langle m,\sigma\rangle$.

Configurations in $\tilde{M}$ have the form $\{\langle m,\tau(\sigma)\rangle,\delta\}$. The stack δ is said to be <u>well formed</u> if its projection $p(\delta)$ is a well formed Γ-stack and it has the form:

$$\delta = [X_1,t_1][X_2,t_2] \ldots [X_k,t_k]$$

such that for each $j = 1,\ldots,k$, $t_j = \tau(X_{j+1},\ldots,X_k)$. Under the assumption of <u>well-formedness</u> the projection $p\colon \tilde{\Gamma}^* \to \Gamma^*$ is invertible by defining

$$p^{-1}(X_1 \ldots X_k) = [X_1,\tau(X_2 \ldots X_k)][X_2,\tau(X_3 \ldots X_k)] \ldots [X_k,\tau(\Lambda)].$$

Lemma E4

All attainable configurations of $\widetilde{M}$ have the form $\{<m,t>,\delta\}$ where δ is well formed and $t = \tau(p(\delta))$.

The lemma is proved by induction on the length of the path to an attainable configuration in $C(\widetilde{M})$. Certainly the base configurations have the form $\{<m,\tau(\Lambda)>,\Lambda\}$ which satisfies both requirements. By considering the different edge types we show that the two requirements are preserved by the transitions effected by these edges. For edges leading to shallow configurations (edge types A.1, A.2, B.1, B.2 and C) the result is a direct consequence of the edge definitions.

Consider therefore an A.3 edge connecting the following configurations:

$$\{<m,\tau(\sigma)>,\delta\} \xrightarrow{A/+[X,\tau(\sigma)]} \{<m',\tau(X\cdot\sigma)>,\ [X,\tau(\sigma)]\cdot\delta\}.$$

By the induction hypothesis $\tau(\sigma) = \tau(p(\delta))$, and δ is well formed. Consequently $\delta' = [X,\tau(\delta)]\cdot\delta$ is also well formed. An immediate consequence of lemmas E1-E3 is that $\tau(\sigma_1) = \tau(\sigma_2) \Rightarrow \tau(X\cdot\sigma_1) = \tau(X\cdot\sigma_2)$. We apply this to conclude that $\tau(X\cdot\sigma) = \tau(p(\delta')) = \tau(X\cdot p(\delta))$.

Consider next a B.3 edge connecting the configurations:

$$\{<m,\tau(X\cdot\sigma)>,[X,\tau(\sigma)]\cdot\delta\} \xrightarrow{B/-[X,\tau(\sigma)]} \{<m',\tau(\sigma)>,\delta\}.$$

By the induction hypothesis $[X,\tau(\sigma)]\cdot\delta$ is well formed. Hence δ is well formed and also $\tau(\sigma) = \tau(p(\delta))$.

This establishes both requirements for the end configuration of the transition.

□

Lemma E The underlying models for M and $\widetilde{M}$ are isomorphic.

In fact M is isomorphic to the underlying model of $\widetilde{M}$.

Proof:

We establish 1-1 mapping between the attainable configurations of M and the attainable configurations of $\widetilde{M}$. Define the mapping $h: M \to U(\widetilde{M})$ by

$$h(<m,\sigma>) = \{<m,\tau(\sigma)>,p^{-1}(\sigma)\}.$$

This mapping is invertible on attainable configurations of $\widetilde{M}$ by the mapping $g: U(\widetilde{M}) \to M$ defined by:

$$g(\{<m,t>,\delta\}) = <m,p(\delta)>.$$

We show first that $h\circ g = g\circ h = \text{identity}$.

Let $<m,\sigma> \in M$ then

$$gh(<m,\sigma>) = g(\{<m,\tau(\sigma)>, p^{-1}(\sigma)\}) = <m,p(p^{-1}(\sigma))> = <m,\sigma>$$

On the other hand let $\{<m,t>,\delta\} \in U(\widetilde{M})$, which implies that δ is well formed and $t = \tau(p(\delta))$. Then $hg(\{<m,t>,\delta\}) = h(<m,p(\delta)>) = \{<m,\tau(p(\delta))>, p^{-1}(p(\delta))\} = \{<m,t>,\delta\}$.

Next, we have to show that for every two configurations $c_1,c_2 \in M$, $c_1 \xrightarrow{D} c_2$, for $D \in \Sigma_0$, iff $h(c_1) \xrightarrow{D} h(c_2)$ in $U(\widetilde{M})$. By considering each type of edge in M, the edge it induces in $\widetilde{M}$ and the corresponding edge in $C(\widetilde{M})$, it can be shown that the resulting edge indeed connects $h(c_1)$ to $h(c_2)$.

□

We conclude:

Theorem 3

A formula φ is satisfiable iff it has a finite PDM model.

Decidability

In this section we indicate how the finite PDM property implies decidability of the satisfiability problem.

In a subsequent paper we show how to construct a PDM for satisfiable formula directly by a finite tableaux construction. The direct construction method is more efficient than the procedure outlined here.

Given a formula φ to be tested for satisfiablity we construct its small closure $SC(\varphi)$ which is finite, and then its extended small closure $ESC(\varphi)$.

Denote by T the class of all booleanly closed subsets of $ESC(\varphi)$. Thus each $m \in T$ is a booleanly closed subset of $ESC(\varphi)$. Define Γ as $\Gamma = 3 \times 2^{SC(\varphi)} \times 3 \times SC(\varphi)$. Denote by $\tilde{U}$ the set

$$\tilde{U} = \{\langle m,t\rangle \mid m \in t \subseteq T\}.$$

These are all the possible nodes in the PDM $\tilde{M}$ guaranteed by theorem 3.

We check now all the possible PDM's constructed over nodes taken from $\tilde{U}$ that are consistent with the structure $\tilde{M}$. Since their number is finite we will eventually find $\tilde{M}$ or another appropriate PDM for φ if one exists.

A candidate PDM over $\tilde{U}$ consists of the folowing elements:

$\tilde{T} \subseteq T$ - The set of types appearing in $\tilde{M}$.

$\tilde{N} \subseteq \tilde{U}$ - The set of nodes appearing in $\tilde{M}$.
Each node should be of the form $\langle m,t\rangle$ with $m \in t \subseteq \tilde{T}$.

For each $m \in \tilde{T}$, there should be at least one node $\langle m,t'\rangle \in \tilde{N}$.

If $\langle m,t\rangle \in \tilde{N}$ and $m' \in t$ then also $\langle m',t\rangle \in \tilde{N}$.
These requirements are consequences of the fact that each t should be $\tau(\sigma)$ for some stack σ, such that $\langle m,\sigma\rangle \in M$.

$t_\Lambda \subseteq \tilde{T}$ - The set of types corresponding to $\tau(\Lambda)$.

$\tilde{R} = \{\langle m,t_\Lambda\rangle \mid m \in t_\Lambda\}$ the set of roots, must be $\tilde{R} \subseteq \tilde{N}$.

$\tilde{\Gamma} = \Gamma \times 2^{\tilde{T}}$ the stack alphabet.

$\tilde{E}$ - A set of edges connecting the nodes of $\tilde{N}$.
Each edge should be of one of the types A.1-A.3, B.1-B.3 or C and be labelled accordingly, using symbols of $\tilde{\Gamma}$. There are additional integrity constraints implied by the structure of m and the fact that $t = \tau(\sigma)$ that should be checked. We will not enumerate them here.

Apart from the local constraints that are straighforward to check there is a global constraint that requires some more explanation. This is the requirement that each diamond formula in a node be fulfilled by some path in the model.

We start this analysis by computing for each node $\langle m,t\rangle \in \tilde{N}$ the set of all stacks δ such that $\{\langle m,t\rangle,\delta\}$ is an attainable configuration of $\tilde{M}$. This set, for each node, can be shown to be a regular language over $\tilde{\Gamma}$. Denote it by $\Delta_a(m,t)$.

Next, consider any diamond formula $p \in m$, $\langle m,t\rangle \in M$ (including $\hat{d}$, $\langle A^\Delta B^\Delta\rangle\hat{d}$ and $\langle A\rangle\langle A^\Delta B^\Delta\rangle\langle B\rangle\hat{d}$). We can compute for each such p,m and t the set of all stacks δ such that $C(\tilde{M}),\{\langle m,t\rangle,\delta\} \models n(p,\delta)$.

That is, all stacks δ such that the formula p interpreted under δ is fulfilled by the configuration $\{\langle m,t\rangle,\delta\}$ in the configuration graph $C(\widetilde{M})$. This again can be shown to be a regular set for each p,m and t, that we denote by $\Delta_f(p,m,t)$.

It only remains to check for each p,m and t such that $\langle m,t\rangle \in \widetilde{M}$ and $p \in m$ that

$$(*) \quad \ldots \quad \Delta_f(p,m,t) \subseteq \Delta_a(m,t).$$

This implies that for every stack δ attainable at $\langle m,t\rangle$, the diamond formula p (or $n(p,\delta)$ if p contains $\hat{d}$) can be fulfilled by a traversible path.

To support our claim that $\Delta_a(m,t)$ and $\Delta_f(p,m,t)$ are regular sets that can be effectively computed given $\widetilde{M}$, let us consider the problem of computation of $\Delta_a(m,t)$.

For the question of reachability (attainability) in $\widetilde{M}$ we may ignore the Σ_0 labels on the edges. Thus we consider a finite graph with nodes N and edges $\widetilde{E}$ that are labelled by one of the stack actions: c; c,+X; +X; -Y,c; -Y. Some of the nodes are designated as roots $\widetilde{R} \subseteq \widetilde{N}$. We are interestested for each node $n \in \widetilde{N}$ in the set of stacks $\Delta_a(n)$ that can be built up along a path from some $n_0 \in \widetilde{R}$ to n. A preliminary transformation may introduce some additional nodes and split edges with compound labels such as 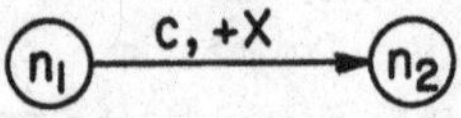

into a structure 

, where n' is a newly introduced node.

Thus we may consider graphs in which the stack actions labelling the edges are c, +X and -X for some $X \in \widetilde{\Gamma}$.

We now apply successively the following transformation steps to the graph until none is applicable any more. Each step adds a labelled edge to an existing configuration of three nodes which need not be distinct.

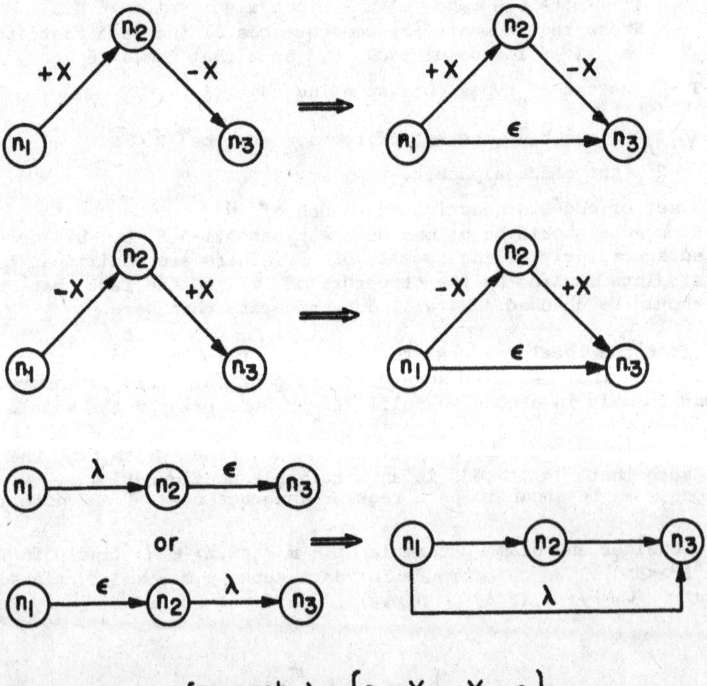

for each $\lambda \in \{c, +X, -X, \epsilon\}$

After all these steps have been taken we may completely ignore the $-X$ edges. We are left with a graph labelled with c and $+X$ actions. It is easy now to construct for each node $n \in \tilde{N}$ the regular expression describing the set of possible stacks constructed along paths from some $n_0 \in \tilde{R}$ to n - $\Delta_a(n)$.

The $\Delta_f(p,m,t)$ can be computed by a very similar procedure.

To check the inclusion $\Delta_f(p,mt) \subseteq \Delta(m,t)$ we have to compare two regular expressions for inclusion which is doable by known efficient algorithms.

The regularity of Δ_a and Δ_f is closely related to the theorem of formal language theory, claiming that the set of possible stacks arising in some state of a pushdown automaton under some input, is regular.

Generalization and Discussion

The method shown above can certainly be extended to the cases of PDL extended by other languages.

For example $PDL_{RG(A_1^\Delta B_1^\Delta, A_2^\Delta B_2^\Delta, \ldots, A_n^\Delta B_n^\Delta)}$ for distinct A_i, B_i, $i = 1,\ldots,n$ would certainly be decidable by the same methods. Another possible extension is the language

$$\{\varphi(W^R)\psi(W) \mid W \in \{0,1\}^*\}$$

with $\varphi(0) = A$, $\varphi(1) = B$, $\psi(0) = C$, $\psi(1) = D$, all distinct.

In fact we suggest the following conjecture:

Let C be a class of languages such that:

1. $RG \subseteq C$, i.e. C contains all the regular languages.
2. $C \subseteq CF$, i.e. every member of C is at most context free.
3. $C \cdot C \subseteq C$, C is closed under concatenation.
4. C is closed under <u>intersection</u>, i.e. for every $L_1, L_2 \in C$, $L_1 \cap L_2 \in C$.

Then PDL_C is decidable. These conditions are certainly satified for $RG_{(A^\Delta B^\Delta)}$ for which decidability has been shown in this paper.

On the other hand, if we consider the counter examples of [HPS1,2] they violate clause 4.

For $RG + A^\Delta B^\Delta + B^\Delta A^\Delta$ we could consider the intersection

$$(A^\Delta B^\Delta)A^* \cap A^*(B^\Delta A^\Delta) = \{A^i B^i C^i \mid i \geq 0\}$$

which is not context free.

Similarly for $RG + A^\Delta BA^\Delta$ the intersection

$$(A^\Delta BA^\Delta)BA^* \cap A^*B(A^\Delta BA^\Delta) = \{A^i BA^i BA^i \mid i \geq 0\}$$

again yields a non-context free language.

Condition 4 may be violated in more subtle ways.

Thus for $RG + A^\Delta B^\Delta + A^\Delta B^{2\Delta}$ we have

$$(A^{\Delta}B^{\Delta})P?B^{*} \cap A^{\Delta}B^{2\Delta} = \{A^{i}B^{i}P?B^{i} \mid i \geq 0\}$$

which again is context sensitive.

Acknowlegement:

We wish to thank Hava Chetrit for a most speedy and dedicated typing of this manuscript. We thank Yehuda Barbut for the lucid diagrams.

We gratefully acknowledge many helpful discussions and illuminating comments by Jonathan Stavi, David Harel and Rivi Sherman.

REFERENCES

[B] Ben Ari, M. - Complexity of Proofs and Models in Programming Languages. Ph.D. Thesis, Tel Aviv University, June 1981.

[FL] Fischer, M.J. and Ladner, R.E. - Propositional Logic of Regular Programs. JCSS 18:2.

[HPS1] Harel, D., Pnueli, A., Stavi, J. - Propositional Dynamic Logic of Nonregular Programs - FOCS 81.

[HPS2] Harel, D., Pnueli, A., Stavi, J. - Further Results on Propositional Dynamic Logic of Nonregular Programs - Workshop on Program Logics, Yorktown Heights, May 1981, Springer Verlag, Ed. D. Kozen.

[PR1] Pratt, V.R. - Sementical Considerations of Floyd-Hoare Logic - Proc. of 17-th FOCS (1976), 109-121.

A DECISION PROCEDURE FOR THE PROPOSITIONAL μ-CALCULUS

Dexter Kozen
Mathematical Sciences Department
IBM Research
Yorktown Heights, NY 10598

Rohit Parikh
Dept. of Computer and Information Sciences
Brooklyn College
Brooklyn, NY 11210

1. INTRODUCTION

Lμ is a propositional μ- or least fixpoint-calculus related to systems of Scott and DeBakker [SDeB] and Pratt [P]. It is strictly more expressive than Propositional Dynamic Logic (PDL) [FL]. In [K], an exponential-time decision procedure and complete finitary deductive system were given for a restricted version of Lμ. In this paper we show that unrestricted Lμ is decidable by reducing it to SnS, the second-order theory of n successors, shown decidable by Rabin [R]. This gives a nonelementary decision procedure. It is unknown whether Lμ can be decided in elementary time.

The key lemma in the reduction is that every satisfiable formula is satisfied in a tree model of finite degree. This construction is fairly straightforward in PDL: first, unwind a model into a tree model, then prune edges according to certain rules to give a tree of finite out-degree. Moreover, a bound can be obtained on the out-degree at any node in the tree. The construction is less straightforward in full Lμ, because of the more powerful iteration construct μ. It is still straightforward to unwind a model into a tree model (Lemmas 1 and 2), but the pruning (Lemmas 3 and 4) must be done with some care, because the truth of a formula μX.pX in a state s depends on the entire subtree under s, whereas in PDL, the truth of a formula <α*>p at s depends only on a single α* path out of s. We are not able to give a bound on the out-degree of the final tree, and suspect that such a bound would be tantamount to an elementary decision procedure.

2. DEFINITION OF Lμ AND Lμ+

The systems Lμ and Lμ+ were defined in [K]. We review the definitions briefly, referring the reader to [K] for a more detailed presentation.

2.1 SYNTAX

The primitive nonlogical symbols of Lμ and Lμ+ consist of <u>propositional letters</u> P,Q,..., including the constants 0,1; <u>propositional variables</u> X,Y,...; and <u>program letters</u> a,b,... . <u>Formulas</u> p,q,... are defined inductively:

(1) X

(2) P

(3) $p \vee q$

(4) $\neg p$

(5) $\langle a \rangle p$

(6) $\alpha X.pX$, α an ordinal

(7) $\mu X.pX$

In (6) and (7), pX is a formula with a distinguished variable X, all of whose free occurrences are positive. Intuitively, $\alpha X.pX$ represents the α-fold composition of the operator $\lambda X.pX$ applied to 0. Lμ+ is the infinitary language defined by (1)-(7). Lμ is the countable sublanguage obtained by deleting (6).

In addition to the above primitive operators, we will use defined operators

$$p \wedge q = \neg(\neg p \vee \neg q)$$

$$[a]p = \neg\langle a \rangle \neg p$$

$$\nu X.pX = \neg \mu X.\neg p \neg X \; .$$

The operator ν is the <u>greatest fixpoint operator</u>. Every Lμ formula is equivalent to a formula over ∨, ∧, μ, ν, <>, [], and ¬ in which ¬ is applied to primitive P and X only.

A variable X is <u>bound</u> if it occurs within the scope of a μX or αX, otherwise it is <u>free.</u> A formula with no free variables is called <u>closed.</u>

2.2 SEMANTICS

A <u>model</u> is a structure $M = (S^M, I^M)$, where $S = S^M$ is a set of <u>states,</u> and $I = I^M$ is an interpretation of the propositional letters and program letters as, respectively, subsets of S and binary relations on S. We require that $I(0) = \emptyset$ and $I(1) = S$. A formula $p(\bar{X})$ with free variables among $\bar{X} = X_1, \ldots, X_n$ is interpreted in M as an operator p^M which maps any valuation $\bar{A} = A_1, \ldots, A_n$ of $\bar{X}$ over subsets of S to a subset $p^M(\bar{A})$ of S. The operator p^M is defined by induction on the complexity of p:

(1) $X_i^M(\bar{A}) = A_i$

(2) $P^M(\bar{A}) = I(P)$

(3) $(p \vee q)^M(\bar{A}) = p^M(\bar{A}) \cup q^M(\bar{A})$

(4) $(\neg p)^M(\bar{A}) = S - p^M(\bar{A})$

(5) $(\langle a \rangle p)^M(\bar{A}) = \langle a^M \rangle (p^M(\bar{A}))$

where in (5),

$$\langle a^M \rangle (B) = \{s \mid \exists t \in B \ (s,t) \in I(a)\} .$$

In order to define (6) and (7), let pX be a formula with distinguished free variable X occurring only positively. Let $\bar{X}$ denote the other free variables in p. Thus pX =

$p(X,\bar{X})$. We assume by induction hypothesis that the operator p^M has already been defined.

(6.1) $0X.pX^M(\bar{A}) = 0^M = \emptyset$

(6.2) $(\alpha+1)X.pX^M(\bar{A}) = p^M(\alpha X.pX^M(\bar{A}),\bar{A})$

(6.3) $\delta X.pX^M(\bar{A}) = \cup_{\beta<\delta}\ \beta X.pX^M(\bar{A})$, δ a limit ordinal

(7) $\mu X.pX^M(\bar{A}) = \cup_{\beta}\ \beta X.pX^M(\bar{A})$

where in (7), the union is over all ordinals β. Taking $\mu > \alpha$ for any ordinal α, (6.1-3) and (7) can be combined into the single definition

(8) $\alpha X.pX^M(\bar{A}) = \cup_{\beta<\alpha}\ p^M(\beta X.pX^M(\bar{A}),\bar{A})$

where α is either an ordinal or μ.

Because p is positive in X, the operator p^M is monotone, therefore

$$\alpha X.pX^M(\bar{A}) \subseteq \beta X.pX^M(\bar{A})$$

for $\alpha \leq \beta$, and $\mu X.pX^M(\bar{A})$ is the least fixpoint of the operator $\lambda X.p^M(X,\bar{A})$.

If p is closed, then p^M is a constant function, i.e. $p^M(\bar{A})$ is a fixed set of states independent of $\bar{A}$. In this case, we say s satisfies p (notation: $M,s \models p$ or $s \models p$) if $s \in p^M(\bar{A})$.

3. FINITE BRANCHING TREE MODELS

Let $M = (S^M,I^M)$ be any model. We can unwind M to get an infinite-branching tree model $N = (S^N,I^N)$, as follows:

$$S^N = \{s_0a_1s_1a_2s_2\ldots a_ns_n \mid n < \omega,\ s_i \in S^M,\ a_i \text{ a program letter}\}$$
$$I^N(a) = \{(\sigma,\sigma as) \mid \sigma \in S^N,\ (\text{last}(\sigma),s) \in I^M(a)\}$$
$$I^N(P) = \{\sigma \in S^N \mid \text{last}(\sigma) \in I^M(P)\}$$

where $\text{last}(s_0a_1s_1\ldots a_ns_n) = s_n$. If $\bar{A} = A_1,\ldots,A_n$ is a valuation over M, let $\text{last}^{-1}(\bar{A})$ denote the valuation $\text{last}^{-1}(A_1),\ldots,\text{last}^{-1}(A_n)$ over N.

Lemma 1. $p^N(\text{last}^{-1}(\bar{A})) = \text{last}^{-1}(p^M(\bar{A}))$.

Proof. The proof is by induction on the structure of p. The cases below correspond to the cases in the definition of Lμ+ in the last section.

(1) $$X_i^N(\text{last}^{-1}(\bar{A})) = \text{last}^{-1}(A_i) = \text{last}^{-1}(X_i^M(\bar{A}))\ .$$

(2) $$P^N(\text{last}^{-1}(\bar{A})) = I^N(P) = \text{last}^{-1}(I^M(P)) = \text{last}^{-1}(P^M(\bar{A}))\ .$$

The cases (3), (4) for $\vee$ and $\neg$ follow from the induction hypothesis and the fact that last^{-1} commutes with set union and complementation.

(5) $$(\langle a\rangle p)^N(\text{last}^{-1}(\bar{A})) = \langle a^N\rangle(p^N(\text{last}^{-1}(\bar{A})))$$
$$= \langle a^N\rangle(\text{last}^{-1}(p^M(\bar{A}))) \quad \text{(induction hypothesis)}$$
$$= \{\sigma \in S^N \mid \exists\tau \in \text{last}^{-1}(p^M(\bar{A}))\ (\sigma,\tau) \in I^N(a)\}$$
$$= \{\sigma \in S^N \mid \exists t \in p^M(\bar{A})\ (\text{last}(\sigma),t) \in I^M(a)\}$$
$$= \{\sigma \in S^N \mid \text{last}(\sigma) \in \langle a^M\rangle p^M(\bar{A})\}$$
$$= \text{last}^{-1}(\langle a\rangle p^M(\bar{A}))\ .$$

(8) $$\alpha X.pX^N(\text{last}^{-1}(\bar{A})) = \cup_{\beta<\alpha}\ p^N(\beta X.pX^N(\text{last}^{-1}(\bar{A})),\text{last}^{-1}(\bar{A}))$$

$= \cup_{\beta<\alpha}\ p^N(\mathrm{last}^{-1}(\beta X.pX^M(\bar{A})),\mathrm{last}^{-1}(\bar{A}))$ (ind. hyp. on β)

$= \cup_{\beta<\alpha}\ \mathrm{last}^{-1}(p^M(\beta X.pX^M(\bar{A}),\bar{A}))$ (ind. hyp. on p)

$= \mathrm{last}^{-1}(\cup_{\beta<\alpha}\ p^M(\beta X.pX^M(\bar{A}),\bar{A}))$ (last^{-1} commutes with $\cup$)

$= \mathrm{last}^{-1}(\alpha X.pX^M(\bar{A}),\bar{A})$.

(6.1-3) and (7) are special cases of (8). □

<u>Lemma 2.</u> State s of M and state (s) of N satisfy the same closed formulas.

<u>Proof.</u> Let $\bar{A}$ be any valuation over M.

$$\begin{aligned} M,s \models p \ \text{ iff } & \ s \in p^M(\bar{A}) \\ \text{iff } & \ (s) \in \mathrm{last}^{-1}(p^M(\bar{A})) \\ \text{iff } & \ (s) \in p^N(\mathrm{last}^{-1}(\bar{A})) \quad \text{(by Lemma 1)} \\ \text{iff } & \ N,(s) \models p\ . \quad \square \end{aligned}$$

We wish now to show that we can restrict our attention to finite-branching tree models (though not necessarily bounded-branching). Suppose $s_0 \in S^N$ and $N,s_0 \models p_0$, where p_0 is a closed formula of Lμ. Thus p_0 contains no subformula of the form αX.pX. Assume p is expressed in terms of the operators μ, ν, <>, [], ∨, ∧, and ¬, such that all occurrences of ¬ are to primitive P and X. Replace all subformulas μX.pX with κX.pX, where $\kappa = |S^N|$. Note that $\kappa = \omega$ will not suffice here. Leave all subformulas νX.pX as they are.

Now label each state $s \in S^N$ with a finite set Φ_s of closed formulas, such that $s \models \Phi_s$. Initially, set $\Phi_s := \emptyset$ for all $s \in S^N$, $s \neq s_0$, and $\Phi_{s_0} := \{p_0\}$, with p_0 unmarked in Φ_s. Now suppose that state t has been labeled Φ_t.

(1) If $p \vee q \in \Phi_t$, $p \vee q$ unmarked, then $t \models p \vee q$, so either $t \models p$ or $t \models q$. Without loss of generality, suppose the former. Set $\Phi_t := \Phi_t \cup \{p\}$, and mark $p \vee q$ in Φ_t.

(2) If $p \wedge q \in \Phi_t$, $p \wedge q$ unmarked, mark $p \wedge q$ and set $\Phi_t := \Phi_t \cup \{p,q\}$.

(3) If P or $\neg P \in \Phi_t$ unmarked, mark it.

(4) If $[a]p \in \Phi_t$ unmarked, mark it.

(5) If $\nu X.pX \in \Phi_t$ unmarked, mark it and set $\Phi_t := \Phi_t \cup \{p(\nu X.pX)\}$.

(6) If $\alpha X.pX \in \Phi_t$ unmarked, since $t \models \alpha X.pX = \cup_{\beta<\alpha} p(\beta X.pX)$, there must be a least $\beta < \alpha$ such that $t \models p(\beta X.pX)$. Mark $\alpha X.pX$ and set $\Phi_t := \Phi_t \cup \{p(\beta X.pX)\}$.

Repeat (1)-(6) on state t until the only unmarked formulas remaining in Φ_t are of the form <a>p. This must happen after a finite time, by the well-foundedness of the ordinal numbers, and by the fact that if all ordinals appearing in formulas of Φ_t are replaced by μ, the resulting set of formulas is a subset of $CL(p_0)$, the <u>closure</u> of p_0 [K], and is therefore finite. Thus Φ_t itself is finite. Moreover, $t \models \Phi_t$, since this fact is preserved by (1)-(6).

(7) For each unmarked $<a>p \in \Phi_t$, since $t \models <a>p$, there must be a state $u \in S^N$ such that $(t,u) \in I^N(a)$ and $u \models p$. Pick one such u and set

$$\Phi_u := \Phi_u \cup \{p\} \cup \{q \mid [a]q \in \Phi_t\} .$$

Mark <a>p in Φ_t.

A descendant u of t may be picked more than once by (7), due to different formulas of the form <a>p in Φ_t, but only finitely many times. Thus Φ_u is finite. After all $<a>p \in \Phi_t$ are marked, u will never again be picked by (7).

After all formulas of Φ_t are marked, (1)-(7) no longer apply. Repeat the process on immediate descendants of t, and so on all the way down. In the sequel, the notation Φ_t refers to the final value of Φ_t obtained by this process. This final value of Φ_t is finite and $t \models \Phi_t$ for all $t \in S^N$.

Define a new model T as follows:

$$S^T = \{s \in S^N \mid \Phi_s \neq \emptyset\}$$
$$I^T(P) = I^N(P) \cap S^T$$
$$I^T(a) = I^N(a) \cap (S^T \times S^T) .$$

Then T is a countable, finite-branching tree model with root s_0. Define, for closed formula p, the set

$$p^L = \{s \mid p \in \Phi_s\} .$$

Thus $p^L \subseteq S^T$ and $p^L \subseteq p^N$. Let $p(\bar{X})$ be any formula in positive form with free variables $\bar{X} = X_1,\ldots,X_n$, and $\bar{q} = q_1,\ldots,q_n$ a list of closed formulas, $\bar{q}^L = q_1^L,\ldots,q_n^L$.

<u>Lemma 3.</u> $p(\bar{q})^L \subseteq p^T(\bar{q}^L)$.

<u>Proof.</u> The proof is by induction on the structure of p.

(i) $P^L \subseteq P^N \cap S^T = P^T$.

(ii) $\neg P^L \subseteq \neg P^N \cap S^T = \neg P^T$.

(iii) $X_i(\bar{q})^L = q_i^L = X_i^T(\bar{q}^L)$.

(iv) $(p \vee q)(\bar{q})^L \subseteq p(\bar{q})^L \cup q(\bar{q})^L$ (by rule 1)

$\subseteq p^T(\bar{q}^L) \cup q^T(\bar{q}^L)$ (by induction hypothesis)

$= (p \vee q)^T(\bar{q}^L)$.

(v) $(p \wedge q)(\bar{q})^L \subseteq p(\bar{q})^L \cap q(\bar{q})^L$ (by rule 2)

$\subseteq p^T(\bar{q}^L) \cap q^T(\bar{q}^L)$ (by induction hypothesis)

$= (p \wedge q)^T(\bar{q}^L)$.

(vi) $s \in \langle a \rangle p(\bar{q})^L \rightarrow \exists t\ (s,t) \in I^T(a) \wedge t \in p(\bar{q})^L$ (rule 7)

$\rightarrow \exists t\ (s,t) \in I^T(a) \wedge t \in p^T(\bar{q}^L)$ (induction hyp.)

$\rightarrow s \in \langle a^T \rangle p^T(\bar{q}^L)$

$\rightarrow s \in (\langle a \rangle p)^T(\bar{q}^L)$.

(vii) $s \in [a]p(\bar{q})^L \rightarrow \forall t\ (s,t) \in I^T(a) \rightarrow t \in p(\bar{q})^L$ (rule 7)

$\rightarrow \forall t\ (s,t) \in I^T(a) \rightarrow t \in p^T(\bar{q}^L)$

$\rightarrow s \in [a^T]p^T(\bar{q}^L)$

$\rightarrow s \in ([a]p)^T(\bar{q}^L)$.

(viii) $\alpha X.pX(\bar{q})^L \subseteq \cup_{\beta<\alpha}\ p(\beta X.pX(\bar{q}),\bar{q})^L$ (rule 6)

$\subseteq \cup_{\beta<\alpha}\ p^T(\beta X.pX(\bar{q})^L,\bar{q}^L)$ (induction hypothesis on p)

$\subseteq \cup_{\beta<\alpha}\ p^T(\beta X.pX^T(\bar{q}^L),\bar{q}^L)$ (ind. hyp. on β, monotonicity of p^T)

$= \alpha X.pX^T(\bar{q}^L)$.

(ix) $\nu X.pX(\bar{q})^L \subseteq p(\nu X.pX(\bar{q}),\bar{q})^L$ (rule 5)

$\subseteq p^T(\nu X.pX(\bar{q})^L,\bar{q}^L)$ (induction hypothesis on p);

but $\nu X.pX^T(\bar{q}^L)$ is the greatest subset A of S^T such that

$$A \subseteq p^T(A,\bar{q}^L) .$$

This follows from the definition of ν and the Knaster-Tarski theorem. Therefore

$$\nu X.pX(\bar{q})^L \subseteq \nu X.pX^T(\bar{q}^L) . \quad \square$$

In particular, ${p_0}^L \subseteq {p_0}^T$, therefore $T,s_0 \models p_0$. We have proved

Lemma 4. If p is satisfiable, then it is satisfied at the root of a countable tree model with finite (but not necessarily bounded) out-degree. □

4. CODING OF Lμ INTO SnS

We will encode formulas of Lμ into formulas of the second order theory of n successors. The n successor functions are denoted by $\Sigma = \{a_1,\ldots,a_{n-1},b\}$ where the a_i correspond to the n-1 primitive programs of Lμ and b is a new symbol. Let $X,X_1,\ldots,\ P,P_1,\ldots$ denote set (unary relation) parameters. Let x,y,z,... denote elements of Σ^*. λ denotes the empty string. We write $x \in X$ and $X(x)$ interchangeably. Define the following formulas of SnS:

"$y = xa_jb^i$, some $i \geq 0$" =

$$\forall X\ (xa_j \in X \wedge \forall z\ z \in X \rightarrow zb \in X) \ \rightarrow\ y \in X$$

$x \leq y$ ("x is an initial substring of y") =

$$\forall X\ (x \in X \wedge \forall z\ z \in X \rightarrow zb \in X \wedge \wedge_i\ za_i \in X) \ \rightarrow\ y \in X)$$

"M is closed under ≤" =

$$\forall x\ \forall y\ \ y \in M \wedge x \leq y \rightarrow x \in M$$

Let $\sigma(x,X,\ldots)$ be a formula of SnS with a distinguished free set variable X and a distinguished free individual variable x. Given fixed interpretations for the other free variables, σ represents a set operation

$$X \rightarrow \{x \in \Sigma^* | \sigma(x,X,\ldots)\}\ .$$

For any such σ, we can express the property "X is closed under the operation σ" by

$$\forall x\ \sigma(x,X,\ldots) \rightarrow x \in X .$$

Let ϕ be the following translation from formulas of $L\mu$ to formulas of SnS with one free variable x:

(1) $\phi(X_i)(x) = X_i(x) \wedge M(x)$

(2) $\phi(P_i)(x) = P_i(x) \wedge M(x)$

(3) $\phi(p\vee q)(x) = \phi(p)(x) \vee \phi(q)(x)$

(4) $\phi(\neg p)(x) = \neg\phi(p)(x) \wedge M(x)$

(5) $\phi(\langle a\rangle p)(x) = \exists y\ M(y) \wedge (y = xab^i, \text{ some } i \geq 0) \wedge \phi(p)(y)$

(6) $\phi(\mu X.pX)(x) = \forall X\ (X \text{ is closed under } \phi(pX)) \rightarrow x \in X .$

Finally, for p closed (no free X_i), define the formula

$$\begin{aligned}\psi(p) = \exists M\ \exists P_1{\subseteq}M \ldots \exists P_n{\subseteq}M\ \ &\lambda \in M\\ &\wedge (M \text{ is closed under } \leq)\\ &\wedge \phi(p)(\lambda) .\end{aligned}$$

<u>Lemma 5.</u> $\psi(p)$ is true in SnS iff p is satisfiable at the root of some countably branching tree model.

<u>Proof.</u> ($\rightarrow$) Suppose $\psi(p)$ is true. Let $M,P_1^M,\ldots,P_n^M$ be subsets of Σ^* satisfying $\psi(p)$. Then $P_i^M \subseteq M$. Define a model N with

$$\begin{aligned}&S^N = M\\ &I^N(a_j) = \{(x,xa_jb^i) \mid xab^i \in M\}\\ &I^N(P_j) = P_j^M .\end{aligned}$$

Then N is a countably branching tree model with root λ. It follows by induction on the structure of q that for any $x \in M$ and instantiation $\bar{A}$ of variables $\bar{X}$ over subsets of M,

$$\phi(q)(x) \text{ iff } x \in q^N(\bar{A}) ,$$

and the result follows by taking $q = p$ and $x = \lambda$.

($\leftarrow$) Suppose p is satisfied in a countably branching tree model N. Order the a_j-successors of any node in an arbitrary but fixed order. To each state $s \in N$ there corresponds a unique string x(s), defined inductively: if r is the root, $x(r) = \lambda$; and if t is the kth a_j-successor of state s, then $x(t) = x(s)a_jb^k$. Take

$$M = \{x(s) | s \in S^N\}$$
$$P_j^M = \{x(s) | s \in P^N\} .$$

M is nonempty since it contains λ, and M is closed under substrings. Again by induction on the structure of q,

$$\phi(q)(x(s)) \text{ iff } x(s) \in q^N(\bar{A}) ,$$

and taking $q = p$ and $s = r$, we have that $\phi(p)(\lambda)$ holds. This establishes the result. □

Combining Lemmas 4 and 5, and using the fact that SnS is decidable [R], we get

Theorem 1. Lμ is decidable. □

REFERENCES

[FL] Fischer, M.J. and R.E.Ladner, "Propositional Dynamic Logic of Regular Programs," J. Comput. Syst. Sci. 18:2 (1979), 194-211.

[K] Kozen, D., "Results on the propositional μ-calculus," Proc. 9th Int. Colloq. on Automata, Languages, and Programming, 1982, Springer-Verlag, 348-359.

[P] Pratt, V.R., "A Decidable μ-calculus (preliminary report)," Proc. 22nd IEEE Symp. on Foundations of Computer Science, 1981, 421-427.

[R] Rabin, M.O., "Decidability of second-order theories and automata on infinite trees," Trans. Amer. Math. Soc. 141 (1969), 1-35.

[S] Streett, R., "Propositional Dynamic Logic of looping and converse," Proc. 13th ACM Symp. on Theory of Computing, 1981, 375-383.

[SDeB] Scott, D. and J. de Bakker, "A theory of programs," unpublished, Vienna, 1969.

A VERIFIER FOR COMPACT PARALLEL COORDINATION PROGRAMS*

B. D. Lubachevsky
Courant Institute of Mathematical Sciences
New York University
251 Mercer Street, New York, NY 10012/USA

1. The class of programs considered here is being developed for the "NYU-Ultracomputer," a shared-memory asynchronous parallel processor. These programs are characterized by the following two properties: 1) they are to be executed by a computer system which includes thousands of processing elements (PEs); 2) they use the basic primitive Fetch&Add. The format of the Fetch&Add (which will be abbreviated as F&A) is

PRIVATE_RESULT <- F&A (SHARED, INCREMENT). (1)

When a single PE executes (1) its PRIVATE_RESULT becomes equal to the old contents of the location SHARED, while the contents of SHARED are replaced by SHARED + INCREMENT.

The following example demonstrates both the indivisibility and the efficiency of F&A when executed by many PEs concurrently. Let the number of PEs in the Ultracomputer be 4096, SHARED be initially 1. We assume that each PE's private memory contains a location named MY_INDEX, while SHARED is a unique location in the shared memory. If, at the same instant, each PE starts executing the code

```
MY_INDEX <- F&A (SHARED,1)
CALL TASK (MY_INDEX)
```

Program 1. Task distribution.

then after very few (8) cycles each PE obtains its own unique invocation of TASK (MY_INDEX), $1 \leq$ MY_INDEX ≤ 4096 (it is not specified which PE gets which value of MY_INDEX). The final value of SHARED will be 4097. Note that if in the above example the distribution of the tasks between the PEs had been conducted using a critical section of only one instruction, then, on average, more than 2000

*This work was supported in part by the Applied Mathematical Sciences Program of the U.S. Department of Energy under Contract No. DE-AC02-76ER03077, and in part by the National Science Foundation under Grant No. NSF-MCS79-21258.

instructions would have been spent by each PE to obtain an available task for execution.

An Ultracomputer program can also use the conventional READ and WRITE, which possess a similar efficiency.

The existence of the powerful primitive F&A introduces a programming style whose distinctive feature is the avoidance of critical sections that are not implied by the programming problem.

2. A short F&A-program which is difficult to verify: "readers" and "writers." The following example of the Ultracomputer programming style (program 2) is an efficient solution to the "readers" and "writers" problem. Note that in this solution an individual process may "starve," i.e. never be granted access to the section it is bound for. This starvation is not dangerous in some applications, however.

For simplicity we identify PEs with processes. (Thus each PE always carries one and always the same process.) OR in statement P1 of program 2 represents an arbitrary law, not visible to this program, by which an external program transfers control of a PE to the "read" or to the "write" section.

```
COMMENT: CONSTANT B ≥ TOTAL NUMBER OF PES; INITIALLY COUNT = B

             P1:  GO TO P2 (TO "READ") OR TO P5 (TO "WRITE")

P2:  IF (F&A (COUNT,-1) ≥ 1)      |  P5:  IF (COUNT < B)
     THEN GO TO P4                |       THEN GO TO P5
                                  |
P3:  F&A (COUNT,1)                |  P6:  IF (F&A (COUNT, -B) ≥ B)
     GO TO P2                     |       THEN GO TO P8
                                  |
P4:  {"READ" SECTION}             |  P7:  F&A (COUNT,B)
     F&A (COUNT, 1)               |       GO TO P5
     GO TO P1                     |
                                  |  P8:  {"WRITE" SECTION}
                                  |       F&A (COUNT,B)
                                  |       GO TO P1
```

Program 2. "Readers" and "writers."

We argue that program 2 is difficult to verify, and that such difficulties are specific to even short F&A-programs. A liveness property of program 2 which, in our opinion, is difficult to prove is:

(LWR) For any time t, there exists time $t' \geq t$, such that one PE is at P4 ("reading") or at P8 ("writing").

One may assume the following conditions when proving (LWR):

(i) N (= 4096) PEs execute program 2 in parallel starting from statement P1.

(ii) Time is discrete, t = 0,1,2,...; each statement Pi takes one time step to execute.

(iii) At each time step t each PE may or may not execute its current statement.

(iv) (Fairness) Each PE eventually completes execution of its current statement.

(v) (Serialization principle) If several PEs at the same time step execute their current statements Pi involving the same memory location then the effect of this execution is the same as if each PE were to execute its statement Pi indivisibly, with these executions forming an (unspecified) serial order.

A verifier system has been designed for checking and proving the correctness of Ultracomputer programs. Produced by this verifier, a complete proof of (LWR) and other properties of program 2 occupies about four pages of text.

3. <u>A simpler program, "critical section,"</u> may be obtained from program 2 if one excludes the possibility of GO TO P2 in statement P1. Then COUNT only takes values that are multiples of B, P2-P4 are never executed, and P1 becomes redundant.

After the proper reenumeration and the substitution COUNT = B × SEM, one obtains the following efficient F&A-implementation of the critical section (which is still not free from starvation for an individual PE).

```
COMMENT: INITIALLY SEM = 1

    P1:  IF (SEM < 1) THEN GO TO P1

    P2:  IF (F&A (SEM, -1) ≥ 1) THEN GO TO P4

    P3:  F&A (SEM,1)
         GO TO P1

    P4:  {CRITICAL SECTION}
         F&A (SEM,1)
         GO TO P1
```

Program 3. Critical section.

In this case (LWR) reduces to the following liveness property:

(LCS) For any time t, there exists time $t' \geq t$, such that one PE is in the CS.

To emphasize a difficulty involved in proving (LCS) we mention that it is not sufficient to establish that a PE eventually accesses the CS. Note that this latter property holds for the following "naive" implementation of the CS (program 4).

```
COMMENT: INITIALLY SEM = 1

   P1:  IF (F&A (SEM,-1) ≥ 1) THEN GO TO P3

   P2:  F&A (SEM,1)
        GO TO P1

   P3:  {CRITICAL SECTION}
        F&A (SEM,1)
        GO TO P1
```

Program 4. "Naive" implementation of the critical section.

However, the following counter-example shows that (LCS) does not hold for program 4: PE1 and PE2 execute program 4. PE1 enters the CS, SEM changing from 1 to 0. Then PE2 goes to P2, SEM changing to -1. PE1 returns to P1 while PE2 is still at P2, SEM changing to 0. Starting from this state a "livelock" is possible: PE1 goes to P2, then PE2 goes to P1 exchanging its role with PE1, and so on.

4. <u>The proof of (LCS)</u> for program 3 produced by the verifier consists of the four descriptions given below, in which N and Mi (i = 1,2,3,4) denote, respectively, the number of PEs in the Ultracomputer and at positions Pi of program 3.

```
S2  M1 + M2 = N, SEM = 1
    MOVES FROM P1 TO P2 LEAD TO S2
    MOVES FROM P2 TO P4 LEAD TO S5

S5  M1 + M2 + M3 + M4 = N, M4 ≤ 1,
    M1 + M4 ≥ 1, M3 + M4 ≥ 1, SEM = 1 - M3 - M4
    MOVES FROM P1 TO P1 LEAD TO S5
    MOVES FROM P2 TO P3 LEAD TO S5
    MOVES FROM P3 TO P1 LEAD TO S5, IF M4 = 1 OR M3 ≥ 1
                        LEAD TO S2, IF M3 = M4 = 0
    MOVES FROM P4 TO P1 LEAD TO S5, IF M3 ≥ 1
                        LEAD TO S2, IF M3 = 0
```

Descr. 1. Reachability set description for program 3.

Descr. 1 is the <u>reachability set description</u> (RSD). This RSD consists of two predicates on the program state, S2 and S5, called <u>metastates</u>, and a number of <u>directing phrases</u> attached to the metastates. As usual, each predicate may be identified with the set of states for which it is valid. (For example, S2 may be thought of as the set of all states for which no PE is at P3 nor at P4 and the value of SEM is 1.) The RSD is a compact representation of all states reachable by the program in executing all possible sequences of transitions. The phrases attached to some of the directing phrases (like the phrase "IF M4 = 1 OR M3 $\geq$ 1" attached to the directing phrase "MOVES FROM P3 TO P1 LEAD TO S5") are understood <u>after</u> the move.

The validity of the following two statements is implied by the RSD:
(I) if a state s of the program is reachable from the initial state s_0 in which all PEs are at P1, then s is represented in the RSD;
(II) if a state s belongs to S2 or S5, then s is reachable from s_0.

Another way of expressing (I) and (II) is to say that set (S2 U S5) is the transitive closure of the set $\{s_0\}$ with respect to the relation $s\nabla s'$ between the program states s and s', where
∇ = {s' is obtained from s by a PE executing its current statement}.

The text of the RSD serves as a proof for (I) since s_0 belongs to S2 and all possible transitions $s\nabla s'$ are represented in the directing phrases and LEAD TO S2 or S5. The proof of (II) is descr. 2, which represents the <u>reachability tree</u>.

```
S1   M1 = N, SEM = 1
     MOVES FROM P1 TO P2 LEAD TO S2

S2   M1 + M2 = N, SEM = 1
     MOVES FROM P2 TO P4 LEAD TO S3

S3   M1 + M2 + M4 = N, M4 = 1, SEM = 0
     MOVES FROM P2 TO P3 LEAD TO S4

S4   M1 + M2 + M3 + M4 = N, M4 = 1, SEM = 1 - M3 - M4
     MOVES FROM P4 TO P1 LEAD TO S5, IF M3 ≥ 1

S5   M1 + M2 + M3 + M4 = N, M4 ≤ 1,
     M1 + M4 ≥ 1, M3 + M4 ≥ 1, SEM = 1 - M3 - M4
```

Descr. 2. Reachability tree for program 3.

```
S2&Θ  M1 + M2 = N, SEM = 1
      MOVES FROM P1 TO P2 LEAD TO S2&Θ

S5&Θ  M1 + M2 + M3 = N, M1 ≥ 1, M3 ≥ 1, SEM = 1 - M3
      MOVES FROM P1 TO P1 LEAD TO S5&Θ
      MOVES FROM P2 TO P3 LEAD TO S5&Θ
      MOVES FROM P3 TO P1 LEAD TO S5&Θ, IF M3 ≥ 1
                          LEAD TO S2&Θ, IF M3 = 0
```

Descr. 3. Subgraph generated by the predicate Θ = {M4 = 0}.

Descr. 2 obviates (II) since S1 = $\{s_0\}$ and each Si, i = 1,...5, is reachable from the previous Si's, S2 and S5 being among them. Note that the verifier generates descr. 1 after descr. 2. Descriptions 3 and 4 complete the proof of (LCS). By discarding all the directing phrases that refer to P4 and by imposing the predicate $\Theta = \{M4 = 0\}$ one produces a description of a subgraph Γ of the reachability graph (see descr. 3). Staying in Γ means "no PE is in the CS."

S5&Θ M1 + M2 + M3 = N, M1 $\geq$ 1, M3 $\geq$ 1, SEM = 1 - M3
MOVES FROM P1 TO P1 LEAD TO S5&Θ

Descr. 4. Subgraph in Γ that represents all cycles when M4 = 0.

Our next goal is to derive from descr. 3 a compact description of all possible cycles in Γ. Being on such a cycle, the state can not "jump" from S2&Θ to S5&Θ or back. The set S2&Θ carries no cycles since the graph P1->P2 carries no cycles. Since P1->P1 is the only strongly connected component (SCC) in the graph P2->P3->P1->P1, set S5&Θ can carry only cycles presented in descr. 4. Staying in such an SCC is the only way not to satisfy (LCS). It is clear though that the fairness property (iv) of section 2 can be satisfied for no cycle presented in descr. 4, since a positive number M3 of PEs at P3 never move on such a cycle. This completes the proof of (LCS) for program 3.

The verifier program spent about 5 seconds (on a VAX 11/780) in producing the reachability tree and the RSD. The subsequent reductions to descriptions 3 and 4 were done with pencil and paper. A text editor was used to reduce larger RSDs. While it is known how to automate the reduction phase, in all the considered examples it was not difficult to perform this phase manually. By contrast, the phases of building the reachability tree and RSD were difficult to perform manually; for this reason these phases were automated. In the absence of the verifier, the author spent several hours building the RSD for an example similar to program 2. Later, a comparison of the "manual" RSD with the one produced by the verifier revealed a mistake in the former.

5. Compactness. A necessary condition for the termination of the verifier when building an RSD for a given parallel program is the compactness of the program.

We define compactness in several stages:

5.1. Progress functional. If s is a state of the program C, then the value $F_C(s)$ of the progress functional F_C on s is the set of states obtained by each PE performing at most one atomic action Pi. If $S = \{s\}$ is a set of program states, then $F_C(S) \overset{Df}{==} \bigcup_{s \in S} F_C(s)$.

5.2. A representation of the reachability set of a program. Note that if S is a set of states of a program C, then

$$S \subset F_C(S) \subset F_C^2(S) \subset \dots \tag{2}$$

For the set R(S) of all states reachable from a state in S the following presentation takes place

$$R(S) = \lim_{t \to +\infty} F_C^t(S). \tag{3}$$

The limit in (3) exists by virtue of (2). For a finite set S, the following are equivalent: (a) the monotonic sequence (2) stabilizes, i.e. $F_C^t(S) = F_C^{t+1}(S)$ for some t, (b) (3) converges finitely, (c) the reachability set R(S) is finite.

5.3. Parametric case: $C = C_N$ and $S = S_N$ depend on a parameter $N = 1,2,\dots$

5.4. Definiton of compactness. C_N is compact with respect to the parameter N and the set S_N if there exists T independent of N such that for all N

$$F_{C_N}^T(S_N) = F_{C_N}^{T+1}(S_N) \tag{4}$$

We give another form of this definition: C_N is compact with respect to N and S_N if the sequence $F_{C_N}^t$ in (3) converges finitely, uniformly with respect to N.

Program 3 is compact with respect to its initial state s_0 by virtue of the existence of the finite reachability tree (descr. 2). It is easy to modify program 3 so that it becomes non-compact with respect to s_0 (program 5).

```
COMMENT: INITIALLY SEM = 1

    P1:  IF (SEM ≤ 0) THEN GO TO P1

    P2:  IF (F&A (SEM, -1) ≥ 1) THEN GO TO P4

    P3:  F&A (SEM,1)
         GO TO P1

    P4:  {CRITICAL SECTION}
         F&A (SEM,1)

    P5:  STOP
```

Program 5. Critical section: terminating version.

When the verifier is applied to program 5, it does not terminate and produces an endless description of the reachability tree. On observing the initial segments of this description, the author realized that each set W_r = {M1 + M2 + M5 = N, M5 = r, SEM = 1}, r = 0, 1,...., appeared in it as a certain metastate: W_0 = S2, W_1 = S7,....W_r = S(2+5r),... This gave an intuitive explanation of the non-compactness of program 5: r PEs have to go through the "bottleneck" P4, one PE at a time. If one interprets index t in (3) as the time, then it is clear that the time required to reach W_r from s_0 is no less than r. Since r may be as large as N, $F^t_{C_N}$ does not stabilize uniformly for all N.

Since the compactness property is not absolute to a program and depends also on the choice of the initial set, by playing with this choice one can satisfy this property. Program 5 can be made compact by taking the initial set to be S_N = {M1 + M5 = N, SEM = 1}.

7. Bose and Boltzmann semantics. Observe that the representation of a program state in descriptions 1 - 4 is symmetrized in the following sense. An instance of the vector (M1, M2, M3, M4, SEM) indicates how many PEs are at each position Pi in program 2 but gives no identification of these PEs. The PEs remain indistinguishable ("anonymous" so to say). In statistical physics, there exist Bose statistics and Boltzmann statistics which describe ensembles of particles. The difference between these two statistics is similar to the difference between the two ways of representing a state of a parallel program. Bose statistics describes systems with the indistinguishable particles; in Boltzmann statistics each particle is distinguishable from the others. We will use the same nomenclature with respect to the program states. Note that the representation of the program state in Bose semantics may hide the starvation of an individual PE. The starvation can be identified, though, if one replicates the program section in question. For example, if one duplicates the code of program 3 (statements P1-P4 of the first replica become P5-P8, respectively, in the second one) and assumes the initial state of the so obtained program to be {M1 = N-1, M5 = 1, SEM = 1}, then starvation reveals itself as a certain SCC in the subgraph of the reachability graph generated by the predicate {M8 = 0}. A similar procedure, when applied to program 5, proves the absence of starvation.

An advantage of representing the reachability graph in Bose semantics is the reduction of its complexity. The number of all possible distributions of N particles (PEs) among k possible states (statements of a program) in Boltzmann statistics is k^N which is the sum of all terms N!/(M1!...Mk!) restricted to all (integer non-negative) solutions of the equation

$$M1 + ... + Mk = N, \qquad (5)$$

and is thus exponential with respect to N, given a fixed k (size of the program). In Bose statistics (with indistinguishable particles) all states corresponding to a solution of (5) reduce to a single state. Hence their total becomes the number of different solutions of (5), i.e.

$$\frac{(N + k - 1)!}{N! \times (k - 1)!} = \frac{N^{k-1}}{(k - 1)!} + O(N^{k-2}). \tag{6}$$

This is a polynomial with respect to N given a fixed k. Of course, k^N and (6) are only rough estimates. The concrete figures depend on the program. Given the RSD it is easy to produce the formula (even automatically) for the number of states in the reachability graph under its two representations. For program 2, for example, this graph has $N^2 + N + 1$ nodes in Bose representation and $N \times 3^{N-1} + 3^N - 2^N + 1$ nodes in Boltzmann representation.

8. A geometric interpretation of the reachability tree and the RSD. For a given N, consider the 3-dimensional grid H formed in the 4-dimensional space of vectors (M1, M2, M3, M4) by all non-negative integer solutions of equation (5) for k = 4.

Since program 3 possesses the invariant q = {SEM = 1 - M3 - M4}, a state (in Bose semantics) of this program may be uniquely identified by a point of H. (We call q an invariant of a program C if F_C (CAR(q)) $\subset$ CAR(q), where CAR(q) denotes carrier of q, CAR(q) = {s ε U | q(s) = TRUE}, U being the universe, here U = H.)

We introduce the bundle of possible transitions (or simply the bundle) corresponding to each s ε H. This bundle will be denoted as B(s). B(s) is a set of transitions. A transition of B(s) may be thought of as a 4-dimensional integer vector m such that vector s+m is a state resulting from a PE completing execution of a statement, if the starting state was s. We denote by m_{ij} the transition vector corresponding to a PE moving from Pi to Pj. Hence m_{ii} = 0 and if i ≠ j, m_{ij} is a vector all of whose components are zero, save the i-th which is -1 and the j-th which is 1.

We now investigate the reasons why the bundles B(s) of different states s can differ. It follows that if there is no PE at Pi in state s (the i-th coordinate of s is 0), then B(s) contains no m_{ij} for any j. This is one reason why B(s) can differ from B(s'). Were this the only reason, then our geometrical construction might be qualified as a vector addition system (VAS).

In a VAS a state freely migrates from a grid point s to a grid point s' providing that the vector s'-s is a multiple of a transition from a bundle. The only obstacle which may prevent such moving is an "outside boundary" which represents the condition of non-negativity of a coordinate of the state vector.

There exists another reason why B(s) can differ from B(s′) in the system we describe. This reason may be interpreted geometrically as an "inside boundary." This boundary may be thought of as a plane L with the equation $M3 + M4 = 1/2$. L divides H into two _regions_, region H1, inside which $M3 + M4 \leq 0$, and region H2, inside which $M3 + M4 \geq 1$.

If $s \in H1$ then sem ≥ 1. This means that no PE can move from P2 to P3, or else B(s) cannot contain vector m_{23} (but may contain vector m_{24}).

If $s \in H2$ then sem ≤ 0. This means that no PE can move from P2 to P4, or else B(s) cannot contain vector m_{24} (but may contain vector m_{23}).

The structure thus obtained is an example of a _controlled vector addition system_ (CVAS). A state may move in the state-space H of the CVAS along a given direction defined by a transition until an obstacle is met. If the obstacle is an outside boundary then further moves in this direction are impossible. If the obstacle is an inside boundary then one more transition is effected in the given direction. If the bundle of the current point of the new region does not include this transition then further moves in this direction are impossible.

Now we can give the following geometrical interpretation of the process of producing the RSD and the reachability tree for program 3 by the verifier.

Metastate S1 reduces to a single state s_1. $B(s_1)$ contains the only transition m_{12}. The state moves along m_{12} as far as possible and thus creates metastate S2.

Bundles of the states of S2 contain at most two transitions: m_{12} and m_{24}. The verifier checks transition m_{12}, although it says nothing about this transition, since it generates no new state. When the verifier tries to apply transition m_{24} to the states of S2, the moving states immediately cross L, and, since bundles in H2 do not include m_{24}, the moving stops. As a result, metastate S3 is generated in H2.

Bundles of the states of S3 contain m_{11}, m_{23}, m_{41}. The verifier first tries m_{11} which does not produce anything new. Then it tries to apply transition m_{23} to states of S3, and the moving states produce S4 without crossing L. The verifier realizes that S3 $\subset$ S4. Hence it does not try the remaining m_{41} for metastate S3 but instead starts working with S4.

Bundles of the states of S4 contain m_{11}, m_{23}, m_{31}, m_{41}. The verifier tries m_{11}, m_{23}, m_{31} without producing anything new. When it tries to apply transition m_{41} to the states of S4, the moving states produce S5 without crossing L.

Working with all possible transitions at S5, the verifier realizes that no more states can be produced. This terminates the phase of building the reachability tree.

Once the reachability tree is produced, the verifier reduces the set of all metastates as follows. The verifier scans each metastate Si and discards it if Si is a subset of the union of other metastates remaining at the time of this scanning. (This is an easier way to think about this reduction. In the existing program, however, this reduction interleaves the process of building the reachability tree.)

Two metastates, S2 and S5, remain after the reduction. The verifier completes the obtained description with all possible directing phrases by trying all possible transitions for both S2 and S5 and thus produces the RSD.

9. <u>Indivisibility by virtue of the program</u>. Program 6 is an implementation [17] of the general CS with the restriction that at most K PEs execute within the CS. It is

```
COMMENT: INITIALLY G = K, M = 1, D = 0;

P1:   P(M);
P2:       G <- G-1;
P3:       IF  G ≤ -1  THEN
                           BEGIN
P4:                           V(M);
P5:                           P(D)
                           END;
P6:   V(M);

P7:  {CRITICAL SECTION}

      P(M);
P8:       G <- G+1;
P9:       IF  G ≤ 0  THEN
P10:                    V(D);
                     ELSE
P11:                    V(M);

      GO TO P1
```

Program 6. General critical section.

not an Ultracomputer program; the parallel processor is expected to support only the indivisibility of binary P and V operations. Thus the indivisibility of statements P2, P3, P8, and P9 is not supposed to take place <u>a priori</u>. This property is, seemingly, a precondition for studying any property of this program including this indivisibility itself. If, for example, statements P2 and P8 are not indivisible, then, without detail information of the device that executes program 6 one does not know what is going to happen with the variable g.

To emphasize a subtle point inherent in the proof of indivisibility of statements P2, P3, P8, and P9, we compare this problem with the one of proving the indivisibility of the CS in program 3. Since program 3 "serves" indivisibility of the CS for some other routine, one can ignore the contents of the CS when proving this indivisiblity. Program 6 is supposed to "serve" indivisibility of the statements refering g to itself. One can not ignore the contents of statements in question when proving the indivisibility. (If this content is ignored, how can one deal with statements P3 and P9 which contain test-branching depending on the value of g?)

We now describe a simple solution to this problem.
We say that a computer supports <u>total indivisibility</u> with respect to a given program if any possible combination of statements Pi of this program is executed by the computer in a way equivalent to some serial execution of these statements.

Let $p = p(s)$ be a predicate on a program state s and let our computer only support indivisibility in those combinations of statements Pi for which the state s satisfies the predicate p. Then we say that the computer supports the <u>partial indivisibility with respect to the predicate p</u>.

<u>Proposition</u>. Let Δ be the reachability graph of a program built under the assumption of total indivisibility, and let p be a predicate valid for any reachable state in Δ. Then it is possible to build the reachability graph Δ' of this program under the assumption of partial indivisibility with respect to p and $\Delta' = \Delta$.

According to this proposition one can use the following procedure to verify indivisibility of statements refering to g in program 6.
Step 1. Build the reachability graph under the assumption of total indivisibility.
Step 2. Verify the predicate p = {no more than 1 PE may access the critical sections in question} in the reachability graph. (Note that in program 6 the predicate p may also be expressed as: {no more than 1 PE may access g}.)
Step 3. If there is a state which violates property p, then the required indivisibility is not obtained (and one should fix the bug before verifying any other property). Otherwise, the indivisibility is supported by virtue of the program itself.

It was possible to analyse program 6 using the verfier. This program appears compact with respect to the initial set $S_N = \{M1 + M5 + M7 = N, M7 = K, M = 1, D = 0\}$ for fixed values of K.

10. Further comments and bibliography notes. An extended description of the verifier is given in [10]. In particular, [10] contains the mechanically produced proof of (LWR), and a detailed discussion of the notion of CVAS. The notion of VAS is introduced in [7].

Note that the reachability tree is not unique given a program and an initial set of states and depends on some set-up parameters of the verifier. Suppose the verifier does not terminate for a given set-up. Is it then hopeless to play with this set-up? This question may be transformed into the following: does compactness suffice for termination? (Necessity of compactness for the termination follows directly.) A class of program is specified in [10] for which compactness is the sufficient condition of termination for the verifier.

In developing the RSD, the verifier uses a projection algorithm communicated to the author by Robert Thau. For an extended discussion of the Ultracomputer see [4, 5]. [5] and [15] contain a number of F&A-solutions to parallel coordination problems.

We understand the "readers" and "writers" problem [2] to be that of providing a specific parallel coordination pattern in which concurrent "read/write" and "write/write" are excluded by definition. "Read" and "write" thus are just labels of the programming sections (enclosed in the quotation marks to distinguish them from actual read and write). This is different from [9, 13] where these operations are understood as actual read or write of data and sometimes concurrent read/write is possible and even desirable. The following are advantages of the solution presented here (program 2): in the absence of the "writers" a small amount of instructions is required by the "reader" to get to its "read" section (the instructions implied in the execution P2); shared memory requirements are extremely modest (one location COUNT); both these requirements are independent of the number of executing processes. Starvation-free and fair F&A-solutions to this problem also exist [15].

Note that one can easily rewrite program 2 without so many GO TO's and labels Pi by employing programming constructs which use WHILE. P6 in program 2 seems to be redundant even in the given presentation, since there is no GO TO P6 in this code. These GO TO's and Pi's are only introduced for the verification purposes and are not a part of the Ultracomputer programming style. A rule for inserting Pi's is described in [10].

Various methods of parallel program verification are developed in [1, 6, 8, 11, 12, 14, 16]. The case of the number of processes being a parameter seems, however, to not have been explicitly studied. Note that N = 2 PEs is enough to expose the livelock in program 4. The terminating counter-part of program 4 (which may be obtained from program 4 in a way similar to that of obtaining program 5 from program 3) exposes the same livelock for N = 3 but not for N = 2. One may expect that more complex programs and properties might require a larger "representative" N. The author does not know of any work which determines the minimal representative number of processes. (After an RSD is built such N can of course be determined.)

While liveness properties were our concern in the above examples, the RSD being the strongest invariant implies that it is not difficult to study safeness properties once an RSD has been obtained. However, all the interesting safeness properties for the above example can be inferred without the RSD from the existence of invariants introduced in [6]. The latter can be generated mechanically. For example, to prove that no more than 1 PE can execute the CS in program 3, one invokes the invariant q = {SEM = 1 - M3 - M4} and the method of [11]. The required property can be expressed as the predicate r = {M4 $\leq$ 1}, and since (q & r) is an invariant, r holds for any reachable state of program 2.

But this method does not explain how to find a proper q for a given r in a general case. The invariant q which appeared useful in this particular case does not work for r_* = {M3 $\neq$ N}. Indeed, q(s) = r_*(s) = TRUE for the state s = {M2 = 1, M3 = N-1, SEM =2-N}, state s′ = {M3 = N, SEM = 1-N} belongs to F_C(s), but r_*(s′) = FALSE. Meanwhile, the property r_* is immediate from the RSD. A similar example of the incompletness of the invariants of [6] is given in [1].

The operation "add to store" which is equivalent to the F&A was considered and the livelock in the "naive" critical section implementation was exposed in [3] (p.122) without discussing a possible cure for it in the class of F&A-programs (another primitive was suggested instead). At p.129-130 of [3], a description slightly similar to the RSD was considered. However no discussion was given of the possibilities of mechanically producing such a description or using it to prove liveness properties.

The RSD serves as a solution to the problem of finding the strongest invariant for a program. The latter problem is also considered in [1] where only the problem of proving safeness properties was discussed (our "progress functional" is the "program functional" in [1]). A mechanical method (different from ours) for generating the strongest invariant for a fixed number of concurrent processes was suggested in [1].

11. <u>Acknowledgement</u>. I would like to thank G. O. Williams for reading the manuscript.

REFERENCES

1. Clarke, E.M.: Synthesis of resource invariants for concurrent programs. ACM TOPLAS, Vol.2, No.3, July 1980, p. 338-358.

2. Courtois, P.J., Heymans, F., Parnas, D.L.: Concurrent control with "readers" and "writers." Comm. ACM, Vol. 14, No.10 (October 1971), 667-668.

3. Dijkstra, E.M.: Hierarchial orderings of sequential processes. Acta Inf., Vol.1, p. 115-138 (1971).

4. Gottlieb, A., Grishman, R., Kruskal, C.P., McAuliffe, K.P., Rudolph, L., and Snir, M.: The NYU ultracomputer-designing an MIMD shared memory parallel machine. IEEE Trans. on Computer, C-32, No.2 (Feb. 1983).

5. Gottlieb, A., Lubachevsky, B.D., Rudolph, L.: Basic techniques for the efficient coordination of very large numbers of cooperating sequential processors. ACM TOPLAS, Vol.5, No.2, April 1983, p. 164-189.

6. Habermann, A.N.: Synchronization of communicating processes. Comm. ACM, Vol. 15, No. 3 (March 1972), p. 171-176.

7. Karp, R.M., Miller, R.E.: Parallel program schemata. J. Comp. Syst. Sci. 3., 147-195 (1969).

8. Lamport, L.: Proving the correctness of multiprocess programs. IEEE Trans. Softw. Eng. 3, 125-143 (1977).

9. Lamport, L: Concurrent reading and writing. Comm. ACM, Vol. 20, No. 11, (November 1977), p. 806-811.

10. Lubachevsky, B.D.: An approach to automating the verification of compact parallel coordination programs. Submitted to publication.

11. Owicki, S., Gries, D.: An axiomatic proof technique for parallel programs.I, Acta Inf. 6, p. 319-340, (1976).

12. Owicki, S. Lamport, L.: Proving liveness properties of concurrent programs. ACM TOPLAS, 3, Vol.4 (July 1982).

13. Peterson, G.L.: Concurrent reading while writing. ACM TOPLAS, 1, Vol.5 (January 1983), p. 46-55.

14. Pnueli, A.: The temporal semantics of concurrent programs. Theoretical Comp. Sci., Vol.13 (1981), p. 45-60. 1980, PP. 484-521.

15. Rudolph, L.: Software structures for ultraparallel computings. Ph.D. Thesis, Courant Inst., NYU, 1982.

16. Schwartz, R.L., Melliar-Smith, P.M.: Temporal logic specification of distributed systems. Proc. 2-nd Int. Conf. on Distributed Computing Systems, Paris, April 1981, p. 446-454.

17. Shaw, A.C.: The logical design of operating systems. Prentice-Hall, Englewood, New Jersey, 1974.

Information Systems, Continuity and Realizability

Charles McCarty
Carnegie-Mellon University, Pittsburgh, PA

There is a widespread and injurious impression—that working in constructive rather than in classical mathematics is ***mathematically expensive***. Perhaps, the impression derives from the feeling that one pays too high a price for relinquishing those logical laws, like excluded third:

$$\phi \vee \neg \phi$$

that lapse on the passage into constructivism. Usually, that price is quoted in terms of the comforting theorems from analysis, like the mean value theorem, that lapse along with classical logic. A benefit of working in realizability is the perception that this impression is truly a prejudice, one fostered by lingering over invidious comparisons between constructive and certain classical theories.

With realizability, one finds that the initial price of constructivism brings considerable profit. Net gain accrues from the fact that lost mathematics is more than countered by an ***axiomatic freedom*** that attends intuitionistic logic. Granted, intuitionistic logic is, when measured along certain dimensions, weaker than its classical counterpart. This very weakness, however, holds tremendous potential value. Axiomatic freedom is the recognition that intuitionistic logic allows axioms which are classically false but mathematically efficient to be consistent with powerful theories.

The results of this paper afford a case study in and demonstration of axiomatic freedom. First, full intuitionistic set theory (IZF) is proved consistent with the assumption that there is an extensive category of information systems, $\underline{ISys}$, in which ***every*** function and ***every*** functor is approximable. As you might imagine, the assumption that every function on information systems is approximable becomes an extremely useful nonclassical axiom for the theory of domains. Its presence in constructive set theory turns some moderately difficult results in the theories of domains and effective domains into trivialities. Next, we show that it is consistent with IZF to assume that $\underline{ISys}$ is at the same time the category of effectively given information systems (eg systems) with computable maps. In each case, consistency comes by working over the realizability model $\mathbf{V}(Kl)$ of IZF. Truth over $\mathbf{V}(Kl)$ represents the extension to set theory of Kleene's original notion of realizability for arithmetic. Finally, the profit in our venture is revealed when $\underline{ISys}$, as interpreted over $\mathbf{V}(Kl)$, is examined from the conventional mathematical standpoint of $\mathbf{V}$. So seen, $\underline{ISys}$ is precisely the external category $\underline{ESys}$ of eg information systems, computable elements and computable morphisms. This ontic correspondence extends to one between the respective theories: the $\mathbf{V}(Kl)$-theory of $\underline{ISys}$ incorporates all the usual theory of classical eg systems. Consequently, the burden of working constructively with axioms true in $\mathbf{V}(Kl)$ is pure profit; the theory of effectively given domains is captured in a streamlined theory of purely intutionistic sets ***without effective superstructure***.

These are not the only benefits to axiomatic freedom; there are some mathematical benefits that fall out along the way. Incidental to the representation of $\underline{ESys}$ as $\underline{ISys}$ is a complete answer to a question of G. Plotkin. Plotkin asked (in [7]) whether the tedious calculations characteristic of work over eg systems–the calculations of recursive indices of products, of exponentials and of other domain constructs in terms of their components' indices–are eliminable in favor of constructive mathematics over some form of realizability. Our answer is affirmative and uniform for a variety of domain constructs that includes all those conventionally considered.

Limitations of space prohibit us from giving much more than a quick sketch of the proofs of many of our theorems. We apologize for the telegraphic style of this report and refer any disgruntled reader to [6], where there is a more leisurely exposition.

Section 1: Wouldn't it be lovely?

Wouldn't it be lovely if the cartesian closed category of information systems and approximable maps (à la Scott [8]) were a *full* subcategory of the category of sets? Proofs in denotational semantics would be much easier (and shorter) if the semanticist could freely assume that every map is continuous and monotone. To take a simple example, it would be trivial to show that the fixed-point operator, **fix**, is approximable as a function from $\underline{A} \Rightarrow \underline{A}$ into $\underline{A}$. If morphisms of information systems were just set maps, it would suffice to prove that **fix** provides a map. More generally, it would be child's play to prove that every term of the typed λ-calculus defines an approximable map; one need only check that each term defines a function.

Once one assumes that there is such a lovely category and that it is cartesian closed, there is a simple proof that the loveliness extends from the morphisms in the category to the endomorphisms of the category. Specifically, *every endofunctor* on the correlative category of systems and embeddings is provably approximable.

1.1. Assumption. $\underline{ISys}$ is a cartesian closed category of information systems in which every set map is approximable. ∎

1.2. Definition. If $\underline{ISys}$ is a category of information systems, $\underline{ISys}^E$ is the category of systems with embeddings. $\prec^i_j$ is an *embedding* of system $\underline{A}$ into system $\underline{B}$ just in case i and j are approximable maps, $i : \underline{A} \to \underline{B}$ and $j : \underline{B} \to \underline{A}$, such that $j \circ i = id_{\underline{A}}$ and $i \circ j \subseteq id_{\underline{B}}$. ∎

1.3. Definition. A (unary) endofunctor $F : \underline{ISys}^E \to \underline{ISys}^E$ is *approximable* whenever it is continuous and monotone on $\underline{ISys}^E$. F is *monotone* when it carries embeddings into embeddings, i.e., $\underline{A} \prec^i_j \underline{B}$ implies that $F(\underline{A}) \prec^{F(i)}_{F(j)} F(\underline{B})$. F is *continuous* when it commutes with direct limits: $F(lim\langle \underline{A}_i, e_{ij}\rangle) = lim\langle F(\underline{A}_i), F(e_{ij})\rangle$. ∎

1.4. Theorem. *Given the assumption, every endofunctor of $\underline{ISys}^E$ is approximable.*

Proof. To prove that every functor F is monotone and continuous, assume that $i : \underline{A} \to \underline{B}$ and $j : \underline{B} \to \underline{A}$, such that $j \circ i = id_{\underline{A}}$ and $i \circ j \subseteq id_{\underline{B}}$. First, F is a functor, so $F(i) : F(\underline{A}) \to F(\underline{B})$, $F(j) : F(\underline{B}) \to F(\underline{A})$ and $F(j) \circ F(i) = id_{F(\underline{A})}$. But F is also a map on function spaces; in particular, $F : (\underline{A} \Rightarrow \underline{B}) \to (F(\underline{A}) \Rightarrow F(\underline{B}))$. By assumption, $\underline{ISys}$ is cartesian closed and every map is monotone. Therefore, $F(i) \circ F(j) \subseteq id_{F(\underline{B})}$ and, consequently, F is itself monotone.

Next, if $\mathrm{Lim} = lim\langle \underline{A}_i, e_{ij}\rangle$ is a direct limit, then $id_{\mathrm{Lim}} = \bigcup(f_i \circ f_i^r)$, where, for each i,

$$\underline{A}_i \prec^{f}_{f^r} \mathrm{Lim}$$

Since F is approximable as a mapping from $\mathrm{Lim} \Rightarrow \mathrm{Lim}$ into $F(\mathrm{Lim}) \Rightarrow F(\mathrm{Lim})$,

$$id_{F(\mathrm{Lim})} = F(\bigcup(f_i \circ f_i^r)) = \bigcup F(f_i) \circ F(f_i^r).$$

It follows (cf. [7]) that $F(\mathrm{Lim})$ is the direct limit of $\langle F(\underline{A}_i), F(e_{ij})\rangle$. Therefore, the functor F is continuous. Consequently, even though $\underline{ISys}^E$ is nothing more than a category of sets and set maps, there are solutions to recursive domain equations defined over it. ∎

Once we've come this far, not even propriety prohibits us from becoming even more *imaginative*. Can we also assume that $\underline{ISys}$ coincides with the category of effectively given information systems with computable maps? If there were such a category, all manner of tiresome calculations become superfluous. Dispensible would be the check that λ-terms always define computable maps on eg systems. Also, the knowledge that recursive domain equations are solvable over the eg systems would come automatically from the elementary considerations of the preceding theorem.

Section 2: The intuitionistic set theory IZF

If one insists on ordinary set theory in classical logic, the category *ISys* is a pure fancy; our assumption is outrageously false. Even in classical arithmetic, one can define demonstrably nonapproximable maps on information systems. However, in intuitionistic set theory, we attain axiomatic freedom: there are no *counterexamples* to our assumption. In fact,the requisite intuitionistic set theory is nowise nonstandard. Once ordinary set theory is "minimally constructive," that is, once it is formulated independently of the excluded third, one can show that it is consistent with the axiom that there is a sizeable category of information systems in which every function is approximable.

A minimally constructive set theory is even, as far as axioms are concerned, quite familiar; it is IZF, a version of Zermelo-Fraenkel set theory in intuitionistic logic. IZF is formulated in a single-sorted first-order language with $\in$ and $=$ as its only primitive nonlogical predicates. The axioms of IZF are all instances of [1] through [8]:

[EXT]	$\forall x \forall y(\forall z(z \in x \leftrightarrow z \in y) \rightarrow x = y)$	[1]
[PAIR]	$\forall x \forall y \exists z(x \in z \wedge y \in z)$	[2]
[UN]	$\forall x \exists y \forall z \forall u((z \in u \wedge u \in x) \rightarrow z \in y)$	[3]
[SEP]	$\forall x \exists y \forall z(z \in y \leftrightarrow (z \in x \wedge \phi))$	[4]
[POW]	$\forall x \exists y \forall z(\forall u(u \in z \rightarrow u \in x) \rightarrow z \in y)$	[5]
[INF]	$\exists x(\exists u(\forall y\ y \notin u \wedge u \in x) \wedge \forall y(y \in x \rightarrow \exists z(y \in z \wedge z \in x)))$	[6]
[COLL]	$\forall x(\forall y(y \in x \rightarrow \exists z \phi) \rightarrow \exists u \forall y(y \in x \rightarrow \exists z(z \in u \wedge \phi)))$	[7]
[IND]	$\forall x(\forall y \in x \phi(y) \rightarrow \phi) \rightarrow \forall x \phi$	[8]

In classical logic, the axioms of IZF are equivalent to traditional Zermelo-Fraenkel. In intuitionistic logic, this equivalence fails; IZF does not derive the general law of excluded third.

Section 3: Kleene realizability for set theory

There is an intuitively appealing model of IZF that comes from extending the idea of Kleene realizability up the hierarchy of well-founded sets. It was Kleene's original insight, in [5], that constructive proofs (in arithmetic) are sufficiently algorithmic to be coded without loss as natural numbers. In the 1970's several researchers discovered that the insight could be applied as well and with happy effect to set theory. (cf. [1] and [3]) The foundation of the realizability idea, as applied to set theory, lies in the replacement of quantification over ordinary sets by quantification over "realizability sets."

To be precise, a realizability set is a collection which is hereditarily a realizability set, a collection of number-realizability set pairs $\langle n, b\rangle$, where n is conceived as a natural number that "proves" $b \in a$. $\mathbf{V}(Kl)$, the universe of hereditarily realizability sets, is the least class closed under the formation of realizability sets, and, as befits a least fixed point, it is defined inductively:

3.1. Definition.

$$\mathbf{V}(Kl)_0 = \emptyset$$

$$\mathbf{V}(Kl)_\alpha = \bigcup_{\beta<\alpha} \mathrm{P}(\omega \times \mathbf{V}(Kl)_\beta)$$

$$\mathbf{V}(Kl) = \bigcup_\alpha \mathbf{V}(Kl)_\alpha$$

∎

The sentences of IZF can now be interpreted over $\mathbf{V}(Kl)$ much as Kleene interpreted formal arithmetic over the natural numbers. The senses of the intuitionistic connectives, as specified by Heyting's interpretation ([4]), are approximated by *realizing* them as recursive operations. The interpretation is smoother if we extend the language of set theory by the addition of constants for each $a \in \mathbf{V}(Kl)$ and then use the constants autonymously. Let a, b, c and d stand for elements of $\mathbf{V}(Kl)$ and let e, f and g range over ω. We presuppose a primitive recursive surjective pairing function on ω for which x_0 and x_1 are the unpairing functions. As usual, '$\{e\}(n)$' represents the result of applying the Turing machine with index e to numeral n. In giving the interpretation, we assume that, whenever we write an application term, it is defined. For sentences ϕ of the extended language, read $e \Vdash \phi$ as "e realizes ϕ."

3.2. Definition.

$$e \Vdash a \in b \text{ iff } \exists c\, (\langle e_0, c\rangle \in b \text{ and } e_1 \Vdash c \in b) \quad [1]$$

$$e \Vdash a = b \text{ iff } \forall c, f\, (\langle f, c\rangle \in a \text{ implies that } \{e_0\}(f) \Vdash c \in b \text{ and } \langle f, c\rangle \in b \text{ implies that } \{e_1\}(f) \Vdash c \in a) \quad [2]$$

$$e \Vdash \phi \wedge \psi \text{ iff } e_0 \Vdash \phi \text{ and } e_1 \Vdash \psi \quad [3]$$

$$e \Vdash \phi \vee \psi \text{ iff either } e_0 = 0 \text{ and } e_1 \Vdash \phi \text{ or } e_0 \neq 0 \text{ and } e_1 \Vdash \psi \quad [4]$$

$$e \Vdash \phi \rightarrow \psi \text{ iff } \forall f\, (f \Vdash \phi \text{ implies that } \{e\}(f) \Vdash \psi) \quad [5]$$

$$e \Vdash \neg \phi \text{ iff } \forall f\ \neg f \Vdash \phi \quad [6]$$

$$e \Vdash \forall x\, \phi \text{ iff } \forall a\ e \Vdash \phi(a) \quad [7]$$

$$e \Vdash \exists x\, \phi \text{ iff } \exists a\ e \Vdash \phi(a) \quad [8]$$

We say that $\mathbf{V}(Kl)$ satisfies ϕ (in symbols, $\mathbf{V}(Kl) \models \phi$) whenever $\exists n\ n \Vdash \phi$. ∎

Section 4: On the internal mathematics of realizability

Just as Kleene proved that HA, the system of first-order intuitionistic arithmetic, is sound with respect to his original conception, one can prove that IZF holds in $\mathbf{V}(Kl)$. Here, $\overline{\forall x}\, \phi$ is a universal closure of ϕ.

4.1. Theorem. *If* IZF $\vdash \phi$, *then* $\mathbf{V}(Kl) \models \overline{\forall x}\, \phi$.

Proof. The proof is nothing more than a straightforward inductive check. For the details, consult [1]. ∎

Besides all the axioms of "pure" constructive mathematics, $\mathbf{V}(Kl)$ also satisfies statements reminiscent of recursive mathematics, among them *Church's Thesis*, CT.

4.2. Theorem. $\mathbf{V}(Kl) \models$CT

CT is the statement that every number-theoretic function is general recursive:

$$f \in (\omega \Rightarrow \omega) \rightarrow \exists e \in \omega\, \forall x \in \omega\, \exists y, u \in \omega\, (T(e, x, u) \wedge U(u, y) \wedge f(x) = y)$$

T represents the Kleene "T" predicate and U is the upshot function.

The proof that there is an *ISys*-like category in $\mathbf{V}(Kl)$ requires no very esoteric knowledge. CT is helpful, as is the fact that the set-theoretic operation of ordered pairing has a straightforward internal representation in $\mathbf{V}(Kl)$. There is a binary function $\overline{\langle a, b\rangle} : \mathbf{V}(Kl) \times \mathbf{V}(Kl) \rightarrow \mathbf{V}(Kl)$ with the property that, in the eyes of $\mathbf{V}(Kl)$, $\overline{\langle a, b\rangle}$ is the ordered pair of sets a and b:

$$\mathbf{V}(Kl) \models \overline{\langle a, b\rangle} = \overline{\langle c, d\rangle} \leftrightarrow a = c \wedge b = d$$

Also, the axiom of infinity is obviously true in $V(Kl)$, thanks to the fact that ω has a particularly salient internal representation as the realizability set $\overline{\omega}$. For each $n \in \omega$, let $\overline{n} = \{\langle m, \overline{m}\rangle : m \in n\}$. Then,

$$\overline{\omega} = \{\langle n, \overline{n}\rangle : n \in \omega\}$$

In describing the consistency proof, we will have reference to the following fact about $\overline{\omega}$: that there is an index i such that, whenever f is a total recursive function with index e, $\{i\}(e) \Vdash \overline{f} \in (\omega \Rightarrow \omega)$. $\overline{f}$ is an internal representation of f defined in terms of pairing:

$$\overline{f} = \{\langle n, \overline{\langle \overline{n}, \overline{m}\rangle}\rangle : f(n) = m\}$$

Finally, one needs to recognize that $V(Kl)$ mediates a strict correspondence between relations which are classically recursive and those which the intuitionist would call 'decidable'.

4.3. Definition. A subset B of A is *decidable* on A iff $\forall x \in A\ (x \in B \vee x \notin B)$.

∎

Since the law of excluded middle fails of universal validity, the assumption of decidability is a significant *mathematical constraint* on the structure of a set. Indeed, we have

4.4. Proposition. *A subset of the internal natural numbers is decidable in* $V(Kl)$ *just in case, when viewed from without, it is recursive.*

Proof. To see this, assume that $V(Kl) \models Y \subseteq \overline{\omega}$ is decidable. This means that there is an index e such that $e \Vdash \forall x \in \overline{\omega}\ (x \in Y \vee x \notin Y)$. By clauses [4] and [6] of 3.2, e decides, for each internal number $\overline{n}$, which of $\overline{n} \in Y$ or $\overline{n} \notin Y$ holds. Hence, we can assume that $\{e\}$ is total, $\{e\} : \omega \to 2$ and

$$V(Kl) \models \overline{n} \in Y \text{ if } \{e\}(n) = 0, \text{ while}$$
$$V(Kl) \models \overline{n} \notin Y \text{ if } \{e\}(n) = 1.$$

Conversely, every recursive set can be injected into $V(Kl)$ as a decidable set. This follows directly from our remarks on the internalization of recursive functions. If (external) Y is recursive, just internalize its characteristic function, c_Y. Then, $V(Kl) \models \overline{c_Y} : \overline{\omega} \rightarrowtail 2$. Therefore,

$$V(Kl) \models \forall x \in \omega\ (\overline{c_Y}(x) = 0 \vee \overline{c_Y}(x) = 1)$$

and $V(Kl) \models (\overline{c_Y})^{-1}(0)$ is decidable. ∎

Section 5: A category of constructive information systems

Just as IZF is in many ways a natural set theory, so is *ISys* a quite natural category of information systems. In fact, *ISys* is properly conceived as the result of a straightforward constructivization of Scott's notion of an information system. And that is just how we conceive it and how we will motivate its definition, starting from the conventional definition of a system:

5.1. Definition. Let $P^{<\omega}(A)$ be the finite powerset of A. A quadruple $\underline{A} = \langle A, \mathrm{Cons}_A, \vdash_A, \Delta_A\rangle$ is an *information system* iff Cons_A is a unary relation on $P^{<\omega}(A)$ and $\vdash_A$ is a binary relation on $P^{<\omega}(A) \times P^{<\omega}(A)$ such that

whenever $u \subseteq v$ and $\mathrm{Cons}_A(v)$, $\mathrm{Cons}_A(u)$	[1]
for all $x \in$A, $\mathrm{Cons}_A(\{x\})$	[2]
whenever $u \vdash_A v$ and $\mathrm{Cons}_A(u)$, $\mathrm{Cons}_A(u \cup v)$.	[3]

And, whenever, $\text{Cons}_A(u)$ and $\text{Cons}_A(v)$,

$$u \vdash_A \{\Delta\} \qquad [4]$$

$$u \vdash_A v \text{ if } v \subseteq u \qquad [5]$$

$$u \vdash_A v \text{ and } v \vdash_A w \text{ implies that } u \vdash_A w, \text{ and} \qquad [6]$$

$$u \vdash_A v \text{ and } u \vdash_A w \text{ implies that } u \vdash_A v \cup w. \qquad [7]$$

∎

When $\underline{A}$ is an information system, A is thought of as the set of tokens or "atomic bits of information" about some interpreted computations. Con_A and $\vdash_A$ are, respectively, a notion of consistency on the finite subsets of A and a relation of entailment holding between the finite subsets. Δ_A is the null bit, the token incorporating no information. One can think of A as a "space" of all possible propositions or coherent bits of information, about a collection of computations. The reasonably complete collections of bits are the elements of $\underline{A}$ and these are collected into the set A^*. Officially, $x \in A^*$ iff $x \subseteq A$, all finite subsets of x satisfy Cons_A and whenever $u \subseteq x$ and $u \vdash v$, then $v \subseteq x$. By analogy with consistency in logic, any subset of A all of whose finite subsets are consistent is also called consistent. Moreover, as far as the elements of $\underline{A}$ are concerned, such consistent sets are all that matter. The members of A^* are precisely the closures of consistent sets under $\vdash_A$. Hence, we can refer to each consistent subset of A, finite or otherwise, as a *basis* (for some element). Furthermore, if A is countable, so is every basis, as is the set of all finite subsets of the basis.

The move from this basic notion of information system to the notion appropriate for constructive contexts calls for the addition to the basic notion of some extra structure. This is no cause for alarm, the weakness of intuitionistic logic itself issues a general permit for structural improvements. (cf. [2]) But aside from this, one can offer good reasons, both prudential and philosophical, for the structure we propose to add.

The first addition belongs to the notion of element of an *ISys* system. We will identify elements with countable bases. In constructive contexts, it is generally a matter of prudence to refrain from talk about arbitrary subsets of (even finite) structures. So, one should avoid arbitrary elements of systems. The IZF axioms exert even less control over powersets than do their classical counterparts. This is apparent from realizability: $\mathbf{P}(\omega)$ in $\mathbf{V}(Kl)$ contains cardinal numbers up to (a version of) ω_{ω_1}. On the philosophical side, insisting that bases be enumerable preserves the computational metaphors that enliven Scott's ideas. When the basis is enumerable, the finite consistent subsets of it literally form a *series* of approximations to the corresponding element.

Second, in *ISys*, Cons_A and $\vdash_A$ are assumed to be decidable relations. This restriction shares its prudential motivation with the first: arbitrary relations on a structure are just too hairy. But again, decidability seems mandated if we're to follow the advice of Scott in conceiving of the building blocks of systems:

The best advice is to think of the members of $[A]$ *as consisting of* finite *data objects, some of which are more informative than others. The word "finite" should be taken in the sense of "fully circumscribed"—as regards what is given in* $[A]$ *these data objects can be comprehended in "one step."*

If the tokens are *thoroughly finite* informational bits, one should be able to determine, in a finite number of steps, the entailment and consistency relations holding on finite collections of them. Hence, the decidability requirement is extremely natural.

Lastly, we assume that the set of tokens of an *ISys* system is an ω-retract.

5.2. Definition. A set S is an ω-retract whenever there are functions $i : S \rightarrowtail \omega$ and $j : \omega \rightarrowtail S$ such that $j \circ i = id_S$. ∎

Admittedly, this is a nontrivial constraint. In the presence of the axiom of choice (AC), even in intuitionistic logic, all and only countable sets are ω-retracts. As it happens, full choice is not constructively consistent with IZF: IZF+AC $\vdash \phi \vee \neg\phi$. However, the connection with AC points the way to an acceptable motivation for the requirement, for one can prove that

5.3. Proposition. $V(Kl) \models$ *For S countable, S is an ω-retract iff equality is decidable on S iff AC holds on S.*

Proof. See [6] ∎

Insisting on ω-retracts, then, is in keeping with Scott's advice; it guarantees that identity on the sets of bits is decidable. Also, AC will make sure that functions exist over the system whenever they are needed. It is a simple consequence of this characterization that, for subsets of ω, ω-retraction is no restriction beyond countability.

5.4. Corollary. $V(Kl) \models$ *For $S \subseteq \omega$, S is countable iff S is an ω-retract.*

Proof. See [6] ∎

A point worth noting: to the classical mathematician schooled in AC, all this extra structure is nugatory. In ZF+AC, *ISys* is merely the category of countable information systems.

Now that all the conceptual software is mounted, we can give the official description of *ISys*.

5.5. Definition. $\underline{A}$ is an object of *ISys* iff $\underline{A} = \langle A, \mathrm{Cons}_A, \vdash_A, \Delta_A \rangle$ is an information system, Cons_A and $\vdash_A$ are decidable on $P^{<\omega}(A)$ and $P^{<\omega}(A) \times P^{<\omega}(A)$, respectively, and A is an ω-retract. ∎

5.6. Definition. f is an *element* of $\underline{A}$ iff $f \in (\omega \Rightarrow P^{<\omega}(A))$, and $\forall n\ \mathrm{Cons}_A(f(0) \cup f(1) \cup \ldots \cup f(n))$. The set of elements of $\underline{A}$ is denoted A^*.

∎

Intuitively, equality on bases should be equality on elements, and this is what the next definition provides. When f is equal to g as elements, we will say that $f \approx_A g$.

5.7. Definition. For $f, g \in A^*$, $f \subseteq_A g$ iff

$$\forall n\ \exists m\ g(0) \cup g(1) \cup \ldots \cup g(m) \vdash_A f(n)$$

and $f \approx_A g$ iff

$$f \subseteq_A g \text{ and } g \subseteq_A f.$$

∎

Strictly speaking, the set of elements of $\underline{A}$ is the collection of bases, plus the appropriately defined equality:

5.8. Definition. If $\underline{A}$ is an object of *ISys*, the *set of elements* of $\underline{A}$ is the pair $\langle A^*, \approx_A \rangle$. ∎

Finally, there is no difficulty in proving constructively that *ISys* is truly a category of domains:

5.9. Proposition. *For $\underline{A}$ from ISys, $\langle A^*, \subseteq_A, \approx_A \rangle$ is a consistently complete, ω-algebraic cpo.*

Proof. ∎

As an ω-algebraic cpo, $\underline{A}$ has finite elements. These are sequences of finite consistent subsets from A which are, up to $\approx_A$, constant.

5.10. Definition. $f \in A^*$ is *finite* iff $\exists g \in A^*$ g is constant and $f \approx_A g$. ∎

As a category, *ISys* has a perspicuous and useful skeleton–the collection of *presented information systems.* Rougly, the presented systems are those having ω itself as a set of tokens. Let $\{x_0, x_1, \ldots x_n\}$

represent a surjective primitive recursive coding into ω of finite subsets $x_0, x_1, \dots x_n$ of ω. Under this coding, $n \cup m$ represents the code of the finite set which is the union of the set coded by n with that coded by m. $n \subseteq m$ is the primitive recursive relation of set-theoretic inclusion holding between the sets coded by n and by m.

5.11. Definition. A pair $\langle \text{Cons}, \vdash \rangle$ is an ***presentation*** iff Cons is a decidable unary relation on ω and $\vdash$ is a decidable binary relation such that

whenever $n \subseteq m$ and Cons(m), Cons(n) [1]

for all n, Cons($\{n\}$), and [2]

whenever $n \vdash m$ and Cons(n), Cons($n \cup m$). [3]

And, whenever, Cons(n) and Cons(m),

$n \vdash 0$ [4]

$n \vdash p$ if $p \subseteq n$ [5]

$m \vdash n$ and $n \vdash p$ implies that $m \vdash p$, and [6]

$n \vdash m$ and $n \vdash p$ implies that $n \vdash m \cup p$. [7]

∎

This definition just makes explicit what it takes to be an information system in terms of the coding on the natural numbers. Note that, in presented systems, 0 always plays the role of $\{\Delta\}$. The constant m-valued ω-sequence is denoted '$[m]$' and finite elements are specified in accord with this notational convention. Again, this is merely a restatement, in terms of natural number codes, of our earlier definition of finite element. Hence, if $\underline{S}$ is presented, then $f \in S^*$ is finite iff $\exists m \in \omega\ f \approx_S [m]$.

One readily sees that the presented systems really do provide a domain-theoretic skeleton for $\underline{\mathit{ISys}}$.

5.12. Definition. Information systems $\underline{A}$ and $\underline{B}$ are equivalent iff $\langle A^*, \subseteq_A, \approx_A \rangle$ is isomorphic (in the order-theoretic sense) to $\langle B^*, \subseteq_B, \approx_B \rangle$. ∎

5.13. Theorem. ***Every object of $\underline{ISys}$ is equivalent to some presented system.***

Proof. Given $\underline{A}$ in $\underline{\mathit{ISys}}$, A is an ω-retract. Hence, there are functions $i : A \rightarrowtail \omega$ and $j : \omega \twoheadrightarrow A$ such that $j \circ i = id_A$. Define a presentation on ω so that it accords with consistency and entailment in A, as mediated by the pair $\langle i, j \rangle$. Specifically, let

$$\text{Cons}(n) \text{ iff } \text{Cons}_A\{j(m) : m \in n\} \text{ and}$$

$$m \vdash n \text{ iff } \{j(p) : p \in m\} \vdash_A \{j(q) : q \in m\}.$$

It is a simple matter to show that this presented system is equivalent to $\underline{A}$. ∎

Section 6: Consistency theorems

This section is devoted to proving, in some detail, that, in the case of intuitionistic information systems, axiomatic freedom is attainable. We will prove that, in $\mathbf{V}(Kl)$, the assumption that every set map in $\underline{\mathit{ISys}}$ is approximable is true along with all the axioms of IZF. In keeping with the set-theoretic paradigm, a map between objects of $\underline{\mathit{ISys}}$ is just a binary relation that is single-valued on its second place and respects the relevant equalities. More formally,

6.1. Definition. If $\underline{A}$ and $\underline{B}$ are in $\underline{ISys}$, and $\approx_A$ and $\approx_B$ are the respective equalities, F is a function from $\underline{A}$ to $\underline{B}$ ($F : \underline{A} \to \underline{B}$) iff $F \subseteq \overline{A^* \times B^*}$ which is invariant under $\approx_A$ in its first coordinate, invariant with respect to $\approx_B$ in its second, and which is total and functional:

$$\langle a, b\rangle \in F \wedge \langle a, c\rangle \in F \to b \approx_B c$$

▮

It is also worth recalling the definitions of monotonicity and of continuity for systems maps. Again, these are written in "set-theoreticalese."

6.2. Definition. For $\underline{A}$ and $\underline{B} \in \underline{ISys}$, $F : \underline{A} \to \underline{B}$ is *monotone* iff

$$\forall a, c \in A^* \; (a \subseteq_A c \to \forall b, d \in B^* \; ((\langle a, b\rangle \in F \wedge \langle c, d\rangle \in F) \to b \subseteq_B d))$$

▮

6.3. Definition. $F : \underline{A} \to \underline{B}$ is *continuous* iff

$$\forall n \, \forall a \in A^* \; (\forall b \in B^* \; (\langle a, b\rangle \in F \to [n] \subseteq_B b) \to$$
$$\exists m \; ([m] \subseteq_A a \wedge \forall b \in B^* \; (\langle [m], b\rangle \in F \to [n] \subseteq_B b)))$$

▮

In giving the definitions, we have taken an excusable liberty. Strictly speaking, an arbitrary $\underline{A}$ from $\underline{ISys}$ does not *contain* the finite elements $[n]$ of a presented system. But, since every object of $\underline{ISys}$ is equivalent to a presented system, we can use the same notation for the finites of any system. Conjoining the two definitions gives the definition of systems morphism:

6.4. Definition. $F : \underline{A} \to \underline{B}$ is *approximable* iff F is continuous and monotone. ▮

All the machinery is now in place for the proofs of the consistency theorems.

6.5. Theorem. $\mathbf{V}(Kl) \models$ *If* $F : \underline{A} \to \underline{B}$, *then* F *is continuous.*

Proof. Since every member of $\underline{ISys}$ is equivalent to a presented system, we are free to restrict consideration to $\underline{A}$ and $\underline{B}$ presented. There will be no notational distinction made between the basic relations Cons and $\vdash$ for $\underline{A}$ and the corresponding relations for $\underline{B}$. This will not be a source of confusion.

F is, by definition, total on A^*, so we can assume that there is an e_1 such that

$$e_1 \Vdash \forall f \; (f \in A^* \to \exists g \; (g \in B^* \wedge \langle f, g\rangle \in F)).$$

Now, we evaluate the definition of continuity over $\mathbf{V}(Kl)$: let $e_3 \Vdash f \in A^*$ while

$$\{e_2\}(\langle n, e_3\rangle) \Vdash \forall g \; (\langle f, g\rangle \in F \to \exists m \in \omega \; g^*(m) \vdash \overline{n}) \qquad [1]$$

Here, we are abbreviating $g(0) \cup \ldots \cup g(m)$ as $g^*(m)$.

Now, think of i as an index for a Turing machine. Take ϕ to be a total recursive function for which $\{\phi(i)\}$ outputs 0 on 0 and such that, for $n > 0$,

$$\{\phi(i)\}(n) \simeq \begin{cases} \{i\}(n) & \text{if } \forall x \leq n \; \{i\}(x) \downarrow \wedge \mathbf{V}(Kl) \models \text{Cons}\, \overline{\{i\}}^*(n) \\ \uparrow & \text{if } \forall x \leq n \; \{i\}(x) \downarrow \wedge \neg \mathbf{V}(Kl) \models \text{Cons}\, \overline{\{i\}}^*(n) \\ \uparrow & \text{if otherwise} \end{cases}$$

From what was said in the preceeding section—that $\mathbf{V}(Kl)$ mediates a close relation between decidability and necessity—it is clear that ϕ exists. Let $\psi(i)$ index the total recursive function enumerating the range of $\{\phi(i)\}$ by dovetailing. Because of the way $\phi(i)$ is defined, there is a total recursive θ such that

$$\theta(i) \Vdash \overline{\{\psi(i)\}} \in A^*$$

Use clause [5] of the definition of $\Vdash$ to infer that

$$\{e_1\}(\theta(i)) \Vdash \exists g\, (g \in B^* \wedge \langle \overline{\{\psi(i)\}}, g\rangle \in F)$$

Because total functions on ω in $\mathbf{V}(Kl)$ are recursive, there are partial recursive ρ, σ_1, σ_2 such that

$$\{\rho(i)\} \text{ is total,}$$
$$\sigma_1(i) \Vdash \overline{\{\rho(i)\}} \in B^*, \text{ while}$$
$$\sigma_2(i) \Vdash \overline{\langle \overline{\{\psi(i)\}}, \overline{\{\rho(i)\}}\rangle} \in F$$

From [1] we have that

$$\{\{e_2\}(\langle n, e_3\rangle)\}(\sigma_2(i)) \Vdash \exists m\ \overline{\{\rho(i)\}}^*\ (m) \vdash \overline{n}$$

For each $n \in \omega$, let

$$U_n = \{i : \mathbf{V}(Kl) \models \exists m\ \overline{\{\rho(i)\}}^*\ (m) \vdash \overline{n}\}$$

Our intention to to apply the classical Rice-Shapiro theorem to U_n. For that purpose, we have to check that U_n is r.e. and extensional in indices. Because $\underline{A}$ is presented and $\vdash$ is decidable in $\mathbf{V}(Kl)$, U_n is clearly r.e. For extensionality, assume that $\{i\} \simeq \{j\}$. Then $\{\phi(i)\} \simeq \{\phi(j)\}$ and

$$\mathbf{V}(Kl) \models \overline{\{\psi(i)\}} \approx \overline{\{\psi(j)\}}.$$

As $F : \underline{A} \to \underline{B}$ is a function in $\mathbf{V}(Kl)$,

$$\mathbf{V}(Kl) \models \overline{\{\rho(i)\}} \approx \overline{\{\rho(j)\}}.$$

This asserts that $\{\rho(i)\}$ and $\{\rho(j)\}$ determine bases generating the same element of $\underline{B}$. Hence, if $i \in U_n$, then so is j. Note that an r.e. index for U_n can be calculated uniformly in n.

Now, suppose that $i \Vdash f \in A^*$. Without loss of generality, we can assume that $\mathbf{V}(Kl) \models f = \overline{\{i\}}$. From our work above, it follows that

$$\theta(i) \Vdash \overline{\{\psi(i)\}} \in A^*,$$

and that there is a σ_3 such that

$$\sigma_3(i) \Vdash \overline{\{\psi(i)\}} \approx f.$$

Working just as above and using [1], we get

$$\{\{e_2\}(\langle n, \theta(i)\rangle)\}(\sigma_2(i)) \Vdash \exists m\ \overline{\{\rho(i)\}}^*\ (m) \vdash \overline{n}.$$

Therefore, every index for $\{i\}$ lies in U_n. By the Rice-Shapiro theorem, there is a finite subfunction g of $\{i\}$ which is defined on an initial segment of ω and which has an index in U_n. Given the conditions on i and n, one can find, effectively in i and n, a canonical index for g. Consequently, there is available a partial recursive π such that $\pi(i, n)$ indexes the total constant function whose value is $m = \bigcup_{i \in Dom(g)} g(i)$.

Since $\mathbf{V}(Kl) \models \overline{\{i\}} \in A^*$, $\mathbf{V}(Kl) \models \mathrm{Cons}(\overline{m})$. Also, there is an effective routine which, from i and n, calculates a j such that

$$j \Vdash [\overline{m}] \subseteq f.$$

If k is an Turing index for g, calculable from i and n, then $k \in U_n$ or

$$V(Kl) \models \exists m\ \overline{\{\rho(k)\}}^*(m) \vdash \overline{n}.$$

Again, it is easy to calculate a realizing number for the statement above. To complete the proof, it suffices to calculate a witness for the assertion

$$\overline{\langle[\overline{m}], \overline{\{\rho(k)\}}\rangle} \in F \qquad [2]$$

This will suffice, since we already know that, in $V(Kl)$,

$$\overline{n} \subseteq \overline{\{\rho(k)\}}.$$

To find a realizing number for [2], it is sufficient to find one for

$$[\overline{m}] \approx \overline{\{\psi(k)\}}.$$

But that is easy—just run through the dovetailing procedure that specifies $\overline{\{\psi(k)\}}$. The proof is now complete. ∎

6.6. Theorem. $V(Kl) \models$ *If $F : \underline{A} \to \underline{B}$, then F is monotone.*

Proof. Assume that $V(Kl) \models F : \underline{A} \to \underline{B}$. Take $e_1, e_2, e_3, e_4 \in \omega$ such that

$$e_1 \Vdash \forall f \in A^* \ \exists h \in B^* \ (\langle f, h\rangle \in F)$$
$$e_3 \Vdash f \in A^*$$
$$\{e_2\}(\langle n, e_3\rangle) \Vdash \forall h\ (\langle f, h\rangle \in F \to \exists m\ h^*(m) \vdash \overline{n})$$
$$e_4 \Vdash \forall n\ \exists m\ g^*(m) \Vdash f(n)$$

e_1 realizes that F is total, $e_2(\langle n, e_3\rangle)$ realizes that $[\overline{n}] \subseteq F(f)$ and e_3 realizes that $f \subseteq g$. The plan is to prove monotonicity for F in $V(Kl)$ by checking that

$$V(Kl) \models ((f \subseteq g \wedge [\overline{n}] \subseteq F(f)) \to [\overline{n}] \subseteq F(g)).$$

e_1 is used to instigate the same construction as that of of the preceding theorem. As before, we form the collection

$$U_n = \{i : V(Kl) \models \exists m\ \overline{\{\rho(i)\}}^*(m) \vdash \overline{n}\}$$

Again, it's easily provable that, if $i \Vdash f \in A^*$, then $i \in U_n$. By the Rice-Shapiro theorem, there is a finite subfunction g_1 of $\{i\}$ all of whose indices belong to U_n. Continue as in 6.5 to find an $m \in \omega$ and a realizing number for $[\overline{m}] \subseteq g$. To complete the proof, it will suffice to show that there is a $j \in \omega$ such that $j \Vdash g \in A^*$ and $j \in U_n$.

To that end, assume that $j \Vdash g \in A^*$ and $V(Kl) \models g = \overline{\{j\}}$. We will locate a function h and a subfunction h_1 such that $V(Kl) \models h \approx g$ and h_1 has its indices in U_n. Again, this is very easy:

$$V(Kl) \models [\overline{m}] \subseteq g$$

This means that

$$V(Kl) \models \exists k\ g^*(k) \vdash \overline{m}$$

Let h be a function on ω such that for all $p \in \omega$,

$$h(p) = \begin{cases} m & \text{if } p \leq k \\ \{i\}(p-(k+1)) & \text{if } p > k \end{cases}$$

Obviously, $\mathbf{V}(Kl) \models \overline{h} \approx g$. Take $h_1 = h \upharpoonright (k+1)$ and let r be an index for this finite function. It follows from all this that

$$\mathbf{V}(Kl) \models \exists k\, \overline{\{\rho(r)\}}^* (k) \vdash \overline{m}$$

and, hence, that r has an index for h_1 that falls into U_n. ∎

In the eyes of $\mathbf{V}(Kl)$, every set map between members of $\underline{ISys}$ is continuous and monotone. Therefore, the category of $\underline{ISys}$ objects and set maps is precisely a category of information systems and approximable maps. Now, IZF can take over almost entirely; from the definitions and these nonstandard axioms one can show that $\underline{ISys}$ has all the properties of a rich collection of computational domains. In fact, we catalogue some of these properties in the following section.

6.7. Note. Certainly other proofs of the consistency theorems are available. We opted to present that which employs the Myhill-Shepherdson explicitly to emphasize the accord (which will be plainly apparent from later sections) between the objects of $\underline{ISys}$ and classically eg systems. Using the Myhill-Shepherdson theorem in this way shows that the consistency theorems derive from a realizability-theoretic application of known results about effective domains, specifically the Myhill-Shepherdson for eg systems. (cf. [7]) ∎

Section 7: Properties of the category

Every map between $\underline{A}$ and $\underline{B}$ in $\underline{ISys}$ is determined by its graph:

7.1. Definition. For $F : \underline{A} \to \underline{B}$, $gh(F)$, the *graph* of F, is the binary relation on ω for which $\langle m, n\rangle \in gh(F)$ iff $[n] \subseteq_B F([m])$. ∎

7.2. Theorem. $\mathbf{V}(Kl) \models$ *If* $F : \underline{A} \to \underline{B}$, *then* F *is uniquely determined by* $gh(F)$.

Proof. Assume that both $\underline{A}$ and $\underline{B}$ are presented and take F approximable. For each $f \in A^*$, let $H(f)$ enumerate

$$\{n \in \omega : \exists m\, [m] \subseteq_A f \wedge \langle m, n\rangle \in gh(F)\}$$

Since all the basic relations are decidable, $H(f)$ exists. It will do to show that $\langle f, H(f)\rangle \in F$, and, for that, it will suffice to prove that, if $\langle f, g\rangle \in F$, then $g \approx_B H(f)$.

By continuity of F, if $[n] \subseteq_B y$ and $\langle f, g\rangle \in F$, then $H(f)$ eventually outputs n. Hence, $g \subseteq_B H(f)$. On the other hand, let $[n] \subseteq_B H(f)$. From the definition of $H(f)$ and the monotonicity of F, $[n] \subseteq_B g$. Therefore, $g \approx_B H(f)$. ∎

7.3. Theorem. $\mathbf{V}(Kl) \models$ *If* $F : \underline{A} \to \underline{B}$, *then* $gh(F)$ *is countable.*

Proof. This is immediate, in IZF, from the decidability of Cons and $\vdash$. ∎

Thanks to the recursion theory which is "built into" realizability, $\underline{ISys}$ is, in $\mathbf{V}(Kl)$, precisely the category of effectively given domains. First, the fact that decidable and recursive relations coincide in $\mathbf{V}(Kl)$ has already received considerable play. Moreover, since CT holds in $\mathbf{V}(Kl)$, every countable set of natural numbers is re. It follows directly from this that $\underline{ISys}$ coincides with $\underline{ESys}$ and that every $\underline{ISys}$ morphism is computable.

7.4. Corollary. $\mathbf{V}(Kl) \models$ $\underline{ISys}$ *coincides with the category of eg information systems and computable morphisms.*

Again, because of CT, only the computable elements of a system exist in $\mathbf{V}(Kl)$:

7.5. Corollary. $\mathbf{V}(Kl) \models$ *If* $\underline{A} \in \underline{ISys}$ *and* $f \in A^*$, *then* f *is computable.*

The standard proof that $\underline{Sys}$, the classical category of information systems, is cartesian closed is fully constructive. Hence, it is reproducible in IZF and, to show that $\underline{ISys}$ is cartesian closed, it suffices to show that products and exponentials of presented systems are presented. In truth, one can show that the category is closed under many of the usual constructs.

7.6. Theorem. $\mathbf{V}(Kl) \models$ *$\underline{ISys}$ is closed under products, sums, exponentiation, and the formation of Hoare and of Smyth powerdomains.*

Proof. All the requisite verifications are obtainable in IZF. We restrict ourselves here to proving closure under products.

Recall that $\langle\ ,\ \rangle$ is a surjective p.r. pairing function with x_0 and x_1 as the corresponding projections. Let m^0 and m^1 be the p.r. functions defined by

$$m^0 = \{n_0 : n \in m\} \text{ and}$$
$$m^1 = \{n_1 : n \in m\}.$$

We assume that $0^0 = 0 = 0^1$. Let $\underline{A}$ and $\underline{B}$ be presented elements of $\underline{ISys}$. We define relations $\mathrm{Cons}_{A\times B}$ and $\vdash_{A\times B}$ as follows:

$$\mathrm{Cons}_{A\times B}(n) \text{ iff } \mathrm{Cons}_A(n^0) \text{ and } \mathrm{Cons}_B(n^1)$$
$$m \vdash_{A\times B} \text{ iff } m^0 \vdash_A n^0 \text{ and } m^1 \vdash_B n^1$$

These new relations are clearly decidable and satisfy the conditions on presentations. It is easy to check that $\langle \mathrm{Cons}_{A\times B}, \vdash_{A\times B}, 0\rangle$ is a presentation for $\underline{A} \times \underline{B}$. ▮

Section 8: On eg systems: a question of Plotkin

8.1. Note. For the last two sections, considerations of space will prohibit us from giving much more than statements of theorems and the merest indications of their proofs. ▮

In $\mathbf{V}$, $\underline{ESys}$ is the category whose objects are the eg information systems and whose morphisms are the computable approximable maps. Specifically,

8.2. Definition. $\underline{S} = \langle \omega, \mathrm{Cons}_S, \vdash_S, 0\rangle$ is an *eg information system* (an object of $\underline{ESys}$) iff $\underline{S}$ is an information system and Cons_S and $\vdash_S$ are recursive relations on (coded) $\mathrm{P}^{<\omega}(\omega)$ and on $\mathrm{P}^{<\omega}(\omega)\times\mathrm{P}^{<\omega}(\omega)$, respectively. As is the case with $\underline{ISys}$, when $\underline{S}$ is in $\underline{ESys}$, we say that $\langle \mathrm{Cons}_S, \vdash_S\rangle$ is a presentation of $\underline{S}$. ▮

8.3. Definition. $i \in \omega$ indexes $\underline{S}$ in $\underline{ESys}$ iff i_0 in an index for Cons_S and i_1 is an index for $\vdash_S$. ▮

The proof of the last theorem of Section 7, not to mention the effectiveness of all set maps of $\underline{ISys}$ in $\mathbf{V}(Kl)$, point to the existence of a close connection between $\underline{ISys}$ and $\underline{ESys}$. As a first step toward illuminating the connection, we note that the objects of $\underline{ISys}$ in $\mathbf{V}(Kl)$ stand in a correspondence with the objects of $\underline{ESys}$ given by the respective presentations. The injection $\underline{S} \mapsto \overline{\underline{S}}$ takes each presentation from $\underline{ESys}$ into the presentation of a presented system of $\underline{ISys}$.

8.4. Definition. Let $\langle \mathrm{Cons}_S, \vdash_S\rangle$ be a presentation from $\underline{ESys}$. Then, $\overline{\langle \mathrm{Cons}_S, \vdash_S\rangle} = \langle \overline{\mathrm{Cons}_S}, \overline{\vdash_S}\rangle$ where

$$\overline{\mathrm{Cons}_S} = \{\langle n, \overline{n}\rangle : n \in \mathrm{Cons}_S\} \text{ and}$$
$$\overline{\vdash_S} = \{\langle\langle n, m\rangle, \overline{\langle \overline{n}, \overline{m}\rangle}\rangle : n \vdash_S m\}.$$

▮

Of equal note is the fact that the correspondence is effective:

8.5. Lemma. *There is an $e \in \omega$ with the property that, if i indexes $\underline{S}$, then $\{e\}(i)\downarrow$ and*

$$\{e\}(i) \Vdash \overline{\langle Cons_S, \vdash_S\rangle} \text{ is a presentation in } \underline{ISys}.$$

Conversely, there is an $h \in \omega$ with the property that, if

$$j \Vdash \overline{\langle Cons_S, \vdash_S\rangle} \text{ is a presentation in } \underline{ISys},$$

then $\{h\}(j)\downarrow$ and $\{h\}(j)$ indexes $\overline{S}$.

Proof. ▮

With this information, we propose to answer the question of Plotkin in a simple case, that of products. Then, from the simple case, we derive a general answer. Since the usual proof of the closure of $\underline{ESys}$ under products is constructive, there is no need to calculate on indices to insure that the product construct is effective. The realizability interpretation of intuitionistic logic gives the indexing calculations automatically.

The mathematical core of the proof that $\underline{ISys}$ is, intuitionistically, closed under products is the provision of a presentation for the product, $\langle \mathrm{Cons}_{A\times B}, \vdash_{A\times B}\rangle$, in terms of the presentations $\langle \mathrm{Cons}_A, \vdash_A\rangle$ and $\langle \mathrm{Cons}_B, \vdash_B\rangle$ of its component systems. This same construction is also the mathematical core of the proof that $\underline{ESys}$ is closed under products. The very identification of these two "cores" has itself a mathematical content, which is expressed in the proof that, over $\mathbf{V}(Kl)$, the results of the two constructions are identical. Let $\underline{A}$ and $\underline{B}$ belong to $\underline{ESys}$. Let $\mathrm{Cons}_A \times \mathrm{Cons}_B$ represent $\mathrm{Cons}_{A\times B}$ as it is defined arithmetically in terms of Cons_A and Cons_B. Similarly for $\vdash_A \times \vdash_B$.

8.6. Lemma. *Let $\langle Cons_A, \vdash_A\rangle$ and $\langle Cons_B, \vdash_B\rangle$ present $\underline{A}$ and $\underline{B}$ as objects from $\underline{ESys}$.* $\mathbf{V}(Kl)$ *satisfies*

$$\langle \overline{Cons_{A\times B}}, \overline{\vdash_{A\times B}}\rangle = \langle \overline{Cons_A} \times \overline{Cons_B}, \overline{\vdash_A} \times \overline{\vdash_B}\rangle.$$

A realizability witness can be found for the latter statement independently of $\underline{A}$, $\underline{B}$ and of their respective presentations.

Proof. ▮

With lemmas 8.4 and 8.5 in place, the elimination of indices for products is an easy exercise:

8.7. Theorem. *The explicit calculation of indices is eliminable from a complete proof that $\underline{ESys}$ is closed under products. The calculation is eliminated in favor of working constructively over* $\mathbf{V}(Kl)$.

Proof. Assume that $\langle \mathrm{Cons}_A, \vdash_A\rangle$ and $\langle \mathrm{Cons}_B, \vdash_B\rangle$ present $\underline{A}$ and $\underline{B}$ as objects of $\underline{ESys}$ and have indices i_A and i_B, respectively. Thanks to Lemma 8.4, for $X = A, B$, $\{e\}(i_X)\downarrow$ and

$$\{e\}(i_X) \Vdash \langle \overline{\mathrm{Cons}_X}, \overline{\vdash_X}\rangle \text{ is a presentation of an object of } \underline{ISys}.$$

As we have seen IZF $\vdash$ $\underline{ISys}$ is closed under $\times$, so the soundness of realizability gives a j such that $j \Vdash$ "$\langle\overline{\mathrm{Cons}_A}, \overline{\vdash_A}\rangle$ and $\langle\overline{\mathrm{Cons}_B}, \overline{\vdash_B}\rangle$ are presentations from $\underline{ISys}$ only if $\langle \overline{\mathrm{Cons}_A} \times \overline{\mathrm{Cons}_B}, \overline{\vdash_A} \times \overline{\vdash_B}\rangle$ presents their product."

By the definition of realizability for $\rightarrow$,

$$\{j\}((\{e\}(i_A), \{e\}(i_B))) \Vdash \langle \overline{\mathrm{Cons}_A} \times \overline{\mathrm{Cons}_B}, \overline{\vdash_A} \times \overline{\vdash_B}\rangle \text{ presents their product.}$$

By lemma 8.5, there is a $k \in \omega$ such that $\{k\}(\{j\}((\{e\}(i_A), \{e\}(i_B))))$ realizes $\langle\overline{\mathrm{Cons}_{A\times B}}, \overline{\vdash_{A\times B}}\rangle$ presents the product of $\overline{A}$ and $\overline{B}$ in $\underline{ISys}$.

Finally, apply the second half of the first lemma to obtain the result that

$$\{h\}(\{k\}(\{j\}((\{e\}(i_A), \{e\}(i_B)))))$$

indexes $\langle \mathrm{Cons}_{A\times B}, \vdash_{A\times B}\rangle$ in $\underline{ESys}$.

∎

Theorem 8.6 is among the most instructive elementary indications of the profits of constructivity. The only price for automatic index calculation is the observation that the conventional proof of closure is constructive and that constructive mathematics is sound with respect to realizability. But that's not all: the pleasures of realizability are not limited to products. Any of the conventional operations on $\underline{ESys}$ admit of the same treatment because the definitions of the operations can take a particularly simple form. The form in question is that which allows, for each operation, a version of Lemma 8.5 to go through.

8.8. Definition. Let **P** be a set of decidable number-theoretic predicates. Let L^P be the language of Peano arithmetic with the predicates from **P**. $\phi \in$**Form**(L^P) is *almost negative* (a.n.) in **P** iff $\vee$ does not occur in ϕ and $\exists x$ occurs only preceding decidable subformulae of ϕ. ∎

This definition should be compared with that of "almost negative" formulae as it appears in [11]. For purposes of exposition, we pretend that the predicates of **P** are all binary.

8.9. Definition. For $\phi \in$**Form**(L^P), $\overline{\phi}$ is obtained by replacing each appearance of any P from **P** in ϕ by $\overline{\mathrm{P}}$ where $\overline{\mathrm{P}} =$

$$\{\langle\langle m, n\rangle, \overline{\langle \overline{m}, \overline{n}\rangle}\rangle : \mathrm{P}(m) \text{ holds }\},$$

and then by expressing ϕ "in the natural way" in set theory. ∎

For purposes of exposition in the next lemma, we assume that ϕ has at most two free variables.

8.10. Lemma. *If ϕ is a.n. in the* **P**, *then there is an $e_\phi \in \omega$ such that if* $\mathbf{V} \models \phi(m,n)$, *then* $\{e_\phi\}(m,n)\downarrow$ *and* $\{e_\phi\}(m,n) \Vdash \overline{\phi}(\overline{m},\overline{n})$. *Also, if* $\mathbf{V}(Kl) \models \overline{\phi}(\overline{m},\overline{n})$, *then* $\mathbf{V} \models \phi(m,n)$.

Proof. ∎

Again, it is ease of exposition only that motivates our upcoming use of a binary, rather than an arbitrary, operation on $\underline{ESys}$.

8.11. Lemma. *Let $F(\underline{A},\underline{B})$ be an operation on $\underline{ESys}$ such that the presentation of $F(\underline{A},\underline{B})$ is a.n. in the presentations of $\underline{A}$ and of $\underline{B}$. Specifically, let ϕ_0 be an a.n. formula defining $Cons_{F(A,B)}$ in terms of $Cons_A$, $Cons_B$, $\vdash_A$ and $\vdash_B$ and let ϕ_1 do the same for $\vdash_{F(A,B)}$. Then*

$$\mathbf{V}(Kl) \models \overline{Cons_{F(A,B)}} = \overline{\phi_0} \text{ and}$$
$$\overline{\vdash_{F(A,B)}} = \overline{\phi_1}.$$

Also, realizability witnesses for each of the above is obtainable independently of $\underline{A}$ and $\underline{B}$.

Proof. ∎

8.12. Theorem. *Assume that $F(\underline{A},\underline{B})$ is an operation on $\underline{ESys}$ such that a presentation of $F(\underline{A},\underline{B})$ is a.n. in those of $\underline{A}$ and $\underline{B}$. Let T be any extension of IZF such that both* $\mathbf{V} \models T$ *and* $\mathbf{V}(Kl) \models T$ *and assume that* $T \vdash \underline{ESys}$ *is closed under F. Then,* $\mathbf{V}(Kl) \models \underline{ISys}$ *is closed under F and all the relevant indexing calculations are effective and eliminable in favor of realizability.*

Proof. Use the Lemmas 8.5 and 8.10 and work just as in the case of products. ∎

The following corollary provides a general answer to Plotkin's question.

8.13. Corollary. *In* V(*Kl*), $\underline{ISys}$ *is closed under products, exponentials, sums, Hoare powerdomains, and Smyth powerdomains. The operations corresponding to the constructions are effective and all the indexing calculations are eliminable.*

Proof.

Just check that all the operations give presentations which are a.n. in those of their components and that all the relevant proofs can be carried out in IZF. ∎

Section 9: Eliminating the first-order theory of eg systems

One might say that, in eliminating index calculations, we have shown that the effective *form* of the theory of eg systems is fully captured by the logic of the theory of $\underline{ISys}$. By 'eliminating the theory of $\underline{ESys}$', we mean to suggest that the mathematical *content* of the theory of eg systems can be replaced by that of $\underline{ISys}$ over V(*Kl*). As rationale for the suggestion, we give a "small scale" isomorphism result linking $\underline{ESys}$ with $\underline{ISys}$. The result shows that, mathematically speaking, nothing will be lost in taking up the suggestion. The isomorphism is "small scale" because it does not treat of logical features, like quantification over objects from the categories, which will be considered in a later publication. The section closes with a demonstration of the ease with which the suggestion can be applied; we see that the effective fixed-point theorem comes directly from its noneffective version.

9.1. Definition. For $\underline{A}$ from $\underline{ESys}$, the language $\mathbf{L}^e$ ('*e*' for 'effective') is a two-sorted first-order language with sorts E and M and with the following predicates as primitive:

$$\subseteq \text{ of sort } E \times E$$

$$\text{App of sort } M \times E \times E$$

As a matter of convenience, assume that each computable $f \in A^*$ and computable $F : \underline{A} \to \underline{A}$ appears in $\mathbf{L}^e$ as an autonymous name. ∎

Under the natural interpretation of $\mathbf{L}^e$ over $\underline{ESys}$, E represents the collection of computable elements of $\underline{A}$ and M the collection of computable morphisms from $\underline{A}$ into $\underline{A}$. $\underline{ESys} \models f \subseteq g$ iff computable f is contained in computable g as $\underline{A}$-elements and $\underline{ESys} \models \mathrm{App}(F, f, g)$ iff $F : \underline{A} \to \underline{A}$ and f are computable and $F(f) = g$.

Each of the objects of the interpreted sorts is injected into V(*Kl*) and there reappears, under the appropriate description, as a feature of $\overline{\underline{A}}$ in $\underline{ISys}$. In the following, let e_f be any index for recursive f.

9.2. Definition. For $f \in (\omega \Rightarrow \omega)$, let

$$\overline{f} = \{\langle n, \overline{\langle \overline{n}, \overline{m} \rangle} \rangle : \langle n, m \rangle \in f\}.$$

For $F : \underline{A} \to \underline{A}$, and F computable let

$$\overline{F} = \{\langle e_f, \overline{\langle \overline{f}, \overline{g} \rangle} \rangle : \langle f, g \rangle \in F\}.$$

∎

The next lemma is intended to show that the "overlining" injection underlies a perfect semantic accord–at least as far as the sorts and atomic sentences are concerned–between $\underline{ESys}$ and $\underline{ISys}$ over V(*Kl*).

9.3. Lemma.

$$\underline{ESys} \models E(f) \quad \textit{iff } \mathrm{V}(Kl) \models \overline{f} \in \overline{\underline{A}}^* \quad [1].$$

$$\underline{ESys} \models M(F) \quad \textit{iff } \mathrm{V}(Kl) \models \overline{F} : \overline{\underline{A}} \to \overline{\underline{A}} \quad [2]$$

$$\underline{ESys} \models f \subseteq g \quad \textit{iff } \mathrm{V}(Kl) \models \overline{f} \subseteq_{\mathbf{A}} \overline{g} \quad [3]$$

$$\underline{ESys} \models \mathrm{App}(F, f, g) \quad \textit{iff } \mathrm{V}(Kl) \models \langle \overline{f}, \overline{g} \rangle \in \overline{F} \quad [4]$$

Proof. [1] and [3] follow immediately from the definitions of the pertinent notions and from our oft cited reflections on decidability in $\mathbf{V}(Kl)$ and recursivity in $\mathbf{V}$. [2] follows from [1] and [3]. Concerning [4]:

If $\mathrm{App}(F,f,g)$ holds in $\underline{ESys}$, then F is computable and takes f into g. By the definition of $\overline{F}$, $\langle e_f, i\rangle \Vdash \overline{\langle \overline{f}, \overline{g}\rangle} \in \overline{F}$. Conversely, if $e \Vdash \overline{\langle \overline{f}, \overline{g}\rangle} \in \overline{F}$, then

$$e_0 = e_h \text{ and } e_1 \Vdash \overline{\langle \overline{f}, \overline{g}\rangle} = \overline{\langle \overline{h}, \overline{k}\rangle}$$

where $\langle h,k\rangle$ is in F. By the absoluteness properties for the natural numbers, $f = h$ and $g = k$, so $\langle f,g\rangle \in F$. ∎

The neat correspondence of this lemma extends to a full translation ϕ^{tr}. Let $\mathbf{S}^e$ be the set of sentences of $\mathbf{L}^e$.

9.4. Definition. ϕ^{tr} is defined for ϕ from $\mathbf{S}^e$. If ϕ is atomic, let ϕ^{tr} be given by the correspondence of the preceding lemma. ϕ^{tr} commutes with $\wedge$, $\vee$, $\neg$, $\rightarrow$. For X and x ranging, respectively, over the computable morphisms and elements of $\underline{A}$,

$$(\forall X\, \phi)^{tr} = \forall X\, (X : \overline{\underline{A}} \rightarrow \overline{\underline{A}} \rightarrow \neg\neg \phi^{tr})$$
$$(\forall x\, \phi)^{tr} = \forall x\, (x \in \overline{A}^{*} \rightarrow \neg\neg \phi^{tr})$$
$$(\exists X\, \phi)^{tr} = \exists X\, (X : \overline{\underline{A}} \rightarrow \overline{\underline{A}} \wedge \phi^{tr})$$
$$(\exists x\, \phi)^{tr} = \exists x\, (x \in \overline{A}^{*} \wedge \phi^{tr}).$$

∎

9.5. Theorem. *For $\phi \in \mathbf{S}^e$, $\underline{ESys} \models \phi$ iff $\mathbf{V}(Kl) \models \phi^{tr}$.*

Given the previous lemmas and the properties of realizability, there is no difficulty in proving that if ϕ is quantifier-free, then the theorem holds. For quantified expressions, the following lemmas are necessary

9.6. Lemma. *For $f \in \mathbf{V}(Kl)$, if $\mathbf{V}(Kl) \models f \in \overline{A}^{*}$, then, for some $g \in A^{*}$, $\mathbf{V}(Kl) \models f = \overline{g}$.*

9.7. Lemma. *For $F \in \mathbf{V}(Kl)$, if $\mathbf{V}(Kl) \models F : \overline{\underline{A}} \rightarrow \overline{\underline{A}}$, then $\mathbf{V}(Kl) \models F = \overline{G}$, for some computable $G : \underline{A} \rightarrow \underline{A}$.*

Proof. The essential idea can be conveyed by presenting the proof for one of the universal quantifiers.

Assume that $\underline{ESys} \models \forall X\, \phi$ and suppose that $\mathbf{V}(Kl) \models F : \overline{\underline{A}} \rightarrow \overline{\underline{A}}$. By the lemma, there is a $G : \underline{A} \rightarrow \underline{A}$ such that, in $\mathbf{V}(Kl)$, $F = \overline{G}$. $\phi(X/G)$ holds in $\underline{ESys}$, so

$$\mathbf{V}(Kl) \models \phi^{tr}(X/F) \text{ and } 0 \Vdash \neg\neg\phi^{tr}(X/F).$$

On the other hand, if

$$\mathbf{V}(Kl) \models \forall X\, (X : \overline{\underline{A}} \rightarrow \overline{\underline{A}} \rightarrow \neg\neg\phi^{tr}),$$

and $F : \underline{A} \rightarrow \underline{A}$ in $\mathbf{V}$ is computable, then

$$\mathbf{V}(Kl) \models \overline{F} : \overline{\underline{A}} \rightarrow \overline{\underline{A}}.$$

It follows that $\mathbf{V}(Kl) \models \phi^{tr}(X/\overline{F})$ and, hence, by the inductive hypothesis, $\underline{ESys} \models \phi(X/F)$. ∎

The theorem on ϕ^{tr} shows that, in studying the effective aspects of $\underline{ESys}$, nothing is ever lost by restricting our researches to $\underline{ISys}$ and using the mathematical principles holding over $\mathbf{V}(Kl)$. The next theorem, a straightforward preservation result, shows the ease with which constructive truth about $\underline{ISys}$ can be transformed into classical truth for $\underline{ESys}$. First, we pick out those formulae of $\mathbf{L}^e$ which are naturally preserved in this transition.

9.8. Definition. A formula ϕ of $\mathbf{L}^e$ is in Γ iff $\phi \in \mathbf{S}^e$, and, in ϕ, occurrences of $\forall$ appear neither in the scope of $\neg$ nor in the antecedent of $\to$. ∎

9.9. Definition. The translation ϕ^{pr} is defined just as ϕ^{tr}, except that the double negatives are removed from the cases governing the quantifiers. ∎

9.10. Theorem. *For* $\phi \in \Gamma$, $\mathbf{V}(Kl) \models \phi^{pr}$ *only if* $\underline{ESys} \models \phi$.

Proof. This is immediate by induction on the structure of ϕ. ∎

Nothing stands in the way of giving elegant and informative but decidedly "nonstandard" derivations of classical results about $\underline{ESys}$. For example, the usual proof of the (noneffective) fixed point theorem is fully constructive, so there is no difficulty in carrying it out over $\mathbf{V}(Kl)$. It is an immediate consequence of this trivial remark that the following holds in $\mathbf{V}(Kl)$ for every $\underline{A}$ from $\underline{ESys}$:

$$\forall X\ (X : \overline{\underline{A}} \to \overline{\underline{A}} \to \exists y \in \overline{\underline{A}}^*\ (X(y) = y \wedge \forall z \in \overline{\underline{A}}^*\ (X(z) = z \to y \subseteq_A z))).$$

Since this expression of the fixed point result is formulable in $\mathbf{L}^e$ as a sentence in Γ, the *effective* fixed-point theorem holds automatically and without further ado in $\underline{ESys}$, thanks to the last theorem.

Moreover, because the constructive proof of the fixed-point theorem is interpreted over realizability, more information is forthcoming. The realizability conditions for $\to$ show that there is a uniform effective procedure which, given an index for computable $F : \underline{A} \to \underline{A}$ in $\underline{ESys}$, outputs an index of the computable fixed point of F. Moreover, the proof of the soundness theorem for realizability gives one even more: an index for this procedure is itself effectively calculable from the code of a constructive proof of the fixed-point theorem together with the index of a presentation of $\underline{A}$.

Section 10: Conclusion and prospectus

In $\mathbf{V}(Kl)$, $\underline{ISys}$ represents exactly what one would want from a constructive category of information systems. First, we've seen that $\underline{ISys}$ has a kind of domain-theoretic Brouwer's Theorem: every set map of systems is continuous. It also satisfies a kind of Church's Thesis, that every set map is computable. These highly nonclassical axioms make for the axiomatic freedom encouraged earlier; in $\mathbf{V}(Kl)$, domain-theoretic life is blissful. But that's not all. Since set theory is interpreted over $\mathbf{V}(Kl)$ as realizability, $\underline{ISys}$ stands in an illuminating semantical relationship with the classical category $\underline{ESys}$. Thanks to this relationship, proofs of "effective facts" about $\underline{ESys}$ can be obtained from simpler, noneffective set-theoretic arguments over $\underline{ISys}$. In this way, the theory of $\underline{ESys}$ is eliminated, and all that remains are realizability and the constructive mathematics of $\underline{ISys}$.

Of course, a portion of this is still programmatic. We have said nothing about universal domains for $\underline{ISys}$. Nor have we tried to eliminate the higher-order or functorial aspects of $\underline{ESys}$. There are certainly suggestions in this report as to how that elimination should go and that it will be successful. For one thing, it's easy to see that the notion of endofunctor in $\underline{ISys}$ is, under realizability, identified with that of *computable* endofunctor of $\underline{ESys}$. Under this identification, the "imaginary theorem," Theorem 1.4, turns into the world's shortest proof that computable endofunctors on $\underline{ESys}$ are continuous.

10.1. Acknowledgments. The results of this report were obtained during March and April of 1983. Theorem 6.5 was conjectured and an outline of its proof predicted by Dana Scott. Our thanks also to Glynn Winskel for his helpful comments and suggestions. ∎

Section 11: References

[1] Beeson, M. *Continuity in intutionistic set theories.* **Logic Colloquium '78 (1979)**

[2] Bishop, E. **Foundations of Constructive Analysis.** McGraw-Hill (1967)

[3] Friedman, H. *Some applications of Kleene's methods for intuitionistic systems.* **Cambridge Summer School in Mathematical Logic** (1973). pp.113–170

[4] Heyting, A. *Mathematische Grundlagenforschung. Intuitionismus. Beweistheorie.* Springer, Berlin (1934) iv+74 pp.

[5] Kleene, S. C. *On the interpretation of intuitionistic number theory.* **Journal of Symbolic Logic** Volume 10 (1945) pp. 109–124

[6] McCarty. D. C. *D. Phil Thesis.* Oxford University (1983)

[7] Plotkin, G. D. *Lectures on the theory of domains.* manuscript.

[8] Scott, D. S. *Domains for denotational semantics.* **Proceedings of the ICALP '82** Lecture Notes in Computer Science 140 (1982)

[9] Scott, D. S. *Data types as lattices.* **SIAM Journal of Computing** Volume 5 (1976) pp. 522–587

[10] Scott, D.S. **Lectures on a Mathematical Theory of Computation.** Oxford University Computing Laboratory, Programming Research Group (1981) 148 pp.

[11] Troelstra, A. S. *Notions of realizability for intuitionistic arithmetic and intuitionistic arithmetic in all finite types.* **Proceedings of the Second Scandinavian Logic Symposium** (1971) pp. 369–405

A Complete System of Temporal Logic for Specification Schemata

John McLean

Computer Science and Systems Branch
Naval Research Laboratory
Washington, D.C. 20375 USA

1. Introduction

A software specification should be both formal and abstract.[1] The use of a formal language avoids ambiguity, aids the development of software support, and simplifies proofs of consistency, totalness, and correctness. Abstract specifications, i. e. specifications that are based on truth conditional assertions rather than on paradigm implementations, simplify proofs by eliminating nonessential clutter from the specification and help to eliminate ambiguities that result from the attempted gleaning of essential program features from such clutter.

First order logic provides an ideal framework for formal, abstract software specification because of its soundness and completeness properties. For example, a first order formalization of the trace method for software specification is contained in [3,4]. Procedure calls and domain elements are introduced as terms, and a concatenation function permits the forming of sequences of procedure calls, called *traces*. A legality predicate characterizes those traces that are *legal* (i. e., do not result in error), and a function from traces to domain values characterizes the return values of legal traces that end in a function call. A semantics and a sound, complete derivation system are given. This allows for coextensive syntactic and semantic definitions of both consistency and totalness. It also serves as a basis for a quick implementation system [1].

However, it is not clear how to specify asynchronous processes in such a framework. Although constraints on *relative* time (i. e., the occurrence of events relative to each other) are easily specified with the trace method, constraints on *absolute* time (i. e., the occurrence of events on an absolute time scale) are not. To specify absolute time constraints on a system, it may be

1. See [3,4] for a more detailed presentation of the issues discussed in this paragraph.

necessary to extend first order logic by introducing new operators.

An extension advocated by many to specify time (both relative and absolute) is the use of temporal sentential logic. I am not sure that adding temporal operators to a specification language is the right route to take. One problem with introducing temporal operators is that they lead to a loss of extensionality -- the principle that the truth value of a compound sentence is determined by the truth value of its sentential components (which are, in turn, determined by the denotations of their parts). For example, consider the specification method obtained by adding a $\Box$ operator to the trace language described above, where $\Box\varphi$ means that φ is true now and for all future system states, and assume that we want to specify a system that contains the predicates $\Phi STAT$ and $\Pi STAT$ to indicate the readiness of the corresponding procedures Φ and Π, respectively. In other words, Φ can be used if $\Phi STAT$ is *true*. We have as a formula in our specification $\Box(\Phi STAT \rightarrow L(\Phi))$ where $L(\Phi)$ means that a call can legally be made on Φ. If our system preserved extensionality, we should be able to infer $\Pi STAT \rightarrow \Box((\Phi STAT \equiv \Pi STAT) \rightarrow L(\Phi))$, which is clearly false. The loss of extensionality is unappealing for both intuitive and theoretical reasons.

In this paper we examine a more severe problem with temporal logic that emerges on getting a clear understanding of what is involved in using temporal logic as a specification language. When specifying programs, it is often convenient to use schemata to make assertions about program properties. Specifications containing such schemata are most simply viewed as containing an infinite number of assertions. However, extending systems of temporal logic to include schemata causes problems since some of the resulting specifications have semantic consequences that are not derivable. This paper presents a simple system of temporal logic and shows how the system must be modified if it is to remain complete when supplemented by schemata. A final section evaluates the modified system.

2. A System of Temporal Logic

The following system of temporal logic, *TL*, is minimal in that it is contained, in some form, as a subset of most proposed systems of linear (nonbranching) time, although it is derived from [5]. I have kept the system simple to bring out the issues clearly.

TL consists of a standard system of sentential calculus (e. g., the system consisting of parentheses, the sentence letters p, q, r, s, t, possibly subscripted, and the connectives $-$, and $\rightarrow$ for *not*, and *if...then...*, respectively), supplemented by the sentential operators $\Box$ and $\bigcirc$ for *future* and *next*, respectively. More formally, *TL* is the smallest set that contains its sentence letters and is closed under the following formation rule: if φ and ψ are in *TL*, then so are $-\varphi$, $(\varphi\rightarrow\psi)$, $\Box\varphi$, and $\bigcirc\varphi$. An element of *TL* is called a *formula*. For convenience, we abbreviate $-(\varphi\rightarrow-\psi)$ by $(\varphi\&\psi)$ and $(\varphi\rightarrow\psi)\&(\psi\rightarrow\varphi)$ by $(\varphi\equiv\psi)$, and we drop parentheses when no ambiguity results.

A *model* for *TL* is an ω-sequence of functions (called *states*), $\sigma=<s_0,s_1,\cdots>$, from *TL* to the set $\{true, false\}$ such that for all i, $s_i[-\varphi]=true$ *iff* $s_i[\varphi]=false$, $s_i[(\varphi\rightarrow\psi)]=false$ *iff* $s_i[\varphi]=true\neq s_i[\psi]$, $s_i[\Box\varphi]=true$ *iff* for all $j\geq i$, $s_j[\varphi]=true$, and $s_i[\bigcirc\varphi]=true$ *iff* $s_{i+1}[\varphi]=true$. When $s_0[\varphi]=true$, we write $\sigma\models\varphi$. For any set of formulae Σ, if for all σ, $\sigma\models\varphi$ whenever $\sigma\models\psi$ for all $\psi\in\Sigma$, we write $\Sigma\models\varphi$. If $\phi\models\varphi$, we write $\models\varphi$.

A *derivation* from a set of formulae Σ is a finite sequence of *TL* formulae (called lines) such that each member of the sequence is an *axiom* or follows from previous members of the sequence by a *rule of inference*, where the axioms and rules of inference are listed below.

Axiom Schemata:

1. $\Box(\varphi\rightarrow\psi)\rightarrow(\Box\varphi\rightarrow\Box\psi)$
2. $\bigcirc-\varphi\equiv-\bigcirc\varphi$
3. $\bigcirc(\varphi\rightarrow\psi)\rightarrow(\bigcirc\varphi\rightarrow\bigcirc\psi)$
4. $\Box\varphi\rightarrow(\varphi\&\bigcirc\varphi\&\bigcirc\Box\varphi)$
5. $(\varphi\&\Box(\varphi\rightarrow\bigcirc\varphi))\rightarrow\Box\varphi$

Rules of Inference:

T: If φ is a tautological consequence of a (possibly empty) set Λ of previous lines in a derivation, then φ may be written down as a line in the derivation.

F: If φ is a previous line in a derivation, then $\Box\varphi$ may be written down as a line in the derivation.

If there is a derivation whose last line is φ, we write $\vdash\varphi$. If $\vdash(\psi\rightarrow\varphi)$ where ψ is a conjunction of formulae contained in some set Σ, we write $\Sigma\vdash\varphi$.

3. A System with Schemata

A program specification is a set of *TL* statements that any implementation must satisfy. As argued in [3,4] schemata are necessary if we are to be able to specify programs that contain procedures that take a variable number of parameters. Temporal logic, in particular, also requires schemata to force, e. g., a particular formula φ to be *true* in all and only states s_i such that i is a prime number.[2] Such schemata may be introduced by allowing temporal operators to be replaced by strings such as $\Box \cdots \Box$ or $\bigcirc \cdots \bigcirc$ where an accompanying text or grammer gives the intended translation. In the present example, our specification would consist of the single schemata $\bigcirc \cdots \bigcirc\varphi$ where φ is the desired formula and $\bigcirc \cdots \bigcirc$ is interpreted as a string of a prime number of $\bigcirc$'s. Such schemata do not extend the language in any real sense since they can be interpreted as denoting an infinite set of formulae (in this example the set $\{\bigcirc\bigcirc\varphi, \bigcirc\bigcirc\bigcirc\varphi, \bigcirc\bigcirc\bigcirc\bigcirc\bigcirc\varphi, \cdots\}$).

As soon as we allow such specifications, we see that *TL* is inadequate. Call a language *compact* if for every set of formulae Σ, Σ is true in some model if every finite subset of Σ is true in some model. *TL* is not compact as can be seen by considering the set $\Sigma=\{p, \bigcirc p, \bigcirc\bigcirc p, \cdots, -\Box p\}$. For any finite set of formulae from Σ, there is an n such that no formula in the set has more than n occurrences of $\bigcirc$. Such a set is true in the sequence whose first n members assign true to p and whose other members assign false to p. Hence, every finite set of Σ has a model. But Σ, itself, has no model since for a sequence to make it true, each member, s_n, must assign true to p to render the formula that contains exactly n occurrences of $\bigcirc$ true, yet there must also be an n such that s_n assigns false to p to render $-\Box p$ true. This is impossible.

The failure of compactness has dire consequences for our proof theory since by definition, a proof contains only a finite number of lines. Hence, we have sets Σ and formulae φ such that $\Sigma \models \varphi$, yet it is not the case that $\Sigma \vdash \varphi$ if our system is sound. For the case in question, we have $\Sigma \models p\&-p$ although there is no derivation of $p\&-p$ from Σ. As a result, syntactic conceptions of consistency and totalness no longer coincide with their semantic counterparts.

Once we allow schemata and the infinite specifications they generate, we

---

2. Wolper [5] claims that there is no formula that forces p to be true in every even state (requiring nothing in odd states). This is false, as can be clearly seen by considering the formula $p\&\Box(p \rightarrow \bigcirc\bigcirc p)$.

must modify *TL*. *TL** resembles *TL*, but it allows for derivations from an infinite number of premises. To this end, we introduce the term *assumption set* to refer to the set of formulae that are assumed in a derivation.

As in *TL*, a derivation in *TL** is a finite sequence of formulae such that each member of the sequence is an axiom or a rule of inference. Further, the axioms of *TL** are those of *TL*. Unlike *TL*, the basic sense of *derivation* in *TL** is a derivation from a set of formulae. Any line in a derivation that is an axiom is said to have ϕ for an assumption set. The assumption set of a formula inferred by applying *T* to a set of earlier lines is the union of the assumption sets of those earlier lines. *F* can be applied only to formulae with ϕ for an assumption set; the result also has ϕ for an assumption set. Finally, we need two new rules of inference.

A: φ may be written down as a line in a derivation with $\{\varphi\}$ as an assumption set.

W: If there is an w-series of derivations whose last lines are $\psi\to\varphi$, $\psi\to\bigcirc\varphi$, $\psi\to\bigcirc\bigcirc\varphi$, $\cdots$, then $(\psi\to\Box\varphi)$ can be entered as a new line in a derivation. $(\psi\to\Box\varphi)$'s assumption set is the union of the assumption sets of the last lines of the derivation in the series.

Note that in *W*, we do not assume that the formulae are written in primitive terms. This is to avoid the complication of nested conditionals. Hence, if we have derivations of $\gamma\to(\psi\to\varphi)$, $\gamma\to(\psi\to\bigcirc\varphi)$, $\gamma\to(\psi\to\bigcirc\bigcirc\varphi)$, $\cdots$, we can use *T* to extend them to derivations of $(\gamma\&\psi)\to\varphi$, $(\gamma\&\psi)\to\bigcirc\varphi$, $(\gamma\&\psi)\to\bigcirc\bigcirc\varphi$, $\cdots$ and *W* to derive $(\gamma\&\psi)\to\Box\varphi$. Another application of *T* allows us to derive $\gamma\to(\psi\to\Box\varphi)$. For simplicity we restrict *W* so that it is *well-founded* in the sense that it can be applied only if it does not presuppose an infinite chain of derivations. That is, *W* can be applied only if there is an integer n that bounds the level of nesting of derivation series that must be appealed to in using *W*. We cannot use *W* on the basis of a derivation series that contains a derivation that uses *W* on the basis of a derivation series that contains a derivation that uses *W* on the basis $\cdots$.

If there is a *TL**-derivation whose last line is φ, where φ has for its assumption set some set Λ, we say that the assumption set of the derivation is Λ, and for any set Σ such that $\Lambda\subseteq\Sigma$, write $\Sigma\vdash\varphi$. If $\phi\vdash\varphi$, we write $\vdash\varphi$. Σ is *consistent* if it is not the case that there is a formula φ such that $\Sigma\vdash\varphi\&-\varphi$.

*TL** solves the particular problem since there are *TL*-derivations of $(p\&(p\to p))\to p$, $(\bigcirc p\&(p\to p))\to\bigcirc p$, $(\bigcirc\bigcirc p\&(p\to p))\to\bigcirc\bigcirc p$, $\cdots$, and hence, a *TL**-

derivation of $(p \to p) \to \Box p$ from $\{p, \bigcirc p, \bigcirc\bigcirc p, \cdots\}$. Using T, we derive $\Box p$. However, if TL^* is to be useful, it must not allow us to prove too much. Hence, our next step is to prove the soundness of TL^*.

Theorem: For any formula φ, there is a derivation of φ with assumption set Σ only if $\Sigma \models \varphi$.

Proof: Order all derivations that do not use W alphabetically or in any other way that has the property that if one derivation is the initial segment of another, the former occurs before the latter in the ordering. Assign the *ith* derivation in the ordering the ordinal $i-1$. Now, order those remaining derivations that use W applied only to derivations that appear in the first ordering and assign the *ith* derivation in this ordering to the ordinal $w+i-1$. Continue this process, collecting at each stage those derivations that have not been assigned an ordinal and that apply W only to derivations that appear in previous orderings, assigning to the *ith* derivation of this collection the ordinal $nw+i-1$ where the first derivation of the previous stage was assigned to the ordinal $(n-1)w$. Call the ordinal assigned to a derivation the *order* of the derivation. Since uses of W in a derivation must be well-founded, each derivation is assigned an order by the above process.

The proof proceeds by transfinite induction on the order of derivations. We assume the hypothesis for all derivations of order less than some ordinal n and prove it for the derivation, say δ, of order n. Since any initial segment of δ is, itself, a derivation of order less than n, the theorem holds for all but δ's last line by assumption. The case where δ's last line, φ, is an axiom is straight forward and left to the reader. If φ is inferred by A, the theorem is trivial. If φ is inferred by T, then the theorem follows since our definition of *model* validates all tautologies. If φ is inferred by F, then it is of the form $\Box\psi$ where ψ is a previous line in the derivation. By hypothesis, ψ is true whenever its assumption set is true. But its assumption set is ϕ, so ψ is true in all states, and hence, so is φ. If φ is inferred by W, it is of the form $(\beta \to \Box\psi)$. By hypothesis we know that the theorem holds for the derivations of $\beta \to \psi$, $\beta \to \bigcirc\psi$, $\beta \to \bigcirc\bigcirc\psi$, $\cdots$. The theorem holds for φ since these conditionals are true in a state only if $(\beta \to \Box\psi)$ is true, and we are done.

The next question we must face is whether TL^* really allows us to prove enough. We can derive $\Box p$ from $\{p, \bigcirc p, \bigcirc\bigcirc p, \cdots\}$, but can we derive, e. g., $\Box(p \to \bigcirc\bigcirc p)$ from $\{p, \bigcirc\neg p, \bigcirc\bigcirc p, \bigcirc\bigcirc\bigcirc\neg p, \cdots\}$? In other words, we must show that W covers all problematic cases. Note, for example, that if instead of W, we had the simpler rule that we could infer $\Box\varphi$ whenever $\vdash \varphi, \vdash \bigcirc\varphi, \cdots$, we still could not derive $p \rightarrow \Box q$ from $\{p \rightarrow q, p \rightarrow \bigcirc q, \cdots\}$.

Call a system *complete* if for any formula φ and set of formulae Σ, $\Sigma \models \varphi$ only if $\Sigma \vdash \varphi$.[3] We wish to establish that TL^* is complete, i. e., that it eliminates not just the particular troubling Σ we looked at, but all such Σ. As a first step we prove a deduction theorem that is useful in establishing completeness.

Theorem: If $\Sigma \vdash \varphi$, then $\Sigma \sim \{\beta\} \vdash (\beta \rightarrow \varphi)$ where β is any TL formula.

Proof: As for soundness, proof proceeds by transfinite induction on the order of derivations. Assuming the theorem for derivations of order less than n, we prove it for the derivation δ whose order is n. Let φ be δ's last line. Without loss of generality, assume that Σ is the assumption set of the derivation of φ. If φ is an axiom, then we use T to enter $(\beta \rightarrow \varphi)$ as the next line in the derivation with assumption set $\Sigma = \phi$. If φ is entered by A, then $\Sigma = \{\varphi\}$. If $\varphi \neq \beta$, then we use A to enter φ with the same assumption set (which does not contain β). T then yields $\{\varphi\} \vdash (\beta \rightarrow \varphi)$. If $\varphi = \beta$, then we use T to yield $\phi \vdash (\beta \rightarrow \varphi)$. If φ was entered by T, then it is a consequence of earlier lines $L_1, \cdots, L_m$. By hypothesis, $\Sigma_i \sim \{\beta\} \vdash (\beta \rightarrow L_i)$ for $1 \leq i \leq m$, where Σ_i is the assumption set of L_i. By T, $\Sigma \sim \{\beta\} \vdash (\beta \rightarrow \varphi)$. If φ was entered by F, then it is of the form $\Box\psi$ and $\Sigma = \phi$. By T, $\phi \vdash (\beta \rightarrow \varphi)$. If φ was entered by W, then it is of the form $(\gamma \rightarrow \Box\psi)$ and $\Sigma_0 \vdash (\gamma \rightarrow \psi), \Sigma_1 \vdash (\gamma \rightarrow \bigcirc\psi), \Sigma_2 \vdash (\gamma \rightarrow \bigcirc\bigcirc\psi), \cdots$ where $\Sigma = \bigcup \Sigma_i$ and each derivation is of order less than n. By hypothesis, we know that $\Sigma_0 \sim \{\beta\} \vdash (\beta \rightarrow (\gamma \rightarrow \psi))$, $\Sigma_1 \sim \{\beta\} \vdash (\beta \rightarrow (\gamma \rightarrow \bigcirc\psi))$, $\Sigma_2 \sim \{\beta\} \vdash (\beta \rightarrow (\gamma \rightarrow \bigcirc\bigcirc\psi)), \cdots$. By T, $\Sigma_0 \sim \{\beta\} \vdash ((\beta \& \gamma) \rightarrow \psi)$, $\Sigma_1 \sim \{\beta\} \vdash ((\beta \& \gamma) \rightarrow \bigcirc\psi)$, $\Sigma_2 \sim \{\beta\} \vdash ((\beta \& \gamma) \rightarrow \bigcirc\bigcirc\psi), \cdots$, By W, $\Sigma \sim \{\beta\} \vdash ((\beta \& \gamma) \rightarrow \Box\psi)$, and by T, $\Sigma \sim \{\beta\} \vdash (\beta \rightarrow \varphi)$.

We now establish completeness.

Theorem: TL^* is complete, i. e., for any set of formulae Σ, if $\Sigma \models \varphi$, then $\Sigma \vdash \varphi$.

Proof: If $\Sigma \models \varphi$, then $\Sigma \cup \{-\varphi\}$ has no model. Assuming that every consistent set of formulae has a model, we can conclude that $\Sigma \cup \{-\varphi\} \vdash p \& -p$. By the deduction theorem, $\Sigma \vdash -\varphi \rightarrow (p \& -p)$, and by T, $\Sigma \vdash \varphi$. Hence, completeness follows if we prove that every consistent set of formulae has a model.

Let Σ be any consistent set of formulae. Our proof that Σ has a model is based on the notion of a maximally consistent set as described in [2]. Enumerate all formulae of TL^*, and let φ_i be the *ith* formula of the enumeration. We construct a sequence of sets $\Gamma = \langle \Gamma_0, \Gamma_1, \cdots \rangle$ that determine a model.

---

3. This sense of *completeness* is often referred to as *strong-completeness*.

Note that in the construction whenever a set $\Lambda\cup\{-\Box\varphi\}$ is consistent, then there is some string α of $\bigcirc$'s such that $\Lambda\cup\{-\Box\varphi,\alpha-\varphi\}$ is consistent. If there were no such string, the deduction theorem implies that we could derive a contradiction from the first set using axiom (2) with T and W since we would have $\Lambda\vdash-\Box\varphi\rightarrow\varphi$, $\Lambda\vdash-\Box\varphi\rightarrow\bigcirc\varphi$, $\Lambda\vdash-\Box\varphi\rightarrow\bigcirc\bigcirc\varphi,\cdots$, and hence $\Lambda\vdash-\Box\varphi\rightarrow\Box\varphi$. We begin our construction by building Γ_0 from a sequence of sets Γ^i.

$\Gamma^0=\Sigma$

$\Gamma^i=\Gamma^{i-1}\cup\{\varphi_i\}$ if φ_i is not of the form $-\Box\psi$ and the resulting set is consistent.

$\Gamma^i=\Gamma^{i-1}\cup\{\varphi_i,\alpha-\psi\}$ if φ_i is of the form $-\Box\psi$ and can be consistently added to Γ^{i-1}, and where α is the shortest string of $\bigcirc$'s such that $\alpha-\psi$ can be consistently added to Γ^{i-1}.

$\Gamma^i=\Gamma^{i-1}$ otherwise.

$\Gamma_0=\Gamma^\omega$.

Given Γ_i, we construct Γ_{i+1} exactly as we constructed Γ_0 except that instead of using Σ for our base set Γ^0, we use $\{\varphi\colon \bigcirc\psi \text{ is in } \Gamma_i\}$. Note that this set is consistent if Γ_i is for consider any derivation $L_1,L_2,\cdots,L_n$ where L_n is $\varphi\&-\varphi$. Replace each L_i that is an axiom by the sequence of lines $<L_i,\Box L_i,A4,\bigcirc L_i>$, where $A4$ is axiom (4) with L_i substituted for φ; replace each L_i that is inferred by A by $\bigcirc L_i$; replace each L_i that is inferred by T by $<A2\text{–}3,\bigcirc L_i>$, where $A2\text{–}3$ is a sequence of applications of T and axioms (2) and (3) on the premises of the original inference to convert formulae of the form $\bigcirc-\psi$ and $\bigcirc(\psi\rightarrow\gamma)$ to $-\bigcirc\psi$ and $(\bigcirc\psi\rightarrow\bigcirc\gamma)$, respectively; replace each L_i that is inferred by F by $<L_i,A4,\bigcirc L_i>$, where $A4$ is as above; and replace each L_i that is inferred by W by the sequence $<\beta\rightarrow\Box\bigcirc\psi,\cdots,\beta\rightarrow\bigcirc\Box\psi>$ where $L_i=\beta\rightarrow\Box\psi$ and the string of dots is a derivation of the last member of the sequence from the first.[4] If the original sequence is a derivation of $(\varphi\&-\varphi)$ from our new Γ^0, then the result is a derivation of $\bigcirc(\varphi\&-\varphi)$ from Γ_i. But this means that Γ_i is inconsistent since $\vdash-\bigcirc(\varphi\&-\varphi)$ by T, F, and axioms (2) and (4). Since by hypothesis, Σ is consistent and no formula was added to Σ to render it inconsistent, we conclude that each Γ_i is consistent.

We define our model σ in terms of the sequence Γ. For any sentence letter φ, φ is true in s_i if $\varphi\in\Gamma_i$, and false otherwise. We show that for any formula φ, φ is true in s_i *iff* $\varphi\in\Gamma_i$. This shows that Σ has a model since $\Sigma\subset\Gamma_0$. To this end, define the *order* of a TL^* formula as follows:

---

4. Such a derivation is straight forward, but long. It is left to the reader.

$O[\varphi]=0$ if φ is a sentence letter.

$O[\varphi]=O[\psi]+1$ if φ is of the form $-\psi$, $\Box\psi$ or $\bigcirc\psi$.

$O[\varphi]=max[O[\psi],O[\gamma]]+1$ if φ is of the form $(\psi\rightarrow\gamma)$.

We prove that for all i and φ, φ is true in s_i *iff* $\varphi\in\Gamma_i$ by induction on the order of formulae. Assume that for all formulae of order less than n the hypothesis holds. We show that it holds for any formula φ of order n. φ has one of five forms:

1. If φ is a sentence letter than the hypothesis holds by construction.
2. If φ is of the form $-\psi$, then ψ falls under the induction hypothesis, i. e., ψ is true in s_i *iff* $\psi\in\Gamma_i$. Assume that $\varphi\in\Gamma_i$. If ψ were in Γ_i then Γ_i would be inconsistent. Hence, $\psi\notin\Gamma_i$ and by hypothesis, ψ is false in s_i. Therefore, φ is true. Going the other direction, assume that $\varphi\notin\Gamma_i$. If neither ψ nor $-\psi$ were in Γ_i, then it must be that neither could have been consistently added during construction. Assume that ψ occurs later than $-\psi$ in our enumeration of formulae. If ψ is our *mth* formula, then Γ^m is inconsistent with both ψ and $-\psi$, where Γ^m is Γ_i at stage m in its construction. But by T and the deduction theorem, this means that Γ^m is inconsistent, which is impossible. Hence, either ψ or $-\psi$ is in Γ_i, and if $\varphi\notin\Gamma_i$, then $\psi\in\Gamma_i$. But by hypothesis, $\psi\in\Gamma_i$ *iff* ψ is true in s_i. Therefore, if $\varphi\notin\Gamma_i$, then φ is false in s_i.
3. If φ is of the form $\psi\rightarrow\gamma$, then both ψ and γ fall under the induction hypothesis. Assume that $\varphi\in\Gamma_i$. If $\psi\notin\Gamma_i$, then ψ is false in s_i by hypothesis. Hence, φ is true. If $\psi\in\Gamma_i$, then $\gamma\in\Gamma_i$ since as shown in case (2) above if $\gamma\notin\Gamma_i$, then $-\gamma\in\Gamma_i$, rendering Γ_i inconsistent by T. By hypothesis, if ψ and γ are in Γ_i, then they are true. Therefore, φ is true. In the other direction, assume that $\varphi\notin\Gamma_i$. Hence, $-\varphi\in\Gamma_i$ as shown in case (2) above. Similarly, if $\psi\notin\Gamma_i$, then $-\psi\in\Gamma_i$, and Γ_i would be inconsistent. Hence, $\psi\in\Gamma_i$. If $\gamma\in\Gamma_i$, then Γ would also be inconsistent. So, $\gamma\notin\Gamma_i$. Hence, by hypothesis, ψ is true and γ is false in s_i. Hence, φ is false.
4. If φ is of the form $\Box\psi$, then ψ falls under the induction hypothesis. Assume that $\varphi\in\Gamma_i$. If there is a $j\geq i$ such that $\psi\notin\Gamma_j$, then let $n=j-i$ and let α be a (possibly empty) string of n O's. As above, if $\alpha\psi\notin\Gamma_i$, then $-\alpha\psi\in\Gamma_i$. But this would render Γ_i inconsistent by (repeated) application of axiom (4). Hence, $\alpha\psi\in\Gamma_i$, and by construction, $\psi\in\Gamma_j$. Therefore, $\psi\in\Gamma_j$

for all $j \geq i$, and by hypothesis, ψ is true in all s_j. This makes φ true in s_i. For the other direction, assume that $\varphi \notin \Gamma_i$. As above, $-\varphi \in \Gamma_i$. By construction, $\alpha - \psi \in \Gamma_i$ for some string of n O's α, and $-\psi \in \Gamma_{i+n}$. Since Γ_{i+n} is consistent, $\psi \notin \Gamma_{i+n}$. By hypothesis, ψ is false in s_{i+n}, and therefore, φ is false in s_i.

5 If φ is of the form $\bigcirc\psi$, then ψ falls under the induction hypothesis. Assume that $\varphi \in \Gamma_i$. By construction, $\psi \in \Gamma_{i+1}$. By hypothesis, ψ is true in s_{i+1}, and therefore, φ is true in s_i. In the other direction, assume that $\varphi \notin \Gamma_i$. As above, $-\varphi \in \Gamma_i$. Hence, by axiom (2) $\bigcirc - \psi \in \Gamma_i$, and by construction $-\psi \in \Gamma_{i+1}$. Since, Γ_{i+1} is consistent, $\psi \notin \Gamma_{i+1}$. By hypothesis, ψ is false in s_{i+1} and so φ is false in s_i.

4. Temporal Logic as a Specification Language

We have built a sound, complete system of temporal logic that includes schemata. Such a system allows us to freely use both syntactic and semantic considerations in reasoning about consequence, consistency, and totalness. However, before advocating an unbridled use of the system, an issue must be addressed.

As argued above, any system of temporal logic with schemata must have a derivation rule such as W if we are to be able to use the system for program specification. This is unfortunate since applications of W involve an infinite number of premises. As a consequence, quick implementation systems based on derivation, such as described in [1], are not likely to be developed for a useful system of temporal logic. Such implementation systems would have to be capable of independently preforming inductions that involve demonstrating, e. g., that $\Sigma \vdash p$ and that $\Sigma \vdash \alpha p$ implies that $\Sigma \vdash \alpha\bigcirc p$, where α is a (possibly empty) string of O's, and inferring that $\Sigma \vdash \Box p$. However, theorem provers are not yet that independent.

The moral seems clear. When dealing with absolute temporal constraints, the system of temporal logic developed here offers a viable approach. Unless we have absolute time constraints, however, we should make do without temporal operators. Talk of something holding in all future states in such a system is to be interpreted as saying that it holds at the end of any legal string of procedure calls. To say that something holds in the next state is to say that it holds after the next procedure call. Temporal logic should be reserved only for use as a last resort.

References:

1. J. Dixon, J McLean, and D. Parnas, "Rapid Prototyping by Means of Abstract Module Specifications Written as Trace Axioms," *ACM SIGSOFT Engineering Notes* **7** pp. 45-49 (1982).
2. L. Henkin, "The Completeness of First Order Functional Calculus," *Journal of Symbolic Logic* **14** pp. 159-166 (1949).
3. J. McLean, "A Formal Foundation for the Trace Method of Software Specification," NRL Report 4878, Naval Research Laboratory, Washington, D. C. 20375 (1982).
4. J. McLean, "A Formal Method for the Abstract Specification of Software," *Journal for the Association of Computing Machinery*, forthcoming.
5 P. Wolper, "Temporal Logic Can Be More Expressive," *IEEE Symposium on the Foundations of Computer Science* pp. 40-348 (1981).

Reasoning in Interval Temporal Logic

by

Ben Moszkowski[1,2] and Zohar Manna[1,3]

[1]Department of Computer Science, Stanford University, Stanford, CA 94305, USA

[2]From July, 1983: Computer Lab., Corn Exchange St., Cambridge Univ., England

[3]Applied Mathematics Deparment, Weizmann Institute of Science, Rehovot, Israel

Abstract

Predicate logic is a powerful and general descriptive formalism with a long history of development. However, since the logic's underlying semantics have no notion of time, statements such as "*I increases by* 2" cannot be directly expressed. We discuss *interval temporal logic* (ITL), a formalism that augments standard predicate logic with operators for time-dependent concepts. Our earlier work used ITL to specify and reason about hardware. In this paper we show how ITL can also directly capture various control structures found in conventional programming languages. Constructs are given for treating assignment, iteration, sequential and parallel computations and scoping. The techniques used permit specification and reasoning about such algorithms as concurrent Quicksort. We compare ITL with the logic-based programming languages Lucid and Prolog.

§1 Introduction

As a tool for specification and reasoning, predicate logic has many attractive features. Here are a few:

- Every formula and expression has a simple semantic interpretation
- Concepts such as recursion can be characterized and explored.
- Subsets can be used for programming (e.g., Prolog [5]).
- Theorems about formulas and expressions can themselves be stated and proved within the framework of predicate logic.
- Reasoning in predicate logic can often be reduced to propositional logic.
- Decades of research lie behind the overall formalism.

However, predicate logic has no built-in notion of time and therefore cannot directly express such dynamic actions as

"*I increases by* 2"

or

"*The values of A and B are exchanged.*"

We get around this limitation by using an extension of linear-time temporal logic [6,10] called *interval temporal logic* (ITL). The behavior of programs and hardware devices can often be decomposed into successively smaller periods or intervals of activity. These intervals provide a convenient framework for introducing quantitative timing details. State transitions can be characterized by properties relating the initial and final values of variables over intervals of time.

We originally used ITL to specify and reason about timing-dependent hardware. Moszkowski, Halpern and Manna [4,7,8] give details about ITL's syntax and semantics and also show how to describe hardware ranging from delay elements up to a clocked multiplier and an ALU bit slice. In this paper we show how ITL can also directly capture various control structures found in programming languages. Constructs are given for treating assignment, iteration, sequential and parallel computations and scoping.

This work was supported in part by the National Science Foundation under a Graduate Fellowship, Grants MCS79-09495, MCS80-06930 and MCS81-11586, by DARPA under Contract N00039-82-C-0250, and by the United States Air Force Office of Scientific Research under Grant AFOSR-81-0014.

§2 Expressing Programming Concepts in ITL

This section will show how ITL can express a variety of useful programming concepts. We assume that the reader is familiar with the syntax and semantics of first-order ITL as described by us in [4] and [8]. Upper-case variables such as A and I are signals and vary over states. Lower-case variables such as b and i are static and thus time-invariant. In general, variables such as A and b can range over all the elements of the underlying data domain. On the other hand, J and n range over natural numbers. The variable X always equals one of the truth values *true* and *false*.

Assignment

The assignment $A \rightarrow B$ is true for an interval if the signal B ends up with the signal A's initial value. If desired, we can reverse the direction of the arrow:

$$B \leftarrow A \quad \equiv_{\text{def}} \quad A \rightarrow B.$$

Assignment in ITL only affects variables explicitly mentioned; the values of other variables do not necessarily remain fixed. For example, the formulas

$$I \leftarrow (I+2)$$

and

$$[I \leftarrow (I+2)] \wedge [J \leftarrow J]$$

are not equivalent.

Example (Leaving the elements of a vector unchanged):

A vector U ends up unchanged iff all of its elements end up unchanged:

$$\models \quad (U \leftarrow U) \equiv \forall 0 \leq i < |U|. (U[i] \leftarrow U[i]).$$

For example, if U has 3 elements, the following formula leaves U unchanged:

$$(U[0] \leftarrow U[0]) \wedge (U[1] \leftarrow U[1]) \wedge (U[2] \leftarrow U[2]).$$

This illustrates a simple form of parallel processing.

Example (Swapping two variables):

We define the predicate $A \leftrightarrow B$ to be true iff the values of the parameters A and B are swapped:

$$A \leftrightarrow B \quad \equiv_{\text{def}} \quad [(A \leftarrow B) \wedge (B \leftarrow A)]$$

A variable is swapped with itself iff it ends up unchanged:

$$\models \quad (A \leftrightarrow A) \equiv (A \leftarrow A).$$

If U and V are both vectors of length n then U and V are swapped iff their corresponding elements are swapped:

$$\models \quad (U \leftrightarrow V) \equiv \forall 0 \leq i < n. (U[i] \leftrightarrow V[i]).$$

Example (In-place computation of maximum of two numbers):

Let the function $max(i,j)$ equal the maximum of the two values i and j. We can define $max(i,j)$ by means of a condition expression:

$$max(i,j) \quad =_{\text{def}} \quad \textit{if } i \geq j \textit{ then } i \textit{ else } j.$$

The following two ITL formulas are then semantically equivalent:

$$I \leftarrow max(I,J)$$

$$\textit{if } I \geq J \textit{ then } (I \leftarrow I) \textit{ else } (I \leftarrow J)$$

Example (*In-place sorting*):

Suppose we have a function $sort(U)$ that given a list U equals U in sorted order. The following predicate $Sort(U)$ then expresses that U is sorted in place:

$$Sort(U) \quad \equiv_{\text{def}} \quad U \leftarrow sort(U).$$

This is not the only way to express *Sort*. Let $bagval(U)$ be a function that gives the bag (multiset) containing exactly the elements of U and let the predicate $sorted(U)$ be true of U iff the U's elements are sorted. An alternative way to express *Sort* can then be given by the following property:

$$\models \quad Sort(U) \equiv \big([bagval(U) \leftarrow bagval(U)] \land fin[sorted(U)]\big).$$

This says that a list is sorted in place iff the list's elements remain unchanged but end up in order.

Example (*In-place parallel doubling of the values of a vector's elements*):

Here is a formula that represents the parallel doubling of the elements of a vector U:

$$Double(U) \quad \equiv_{\text{def}} \quad \forall\, 0 \le i < |U|.\, (U[i] \leftarrow 2U[i]).$$

The property below expresses *Double* recursively:

$$\models \quad Double(U) \quad \equiv \quad if\ |U| > 0\ then\big[(head(U) \leftarrow 2head(U)) \land Double(tail(U))\big].$$

Here the function $head(U)$ always equals U's leftmost element and $tail(U)$ equals the remainder of U:

$$head(U) =_{\text{def}} U[0] \qquad tail(U) =_{\text{def}} U[1 \text{ to } |U| - 1].$$

For example,

$$head(\langle 1,3,0\rangle) = 1, \quad tail(\langle 1,3,0\rangle) = \langle 3,0\rangle.$$

The behavior of *head* and *tail* on the empty list $\langle\ \rangle$ is left unspecified. The logical construct *if* w_1 *then* w_2 is the same as the implication $w_1 \supset w_2$.

Example (*In-place parallel reversal of vector elements*):

The predicate $Rev(U)$ specifies an in-place reversal of the vector U's elements:

$$Rev(U) \quad \equiv_{\text{def}} \quad \forall\, 0 \le i < n.(U[i] \leftarrow U[n-i-1]),$$

where $n = |U|$. If the function $reverse(U)$ equals the reverse of the vector U, we can describe *Rev* as shown below:

$$\models \quad Rev(U) \equiv [U \leftarrow reverse(U)]$$

The following property expresses $Rev(U)$ by symmetrically exchanging pairs of U's elements in parallel:

$$\models \quad Rev(U) \equiv \forall\, 0 \le i < \lceil n \div 2\rceil.\, (U[i] \leftrightarrow U[n-i-1])$$

For example, if the vector U has 5 elements, then $Rev(U)$ is equivalent to the formula

$$(U[0] \leftrightarrow U[4]) \land (U[1] \leftrightarrow U[3]) \land (U[2] \leftrightarrow U[2]).$$

The *gets* Construct

We now introduce the *gets* construct, which is used for repeatedly assigning one expression to another:

$$A\ gets\ B \quad \equiv_{\text{def}} \quad keep(B = \bigcirc A),$$

where the operator *keep* is defined as

$$keep\ w \quad \equiv_{\text{def}} \quad \boxdot(\neg empty \supset w).$$

The effect of *gets* is that B's current value always equals A's next value. The *keep* construct ensures that we don't "run off" the end of the interval. Note that *gets* is semantically equivalent to the unit delay

$$B\ del\ A$$

described by us in [4,7,8]. It is also similar to the operator "*followed by*" in the programming language Lucid [2].

Example (*Synchronous incrementing of a variable*):

The predicate $gen^n\, I$ initializes I to 0 and then repeatedly increments I by 1 until I equals n:

$$gen^n\, I \quad \equiv_{\mathrm{def}} \quad beg(I = 0) \wedge (I \; gets \; I + 1) \wedge halt(I = n).$$

Example (*Strength reduction*):

The next formula has J run through $0^2, 1^2, \ldots, n^2$.

$$gen^n\, I \wedge J \approx I^2.$$

Rather that compute I^2 at each step, we can initialize J to 0 and continuously add $2I + 1$ to it:

$$gen^n\, I \wedge beg(J = 0) \wedge J \; gets \; (J + 2I + 1).$$

This is semantically equivalent to the previous formula but uses simpler operators. These formulas illustrate a way of treating *strength reduction* in ITL. The expression $2I+1$ can itself be strength-reduced if desired.

Example (*Assigning a list the sequence* $\langle 0, \ldots, 2n-1 \rangle$):

The combined formula

$$(gen^{2n}\, I) \wedge (L = \langle\,\rangle) \wedge (L \; gets \; [L \,\|\, \langle I \rangle])$$

has the list variable L end up equal to the value $\langle 0, \ldots, 2n-1 \rangle$. We use the operator $\|$ to append two lists together. Here is an example:

$$\langle 1, 2 \rangle \,\|\, \langle 5, 0 \rangle \quad = \quad \langle 1, 2, 5, 0 \rangle.$$

Example (*Simple pipeline*):

If U is a numerical vector of length $m + 1$, the following formula sends twice the value of each element of U to the next:

$$\forall 0 \le i < m. \, (U[i+1] \; gets \; 2U[i]).$$

For example, if m equals 3, this is equivalent to the formula

$$(U[1] \; gets \; 2U[0]) \wedge (U[2] \; gets \; 2U[1]) \wedge (U[3] \; gets \; 2U[2]).$$

This illustrates a way of expressing highly parallel pipelines in ITL. By using the quantifier $\forall$, we can obtain an arbitrary number of simultaneously executing processes.

Example (*Keeping a variable stable*):

The predicate $stb\, A$ is true if the variable A has a fixed value throughout the entire interval:

$$stb\, A \quad \equiv_{\mathrm{def}} \quad \exists b. \, (A \approx b).$$

We can achieve *stb* by means of *gets*:

$$\models \quad stb\, A \equiv (A \; gets \; A).$$

Example (*Greatest common divisor*):

The predicate *GetsGcd* computes the greatest common divisor of two numbers:

$$GetsGcd(M, N) \quad \equiv_{\mathrm{def}} \quad M \; gets \; (N \bmod M) \wedge N \; gets \; M \wedge halt(M = 0),$$

where the construct $halt\, w$ is true for intervals that terminate the first time the formula w is true:

$$halt\, w \quad \equiv_{\mathrm{def}} \quad \boxdot(w \equiv empty).$$

Thus $halt\, w$ can be thought of as a kind of wait-statement. Here is a corresponding correctness property for *GetsGcd*:

$$\models \quad GetsGcd(M, N) \supset [N \leftarrow gcd(M, N)],$$

where the function $gcd(i, j)$ equals the greatest common divisor of i and j. The following property shows that throughout the computation, M and N's *gcd* remains stable:

$$\models \quad GetsGcd(M, N) \supset stb[gcd(M, N)].$$

Measuring the length of an interval

We can view the formula

$$len = e$$

as an abbreviation for

$$\exists I.[beg(I = e) \wedge (I \; gets \; [I - 1]) \wedge halt(I = 0)].$$

The formula is true exactly of intervals with length e and illustrates how to localize or "hide" a variable such as I by means of existential quantification. This is similar to a *begin-block* in conventional block-structured programming languages. No conflicts arise when such a formula is combined with others containing variables named I. We use this technique elsewhere in this work.

Example (*Constraining the length of a computation*):

By using the construct *len*, we can look at the length of computations. For example, the formula

$$(I \leftarrow I^2) \wedge (len \leq I)$$

specifies that I is squared in at most I steps.

Iteration

An interval can be broken up into an arbitrary number of successive subintervals, each satisfying some formula w. For example, we use the construct w^3 as an abbreviation for

$$w; w; w$$

We can extend ITL to include formulas of the form w^*; this is the Kleene closure of *semicolon*. Other constructs such as while-loops are also expressible within ITL:

$$while \; w_1 \; do \; w_2 \quad \equiv_{def} \quad [(beg[w_1] \wedge w_2)^* \wedge fin(\neg w_1)]$$

ITL can also be augmented with iteration of the form w^e where w is a formula and e is an arithmetic expression. This repeats w for e times in succession.

For-loops are expressible by means of while-loops. For example, the construct

$$for \; 0 \leq I < n \; do \, (J \leftarrow J + I)$$

can be expanded to

$$beg(I = 0) \wedge while \, (I < n) \; do \, ([J \leftarrow J + I] \wedge [I \leftarrow I + 1])$$

Example (*Sequential doubling of the values of a vector's elements*):

The following formula achieves the predicate *Double*(U) by sequentially running through the elements of the vector U and doubling each:

$$\models \quad [for \; 0 \leq K < |U| \; do \; Alter(U, K, 2U[K])] \supset Double(U)$$

The predicate $Alter(U, i, a)$ sets the i-th element of U to the value a and leaves the other elements unchanged. We can define *Alter* in various ways. Here is one:

$$Alter(U, i, a) \quad \equiv_{def} \quad \forall 0 \leq j < |U|. [if \; i = j \; then \; (U[j] \leftarrow a) \; else \; (U[j] \leftarrow U[j])].$$

Sometimes a formal parameter of a predicate such as *Alter* has behavior that is slightly incompatible with that of the corresponding actual parameter. For example, the formula

$$Alter(U, K, 2U[K])$$

contains the signals K and $2U[K]$ where static objects are expected. We therefore view the formula as an abbreviation for

$$\exists i, a. [beg(i = K \wedge a = 2U[K]) \wedge Alter(U, i, a)].$$

This form of *temporal conversion* corresponds to *call-by-value* in conventional programming languages.

Example (In-place sequential reversal of a vector):

The next formula reverses U by serially swapping pairs of U's elements:

$$for\, 0 \le K < \lfloor |U| \div 2 \rfloor \; do \; Swap(U, K, |U| - K - 1),$$

where the predicate $Swap(U, i, j)$ exchanges the i-th and j-th elements of U, leaving the other elements unchanged. We can define *Swap* in a manner similar to the predicate *Alter* shown above. Note that sequential reversal provides one way to implement the parallel reversal computation discussed earlier.

Example (Computation of greatest common divisor using while-loop):

As mentioned previously, we can specify the in-place computation of the greatest common divisor of two variables M and N as follows:

$$N \leftarrow gcd(M, N).$$

The while-loop below implies this:

$$\begin{array}{l} while\,(M \neq 0)\; do \\ \qquad if\,(M > N)\; then\,(M \leftrightarrow N)\; else\,([M \leftarrow M] \wedge [N \leftarrow N - M]). \end{array}$$

Example (Expressing gets using a loop):

The construct *gets* can be expressed using iteration:

$$\models \quad (A\; gets\; B) \equiv (skip \wedge [A \leftarrow B])^*.$$

Based on the semantics of while-loops and the predicate *gets*, we can rewrite the while-loop

$$while\,(I \neq 0)\; do\,(skip \wedge [I \leftarrow I - 1] \wedge [J \leftarrow J + I])$$

as

$$halt(I = 0) \wedge (I\; gets\; I - 1) \wedge (J\; gets\; J + I).$$

This gives us a decentralized, concurrent view of the computation.

Example (In-place partitioning of a vector):

The predicate $Partition(U, I)$ specifies that the vector U of numbers is reorganized in place so that all elements in positions less than the variable I are less than $U[I]$ and the elements in higher positions are at least as large as $U[I]$:

$$Partition(U, I) \quad \equiv_{def} \quad ([bagval(U) \leftarrow bagval(U)] \wedge fin[partition(U, I)])$$

where the predicate $partition(u, i)$ is true iff u is partitioned about the i-th element:

$$partition(u, i) \quad \equiv_{def} \quad \forall 0 \le j < |u|. [(j \ge i) \equiv (u[j] \ge u[i])].$$

The following property shows how to achieve *Partition* in an algorithmic manner:

$$\models \quad [if\, |U| > 0 \; then \; (Part(U, I); [Swap(U, 0, I) \wedge (I \leftarrow I)])] \supset Partition(U, I).$$

We use *Part* to partition $tail(U)$ into elements $< U[0]$ and $\ge U[0]$:

$$\begin{array}{l} Part(U, I) \quad \equiv_{def} \\ \qquad \exists J. \left[beg(I = 1 \wedge J = |U| - 1) \wedge while\,(I \le J)\; do\; PartitionStep(U, I, J)\right]. \end{array}$$

Note that *Part* uses a localized variable J. Each iteration step of the while loop refers to $Partition(U, I, J)$, which either leaves U unchanged or swaps $U[I]$ with $U[J]$:

$$\begin{array}{l} PartitionStep(U, I, J) \quad \equiv_{def} \\ \qquad if\,(U[I] \ge U[0])\; then\, \left[(I \leftarrow I) \wedge (J \leftarrow J - 1) \wedge Swap(U, I, J)\right] \\ \qquad else\, \left[(I \leftarrow I + 1) \wedge (J \leftarrow J) \wedge (U \leftarrow U)\right]. \end{array}$$

Example (*Parallel Quicksorting of a vector*):

Using the predicate *Partition*, we can describe an in-place Quicksort algorithm that partitions a vector U and recursively sorts the resulting sections in parallel. The following property of in-place sorting is used.

$$\models \quad (\textit{if } |U| > 0 \textit{ then } \exists I.\, [\textit{Partition}(U,I); \textit{SortParts}(U,I)]) \supset \textit{Sort}(U),$$

where the predicate *SortParts* recursively sorts the two partitions of U in parallel:

$$\textit{SortParts}(U,j) \quad \equiv_{\text{def}} \quad \textit{Sort}(U[0 \text{ to } j-1]) \wedge \textit{Sort}(U[j+1 \text{ to} |U|-1]) \wedge (U[j] \leftarrow U[j]).$$

Here, for example, the expression $U[0 \text{ to } j-1]$ equals the list

$$\langle U[0], \ldots, U[j-1] \rangle.$$

We leave the "pivot" element $U[j]$ unchanged. An actual implementation of this form of sorting might execute more sequentially.

§3 Markers

As mentioned earlier, we can iterate a temporal formula w by means of the construct

$$w^*.$$

A useful variant of this has an explicit Boolean flag X that is true exactly at the end-points of the individual iterative steps:

$$\textit{beg}\, X \wedge ([\bigcirc\, \textit{halt}\, X] \wedge w)^*.$$

Variables such as X are called *markers* since they mark off the loop's steps. We abbreviate the above form of looping by means of the operator *cycle*:

$$\textit{cycle}_{w_1}\, w_2 \quad \equiv_{\text{def}} \quad [\textit{beg}\, w_1 \wedge ([\bigcirc\, \textit{halt}\, w_1] \wedge w_2)].$$

Here the formula w_1 represents the marker and w_2 gives the individual iterative steps. From the semantics of ITL, every loop has an implicit marker. For example, the formulas

$$(I \leftarrow I+1)^* \qquad \text{and} \qquad \exists X.\, \textit{cycle}_X(I \leftarrow I+1)^*$$

are semantically equivalent.

When a loop's marker is made explicit, we can sometimes express the loop as smaller mutually synchronized loops that operate in parallel. For example, the loop

$$\textit{cycle}_X([I \leftarrow I-1] \wedge [J \leftarrow J+I])$$

can be represented as

$$\textit{cycle}_X(I \leftarrow I-1) \wedge \textit{cycle}_X(J \leftarrow J+I).$$

The individual steps of the loops start and end at the same times. This demonstrates one use of markers since, for instance, the loop

$$([I \leftarrow I-1] \wedge [J \leftarrow J+I])^*$$

is not readily decomposible without some additional means of synchronization.

If the marker X is identically *true*, then each step of the loop is reduced to having unit length. Thus, the construct

$$\textit{cycle}_{\textit{true}}(I \leftarrow I-1)$$

is equivalent to the formula

$$(\textit{skip} \wedge [I \leftarrow I-1])^*$$

and therefore has the same meaning as

$$I \textit{ gets } (I-1).$$

Markers can also be used with while-loops. We define a while-loop with an explicit marker formula w_1 as follows:

$$\textit{while}_{w_1}\, w_2 \textit{ do } w_3 \quad \equiv_{\text{def}} \quad \textit{beg}\, w_1 \wedge \textit{while } w_2 \textit{ do } ([\bigcirc\, \textit{halt}\, w_1] \wedge w_3).$$

For instance, the loop

$$\textit{while}_X\, (I \neq 0) \textit{ do } ([I \leftarrow I-1] \wedge [J \leftarrow J+I])$$

can be alternatively expressed by means of the following conjunction of three formulas:

$$\textit{halt}(I=0) \wedge \textit{cycle}_X(I \leftarrow I-1) \wedge \textit{cycle}_X(J \leftarrow J+I).$$

§4 Data Transmission

In ITL we can use shared variables for communication between different processes. Given an interval and some variable A, it is convenient to speak of the *trace* of A. We define the function $tr(A)$ to be the sequence of A's values in all but the last state of the interval:

$$tr(A) \quad =_{\text{def}} \quad \langle (\bigcirc^j A) : 0 \leq j < len \rangle.$$

Thus, in an interval of length 2, the value of $tr(A)$ is the sequence

$$\langle A, \bigcirc A \rangle.$$

Note that in an interval of length 0, $tr(A)$ equals the empty sequence $\langle\,\rangle$. A variant of $tr(A)$ that doesn't ignore that interval's last state can also be defined.

Example (*Transmitting the elements of a list*):

The formula $WriteList_I(L)$ outputs the contents of the list L from left to right into the variable I:

$$WriteList_I(L) \quad \equiv_{\text{def}} \quad [tr(I) = L].$$

The next property shows a constructive way to achieve *WriteList*:

$$\models \quad (keep[I = head(L)] \wedge L \; gets \; [tail(L)] \wedge halt[L = \langle\,\rangle]) \supset WriteList_I(L).$$

The predicate $ReadList_I(L)$ is similar to $WriteList_I(L)$ but requires that L end up with I's trace:

$$ReadList_I(L) \quad \equiv_{\text{def}} \quad [L \leftarrow tr(I)].$$

Example (*Writing a set in sorted order*):

The predicate $WriteSorted_I(S)$ outputs the elements of the finite set S in sorted order to the variable I:

$$WriteSorted_I(S) \quad \equiv_{\text{def}} \quad WriteList_I(sort(S)).$$

For simplicity, we assume that S contains only numbers. The following formula gives a way to achieve *WriteSorted*:

$$keep(I = \min S) \wedge S \; gets \; (S \sim \{I\}) \wedge halt(S = \{\,\}).$$

The ITL *keep* construct ensures that the variable I always equals the minimum element of S except perhaps in the computation's last state. The *gets* subformula continually deletes I's value from S. As the computation runs, S is reduced to being empty. In the combined formula

$$WriteSorted_I(S) \wedge ReadList_I(L),$$

the list L ends containing the initial elements of S in sorted order:

$$\models \quad [WriteSorted_I(S) \wedge ReadList_I(L)] \supset [L \leftarrow sort(S)].$$

For example, if S initially equals the set $\{3, 5, 1\}$ then upon termination, L equals $\langle 1, 3, 5 \rangle$. Note that bags (multisets) can be used instead of sets if duplicate data values arise.

Example (*Synchronous walk through an S-expression*):

An *S-expression* is either an *atom* or a pair $\langle a, b \rangle$ where a and b are themselves S-expressions. For our purposes, we restrict atoms to being nonnegative integers. Here are some simple S-expressions:

$$3, \quad \langle 4, 1 \rangle, \quad \langle \langle 2, 3 \rangle, 5 \rangle.$$

The predicate $atom(t)$ is true iff the S-expression t is an atom. If t is not atomic then $left(t)$ and $right(t)$ access t's two parts. We can inductively define the *frontier* of an S-expression as follows:

$$frontier(t) \quad \equiv_{\text{def}} \quad if \; atom(t) \; then \; \langle t \rangle \; else \; [frontier(left(t)) \,\|\, frontier(right(t))].$$

For instance, the frontiers of the S-expressions given above are respectively

$$\langle 3\rangle, \quad \langle 4,1\rangle, \quad \langle 2,3,5\rangle.$$

The predicate *WriteFrontier* specifies that the frontier of the S-expression T is output to the variable I:

$$WriteFrontier_I(T) \quad \equiv_{\text{def}} \quad WriteList_I(frontier(T)).$$

The following property shows how to recursively use *WriteFrontier* to output the frontier of a static S-expression t:

$$\begin{aligned}\models\quad & WriteFrontier_I(t) \equiv \\ & \quad \textit{if}\; atom(t)\; \textit{then}\,[beg(I=t) \wedge skip] \\ & \quad \textit{else}\,\big[WriteFrontier_I(left(t));\; WriteFrontier_I(right(t))\big].\end{aligned}$$

An S-expression T's frontier can for example be entered into a list L as shown by the property

$$\models \quad [WriteFrontier_I(T) \wedge ReadList_I(L)] \supset [L \leftarrow frontier(T)].$$

§5 Comparison with the Programming Languages Lucid and Prolog

The innovative programming language *Lucid* developed by Ashcroft and Wadge [1,2,3] is similar to parts of ITL. For example, the ITL formula

$$beg(I=0 \wedge J=0) \wedge I \; gets \; (I+1) \wedge J \; gets \; (J+I)$$

roughly corresponds to the Lucid program

$$\begin{aligned} I &= 0 \; fby \; (I+1) \\ J &= 0 \; fby \; (J+I). \end{aligned}$$

Not surprisingly, many properties of *gets* involving such concepts as strength reduction can also be handled in Lucid. On the other hand, the Algol-like ITL formula

$$while\,(I \neq 0)\; do\,([I \leftarrow I-1] \wedge [J \leftarrow J+I])$$

has no direct analog in Lucid. Lucid's underlying semantics are rather different from ITL's since Lucid uses a three-valued logic and has no notion of global state. Instead, each variable has an infinite sequence of values.

Prolog [5] is based on an interesting subset of predicate logic in which formulas can be interpreted as applicative programs. Because Prolog has no sense of time, ITL formulas cannot in general be directly expressed in it. For example, there is nó true analog in Prolog to ITL's while-loops and assigments. In practice, side effects are permitted in Prolog, although the language's core is not really designed to handle them.

§6 Future Research Directions

Let use now consider some aspects of ITL that require further investigation.

Temporal types and higher-order objects

A theory of temporal types needs to be developed. This should provide various ways of constructing and comparing types. Given two predicates p and q, we form the predicate $p \times q$ which is true for any pair whose first element satisfies p and whose second element satisfies q. For example, the formula

$$(nat \times bool)(\langle 3, true\rangle)$$

is true. In general, we write such a test as

$$\langle 3, true\rangle\colon (nat \times bool).$$

The operator $\times$ extends to n-element tuples:

$$p_1 \times \cdots \times p_n,$$

where $p_1, \ldots, p_n$ are unary predicates. In addition, the construct p^n is equivalent to n repetitions of p. For instance, the test

$$a\colon nat^3$$

is true if a is a triple of natural numbers. The predicate p^* is true for vectors of arbitrary, possibly null length, whose elements all satisfy p. Thus, the type $bool^*$ is true for all vectors of truth values. The type $sig(bool^*)$ is true for any Boolean vector signal with a possibly varying length.

The predicate $struct(X_1\colon p_1, \ldots, X_n\colon p_n)$ checks for tuples whose elements have field names $X_1, \ldots, X_n$ and satisfy the respective types $p_1, \ldots, p_n$. For example, the predicate

$$struct(X\colon nat, Y\colon bool^2)$$

is true for the tuple

$$\langle X\colon 3, Y\colon \langle true, false\rangle\rangle.$$

Note that two types can be semantically equivalent. For example, the types $sig(bool^2)$ and $[sig(bool)]^2$ have the same meaning. On the other hand, the types $sig(bool^*)$ and $[sig(bool)]^*$ are not equivalent. The type $sig(bool^*)$ is true for any object that is always a Boolean vector signal with a possibly varying length. In contrast, the type $[sig(bool)]^*$ requires that the object's length be fixed over time:

$$\models \quad A\colon [sig(bool)]^* \;\equiv\; [A\colon sig(bool^*) \;\wedge\; stb|A|].$$

Type constructs of the form p^* have other uses. For example, we can define the predicate *incr* to increment a variable I by 1:

$$incr(I) \quad \equiv_{\text{def}} \quad (I \leftarrow I+1).$$

Then given a vector U, the formula

$$U\colon incr^*$$

specifies that each element of U is incremented by 1 in parallel. This technique is similar to the *mapcar* function of Lisp.

It would be interesting to have a semantics of higher-order temporal objects such as time-dependent functionals. Perhaps a suitable variant of proposition ITL can facilitate some sort of Gödelization by representing all values as temporal formulas. Alternatively, an encoding like that used by Scott [11,12] in developing a model of the typeless lambda calculus might work. However, we wish to strongly resist the introduction of partial values. One concession we make in this direction is to not require that every function have a fixed point.

Projection

Sometimes it is desirable to examine a computation at certain points in time and ignore all intermediate states. This can be done using the *temporal projection* construct $w_1 \,\Pi\, w_2$. For example, the formula

$$X \,\Pi\, (I \; gets \; [I+1])$$

is true if I increments by 1 over each successive pair of the states where X is true. Variables like X serve as markers for measuring time and facilitate different levels of atomicity. If two parts of a system are active at different times or are running at different rates, markers can be constructed to project away the asynchrony.

Other definitions of projection are also possible. For example, a *synchronous* form can be defined as follows:

$$w_1 \; sim \; w_2 \quad \equiv_{\text{def}} \quad (beg\, w_1 \;\wedge\; fin\, w_1 \;\wedge\; [w_1 \,\Pi\, w_2]).$$

This forces the marker formula w_1 to be true in an interval's initial and final states. We can view this construct as *simulating* the formula w_2 at at rate given by w_1; hence the name "*sim*." For example, the formula

$$X \; sim \; [ReadList_I(L)]$$

reads the variable I into the list L at the rate indicated by X.

In section 3, we showed how to express iterative constructs by means of markers: For example, the following loop has X as a marker:

$$cycle_X([I\ gets\ I+1] \wedge [J\ gets\ J+I]).$$

All loops have implicit markers that are accessible through existential quantification. This provides a general means for identifying the end points of the iteration steps and extracting them using projection. We feel that markers and projection provide a way to decoupled low-level computational details from high-level ones.

Tempura, a prototype programming language based on ITL

Moszkowski and Manna [9] present a prototype programming language called *Tempura* that is based on ITL. Along with the programming languages Lucid and Prolog, Tempura has the property of having a semantics based on logic. Much work remains ahead in exploring this temporal approach to language design and developing practical techniques for specifying, executing, transforming, synthesizing and verifying Tempura programs. Perhaps the state sequences of temporal logic can also be used as a convenient basis for logics of, say, formal languages, typesetting and music. More generally, temporal logic may provide a semantics of both time and space.

§7 Conclusions

Interval temporal logic has constructs for dealing with such programming concepts as assignment, iteration and computation length. Because ITL is a logic, programs and properties can be stated in the same formalism. Unlike conventional first-order logic, ITL can directly express computations requiring a notion of change. Moszkowski, Halpern and Manna [4,7,8] have shown that ITL also provides a basis for describing timing-dependent hardware involving clocking and propagation delay. ITL-based programming languages such as Tempura [9] will be able to take advantage of this versatility. Thus, ITL appears to have a wide range of application.

Acknowledgements

We wish to thank Martin Abadi, Joe Halpern, John Hobby and Yoni Malachi for stimulating conversations and suggestions.

References

1. E. A. Ashcroft and W. W. Wadge. "Lucid: A formal system for writing and proving programs." *SIAM Journal of Computing 5*, 3 (Sept. 1976), 336–354.
2. E. A. Ashcroft and W. W. Wadge. "Lucid, a nonprocedural language with iteration." *Communications of the ACM 20*, 7 (July 1977), 519–526.
3. E. A. Ashcroft and W. W. Wadge. *Lucid, the Data Flow Programming Language.* To be published.
4. J. Halpern, Z. Manna and B. Moszkowski. A hardware semantics based on temporal intervals. Proceedings of the 10-th International Colloquium on Automata, Languages and Programming, Barcelona, Spain, July, 1983.
5. R. Kowalski. *Logic for Problem Solving.* Elsevier North Holland, Inc., New York, 1979.
6. Z. Manna and A. Pnueli. Verification of concurrent programs: The temporal framework. In R. S. Boyer and J. S. Moore, editors, *The Correctness Problem in Computer Science*, pages 215–273, Academic Press, New York, 1981.
7. B. Moszkowski. A temporal logic for multi-level reasoning about hardware. Proceedings of the 6-th International Symposium on Computer Hardware Description Languages, Pittsburgh, Pennsylvania, May, 1983, pages 79–90.

8. B. Moszkowski. *Reasoning about Digital Circuits.* PhD Thesis, Department of Computer Science, Stanford University, 1983.

9. B. Moszkowski and Z. Manna. Temporal logic as a programming language. In preparation.

10. N. Rescher and A. Urquart. *Temporal Logic.* Springer-Verlag, New York, 1971.

11. D. Scott. "Data types as lattices." *SIAM Journal of Computing 5*, 3 (Sept. 1976), 522–587.

12. J. E. Stoy. *Denotational Semantics: The Scott-Strachey Approach to Programming Language Theory.* MIT Press, Cambridge, Masachusetts, 1977.

HOARE'S LOGIC FOR PROGRAMS WITH PROCEDURES -
WHAT HAS BEEN ACHIEVED ?

Ernst-Rüdiger Olderog
Institut für Informatik, Universität Kiel
Programming Research Group, Oxford University

1. Introduction

Many different formalisms or logics have been developed for proving programs correct (cf. e.g. [Ko]). This paper looks at the traditional Hoare's logic for partial correctness and tries to assess what has been achieved over the past years. This review is done for programs with procedures because they require the most sophisticated arguments in Hoare's logic and still offer challenging questions (see Sec. 10).

The idea of Hoare's logic [Ho 1] is to find a formal proof system $\mathcal{H}$ which captures the true partial correctness formulas $\{P\}\pi\{Q\}$. Here P,Q are logical formulas taken from some assertion language LF and π is a program in the considered programming language L. $\mathcal{H}$ should be a *Hoare calculus*, i.e. its proof rules should be

- decidable,
- syntax-directed, and
- work schematically,

i.e. independently of the underlying data structures. The concept of *capturing* the true partial correctness formulas is formalized by requiring that $\mathcal{H}$ should be

- sound and
- relatively complete

for L [Co]. Since soundness of $\mathcal{H}$ is usually easy to establish, the main concern has to be about completeness.

In this paper we show how recent completeness (incompleteness) results on Hoare's logic for programs with procedures can be explained, in fact visualized, by looking at the *structure trees* of theses programs. We argue that attempts to find complete Hoare calculi can be considered as attempts to understand the construction principles of the structure trees. Once these principles are understood, seemingly unrelated issues such as runtime behaviour and partial correctness can be treated on a uniform basis.

2. Basic Concepts

We start from a *signature* Sig with function and relation symbols and (simple) variables $x,y,\ldots \in$ SV. Sig determines *expressions* $e \in$ EX, *Boolean expressions* $b \in$ BE, and *(logical) formulas* $P,Q,\ldots \in$ LF. At the moment these are all first-order constructs, but later we will add (weak) *second-order* formulas to LF.

Since the syntax of our programming languages L depends on EX and BE, the *semantics* $\Sigma_{\mathcal{I}}$ of L involves an *interpretation* $\mathcal{I}$ of Sig. $\mathcal{I}$ consists of a domain $\mathcal{D}_{\mathcal{I}}$, assigns meanings to function and relation symbols in Sig, and induces the set $\mathcal{St}_{\mathcal{I}}$ of states. Then $\Sigma_{\mathcal{I}}$ assigns a relation $\Sigma_{\mathcal{I}}(\pi) \subseteq \mathcal{St}_{\mathcal{I}} \times \mathcal{St}_{\mathcal{I}}$ to every program $\pi \in$ L.

Partial correctness of programs $\pi \in$ L is described using the set CF of *correctness formulas* $\{P\}\pi\{Q\}$ with $P,Q \in$ LF. Analogously to $\models_{\mathcal{I}} P$ we say that $\{P\}\pi\{Q\}$ is true and write

$$\models_{\mathcal{I}} \{P\}\pi\{Q\}$$

Author's address from Oct. 1983: Institut für Informatik und Praktische Mathematik, Christian-Albrechts-Universität Kiel, Olshausenstr. 40 - 60, D-2300 Kiel 1 if π is partially correct w.r.t. precondition P and postcondition Q, i.e. if $\Sigma_{\mathcal{J}}(\pi)(P_{\mathcal{J}}) \subseteq Q_{\mathcal{J}}$ holds where $P_{\mathcal{J}}$, $Q_{\mathcal{J}}$ denote the set of states expressed by P,Q. A *Hoare calculus* is a formal proof system $\mathcal{H}$ for correctness formulas consisting of finitely many proof rules (satisfying the conditions stated in Sec. 1) and an *oracle* $\mathcal{O} \subseteq LF$ for checking logical consequences. Usually the full theory Th($\mathcal{J}$), consisting of all true formulas P under $\mathcal{J}$, is taken as oracle. We write

$$A \vdash_{\mathcal{H},\mathcal{O}} \{P\}\,\pi\,\{Q\}$$

if $\{P\}\,\pi\,\{Q\}$ is *deducible* in $\mathcal{H}$ with $\mathcal{O}$ from the assumption set $A \subseteq CF$. If A is empty, $\{P\}\,\pi\,\{Q\}$ is *formally provable*:

$$\vdash_{\mathcal{H},\mathcal{O}} \{P\}\,\pi\,\{Q\}\,.$$

$\mathcal{H}$ is *sound* for a programming language L if for every interpretation $\mathcal{J}$ and $\pi \in L$, $P,Q \in LF$

$$\vdash_{\mathcal{H},Th(\mathcal{J})} \{P\}\,\pi\,\{Q\} \quad \text{implies} \quad \models_{\mathcal{J}} \{P\}\,\pi\,\{Q\}\,.$$

And $\mathcal{H}$ is *relatively complete* (in the sense of Cook [Co]) for L if for every *expressive* [Co] interpretation $\mathcal{J}$ and $\pi \in L$, $P,Q \in LF$

$$\vdash_{\mathcal{J}} \{P\}\,\pi\,\{Q\} \quad \text{implies} \quad \vdash_{\mathcal{H},Th(\mathcal{J})} \{P\}\,\pi\,\{Q\}\,.$$

Relative completeness means schematic completeness, independent of the underlying interpretation $\mathcal{J}$; in particular there is no powerful data structure assumed as in *arithmetical completeness* [Ha] .

3. While-Programs

We start with the language L_1 of *while-programs* π , i.e. statements π = S defined as follows:

S ::= x:=e | S_1;S_2 | <u>if</u> b <u>then</u> S_1 <u>else</u> S_2 <u>fi</u> | <u>while</u> b <u>do</u> S_1 <u>od</u> .

The semantics $\Sigma_{\mathcal{J}}$ of L_1 is as usual. To investigate the computational behaviour of while-programs π independently of the actual interpretation $\mathcal{J}$, we introduce the following *parsing relation* $\longrightarrow$ between statements:

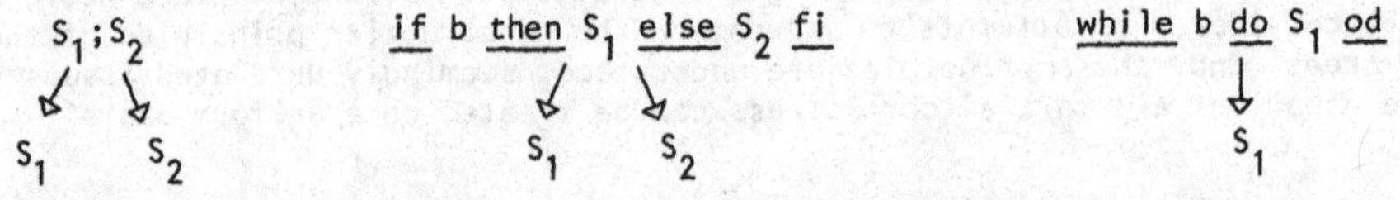

Systematic application of $\longrightarrow$ to a while-program π yields a set of parsing paths

$$p : \pi \longrightarrow S_1 \longrightarrow S_2 \longrightarrow \ldots$$

which can be represented as a parsing tree T_π , called the *structure tree* of π . For example,

π = x:=e_1 ; <u>while</u> b <u>do</u> x:=e_2 <u>od</u>

has the structure tree

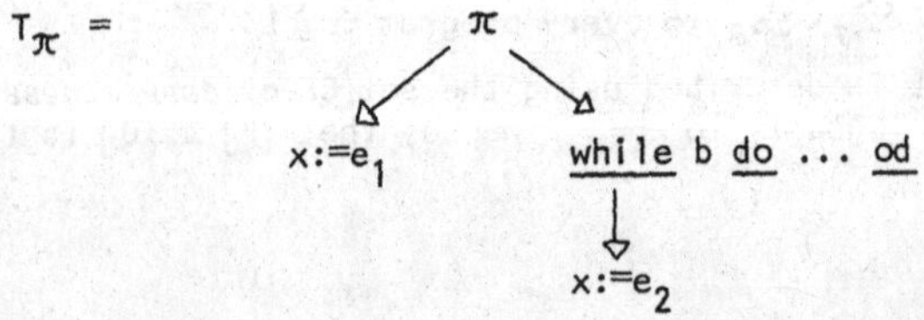

Because while-programs generate only *finite* structure trees, L_1 is easy to analyze in terms of Hoare's logic.

In fact, the semantics of every language constructor

$C(S_1,\dots,S_m)$ with $m \geq 0$

in L_1 can be fully described by a corresponding proof rule

$$(*)\qquad \frac{\{P_i\}\ S_i\ \{Q_i\},\ i=1,\dots,m\ ,\quad R_j\ ,\ j=1,\dots,n}{\{P\}\ C(S_1,\dots,S_m)\ \{Q\}}$$

satisfying the conditions stated in Sec. 1. "Fully describing" the semantics means that the rules (*) themselves are *sound*, i.e. whenever $\models_{\mathcal{I}} \{P_i\}\ S_i\ \{Q_i\}$ and $\models_{\mathcal{I}}\ R_j$ hold for $i=1,\dots,m$ and $j=1,\dots,n$ then also $\models_{\mathcal{I}}\ \{P\}\ C(S_1,\dots,S_m)\{Q\}$ holds, and *relatively complete*, i.e. whenever $\models_{\mathcal{I}}\ \{P\}\ C(S_1,\dots,S_m)\{Q\}$ holds, we can find formulas P_i, Q_i, $R_j \in LF$ satisfying (*) with $\models_{\mathcal{I}} \{P_i\}\ S_i\ \{Q_i\}$ and $\models_{\mathcal{I}} R_j$.

Thus the set $\mathcal{H}_1$ of proof rules (*) forms a sound Hoare calculus for L_1 [Ho 1]. Relative completeness of $\mathcal{H}$ follows immediately from the finiteness of the structure trees [Co]. Indeed, every formal proof Δ of a true correctness formula $\models_{\mathcal{I}}\ \{P\}\ \pi\ \{Q\}$ about some $\pi \in L_1$ can be obtained from the finite structure tree T_π by decorating its nodes S with appropriate pre- and postconditions:

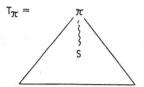

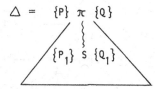

This explains Cook's completeness result [Co]. Note that it does not depend on the precise syntax of L_1 , but only on the fact that sound and complete proof rules (*) exist.

4. Fixed Systems of Procedures

We extend L_1 to a language L_2 by adding a simple form of recursive procedures. Taking procedure identifiers $p,q,\dots \in PI$, we add parameterless procedure calls to the set of statements:

$S ::= \dots$ as before $\dots \mid p$.

The meaning of such procedure calls is given by *(procedure) environments*

$E ::=$ proc p_1; S_1 ; ... ; proc p_n; S_n ; .

Note that *procedure bodies* S_i may contain recursive calls p_j. Programs $\pi \in L_2$ are now *closed* pairs

$\pi = E|S$,

i.e. every procedure identifier p in π has a corresponding declaration proc p; S_1 ; in E. Thus programs have only one fixed system E of mutually recursive procedures. The semantics $\Sigma_{\mathcal{I}}$ of L_1 can conveniently be extended to L_2 in a *copy rule style* using approximations $\Sigma^j_{\mathcal{I}}$ of $\Sigma_{\mathcal{I}}$ which depend on the copy depth $j \geq 0$ [La 1, Ol 1, Ap 2, DJ].

To analyze the computational behaviour of programs in L_2 , we extend the parsing relation $\longrightarrow$ from L_1 to L_2. For Programs $\pi = E|S$ with $S \neq p$ this is done simply by attaching the new environment E everywhere. For example,

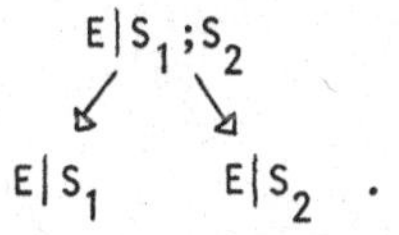

For procedure calls $E|p$ we define $\longrightarrow$ by using the *copy rule*:

$$\begin{array}{c} E|p \\ \downarrow \\ E|S_1 \end{array}$$

where proc p; S_1 ; is in E. The structure trees T_π of programs $\pi = E|S$ are again obtained by systematic application of $\longrightarrow$ to π. But in the presence of recursive procedure calls T_π may be infinite now. Thus the simple completeness argument of transforming finite structure trees into finite formal correctness proofs as used in Sec. 3 does not work any longer.

The solution to this problem is to realize that programs $\pi \in L_2$ can generate only *regular structure trees* T_π . Remember that a tree T is called *regular* if its path set is a regular language in the Chomsky hierarchy, or equivalently, if there are only finitely many different patterns of subtrees in T [CN].

More specifically, whenever we pursue an infinite path in T_π starting at the root π, we will encounter a *repetition*, i.e. two successive nodes are marked with the same procedure call $E|p$ such that the corresponding subtrees T_p and T_{pp} are *identical*.

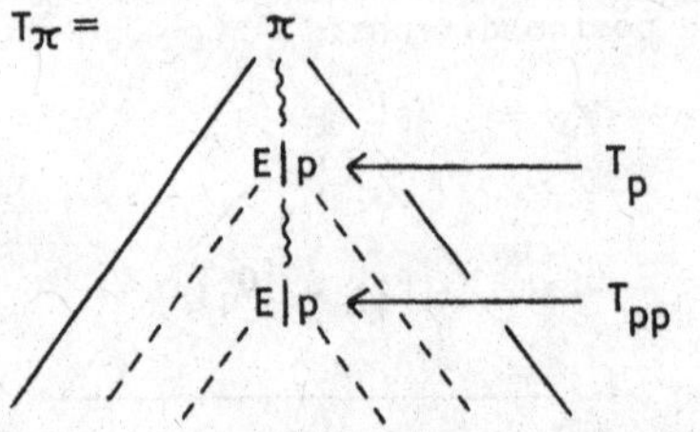

Let now U_π be the smallest initial segment of T_π such that every leaf in U_π is either a leaf in T_π too or that it is a procedure call $E|p$ with an *identical* predecessor node $E|p$. Since T_π is regular, U_π is *finite* and fully characterizes T_π :

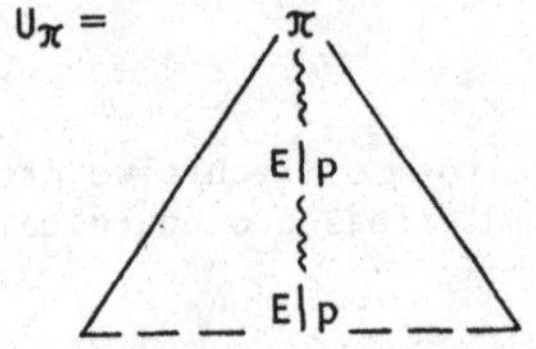

The idea of Hoare's logic for L_2 is now to exploit this finite initial segment U_π as a skeleton for formal proofs Δ of true correctness formulas $\{P_0\}\,\pi\,\{Q_0\}$. Except for procedure calls, Δ can be constructed in much the same way as in Sec.3. In fact, we can simply adopt the proof rules of $\mathcal{H}_1$ by attaching the environment E as done for th parsing relation. Repetitive procedure calls $E|p$ are dealt with by the *Recursion Rule* [Ho 2]:

$$\text{(R)} \qquad \frac{\{P\}\ E|p\ \{Q\} \vdash \{P\}\ E|S_1\ \{Q\}}{\{P\}\ E|p\ \{Q\}}$$

where proc p; S_1 ; is the declaration of p in E. This is a deduction rule in the sens of Prawitz [Pr] ; it says that whenever we can deduce $\{P\}\ E|S_1\ \{Q\}$ from the assumpti of $\{P\}\ E|p\ \{Q\}$, we have proved $\{P\}\ E|p\ \{Q\}$ without this assumption. We say the assum tion $\{P\}\ E|p\ \{Q\}$ is discharged. The following diagram shows the correspondence betwee U_π and the formal proof Δ using (R).

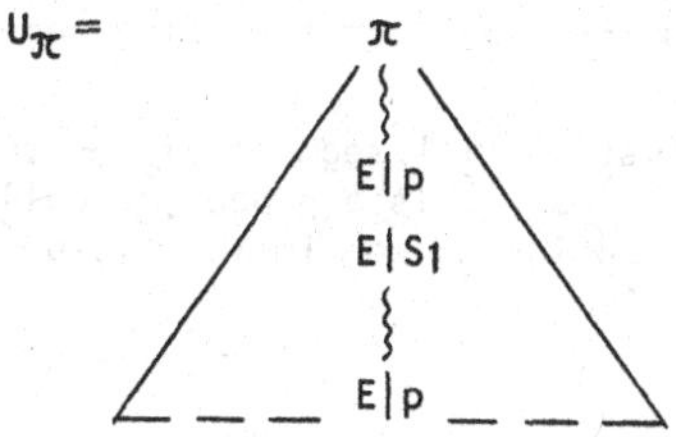

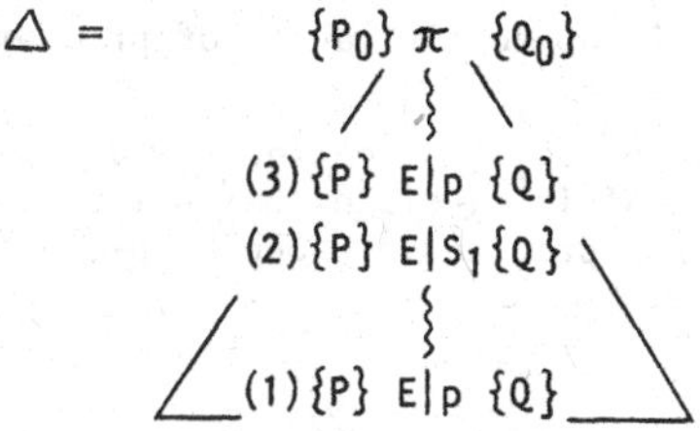

The idea is that Δ starts off with the assumption (1). When it reaches the procedure body (2), we apply the Recursion Rule (R) to prove (3) with assumption (1) discharged. This idea works for expressive interpretations provided we add two further auxiliary rules, the Invariance Rule and the Variable Substitution Rule [Go]: the resulting proof system $\mathcal{H}_2$ is sound and relatively complete for L_2 [Go].

5. Local Declarations of Variables and Procedures

We extend L_2 to a language L_3 by adding block structure to statements and procedure environments:

S ::= ... as before ... | begin var x; S end | begin var x; E_1 S end

E ::= proc p_1; S_1 ; ... ; proc p_n; S_n ;

Programs $\pi \in L_2$ are again closed pairs

π = E|S ,

but now local variables and procedure nestings are allowed. Again, the semantics $\Sigma_{\mathcal{J}}$ of L_1 can be extended in a copy rule style to cover L_3.

The parsing relation $\longrightarrow$ is extended to handle block structure:

$$E \mid \text{begin var } x;\ E_1\ S \text{ end}$$
$$\downarrow$$
$$E \cup E_1^* \mid S^*$$

where E_1^* , S^* result from E_1 , S by renaming x and every procedure identifier p declared in E_1 into a fresh simple variable x^* resp. a fresh procedure identifier p^* not present in E , E_1 and S. These renamings reflect the assumption of *static scoping* in $\Sigma_{\mathcal{J}}$ and add a further complexity to the induced structure trees T_π : in general they are not regular any more.

However, whenever we pursue an infinite path in the structure tree T_π of a program π we will encounter a *repetition up to similarity*, i.e. two successive nodes are marked with similar procedure calls $E_1|p_1 \approx E_2|p_2$ such that the corresponding subtrees T_1 and T_2 are similar as well: $T_1 \approx T_2$. We say that T_π is *regular up to similarity*.

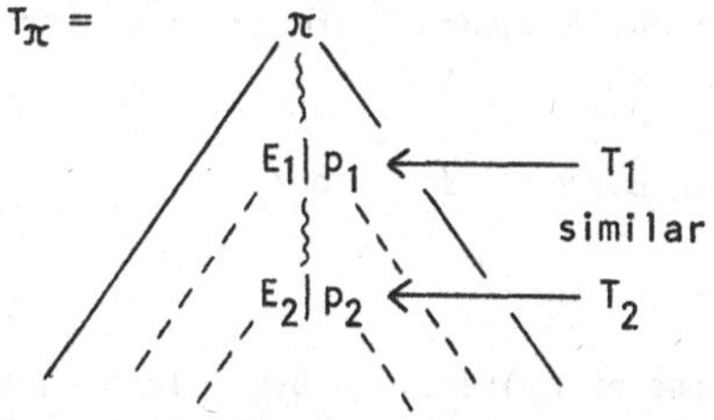

Here two programs $E_1|S_1$ and $E_2|S_2$ are called *similar* if there are (sub-) environments $E_1^* \subseteq E_1$ and $E_2^* \subseteq E_2$ such that the programs $E_1^*|S_1$ and $E_2^*|S_2$ differ only by a one-one substitution σ of variables and procedure identifiers [Ol 1]. We write $E_1|S_1 \approx E_2|S_2$ or more precisely $E_1|S_1 \ {}_\sigma\!\!\approx E_2|S_2$. This notion of similarity is extended to structure trees $T_1 \approx T_2$ by requiring that T_1 and T_2

are isomorphic up to similarity of programs $E_1|S_1$ and $E_2|S_2$ at corresponding nodes in T_1 resp. T_2.

Analogously to Sec. 4 we define now U_π as the smallest initial segment of T_π such that every leaf in U_π is either a leaf in T_π too or that it is a procedure call $E_2|S$ with a *similar* predecessor node $E_1|p_1$. Since T_π is regular up to similarity, U_π is again finite.

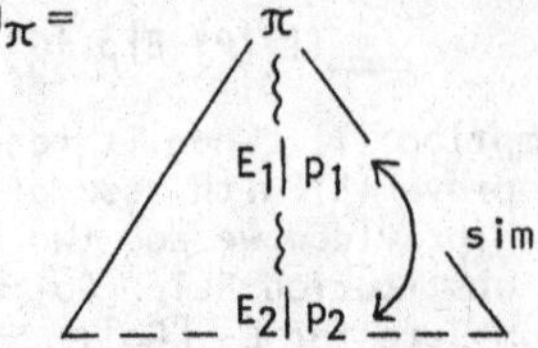

Following the spirit of Sec. 4, a Hoare calculus for L_2 should again use U_π as a skeleton for formal correctness proofs Δ. To achieve this goal, we augment the previous Hoare calculus $\mathcal{H}_2$ by the Block Rule [dB, Ap 2] and the following *Similarity Rul* [Ol 1]:

$$\text{(SIM)} \qquad \frac{\{P\}\ E_1|S_1\ \{Q\}}{\{P\sigma\}\ E_2|S_2\ \{Q\sigma\}}$$

where σ is a one-one substitution with $E_1|S_1 \ {}_\sigma\!\approx\ E_2|S_2$. The resulting Hoare calculu $\mathcal{H}_3$ is sound and relatively complete for L_3 [Ap 1, Ol 1]. The correspondence between U_π and formal proofs Δ in $\mathcal{H}_3$ is shown in the following diagram:

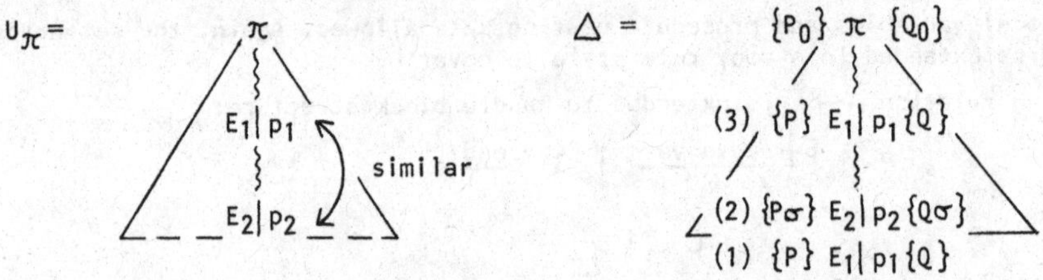

Δ starts off with an assumption (1) about the similar predecessor node $E_1|p_1$. Applying the Similarity Rule (SIM), we obtain a correctness formula (2) about the leaf $E_2|p$ of U_π. We then follow the structure of U_π. Eventually we hit the predecessor $E_1|p_1$. An application of the Recursion Rule (R) yields (3) with assumption (1) discharged.

6. Adding Parameters to the Procedures

Recursion and Similarity are the principle rules of a complete Hoare's logic for the language L_3. To push these principles to their limits, we extend L_3 to a language L_{Algol} of *Algol-like programs* by allowing in environments E procedure declarations

$$E = \ldots\ \underline{\text{proc}}\ p(\bar{x}_f : \bar{q}_f);\ S_1\ ;\ \ldots$$

with two lists of distinct formal name parameters: procedure identifiers $\bar{q}_f$ and variables $\bar{x}_f$. Procedure calls

$$S = p(\bar{x}_a : \bar{q}_a)$$

have corresponding lists of actual name parameters. To avoid talking about *sharing* or *aliasing* [Ol 1/2, THM] in this paper, we assume that the actual variables $\bar{x}_a$ are all distinct. Programs are again closed pairs

$$\pi = E|S\ .$$

For procedure calls the parsing relation $\longrightarrow$ of L_{Algol} uses now the *full copy rule* substituting actual for formal parameters:

$$E \mid p(\bar{x}_a : \bar{q}_a)$$
$$\downarrow$$
$$E \mid S_1[\bar{q}_a, \bar{x}_a / \bar{q}_f, \bar{x}_f]$$

In general Algol-like programs π do not generate structure trees T_π which are regular up to similarity. This is also clear from the fact that there exists no sound and relatively complete Hoare calculus for L_{Algol} [Cl].

But most completeness results in Hoare's logic for programs with procedures can be understood as looking for restrictions $L \subseteq L_{Algol}$ where regularity (up to similarity) of the structure trees is preserved. Typical restrictions are:

L_{pp}: no procedures as parameters; this works not only for

- simple name variables as assumed here [Cl, Ol 1] , but also for
- value expressions [Go] and
- value and reference array variables [dB, Ap 2]

as non-procedure parameters.

L_{pnes}: no procedure nestings [Cl, Ol 1]

L_{gf}: no *global formal procedure identifiers* [Ol 1], i.e. no procedure identifiers f which are declared as a formal parameter and used globally in some local procedure q:

```
                                  global formal
proc p(... : f ); begin proc q; ... f ... ; ... h(:q) ... end
                                  q-body
                                  p-body
```

Lcgf: no *critical occurrences* of global formal procedure identifiers [THM], i.e. procedures q containing a global formal procedure identifier f must not occur as actual parameters of another call as for example in h(:q) above.

Except for the Recursion Rule which has to be modified to

$$\text{(REC)} \quad \frac{\{P\}\ E|p(\bar{x}_a : \bar{q}_a)\ \{Q\} \vdash \{P\}\ E|S_1[\ldots]\ \{Q\}}{\{P\}\ E|p(\bar{x}_a : \bar{q}_a)\ \{Q\}}$$

to allow for parameters, the Hoare calculus $\mathcal{H}_3$ of Sec. 5 remains sound and relatively complete for all these sublanguages $L \subseteq L_{Algol}$.

7. Run Time Behaviuor

As demonstrated in the previous sections, Hoare's logic forces us to analyze the structure trees of programs precisely. We will now indicate that this sort of analysis is not only interesting for constructing formal proofs for partial correctness formulas, but also for deciding various questions linked with the *run time behaviour* of programs [La 2/3] such as:

(1) Does a program π terminate formally ?

(2) Is a procedure p in a program π formally recursive ?

(3) Is a procedure p in a program π formally reachable ?

(4) Is a program π implementable by formal macro-expansions ?

"Formal" means that we consider these questions schematically, i.e. independently of any input data. The idea of these questions is that depending on their answers the *standard run time system* for Algol-like programs [Di, RR, GHL] can apply simplified working techniques.

We concentrate on Question (3) and explain its decidability for programs $\pi \in L_{Algol}$ whose structure trees T_π is regular up to similarity. By definition, a procedure p in π is *formally reachable* if there is a node $E|p^*(...)$ in T_π with p^* being a *copy* of p [La 1]. (Recall the renaming convention for parsing blocks.)

To decide this we first construct the initial segment U_π of T_π defined in Sec. 5. Since U_π is finite, this can be done effectively. The desired decidability result follows from:

(*) If p is formally reachable in T_π then already in U_π.

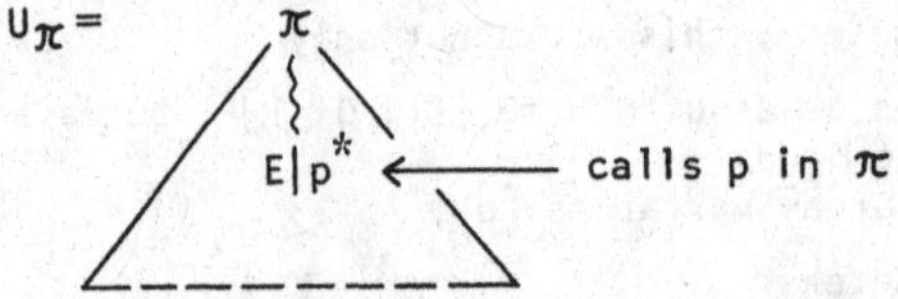

Decidability of the remaining questions requires an analogous argument. The complexity of such decision procedures has been studied in [Wi].

8. Regular Formal Call Trees

So far we have seen how Hoare's logic can deal with certain classes of programs generating regular tree structures. The question arises whether regularity is in some sense also a *necessary* condition for the existence of a complete Hoare calculus. To answer this question we first extend the present notion of regularity by introducing the notion of formal call trees.

The *formal call tree* of a program π records only in which order the procedures of π are called [Ol 3/4]. It is the homomorphic image of the more detailed structure tree T_π under a mapping call which takes a parsing path

$$p:\ \pi \longrightarrow \ \dots \longrightarrow \ E_1|\tilde{p}_1(\dots) \longrightarrow \ \dots \longrightarrow E_n|\tilde{p}_n(\dots)$$

in T_π and yields a *formal call path* call p, built up from a special symbol main (for main program) and the procedure identifiers in π.

The precise definition of call p is as follows: let us assume that $E_1|\tilde{p}_1(\dots),\dots,E_n|\tilde{p}_n(\dots)$ are *all* procedure calls in p. Every of these called procedures $\tilde{p}_i$ is a copy of exactly one original procedure proc $p_i(\dots);\ S_i$; in π. Taking the identifiers p_i, we define

$$\text{call}\ p:\ \text{main} \longrightarrow p_1 \longrightarrow \dots \longrightarrow p_n\ .$$

The formal call tree call T_π represents the set of all these formal call paths. (See [Ol 4] for examples.)

Let $L_{regular}$ denote the set of all programs $\pi \in L_{Algol}$ with a regular call T_π. In [Ol 3/4] the following *characterization* of Hoare's logic has been proved for a rich class $\mathcal{L}$ of languages $L \subseteq L_{Pas}$ which allow programs with global variables (side effects):

(1) There exists a Hoare calculus $\mathcal{H}$ which is sound and relatively complete for $L_{regular} \in \mathcal{L}$.

(2) Whenever a language $L \in \mathcal{L}$ contains a program $\pi \in L$ with a non-regular formal call tree call T_π then there is *no* sound and relatively complete Hoare calculus for L.

$L_{Pas} \subseteq L_{Algol}$ is defined in Sec. 9. By a *global variable (side effect)* we mean a variable x which occurs in the body S of a procedure p, but is neither a formal parameter of p nor locally declared in S:

$$\underline{\text{proc}}\ p(\ldots);\ \underbrace{\ldots\ldots\ x{:=}e\ \ldots\ldots}_{S}\ ;$$

Because of

$$\mathcal{L} \ni L_1, L_2, L_3, L_{pp}, L_{pnes}, L_{gf}, L_{cgf} \subsetneq L_{regular}$$

the calculus $\mathcal{H}$ generalizes all previously discussed Hoare calculi. In fact, $\mathcal{H}$ uses besides Recursion and Similarity the concept of "depth" as a third essential principle to analyze the structure trees T_π of programs in $L_{regular}$.

Informally (2) states that if we allow arbitrary global variables (side effects), there is no way to reason schematically, i.e. independently of the underlying interpretation $\mathcal{J}$, about partial correctness of programs with a non-regular formal call tree. This is remarkable since all questions on *run time behaviour* stated in Sec. 7 remain decidable for L_{Pas}. This shows that Hoare's logic forces us to a *finer analysis* of the structure trees as decidability questions concerning run time behaviour do. It also shows that questions on completeness of Hoare's logic can very well identify problematic language constructs such as side effects of procedures.

9. Programs without Global Variables: The Pascal Case

From the previous section we know that in the presence of global variables there is not much hope for getting a schematically working Hoare's logic for programs with non-regular structure trees. But once we disallow global variables, we can go beyond this limit. We show this for the language $L_{Pas} \subseteq L_{Algol}$ of programs with Pascal-like procedures.

L_{Pas} is defined by requiring that every procedure identifier p in a program $\pi \in L_{Pas}$ is used in accordance with a fixed *Pascal-like mode* or *type* μ_p which can be either of level 1:

(i) $\underline{\text{proc}}(\underline{\text{var}}, \ldots, \underline{\text{var}}\ :)$,

$n \geq 0$ times $\underline{\text{var}}$, or of level 2:

(ii) $\underline{\text{proc}}(\underline{\text{var}}, \ldots, \underline{\text{var}}\ : \mu_1, \ldots, \mu_m)$,

$n \geq 0$ times $\underline{\text{var}}$, where $\mu_1, \ldots, \mu_m, m \geq 1$, are modes of level 1.

A mode μ_p = (i) means that p always takes n variables and no procedures as parameters, and μ_p = (ii) means that p always takes n variables and m procedures of modes $\mu_1, \ldots, \mu_m$ of level 1 as parameters. These two possibilities are typical for Pascal [JW].

We now explain how to develop a Hoare calculus for $L_{Pas} \cap L_{gv}$, the set of all $\pi \in L_{Pas}$ without global variables. For $L_{Pas} \cap L_{gv}$ none of the previously introduced Hoare calculi is relatively complete. This is because programs $\pi \in L_{Pas} \cap L_{gv}$ generate non-regular structure trees of the form:

(*) $T_\pi =$

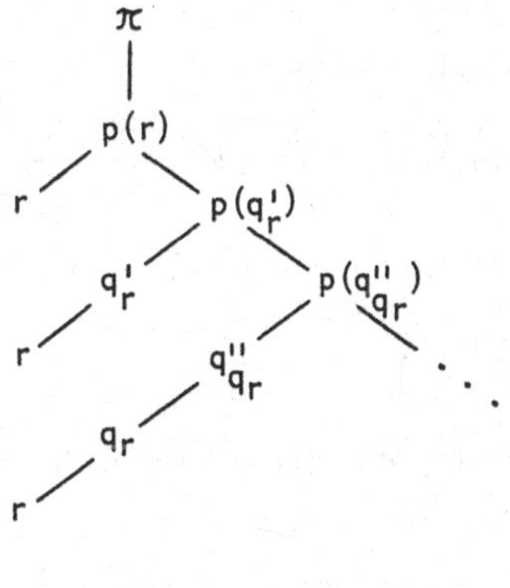

(For simplicity environments E and programs $E|S$ where S is not a procedure call are dropped in this diagram.) Note that call T_π remains non-regular as well; so the calculus $\mathcal{H}$ mentioned in Sec. 8 is of no help either.

However, we can transform the non-regular tree T_π into a regular one by introducing a new parsing relation $\Longrightarrow$ for $L_{Pas} \cap L_{gv}$. This transformation relies on *second-order* concept of relation variables which are needed to deal properly with procedures as parameters.

More precisely, we extend both the programming language $L_{Pas} \cap L_{gv}$ and the assertion language LF by allowing free *relation variables* $\varphi, \psi, \ldots \in$ RV each with a certain mode

$$\mu_\varphi = \underline{\text{proc}}(\underline{\text{var}}, \ldots, \underline{\text{var}} :),$$

$n \geq 0$ times var, of level 1. Thus the semantics of $L_{Pas} \cap L_{gv}$ and LF is not any more fixed by the interpretation $\mathcal{J}$, but it depends also on *valuations* $\mathcal{V}$ which assign to every relation variable φ of mode μ_φ a 2n-ary (!) relation

$$\mathcal{V}(\varphi) \subseteq \mathcal{D}_{\mathcal{J}}^{2n}$$

over the domain $\mathcal{D}_{\mathcal{J}}$ of $\mathcal{J}$.

The programming language $L_{Pas} \cap L_{gv}$ uses relation variables φ as procedure calls

$$S = \varphi(x_1, \ldots, x_n :)$$

with n simple variables as actual parameters. Informally $\varphi(x_1, \ldots, x_n :)$ denotes a *nondeterministic assignment* of values determined by $\mathcal{V}(\varphi)$ to $x_1, \ldots, x_n$. The assertion language LF uses φ as an uninterpreted relation symbol of arity 2n:

$$P ::= \ldots \mid \varphi(e_1, \ldots, e_{2n}) .$$

The link between both applications is that the *graph* of an assignment to n variables is described by a 2n-ary relation.

Furthermore, we extend the concept of substitution to relation variables. Let $G \in$ LF, $\bar{x}$ be a list of length 2n containing all free simple variables of G, and $\varphi \in$ RV of mode μ_φ. Then

$$P[G_{\bar{x}}/\varphi]$$

denotes the result of replacing every occurrence of $\varphi(\bar{e})$ in P by $G[\bar{e}/\bar{x}]$ which describes the usual substitution of expressions $\bar{e}$ for free variables $\bar{x}$ in G.

Now we define the new parsing relation $\Longrightarrow$ for $L_{Pas} \cap L_{gv}$. If $E|S$ is not a procedure call, $\Longrightarrow$ coincides with the old relation $\longrightarrow$. For procedure calls $E|p(\ldots)$ we distinguish between two cases:

(1) If there is at least one procedure identifier q as actual parameter of p, we *separate concerns* about q and p by calling q in advance and separately calling p with a fresh relation variable φ instead of q:

$$E \mid p(\bar{x} : \ldots q \ldots)$$

$$\swarrow \qquad \searrow$$

$$E|q(\bar{b}:) \qquad\qquad E \mid p(\bar{x} : \ldots \varphi \ldots)$$

(2) This separation process eventually leads to procedure calls where all actual parameters are relation variables. Only then we apply the copy rule as before:

$$E \mid p(\bar{x}_a : \bar{\varphi})$$

$$\Downarrow$$

$$E \mid S_1[\bar{x}_a, \bar{\varphi} / \bar{x}_f, \bar{q}_f] .$$

To understand the impact of this new parsing relation, let us look at the induced new T_π of Example (*) above:

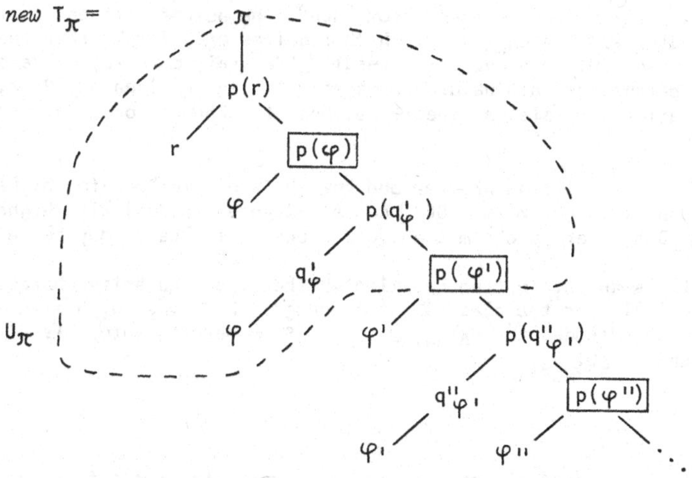

The transformed structure tree *new* T_π has now become *regular up to similarity*: the marked procedure calls $p(\varphi)$, $p(\varphi')$, $p(\varphi'')$, ... are all similar in the sense of Sec. 5. Thus *new* T_π can be fully characterized by a finite initial segment U_π.

The idea of Hoare's logic for programs $\pi \in L_{Pas} \cap L_{gv}$ is once again to exploit the finite U_π as a skeleton for formal correctness proofs $\{P_0\}\pi\{Q_0\}$. But since U_π is obtained with the stronger parsing relation $\Longrightarrow$, we need now a stronger rule for procedure calls. This is the *Separation Rule* [Ol 2] which directly reflects clause (1) of the definition of $\Longrightarrow$:

$$\text{(SEP)}\quad \frac{\{\bar{a}=\bar{b}\}\ E|q(\bar{b}:)\ \{G\}\ ,\ \{P\}\ E|p(\bar{x} : \dots \varphi \dots)\ \{Q\}}{\{P[G_{\bar{a},\bar{b}}/\varphi]\}\ E|p(\bar{x} : \dots q \dots)\ \{Q[G_{\bar{a},\bar{b}}/\varphi]\}}$$

where $\bar{a},\bar{b}$ contains all free simple variables of G and φ is a fresh relation variable with $mode_\varphi = mode_q$.

Augmenting $\mathcal{H}_3$ with (SEP) and a rule covering nondeterministic assignments $E|\varphi(\bar{x}:)$ yields indeed a sound and relatively complete Hoare calculus $\mathcal{H}_4$ for $L_{Pas} \cap L_{gv}$ [Ol 2]. In [DJ] it is shown that these arguments can be extended in a natural way to deal with procedures allowing modes (types) of arbitrary level.

We remark that the run time questions of Sec. 7 can again be proved decidable for $L_{Pas} \cap L_{gv}$, in fact for all programs with procedures of finite modes, by using the initial segment U_π of *new* T_π analogously to Sec. 7 (cf. [Da, La 3]).

10. Open Questions

(1) The calculus $\mathcal{H}_4$ for $L_{Pas} \cap L_{gv}$ is complete only

- relative to second-order theories $Th(\mathcal{J})$ as oracles and
- relative to second-order expressiveness.

The question arises whether "second-order" is really needed when dealing with $L_{Pas} \cap L_{gv}$.

In [Jo] it has been shown that at least in case of *Herbrand-expressive* [CGH] interpretations $\mathcal{J}$ second-order expressiveness can be eliminated in favour of first-order expressiveness. But it remains an open question whether the calculus $\mathcal{H}_4$ can be refined in such a way that only first-order theories are needed as an oracle.

Hope for a positive answer stems from [GCH]: the authors present a different Hoare calculus $\mathcal{H}^*$ for $L_{Pas} \cap L_{gv}$ which requires only first-order theories and expressiveness. But to prove their result [GCH] rely on a technique of *coding* procedure parameters into natural numbers. We find the idea of [Ol 2, DJ, ENO] to use relation variables as specifications of unknown procedure parameters more attractive.

(2) Also open is the question whether and how the proof methods for higher type procedures used in [Ol 2, DJ, GCH] can be extended to deal with higher type *functions* [BKM]. Here program transformations as in [La 4] may be helpful.

(3) Thirdly, it is an interesting question whether the regularity characterization of Hoare's logic for the class $\mathcal{L}$ of languages $L \subseteq L_{Pas}$ with side effects [Ol 4] can be extended to $L_{Algol} \supseteq L_{Pas}$. Some results into this direction can be found in [Ol 3].

References

[Ap 1] Apt, K.R., A sound and complete Hoare-like system for a fragment of Pascal, Report IW 96/78, Mathematisch Centrum, Amsterdam, 1978.

[Ap 2] Apt, K.R., Ten years of Hoare's logic, a survey-part I, ACM TOPLAS 3 (1981) 431-483.

[dB] de Bakker, J.W., Mathematical theory of program correctness (Prentice Hall International, London, 1980).

[BKM] de Bakker, J.W., Klop, J.W., Meyer, J.-J.Ch., Correctness of programs with function procedures, in: [Ko] 94-112.

[Cl] Clarke, E.M., Programming language constructs for which it is impossible to obtain good Hoare-like axioms, J.ACM 26 (1979) 129-147.

[CGH] Clarke, E.M., German, S.M., Halpern, J.Y., On effective axiomatizations of Hoare logics, Tech. Report TR-14-82, Aiken Computation Laboratory, Harvard Univ., 1982 (to appear in J.ACM).

[Co] Cook, S.A., Soundness and completeness of an axiom system for program verification, SIAM J. Comput. 7 (1978) 70-90.

[CN] Cousineau, G., Nivat, M., On rational expressions representing infinite rational trees: application to the structure of flowcharts, in: J. Becvar, Ed., Proc. 8th Math. Found. of Comput. Sci., Lecture Notes in Computer Science 74 (1979) 567-580.

[Da] Damm, W., The IO- and OI-hierarchies, Theoret. Comput. Sci. 20 (1982) 95-207.

[DJ] Damm, W., Josko, B., A sound and relatively* complete Hoare-logic for a language with higher type procedures, Schriften zur Informatik und Angew. Math. Nr. 77, RWTH Aachen, 1982 (to appear in Acta Inform.).

[Di] Dijkstra, E.W., Recursive programming, Numer. Math. 2 (1960) 312-318.

[ENO] Ernst, G.W., Navlakha, J.K., Ogden, W.F., Verification of programs with procedure type parameters, Acta Inform. 18 (1982) 149-169.

[GCH] German, S.M., Clarke, E.M., Halpern, J.Y., A stronger axiom system for reasoning about procedures as parameters, in: E.M. Clarke, D. Kozen, Eds., Proc. Logics of Programs 1983 (to appear in Lecture Notes in Computer Science).

[Go] Gorelick, G.A., A complete axiomatic system for proving assertions about recursive and non-recursive programs, Tech. Report 75, Dept. of Comput. Sci., Univ. of Toronto (1975).

[GHL] Grau, A.A., Hill, U., Langmaack, H., Translation of ALGOL 60. Handbook for automatic computation, Vol. Ib (Springer, Berlin-Heidelberg-New York, 1967).

[Ha] Harel, D., First-order dynamic logic, Lecture Notes in Computer Science 68 (1979).

[Ho 1] Hoare, C.A.R., An axiomatic basis for computer programming, Comm. ACM 12 (1969) 576-580, 583.

[Ho 2] Hoare, C.A.R., Procedures and parameters: an axiomatic approach, in: E. Engeler, Ed., Symposium on semantics of algorithmic languages, Lecture Notes in Mathematics 188 (Springer, Berlin, 1971) 102-116.

[JW] Jensen, K., Wirth, N., Pascal user manual and report (Springer, Berlin, 1975).

[Jo] Josko, B., On expressive interpretations of a Hoare-logic for a language with higher type procedures, Schriften zur Informatik und Angew. Math., RWTH Aachen (1983).

[Ko] Kozen, D., Ed., Proc. Logics of Programs 1981, Lecture Notes in Computer Science 131 (1982).

[La 1] Langmaack, H., On correct procedure parameter transmissions in higher programming languages, Acta Inform. 2 (1973) 110-142.

[La 2] Langmaack, H., On procedures as open subroutines, Acta Inform. 2 (1973) 311-333, and Acta Inform. 3 (1974) 227-241.

[La 3] Langmaack, H., On termination problems for finitely interpreted ALGOL-like programs, Acta Inform. 18 (1892) 79-108.

[La 4] Langmaack, H., Aspects of programs with finite modes, in: Proc. Foundations of Computation Theory, Sweden, 1983 (to appear in Lecture Notes of Computer Science).

[LO] Langmaack, H., Olderog, E.-R., Present-day Hoare-like systems for programming languages with procedures: power, limits and most likely extensions, in: J.W. de Bakker, J. van Leeuwen, Eds., Proc. 7th Coll. Automata, Languages and Programming, Lecture Notes in Computer Science 85 (1980) 363-373.

[Ol 1] Olderog, E.-R., Sound and complete Hoare-like calculi based on copy rules, Acta Inform. 16 (1981) 161-197.

[Ol 2] Olderog, E.-R., Correctness of programs with Pascal-like procedures without global variables, revised version of Bericht Nr. 8110, Institut für Informatik und Prakt. Math., Univ. Kiel, 1981 (to appear in Theoret. Comput. Sci.).

[Ol 3] Olderog, E.-R., Charakterisierung Hoarescher Systeme für Algol-ähnliche Programmiersprachen, Dissertation, Univ. Kiel (1981).

[Ol 4] Olderog, E.-R., A characterization of Hoare's logic for programs with Pascal-like procedures, in: Proc 15th ACM Symp. on Theory of Computing (Boston, Mass., 1983) 320-329.

[RR] Randell, B., Russell, L.J., ALGOL 60 implementation (Academic Press, London, 1964).

[Pr] Prawitz, D., Natural deduction - a proof-theoretic study (Almqvist and Wiksell, Stockholm, 1965).

[THM] Trakhtenbrot, B.A., Halpern, J.Y., Meyer, A.R., Denotational semantics and partial correctness for an Algol-like language with procedure parameters and sharing, Tech. Report, Laboratory for Computer Science,MIT (1982).

[Wi] Winklmann, K., On the complexity of some problems concerning the use of procedures, Acta Inform. 18 (1982) 299-318, and Acta Inform. 18 (1983) 411-430.

A THEORY OF PROBABILISTIC PROGRAMS

Rohit Parikh
Department of Computer Science
Brooklyn College of CUNY
Brooklyn, NY, 11210

and

Anne Mahoney

Mathematics Department
Boston University
Boston, Mass, 02215

Abstract: We define a propositional programming language for probabilistic program schemes and study the equational properties of the programs thus arising.

Introduction: There has been a great deal of activity of late in the Complexity theory of probabilistic programs. We also have some very nice probabilistic algorithms for primality testing, dining philosophers and other matters. Recently, there has also been some progress in logic for probabilistic programs. We have the very pretty semantics for probabilistic programs defined by Kozen [K1], and in [K2] a decidability result for a Propositional PDL (PPDL) is proved. in [FH] Feldman and Harel define a PROB-DL (A probabilistic dynamic logic) which is Cook-complete, but it needs an oracle for full analysis to decide it. A more recent paper by Feldman alone [F] gives a decision procedure. His logic is propositional in only a partial sense. Real numbers enter explicitly, and can be quantified over. Reif [R] contains an attempt to construct a probabilistic propositional dynamic logic, but not all of his axioms are sound. For example his axiom A2 fails. None of the authors mentioned consider recursive calls.

In this paper we define a propositional (equational, to be specific) language for talking about probabilistic programs, which allows certain recursive calls and show that the finite model property holds. We do not know whether this logic is decidable, but at worst it can only be co-RE and thus it is much easier than CFDL which is Π^1_1-complete.

One difficulty with the whole of probabilistic logic is that after you assign probabilities to formulae, you are stuck with the fact that probabilities do not obey the laws of boolean algebra that truth values obey. E.g. the formula $A \vee \neg A$ does not have probability 1 in general, no matter how you interpret $\vee$ and $\neg$ as functions from [0,1] to [0,1] Moreover, there is no way to calculate the probability of, say, $A \vee B$ from those of A and B. It can be done if we know, say, that A and B are independent, but usually that is itself a hard question, and the answer is not always yes. There is also another problem with rules of inference. For example, if α is a probabilistic program of the form "while A do β" where A is probabilistic, then we cannot be certain on termination of α that A is false, but only that $\neg A$ has a non-zero probability. Similarly, the partial correctness assertions $\{A\}\alpha\{B\}$ and $\{B\}\beta\{C\}$ can be true with high probability and yet, $\{A\}\alpha;\beta\{C\}$ be simply false. Surprisingly, program constructs are much better behaved, and for the present, we have confined ourselves to studying these.

We start by describing our programming language. We have some atomic program symbols $a_1, \ldots, a_n$ and a certain number of atomic predicates $P_1, \ldots, P_m$. We define the class of programs and formulae by simultaneous recursion.

Definition 1:

1. Each a_i is a program, each P_j is a formula.
2. If A is a formula, then so is $\neg A$, and A? is a program
3. If α and β are programs, then so is $\alpha;\beta$
4. If A is a formula and α and β are programs, then "while A do α" and "if A then α else β" are programs.
5. If α is a program and A is a formula then $(\alpha)A$ is a formula.
6. If α and β are programs and $0 < p < 1$, then $p\alpha + (1-p)\beta$ is a program. (Intuitively, do a with probability p and β with probability 1-p)
7. Allow certain strings as labels. If b is a label and α is an (unlabelled) program, then b:α is a program, and α can be called within another program by the instruction "call(b)". We are assuming that each label is used only once. Mutual recursion and self-recursion are allowed.

To give the semantics of this language we take a state space W, and to each program a we assign a function from $W \times W$ to [0,1], the closed unit interval satisfying the condition: $\sum a(s,t):t \in W \leq 1$. $a(s,t)$ is of course the probability that the program a takes us from state s to state t. Similarly, for each P we have P(s), the probability that P tests true at s, a number in [0,1]. Now we compute $\alpha(s,t)$ and A(s) for more complex α and A as follows:

Definition 2:

1) $(\alpha;\beta)(s,t) = \sum\alpha(s,u);\beta(u,t):u\in W$
2) $(\neg A)(s) = 1-A(s)$. $(A?)(s,t) = A(s)\delta(s,t)$.
   where $\delta(s,t) = 1$ if $s=t$ and 0 otherwise.
3) (if A then α else β)(s,t)
   $= A(s)\alpha(s,t)+(1-A(s))\beta(s,t)$
4) If α is "while A do β"
   then $\alpha(s,t) = (1-A(s))\delta(s,t) + \sum A(s)\beta(s,u)\alpha(u,t):u\in W$
   where the smallest solution α to the equation is intended.
5) $((\alpha)A)(s) = \sum\alpha(s,t)A(t):t\in W$
6) $(p\alpha + (1-p)\beta)(s,t) = p.\alpha(s,t) + (1-p).\beta(s,t)$
7) In case of recursive calls, the minimum solution to the obvious equations can be shown to exist. To give an example, if α is label:(a;call(label);c), then the minimal solution to the equation $\alpha(s,t) = \sum a(s,u)\alpha(u,v)c(u,t):u,v\in W$ is 0, but if call(label) were replaced by "if A then call(label) else d" then a nontrivial minimal solution will exist.

Remark: The semantic meaning of a program in our model can really be thought of as a sub-stochastic matrix, i.e. one satisfying the inequality

$\sum\alpha(s,t):t\in W \leq 1$

It is easy to check that this inequality is preserved under sequencing and if then else. For example we have

$$\begin{aligned}\sum(\alpha;\beta)(s,t):t\in W &= \sum\alpha(s,u)\beta(u,t):u,t\in W\\ &= \sum\alpha(s,u)(\sum\beta(u,t):t\in W):u\in W\\ &\leq \sum\alpha(s,u):u\in W \leq 1.\end{aligned}$$

This property is preserved also under while dos and recursive calls. For example, if α were defined by lab:if P then β els b;call(lab);c, where β is a previously defined program and b,c ar atomic then we have

$$\sum\alpha(s,t):t\in W =$$
$$\sum(P(s)\beta(s,t)+\sum(1-P(s))b(s,u)\alpha(u,v)c(v,u):u,v\in W):t\in W$$

If we replace the α to the right of the = sign by α_n and that to the left by α_{n+1} then we get a series of equations $\alpha_{n+1} = \phi(\alpha_n)$, with α_0 being 0.

It is straightforward that α_{n+1} is sub-stochastic if α_n is and hence so is the limit α which is the semantic meaning of the label lab. Indeed, the maps from WxW to [0,1] are a CPO under the obvious ordering and we are merely solving equations in it. However, this machinery of CPOs will not be of much use to us.

Recursive calls are associated with context free languages in that there is an obvious association of recursive definitions with context free languages. In our considerations below we shall sometimes need to impose the requirement of linearity. I.e. we shall impose the requirement that the context free constructions involved in these recursive calls be *linear*. Thus, for example, we shall allow the definition

b:if A then α else β;call(b);δ

but *not*

b:if A then α else β;call(b);call(b);δ.

More formally, we could define the notion of a probabilistic context free language. As usual, we have terminals and nonterminals. A production is a string of terminals and non-terminals and is linear if there is at most one non-terminal in it. A grammar will then be defined by a series of equations of the form

$(e_i) \quad A_i = \sum c_{i,j} p_{i,j} : j=1...m_i$

where the A_i are all the non-terminals, the $p_{i,j}$ are productions. The m_i depends on i, the $c_{i,j}$ are reals in [0,1] and finally, $\sum c_{i,j} : j=1..m_i \leqslant 1$.

If Σ is the set of terminals then such a grammar defines a set of functions ϕ_i from Σ^* to [0,1] which are the minimal solutions of the equations (e_i) above, with ϕ_i corresponding to A_i. More generally, if the terminals also are not elements of Σ but are themselves such functions from Σ^* to [0,1] then the grammar defines new functions. In any case, once we have defined the syntactic object corresponding to a program to be a probabilistic context free language with Σ as the atomic programs, then assignment of sub-stochastic matrices to the atomic programs automatically yields one for all probabilistic languages. The situation becomes somewhat more complex when tests are present. I.e. the total probability 1 may be divided not between say 1/3 and 2/3, but between, say, P;Q, P;¬Q, and ¬P. The proper definition must then account for the interaction between the real and boolean divisions that are present here. We postpone the full details to the journal version of this paper.

We shall describe as "regular" that part of our programming language which does not involve recursive calls, and "poor-test" if the formula A in the "if A then ... else ..." and "while A do ..." constructs does not involve programs.

Results

We assume in theorem 1 below that the p used in case 6 of definition 1 is always rational and that the recursive calls are all linear.

We shall describe a model as being countable or finite according as its state space is countable or finite respectively. A model will be described as rational if all the basic probabilities P(s) and a(s,t) are rational.

Theorem 1: In a rational, finite model M, all probabilities $\alpha(s,t)$ are rational.

Proof: By induction on the complexity of α. It is clear that cases 1-3 and 5-6 of definitions 1,2 do not give any trouble. We consider case 7. Case 4 is similar. Consider for example the definition of a program α with label lab.

lab:If A then β else b;call(lab);c

where b,c are atomic programs and β has complexity less than α. Let $W = \{s_1,...,s_n\}$ and let $\alpha(i,j)$ be the probability of the program α taking us from state s_i to s_j. Similarly for b,c,β. A(i) is the probability that A is true at s_i. All these numbers with the possible exception of $\alpha(i,j)$ are rational by induction hypothesis or because the model is rational. The definition of α translates into the equation

(*) $\alpha(i,j) = A(i)\beta(i,j)+\sum b(i,k)\alpha(k,m)c(m,j):k,m \leq n.$

If we now think of α as an n^2-dimensional vector, then (*) is a linear non-homogeneous equation satisfied by α. If the solution were unique, it would be rational. But of course it need not be unique. However, it is sufficient to notice that when such an equation has a *least* non-negative solution, then it must be rational.

Let α be the intended solution of the equation (*) which can be written $\alpha = \phi(\alpha) = B\alpha + w$, where B is a non-negative linear operator on this n^2-dimensional space, and $w(i,j)=A(i)\beta(i,j)$. Then α is the increasing limit of the vectors α_k where α_0 is 0 and α_{k+1} is $\phi(\alpha_k)$. If α' is non-negative and satisfies the same equation, then since $0 \leq \alpha'$, applying ϕ repeatedly yields $\alpha \leq \alpha'$. Hence, if for some particular i,j, $\alpha'(i,j)=0$, then $\alpha(i,j)=0$.

Suppose now that there were α' distinct from α such that $\alpha(i,j)=0$ implies $\alpha'(i,j)=0$ for all i,j. Then the line $\lambda\alpha+\mu\alpha'$ with $\lambda+\mu=1$ consists of solutions of the equation $\gamma=\phi(\gamma)$ and the point where this line would leave the non-negative cone would be an α'' which vanishes for some pair i,j for which α did not vanish. But this is impossible. Hence $\alpha=\alpha'$ and α is the *unique* solution of the equation $\alpha=\phi(\alpha)$ and a finite number of other equations $\alpha(i,j)=0$. Hence α is rational. QED.

Note incidentally, that the argument above also gives us a method for calculating α. While solving linear equations with a unique solution can be done in polynomial time, it would appear that guessing the pairs (i,j) such that $\alpha(i,j)=0$ might make the problem NP-hard. That this is not so follows easily from the following observation. Define $\alpha_0=0$ and $\alpha_{k+1}=\phi(\alpha_k)$. Let $\beta=\alpha_m$ where $m=n^2$. Then the set $\{(i,j) \mid \alpha(i,j)=0\} = \{(i,j) \mid \beta(i,j)=0\}$ and can be calculated in polynomial time. Thus we can in fact calculate α itself in polynomial time.

In the following theorem we assume that the formulae A involved in programs are all atomic. I.e. we are considering the "poor-test" case.

Theorem 2: If two programs α and β always have the same behaviour (assignment of probabilities) over rational, finite models then they have the same behaviour over all models.

Proof: Suppose that they do not. Then there exists a model M and states s_0,t_0 such that $\alpha(s_0,t_0)\neq\beta(s_0,t_0)$.

We can assume without loss of generality that the universe W of M is countable.

For consider, for any state s, the set of all states t such that for some atomic program a, $a(s,t)>0$. There can only be countably many such t for each a and hence only countably many in all. Let W_s be the set of all these t. Define sets W_n as follows. W_0 is $\{s_0\}$ and W_{n+1} is the union of all W_u where $u\in W_n$. Let W' be the union of all W_n. Then if M' is the model M restricted to W', we have,

(1) For all t, if $\gamma(s_0,t)>0$, then $t\in W'$ and moreover, for all $s,t\in W'$, $\gamma(s,t)$ is the same in both M and M'.

(2) More generally, a formula $A(s')$ with $s'\in W'$ has the same probability in M and M'.

Thus we can assume without loss of generality that M itself was countable. Note that for (1) and (2) above, we do not need to assume that we are looking at atomic-test programs and or formulae. However, we do for the following observation.

Let U_n be a sequence of finite universes whose union is W and for a fixed poor-test program γ and states s,t in W_1, $\gamma_n(s,t)$ is the probability that γ takes us from s to t in M_n. Then $\gamma_n(s,t)$ approaches $\gamma(s,t)$ where the last is the probability in the full model M. (This fact can be proved by induction on the compexity of γ)

It follows that there is a finite model M_n such that $\alpha(s,t)$ and $\beta(s,t)$ are distinct in M_n. Otherwise they would have been the same in M.

Thus we can also assume, again without loss of generality, that our original M was finite.

Finally, we use the folllowing fact. Suppose that a finite universe W is fixed, Models M_i, M are such that the basic probabilities $a^i(s,t)$ in M_i for the atomic programs a, approach the probabilities a(s,t) in M for the same programs, then all probabilities $\alpha^i(s,t)$ approach $\alpha(s,t)$. Hence there must be a finite rational model M_i in which α and β are distinct. QED.

We say that the equation $\alpha=\beta$ is *valid* and write $\alpha\equiv\beta$ to mean that $\alpha(s,t)$ and $\beta(s,t)$ are always equal for all s,t over all models.

Theorem 3: For the poor-test programming language where all recursive calls are linear, the set of valid equations is co-r.e.

Proof: Immediate from theorems 1 and 2 above. If $\alpha\not\equiv\beta$ then there is, by theorem 2, a finite rational model in which they differ, and by theorem 1 (or rather the argument just after it) we can calculate the probabilities in that model, thereby discovering that they are distinct.

We conjecture that this set is decidable and in poly-space. However, proving this fact will need better control on the size of the rational model than that provided by theorem 2.

References

[FH] Y. Feldman and D. Harel, "A Probabilistic Dynamic Logic", *Proceedings of the 14th STOC,* (1982) pp.181-195.

[F] Y. Feldman, "A Decidable Prpositional Probabilistic Dynamic Logic", *Proceedings of the 15th STOC* (1983) pp 298-309.

[K1] D. Kozen, "Semantics of Probabilistic Programs", *20th IEEE-FOCS* (1979) pp 101-114. Also JCSS vol 22 (1981) pp 328-350.

[K2] D. Kozen, "A Probabilistic PDL", *15th ACM-STOC* 1983, pp. 291-297.

[P] R. Parikh, "Propositional Logics of Programs: A Survey", *Logic of Programs* Ed. E. Engeler, Springer LNCS 125, pp 102-144

[R] J. Reif, "Logics for Probabilistic Programming", *12th ACM-STOC* (1980) pp 8-13

A Low Level Language for Obtaining Decision Procedures for Classes of Temporal Logics

David A. Plaisted
SRI International
333 Ravenswood Avenue
Menlo Park, California 94025
(on leave from University of Illinois)

1. Introduction

We present a low level language which has been found convenient for obtaining a decision procedure for the interval logic of Schwartz, Melliar-Smith, and Vogt [7]. This language is a generalization of regular expressions, and is expressive enough so that there are easy translations of other temporal logics into the low level language. We give a non-elementary decision procedure for the language with a certain syntactic restriction. This procedure requires that eventualities be treated in a nonstandard way; the reason seems to be that this language deals with concatenation of sequences as well as with the usual temporal connectives. The low level language is convenient for expressing synchronization constraints such as mutual exclusion and thus may have applications to automatic generation of concurrent programs as described in Manna and Wolper[3]. It would also be interesting to investigate relationships of this language to the path expressions of [1].

1.1 Sets of computations

The most natural way to view the language is that each expression represents a set of computation sequence constraints. A ***computation sequence constraint*** is a sequence of sets of permitted and forbidden events, specifying which events may or may not occur at various instants of time. For example, we specify that event x is permitted and events y and z are forbidden at a given instant of time by the conjunction $x \wedge \bar{y} \wedge \bar{z}$, where x, y, and z are propositional variables. Thus a computation sequence constraint may be represented by a sequence of conjunctions of propositional variables and negations of propositional variables. A *computation sequence* over a given set X of events is a sequence of conjunctions C in which for each x in X, either x occurs in C or $\bar{x}$ occurs in C but not both. This represents the computation in which event x occurs at time i if x is in the ith conjunction, and event x does not occur at time i if $\bar{x}$ is in the ith conjunction. Such a computation sequence satisfies a constraint if permitted events occur when specified by the constraint and forbidden events do not occur when forbidden by the constraint. Sets of such constraints represent the disjunction of their elements; that is, a computation sequence satisfies a set S of constraints if the computation sequence satisfies some element of S. The language has connectives for expressing concurrency, nondeterministic choice, iteration, concatenation, "hiding" of events, and "exceptional events" which are false unless specified to be true, or true unless specified to be false. Note that this language differs from dynamic logic[6] in that we consider computation sequences rather than just input-output relations of programs.

2. Syntax

The language consists of well-formed expressions built up from propositional variables and their negations, the following constants:

T (True), F(False), T^*,

the following unary operations:

infloop, $\exists x$, Fx, Tx (for propositional variable x),

the following binary connectives:

$\wedge$ (conjunction), $\vee$ (disjunction), as, concatenation, ";", iter*, iter(*)

Expressions in the language are denoted by α, β, γ, δ. The concatenation of α and β is written as $\alpha\beta$. Also, infloop(α) is sometimes written α^∞. Thus $(\exists x)[y \wedge (Fx)(T^*x)]$ is an example of a formula. The quantifier $\exists x$ binds the variable x according to the usual scope rules; Fx and Tx do not bind x, although they can also be viewed as quantifiers. Thus in the formula $(Fx)(x \wedge y)$, both x and y are free variables; in the formula $(\exists x)(x \wedge y)$, y is free but x is not free. Therefore in the formula $(\exists x)(y \wedge (Fx)x)$, the same x is referred to by $(\exists x)$ and by (Fx). Negation can only be applied to propositional variables; this restriction seems natural for the examples we have considered.

3. Semantics

Our method of defining semantics is nonstandard, but seems most convenient for this language. With each formula α we associate a set $\Psi(\alpha)$ of ***partial interpretations,*** where a partial interpretation is a finite or infinite sequence of conjunctions of propositional variables and negations of propositional variables. These are the same as the "computation sequence constraints" introduced in section 1.1. Thus a formula represents a set of constraints; later we introduce another semantics in which a formula represents the set of computations satisfying at least one of these constraints. This is an example of a partial interpretation:

$$P, \ \overline{P} \wedge Q, \ \overline{R}, \ F, \ T, \ R$$

If I is a partial interpretation then |I| is the length of I (so the length of the above example is 6). The letters I and J will be used for partial interpretations. A formula α is ***satisfiable*** if there exists I in $\Psi(\alpha)$ such that no conjunction of I is contradictory.

Intuitively, propositional variables x represent computation sequences consisting of the single event x, negations $\overline{x}$ of propositional variables represent computation sequences consisting of a single time instant in which x does not occur, T represents any computation sequence of length one (that is, consisting of one instant of time), F represents no computation sequence, T^* represents any finite or infinite computation sequence, $\alpha \vee \beta$ represents the nondeterministic choice of α or β, $\alpha \wedge \beta$ represents concurrent execution of α and β, with the longer computation extended past the shorter one, as represents concurrent execution for sequences of the same length, $\alpha;\beta$ represents serial composition of α and β, $\alpha\beta$ represents serial composition of α and β in which the last state of α is concurrent with the first state of β, and $(\exists x)\alpha$ represents the computation of α with the events x "hidden;" this permits "local events" not visible outside of $(\exists x)\alpha$. Such local events can be used for message passing or synchronization within a subcomputation, for example. Also, $(Fx)\alpha$ represents computations of α in which the event x is made false everywhere except where it is specified to be true, and $(Tx)\alpha$ represents computations of α in which the event x is made true everywhere except where it is specified to be false. In addition, α^{∞} represents computation sequences in which a copy of α is begun at each successive time instant from now on, $iter(*)(\alpha, \beta)$ represents computation sequences in which copies of α are begun at successive time instants until possibly some future time, at which β is begun; and $iter*(\alpha, \beta)$ is the same except that β must eventually be started, and up to that time, copies of α are begun. Furthermore, these last three "iteration" operators require that all relevant α and β computations end at the same time. Possibly this simultaniety requirement can be dropped. We could add a constant ϵ to the language, representing a sequence of length zero, but this has not been necessary.

We give an example to show how the language can express synchronization constraints. Let α and β be formulae of the language in which neither of the propositional variables x or y occur free. Consider the expression

$$(Fx)(T^*x\alpha) \wedge (Fy)(T^*y\beta) \wedge (Fx)(Fy)(T^*xT^*y).$$

The first part of the formula $(Fx)(T^*x\alpha)$ specifies x as an event that occurs at the beginning of the α computation, but nowhere else until α ends. The second part of the formula specifies that y is an event that occurs at the beginning of the β computation, but nowhere else until β ends. The third part $(Fx)(Fy)(T^*xT^*y)$ specifies that the first time x becomes true is no later than the first time y becomes true. The whole formula therefore specifies that α begins no later than β begins. The formula

$$(\exists x)(\exists y)[(Fx)(T^*x\alpha) \wedge (Fy)(T^*y\beta) \wedge (Fx)(Fy)(T^*xT^*y)].$$

is the same except that the events x and y used to communicate between α and β have been hidden, and are no longer part of the computation sequences.

It is useful to define some operations on partial interpretations in order to give a formal semantics of the language.

$I \wedge J$ is defined by

1. $|I \wedge J| = max(|I|, |J|)$ and
2. if $i \leq |I|$, $i \leq |J|$ then $|I \wedge J|_i = I_i \wedge J_i$;
   if $i \leq |I|$, $i > |J|$ then $|I \wedge J|_i = I_i$;
   if $i > |I|$, $i \leq |J|$ then $|I \wedge J|_i = J_i$.

IJ (the concatenation of I and J) is defined by

1. $|IJ| = |I| + |J| - 1$ where $\infty + x = x + \infty = \infty$, and
2. $IJ_i = I_i$ if $i < |I|$,
   $IJ_i = I_i \wedge J_1$ if $i = |I|$,
   $IJ_i = J_{i+1-|I|}$ if $i > |I|$.

Thus there is a one element overlap between I and J.

$I;J$ is concatenation without overlap, and is defined by

1. $|I;J| = |I| + |J|$ and
2. $(I;J)_i = I_i$ if $i \leq |I|$,
   $(I;J)_i = J_{i-|I|}$ if $i > |I|$.

$(\exists x)I$ is I with x and $\bar{x}$ deleted from all conjunctions.

$(Fx)I$ is I with $\bar{x}$ added to all conjunctions not containing x or $\bar{x}$. Thus x is made false except where a value for x is already specified.

$(Tx)I$ is I with x added to all conjunctions not containing x or $\bar{x}$. Thus x is made true except where a value for x is already specified.

The semantics of formulae are defined as follows:

$\Psi(p) = \{p\}$ for propositional variable p
$\Psi(\bar{p}) = \{\bar{p}\}$
$\Psi(T) = \{T\}$
$\Psi(F) = \{F\}$
$\Psi(T^*) = \{T,\ \ T;T,\ \ T;T;T,\ \ \cdots,\ \ T^\infty\}$
$\Psi(\alpha \ \bigvee \ \beta) = \Psi(\alpha) \cup \Psi(\beta)$
$\Psi(\alpha \ \bigwedge \ \beta) = \{I \ \bigwedge \ J \ : \ I \in \Psi(\alpha),\ J \in \Psi(\beta)\}$
$\Psi(\alpha \ as \ \beta) = \{I \ \bigwedge \ J \ : \ I \in \Psi(\alpha),\ J \in \Psi(\beta),\ |I| = |J|\}$
$\Psi(\alpha;\beta) = \{I;J \ : \ I \in \Psi(\alpha),\ J \in \Psi(\beta)\}$
$\Psi(\alpha\beta) = \{IJ \ : \ I \in \Psi(\alpha),\ J \in \Psi(\beta)\}$
$\alpha^\infty \equiv \alpha \ \bigwedge \ (T;\alpha) \ \bigwedge \ (T;T;\alpha) \ \bigwedge \ (T;T;T;\alpha) \ \bigwedge \ \cdots$
$iter*(\alpha,\ \beta) \equiv \bigvee_{k \geq 0}[\alpha \ as \ (T;\alpha) \ as \ (T^2;\alpha) \ as \ \cdots \ as \ (T^k;\alpha) \ as \ (T^{k+1};\beta)]$
where T^2 is $T;T$ and T^3 is $T;T;T$, et cetera.
$iter(*)(\alpha,\ \beta) \equiv \alpha^\infty \ \bigvee \ iter*(\alpha,\ \beta)$
$\Psi(\exists x\alpha) = \{\exists xI \ : \ I \in \Psi(\alpha)\}$
$\Psi(Fx\alpha) = \{FxI \ : \ I \in \Psi(\alpha)\}$
$\Psi(Tx\alpha) = \{TxI \ : \ I \in \Psi(\alpha)\}$

3.1 Restrictions on the Quantifiers

Note that Fx and Tx are non-monotone. They must therefore be used with care. Let L be the language defined above. Let L_1 be L with the following restriction added:

The quantifiers Tx and Fx may only be applied to a formula α which is composed of

a) formulae in which x does not occur free

b) x

c) the connectives concatenation, ";", $\bigwedge$, as, $\exists y$, Fy, Ty for $y \neq x$.

If these restrictions are relaxed, then one can construct formulae which can count arbitrarily high, and the tableau like decision procedure does not work correctly. In fact, satisfiability of formulae in L may even be undecidable.

4. A Decision Procedure

The decision procedure for L_1 is complicated by the fact that eventualities do not behave in the usual way. The connective iter* is the only connective introducing an eventuality: iter*(α, β) implies that eventually β will be true (considering the interpretations as representing sequences of formulae which must be true at successive instants of time). Also, the formula $iter*(\alpha, \beta);\gamma$ implies that eventually $\beta;\gamma$ will be true. We express an eventuality $\Diamond\delta$ as $\bigvee_k(T^k;\delta)$. We would like to find some eventuality δ such that

$$iter*(\alpha, \beta);\gamma \equiv [iter(*)(\alpha, \beta);\gamma] \wedge \Diamond\delta$$

or such that

$$iter*(\alpha, \beta);\gamma \equiv [iter(*)(\alpha, \beta);\gamma] \text{ as } \Diamond\delta$$

Now, letting δ be $\beta;\gamma$ will not work because we need to know that the β in $\beta;\gamma$ ends the same time $iter(*)(\alpha, \beta)$ ends. In fact, we have the following result:

Proposition 4.1. There does not exist a formula δ depending on α, β, γ such that for all α, β, γ,

$$iter*(\alpha, \beta);\gamma \equiv [iter(*)(\alpha, \beta);\gamma] \wedge \Diamond\delta$$

or such that for all α, β, γ,

$$iter*(\alpha, \beta);\gamma \equiv [iter(*)(\alpha, \beta);\gamma] \text{ as } \Diamond\delta$$

Proof. Let α be $PT^\infty \vee \bar{P}T^*$, let β be $\bar{P}$, and let γ be $\bar{P}^\infty$. Then $P;\bar{P}^\infty$ is a model of iter$(*)(\alpha, \beta);\gamma$ but not a model of iter*$(\alpha, \beta);\gamma$. Therefore if such a δ exists, $\Diamond\delta$ must be false in the interpretation $P;\bar{P}^\infty$. However, $\bar{P}^\infty$ is a model of iter*(α, β) so $\Diamond\delta$ must be true in the interpretation $\bar{P}^\infty$. But if $\bar{P}^\infty \models \Diamond\delta$ then $T;\bar{P}^\infty \models \Diamond\delta$ hence $P;\bar{P}^\infty \models \Diamond\delta$, contradiction.

Because of this result, we give a decision procedure in which eventualities are treated in a nonstandard way. The decision procedure is graph oriented and model theoretic in nature; it may be possible to convert it to a syntactic nondeterministic tableau-like decision procedure. We first give another definition of the semantics of a formula of L.

Definition. A ***standard temporal interpretation*** is an infinite sequence of interpretations of propositional variables in a given set X of propositional variables. This is the same as the "computation sequence" introduced in section 1.1.

Definition. If I is a partial interpretation $c_1, c_2, c_3, \cdots$, let $\Psi_1(I)$ be the set of standard temporal interpretations I' such that c_i is true in the ith element of I' for $1 \leq i \leq |I|$.

Definition. If α is a formula of L_1 then $\Psi_1(\alpha) = \cup\{\Psi_1(I) : I \in \Psi(\alpha)\}$. This is the set of computation sequences satisfying at least one of the constraints in $\Psi(\alpha)$.

Note that α is consistent iff $\Psi_1(\alpha) \neq \emptyset$. For each formula α of L_1, the decision procedure constructs a graph G_α and provides a semantics $\Psi_1(G_\alpha)$ for G_α such that $\Psi_1(G_\alpha) = \Psi_1(\alpha)$. An iteration procedure applied to G_α decides if $\Psi_1(G_\alpha) = \emptyset$.

4.1 Graph construction

We construct graphs G_α such that G_α represents the set of computation sequences specified by α. The nodes in the graphs represent states, and the edges represent transitions from one state to another. Successive states in a path through the graph represent successive instants of time in a computation sequence. If there is an edge from node m to node n, then this edge specifies the events (propositional variables) that must occur or not occur in state m, if the transition from m to n is taken. Also, this edge may have a set of *eventualities*, representing events that must occur at some future time, and a set of *satisfied eventualities*, representing events that occur at state m and satisfy some previous eventuality. It is necessary to associate eventualities with nodes (actually, node basis elements, see below) in the graph. The reason is that if two processes are running concurrently, and they both require that some eventuality be satisfied, it is sometimes necessary to know for which of the two processes the eventuality has been satisfied. It may not be enough just for an eventuality to be satisfied; it may have to be satisfied at a particular time in the computation. For this reason, eventualities also contain information about which node they are associated with. We let the nodes in a graph be sets of elements of the *node basis*, which is some set disjoint from the set of eventualities. The reason for using subsets of the node basis as nodes of the graph, is that we can represent states s1 and s2 occurring concurrently by a node which is the union of the node basis elements of s1 and s2. However, if s1 and s2 have common elements, the semantics can become confused; eventualities are associated with node basis elements, and it may be necessary to distinguish which node the eventuality came from. Therefore we require that the node basis elements of s1 and s2 be disjoint whenever such a union is done. If this disjointness property does not already hold, then we define a *disjoining* operation and a *separation* property on graphs, which insure that the disjointness property does hold.

We define the graphs as follows. Each node is a subset of the ***node basis*** NB. One node of the graph is distinguished as the ***initial node*** of G, written init(G). The edges e have, in addition to an initial node init(e) and a final node fin(e), a set ev(e) of ***eventualities*** and a set se(e) of ***satisfied eventualities.*** Each eventuality and satisfied eventuality is an ordered pair <v, n> where n is a subset of NB and v is an ***eventuality primitive.*** The eventuality primitives are elements of the set EP; we assume the set EP is specified in some way and is disjoint from NB. An edge e also has a ***propositional part*** prop(e), which is a conjunction of propositional variables and their negations. Associated with each edge e of a graph G there is a ***node relation*** R_e between subsets of NB and subsets of NB. We consider such a relation R to be the set $\{<x, y> : R(x, y)\}$. Thus $\emptyset$ is the totally undefined relation. Also, for nodes m and n, let $g_{m,n}$ be the relation $\{<m, n>\}$ between m and n. We write the edge e as the tuple <init(e), fin(e), prop(e), ev(e), se(e), R_e>. Let N(G) be the nodes of graph G and E(G) be the edges. Each graph may have a distinguished END node. This indicates the end of the partial interpretation.

The graphs G_α for various α are defined as follows. We give the easy cases first.

If α is T, F, x, or $\bar{x}$ for propositional variable x, then G_α is defined by $N(G_\alpha) = \{m, END\}$, init(G_α) = m, and $E(G_\alpha) = \{<m, END, \alpha, \emptyset, \emptyset, \emptyset>\}$. Here m is some singleton subset of NB. Note that f_e is totally undefined for the edge e of G.

If α is T' then G_α is defined by $N(G_\alpha) = \{m, END\}$, init(G_α) = m, and $E(G_\alpha) = \{<m, m, T, \emptyset, \emptyset, g_{m,m}>, <m, END, T, \emptyset, \emptyset, empty>\}$, where m is some singleton subset of NB.

$G_{\exists x\alpha}$ is G_α with x and $\bar{x}$ deleted from the propositional parts of all edges (and node relations unchanged).

$G_{Fx\alpha}$ is G_α with $\bar{x}$ added to the propositional parts of all edges not containing x or $\bar{x}$ in the propositional part (and node relations unchanged).

$G_{Tx\alpha}$ is G_α with x added to the propositional parts of all edges not containing x or $\bar{x}$ in the propositional part (and node relations unchanged).

Definition. Two graphs G_α and G_β are ***separated*** if they have no common node basis elements or eventuality primitives. That is, if $m_1 \in Nodes(G_\alpha)$ and $m_2 \in Nodes(G_\beta)$ then $m_1 \cap m_2 = \emptyset$, and if $<v_1, m_1>$ is an eventuality or satisfied eventuality of G_α, and $<v_2, m_2>$ is an eventuality or satisfied eventuality of G_β, then $v_1 \neq v_2$.

In the following definitions of graphs, assume that G_α and G_β are separated. If they are not, then assume node basis elements and eventuality primitives have been systematically renamed so that G_α and G_β are separated. Note that this also requires modifying the node relations in a corresponding way.

$G_{\alpha \vee \beta}$ is defined as follows: Let m be a new node not in N(G_α) or N(G_β). That is, m is {b} for some node basis element b which does not appear in G_α or G_β. Then

$N(G_{\alpha \vee \beta}) = N(G_\alpha) \cup N(G_\beta) \cup \{m\}$,

$init(G_{\alpha \vee \beta}) = m$, and

$E(G_{\alpha \vee \beta}) = E(G_\alpha) \cup E(G_\beta) \cup$

$\{<m,\ n,\ C,\ ev,\ se,\ g_{m,n}> :$

$<init(G_\alpha),\ n,\ C,\ ev,\ se,\ R_1> \in E(G_\alpha)\} \cup$

$\{<m,\ n,\ C,\ ev,\ se,\ g_{m,n}> :$

$<init(G_\beta),\ n,\ C,\ ev,\ se,\ R_2> \in E(G_\beta)\}$.

$G_{\alpha;\beta}$ is defined as follows: $N(G_{\alpha;\beta}) = N(G_\alpha) \cup N(G_\beta)$, $E(G_{\alpha;\beta}) = E(G_\alpha) \cup E(G_\beta)$ except that edges of G_α of the form $<m,\ END,\ C,\ ev,\ se,\ R_e>$ are replaced by $<m,\ init(G_\beta),\ C,\ ev,\ se,\ g_{m,\ init(G_\beta)}>$. Also, $init(G_{\alpha;\beta}) = init(G_\alpha)$.

$G_{\alpha\beta}$ is defined as follows: $N(G_{\alpha\beta}) = N(G_\alpha) \cup N(G_\beta)$, $init(G_{\alpha\beta}) = init(G_\alpha)$, and $E(G_{\alpha\beta}) = E(G_\alpha) \cup E(G_\beta)$ except that an edge $<m,\ END,\ C,\ ev,\ se,\ R_e>$ of G_α is replaced by $\{<m,\ n,\ C \wedge D,\ ev',\ se,\ g_{m,n}> \ :\ <init(G_\beta),\ n,\ D,\ ev',\ se',\ R'> \in E(G_\beta)\}$.

For the remaining cases we need to define operations on edges. Suppose $e_1 \cdots e_k$ are edges, and either $fin(e_i) = END$ for all i or $fin(e_i) \neq END$ for all i. Then $as(e_1,\ \cdots,\ e_k)$ is the edge e such that

$init(e) = \cup_i init(e_i)$,

$fin(e) = \cup_i fin(e_i)$ unless $fin(e_i) = END$ for all i,

in which case $fin(e) = END$;

$prop(e) = \bigwedge_i prop(e_i)$,

$ev(e) = \cup_i ev(e_i)$,

$se(e) = \cup_i se(e_i)$, and

$R_e = \cup_i R_{e_i}$.

Also, $and(e_1,\ \cdots,\ e_k)$ is defined similarly except that the condition on $fin(e_i)$ and END need not hold, and if $fin(e_i) = END$ for all i then $fin(and(e_1,\ \cdots,\ e_k)) = END$, but otherwise $fin(and(e_1,\ \cdots,\ e_k)) = \cup\{fin(e_i)\ :\ fin(e_i) \neq END\}$.

$G_{\alpha \wedge \beta}$ is defined as follows: $N(G_{\alpha \wedge \beta})=\{m \cup n \ : \ m \in N(G_\alpha), \ n \in N(G_\beta)\} \cup N(G_\alpha) \cup N(G_\beta)$, $E(G_{\alpha \wedge \beta})=\{and(e_1, \ e_2) \ : \ e_1 \in E(G_\alpha), \ e_2 \in E(G_\beta)\}$, and $init(G_{\alpha \wedge \beta})=init(G_\alpha) \cup init(G_\beta)$.

$G_{\alpha \, as \, \beta}$ is defined as follows: $N(G_{\alpha \, as \, \beta})=\{m \cup n \ : \ m \in N(G_\alpha), \ n \in N(G_\beta)\}$, $E(G_{\alpha \, as \, \beta})=\{as(e_1, \ e_2) \ : \ e_1 \in E(G_\alpha), \ e_2 \in E(G_\beta), \ as(e_1, \ e_2) \textit{ is defined}\}$, and $init(G_{\alpha \, as \, \beta})=init(G_\alpha) \cup init(G_\beta)$.

The remaining connectives are iter*, iter(*), and infloop. For these iteration primitives, it is necessary to require that some of the graphs be node disjoint. We say that a graph G is *node disjoint* if for any two distinct nodes m and n of G, $m \cap n = \emptyset$. We define the operation of *disjoining* a graph G_1 to produce an "equivalent" graph G_2 which is node disjoint. This consists essentially in renaming node basis elements in each node so that distinct nodes will be disjoint, and also adjusting eventualities, satisfied eventualities, and node relations in an appropriate way. Formally, for each node n we find a 1-1 function θ_n whose domain is n and such that for distinct nodes m and n of G_1, $\theta_m(m)$ and $\theta_n(n)$ are disjoint. Note that we are extending θ_m and θ_n to sets of elements in the node basis, in the usual way. Then G_2 is defined by Nodes(G_2) $=$ $\{\theta_n(n) \ : \ n \in Nodes(G_1)\}$, Init($G_2$) $=$ $\theta_{Init(G_1)}(Init(G_1))$, and Edges($G_2$) $=$ $\{<\theta_m(m), \ \theta_n(n), \ C, \ ev', \ se', \ R'> \ : \ <m, \ n, \ C, \ ev, \ se, \ R> \in Edges(G_1)\}$, where ev' $=$ $\{<v, \ \theta_m(r)> \ : \ <v, \ r> \in ev\}$, se' $=$ $\{<v, \ \theta_m(r)> \ : \ <v, \ r> \in se\}$, and R' $=$ $\{<\theta_m(x), \ \theta_n(y)> \ : \ <x, \ y> \in R\}$. It is this operation of disjoining graphs that leads to the nonelementary performance of the satisfiability algorithm. It is not really necessary to do this operation in all cases, but we specify it for all cases for simplicity. When defining graphs for $iter*(\alpha, \ \beta)$, $iter(*)(\alpha, \ \beta)$, and $infloop(\alpha)$, we assume that α and β are separated as before, and also that α is node disjoint.

$G_{iter(*)(\alpha, \ \beta)}$ is defined using $G_{\alpha \vee \beta}$ in the following way: $N(G_{iter(*)(\alpha, \ \beta)})=\{\cup S \ : \ S$ is a subset of $N(G_{\alpha \vee \beta})$ not containing END and containing at most one node in $N(G_\beta)\} \cup \{END\}$, $init(G_{iter(*)(\alpha, \ \beta)})=\{init(G_{\alpha \vee \beta})\}$, and $E(G_{iter(*)(\alpha, \ \beta)})=E1 \cup E2$ where E1 and E2 are as follows:

$E1=\{ \ as \ (e_1, \ \cdots, \ e_k, \ <init(G_{\alpha \vee \beta}), \ init(G_{\alpha \vee \beta}), \ T, \ \emptyset, \ \emptyset, \ g_{init(G_{\alpha \vee \beta}), \ init(G_{\alpha \vee \beta})}>) \ :$ this is defined and $e_i \in E(G_{\alpha \vee \beta})$ all i, no e_i in $E(G_\beta)$, $init(e_1)=init(G_{\alpha \vee \beta})$, and $init(e_i)$ are all distinct$\}$

$E2=\{ \ as \ (e_1, \ \cdots, \ e_k) \ : \ as \ (e_1, \ \cdots, \ e_k)$ is defined and $e_i \in E(G_{\alpha \vee \beta})$ with exactly one e_i in $E(G_\beta)$ and $init(e_i)$ are all distinct$\}$

The edges E1 represent repeated iterations of α and the edges E2 represent the time after β has begun.

$G_{iter*(\alpha,\ \beta)}$ is the same as $G_{iter(*)(\alpha,\ \beta)}$ except that there is a new eventuality $<v,\ init(G_{\alpha\ \vee\ \beta})>$ added to edges e such that $init(G_{\alpha\ \vee\ \beta}) \in init(e)$ and $init(G_{\alpha\ \vee\ \beta}) \in fin(e)$. Also, edges e in $G_{iter*(\alpha,\ \beta)}$ have satisfied eventuality $<v,\ init(G_{\alpha\ \vee\ \beta})>$ added if $init(G_{\alpha\ \vee\ \beta}) \in init(e)$ but not $init(G_{\alpha\ \vee\ \beta}) \in fin(e)$. Intuitively, v represents the eventuality that β must eventually be true.

Finally, $G_{infloop(\alpha)}$ is like $G_{iter(*)(\alpha,\ \beta)}$ except that the edges in E2 and nodes having subsets in N(G_β) are omitted.

4.2 Semantics of graphs

With a graph G as above we associate a semantics $\Psi_1(G)$ representing the set of standard interpretations satisfying G. A standard interpretation I is in $\Psi_1(G)$ if there is an infinite sequence $e_1,\ \ e_2,\ \ \cdots$ of edges of G such that

a) init(e_1) = init(G)
b) $fin(e_i) = init(e_{i+1})$ for all i $\geq$ 1
c) $I_i \models prop(e_i)$ for all i, where I_i is the interpretation I specifies at the ith instant of time
d) all eventualities in the path $e_1,\ \ e_2,\ \ \cdots$ are satisfied.

The satisfaction of eventualities is defined in a nonstandard way. We extend the node relations R to eventuality relations by R(<v, m>, <w, n>) iff v = w and R(m, n). An eventuality ev in $ev(e_i)$ is satisfied in the path if there exist $ev_i,\ \ ev_{i+1},\ \ \cdots,\ \ ev_{i+k}$ such that ev = ev_i and $ev_{i+k} \in se(e_{i+k})$ and for all j, $0 \leq j < k$, $R_{e_{i+j}}(ev_{i+j},\ \ ev_{i+j+1})$. Thus the eventualities may be transformed at each edge in the path, and they are satisfied if at some future time, some such transformed eventuality is satisfied. We claim that $\Psi_1(\alpha) = \Psi_1(G_\alpha)$ for all formulae α in L_1. Thus the semantics of graphs agree with those of the formulae of the low level language.

4.3 Example

We now give an example of a formula and the graph constructed from it. First we give an intuitive explanation of the construction for iter*(α, β). Consider the graph G = $G_{\alpha\ \vee\ \beta}$ for $\alpha\ \vee\ \beta$. We construct the graph for $G_{iter*(\alpha,\ \beta)}$ from G by permitting the nodes of G to have "markers." These markers can travel along edges of G. The current state of the graph is determined by which nodes have markers on them. At the start, only the initial node of G has a marker. Thereafter, markers travel along edges in one of two ways: a) The marker from the initial node travels to some node in G_α along an edge, and also reproduces a copy of itself which remains on the initial node. All other markers travel along some edge; if there is an edge e and a marker on node init(e), this marker can travel to node fin(e). This marker is then removed from init(e). A marker can only travel to one other node in one time instant (except that the marker on the initial node also may reproduce a copy of itself on the initial node). If a marker is on a node with no outgoing edges, this marker is deleted; this will happen for markers on the END node, for example. b) The marker from the initial node travels to some node in G_β, but does not reproduce a copy of itself on the initial node. Other markers may travel along edges as in a).

In both cases, if a node ends up with more than one marker on it, all but one of these markers are removed. The collection of marked nodes may be considered as the "current node" of the graph G. A transition as in a) corresponds to the part of the iteration in which α is being repeated; a transition as in b) corresponds to the beginning of the β part of the iteration. Let us call these transitions *a-transitions* and *b-transitions,* respectively. These transitions are the edges of G. The propositional part of such a transition is the conjunction of the propositional parts of the edges of $G_{\alpha \vee \beta}$ traversed during the transition. The a-transitions have a new eventuality associated with them; the b-transitions have this eventuality satisfied. This corresponds to the fact that there must eventually be a b-transition. In the formal definition of G, the nodes of G are unions of the node basis elements in the marked nodes of $G_{\alpha \vee \beta}$, with the END node ignored in such unions. However, if only END is marked, this corresponds to the END node of G. The graph $G_{iter(*)(\alpha,\ \beta)}$ is similar except that there is no eventuality for a b-transition to occur. The graph G_{α^∞} is similar except that there are no b-transitions and no eventuality for a b-transition to occur.

Consider the formula iter*(P, Q). Since all the partial interpretations P must end at the same time as Q does, this formula is equivalent to Q. To get a nontrivial use of iter*, we need to use the T^* constant. Consider the formula iter*(PT^*, Q). This is equivalent to $\bigvee_i P^i;Q$. To represent graphs pictorially, we draw a node as a circle or oval containing its node basis elements. The edges are drawn as arrows from their initial node to their final node. The propositional parts of edges are drawn next to the edges. The eventualities, satisfied eventualities, and eventuality transforms are not given in the picture but are specified separately for simplicity. The initial node is indicated by a minus sign next to the node; the end node, if any, is indicated by END. This graph, with nodes deleted that are not reachable from the initial node, is as follows. Note that it is also permissible to delete edges whose propositional part is contradictory.

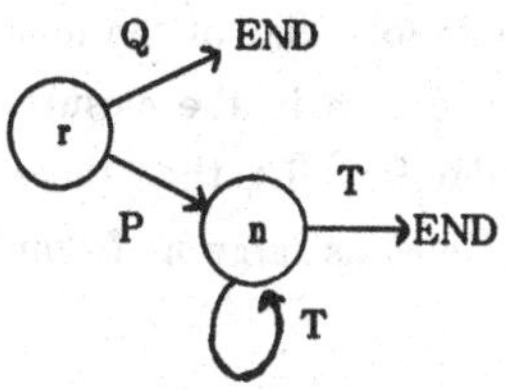

Graph for the formula $PT^{*} \vee Q$

Now, whenever there is an a-transition, P will be true and markers will remain on nodes {r} and {n} and possibly END; when there is a b-transition, Q will be true. Thus this graph specifies $\bigvee_i P^i;Q$.

4.4 Iteration method

An iteration method is applied to the graph G_α to determine if α is satisfiable. The idea is to repeatedly delete edges having eventualities that cannot be satisfied by any path in the graph, and to delete nodes having no outgoing edges (except for the END node). Also, edges whose propositional part is contradictory may be deleted. The formula α is satisfiable iff the initial node of G_α remains after this iteration is completed. When searching for paths satisfying eventualities, the eventuality transforms have to be considered as indicated above. The techniques described in [5] for obtaining decision procedures for combinations of temporal logic and other specialized theories, can also be applied. Finally, as in [5], it is possible to permit an arbitrary combination of state variables, whose values change with time, and free variables, whose values do not. For a discussion of these concepts see [5].

4.5 Complexity

This decision procedure is of nonelementary complexity since $|N(G_{iter*(\alpha,\ \beta)})|$ is exponential in $|N(G_\alpha)|$, and the node disjoining procedure can then lead to an exponential number of node basis elements in the graph. There may be an arbitrarily deep nesting of the iter* and iter(*) and infloop connectives, leading to nonelementary behavior. The following example may give some syntactic insight as to why the closure of the formulae in L_1 can be so large: Let A_1 be the formula

$$infloop(\exists x(iter(*)(\alpha_1,\ \beta_1)\ as\ \cdots\ as\ iter(*)(\alpha_n,\ \beta_n)))$$

The closure of this formula will include formulae of the form γ_1 *as* γ_2 *as* $\cdots$ *as* γ_k where γ_i is of the form $\exists x(\delta_1$ *as* $\cdots$ *as* $\delta_n)$ and δ_i is in the closure of $iter(*)(\alpha_i,\ \beta_i)$. If the closure of $iter(*)(\alpha_i,\ \beta_i)$ has at least two formulae for all i, then there can be 2^n formulae γ_i and the closure of A_1 can contain formulae 2^n times as large as formulae in the closure of $iter(*)(\alpha_i,\ \beta_i)$. Similarly, let A_2 be

$$infloop((iter(*)(\alpha_1,\ \beta_1)\ as\ \cdots\ as\ iter(*)(\alpha_n,\ \beta_n));\gamma)$$

The closure of A_2 includes formulae of a similar form except that γ_i is of the form $(\delta_1$ *as* $\cdots$ *as* $\delta_n);\gamma$. Finally, let A_3 be the formula

$$infloop(\gamma\ \wedge\ (iter(*)(\alpha_1,\ \beta_1)\ as\ \cdots\ as\ iter(*)(\alpha_n,\ \beta_n)))$$

The closure of A_3 is similar except that γ_i is of the form $\gamma\ \wedge\ (\delta_1$ *as* $\cdots$ *as* $\delta_n)$. Intuitively, the closure of a formula A represents the set of formulae B which may be true at future times if A is true now.

5. Interval logic

We now give some examples to illustrate how the interval logic of Schwartz, Melliar-Smith, and Vogt[7] may easily be translated into the low level language. In fact, this translation was the original motivation for developing the low level language, since it seemed much simpler to program a decision procedure for the low level language than for interval logic.

Interval logic was developed to permit convenient reasoning about intervals of time. An interval *formula* is a formula of interval logic and has a Boolean truth value in any interpretation. An interval *term* is an expression of interval logic whose value is a time interval. Without going into details, let Expr(α)(z) be the translation of interval formula α in context z, and let Int(α)(x y z d) be the translation of interval term α in context z, where the interval begins at x and ends at y. Here d is the direction in which you are looking for the interval, and may be F (forward) or B (backward). For our purposes, x, y, and z are propositional variables which intuitively denote the next state in which they are true. We give a few translations; for an explanation of the notation see [7].

$$Expr([I]\alpha)(z) \equiv \exists x\ \exists y Int(I)(x,\ y,\ z,\ F)\ \wedge\ Fx(T^{*}xExpr(\alpha)(y))$$

$$Int(\alpha\rightarrow\beta)(x,\ y,\ z,\ d) \equiv \exists w Int(\alpha)(w,\ x,\ z,\ d)\ \wedge$$
$$\exists v Fx(T^{*}xInt(\beta)(v,\ y,\ z,\ F))$$

$$Expr(p)(z) = \text{if } z = \infty \text{ then } pT^{\infty} \text{ else } p\ iter*(T^{*},\ z)$$

To decide if an interval formula α is valid, we can convert $\neg\alpha$ to a normal form β and test if $Expr(\beta)(\infty)$ is satisfiable.

6. A PSPACE sublanguage

We originally intended to use the language L_1 to show that interval logic has a PSPACE decision procedure. For this, it is necessary to find a sublanguage of L_1 which can be decided in PSPACE and into which all interval logic expressions may be translated. We have been unable to do this. It seems that preventing α from containing any iteration connectives in expressions of the form $iter*(\alpha,\ \beta)$, $iter(*)(\alpha,\ \beta)$, and $infloop(\alpha)$ would help, but this prevents certain interval logic formulae from being expressed. However, this does not mean that interval logic is not in PSPACE.

7. Other temporal logics

It would be interesting to compare the expressive power of L_1 with other temporal and process logics. One can easily encode the usual discrete linear time temporal logic into L_1 by expressing Until(x, y) as iter(*)(x, y) (with no eventuality implied), "next time x" as T;x, "henceforth x" as infloop(x), "eventually x" as iter*(T^{*}, x), propositional variables p as pT^{*}, $\neg p$ as $\neg pT^{*}$, and Boolean connectives $\wedge$ and $\vee$ as themselves. This requires pushing negations to the bottom, but it is possible to do this; the only slightly hard case is negating "until".

The semicolon operator seems similar to the "chop" operator of dynamic logic [2]; the interval logic of Moszkowski[4] has a slightly similar semicolon operator but is undecidable. We now consider a branching time version of the low level language.

7.1 Branching time syntax

Expressions may be *path expressions* or *state expressions*. Intuitively, the models are trees, and path expressions refer to paths in the tree while state expressions refer to the whole tree. All the previous connectives are still used; they map path expressions to path expressions. Thus if α and β are path expressions, so are $\alpha;\beta$, $\alpha\beta$ et cetera. In addition, if α is a path expression, then $A\alpha$ and $E\alpha$ are state expressions. Also, if α and β are state expressions, then $\alpha \wedge \beta$ and $\alpha \vee \beta$ are state expressions. If α is a state expression, then $\exists x\alpha$, $Fx\alpha$, and

$T x \alpha$ are state expressions. Finally, if x is a propositional variable or its negation, T, or F, then x may be regarded as a state expression. Thus we are overloading certain operators; for example, $\exists x$ maps path expressions to path expressions and state expressions to state expressions. Finally, any state expression can be viewed as a path expression.

7.2 Branching time semantics

The semantics is defined analogously to that for the linear time logic. A *literal* is a propositional variable or its negation. A *partial path interpretation* is a triple (V, L, P) where V is a tree, L is a labeling function mapping nodes of V to conjunctions of literals, and P is a finite or infinite path of V starting at the root and not crossing any node more than once. A *partial state interpretation* is a pair (V, L) with V and L as above. With each path expression α we associate a set $\Psi(\alpha)$ of partial path interpretations, and with each state expression α we associate a set $\Psi(\alpha)$ of partial state interpretations. The expression α is *consistent* if some member of $\Psi(\alpha)$ is a tree having no contradictory conjunctions. Let us call a path P of V as above a *prefix path* of V. By convention, if L is a labeling function of a tree V, and N is a node not in V, then L(N) = T. The semantics is defined as follows.

$(V, L, P) \in \Psi(x)$ for x a literal, T, or F if L(N) = x where N is the root node of V and L(M) = T (True) for $M \neq N$ and P = {N}.

$(V, L, P) \in \Psi(T^*)$ if L(N) = T for all N and P is any prefix path of V.

$(V, L, P) \in \Psi(\alpha \wedge \beta)$ if there exists L1, L2, and P1 such that P1 is a prefix of P and $L \equiv L1 \wedge L2$ and either $(V, L1, P1) \in \Psi(\alpha)$ and $(V, L2, P) \in \Psi(\beta)$ or $(V, L1, P) \in \Psi(\alpha)$ and $(V, L2, P1) \in \Psi(\beta)$.

$(V, L, P) \in \Psi(\alpha \text{ as } \beta)$ if there exist L1, L2 such that $L \equiv L1 \wedge L2$ and $(V, L1, P) \in \Psi(\alpha)$ and $(V, L2, P) \in \Psi(\beta)$.

$(V, L, P) \in \Psi(\alpha \vee \beta)$ if $(V, L, P) \in \Psi(\alpha)$ or $(V, L, P) \in \Psi(\beta)$.

$(V, L, P) \in \Psi(\alpha;\beta)$ if there exist L1, L2, P1, P2 such that $L \equiv L1 \wedge L2$, P = P1 ; P2, $(V, L1, P1) \in \Psi(\alpha)$, and V has a subtree V1 such that $(V1, L2, P2) \in \Psi(\beta)$.

$(V, L, P) \in \Psi(\alpha\beta)$ if there exist L1, L2, P1, P2 such that $L \equiv L1 \wedge L2$, P = P1 P2 (that is, P1 and P2 have a node in common), $(V, L1, P1) \in \Psi(\alpha)$, and V has a subtree V1 such that $(V1, L2, P2) \in \Psi(\beta)$.

$infloop(\alpha) \equiv \alpha \wedge T;\alpha \wedge T^2;\alpha \wedge \cdots \wedge T^k;\alpha \wedge \cdots$

$iter*(\alpha, \beta) \equiv \bigvee_j [\alpha \wedge T;\alpha \wedge \cdots \wedge T^j;\alpha \wedge T^{j+1};\beta]$

$iter(*)(\alpha, \beta) \equiv infloop(\alpha) \vee iter*(\alpha, \beta)$

$(V, L, P) \in \Psi(\exists x \alpha)$ if there is a function L1 such that $(V, L1, P) \in \Psi(\alpha)$ and L is identical to L1 except that L deletes x and $\bar{x}$ from nodes in P.

$(V, L, P) \in \Psi(Fx\alpha)$ if there is a function L1 such that $(V, L1, P) \in \Psi(\alpha)$ and L is identical to L1 except that L adds $\bar{x}$ to nodes of P not containing x or $\bar{x}$.

$(V, L, P) \in \Psi(Tx\alpha)$ if there is a function L1 such that $(V, L1, P) \in \Psi(\alpha)$ and L is identical to L1 except that L adds x to nodes of P not containing x or $\bar{x}$.

$(V, L, \{N\}) \in \Psi(\alpha)$ if α is a state expression, $(V, L) \in \Psi(\alpha)$, and N is the root of V. (This converts state expressions to path expressions.)

If α is a literal, T, F, or T^*, regarded as a state expression, then $\Psi(\alpha)$ is as above except that the path part of interpretations is omitted.

$(V, L) \in \Psi(\exists x \alpha)$ for state expression α if there is a function L1 such that $(V, L1) \in \Psi(\alpha)$ and L is identical to L1 except that L deletes x and $\bar{x}$ from *all* nodes.

The semantics of $Fx\alpha$ and $Tx\alpha$ for state expressions α are defined similarly, modifying *all* conjunctions, not just those on some path.

$(V, L) \in \Psi(A\alpha)$ if for all infinite prefix paths P of V, P has a prefix P1 such that $(V, L, P1) \in \Psi(\alpha)$.

$(V, L) \in \Psi(E\alpha)$ if for some prefix path P of V, $(V, L, P) \in \Psi(\alpha)$.

We do not have any information about the decidability of this branching time version of the low level language, except that the satisfiability problem is at least as hard as that of L_1 since L_1 is a subset of the language. Also, it appears that L_1 is of nonelementary complexity.

7.3 Regular expressions

We could add the star operator α^* to the linear and branching time logics to get a formalism including regular expressions as a syntactic subset. However, this was not necessary for our purposes.

8. Executable specifications

In the style of Manna and Wolper [3] and the "path expressions" of Campbell and Habermann[1], we can use the linear time low level language to construct programs having a specified behavior. Given a low level formula α, we construct the graph G_α which represents the set of models of α; this graph can then be regarded as a program. By adding suitable fairness constraints to certain nodes of G_α, we obtain a program which satisfies all eventualities of α and thus behaves as specified by α. In this way we might consider automatically constructing concurrent programs from their specifications

9. Acknowledgements

This work was initiated by many conversations with Michael Melliar-Smith, Richard Schwartz, and Fritz Vogt at SRI International, relating to the possible implementation of a decision procedure for interval logic. The comments of Richard Schwartz helped in the preparation of this paper.

10. References

1. Campbell, R. and Habermann, A., The specification of process synchronization by path expressions, Lecture Notes in Computer Science, Springer-Verlag, Volume 16, 1974, pp. 89-102.

2. Harel, D, First-order Dynamic Logic, Springer-Verlag Lecture Notes, No. 68, 1979.

3. Manna, Z. and Wolper, P., Synthesis of communicating processes from temporal logic specifications, 253-281 in Proceedings of the Workshop on Logics of Programs, 1981.

4. Moszkowski, B., A temporal logic for multi-level reasoning about hardware, Technical Report STAN-CS-82-952, Computer Science Department, Stanford University, 1982.

5. Plaisted, D., A decision procedure for combinations of propositional temporal logic and other specialized theories, SRI International unpublished report, March, 1983.

6. Pratt, V., Semantical considerations on Floyd-Hoare logic, Proceedings of the 17th Annual IEEE Symposium on Foundations of Computer Science (1976)109-121.

7. Schwartz, R., Melliar-Smith, P. M., and Vogt, F., An interval logic for higher level temporal reasoning: language definition and examples, Computer Science Laboratory, SRI International Tech. Report CSL-138, 1983.

Deriving Efficient Graph Algorithms
(Summary)

John H. Reif[1]
Aiken Computation Laboratory
Harvard University

William L. Scherlis[2]
Department of Computer Science
Carnegie-Mellon University

Abstract. Ten years ago Hopcroft and Tarjan discovered a class of very fast algorithms for solving graph problems such as biconnectivity and strong connectivity. While these depth-first-search algorithms are complex and can be difficult to understand, the problems they solve have simple combinatorial definitions that can themselves be considered algorithms, though they might be very inefficient or even infinitary. We demonstrate here how the efficient algorithms can be systematically *derived* using program transformation steps from the initial definitions. This is the first occasion that these efficient graph algorithms have been systematically derived.

There are several justifications for this work. First, the derivations illustrate several high-level principles of program derivation and suggest methods by which these principles can be realized as sequences of program transformation steps. Second, we believe that the evolutionary approach used in this paper offers more natural explanations of the algorithms than the usual *a posteriori* proofs that appear in textbooks. Third, these examples illustrate how external domain-specific knowledge can enter into the program derivation process. Finally, we believe that future programming tools will be semantically based and are likely to have their foundations in a logic of program derivation. By working through complex examples such as those presented here, we make steps towards a conceptual *and* formal basis for these tools.

1. Introduction.

Discovery of efficient algorithms is a complex and creative task, requiring sophisticated knowledge both of general-purpose algorithm design techniques and of special-purpose mathematical facts related to the problems being solved. While the *process* of algorithm discovery is certain to be exceedingly difficult to mechanize, there is much to be learned—both about algorithms and about programming—from the study of the *structure* of derivations of complex algorithms.

Program derivation techniques provide a natural way of explaining and proving complicated algorithms. Conventional proofs may succeed in convincing a reader of the correctness of an algorithm without supplying any hint of why the algorithm works or how it came about. A derivation, on the other hand, is analogous to a constructive proof; it takes a reader step by step from an initial algorithm he accepts as a specification of the problem to a highly connected and efficient implementation of it. Our approach, then, is to explicate algorithms by *justifying their structure* rather than by merely establishing their correctness.

[1] This research was supported in part by National Science Foundation Grant NSF-MCS79-21024 and in part the Office of Naval Research Contract N00014-80-C-0647.

[2] This research was supported in part by the Defense Advanced Research Projects Agency (DOD), ARPA Order No. 3597, monitored by the Air Force Avionics Laboratory under Contract F33615-81-K-1539, and in part by the U.S. Army Communications R&D Command under Contract DAAK80-81-K-0074. The views and conclusions contained in this document are those of the authors and should not be interpreted as representing the official policies, either expressed or implied, of the Defense Advanced Research Projects Agency or the U.S. Government.

Specifications and algorithms. In this paper we demonstrate how program transformation techniques can be used to derive efficient graph algorithms from intuitive mathematical specifications. These specifications are simple combinatorial definitions that we choose to interpret as algorithms, even though—as algorithms—they might be very inefficient or even infinitary. To illustrate how simple these specifications can be, we give here our specification of the path predicate for directed graphs. Let G be a directed graph with vertices V and adjacency-set function Adj. The predicate $path(u, v)$ is true when there is a path in G from vertex u to vertex v. That is,

$$path(u,v) \Leftarrow \left(u = v \ \textbf{ or } \ (\exists w \in Adj(u))\, path(w,v) \right).$$

Note that this definition—when interpreted as a sequential algorithm in the usual way—does not always terminate.

With this definition, we obtain a straightforward specification of the strongly-connected components of a directed graph. Two vertices u and v are in the same strongly-connected component if there is a path from u to v and a path from v to u. The strongly-connected components of G are thus the elements of the set $strong$, where

$$strong \Leftarrow \bigcup_{r \in V} \{\{s \in V \mid path(r,s) \wedge path(s,r)\}\}.$$

Outline of paper. In Section 2 of this paper we derive a series of simple algorithms leading to a family of depth-first search algorithms. These are generalized and utilized in quite different ways in the derivations of the strong-connectivity algorithms (omitted in this summary) and in derivations of the biconnectivity algorithms of Section 3. These algorithms were discovered by Hopcroft and Tarjan and are (conventionally) presented in [Tarjan72] and [AHU74]. (Similar techniques can be used to derive the almost-linear-time algorithm of [Tarjan73] for flow-graph reducibility.) In the conclusion we discuss further the implications of this work.

The use of combinatorial lemmas. The derivations suggest ways in which programming and algorithm-design techniques separate from domain-specific knowledge. While the depth-first algorithms we derive depend on deep combinatorial properties of depth-first spanning forests, this knowledge can be expressed in the form of a small number of lemmas. These lemmas are used to justify initial specifications of program components and to establish preconditions in later program derivation steps. While we could prove the lemmas entirely in the language of a programming logic, the resulting account of the algorithms would likely be awkward and unnatural. We have thus sought an appropriate balance in our use of facts from graph theory and our use of general-purpose program derivation techniques. (The balance will shift, of course, as our knowledge of programming techniques improves.)

Program transformation techniques. Because we seek to demonstrate how derivations, clearly presented, can lead to a better understanding of the algorithms derived, the emphasis in this paper is primarily on the conceptual structure of the derivations and only secondarily on the actual formal transformation techniques. We make use of transformations for realizing complex recursive control structure as explicit data structure that are similar to those described in [Bird80], [Scherlis80], and [Wand80]. These transformations, which are used to "coerce termination" in infinitary definitions such as specification of $path$ above, are described in a separate report.

In addition, we make use of the transformations of [Scherlis81] (which are similar in spirit to those described in [Burstall77], but for which there is a guarantee of strong equivalence) in order to specialize function definitions and to effect the merging or "jamming" of loops. Discussion of loop jamming techniques also appears in [Paige81]. No prior knowledge of the details of these basic transformation techniques is required for the purposes of this paper.

Programming language for program derivation. The programming language we use is an ML-like applicative language (see [Gordon79]) supplemented with certain imperative features to allow sequencing and reference to state. Because it is hard to reason about and manipulate programs the are overly committed with respect to order of computation and data representation, we have sought to keep the programming language as unconstraining as possible. In addition, certain features that are difficult to implement but which have clear semantics are included because they often allow derivations to be quite straightforward. The infinitary definition of *path* above provides an example of such a feature; it has straightforward fixed-point semantics.

This approach, in which commitments to sequencing and representation are delayed as long as possible, is also vividly illustrated in the case of the SETL language in the derivations of [Paige81]. Another example is the language used in [Scherlis81], which was extended (to include expression procedures—used, for example, in Algorithm 2.3 below) in order to keep the set of transformations simple and yet strong-equivalence preserving. We will explain the unusual features of the language as they are encountered.

Mechanization. We expect that the program derivation techniques such as those refined and applied here and elsewhere will ultimately be of use in practical mechanical programming aids designed to help the programmer in his daily activity.

As in [Clark80], we are deriving a family of related algorithms. Even though the algorithms we derive here do not all have the same specifications, the strong relations between them become manifest in the explicit structure of their derivations. Indeed, it appears that reasoning by analogy will play a very important role in the automation of these techniques.

Other examples and approaches to program derivation are described in [Clark80], [Barstow80], [Green-78], [Manna81], and [Bauer81], among others.

2. Depth-First Search.

We start by deriving a family of simple depth-first search algorithms. These derivations and the algorithms that result will be used, either directly or by analogy, in the later derivations.

The development in the first part of this section is identical for directed and undirected graphs. We therefore carry out the development for directed graphs and consider undirected graphs as a special case.

Let $G = (V, E)$ be a finite directed graph with adjacency list representation—for each $v \in V$, $Adj(v)$ is the set of vertices adjacent to v. For undirected graphs $v \in Adj(u)$ if and only if $u \in Adj(v)$.

Paths. We consider first a simple combinatorial definition of a path in a graph. Let u and v range over vertices.

$$\mathit{path}(u,v) \Leftarrow \big(u = v \;\; \textbf{or} \;\; (\exists w \in Adj(u))\, \mathit{path}(w,v)\big) \tag{2.1}$$

While this definition seems to capture the notion of path, it cannot be interpreted in the usual way—either as a nondeterministic sequential algorithm or as a parallel algorithm—since in certain cases it would have no finite execution paths.

The finite closure transformation. We can, however, distinguish two kinds of infinite execution paths—looping paths and divergent paths. Roughly put, a nonterminating path is a *looping* path if only finitely many distinct recursive calls are made along that path; if the number of distinct calls grows without bound, then the path is *divergent*. In the case of finite graphs (the only graphs we consider) Algorithm 2.1 can exhibit looping, but, because u and v are vertices and the set of vertices is finite, it cannot exhibit divergence.

By framing this as a *finite closure* problem, we can apply transformations that eliminate the looping paths, and hence all non-terminating paths. Suppose a function f over a finite domain is defined recursively

$$f(x) \Leftarrow h(x) \oplus \bigoplus_{z \in g(x)} f(z), \tag{2.2}$$

where h and g do not call f and, in addition, $\oplus$ is a semilattice with identity in which infinite sums are defined (that is, the partial order induced by $\oplus$ is a complete partial order). This definition has a natural, but unconventional, fixed-point semantics in which f is always defined. The transformations allow this definition to be replaced by an equivalent (with respect to the unconventional semantics) but always terminating (with respect to the conventional semantics) definition, essentially by replacing all redundant recursive calls to f by the identity of $\oplus$. (A full account of this technique is beyond the scope of this paper. The transformations, which are related to the closed-world database techniques described in [Clark78] and [Reiter78], are sketched in [Scherlis80].)

In the case of *path*, $\oplus$ is disjunction and has identity (i.e., minimal element) **false**. The effect of the transformation is thus to replace all redundant calls to *path* with **false**.

In order to carry out the transformation, however, it is necessary to introduce mechanism to keep track of the sequencing of computation, collecting values of x as recursive evaluations of f proceed. This forces us to introduce notions of *state* and *state change* into the definition. State changes can be made either implicitly (by introducing imperative operations) or explicitly (by adding a new "memo" parameter to f). More concretely, we introduce explicit data structure to mark vertex pairs as they are considered; by examining this data structure, the program can foreclose any potentially looping execution paths.

It is difficult to manipulate programs involving state, however, so it is best to delay this transformation whenever possible. We will, therefore, postpone the improvement to *path* until the next transformation is complete.

The specialization transformation. Nearly all of the program derivation steps in our derivations are *specialization* steps. This simple technique, which is presented in detail and proved correct in [Scherlis80], is described here informally by means of an example involving the *path* definition.

Suppose we desire to collect the vertices v reachable from a given vertex u.

$$\{v \mid path(u,v)\}$$

If *path* is computable, then the value of this set can be calculated simply by enumerating all vertices v and testing $path(u,v)$ for each. This method is inefficient, however, since it requires multiple traversals of the same graph. We therefore consider *specializing* the definition of *path* to the computational context of the set abstraction.

The transformation has three steps. First, both sides of the definition of *path*

$$path(u,v) \Leftarrow (u = v \ \textbf{ or } \ (\exists w \in Adj(u))\, path(w,v))$$

are *substituted* into the set expression, forming the definition,

$$\{v \mid path(u,v)\} \Leftarrow \{v \mid (u = v) \ \textbf{ or } \ (\exists w \in Adj(u))\, path(w,v)\}\,. \tag{2.3}$$

This definition, called an *expression procedure*, is easily given meaning within the framework of a non-deterministic text-substitution evaluator model; roughly, it denotes a procedure for computing values of instances of its left-hand side.

The second step of the transformation is to *simplify* the right-hand side of the new definition until an instance of the left-hand side appears there. This is accomplished by distributing the set abstraction inward and simplifying.

$$\{v \mid path(u,v)\} \Leftarrow \{u\} \cup \bigcup_{w \in Adj(u)} \{v \mid path(w,v)\} \tag{2.4}$$

Observe now that this definition is recursive, and that it makes exactly one recursive call for each w, rather than one (to *path*) for each w and v pair, as in the earlier version.

The third and final step of the transformation is to ***rename*** all instances of the set expression to a new function name with appropriate parameters. (This has the effect of pruning the tree of nondeterministic computation paths.) The only free variable in the expression is u, so we obtain

$$dfs(u) \Leftarrow \{u\} \cup \bigcup_{w \in Adj(u)} dfs(w). \tag{2.5}$$

(The choice of the name "*dfs*" will be justified shortly.) Now, since

$$path(u,v) = v \in \{v \mid path(u,v)\}, \tag{2.6}$$

we obtain

$$\begin{aligned} path(u,v) &\Leftarrow v \in dfs(u) \\ dfs(u) &\Leftarrow \{u\} \cup \bigcup_{w \in Adj(u)} dfs(w). \end{aligned} \tag{2.7}$$

This new definition of *path* provides a performance advantage over the original definition of *path* if, in a series of computations, u changes infrequently compared with v and $dfs(u)$ is precomputed.

Finite closure revisited. At this point we can make the finite closure transformation that was postponed earlier. Like disjunction, the accumulator function '$\cup$' has the necessary algebraic properties. We thus replace redundant calls to *dfs* by $\emptyset$, which is the identity of union.

$$\begin{aligned} path(u,v) &\Leftarrow \textbf{begin} \\ &\qquad visit[V] \leftarrow \textbf{false}; \\ &\qquad v \in dfs(u) \\ &\quad\ \textbf{end} \\ dfs(u) &\Leftarrow \textbf{begin} \\ &\qquad visit[u] \leftarrow \textbf{true}; \\ &\qquad \{u\} \cup \bigcup_{w \in Adj(u)} (\textbf{if } visit[w] \textbf{ then } \emptyset \textbf{ else } dfs(w)) \\ &\quad\ \textbf{end} \end{aligned} \tag{2.8}$$

(In general, the value of a block is the value of the last expression unless some other expression is marked by the word **value**. In that case, the value of that expression is saved when it is evaluated, and the saved value is returned after evaluation of the remainder of the block is complete; see, for example, Algorithm 2.19. By convention imperative statements are always enclosed in blocks.)

This program requires some explanation. We have made use of implicit state (i.e., imperative operations on global data structure) to keep the "memo" set, representing it in its characteristic-function form by the array *visit*. The definition of *path* has been modified to initialize the memo set by storing **false** in every element of the array; this indicates that initially no vertices have been visited. (We use the word "memo" to draw analogy with the less powerful—since it has no effect on termination—'memo-function' transformation suggested by Donald Michie.)

In spite of the dependence of intermediate values of *visit* on the choice of computation ordering (which is only partially committed above), it is a property of the finite closure method that the ultimate value of *visit* (and, of course, *dfs*) is independent of the order of evaluation of both the binary union and the quantified union. Sequential evaluation of the outer union results in the natural depth-first search ordering.

As noted above, the same effect could be achieved using a purely applicative program. The imperative program has the advantage, however, of using a notation that avoids commitment to a particular order of computing the unions, and thus is more clear for our purposes.

This transformation step and the prior specialization step commute, but, because of the explicit sequencing of computation, it is more difficult to carry out the specialization once state has been introduced by finite closure.

Connected components of undirected graphs. We can now derive a linear-time program for collecting the connected components of an undirected graph.

$$comps \Leftarrow \bigcup_{r \in V} \{\{v \mid path(r,v)\}\} \tag{2.9}$$

(This union of singletons can, of course, also be notated using set abstraction, but the result is less perspicuous.

$$\{\{v \mid path(r,v)\} \mid r \in V\}$$

Tarski's "big-E" notation provides a more succinct, but less widely-known notation for the set.

$$\mathbf{E}_{r \in V}\, \{v \mid path(r,v)\}\ \ )$$

Substitution of the improved definition of *path* above and simplification yield

$$comps \Leftarrow \bigcup_{r \in V} \{\,\mathbf{begin}\ visit[V] \leftarrow \mathbf{false};\ dfs(r)\ \mathbf{end}\,\}\,. \tag{2.10}$$

Many redundant searches are performed, so this definition is not optimal; indeed, its worst case running time is $O(|V|^2)$.

We observe, however, that redundant searches can be avoided by making use of the *visit* array used by *dfs*. Using the specialization technique, we obtain the linear-time program

$$\begin{aligned} comps(V) \Leftarrow\ &\mathbf{begin} \\ &\quad visit[V] \leftarrow \mathbf{false}; \\ &\quad \textstyle\bigcup_{r \in V} (\mathbf{if}\ visit[r]\ \mathbf{then}\ \emptyset\ \mathbf{else}\ \{dfs(r)\}) \\ &\mathbf{end}\,. \end{aligned} \tag{2.11}$$

The edges traversed by this program form a depth-first search forest whose roots are the values of r for which *dfs* is called in the definition of *comps*. It is easy to see that this algorithm runs in time linear in the number of vertices and edges in the graph. This is shown by associating with each vertex and edge of the graph a constant number of program steps. As before, the sequencing of the union affects intermediate states but not the final result, so we need not commit ourselves to an order of consideration of the elements of V.

Trees and tree traversals. The fast depth-first search algorithms rely on subtle combinatorial properties of the depth-first spanning forests implicit in the prior algorithms. We now derive some simple algorithms for trees that will be useful in the later development.

The depth-first search algorithms we derive make extensive use of "non-local" properties of depth-first search trees they induce. In particular, both the biconnectivity and strong connectivity algorithms are based on lemmas that make use of ***ancestor*** or ***descendent*** orderings in the search forest. Both of these orderings relate vertices that may be an arbitrary distance apart in the trees. We make derivation steps here that will enable these relations to be computed efficiently.

A ***tree*** is a directed graph all of whose vertices have indegree one except the ***root*** vertex, which has indegree zero. A vertex with zero outdegree is called a ***leaf***; the others are ***internal nodes.***

The set of vertices of a tree can be enumerated without repetitions by traversing the edges of the tree and recursively enumerating subtrees.

$$\begin{aligned} trav(u) \Leftarrow\ &\mathbf{begin} \\ &\quad examine(u)\ \ //\ \ \mathbf{forpar}\ w\ \mathbf{suchthat}\ u \rightarrow w\ \mathbf{do}\ trav(w) \\ &\mathbf{end} \end{aligned} \tag{2.12}$$

(The symbol '//' indicates parallel execution, which we use (in terminating programs) to indicate explicit avoidance of commitment to computation ordering. Similarly, the notation '**forpar**' indicates parallel (or unordered sequential) execution of all the specified instances of the loop body. In general, explicit sequencing (with ';') will be avoided whenever possible. Finally, the notation '$u \to w$' is shorthand for '$\langle u, w\rangle \in E$', where E is the set of edges in the tree. Note that this program is executed for the side effect of calling *examine*; it has no value.)

If r is the root of the tree T, then *trav*(r) will cause *examine* to be called exactly once for each vertex of T.

Preorder and postorder enumeration are obtained by making differing commitments to computation sequencing in the definition above. Preorder enumeration results, for example, when the instance of '//' is replaced by ';'. For ordered trees, the loop cases must also be evaluated sequentially.

```
trav(u)  ⇐  begin
                examine(u);
                for w suchthat u → w do trav(w)                    (2.13)
            end
```

In the case of binary trees (i.e., all vertices have outdegree either zero or two), inorder can also be easily obtained. In this case, we would need to introduce case analysis on u to determine its outdegree.

Relative preorder position can be tested using an instance of Algorithm 2.13, but more efficient programs can be derived. Both preorder and postorder are (finite) linear orderings, and so can be represented by sequences of vertices. With this representation, two vertices can be compared in pre- or postorder simply by examining their relative positions in the appropriate sequence.

A sequence can be represented as an array mapping vertices to integers representing their positions. Let r be the root of a tree.

```
begin p ← 0;  trav(r);  pre[V] end;

trav(u)  ⇐  begin
                pre[u] ← p ← p + 1;                                (2.14)
                for w suchthat u → w do trav(w)
            end
```

(The first block is a specification of the computation to be performed.) The result of this program is now an array containing the preorder numbers assigned to the vertices of the tree rooted at r. For brevity, we have omitted the intermediate derivation steps by which this imperative algorithm is obtained.

A similar algorithm can be derived for computing the postorder numbering. By merging Algorithm 2.14 with this new algorithm, we obtain

```
begin p ← 0;  e ← 0;  trav(r);  ⟨pre[V], post[V]⟩ end;

trav(u)  ⇐  begin
                pre[u] ← p ← p + 1;
                for w suchthat u → w do trav(w);                   (2.15)
                post[u] ← e ← e + 1
            end.
```

(Again, we omit transformation steps. A detailed example of the merging technique, which is just a special case of the specialization transformation, is presented in a later section.)

Tree orderings. The *descendent* ordering $\succ$ is the transitive closure of the ordering represented by the edges of a tree. That is,

$v \succ u$ if and only if there is a path of tree edges from u to v.

It is undesirable to compute descendency (or ancestry) using a naive implementation of transitive closure, since that would require $O(|V|^3)$ time. We therefore investigate whether we can take advantage of the special properties of trees.

LEMMA 2.1. Let T be a tree with vertices numbered in preorder in array *pre*$[V]$ and in postorder in array *post*$[V]$. Then

$$u \succ v \quad \text{if and only if} \quad pre[u] > pre[v] \ \text{ and } \ post[u] < post[v] .$$

That is, u is a proper descendent of v if and only if both u succeeds v in a preorder traversal and u precedes v in a postorder traversal.

This lemma justifies replacing tests in programs of the form $u \succ v$ by tests of the form

$$pre[u] > pre[v] \quad \wedge \quad post[u] < post[v] ,$$

As shown in the previous section, both numberings can be computed in linear time and in a single tree traversal, so we can now test ancestry in constant time with linear-time precomputation.

Furthermore, u is to the left of v in T if and only if u precedes v in both preorder and postorder. Thus, the relative position of two arbitrary tree vertices can be determined by checking their relative positions in the two orderings.

Depth-first search trees. The depth-first search algorithms on graphs derived earlier impose a natural tree structure on the edges of the graph being searched. That is, the subset of the edges actually traversed forms a forest.

We indicate such facts in our programs by writing ***assertions***, which are expressions enclosed in the special brackets '$[\![\ ]\!]$' and located at points in the program where the facts are true. (This notation is also used to denote preconditions. See, for example, the derivation of Algorithm 2.21.) For example, we can annotate Algorithm 2.8 to obtain

$$
\begin{array}{lll}
path(u,v) & \Leftarrow & \textbf{begin } visit[V] \leftarrow \textbf{false};\ v \in dfs(u) \textbf{ end} \\
dfs(u) & \Leftarrow & \textbf{begin} \\
 & & \quad visit[u] \leftarrow \textbf{true}; \\
 & & \quad \{u\} \ \cup \ \bigcup_{w \in Adj(u)} (\textbf{if } visit[w] \textbf{ then } \emptyset \textbf{ else } [\![u \rightarrow w]\!]\ dfs(w)) \\
 & & \textbf{end}
\end{array}
\qquad (2.16)
$$

In the **else** clause we have asserted that $\langle u, w\rangle \in E$ is a tree edge. This set of tree edges forms the depth-first search forest.

We are now ready to develop an algorithm for carrying out a preorder traversal of a depth-first search tree of a graph. This will be accomplished by deriving a program that simultaneously computes *dfs* and *trav*. We indicate the simultaneous computation by writing a block,

$$\textbf{begin } trav(u);\ \langle dfs(u), pre[V]\rangle \textbf{ end} .$$

Recall that *trav* (see Algorithm 2.14) returns a value—the *pre* array—only implicitly. Thus, the effect of the computation of this block will be to store values into the *pre* array and to return the set of nodes reachable from u. For simplicity, we assume for the moment that the graph is connected.

Let r be a vertex of G. By substituting both definitions into the block and making obvious simplifications, we obtain

$$
\begin{array}{l}
\textbf{begin} \ \ p \leftarrow 0 \ /\!/ \ visit[V] \leftarrow \textbf{false};\ \ (\textbf{begin } trav(r);\ \langle dfs(r), pre[V]\rangle \textbf{ end}) \textbf{ end} \\[1ex]
(\textbf{begin } trav(u);\ dfs(u) \textbf{ end}) \ \Leftarrow \\
\quad \textbf{begin} \\
\quad\quad visit[u] \leftarrow \textbf{true} \ /\!/ \ pre[u] \leftarrow p \leftarrow p+1; \\
\quad\quad \{u\} \ \cup \ (\textbf{begin} \\
\quad\quad\quad\quad \textbf{for } w \textbf{ suchthat } u \rightarrow w \textbf{ do } trav(w); \\
\quad\quad\quad\quad \left(\bigcup_{\substack{w \in Adj(u) \\ \neg visit[w]}} dfs(w) \right) \\
\quad\quad\quad \textbf{end} \\
\quad \textbf{end}
\end{array}
\qquad (2.17)
$$

(We have carried out some trivial transformations on the initial specification in order to bring it into the form of the definition.) Now $u \rightarrow w$ if and only if $w \in Adj(u) \wedge \neg visit(w)$, so the two loops range over the same set. Since they do not interact, this implies that they can be *merged*—the pair of iterations can be combined into a single iteration.

At this point, we can make two further simplifications. First, we *rename* the block being defined to the simple name *dfs* (superseding the previous use of this name), and, second, we observe that if $pre[V]$ is initialized to 0, then

$$visit[u] = \textbf{false} \quad \text{if and only if} \quad pre[u] = 0\,,$$

and we can eliminate the *visit* array and use *pre* instead. The following much shorter program results.

$$\begin{array}{l}
\textbf{begin}\ p \leftarrow 0\ //\ pre[V] \leftarrow 0;\ \ S \leftarrow dfs(r);\ \ \langle S, pre[V]\rangle\ \textbf{end} \\
dfs(u)\ \Leftarrow \\
\quad \textbf{begin} \\
\quad\quad pre[u] \leftarrow p \leftarrow p+1; \\
\quad\quad \{u\} \cup \bigcup_{\substack{w \in Adj(u) \\ pre[w]=0}} dfs(w) \\
\quad \textbf{end}
\end{array} \tag{2.18}$$

The ordering represented by *pre* is called a ***depth-first-search ordering*** of the vertices of the graph.

By a development similar to that for *pre* and a merge step similar to the one just completed, the *post* ordering can be computed as well.

$$\begin{array}{l}
\textbf{begin}\ p \leftarrow 0\ //\ e \leftarrow 0\ //\ pre[V] \leftarrow 0;\ \ S \leftarrow dfs(r);\ \ \langle S, pre[V], post[V]\rangle\ \textbf{end} \\
dfs(u)\ \Leftarrow \\
\quad \textbf{begin} \\
\quad\quad pre[u] \leftarrow p \leftarrow p+1; \\
\quad\quad \textbf{value}\ \{u\} \cup \left(\bigcup_{\substack{w \in Adj(u) \\ pre[w]=0}} dfs(w)\right); \\
\quad\quad post[u] \leftarrow e \leftarrow e+1 \\
\quad \textbf{end}
\end{array} \tag{2.19}$$

Depth-first search in undirected graphs. We now consider the special case of depth-first search in undirected graphs. In this case, the depth-first search divides the edges of a graph into two sets, ***tree edges***, the edges actually traversed during search, and the other edges, which are called ***fronds***. While the tree edges are directed edges, we leave the fronds undirected (for the moment). We use the notation $u \nleftrightarrow v$ to indicate fronds and, as before, $u \rightarrow v$ to indicate tree edges. Thus, every edge $\langle u, v\rangle$ is either a tree edge, a reverse tree edge, or a frond.

We will occasionally need to distinguish the fronds explicitly during search. With respect to Algorithm 2.8, we observe that the fronds are exactly those edges $\langle u, w\rangle$ for which the $visit[w]$ test is true but (since the graph is undirected) such that w is not the father of u in the search tree.

$$\begin{array}{l}
dfs(u)\ \Leftarrow \\
\quad \textbf{begin} \\
\quad\quad visit[u] \leftarrow \textbf{true}; \\
\quad\quad \{u\} \cup \bigcup_{w \in Adj(u)} (\textbf{if}\ visit[w] \\
\qquad\qquad\qquad\qquad \textbf{then}\ (\textbf{if}\ w \neq father(u)\ \textbf{then}\ [\![u \nleftrightarrow w]\!]\,)\ \emptyset \\
\qquad\qquad\qquad\qquad \textbf{else}\ [\![u \rightarrow w \wedge u = father(w)]\!]\ \ dfs(w)) \\
\quad \textbf{end}
\end{array} \tag{2.20}$$

Here we have decorated Algorithm 2.8 with assertions distinguishing the two sets of edges. The *father* function can be considered to be defined implicitly by the assertion. (In the case of a root, *father* can return a special value, say Λ, that will cause the test to fail.)

Observe now that the father of u is known whenever *dfs* is called recursively. Using the specialization technique, we can eliminate all references to the *father* function/array by introducing a new parameter to *dfs* that will be the father of u in the depth-first-search tree being generated. We do this by forming an expression procedure for

$$[\![v = \mathit{father}(u)]\!]\ \mathit{dfs}(u)\,.$$

(In an expression procedure name an assertion denotes a precondition.) We obtain

$$
\begin{array}{l}
[\![v = \mathit{father}(u)]\!]\ \mathit{dfs}(u) \ \Leftarrow \\
\quad \mathbf{begin} \\
\quad\quad \mathit{visit}[u] \leftarrow \mathbf{true}; \\
\quad\quad \{u\} \ \cup \ \bigcup_{w \in Adj(u)} (\mathbf{if}\ \neg \mathit{visit}[w]\ \mathbf{then}\ [\![u \rightarrow w \wedge u = \mathit{father}(w)]\!]\ \mathit{dfs}(w) \\
\quad\quad\quad\quad\quad\quad\quad\quad \mathbf{elseif}\ w \neq \mathit{father}(u)\ \mathbf{then}\ [\![u \nleftrightarrow w]\!]\ \emptyset \\
\quad\quad\quad\quad\quad\quad\quad\quad \mathbf{else}\ [\![w \rightarrow u]\!]\ \emptyset) \\
\quad \mathbf{end}\,.
\end{array}
\tag{2.21}
$$

(For aesthetic reasons we have also reoriented the nested conditionals.) This is simplified by replacing *father*(u) in the test by v. After renaming (again superseding the name *dfs*), we have the definition

$$
\begin{array}{l}
\mathit{dfs}(u,v) \ \Leftarrow \\
\quad \mathbf{begin} \\
\quad\quad \mathit{visit}[u] \leftarrow \mathbf{true}; \\
\quad\quad \{u\} \ \cup \ \bigcup_{w \in Adj(u)} (\mathbf{if}\ \neg \mathit{visit}[w]\ \mathbf{then}\ [\![u \rightarrow w]\!]\ \mathit{dfs}(w,u) \\
\quad\quad\quad\quad\quad\quad\quad\quad \mathbf{elseif}\ w \neq v\ \mathbf{then}\ [\![u \nleftrightarrow w]\!]\ \emptyset \\
\quad\quad\quad\quad\quad\quad\quad\quad \mathbf{else}\ [\![w \rightarrow u]\!]\ \emptyset) \\
\quad \mathbf{end}\,.
\end{array}
\tag{2.22}
$$

Finally, we carry through the transformation steps described earlier to obtain an algorithm similar to Algorithm 2.19.

$$
\begin{array}{l}
\mathbf{begin}\ p \leftarrow 0 \ /\!/ \ e \leftarrow 0 \ /\!/ \ \mathit{pre}[V] \leftarrow 0;\ S \leftarrow \mathit{dfs}(r, \Lambda);\ \langle S, \mathit{pre}[V], \mathit{post}[V] \rangle\ \mathbf{end} \\
\mathit{dfs}(u,v) \ \Leftarrow \\
\quad \mathbf{begin} \\
\quad\quad \mathit{pre}[u] \leftarrow p \leftarrow p+1; \\
\quad\quad \mathbf{value}\ \{u\} \ \cup \ \bigcup_{w \in Adj(u)} (\mathbf{if}\ \mathit{pre}[w] = 0\ \mathbf{then}\ [\![u \rightarrow w]\!]\ \mathit{dfs}(w,u) \\
\quad\quad\quad\quad\quad\quad\quad\quad\quad \mathbf{elseif}\ w \neq v\ \mathbf{then}\ [\![u \nleftrightarrow w]\!]\ \emptyset \\
\quad\quad\quad\quad\quad\quad\quad\quad\quad \mathbf{else}\ [\![w \rightarrow u]\!]\ \emptyset); \\
\quad\quad \mathit{post}[u] \leftarrow e \leftarrow e+1 \\
\quad \mathbf{end}
\end{array}
\tag{2.23}
$$

(We use Λ to stand for a value not equal to any vertex.)

A further specialization. In the biconnectivity algorithm derivation, we will need to classify fronds into *forward fronds* and *reverse fronds.* Observe that if $u \nleftrightarrow w$ then either u is a descendent of w or vice-versa. If $u \succ w$ then $\langle u, w \rangle$ is a reverse frond, notated $u \nrightarrow w$; otherwise the edge is a forward frond, and we write $w \nrightarrow u$.

Lemma 2.1 provides a fast method for distinguishing forward and reverse fronds. It is an immediate consequence of the lemma that

$$\mathit{pre}[u] < \mathit{pre}[w] \quad \text{implies} \quad u \nsucc w\,,$$

and similarly for *post*. Therefore, if it is known that two vertices are related by the descendency relation, but it is not known in which direction, then it suffices to check *either* the preorder *or* the postorder numberings.

On the basis of this fact, we obtain the following depth-first search algorithm.

$$
\begin{array}{l}
\textbf{begin } p \leftarrow 0 \;//\; pre[V] \leftarrow 0;\; S \leftarrow dfs(r,\Lambda);\; \langle S, pre[V]\rangle \textbf{ end} \\
dfs(u,v) \Leftarrow \\
\quad \textbf{begin} \\
\quad\quad pre[u] \leftarrow p \leftarrow p+1; \\
\quad\quad \{u\} \cup \bigcup_{w\in Adj(u)} (\textbf{if } pre[w]=0 \textbf{ then } [\![u \rightarrow w]\!]\; dfs(w,u) \\
\quad\quad\quad\quad \textbf{elseif } w=v \textbf{ then } [\![w \rightarrow u]\!]\; \emptyset \\
\quad\quad\quad\quad \textbf{elseif } pre[u] > pre[w] \textbf{ then } [\![u \twoheadrightarrow w]\!]\; \emptyset \\
\quad\quad\quad\quad \textbf{else } [\![w \twoheadrightarrow u]\!]\; \emptyset\,) \\
\quad \textbf{end}
\end{array}
\tag{2.24}
$$

Observe that the four cases can be distinguished in constant time (given the prior linear-time computation of the *pre* array).

Although this classification of cases clearly does not help solve the immediate problem of collecting reachable vertices, it will be very useful when we use specialization to merge this algorithm with other algorithms obtained in the derivations for biconnectivity in the next section.

3. Biconnected Components.

Let $G=(V,E)$ be an undirected connected graph. An *articulation point* is a vertex whose removal disconnects G. A graph is *biconnected* if it has no articulation point. A *biconnected component* C is a maximal set of edges that contains no vertex whose removal disconnects the vertices contained in the edges of C.

Our specification for the biconnected components of a graph makes use of a modified version of the original *path* definition. Let u, v, and a be vertices in an undirected graph.

$$
\begin{array}{l}
path_a(u,v) \Leftarrow \\
\quad u=v \textbf{ or } (\exists w\in Adj(u))\,(w=v \textbf{ or } (w\neq a \textbf{ and } path_a(w,v)))
\end{array}
\tag{3.1}
$$

There is a path from u to v that *avoids* a if u and v are equal or if there is path avoiding a from a vertex w adjacent to u to v. (The subscripting of the parameter a is for syntactic convenience only.) Observe that

$$path_a(u,v) \quad \text{if and only if} \quad path_a(v,u)\,.$$

There is a natural special case of this definition, obtained by an obvious specialization step.

$$
\begin{array}{l}
[\![u\neq a \wedge v\neq a]\!]\; path_a(u,v) \Leftarrow \\
\quad u=v \textbf{ or } (\exists w\in Adj(u))\,((w\neq a \textbf{ and } [\![w\neq a \wedge v\neq a]\!]\; path_a(w,v)))
\end{array}
\tag{3.2}
$$

Two adjacent edges $\langle u,v\rangle$ and $\langle v,w\rangle$ are *biconnected* if $path_v(u,w)$. Thus, the biconnected component associated with a graph edge $\langle u,v\rangle$ is a set of edges,

$$bc(\langle u,v\rangle) \Leftarrow \{\langle u,v\rangle\} \cup \left(\bigcup_{\substack{\langle v,w\rangle\in E \\ path_v(u,w)}} bc(\langle v,w\rangle)\right). \tag{3.3}$$

(The specialized definition of *path* will suffice in this context.)

Finally, Let $G=(V,E)$ be an undirected graph with no self-loops (edges of the form $\langle u,u\rangle$). Then the set *bcomps* contains the biconnected components of G.

$$bcomps \Leftarrow \bigcup_{\langle u,v\rangle\in E} \{bc(\langle u,v\rangle)\} \tag{3.4}$$

Specialization to depth-first search. The essence of the biconnectivity algorithm is in the definition of *bc*. Our initial goal will be to obtain a finitary—and efficient—version of this definition. We will not apply the finite closure transformation directly, as this would cause us to have to mark ***edges*** as being visited. Rather, we will assume that a depth-first search forest ***already exists***, and ***specialize*** the definition of *bc* to traverse only tree edges and in depth-first search order. That is, we will merge the *bc* definition with a simple depth-first search traversal of the graph.

Note that this merge must actually incorporate a finite closure transformation, as we will be changing the termination properties of *bc*. Rather than carrying this out formally (which would involve going into the technical details of the finite closure transformation method), we will make informal arguments concerning the order of depth-first search traversal. The specialization process will be more difficult than in previous examples because we will need to make use of auxiliary lemmas concerning graphs and trees.

We start by assuming the edge given to *bc* is a tree edge and that previous tree edges have already been traversed in depth-first search order. Our approach will be to consider a variety of cases for the body of the union, depending on the type of the edge $\langle v, w\rangle$. Recall from Section 2 that an undirected graph edge is either a tree edge, a reverse tree edge, a forward frond, or a reverse frond. The first step is to introduce a conditional into the body of the union to distinguish the four cases. Our goal will be to simplify this definition in such a way that *bc* is called recursively for tree edges only ***and*** that the edges are traversed in a depth-first search order.

$$
\begin{aligned}
&[\![u \rightarrow v]\!]\ bc(\langle u,v\rangle) \ \Leftarrow \\
&\quad \{\langle u,v\rangle\} \ \cup \ \textstyle\bigcup_{\langle v,w\rangle \in E}\big(\textbf{if } v \rightarrow w \textbf{ then } (\textbf{if } path_v(u,w) \textbf{ then } bc(\langle v,w\rangle) \textbf{ else } \emptyset) \\
&\qquad\qquad \textbf{elseif } u = w \textbf{ then } (\textbf{if } path_v(u,w) \textbf{ then } bc(\langle v,w\rangle) \textbf{ else } \emptyset) \\
&\qquad\qquad \textbf{elseif } v \nrightarrow w \textbf{ then } (\textbf{if } path_v(u,w) \textbf{ then } bc(\langle v,w\rangle) \textbf{ else } \emptyset) \\
&\qquad\qquad \textbf{else } [\![w \nrightarrow v]\!]\ (\textbf{if } path_v(u,w) \textbf{ then } bc(\langle v,w\rangle) \textbf{ else } \emptyset)\big)
\end{aligned}
\tag{3.5}
$$

We have distributed the *path* test into the four cases. We now consider each of the cases individually.

Suppose $u = w$; that is, w is the father of v. In this case $path_v(u, w)$ is trivially true, so we must compute $bc(\langle v, w\rangle)$. But $\langle v, w\rangle = \langle u, v\rangle$, and we are already computing $bc(\langle u, v\rangle)$, so (by our finite closure argument) we replace the new *bc* call by $\emptyset$. To simplify notation, we also apply transformations so *bc* is passed two adjacent vertices, rather than the edge between them.

$$
\begin{aligned}
&[\![u \rightarrow v]\!]\ bc(u,v) \ \Leftarrow \\
&\quad \{\langle u,v\rangle\} \ \cup \ \textstyle\bigcup_{\langle v,w\rangle \in E}(\textbf{if } v \rightarrow w \textbf{ then } (\textbf{if } path_v(u,w) \textbf{ then } bc(v,w) \textbf{ else } \emptyset) \\
&\qquad\qquad \textbf{elseif } u = w \textbf{ then } \emptyset \\
&\qquad\qquad \textbf{elseif } v \nrightarrow w \textbf{ then } (\textbf{if } path_v(u,w) \textbf{ then } bc(v,w) \textbf{ else } \emptyset) \\
&\qquad\qquad \textbf{else } [\![w \nrightarrow v]\!]\ (\textbf{if } path_v(u,w) \textbf{ then } bc(v,w) \textbf{ else } \emptyset))
\end{aligned}
\tag{3.6}
$$

We next consider the case of a reverse frond $v \nrightarrow w$. In this case, $path_v(u, w)$ is always true since v is a direct descendent of u and w is an ancestor of u. We must therefore include $bc(v, w)$. Now $\langle v, w\rangle$ is not a tree edge, so this recursive call will not be in the specialized form. We therefore expand the definition of *bc* in this context and simplify based on the assumptions. Since w is an ancestor of u and there is an edge adjacent to w already known to be in the same component as $\langle u, v\rangle$, we can (by the finite closure argument and by the assumption of depth-first order of traversal) replace *all* the recursive *bc* calls from w by $\emptyset$ and retain only the single edge $\langle v, w\rangle$. Observe that this implies all reverse fronds from a vertex are collected at that vertex.

The third case, $w \nrightarrow v$, reduces to $\emptyset$. In this case $\langle v, w\rangle$ is a forward frond, and there must be a vertex t such that t is an ancestor of w and such that $v \rightarrow t$ has already been traversed. Now, if $\langle v, w\rangle$ is in the same component as $\langle u, v\rangle$, then it will have been found already (by the immediately preceeding case and by the assumption of depth-first order of traversal). If not, then the *path* test would fail and the result would be $\emptyset$. Thus, the result is $\emptyset$ for both possible eventualities.

The final case turns out to very easy. If $\langle v, w\rangle$ is a tree edge, then the recursive call to *bc* is already in the specialized form.

We thus obtain the following finitary definition.

$$\begin{aligned}
[\![u \to v]\!]\ bc(u,v) \ \Leftarrow\ & \{\langle u,v\rangle\} \ \cup\ \textstyle\bigcup_{\langle v,w\rangle \in E}(\textbf{if } v \to w \textbf{ then } (\textbf{if } path_v(u,w) \textbf{ then } [\![v \to w]\!]\ bc(v,w) \\
& \qquad\qquad\qquad\qquad\qquad\qquad\qquad \textbf{else } \emptyset) \\
& \qquad\qquad \textbf{elseif } u = w \textbf{ then } \emptyset \\
& \qquad\qquad \textbf{elseif } v \not\twoheadrightarrow w \textbf{ then } \{\langle v,w\rangle\} \\
& \qquad\qquad \textbf{else } [\![w \not\twoheadrightarrow v]\!]\ \emptyset)
\end{aligned} \tag{3.7}$$

There are two ways in which the biconnected components algorithm can now be improved. First, the *path* test in *bc* could be made more efficient, and, second, the definition of *bcomps* could be improved to avoid collecting redundant components.

Articulation edges. The improvement of the biconnectivity algorithm *bcomps* depends on the following lemma.

LEMMA 3.1. Let G be an undirected graph with depth-first search forest F. Every biconnected component B contains a unique tree edge $u \to v$, called the ***articulation edge***, such that u is an ancestor of every vertex in the edges of B.

This lemma has two useful consequences.

(1) Every tree edge leaving the roots of the trees in a depth-first search forest is an articulation edge.

(2) If $u \to v$ and $v \to w$, then

$$path_v(u,w) \qquad \text{if and only if} \qquad \langle v,w\rangle \text{ is not an articulation edge.}$$

An immediate application of the lemma is to the original definition of *bcomps*. Since every biconnected component has a unique articulation edge associated with it, *bcomps* can be modified to call *bc* for articulation edges only. Let *aedges* be the set of articulation edges.

$$bcomps \ \Leftarrow\ \textstyle\bigcup_{\langle u,v\rangle \in aedges} [\![u \to v]\!]\ \{bc(u,v)\} \tag{3.8}$$

Note that since every articulation edge is a tree edge and since the set of biconnected components is a partition of the set of edges, the specialized version of *bc* can be applied here.

Collecting biconnected components. Since articulation edges are tree edges, we will attempt to collect them in a single depth-first search. We assume, again, that the tree edges are already so classified and, in addition, we assume that *root*(r) is true if r is a root in the depth-first search forest. The algorithm below reduces the problem to testing individual tree edges using a predicate *aedge*.

$$\begin{aligned}
aedges \ &\Leftarrow\ \textstyle\bigcup_{\substack{root(r)\\ r \to s}} \big(\{\langle r,s\rangle\} \cup ae(r,s)\big) \\
[\![u \to v]\!]\ ae(u,v) \ &\Leftarrow\ \textstyle\bigcup_{\substack{w \in Adj(v)\\ v \to w}} \big(\textbf{if } aedge(v,w) \textbf{ then } \{\langle v,w\rangle\} \cup ae(v,w) \\
& \qquad\qquad\qquad\ \textbf{else } ae(v,w)\big)
\end{aligned} \tag{3.9}$$

The second consequence of the lemma enables replacement of the test '*aedge*(v,w)' by the test '$\neg$***path***$_v(u,w)$.'

It is now a natural step to merge this search for articulation edges with the algorithm *bcomps* for collecting the edges of individual components. The following algorithm results after an obvious specialization step.

$$\begin{aligned}
bcomps \ &\Leftarrow\ \textstyle\bigcup_{\substack{root(r)\\ r \to s}} \big(\{bc(r,s)\} \cup ae(r,s)\big) \\
[\![u \to v]\!]\ ae(u,v) \ &\Leftarrow\ \textstyle\bigcup_{\substack{w \in Adj(v)\\ v \to w}} (\textbf{if } aedge(v,w) \textbf{ then } \{bc(v,w)\} \cup ae(v,w) \\
& \qquad\qquad\qquad\ \textbf{else } ae(v,w))
\end{aligned} \tag{3.10}$$

The function *ae* now returns a set of biconnected components.

It is clear from the structure of this algorithm that it would be advantageous to merge the computations of *ae* and *bc*. We do this by developing an expression procedure for the pair

$$[\![u \to v]\!]\ \langle bc(u,v),\ ae(u,v)\rangle\ .$$

The result of this program will be a pair of sets. The first is the set of edges of the current component accumulated thus far; the second is the set of components accumulated thus far. After substitution and simplification, we obtain

$$
\begin{array}{l}
bcomps \ \Leftarrow\ \bigcup_{\substack{root(r)\\ r\to s}} \big(\{B\}\cup A \ \ \textbf{where}\ \langle B,A\rangle = \langle bc(r,s), ae(r,s)\rangle\big) \\[6pt]
[\![u \to v]\!]\ \langle bc(u,v), ae(u,v)\rangle \ \Leftarrow \\
\quad \langle \{(u,v)\}\cup B, A\rangle \\
\qquad \textbf{where} \\
\qquad\quad \langle B,A\rangle = \langle \bigcup,\bigcup\rangle_{w\in Adj(v)} \\
\qquad\qquad (\textbf{if}\ v\to w\ \textbf{then}\ (\ \textbf{if}\ \neg path_v(u,w) \\
\qquad\qquad\qquad\qquad \textbf{then}\ [\![aedge(v,w)]\!]\ \langle \emptyset, \{B'\}\cup A'\rangle \\
\qquad\qquad\qquad\qquad \textbf{else}\ \langle B',A'\rangle\ ) \\
\qquad\qquad\qquad\qquad \textbf{where}\ \langle B',A'\rangle = [\![v\to w]\!]\ \langle bc(v,w), ae(v,w)\rangle \\
\qquad\qquad\quad \textbf{elseif}\ u = w\ \textbf{then}\ \langle\emptyset,\emptyset\rangle \\
\qquad\qquad\quad \textbf{elseif}\ v \not\to w\ \textbf{then}\ \langle\{(v,w)\},\emptyset\rangle \\
\qquad\qquad\quad \textbf{else}\ \langle\emptyset,\emptyset\rangle)\ .
\end{array}
\tag{3.11}
$$

(We have, in this example, introduced a new notation for the simultaneous accumulation of sets. Suppose the function *f* returns a pair of sets. Then the notation

$$\langle \bigcup,\bigcup\rangle_{w\in S}\ (f(w))$$

describes a pair of sets and yields the same result as

$$\big\langle \bigcup_{w\in S}(first[f(w)]),\ \bigcup_{w\in S}(second[f(w)])\big\rangle\ ,$$

where *first* and *second* select the corresponding elements of a pair.)

We complete the specialization step by renaming the pair to a simple name, *ba*.

$$
\begin{array}{l}
bcomps \ \Leftarrow\ \bigcup_{\substack{root(r)\\ r\to s}} (\{B\}\cup A \ \ \textbf{where}\ \langle B,A\rangle = ba(r,s)) \\[6pt]
ba(u,v) \ \Leftarrow \\
\quad \langle \{(u,v)\}\cup B, A\rangle \\
\qquad \textbf{where}\ \langle B,A\rangle = \langle \bigcup,\bigcup\rangle_{w\in Adj(v)} \\
\qquad\qquad (\textbf{if}\ v\to w \\
\qquad\qquad\quad \textbf{then}\ ((\textbf{if}\ \neg path_v(u,w) \\
\qquad\qquad\qquad\qquad \textbf{then}\ [\![aedge(v,w)]\!]\ \langle \emptyset, \{B'\}\cup A'\rangle \\
\qquad\qquad\qquad\qquad \textbf{else}\ \langle B',A'\rangle\ ) \\
\qquad\qquad\qquad \textbf{where}\ \langle B',A'\rangle = ba(v,w)) \\
\qquad\qquad\quad \textbf{elseif}\ u = w\ \textbf{then}\ \langle\emptyset,\emptyset\rangle \\
\qquad\qquad\quad \textbf{elseif}\ v \not\to w\ \textbf{then}\ \langle\{(v,w)\},\emptyset\rangle \\
\qquad\qquad\quad \textbf{else}\ \langle\emptyset,\emptyset\rangle)\ .
\end{array}
\tag{3.12}
$$

It now remains to derive a method for efficiently testing $\neg path_v(u,w)$.

Finding articulation edges. In order to implement the *path* test efficiently, we need a second technical lemma.

Lemma 3.2. Let G be an undirected graph with depth-first search forest F and let $u \to v$ and $v \to w$ be edges in F. Then

$$\begin{aligned} \mathit{path}_v(u,w) &\equiv (\exists s,t)\,(u \succeq t \wedge t \nleftrightarrow s \wedge s \succeq w) \\ &\equiv (\exists s,t)\,(v \succ t \wedge t \nleftrightarrow s \wedge s \succeq w). \end{aligned}$$

That is, there is a path from u to w avoiding v exactly when there is a frond extending from a descendent s of w to a proper ancestor t of v.

Our goal is to compute this test efficiently in the course of a single depth-first search. The key insight at this point is to represent the *set* of possible values of t such that $t \nleftrightarrow s$ and $s \succeq w$ by a single value—the most remote ancestor found thus far. If this ancestor turns out to be a proper ancestor of v, then there is indeed a path avoiding v from u (the father of v) to w (a son of v).

In other words, we seek to compute something like

$$\mathit{low}(w) \Leftarrow \min_{\succ}(\{t \mid (\exists s)\, s \nrightarrow t \wedge s \succeq w\}) .$$

Unfortunately, because the elements of the set are not always pairwise comparable, this minimum is not well defined. It is the case, however, that each element of the set is either an ancestor or a descendent of w. Furthermore, all ancestors of w are themselves pairwise comparable. Since v is an ancestor of w and since we are only interested in t that are proper ancestors of v, descendents of w can be ignored during search. We implement this improvement by means of a simple modification to the above specification. This modification is easily seen to follow from the lemma.

$$\mathit{low}(w) \Leftarrow \min_{\succ}(\{w\} \cup \{t \mid (\exists s)\, s \nrightarrow t \wedge s \succeq w\}) \tag{3.13}$$

Now, $v \succ \mathit{low}(w)$ if and only if $\mathit{path}_v(u,w)$. In other words, $v \to w$ is an articulation edge if and only if $\mathit{low}(w) \succeq v$.

In order to develop a depth-first search algorithm for computing *low*, we separate the computation into two stages.

$$\begin{aligned} \mathit{low}(w) &\Leftarrow \min_{\succ}(\{w\} \cup \mathit{lowset}(w)) \\ \mathit{lowset}(w) &\Leftarrow \{t \mid (\exists s)\, s \nrightarrow t \wedge s \succeq w\} \end{aligned} \tag{3.14}$$

Lowset computation. We observe first that $\{s \mid s \succeq w\}$ is exactly $\mathit{dfs}(w)$. We recall the definition of *dfs* from Section 2.

$$\begin{aligned} &\textbf{begin } p \leftarrow 0 \;//\; \mathit{pre}[V] \leftarrow 0;\; S \leftarrow \mathit{dfs}(r,\Lambda);\; \langle S, \mathit{pre}[V]\rangle \textbf{ end} \\ &[\![u \to v]\!]\; \mathit{dfs}(u,v) \Leftarrow \\ &\quad \textbf{begin} \\ &\quad\quad \mathit{pre}[v] \leftarrow p \leftarrow p+1; \\ &\quad\quad \{v\} \cup \textstyle\bigcup_{w \in \mathit{Adj}(v)} (\textbf{if } \mathit{pre}[w] = 0 \textbf{ then } [\![v \to w]\!]\; \mathit{dfs}(v,w) \\ &\quad\quad\quad\quad \textbf{elseif } w = u \textbf{ then } [\![w \to v]\!]\; \emptyset \\ &\quad\quad\quad\quad \textbf{elseif } \mathit{pre}[v] > \mathit{pre}[w] \textbf{ then } [\![v \nrightarrow w]\!]\; \emptyset \\ &\quad\quad\quad\quad \textbf{else } [\![w \nrightarrow v]\!]\; \emptyset\,) \\ &\quad \textbf{end} \end{aligned} \tag{3.15}$$

(In order to maintain consistent notation in this section, we are using a slightly different vertex labeling convention that of Section 2.)

Since *dfs* requires a father parameter, we revise slightly our definition of *lowset*.

$$[\![u \to v]\!]\; \mathit{lowset}(u,v) \Leftarrow \{t \mid (\exists s)\, s \nrightarrow t \wedge s \in \mathit{dfs}(u,v)\} \tag{3.16}$$

As before, we assume $u \rightarrow v$. We also assume that a special value Λ is passed for u when v is a root. (We are renaming parameters to be consistent with their subsequent usage.)

Direct substitution for *dfs* in the definition of *lowset* and preliminary simplification yield the expression procedure,

$$
\begin{array}{l}
[\![u \rightarrow v]\!]\ \{t \mid (\exists s)\ s \nrightarrow t \ \wedge\ s \in \mathit{dfs}(u,v)\} \ \Leftarrow \\
\quad \textbf{begin} \\
\quad\quad \mathit{pre}[v] \leftarrow p \leftarrow p+1; \\
\quad\quad \{t \mid (\exists s)\ s \nrightarrow t \ \wedge\ s \in \{v\}\} \\
\quad\quad\quad \cup\ \{t \mid (\exists s)\ s \nrightarrow t \ \wedge\ s \in \bigcup_{w \in Adj(v)} \\
\quad\quad\quad\quad (\textbf{if}\ \mathit{pre}[w] = 0\ \textbf{then}\ [\![v \rightarrow w]\!]\ \mathit{dfs}(v,w) \\
\quad\quad\quad\quad\quad \textbf{elseif}\ w = u\ \textbf{then}\ [\![w \rightarrow v]\!]\ \emptyset \\
\quad\quad\quad\quad\quad \textbf{elseif}\ \mathit{pre}[v] > \mathit{pre}[w]\ \textbf{then}\ [\![v \nrightarrow w]\!]\ \emptyset \\
\quad\quad\quad\quad\quad \textbf{else}\ [\![w \nrightarrow v]\!]\ \emptyset\ )\} \\
\quad \textbf{end}\ .
\end{array}
\tag{3.17}
$$

We now distribute the set abstraction into the union and conditional and simplify.

$$
\begin{array}{l}
[\![u \rightarrow v]\!]\ \{t \mid (\exists s)\ s \nrightarrow t \ \wedge\ s \in \mathit{dfs}(u,v)\} \ \Leftarrow \\
\quad \textbf{begin} \\
\quad\quad \mathit{pre}[v] \leftarrow p \leftarrow p+1; \\
\quad\quad \{t \mid v \nrightarrow t\} \\
\quad\quad\quad \cup\ \bigcup_{w \in Adj(v)} (\textbf{if}\ \mathit{pre}[w] = 0 \\
\quad\quad\quad\quad \textbf{then}\ [\![v \rightarrow w]\!]\ \{t \mid (\exists s)\ s \nrightarrow t \ \wedge\ s \in \mathit{dfs}(v,w)\} \\
\quad\quad\quad\quad \textbf{elseif}\ w = u\ \textbf{then}\ [\![w \rightarrow v]\!]\ \emptyset \\
\quad\quad\quad\quad \textbf{elseif}\ \mathit{pre}[v] > \mathit{pre}[w]\ \textbf{then}\ [\![v \nrightarrow w]\!]\ \emptyset \\
\quad\quad\quad\quad \textbf{else}\ [\![w \nrightarrow v]\!]\ \emptyset\ )\} \\
\quad \textbf{end}\ .
\end{array}
\tag{3.18}
$$

Finally, we can form a recursion. As before, we do this by renaming all instances of the set abstraction to a simple name.

$$
\begin{array}{l}
\mathit{lowset}(u,v) \ \Leftarrow \\
\quad \textbf{begin} \\
\quad\quad \mathit{pre}[v] \leftarrow p \leftarrow p+1; \\
\quad\quad \{t \mid v \nrightarrow t\} \\
\quad\quad\quad \cup\ \bigcup_{w \in Adj(v)} (\textbf{if}\ \mathit{pre}[w] = 0\ \textbf{then}\ [\![v \rightarrow w]\!]\ \mathit{lowset}(v,w) \\
\quad\quad\quad\quad \textbf{elseif}\ w = u\ \textbf{then}\ [\![w \rightarrow v]\!]\ \emptyset \\
\quad\quad\quad\quad \textbf{elseif}\ \mathit{pre}[v] > \mathit{pre}[w]\ \textbf{then}\ [\![v \nrightarrow w]\!]\ \emptyset \\
\quad\quad\quad\quad \textbf{else}\ [\![w \nrightarrow v]\!]\ \emptyset\ )\} \\
\quad \textbf{end}
\end{array}
\tag{3.19}
$$

Now since $\{t \mid v \nrightarrow t\}$ is equivalent to

$$\bigcup_{w \in Adj(v)} (\textbf{if}\ v \nrightarrow w\ \textbf{then}\ \{w\}\ \textbf{else}\ \emptyset),$$

we substitute this into Algorithm 3.19, merge the unions, and simplify on the basis of the assertions to obtain the final *lowset* program.

$$
\begin{array}{l}
\mathit{lowset}(u,v) \ \Leftarrow \\
\quad \textbf{begin} \\
\quad\quad \mathit{pre}[v] \leftarrow p \leftarrow p+1; \\
\quad\quad \bigcup_{w \in Adj(v)} (\textbf{if}\ \mathit{pre}[w] = 0\ \textbf{then}\ [\![v \rightarrow w]\!]\ \mathit{lowset}(v,w) \\
\quad\quad\quad \textbf{elseif}\ w = u\ \textbf{then}\ [\![w \rightarrow v]\!]\ \emptyset \\
\quad\quad\quad \textbf{elseif}\ \mathit{pre}[v] > \mathit{pre}[w]\ \textbf{then}\ [\![v \nrightarrow w]\!]\ \{w\} \\
\quad\quad\quad \textbf{else}\ [\![w \nrightarrow v]\!]\ \emptyset\ )\} \\
\quad \textbf{end}
\end{array}
\tag{3.20}
$$

Low computation. A similar specialization sequence is now used to transform this algorithm into a program for *low*(u, v), defined

$$[\![u \rightarrow v]\!]\ \mathit{low}(u,v) \ \Leftarrow\ \min_{\succ}(\{v\} \cup \mathit{lowset}(u,v)).$$

We obtain

$$
\begin{array}{l}
\mathit{low}(u,v) \ \Leftarrow \\
\quad \textbf{begin} \\
\quad\quad \mathit{pre}[v] \leftarrow p \leftarrow p+1; \\
\quad\quad \min_{w \in Adj(v)}\big(\min(v, (\textbf{if } \mathit{pre}[w] = 0 \textbf{ then } [\![v \rightarrow w]\!]\ \mathit{low}(v,w) \\
\quad\quad\quad\quad \textbf{elseif } w = u \textbf{ then } [\![w \rightarrow v]\!]\ \infty \\
\quad\quad\quad\quad \textbf{elseif } \mathit{pre}[v] > \mathit{pre}[w] \textbf{ then } [\![v \nrightarrow w]\!]\ w \\
\quad\quad\quad\quad \textbf{else } [\![w \nrightarrow v]\!]\ \infty\ ))\big) \\
\quad \textbf{end}
\end{array}
\tag{3.21}
$$

(Here ∞ denotes a maximal vertex value; note that v would do.) An immediate simplification is to distribute the inner 'min' into the conditional.

$$
\begin{array}{l}
\mathit{low}(u,v) \ \Leftarrow \\
\quad \textbf{begin} \\
\quad\quad \mathit{pre}[v] \leftarrow p \leftarrow p+1; \\
\quad\quad \min_{w \in Adj(v)}\big(\textbf{if } \mathit{pre}[w] = 0 \textbf{ then } [\![v \rightarrow w]\!]\ \min(v, \mathit{low}(v,w)) \\
\quad\quad\quad\quad \textbf{elseif } w = u \textbf{ then } [\![w \rightarrow v]\!]\ v \\
\quad\quad\quad\quad \textbf{elseif } \mathit{pre}[v] > \mathit{pre}[w] \textbf{ then } [\![v \nrightarrow w]\!]\ \min(v,w) \\
\quad\quad\quad\quad \textbf{else } [\![w \nrightarrow v]\!]\ v\big) \\
\quad \textbf{end}
\end{array}
\tag{3.22}
$$

Using preorder numbers. Recall that according to the lemma, if *low*(v, w) is a descendent of v, then $v \rightarrow w$ is an articulation edge. Furthermore, it is always the case that the result of *low* is an ancestor or a descendent of v, so we can test the relation using the preorder numbering. This prompts us to specialize the definition of *low* to return preorder numbers rather than vertices. After several straightforward transformations, we obtain

$$
\begin{array}{l}
\mathit{low}(u,v) \ \Leftarrow \\
\quad \textbf{begin} \\
\quad\quad m \leftarrow \mathit{pre}[v] \leftarrow p \leftarrow p+1; \\
\quad\quad \textbf{for } w \in Adj(v) \textbf{ do} \\
\quad\quad\quad \textbf{if } \mathit{pre}[w] = 0 \textbf{ then begin } [\![v \rightarrow w]\!] \\
\quad\quad\quad\quad\quad m \leftarrow \min(m, \ell)\ \ /\!/ \\
\quad\quad\quad\quad\quad (\textbf{if } \ell \geq \mathit{pre}[v] \textbf{ then } [\![\mathit{aedge}(v,w)]\!]\,) \\
\quad\quad\quad\quad \textbf{end} \\
\quad\quad\quad\quad \textbf{where } \ell = \mathit{low}(v,w) \\
\quad\quad\quad \textbf{elseif } w = u \textbf{ then } [\![w \rightarrow v]\!] \\
\quad\quad\quad \textbf{elseif } \mathit{pre}[v] > \mathit{pre}[w] \textbf{ then } [\![v \nrightarrow w]\!]\ m \leftarrow \min(m, \mathit{pre}[w]) \\
\quad\quad\quad \textbf{else } [\![w \nrightarrow v]\!]\ ))) \\
\quad \textbf{end}\ .
\end{array}
\tag{3.23}
$$

(We have aded an assertion noting when articulation edges are found.) Note that there is no action for two branches of the conditional.

Collecting components, revisited. Armed with this efficient method of locating articulation edges, we recall the *bcomps* algorithm derived earlier. That algorithm simultaneously collects the set of biconnected components and the set of edges in the current component. We now show how this algorithm can be merged with *low* to obtain an algorithm that simultaneously collects edges in the current component, collects biconnected components, and keeps track of the current *low* value. The resulting algorithm, while somewhat complicated, is very efficient, requiring time linear in the number of vertices and edges.

We start by substituting to obtain an expression procedure for the expression

$$\langle ba(u,v), low(u,v) \rangle .$$

After simplifying and renaming, we obtain

```
bcomps ⇐
    begin
        pre[V] ← 0 // p ← 0;
        ∪_{root(r), r→s} ({B} ∪ A  where ⟨B,A,ℓ⟩ = balow(r,s))
    end

balow(u,v) ⇐
    begin var m;
        m ← pre[v] ← p ← p + 1;
        ⟨{⟨u,v⟩} ∪ B, A, m⟩
          where ⟨B,A⟩ = ⟨∪,∪⟩_{w∈Adj(v)}
                        ( if pre[w] = 0
                            then ( let ⟨B',A',ℓ⟩ = balow(v,w) in
                                     if ℓ ≥ pre[v]
                                       then begin
                                              m ← min(m,ℓ);
                                              ⟨∅, {B'} ∪ A'⟩
                                            end
                                       else ⟨B',A'⟩ )
                          elseif pre[w] < pre[v]  ∧  w ≠ u
                            then begin
                                   m ← min(m, pre[w]);
                                   ⟨{⟨v,w⟩}, ∅⟩
                                 end
                          else ⟨∅,∅⟩)
    end .
```
(3.24)

(The *balow* algorithm returns a triple instead of two nested pairs.) We now have a linear-time algorithm for computing the set of biconnected components in an undirected graph.

The biconnectivity algorithm. It is traditional in presentations of the biconnected component algorithm that components be emitted as they are found, rather than collected explicitly (as they are in the second component of the result of *balow*). The traditional presentation can be derived easily using transformations that introduce operations on global state and eliminate corresponding operations on explicit results. (The finite closure transformation makes implicit use of such transformations. Again, we do not go into details of the transformation method here; rather, we present this and the next transformation step in an informal manner.)

To carry out the transformation, we distinguish all operations that directly *change* the accumulated value of the second result. There is (essentially) only one place where this happens, which is when B' is added to A' in the innermost conditional. The effect of the transformation is to assert that B' is a biconnected component at that point.

```
bcomps ⇐
    begin
        pre[V] ← 0 // p ← 0;
        for r ∈ V do (if pre[r] = 0 then balow(Λ, r))
    end

balow(u, v) ⇐
    begin var m;
        m ← pre[v] ← p ← p + 1;
        ⟨B, m⟩
          where B = ⋃_{w∈Adj(v)}
                      (if pre[w] = 0
                         then ( let ⟨B', ℓ⟩ = balow(v, w) in
                                let B'' = B' ∪ {⟨u, v⟩} in
                                 if ℓ ≥ pre[v]
                                    then begin ⟦B'' is a component⟧
                                               m ← min(m, ℓ);
                                               ∅
                                         end
                                    else B'' )
                       elseif pre[w] < pre[v]  ∧  w ≠ u
                         then begin
                                m ← min(m, pre[w]);
                                {⟨v, w⟩}
                              end
                       else ∅)
    end                                                          (3.25)
```

(We have, in addition, "rotated" the outermost union to the caller; this allows most of the top-level loop of *bcomps* to be incorporated into *balow*.) In this program, *bcomps* is executed only for its side-effect of emitting components; its value can be is ignored.

A final transformation. Although it is not a necessary part of our development, a similar transformation can be carried out to eliminate the first result. In the prior example, the net effect on state of accumulating the set of biconnected components proved to be very simple; biconnected components were simply added to the set as they were found. In this case, however, the net changes to state corresponding to the way the edge set (viewed globally) is accumulated have a stack-like discipline; this is a result of our transformation of merging *bc* and *ae*. The difficulty here is that it is not known whether the edges found by the innermost call to *balow* are part of the current component until the *low* value is tested. The transformation method provides a means for introducing mechanism (in the form of data structure) to keep track of these changes in values.

There are three places where the accumulated set of edges is modified or used. At two of these, an edge is added to the current set. The third, in the innermost conditional, results in the possible removal of a number of edges from the accumulated set (depending on the *low* value). These edges are those that have been most recently accumulated, however, and they are all distinct. The data structure that results is thus a stack, and the following algorithm is obtained.

```
bcomps ⇐
    begin
        pre[V] ← 0 // p ← 0 // stack←empty;
        for r ∈ V do (if pre[r] = 0 then balow(Λ, r))
    end

balow(u, v) ⇐
    begin var m;
      m ← pre[v] ← p ← p + 1;
      for w ∈ Adj(v) do
        if pre[w] = 0
             then begin
                    Push ⟨v, w⟩;
                    let ℓ = balow(v, w) in
                      if ℓ ≥ pre[v]
                         then begin
                                    m ← min(m, ℓ);
                                    Pop to ⟨v, w⟩
                              end
                  end
           elseif pre[w] < pre[v]  ∧  w ≠ u
             then begin
                    m ← min(m, pre[w]);
                    Push ⟨v, w⟩
                  end;
      m
    end
```
(3.26)

The stack-pop operation, 'Pop to $\langle v, w \rangle$,' pops all edges on the stack up to and including the edge $\langle v, w \rangle$ and emits this set of edges as a biconnected component.

4. Conclusions.

This work is a step towards developing a new paradigm for the presentation and explication of complex algorithms and programs. It seems to us insufficient to simply provide a program or algorithm in final form only. Even with "adequate" documentation and proof, the final code cannot be as revealing to the intuition as a derivation of that code from initial specifications.

Ideally, a mechanical programming environment should support the programmer in the process of building derivations.

In a specific problem domain, such as graph algorithms, certain facts and fundamental algorithms should be available for access. The value of this store of facts should not be underestimated. In our derivations, for example, certain algorithms were repeatedly used as paradigms for the development of other algorithms. This kind of analogical development is similar in heuristic content to the goal-directed transformation of algorithms required to carry out the loop merging optimization or in order to create recursive calls during specialization.

We are still very far from automating the heuristic side of the derivation process. In fact, we argue that at this point our efforts are better directed at discovering and exercising useful transformations, developing foundations for proving their correctness, and developing tools for *interactive* program development that can make appropriate use of outside domain-specific knowledge. For example, it appears that once the necessary outside lemmas are stated and proved, only a modest deduction capability would be required in such a programming environment; it would be used mainly to establish preconditions for transformations and application of lemmas.

Finally, by storing program derivations as data structures in a program development system, ***program modifications*** can be carried out simply by making changes at the appropriate places in the derivation structure; on the other hand, if only the final code is available, the conceptual history of the program must, in effect, be rediscovered.

Bibliography

[AHU74] Aho, A. V., J. E. Hopcroft, and J. D. Ullman, **The Design and Analysis of Computer Algorithms.** Addison-Wesley, 1974.

[AHU83] Aho, A. V., J. E. Hopcroft, and J. D. Ullman, **Data Structures and Algorithms.** Addison-Wesley, 1983.

[Barstow80] Barstow, D. R., *The roles of knowledge and deduction in algorithm design.* Yale Research Report178, April 1980.

[Bauer81] Bauer, F. L., et al., *Programming in a wide spectrum language: a collection of examples.* Science of Computer Programming, Vol. 1, pp. 73–114, 1981.

[Bird80] Bird, R. S., *Tabulation techniques for recursive programs.* Computing Surveys, Vol. 12, No. 4, pp. 403–417, 1980.

[Boyer75] Boyer, R. S. and J. S. Moore, *Proving theorems about LISP functions.* Journal of the ACM, Vol. 22, No. 1, 1975.

[Burstall77] Burstall, R. M. and J. Darlington, *A transformation system for developing recursive programs.* Journal of the ACM, Vol. 24, No. 1, pp. 44–67, 1977.

[Clark78] Clark, K., *Negation as failure.* In: **Logic and Databases.** Gallaire, H., and J. Minker, eds., Plenum, 1978.

[Clark80] Clark, K. and J. Darlington, *Algorithm classification through synthesis.* Computer Journal, Vol. 23, No. 1, 1980.

[Gordon79] Gordon, M. J., Milner, A. J., and C. P. Wadsworth, **Edinburgh LCF.** Springer-Verlag Lecture Notes in Computer Science, 1979.

[Green78] Green C. C. and D. R. Barstow, *On program synthesis knowledge.* Artificial Intelligence, Vol. 10, p. 241, 1978.

[Knuth74] Knuth D. E., *Structured programming with goto statements.* Computing Surveys, Vol. 6, No. 4, pp. 261–301, 1974.

[Manna79] Manna Z. and R. Waldinger, *Synthesis: dreams ⇒ programs.* IEEE Transactions on Software Engineering, Vol. SE-5, No. 4, July 1979.

[Manna81] Manna Z. and R. Waldinger, *Deductive synthesis of the unification algorithm.* Science of Computer Programming, Vol. 1, pp. 5–48, 1981.

[Paige81] Paige, R. and S. Koenig, *Finite differencing of computable expressions.* ACM Transactions on Programming Languages and Systems, Vol. 4, No. 3, pp. 402–454, 1982.

[Reiter78] Reiter, R., *On closed world data bases.* In: **Logic and Databases.** Gallaire, H., and J. Minker, eds., Plenum, 1978.

[Scherlis80] Scherlis, W. L., *Expression procedures and program derivation.* Ph. D. thesis, Stanford University, 1980.

[Scherlis81] Scherlis, W. L., *Program improvement by internal specialization.* Eighth Symposium on Principles of Programming Languages, pp. 41–49, 1981.

[Tarjan72] Tarjan, R. E., *Depth first search and linear graph algorithms.* SIAM Journal of Computing, Vol. 1, No. 2, pp. 146–160, 1972.

[Tarjan73] Tarjan, R. E., *Testing flow graph reducibility.* Fifth ACM Symposium on the Theory of Computing, pp. 96–107, 1973.

[Tarjan77] Tarjan, R. E., *Complexity of combinatorial algorithms.* Stanford Computer Science Report, 1977.

[Wand80] Wand M., *Continuation-based program transformation strategies.* Journal of the ACM, Vol. 27, No. 1, pp. 164–180, 1980.

AN INTRODUCTION TO SPECIFICATION LOGIC†

John C. Reynolds
Syracuse University
Syracuse, NY 13210

ABSTRACT Specification logic is a formal system for proving conditional correctness that is applicable to programming languages whose procedure mechanism can be described by the Algol 60 copy rule. The starting point of its development is the recognition that, in the presence of an Algol-like procedure mechanism, specifications, such as Hoare's {P} C {Q}, must be regarded as predicates about environments. The logic provides additional kinds of specifications describing interference between variables and other entities, and methods for compounding specifications using implication, conjunction, and universal quantification. The result is a system in which one can infer universal specifications that hold in all environments.

Most work on proof methods for procedures has focused on call by reference, and has led to extremely complex inference rules that are incapable of dealing adequately with interference, call by name, statement parameters, or higher-order procedures. In contrast, specification logic is both simpler and more general. Following Algol 60, it avoids the concept of reference, uses call by name, and treats phrase types uniformly. It can be used to reason about procedures involving interfering parameters, e.g. procedures for while and repeat statements, and Jensen's device.

This talk provides a brief introduction to the logic, including a description of specifications and examples of their use. A written version has not been prepared, since the same material is covered in the references given below.

(1) J. C. Reynolds, The Craft of Programming, Prentice-Hall, 1981, Section 3.3 and Chapter 4.

(2) J. C. Reynolds, "Idealized Algol and its Specification Logic", in Tools and Notions for Program Construction, ed. D. Néel, Cambridge University Press, 1982, pp. 121-161.

†Work supported by National Science Foundation Grant MCS 8017577 and U. S. Army Contract DAAK80-80-C-0529.

An Interval-Based Temporal Logic

Richard L. Schwartz, P.M. Melliar-Smith, Friedrich H. Vogt[†]

Computer Science Laboratory
SRI International
Menlo Park, CA 94025

Extended Abstract

1 Introduction

During the last several years, we have explored temporal logic as a framework for specifying and reasoning about concurrent programs, distributed systems, and communications protocols. Previous papers[Schwartz/Melliar-Smith81,82, Vogt82a,b] report on our efforts using temporal reasoning primitives to express very high-level abstract requirements that a program or system is to satisfy. Based on our experiences with those primitives, we have developed an interval logic more suitable for expressing higher-level temporal properties.

In our survey paper[Schwartz/Melliar-Smith82], we examine how several different temporal logic approaches express our conceptual requirements for a simple protocol. Our conclusions were both disappointing and encouraging. On one hand, we saw how our very abstract temporal requirements provided an elegant statement of minimal behavior for implementation conformance. We were able to distill a set of requirements expressing the essence of the desired behavior; stating only requirements without implementation-constraining expedients. Our intention was to specify only the minimum required externally visible behavior, leaving all other aspects to lower levels of description. We have argued that only by doing so can one gain the necessary measure of confidence that a specification reflects the intuitive requirements. Implementation-oriented details, while facilitating verification of *like* implementations, lead to overly detailed and complicated specifications and bias implementation strategies.

While we were happy with the level of *conceptualization* of the specifications, their expression in temporal logic was rather complex and difficult to understand. Because of the relatively low level of the linear-time temporal logic operators ($\Box$, $\Diamond$, **Until**, **Latches-Until**, etc.), we were forced to "encode" many higher-level concepts. To characterize these intervals and any desired properties in temporal logic becomes quite difficult and unwieldy. Intervals in temporal logic are "tail sequence" intervals, always extending from the present state through the remainder of the computation. Temporal logic operators are always interpreted on the *entire* tail sequence. For this reason, unary $\Box$ and $\Diamond$ operators cannot be used to specify invariance and eventuality properties in bounded intervals. The **Until** operator, which does allow one to identify a future point in the computation, must be composed to encode indirectly such properties. This quickly leads to a morass of embedded **Until** formulas.

The impoverished set of temporal abstractions forced us to include state components that were not properly part of our specification. These additional state components were needed to establish the amount of context necessary to express our requirements. Without these components, context could only have been achieved by complex nestings of temporal **Until** constructs to establish a sequence of prior states. Our survey paper highlighted how the introduction of state simplifies the temporal logic formulas at the expense of increasing the amount of "mechanism" in the specification.

---

*This research has been supported by National Science Foundation Grant MCS-8104459.

[†]On leave from the Hahn-Meitner-Institut, Berlin, Federal Republic of Germany.

For our goal of minimal specification of internal behavior, the parameterized event-sequence temporal specification was the most satisfying, and least readable. The difficulty of establishing context by temporal constraint rather than by state function led us to include supplementary state and a slightly lower-level specification.

In this paper, we present an interval logic to provide a higher-level framework for expressing temporal relationships. A higher-level temporal concept that pervades almost all temporal specifications is that of a property being true for an interval. The concept of intervals and interval composition forms the basic structure of our specification and verification method. This allows conceptual requirements to be stated rather directly and intuitively within the logic. For our examples, this new logic has provided concise and workable specifications of the intended semantic requirements.

An informal introduction of the language and logic follows in Section 2. A formal model for the interval logic is given in Section 3, with a selection of valid formulas appearing in Section 4. Several small examples of the use of interval logic are presented in Section 5. Section 6 concludes with a discussion of the current status of the research. Further examples can be found in a companion paper [Schwartz/Melliar-Smith/Vogt83].

2 An Interval Logic

At the heart of our interval logic are formulas of the form:

$$[\, I \,]\alpha$$

Informally, the meaning of this is: "The *next* time the interval I can be constructed, the formula α will 'hold' for that interval." This interval formula is evaluated within the current interval context and is vacuously satisfied if the interval I cannot be found. A formula 'holds' for an interval if it is satisfied by the interval sequence, with the present state being the beginning of the interval.

The unary $\Box$ and $\Diamond$ temporal logic operators retain their intuitive meaning within interval logic. The formula $[\, I \,]\Box\, \alpha$ requires that property α must hold throughout the interval, while $[\, I \,]\Diamond\, \alpha$ expresses the property that sometime during the interval I, α must hold. For simple state predicate P, the interval formula $[\, I \,]P$ expresses the requirement that P be true in the first state of the interval.

Interval formulas compose with the other temporal operators to derive higher-level properties of intervals. The formula

$$[\, I \,][\, J \,]\alpha$$

states that the first J interval contained in the next I interval, if found, will have property α. The property that all J intervals within interval I have property α would be expressed as $[\, I \,]\,\Box[\, J \,]\alpha$. More globally, the formula $\Box[\, I \,]\alpha$ requires all further I intervals to have property α.

Each interval formula $[\, I \,]\alpha$ constrains α to hold only if the interval I can be found. Thus only when the context can be established need the interval property hold. To *require* that the interval occur, one could write $\neg\,[\, I \,]$False. The interval language defines the formula $*\,I$ to mean exactly this.

Thus far, we have described how to compose properties of intervals without discussing how intervals are formed. At the heart of a very general mechanism for defining and combining intervals is the notion of an *event*. An event, defined by an interval formula β, occurs when β changes from False to True, i.e., when it *becomes* true. In the simplest case, β is a predicate on the state, such as $x > 5$ or at Dq . Note that, if the predicate is true in the initial state, the event occurs when it changes from False to True, and thus only after the predicate has become False.

Intervals are defined by a simple or composed interval term. The primitive interval, from which all intervals are derived, is the *event interval*. An event, defined by β, denotes the *interval of change* of length 2 containing the $\neg\beta$ and β states comprising the change. Pictorially, this is represented as

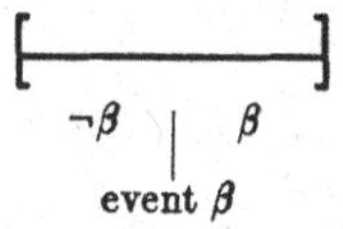

Two functions, begin and end, operate on intervals to extract unit intervals. For interval term I, begin$I$ denotes the unit interval containing the first state of interval I. Similarly, end$I$ denotes the unit interval at the end. Application of the end function is undefined for infinite intervals. Again, pictorially, the intervals selected are

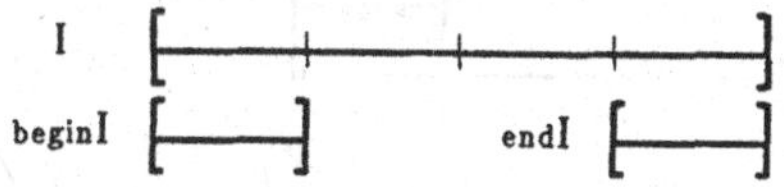

For a P predicate event, the following formulas are valid.

$[\,\text{end}\,P\,]P$

$[\,\text{begin}\,P\,]\neg P$

$[\,P\,]\neg P$

2.1 The Interval Operators $\Rightarrow$ and $\Leftarrow$

Two generic operators exist to derive intervals from interval arguments. We take the liberty of overloading these operators to allow zero, one or two interval-value arguments. Intuitively, the direction of the operator indicates in which direction and in which order the interval endpoints are located. The endpoint at the tail of the arrow is first located, followed by a search in the direction of the arrow for the second endpoint. A missing parameter causes the related endpoint to be that of the outer context.

The interval term $I \Rightarrow$ denotes the interval commencing at the end of the next interval I and extending for the remainder of the outer context. The right arrow operator, in effect, locates the *first* I interval, relative to the outer context, and forms the interval from the *end* of that I interval onward. With only a second argument present, $\Rightarrow J$ denotes the interval commencing with the first state of the outer context and extending to the *end* of the *first* J interval. Thus,

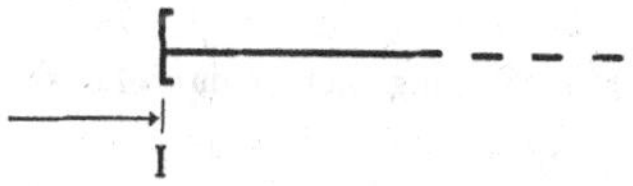

The term $I \Rightarrow J$, with two interval arguments, represents the composition of the two definitions. This constructs the interval starting at the end of interval I and extending to the end of the *next* interval J located in the interval $I \Rightarrow$. Given this definition, the interval formula $[\,I \Rightarrow J\,]\alpha$ is equivalent to

$\left[I \Rightarrow \right]\left[\Rightarrow J \right]\alpha$. Recall that the formula $\left[I \Rightarrow J \right]\alpha$ is vacuously true if the $I \Rightarrow J$ interval cannot be found. Pictorially, the interval selected is

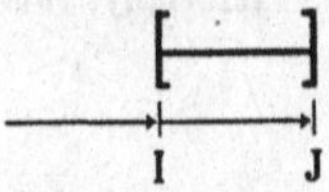

The right arrow operator with no interval arguments selects the entire outer context.

The left arrow operator $\Leftarrow$ is defined analogously. For interval term $I \Leftarrow J$, the first J interval in context is located. From the end of this J interval, the *most recent* I interval is located. The derived interval $I \Leftarrow J$ begins with $\mathrm{end}I$ and ends with $\mathrm{end}J$. Thus,

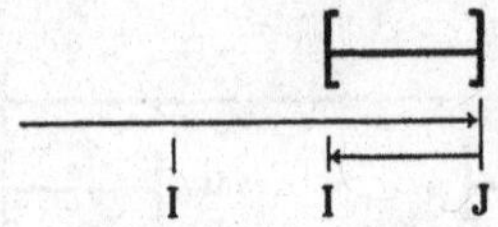

Similarly, the interval term $I \Leftarrow$ selects the interval beginning with the end of the last I interval and extending for the remainder of the context. For a context in which an interval I occurs an infinite number of times, the formula $\left[I \Leftarrow \right]\alpha$ is vacuously true. The interval terms $\Leftarrow$ and $\Leftarrow J$ are strictly equivalent to $\Rightarrow$ and $\Rightarrow J$, respectively.

The following examples illustrate the use of the interval operators.

$$\left[x = y \Rightarrow y = 16 \right] \Box\, x > z \tag{1}$$

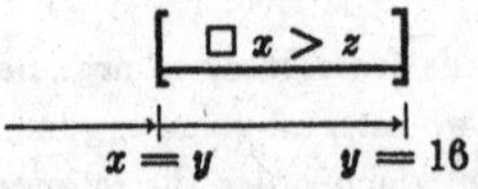

For the interval beginning with the next event of the variable x becoming equal to y and ending with y changing to the value 16, the value of x is asserted to remain greater than z. The first state of the interval is thus the state in which x is equal to y and the last state is that in which y is next equal to 16. Note that the events $x = y$ and $y = 16$ denote the next *changes* from $x \neq y$ and $y \neq 16$.

To modify the above requirement to allow $x > z$ to become False as y becomes 16, one could write

$$\left[x = y \Rightarrow \mathrm{begin}(y = 16) \right] \Box\, x > z \tag{2}$$

Nesting interval terms provides a method of expressing more comprehensive context requirements. Consider the formula

$$\left[(A \Rightarrow B) \Rightarrow C \right] \Diamond D \tag{3}$$

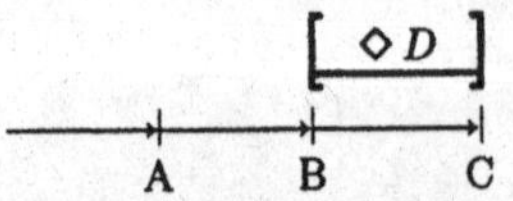

The formula requires that, if an A event is found, the subsequent B to C interval, if found, must sometime satisfy property D. The outer $\Rightarrow$ operator selects the interval commencing at the end of its first argument, in this case, at the end of the selected $A \Rightarrow B$ interval. The interval then extends until the next C event – establishing the necessary context.

In the previous example, the formula was vacuously true if any of the events A,B, or C could not be found in the established context. In order to easily express a requirement that a particular event or interval *must* be found if the necessary context is established, we introduce an interval term modifier $*$. For interval term I, $*I$ adds an additional requirement that B must be found in the designated context. The formula

$$\big[(A \Rightarrow *B) \Rightarrow C\big] \Diamond D \tag{4}$$

strengthens formula (3) by adding the requirement that, if an A event occurs, a subsequent B event *must* occur. This is equivalent to formula (3) conjoined with $\big[A \Rightarrow\big]*B$.

The $*$ modifier can be applied to an arbitrary interval term. The formula $\big[*(A \Rightarrow B) \Rightarrow C\big] \Diamond D$, for example, would be equivalent to (3) conjoined with $*(A \Rightarrow B)$, or equivalently, $*A \;\wedge\; \big[A \Rightarrow\big]*B$. The $*$ modifier adds only linguistic expressive power and can be eliminated by a simple reduction (given in the Appendix).

As an example of specifying context for the end of the interval, consider the formula

$$\big[A \Rightarrow (B \Rightarrow C)\big] \Diamond D \tag{5}$$

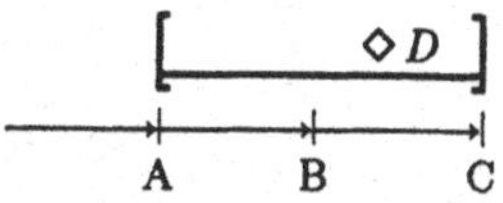

Here, the interval begins with the next occurrence of A and terminates with the first C that follows the next B.

By modifying formula (3) to begin the interval at the beginning of $A \Rightarrow B$, i.e.,

$$\big[\mathrm{begin}(A \Rightarrow B) \Rightarrow C\big] \Diamond D \tag{6}$$

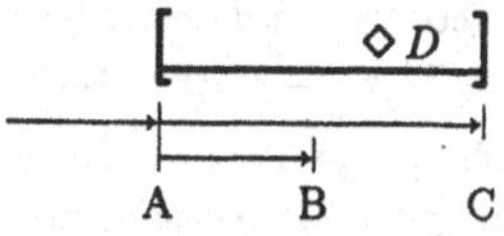

we obtain a requirement similar to that of (5), but allowing events B and C to be ***arbitrarily ordered.***

Introducing the use of backward context, to find the interval $A \Rightarrow B$ in the context of C, we have

$$\big[(A \Rightarrow B) \Leftarrow C\big] \Diamond D \tag{7}$$

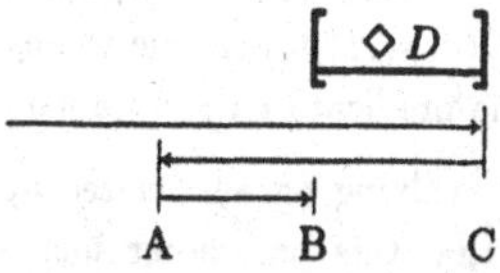

Here the occurrence of the first C event places an endpoint on the context, within which the most recent $A \Rightarrow B$ interval is found. Note the order of search: looking forward, the next C is found, then backward for the most recent A, then forward for the next B. Thus, the formula is vacuously true if no B is found between C and the most recent A.

As a last example, consider

$$\left[\,\text{begin}(A \Leftarrow B) \Leftarrow C\,\right] \Diamond D \tag{8}$$

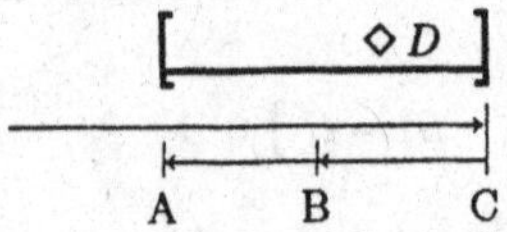

The interval extends back from the first C event to the beginning of the most recent $A \Leftarrow B$ interval.

2.2 Parameterized Operations

Within the language of our interval logic we include the concept of an *abstract operation*. For an abstract operation O, state predicates at$O$, in$O$, and after$O$ are defined. These predicates carry the intuitive meanings of being "at the beginning", "within", and "immediately after" the operation. Formally, we use the following temporal axiomatization of these state predicates.

1. $\left[\,\text{at}O \Rightarrow \text{begin after}O\,\right] \Box\, \text{in}O$
2. $\left[\,\text{after}O \Rightarrow \text{begin at}O\,\right] \Box\, \neg\text{in}O$
3. $\left[\,\neg\text{at}O \Rightarrow \text{after}O\,\right] \Box\, \neg\text{at}O$
4. $\left[\,\neg\text{after}O \Rightarrow \text{at}O\,\right] \Box\, \neg\text{after}O$

Axioms 1 and 2 together define in$O$ to be true exactly from at$O$ to the state immediately preceding after$O$. Axiom 3 allows at$O$ to be true only at the beginning of the operation, and axiom 4 requires that after$O$ be true only immediately following an operation. Note that, in axiom 1 for example, the predicate at$O$ used as an event term defines the interval commencing with the *entry* to the operation.

The axioms do not imply any specific granularity, duration or mapping of the operation symbol to an implementation. *Any interpretation of these state predicate symbols satisying the above axioms is allowed.* In addition, no assumption of operation termination is made. To require an operation to always terminate, one could state as an axiom

$$\left[\,\text{at}O \Rightarrow *\ \text{after}O\,\right]\text{True}$$

Abstract operations may take entry and result parameters. For an operation taking n entry parameters of types $T_1, \ldots, T_n$, and m result parameters of types $T_{n+1}, \ldots, T_{n+m}$, the at and after state predicates are overloaded to include parameter values. at$O(v_1, \ldots, v_n)$ is true in any state in which at$O$ is true and the values of the parameters are $v_1, \ldots, v_n$. The predicate after is similarly overloaded.

As an example of an interval requirement involving parameterized operations, consider an operation O with a single entry parameter. To require that this parameter increase monotonically over the call history, one could state

$$\forall a, b\ \Box\left[\,\text{at}O(a) \Rightarrow \text{at}O(b)\,\right] b > a$$

Since a and b are free variables, for all a and b such that we can find an interval commencing with an $\mathrm{at}O(a)$ and ending with an $\mathrm{at}O(b)$, b must be greater than a. Recall that the formula is vacuously true for any choice of a and b such that the interval cannot be found.

It is also useful to be able to designate the *next* occurrence of the operation call, and to bind the parameter values of that call. The event term $\mathrm{at}O : (a)$ designates the next event $\mathrm{at}O$ and binds the free variable a to the value of the parameter for that call. Thus the previous requirement constraining all pairs of calls, can be restated in terms of successive calls as

$$\Box\Big[\ \mathrm{at}O(a) \Rightarrow \mathrm{at}O : (b)\ \Big]\ b > a$$

The requirement is now that for every a, the call $\mathrm{at}O(a)$ is followed by a call of O whose parameter is greater than a. This parameter binding convention has a general reduction, which we omit here. For this specific formula, the reduction gives

$$\Box\Big[\ \mathrm{at}O(a) \Rightarrow\ \Big]\ \Big(\Big[\mathrm{end\ at}O\ \Big]\mathrm{at}O(b)\Big) \supset \Big[\Rightarrow \mathrm{at}O\ \Big] b > a$$

3 A Formal Model

In this section we give the syntax and model-theoretic semantics for the language of interval logic.

In the following, we will use α, β, γ as logical variables ranging over interval formulas and use I, J, K ranging over interval terms. We use P to range over atomic predicates and A to range over event terms.

Summarizing the language of our logic, we have defined the following syntactic constructs:

<interval formula> α ::

P | $\neg\beta$ | β <propositional connective> γ | $\Diamond\beta$ | $\Box\beta$ | $*\beta$ | $[I]\beta$

<interval term> I ::

A | $\mathrm{begin}\,J$ | $\mathrm{end}\,J$ |

$J \Rightarrow K$ (*with possible omission of one or both arguments*) |

$J \Leftarrow K$ (*with possible omission of one or both arguments*)

<event term> A :: α

As we mentioned earlier, the $*$ interval term modifier is considered as a syntactic abbreviation. Rules for its elimination appear in the Appendix.

For a finite or infinite computation state sequence s, we now define satisfaction of an interval formula α by s. In defining the model, we use the notation $s_{<i,j>}$ to denote the subsequence of s beginning with the ith element of the sequence, and ending with the jth element of the sequence. As a representation for an infinite sequence, we use ∞ as the right endpoint value, as in the subsequence $s_{<i,\infty>}$. For a finite computation, we extend the last state to form an infinite sequence.

The following model defines, for sequence s and interval formula α, the satisfaction relation $s_{<i,j>} \models \alpha$. We say that a sequence s satisfies formula α if $s_{<1,|s|>} \models \alpha$. Since our definition of the satisfaction relation will always be referring to portions of the same s sequence, we will refer to s using only its subsequence denotation, i.e., as $< i, j > \models \alpha$.

The relation $<i,j> \models \alpha$ is defined recursively, based on the structure of the formula, as follows:

$<i,j> \models P \quad \equiv \quad s_i \models P$

$<i,j> \models \neg\alpha \quad \equiv \quad \text{not} <i,j> \models \alpha$

$<i,j> \models \alpha \wedge \beta \quad \equiv \quad <i,j> \models \alpha \text{ and } <i,j> \models \beta$

$<i,j> \models \Box\alpha \quad \equiv \quad \forall k \in <i,j> \; <k,j> \models \alpha$

$<i,j> \models \Diamond\alpha \quad \equiv \quad \exists k \in <i,j> \; <k,j> \models \alpha$

$<i,j> \models [I]\alpha \quad \equiv \quad \mathcal{F}(I, <i,j>, \mathrm{F}) \models \alpha$

$\bot \models \alpha$

The $\mathcal{F}$ function appearing in the definition of $[I]\alpha$ is a interval-valued function from an interval term, an interval, and a direction of search. The direction of search is denoted by F for forward or B for backward - logical variable d ranges over F and B. The function $\mathcal{F}$ denotes the interval I found in the $<i,j>$ context looking in the direction of search. The function is defined to return the null interval value $\bot$ when the interval cannot be constructed. All functions on intervals are strict on $\bot$. By the last clause in the above definition, any formula α is satisfied for such a null interval. This serves as a device to define our partial correctness semantics for interval formulas.

For event term α and interval $<i,j>$ we define

$$\text{changeset}(\alpha, <i,j>) = \left\{ \begin{array}{l} <k-1,k> \mid k \in <i,j> \\ \qquad \wedge <k-1,j> \models \neg\alpha \\ \qquad \wedge <k,j> \models \alpha \end{array} \right\}$$

to define the set of events α occuring in the interval, each event being the interval of change $<k-1,k>$ in which α changes from false to true. With this we next define

$\mathcal{F}(\alpha, <i,j>, \mathrm{F}) = \min(\text{changeset}(\alpha, <i,j>)$

$\mathcal{F}(\alpha, <i,j>, \mathrm{B}) = \max(\text{changeset}(\alpha, <i,j>)$

We assume min and max functions on sets of (interval-valued) pairs are defined in the standard manner (the represented intervals are disjoint). Both min and max return $\bot$ if the set is empty, and max returns $\bot$ for an infinite set. Thus $\mathcal{F}$ returns the interval of change for the first or last event α in the interval $<i,j>$, and returns $\bot$ if that interval cannot be found.

Next we define the interpretation of the interval functions begin and end

$\mathcal{F}(\text{begin}I, <i,j>, d) \quad = \quad <\text{first}(\mathcal{F}(I, <i,j>, d)), \text{first}(\mathcal{F}(I, <i,j>, d))>$

$\mathcal{F}(\text{end}I, <i,j>, d) \quad = \quad <\text{last}(\mathcal{F}(I, <i,j>, d)), \text{last}(\mathcal{F}(I, <i,j>, d))>$

where $\text{first}(<i,j>) = i$, $\text{last}(<i,j>) = j$ and $\text{last}(<i,\infty>)$ is defined to return $\bot$.

We now define our forward and backward interval construction functions through a recursive interpretation for $\mathcal{F}$ based on the structure of the interval-term argument.

$\mathcal{F}(\Rightarrow, <i,j>, d) \quad = \quad \mathcal{F}(\Leftarrow, <i,j>, d) \quad = \quad <i,j>$

$\mathcal{F}(I\Rightarrow, <i,j>, d) \quad = \quad <\text{last}(\mathcal{F}(I, <i,j>, d)), j>$

$\mathcal{F}(I\Leftarrow, <i,j>, d) \quad = \quad <\text{last}(\mathcal{F}(I, <i,j>, \mathrm{B})), j>$

$\mathcal{F}(\Rightarrow J, <i,j>, d) \quad = \quad <i, \text{last}(\mathcal{F}(J, <i,j>, \mathrm{F}))>$

$\mathcal{F}(\Leftarrow J, <i,j>, d) \quad = \quad <i, \text{last}(\mathcal{F}(J, <i,j>, d))>$

We now derive the semantics of the two argument arrow operators as the composition of those above.

$$\mathcal{F}(I{\Rightarrow}J, <i,j>, d) = \mathcal{F}({\Rightarrow}J, \mathcal{F}(I{\Rightarrow}, <i,j>, d), \mathrm{F})$$

$$\mathcal{F}(I{\Leftarrow}J, <i,j>, d) = \mathcal{F}({\Leftarrow}J, \mathcal{F}(I{\Leftarrow}, <i,j>, d), \mathrm{F})$$

This completes our model for interval logic formulas.

Interval logic specifications are divided into two parts: Init and Axioms. An *Init* portion states properties to be satisifed at (from) the beginning of a computation, assuming a distinguished starting state. Formally, using distinguished (uninterpreted) state predicate *start*, each interval formula α within the Init clause is interpreted as an axiom of the form *start* $\supset \alpha$. The interpretation of *start* is a a methodological concern: the predicate will be mapped to the beginning state of the computation sequence when proving that a program satisfies the specification. The assumption of a distinguished starting state will allow us to more completely characterize correct system or program behavior.

4 A Sampling of Valid Formulas

In this section we present a selection of valid formulas. Our intention here is simply to illustrate a style of expression and deduction rather than a more comprehensive list of valid formulas or a complete axiomatization. We are currently incorporating a decision procedure for interval logic[Plaisted83] into our STP deduction system[Shostak/Schwartz/Melliar-Smith82]. We are therefore more concerned about the *style of expression* than an axiomatization of the language or rules of deduction.

As in the previous section, we use α, β, γ as logical variables ranging over interval formulas, and I, J, K ranging over interval terms. Additionally, we use variables ρ, σ to range over interval formulas with only noninterval terms, e.g., $\Diamond \Box x = 14$ or any formula not containing embedded $\big[\, I \,\big]\alpha$ terms.

Interval formulas distribute across intervals, as indicated by the following formulas.

V1. $\big[\, I \,\big]\alpha \;\wedge\; \big[\, I \,\big]\beta \;\equiv\; \big[\, I \,\big](\alpha \wedge \beta)$

V2. $\big[\, I \,\big]\alpha \;\supset\; \big[\, I \,\big]\beta \;\equiv\; \big[\, I \,\big](\alpha \supset \beta)$

Expressing the fundamental case split in interpreting interval formulas, we have

V3. $\big[\, I \,\big]\alpha \;\equiv\; \neg{*}I \;\vee\; \big[\, {*}I \,\big]\alpha$

defining the formula to be true if either the interval cannot be constructed, or if α holds for the constructed interval. Associated with this, we also have

V4. ${*}I \;\equiv\; \neg\big[\, I \,\big]\mathrm{False}$

V5. ${*}\alpha \;\equiv\; \Diamond(\neg\alpha \wedge \Diamond\, \alpha)$

V6. $\neg\big[\, I \,\big]\alpha \;\equiv\; \big[\, {*}I \,\big]\neg\alpha$

Formula V4 derives the meaning of our interval-eventuality operator in terms of an interval formula, while V5 re-expresses this in terms of nested $\Diamond$ eventuality. Formula V6 defines "pushing" interval formula negation into the interval.

For an arbitrary interval α, we have the following formulas illustrating the "promotion" of noninterval properties to interval properties.

V7. $\alpha \;\equiv\; \big[\, \Rightarrow \,\big]\alpha$

V8. $\Box\, \alpha \;\supset\; \Box\big[\, I \Rightarrow \,\big]\alpha$

Formula V7 expresses the fact that the interval (⇒) selects the complete outer context, while V8 expresses the fact that any invariant α of the outer context will apply in any "tail interval" of the context. A consequence of our basic definition of event terms is

V9. $[\alpha \Rightarrow \text{begin}\neg\alpha\ ]\Box\alpha$

That is, for the interval beginning with α becoming true and extending until just prior to α becoming false, α will remain true.

As properties of how intervals are constructed, we have

V10. $[\ \text{begin}\alpha \Rightarrow\ ]*\beta \quad \vee \quad [\ \text{begin}\beta \Rightarrow\ ]*\alpha$

V11. $[\alpha \Leftarrow \beta\ ]\gamma \quad \equiv \quad [\Rightarrow \beta\ ][\neg *\alpha \Rightarrow\ ]\gamma$

V12. $[\Rightarrow I\ ]\neg\Box *J$

Formula V10 expresses a fundamental event-ordering property. For two events designated by α and β, either (1) one or the other event does not occur, (2) α occurs before β, (3) β occurs before α, or (4) both occur at the same time. This case split is often used to prove properties relating multiple events.

For *nonnested* interval terms, formula V11 reduces the semantics of our backward ⇐ operator to an equivalent expression using the forward ⇒ operator. In doing this reduction, we employ a nested interval event formula. The embedded ($\neg *\alpha$) thus begins when the $\neg *\alpha$ formula changes to become true. This will becomes true in the first state when one can no longer find another α event – precisely in the first α state of the last change to α. Of course this kind of "tricky encoding" should be avoided; the backward operator was included in the language to provide a higher-level construct to express this!

Formula V12 expresses the fact that no interval with an upper end point, and therefore finite, can contain an unbounded number of J intervals. This follows from the fact that the occurrence of an event requires a change in predicate value – and thus at least two states. Note that the formula $* \Diamond \alpha$ is satisfiable in a bounded interval. This would be satisfied by any interval state sequence in which α is true in the last state. Thus, the interpretation of $\Box \Diamond$ as "infinitely often" only applies over infinite intervals.

As basic properties of interval partitioning, we have

V13. $[\Rightarrow I\ ]\rho \quad \wedge \quad [I \Rightarrow\ ]\rho \quad \supset \quad \rho$

V14. $\rho \quad \supset \quad [\Rightarrow I\ ]\rho \quad \vee \quad [I \Rightarrow\ ]\rho$

By V13, for any interval term I, if a simple property ρ is true up to I and is true from I onward within the outer context, then ρ is true for the context. Typical use of this would be to establish invariance or eventuality properties for an interval by showing the properties to hold for portions of the interval. Formula V14 expresses the dual of this.

Finally, the following formulas express interval composition.

V15. $[I \Rightarrow J\ ]\rho \quad \wedge \quad [(I \Rightarrow J) \Rightarrow K\ ]\rho \quad \supset \quad [I \Rightarrow (J \Rightarrow K)\ ]\rho$

V16. $[\Rightarrow (J \Rightarrow K)\ ]\alpha \quad \wedge \quad [\Rightarrow *J\ ]\neg *K \quad \supset \quad [\Rightarrow K\ ]\alpha$

Formula V15 defines the composition of two intervals ($I \Rightarrow J$) and (($I \Rightarrow J) \Rightarrow K$) to form the interval ($I \Rightarrow (J \Rightarrow K)$). Pictorially, we have

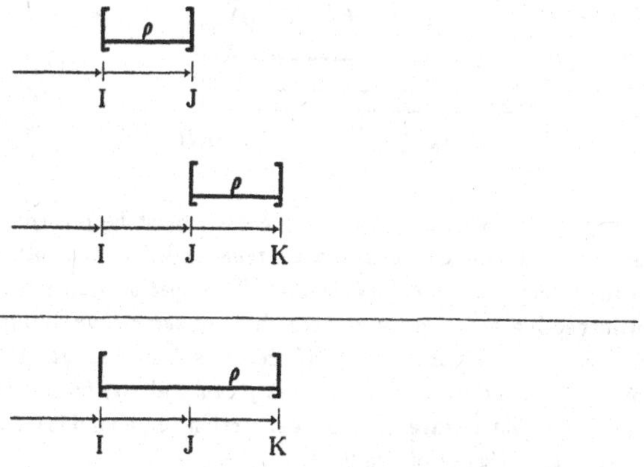

A nonembedded interval property ρ is thus derived for the interval from I to the first K that follows the first J by proving it for the associated I to J and J to K intervals. For the case where one can prove that the first K following I also follows J, formula V16 allows the simplification of $(\Leftarrow (J \Rightarrow K))$ to $(\Rightarrow K)$.

5 Excerpted Examples

Consider a queue with two operations, Enq which takes a single parameter value, which it enqueues, and Dq which removes the value at the front of the queue and returns that value as its result. We assume in this specification that the queue is unbounded, and require that values enqueued must be distinct. No assumptions are made about the atomicity of, or temporal relationships between, the Enq and Dq operations. These operations can overlap in an arbitrary manner. We do assume that at most one instance of the Enq and Dq operations will be active at any given time.

The specification expresses the fundamental first-in first-out behavior that characterizes a queue. It requires that, for all a and b, if we dequeue b, then any other value a will be dequeued in the interim if and only if it was enqueued prior to b. Further axioms are needed to express liveness requirements on the two operations.

$$\text{Queue.} \quad [\Leftarrow \text{afterDq}(b)\,](*\text{afterDq}(a) \quad \equiv \quad *(\text{atEnq}(a) \Leftarrow \text{atEnq}(b)\,))$$

By exchanging atEnq(a) and atEnq(b) terms in the queue axiom above,

$$\text{Stack.} \quad [\Leftarrow \text{afterDq}(b)\,](*\text{afterDq}(a) \quad \equiv \quad *(\text{atEnq}(b) \Leftarrow \text{atEnq}(a)\,))$$

one obtains a last-in first-out queue (i.e., stack).

As a second example, consider a specification to ensure exclusive access to a shared critical section by some set of processes. Each process is to make an independent decision based on a shared global data structure. In stating the specification, we assume a state predicate cs(i) which, for process i, indicates that i is in the critical section. For a shared global data structure, we assume a state predicate x(i) which, for process i, indicates i's intention to enter the critical section. We wish to state minimal requirements on the use of state predicate x by a process to ensure mutual exclusion. Pictorially we represent the required behavior as follows:

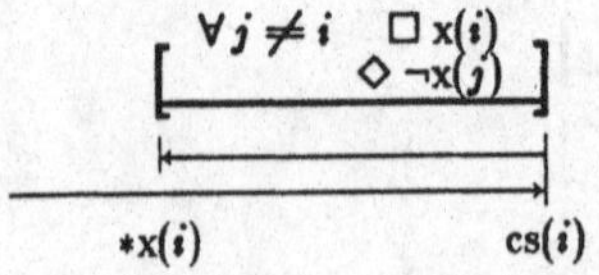

As shown, an entry of the critical section by process i must be preceded by an earlier setting of x(i) to true. Throughout this interval x(i) must remain true, and, for every other process j, there must be some moment within the interval at which x(j) is false. This specification imposes no requirement on the order or frequency of inspecting the x(j)s; it suffices that, *at some time* during the interval, each x(j) is false. Herein lies the basic reason for exclusion. x(i) remains true through the interval, and no other x(j) can be true for that interval. Thus no other process j can find x(i) false between the time that i signals his intention and the time that i leaves the critical section (or abandons his claim). The specification does not, however, ensure the absence of deadlock.

In interval logic, we express these requirements as follows.

Init. $\forall m\ \neg x(m)$

A1. $i \neq j \supset [\, x(i) \Leftarrow cs(i)\,]\ \Diamond \neg x(j)$

A2. $cs(i) \supset x(i)$

Given an initial condition in which all processes have relinquished their claims, axiom A1 expresses our previous pictorial requirement that, if process i enters the critical section, then for the interval back to the most recent setting of x(i), each x(j) must be found to be false. Axiom A2 requires that x(i) remains true while i is in the critical section. We have not needed to state explicitly that there must be a setting of x(i) prior to the entry; this is deducible from the specification. Similarly we can deduce that x(i) remains true through that interval.

From this specification, we can demonstrate (omitted here) the mutual exclusion property that henceforth no pair of processes can both be in the critical section at the same time, i.e.,

$$\forall m\ \neg x(m) \wedge i \neq j \quad \supset \quad \Box \neg(\, cs(i) \wedge cs(j)\,)$$

6 Analysis and Conclusions

We have presented a preliminary version of our interval logic and have illustrated its application to several small examples. We are reasonably satisfied with its success, although we expect further honing of the language as we gain more experience with specification and verification attempts. The language at this point does not address the issue of program correctness. Left for later development is a means to compose multiprocess system semantics from semantics of individual processes. This is, of course, needed to define the semantics of a concurrent programming language as well.

At the heart of our interval logic design is the decision to support a behavioral style of specification and reasoning. A *cause/effect* style pervades our specifications – always of the form "given a particular context, some future behavior of the system must occur". As we discussed in [Schwartz/Melliar-Smith82], we find this form of specification to be closer to our intuitive operational understanding of our requirements, while still managing to avoid details of operational implementation. More history-related specifications, capturing a static view of necessary relationships between different input/output histories, don't seem to provide the same degree of intuition crucial to understanding and reasoning about a system from its specification.

The decision to base interval formation on "state-change events" was motivated by our observation that establishing context almost always required seeing a change in state. Without "anchoring" requirements on properties *becoming* true, one often cannot guarantee that the proper interval has been identified. This is particularly true for eventuality properties.

Two language decisions related to this notion of context establishment are the decisions (1) to make interval formulas vacuously true whenever the context cannot be established, and (2) to interpret interval formulas as properties of the *next time* the context occurs. Both these decisions support an abstract form of operational thinking. Having sufficient expressive power to conveniently establish context requirements either temporally or through the use of state components proved to be an important method of directing the level of abstraction of the specification.

Based on our previous experience with formal specification methods, we do not think *any* specification method for distributed and concurrent systems can be successful without mechanical verification support. The level of process interaction makes it only too easy to make incorrect or incomplete analysis of specifications, regardless of the amount of human care that is taken. Our experiences with informal proof techniques and unverified specifications have led us to include mechanical verification support as a *crucial* part of any specification language design effort. Our emphasis in designing the interval logic was to retain decidability in order to provide a complete decision procedure. Although we believe interval logic has a complete axiomatization, through a reduction to linear-time temporal logic, we do not expect anyone to attempt to use the axiomatization in doing a proof. For this reason, we chose features on the basis of utility rather than mathematical elegance.

One direction for further work that may prove extremely fruitful is development of a formal graphical representation of specifications and proofs. The ability to represent specifications and proof arguments pictorially could greatly enhance intuitive understanding of temporal properties.

Preliminary analysis of the computational complexity of our logic indicates it is P-space complete – the same order of complexity as for linear-time temporal logic. We, with David Plaisted playing the primary role, have developed an experimental decision procedure for interval logic [Plaisted83].

Several other higher-order temporal languages have appeared in the literature. Lamport introduced a Timeset language[Lamport80] for defining properties of intervals. At the heart of the language proposal are terms of the form $[P \Rightarrow Q)$, denoting the set of *all* time intervals starting with a state in which property P is true and extending to *all* points such that Q has remained false. Such all-inclusive terms make it difficult to avoid capturing unexpected and unwanted contexts, and, we believe, result in nonelementary computational complexity.

Wolper[Wolper82] introduced the concept of a regular-expression grammar operator into his Extended Temporal Logic (ETL). These grammar operators are used to define constraints, in the form of regular expressions, on allowable sequences of parameterized operations. This produces very abstract specifications, in much the same style as Hailpern's[Hailpern80] history-based, linear-time temporal logic. Wolper's extension preserves P-space complexity.

With a somewhat different focus, Moszkowski[Moszkowski82] uses a related notion of interval logic to define and prove properties of hardware circuits. Moszkowski integrates specification of quantitative bounds into his hardware description language. While our interval logic is oriented toward identifying properties true of specified contexts, Mozkowski's logic provides interval abstraction, that is, a method to refer to all intervals having a certain property or decomposition. A semicolon operator, similar in spirit to the dynamic logic[Harel79] "chop" operator, allows formulas such as $[\ P\ ;\ Q\ ]$ to refer to all intervals composed from subintervals having properties P and Q. This very powerful concept again leads to nonelementary computational complexity.

Acknowledgments

Discussions with Joe Halpern and David Plaisted have been extremely valuable in helping us to explore the complexity of our logic and to investigate decision procedure support for the logic. Joe Halpern, David Plaisted, Moshe Vardi, Ed Ashcroft, Leslie Lamport, Jan Vitopil, and Rob Shostak have also contributed many valuable suggestions for improving the interval logic and its presentation.

References

[1] Bochmann, G.V., "Hardware Specification with Temporal Logic: An Example", *IEEE Transactions on Computers,* Vol C-31, No. 3, March 1982.

[2] Hailpern, B., "Verifying Concurrent Processes Using Temporal Logic", Technical Report 195, Computer Systems Laboratory, Stanford Univ., August 1980.

[3] Harel, D., "First-Order Dynamic Logic", Springer Verlag Lecture Notes, No. 68, 1979.

[4] International Standards Organization, "Data Processing – Open Systems Interconnection – Basic Reference Model", ISO/DIS 7498, April 1982.

[5] Lamport, L., "Timesets: A New Method for Temporal Reasoning about Programs", *Logics of Programs Conference,* Springer Verlag, Vol. 131, Sept. 1981.

[6] Moszkowski, B., "A Temporal Logic for Multi-Level Reasoning about Hardware", Technical Report STAN-CS-82-952, Computer Science Dept., Stanford Univ., Dec. 1982.

[7] Plaisted, D., "An Intermediate-Level Language for Obtaining Decision Procedures for a Class of Temporal Logics", Computer Science Laboratory, SRI, in preparation, June 1983.

[8] Schwartz, R., P.M. Melliar-Smith, "Temporal Logic Specification of Distributed Systems", *Proceeding of the IEEE Conference on Distributed Systems,* April 1981.

[9] Schwartz, R., P.M. Melliar-Smith, "From State Machines to Temporal Logic: Specification Methods for Protocol Standards", *IEEE Transactions on Communications,* Dec. 1982.

[10] Schwartz, R., P.M. Melliar-Smith, F. Vogt, "An Interval Logic for Higher-Level Temporal Reasoning", *Proceedings of the SIGACT/SIGOPS Conference on Principles of Distributed Computing,* August, 1983.

[11] Seitz, C., "Ideas about Arbiters", *Lambda,* pp. 10-14, First Quarter, 1980.

[12] Shostak, R., R. Schwartz, P.M. Melliar-Smith, "STP: A Mechanized Logic for Specification and Verification", *6th Conference on Automated Deduction,* Springer Verlag Lecture Notes, Vol. 138, June 1982.

[13] Vogt, F., "Entwurf eines Ereignisorientierten Modells zur Spezifikation von Verteilten Systemen Mittels Temporaler Logik", Ph.D. Dissertation, Technische Universität Wien, Austria, Feb. 1982.

[14] Vogt, F., "Event-Based Temporal Logic Specification of Services and Protocols", *Protocol Specificatio Testing and Verification,* North-Holland Publishing, 1982.

[15] Wolper, P., "Synthesis of Communicating Processes from Temporal Logic Specifications", Report No. STAN-CS-82-925, Dept of Computer Science, Stanford University, August 1982.

Reduction of Interval Formulas Containing $*$ Modifier

The $*$ modifier in the interval language is regarded as a linguistic convenience. Below, we give axioms to reduce a formula containing the $*$ modifier to an equivalent formula without the modifier. In this section we denote interval terms possibly containing the $*$ modifier by $\hat{I}$ and $\hat{J}$.

We base the reduction on the following equivalence

$$[\hat{I}]\alpha \quad \equiv \quad [I']\alpha \quad \wedge \quad [\hat{I}]\mathrm{true}$$

where I' is derived from $\hat{I}$ by omitting throughout the $*$ modifiers. We also use the definition of $*\hat{I}$ to reduce the eventuality on intervals to an interval formula

$$*\hat{I} \quad \equiv \quad \neg[\hat{I}]\mathrm{false}$$

For the outer level of interval structure, we use:

$$[*\hat{I}]\mathrm{true} \quad \equiv \quad [\Rightarrow *\hat{I}]\mathrm{true} \quad \equiv \quad *\hat{I}$$

$$[*\hat{I}\Leftarrow]\mathrm{true} \quad \equiv \quad *(\hat{I}\Leftarrow)$$

$$[\mathrm{begin}*\hat{I}]\mathrm{true} \quad \equiv \quad [*\,\mathrm{begin}\hat{I}]\mathrm{true}$$

$$[\mathrm{end}*\hat{I}]\mathrm{true} \quad \equiv \quad [*\,\mathrm{end}\hat{I}]\mathrm{true}$$

and for splitting composite intervals we use:

$$[\hat{I}\Rightarrow\hat{J}]\mathrm{true} \quad \equiv \quad [\hat{I}\Rightarrow][\Rightarrow\hat{J}]\mathrm{true}$$

$$[\hat{I}\Leftarrow\hat{J}]\mathrm{true} \quad \equiv \quad [\Leftarrow\hat{J}][\hat{I}\Rightarrow]\mathrm{true}$$

Finally we give reduction rules for the four composite intervals that cannot be reduced by simple splitting of an interval.

$$[\Rightarrow(\hat{I}\Rightarrow\hat{J})]\mathrm{true} \quad \equiv \quad [\hat{I}\Rightarrow\hat{J}]\mathrm{true}$$

$$[\Rightarrow(\hat{I}\Leftarrow\hat{J})]\mathrm{true} \quad \equiv \quad [\hat{I}\Leftarrow\hat{J}]\mathrm{true}$$

$$[(\hat{I}\Rightarrow\hat{J})\Leftarrow]\mathrm{true} \quad \equiv \quad [\mathrm{begin}(\hat{I}\Leftarrow)\Rightarrow\hat{J}]\mathrm{true}$$

$$[(\hat{I}\Leftarrow\hat{J})\Leftarrow]\mathrm{true} \quad \equiv \quad [\hat{J}\Leftarrow\mathrm{begin}(\hat{I}\Leftarrow)]\mathrm{true}$$

PROPERTY PRESERVING HOMOMORPHISMS OF TRANSITION SYSTEMS

Joseph Sifakis
IMAG
BP68, 38402 St-Martin d'Hères Cedex, France

Abstract

We study functions preserving properties of transition systems described by formulas of a logic.

Let L be a logic for which transition systems constitute a class of models. A formula F of L defines for a given transition system S and interpretation i, a property ; a state q of S satisfies the property represented by F iff $q \models_i F$. Given two transition systems S_1 and S_2 with sets of states respectively Q_1 and Q_2 and a function f, $f : 2^{Q_1} \to 2^{Q_2}$, we say that f preserves the property represented by F iff

$\forall q_1 \in Q_1 (q_1 \models_i F$ implies $\forall q_2 \in Q_2,\ q_2 \in f(\{q_1\}),\ q_2 \models_{f \circ i} F)$.

The results presented concern the characterization of functions f which preserve properties independently of the particular choice of S_1 and S_2 provided that the transition systems be related via homomorphisms of a certain type.

I. INTRODUCTION

The notion of equivalence between systems is of foundamental importance for their design and analysis. Roughly speaking, we say that a system is equivalent to another system whenever some essential aspects of their behaviour agree. These aspects of the behaviour are usually defined by adopting various criteria such as the equality of the sets of sequences of observable events, the realization of the same input/output relation, the preservation of the validity of a set of assertions.

Equivalence relations of systems have often been introduced by using homomorphisms [Br] [KM] [Miln]. This approach is very attractive as it allows the use of algebraic techniques and reduces the study of a relation on systems to the study of a relation on the elements of their structure.

Using equivalence relations within a proof theory implies that they are compatible with the corresponding notion of correctness in the sense that if a system is correct with respect to some specification then any system equivalent to it is correct too (with respect to this specification).

In this paper we tackle the problem of the preservation of correctness in the case where specifications are properties expressed by formulas of a logic. In particular we address the question : given two transition systems S_1 and S_2 related via homomorphisms of a certain type what are the relations induced on the properties of these systems i.e. are there classes of properties such that if they are satisfied by S_1 then they are satisfied by S_2 due to the existence of homomorphisms ?

The study of this problem brought us to consider functions preserving properties according to the following principle. Let L be a logic used for the description of the properties for which transition systems constitute a class of models. A formula F of L defines for a given transition system and interpretation i a property ; a state q of S satisfies this property iff $q \models_i F$. Given two transition systems S_1, S_2 with sets of states respectively Q_1, Q_2 and a function f, $f : 2^{Q_1} \rightarrow 2^{Q_2}$, we say that f preserves the property represented by F iff,

$\forall q_1 \in Q_1$ $(q_1 \models_i F$ <u>implies</u> $\forall q_2 \in Q_2,\ q_2 \in f(\{q_1\}),\ q_2 \models_{f \circ i} F)$.

The results presented concern the characterization of functions f preserving properties independently of the particular choice of S_1 and S_2 provided that the transition systems be related via homomorphisms of a certain type.

In part II of the paper the notions of homomorphisms and bisimulation of transition systems are presented. As in [BR] and [Miln] we consider homomorphisms allowing to compare transition systems with hidden transitions. Such homomorphisms can be used to characterize observational equivalence relations. In part III the definition of the notion of preservation of properties and general results are given. These results are applied to the cases where the language of description of the properties is a branching time logic and a regular trace logic. In the conclusion two important outcomes of the presented approach are discussed.

II. HOMOMORPHISMS AND BISIMULATIONS OF TRANSITION SYSTEMS

II.1 <u>Definitions</u>

* A <u>labelled transition system</u> is a triple $S_A=(Q,A,\{\overset{a}{\rightarrow}\}_{a\in A}\cup\{\overset{\tau}{\rightarrow}\})$ where Q is a countable set of <u>states</u>, A is a finite vocabulary of names of <u>actions</u> and $\{\overset{a}{\rightarrow}\}_{a\in A}\cup\{\overset{\tau}{\rightarrow}\}$ is a set of binary relations on Q.

  Each one of the relations $\overset{a}{\rightarrow}$ describes the effect of the execution of action a : $q\overset{a}{\rightarrow}q'$ means that q' is a state reachable from q by execution of action a. The special symbol τ is used to denote a <u>hidden</u> or <u>non-observable</u> action.

Whenever we do not want to distinguish between the different actions we use a simpler model S=(Q,R) called <u>transition system</u> where R is a binary relation on Q.

* For a labelled transition system $S_A=(Q,A,\{\overset{a}{\rightarrow}\}_{a\in A}\cup\{\overset{\tau}{\rightarrow}\})$, we define a family of labelled transition systems, called transition structures, which represent the aspects of the functioning of S_A which are relevant from an observational point of view.

  A <u>transition structure</u> on S_A is a triple $TS_A=(Q,A,\{R_a\}_{a\in A}\cup\{R_\varepsilon\})$, with $R_\varepsilon=(\overset{\tau}{\rightarrow})^*$ and $R_a\subseteq(\overset{\tau}{\rightarrow})^*\overset{a}{\rightarrow}(\overset{\tau}{\rightarrow})^*$.

  That is, R_ε is the set of the pairs of states (q,q') such that q' is reachable from q by executing a sequence of hidden actions of arbitrary length. Also, R_a contains a set of pairs of states (q,q') such that q' is reachable from q by executing an a-transition preceded and followed by sequences of hidden transitions.

  The interest of considering transition structures on a given labelled transition system will become evident later. In particular we shall consider three classes of transition structures such that the relations R_a be equal to $(\overset{\tau}{\rightarrow})^*\overset{a}{\rightarrow}(\overset{\tau}{\rightarrow})^*$, $(\overset{\tau}{\rightarrow})^*\overset{a}{\rightarrow}$, $\overset{a}{\rightarrow}(\overset{\tau}{\rightarrow})^*$ respectively.

* Given two transition systems $S_i=(Q_i,R_i)$, i=1,2 and a relation ρ from Q_1 to Q_2 ($\rho\subseteq Q_1\times Q_2$) which is total on both Q_1 and Q_2, ρ is a <u>homomorphism</u> from S_1 to S_2 if,

  $q_1\rho q_2$ <u>implies</u> $\forall q_1'(q_1R_1q_1'$ <u>implies</u> $\exists q_2'$ $(q_2R_2q_2'$ <u>and</u> $q_1'\rho q_2'))$.

  We use the notation $R_1\overset{\rho}{\rightarrow}R_2$.

  A <u>bisimulation</u> between S_1 and S_2 is a relation ρ such that ρ is a homomorphism from S_1 to S_2 and ρ^{-1} is a homomorphism from S_2 to S_1 i.e. $R_1\overset{\rho}{\rightarrow}R_2$ and $R_2\overset{\rho^{-1}}{\rightarrow}R_1$. We use the notation $R_1\overset{\rho}{\rightleftarrows}R_2$

* Given two transition structures $TS_{Ai}=(Q_i,A,\{R_{ai}\}_{a\in A}\cup\{R_{\varepsilon i}\})$, i=1,2, defined on two labelled transition systems S_{Ai}, i=1,2, with the same vocabulary A, we say that ρ is a <u>homomorphism</u> from TS_{A1} to TS_{A2} if, $\forall\lambda\in A\cup\{\varepsilon\}$ $R_{\lambda 1}\overset{\rho}{\rightarrow}R_{\lambda 2}$ and ρ is a <u>bisimulation</u> between TS_{A1} and TS_{A2} if, $\forall\lambda\in A\cup\{\varepsilon\}$ $R_{\lambda 1}\overset{\rho}{\rightleftarrows}R_{\lambda 2}$.

<u>Remark</u> : The notion of homomorphism of transition systems is that one of weak homomorphism of non deterministic automata ([Gi] page 99). The requirement for ρ to be total on Q_1 and Q_2 is not essential for the validity of the results which follow ; however it simplifies considerabl their presentation. The notion of bisimulation is due to D. Park [Pa]. Similar definitions have been given in [BR] and [Miln].

Example 1 : Consider the following programs with guarded commands used to compute the Max of a triple of integers.

```
S1 :: x,y,z := X,Y,Z ;
      do x>y → y := y+1 □
         y>z → z := z+1 □
         z>x → x := x+1 od

S2 :: u,v,w := U,V,W ;
      do u>v → v := v+1 □
         v>u → u := u+1 □
         u=v ∧ v>w → w := w+1 □
         u=v ∧ w>v → v := v+1 od
```

These programs trivially represent transition systems $S_i=(Q_i,R_i)$, $i=1,2$, with $Q_1=Q_2=Z^3$. The relation ρ defined by,

$(x,y,z)\rho(u,v,w)$ iff $Max(x,y,z)=Max(u,v,w)$

is a bisimulation between S_1 and S_2.

Example 2 : Consider the buffer of capacity m+n, B(m)|B(n), obtained by connecting in series two buffers B(m) and B(n) of capacity m and n respectively.

```
B(m) :: x := 0 ;
        do x<m -in1-> x := x+1 □
           x>0 -out1-> x := x-1 od

B(n) :: y := 0 ;
        do y<n -in2-> y := y+1 □
           y>0 -out2-> y := y-1 od

B(m)|B(n) :: x,y := 0,0 ;
             do x<m -in1-> x := x+1 □
                x>0 ∧ y<n -τ-> x,y := x-1,y+1 □
                y>0 -out2-> y := y-1 od
```

We want to compare B(m)|B(n) with the buffer of capacity m+n defined by,

```
B(m+n) :: z := 0 ;
          do z<m+n -in1-> z := z+1 □
             z>0   -out2-> z := z-1 od
```

To do this, it is natural to consider the relation ρ,

$\rho=\{((x,y),z) \mid x+y=z$ and $0\le x\le m$ and $0\le y\le n\}$.

The buffers B(m)|B(n) and B(m+n) can be considered as labelled transition systems S_{A_1} and S_{A_2} respectively on a vocabulary $A=\{in1,out2\}$,
$S_{A_1}=([0,m]\times[0,n],A,\{\xrightarrow[1]{a}\}_{a\in A}\cup\{\xrightarrow[1]{\tau}\})$, $S_{A_2}=([0,m+n],A,\{\xrightarrow[2]{a}\}_{a\in A}\cup\{\emptyset\})$.

Consider the transition structures TS_{A_1} and TS_{A_2} defined on S_{A_1} and S_{A_2} respectively and such that $R_{a_1}=(\xrightarrow[1]{\tau})^*\xrightarrow[1]{a}(\xrightarrow[1]{\tau})^*$ and $R_{a_2}=\xrightarrow[2]{a}$. It can be shown that $TS_{A_1}\overset{\rho}{\rightleftarrows}TS_{A_2}$.

Also, consider the transition structure TS'_{A_1} defined on S_{A_1} by taking $R'_{a_1}=(\xrightarrow[1]{\tau})^*\xrightarrow[1]{a}$. Then, $TS'_{A_1}\overset{\rho}{\rightleftarrows}TS_{A_2}$.

This example makes evident the interest of considering transition structures.

II.2 Properties of homomorphisms and bisimulations

For a relation R denote by $\bar{R}$ and R^{-1} its complement and its converse respectively. The following properties can be shown.

Properties 1 : For arbitrary transition systems, $S_i=(Q_i,R_i)$, i=1,2,3 and relations ρ and ρ',

a) $R_1 \overset{\rho}{\to} R_2$ iff $\rho \subseteq \overline{R_1 \overline{\rho} R_2^{-1}}$ iff $R_1^{-1}\rho \subseteq R_2^{-1}\rho$.

b) $R_1 \overset{\rho}{\to} R_2$ and $R_1 \overset{\rho'}{\to} R_2$ implies $R_1 \overset{\rho \cup \rho'}{\to} R_2$.

c) $R_1 \overset{\rho}{\to} R_2$ and $R_2 \overset{\rho'}{\to} R_3$ implies $R_1 \overset{\rho\rho'}{\to} R_3$.

d) $R_1 \overset{\rho}{\to} R_2$ implies $R_1^* \overset{\rho}{\to} R_2^*$.

Property a) states that homomorphisms can be characterized as fixed points of the monotonic operator $\lambda\rho.\rho \cap \overline{R_1 \overline{\rho} R_2^{-1}}$ and properties b) and c) that the union and composition of homomorphisms is a homomorphism. Similar properties are valid for bisimulations. However, in the case of bisimulations, other interesting properties can be shown.

Properties 2 : For arbitrary transition systems, $S_i=(Q_i,R_i)$, i=1,2, and a relation ρ, $\rho \subseteq Q_1 \times Q_2$,

a) $R_1 \overset{\rho}{\rightleftarrows} R_2$ implies $R_1 \overset{\rho\rho^{-1}}{\rightleftarrows} R_1$ and $R_2 \overset{\rho^{-1}\rho}{\rightleftarrows} R_2$.

b) $R_1 \overset{\rho}{\rightleftarrows} R_2$ implies $R_1 \overset{\rho\rho^{-1}\rho}{\rightleftarrows} R_2$.

Property 2b) is particulary interesting as for any relation ρ, $\rho \subseteq \rho\rho^{-1}\rho$. Thus, if ρ is a bisimulation then it can be obtained by successive application of this property an increasing sequence of bisimulations: $\rho\rho^{-1}\rho$, $(\rho\rho^{-1})^4\rho$, $(\rho\rho^{-1})^{13}\rho$, ... It is easy to show that the limit of this sequence is equal to $\hat{\rho}=(\rho\rho^{-1})^*\rho$. Furthermore, it can be shown by using properties 2a) and 2b) that if ρ is a bisimulation then $\hat{\rho}$ is a bisimulation too.

The following lemmata are used to estiblish some interesting properties of $\hat{\rho}$.

Lemma 1 : Let ρ be a relation from a set Q_1 to a set Q_2. Then, $\hat{\rho}=(\rho\rho^{-1})^*\rho=\rho\ (\rho^{-1}\rho)^*$ is the least relation R such that $\rho \subseteq R$ and $RR^{-1}R=R$.

Proof : $\hat{\rho} \subseteq \hat{\rho}\hat{\rho}^{-1}\hat{\rho}$ is always true.
We have, $\hat{\rho}\hat{\rho}^{-1}\hat{\rho}=(\rho\rho^{-1})^*\rho(\rho^{-1}\rho)^*\rho^{-1}(\rho\rho^{-1})^*\rho=(\rho\rho^{-1})^*(\rho\rho^{-1})^*(\rho\rho^{-1})^*\rho\rho^{-1}\rho=$ $((\rho\rho^{-1})^*\rho\rho^{-1})\rho$. From $(\rho\rho^{-1})^*\rho\rho^{-1} \subseteq (\rho\rho^{-1})^*$ we deduce that $(\rho\rho^{-1})^*\rho\rho^{-1}\rho \subseteq (\rho\rho^{-1})^*\rho$.

Suppose that for some relation R, $\rho \subseteq R$. We have $(\rho\rho^{-1})^k \subseteq RR^{-1}$ for any natural integer k. Thus, $(\rho\rho^{-1})^*\rho \subseteq RR^{-1}R=R$.□

Given a relation ρ, $\rho \subseteq Q_1 \times Q_2$, denote by $[\rho]$ the function $[\rho] : 2^{Q_1} \to 2^{Q_2}$ such that for $Q_1' \subseteq Q_1$, $[\rho](Q_1') = \{q_2 \in Q_2 \mid \exists q_1 \in Q_1' \; q_1 \rho q_2\}$.

Lemma 2 : Let ρ be a relation from a set Q_1 to a set Q_2 total on both Q_1 and Q_2. Then,

a) $\hat{\rho}\hat{\rho}^{-1}$ and $\hat{\rho}^{-1}\hat{\rho}$ are equivalence relations on Q_1 and Q_2 respectively and $Q_1/\hat{\rho}\hat{\rho}^{-1}$ is isomorphic to $Q_2/\hat{\rho}^{-1}\hat{\rho}$.

b) The restriction of $[\rho]$on $\mathrm{Im}[\hat{\rho}^{-1}]$ (image of $\hat{\rho}^{-1}$) is an isomorphism from $\mathrm{Im}[\hat{\rho}^{-1}]$ onto $\mathrm{Im}[\hat{\rho}]$which are isomorphic to $2^{Q_1/\hat{\rho}\hat{\rho}^{-1}}$ and $2^{Q_2/\hat{\rho}^{-1}\hat{\rho}}$.

Proof : These are well-known facts about relations R such that $R=RR^{-1}R$. Such relations are called difunctionals in the literature (see for example [Ma] page 23).□

It can be shown that the relations $\hat{\rho}\hat{\rho}^{-1}$ and $\hat{\rho}^{-1}\hat{\rho}$ are in fact the least equivalence relations on Q_1 and Q_2 respectively which are compatible with ρ in the sense that all the elements of Q_2 related via ρ to some element of Q_1 are equivalent and conversely all the elements of Q_1 related via ρ with some element of Q_2 are equivalent. As a consequence of the above discussion and lemmata we have the following proposition.

Proposition 1 : Let $S_1=(Q_1,R_1)$,$S_2=(Q_2,R_2)$ be two transition systems and ρ a relation, $\rho \subseteq Q_2 \times Q_2$, total on Q_1 and Q_2. If $R_1 \overset{\rho}{\rightleftarrows} R_2$ then $R_1 \overset{\hat{\rho}}{\rightleftarrows} R_2$ where $\hat{\rho}=(\rho\rho^{-1})^{*}\rho$ and $\hat{\rho}$ is the least bisimulation R such that $\rho \subseteq R$ and $RR^{-1}R=R$. Furthermore, $\hat{\rho}\hat{\rho}^{-1}$ and $\hat{\rho}^{-1}\hat{\rho}$ are the least equivalence relations on Q_1 and Q_2 respectively which are bisimulations on S_1 and S_2 compatible with ρ.

Remark : This result can be trivially extended to bisimulations between transition structures.

III. PRESERVATION OF THE PROPERTIES

III.1 The notion of preservation

We suppose that properties can be expressed by the formulas of a logic for which transition systems can be considered as models in the following manner.

For a transition system with set of states Q, a logic L on a set of propositional variables $P=\{P_0,P_1,\ldots,P_j,\ldots\}$ and a mapping $i : P \to 2^{Q}$, a satisfaction relation $\models_i$ is a subset of $Q \times L(P)$ where $L(P)$ is the set of the formulas of L on P. This relation is defined in the standard manner for logical operators and constants and for any propositional variable P_j, $q \models_i P_j$ *iff* $q \in i(P_j)$. A formula F of L defines a property ; a state $q \in Q$

satisfies the property represented by F iff $q \models_i F$.

In the sequel we also denote by $\models_i$ the extension of the satisfaction relation on $2^Q \times L(P)$: for $Q' \subseteq Q$, $Q' \neq \emptyset$ ($Q' \models_i F$ iff $\forall q \in Q'$ $q \models_i F$). For a formula F, $|F|_i$ denotes the set of the states satisfying F i.e. $|F|_i = \{q \mid q \models_i F\}$.

* Given two transition systems with sets of states Q_1, Q_2, a formula F of L(P), a subset $\mathcal{P}$ of 2^{Q_1} and a mapping $f: 2^{Q_1} \to 2^{Q_2}$, we say that,
  - f <u>preserves</u> (<u>strongly preserves</u>) F on $\mathcal{P}$, if for any interpretation $i : P \to \mathcal{P}$ and any state q_1 of Q_1,

    $$q_1 \models_i F \text{ implies (iff) } f\{q_1\} \models_{f \circ i} F.$$

  - f <u>semi-commutes</u> (commutes) with F on $\mathcal{P}$, if for any interpretation $i : P \to \mathcal{P}$,

    $$f|F|_i \subseteq |F|_{f \circ i} \quad (f|F|_i = |F|_{f \circ i}).$$

Clearly, preservation of F by f means that if F is satisfied at some state q_1 under an interpretation i then it is satisfied at any state q_2 belonging to $f\{q_1\}$ under the interpretation $f \circ i$. The notions of commutativity are very useful for proving preservation.

We extend the introduced definitions to operators of L : a function f preserves (strongly preserves, semi-commutes with, commutes with) an n-ary operator op if it preserves (strongly preserves, semi-commutes with, commutes with) the formula $op(P_1, .. P_n)$ where $P_1, .., P_n$ are propositional variables.

In the sequel we constantly refer to two transition systems with sets of states Q_1, Q_2 and a function $i : P \to \mathcal{P}$, $\mathcal{P} \subseteq 2^{Q_1}$. Whenever $\mathcal{P}$ is not explicitely mentionned, it is taken equal to 2^{Q_1}.

<u>Proposition</u> 2 : Let F be a formula of L(P) and $f : 2^{Q_1} \to 2^{Q_2}$. If there exists a formula G, $G \equiv F$, such that f commutes (semi-commutes) with each one of the operators occuring in G, then f commutes (semi-commutes) with F.

<u>Proof</u> : By induction on the structure of the formulas.□

<u>Proposition</u> 3 : Let F be a formula of L(P), f a monotonic function, $f: 2^{Q_1} \to 2^{Q_2}$ and $\mathcal{P}$ a subset of 2^{Q_1}.

a) If f semi-commutes with F on $\mathcal{P}$ then f preserves F on $\mathcal{P}$.

b) If f commutes with F on $\mathcal{P}$, f is one-to-one and f^{-1} is monotonic then f strongly preserves F on $\mathcal{P}$.

Proof : a) $q_1 \models_i F$ is equivalent to $\{q_1\} \subseteq |F|_i$, from which we obtain $f\{q_1\} \subseteq f|F|_i \subseteq |F|_{f \circ i}$. Thus, $f\{q_1\} \models_{f \circ i} F$.

b) It remains to prove that for any $q_1 \in Q_1$, $f\{q_1\} \models_{f \circ i} F$ implies $q_1 \models_i F$. $f\{q_1\} \models_{f \circ i} F$ is equivalent to $f\{q_1\} \subseteq |F|_{f \circ i} = f|F|_i$ by commutativity of f with F. From $f\{q_1\} \subseteq f|F|_i$ we deduce that $\{q_1\} \subseteq |F|_i$.□

Proposition 4 : Let F be a formula of L(P) and ρ a relation, $\rho \subseteq Q_1 \times Q_2$, total on Q_1 and Q_2 such that $\rho\rho^{-1}\rho = \rho$. If [ρ] semi-commutes with F on $Im[\rho^{-1}]$ (image of $[\rho^{-1}]$) and $[\rho^{-1}]$ semi-commutes with F on Im[ρ] then [ρ] strongly preserves F on $Im[\rho^{-1}]$ and $[\rho^{-1}]$ strongly preserves F on Im[ρ].

Proof : It is sufficient to prove that for any state $q_1 \in Q_1$ any interpretation $i : P \to Im[\rho^{-1}]$, $q_1 \models_i F$ iff $[\rho]\{q_1\} \models_{[\rho]\circ i} F$.
By proposition 3, $q_1 \models_i F$ implies $[\rho]\{q_1\} \models_{[\rho]\circ i} F$.
$[\rho]\{q_1\} \models_{[\rho]\circ i} F$ is equivalent to $[\rho]\{q_1\} \subseteq |F|_{[\rho]\circ i}$ which implies, $[\rho^{-1}]\circ[\rho]\{q_1\} \subseteq [\rho^{-1}]\ |F|_{[\rho]\circ i}$. Due to the fact that ρ is total we have, $\{q_1\} \subseteq [\rho^{-1}]\circ[\rho]\{q_1\}$. Thus, $\{q_1\} \subseteq [\rho^{-1}]\ |F|_{[\rho]\circ i} \subseteq |F|_{[\rho^{-1}]\circ[\rho]\circ i}$, by semi-commutativity of $[\rho^{-1}]$with F on Im[ρ]. As $[\rho^{-1}]\circ[\rho]\circ[\rho^{-1}] = [\rho^{-1}]$ and $i : P \to Im[\rho^{-1}]$, we have $|F|_{[\rho^{-1}]\circ[\rho]\circ i} = |F|_i$. Thus, $\{q_1\} \subseteq |F|_i$ which is equivalent to $q_1 \models_i F$.□

Corollary : Let F be a formula of L(P) and ρ a relation, $\rho \subseteq Q_1 \times Q_2$, total on Q_1 and Q_2. If [ρ] semi-commutes with F on $Im[\hat{\rho}^{-1}]$ and $[\rho^{-1}]$ semi-commutes with F on $Im[\hat{\rho}]$ then [ρ] strongly preserves F on $Im[\hat{\rho}^{-1}]$ and $[\rho^{-1}]$ strongly preserves F on $Im[\hat{\rho}]$.

Proof : The same as this of proposition 4 by noticing that $[\rho]\circ[\hat{\rho}^{-1}] = [\hat{\rho}][\hat{\rho}^{-1}]$.□

III.2 Applications

III.2.1 Preservation of formulas of BTL

A Branching Time Logic (BTL)[BMP] and [QS] is an extension of the propositional calculus on a set of variables $P = \{P_0, P_1, .. P_j, ..\}$ by adjunction of unary temporal operators PRE, POT, and INEV.

Given a transition system S=(Q,R) and a function $i: P \to 2^Q$, define a satisfaction relation $\models_i \subseteq Q \times BTL(P)$ where BTL(P) is the set of the formulas of BTL on P.

$q \models_i$ true, always
$q \models_i P_j$ iff $q \in i(P_j)$

$q \models_i F_1 \wedge F_2$ iff $q \models_i F_1$ and $q \models_i F_2$

$q \models_i \neg F$ iff not $q \models_i F$

$q \models PRE(F)$ iff $\exists q'(qRq'$ and $q' \models_i F)$

$q \models POT(F)$ iff $\exists q'(qR^* q'$ and $q' \models_i F)$

$q \models INEV(F)$ iff $\forall s \in EX(q)\ \exists k \in \mathbb{N}\ s(k) \models_i F$, where $EX(q)$ is the set of the maximal execution sequences starting from q ($s(k)$ is the k-th element of s and $s(0)=q$).

Proposition 5 : Given two transition systems $S_1=(Q_1,R_1)$, $S_2=(Q_2,R_2)$ and $\rho \subseteq Q_1 \times Q_2$ such that $R_1 \overset{\rho}{\rightleftarrows} R_2$,

a) $[\rho]$ preserves any formula F such that there exists G, $G \equiv F$, in which only the operators $\vee$, $\wedge$, PRE and POT occur.

b) $[\rho^{-1}]$ preserves any formula F such that there exists G, $G \equiv F$, in whic only the operators $\wedge$ and $\lambda x.\neg POT(\neg x)$ occur.

Proof : a) By using propositions 2 and 3it is sufficient to prove that $[\rho]$ semi-commutes with each one of the operators occuring in a formula.

* For P_1, P_2 propositional variables, $q_1 \models_i P_1 \vee P_2$ iff $\{q_1\} \subseteq |P_1|_i \cup |P_2|_i$ which implies $[\rho]\{q_1\} \subseteq [\rho]|P_1|_i \cup [\rho]|P_2|_i$ ($[\rho]$ is distributive with respect to $\cup$). But $[\rho]|P_1| \cup [\rho]|P_2|_i = |P_1|_{[\rho]\circ i} \cup |P_2|_{[\rho]\circ i} = |P_1 \vee P_2|_{[\rho]\circ i}$.
* $q_1 \models_i P_1 \wedge P_2$ iff $\{q_1\} \subseteq |P_1|_i \cap |P_2|_i$ which implies, $[\rho]\{q_1\} \subseteq [\rho](|P_1|_i \cap |P_2|_i) \subseteq [\rho]|P_1|_i \cap [\rho]|P_2|_i$ because $[\rho]$ is monotonic. Thus, $[\rho]\{q_1\} \subseteq |P_1|_{[\rho]\circ i} \cap |P_2|_{[\rho]\circ i}$ is equivalent to $[\rho]\{q_1\} \models_{[\rho]\circ i} P_1 \wedge P_2$.
* $q_1 \models_i PRE(P_1)$ iff $\{q_1\} \subseteq |PRE(P_1)|_i$ which implies, $[\rho]\{q_1\} \subseteq [\rho]|PRE(P_1)|_i \subseteq |PRE([\rho](P_1))|_i$ by property 1a). Thus, $[\rho]\{q_1\} \models_{[\rho]\circ i} PRE(P_1)$.
* We have $POT(P_1) = \bigvee_{k=0}^{\infty} PRE^k(P_1)$ [QS]. Thus, semi-commututativity of $[\rho]$ with POT can be deduced from semi-commutativity with $\vee$ and PRE.

b) Proof by using propositions 2 and 3. Semi-commutativity of $[\rho^{-1}]$ with $\wedge$ can be proved as in a). The proof for $\lambda x.\neg POT(\neg x)$ is given in [Si]

Proposition 6 : Given two transition systems $S_1=(Q_1,R_2)$, $S_2=(Q_2,R_2)$ and ρ, $\rho \subseteq Q_1 \times Q_2$, such that $R_1 \overset{\rho}{\rightleftarrows} R_2$,

a) $[\rho]$ and $[\rho^{-1}]$ preserve any formula F such that there exists G, $G \equiv F$, in which only the operators $\vee$, $\wedge$, PRE, POT and $\lambda x.\neg POT(\neg x)$ occur.

b) if R_1 and R_2 are image finite, then $[\rho]$ and $[\rho^{-1}]$ preserve any formula F such that there exists G, $G \equiv F$, in which only the operators $\vee$, $\wedge$, PRE, POT, $\lambda x.\neg POT(\neg x)$ and $\lambda x.\neg INEV(\neg x)$ occur.

Proof : a) This is a direct consequence of proposition 5.

b) In order to prove semi-commutativity of $[\rho]$ with formulas of the form $\neg INEV(\neg P_0)$, use the fact that $\neg INEV(\neg P_0)$ is equal to $\bigcap_{k=0}^{\infty} X_k$ where, $X_{k+1}=X_k \cap (PRE(X_k) \cup \neg PRE(\neg X_k))$ with $X_0=P_0$ [QS]. A complete proof is given in [Si]. □

<u>Proposition 7</u> : Given two transition systems $S_1=(Q_1,R_1)$, $S_2=(Q_2,R_2)$ such that R_1, R_2 are image finite and a relation ρ, $\rho \subseteq Q_1 \times Q_2$ such that $R_1 \overset{\rho}{\leftrightarrows} R_2$, $[\rho]$ strongly preserves any formula of BTL(P) on $Im[\hat{\rho}^{-1}]$ and $[\rho^{-1}]$ strongly preserves any formula of BTL(P) on $Im[\hat{\rho}]$.

<u>Proof</u> : Direct application of the corollary of proposition 4 and proposition 6) by using the fact that $[\rho]$ is an isomorphism from $Im[\hat{\rho}^{-1}]$ onto $Im[\hat{\rho}]$. □

As a consequence of proposition 7 we have that if ρ is a bisimulation between S_1 and S_2 then for any pair of states q_1, q_2,

$q_1 \rho q_2$ <u>implies</u> ($q_1 \models_i F$ <u>iff</u> $q_2 \models_{[\rho]\circ i} F$ for any F of BTL(P) on $Im[\hat{\rho}^{-1}]$).

That is, if two states are related via ρ then they are equivalent with respect to any formula of this logic. This implies,

$Q_1 \models_i F$ <u>iff</u> $Q_2 \models_{[\rho]\circ i} F$ for any formula F of BTL(P) on $Im[\hat{\rho}^{-1}]$.

That is, if F is a formula expressing a property globally satisfied by S_1 then F is globally satisfied by S_2 and conversely.

<u>Example</u> 1 (continued) : The bisimulation ρ between S_1 and S_2 is such that $\rho=\hat{\rho}$. Then the equivalence relations on Q_1 and Q_2 respectively induced by ρ are defined by,

$(x,y,z)\rho\rho^{-1}(x',y',z')$ <u>iff</u> $Max(x,y,z)=Max(x',y',z')$
$(u,v,w)\rho^{-1}\rho(u',v',w')$ <u>iff</u> $Max(u,v,w)=Max(u',v',w')$

According to proposition 7 are strongly preserved all the formulas constructed on predicates representing unions of classes of $\rho\rho^{-1}$ (elements of $Im[\rho^{-1}]$). These predicates are combinations of predicates of the general form $(x \le k) \wedge (y \le k) \wedge (z \le k)$ where k is a given constant ($k \in Z$). We have,

$$[\rho](x \le k \wedge y \le k \wedge z \le k) = u \le k \wedge v \le k \wedge w \le k \; .$$

Thus, one can obtain all the formulas preserved due to the fact that ρ is a bisimulation. For example, for any $(X,Y,Z) \in Z^3$ and $(U,V,W) \in Z^3$ such that $Max(X,Y,Z)=Max(U,V,W)$,

$(X,Y,Z) \models \neg POT \neg (x \le k \wedge y \le k \wedge z \le k)$ <u>iff</u>
$(U,V,W) \models \neg POT \neg (u \le k \wedge v \le k \wedge w \le k)$.

This equivalence can be used (by taking $k=Max(X,Y,Z)$) to prove that if S_1 computes $Max(X,Y,Z)$ then S_2 computes the same function.

III.2.2 Preservation of the formulas of RTL

A Regular Trace Logic (RTL) [BR] is an extension of the propositional calculus on a set of propositional variables $P=\{P_0,..P_j,..\}$ by adjunction of unary operators $\forall\alpha<.>$ and $\forall\alpha[.]$ where α is a regular language or a vocabulary A.

Given a transition structure $TS_A=(Q,A,\{Ra\}_{a\in A}\cup\{R_\varepsilon\})$ and a function $i : P\to 2^Q$, define a satisfaction relation $\models_i \subseteq Q\times RTL(P)$ where RTL(P) is the set of the formulas of RTL on P. This relation is defined for logical operators and constants in the standard manner. Furthermore,

$q\models_i P_j$ iff $q\in i(P_j)$

$q\models_i \forall\alpha<F>$ iff $\forall s\in\alpha\ \exists q'(qR(s)q'$ and $q'\models_i F)$

$q\models_i \forall\alpha[F]$ iff $\forall s\in\alpha\ \forall q'(qR(s)q'$ implies $q'\models_i F)$ where,

$R(s)=Ra_1Ra_2...Ra_n$ if $s=a_1a_2...a_n$ and ε represents the empty word of A

Remark : This definition of RTL is more general than the one given in [BR] where the class of models considered are transition structures such that $R_a=(\overset{\tau}{\to})^*\overset{a}{\to}(\overset{\tau}{\to})^*$. Restriction to a particular class of models induces different trace logics. In particular it is interesting to consider the logics RTL_l, RTL_r, RTL_{lr} obtained by taking as models transition structures such that $R_a=(\overset{\tau}{\to})^*\overset{a}{\to}$, $R_a=\overset{a}{\to}(\overset{\tau}{\to})^*$, $R_a=(\overset{\tau}{\to})^*\overset{a}{\to}(\overset{\tau}{\to})^*$, respectively.

Proposition 8 : Given two transition structures $TS_{Ai}=(Q_i,A,\{R_{ai}\}_{a\in A}\cup\{R_{\varepsilon i}\})$ $i=1,2$, and a relation ρ, $\rho\subseteq Q_1\times Q_2$,

a) If ρ is a homomorphism from TS_{A1} to TS_{A2} then $[\rho]$ preserves any formula of F in which only the operators $\vee$, $\wedge$, $\forall\alpha<.>$, $\exists\alpha<.>=\lambda x.\neg\forall\alpha[\neg x]$ occur.

b) If ρ is a bisimulation between TS_{A1} and TS_{A2} then $[\rho]$ preserves any formula F in which only the operators $\vee$, $\wedge$, $\forall\alpha<.>$, $\forall\alpha[.]$, $\exists\alpha<.>=\lambda x.\neg\forall\alpha[\neg x]$, $\exists\alpha[.]=\lambda x.\neg\forall<\neg x>$ occur. Furthermore, $[\rho]$ strongly preserves any formula of RTL(P) on $Im[\hat{\rho}^{-1}]$ and $[\rho^{-1}]$ strongly preserves any formula of RTL(P) on $Im[\hat{\rho}]$

Proof : Notice that,

- $\forall\alpha<F>=\bigwedge_{s\in\alpha}\forall\{s\}<F>$

- $\exists\alpha<F>=\bigvee_{s\in\alpha}\exists\{s\}<F>$

- $\forall\alpha[F]=\bigwedge_{s\in\alpha}\forall\{s\}[F]$

- $\exists\alpha[F]=\bigvee_{s\in\alpha}\exists\{s\}[F]$

- $\forall\{s\}\langle F\rangle = \exists\{s\}\langle F\rangle$ for s a word of A^* ; as quantifiers are irrelevant in this case, we simply write $\{s\}\langle F\rangle$.
- $\forall\{s\}[F]=\exists\{s\}[F]$ for s a word of A ; as quantifiers are irrelevant in this case, we simply write $\{s\}[F]$.
- $\{s\}[F]=\neg\{s\}\langle\neg F\rangle$
- $\{as\}\langle F\rangle=\{a\}(\{s\}\langle F\rangle)$ where $a\in A$ and $s\in A^*$
- $q\models_i\{\lambda\}\langle F\rangle$ iff $q\in[R_\lambda^{-1}]|F|_i$ for $\lambda\in A\cup\{\varepsilon\}$.

To prove a), it is sufficient to prove that $[\rho]$ semi-commutes with the operators $\vee$, $\wedge$, $\forall\alpha\langle.\rangle$ and $\exists\alpha\langle.\rangle$ (propositions 2 and 3). Semi-commutativity with $\vee$ and $\wedge$ can be proved exactly as for proposition 5. As the operators $\forall\alpha\langle.\rangle$ and $\exists\alpha\langle.\rangle$ can be expressed as conjunctions or disjunctions of the operators $\{s\}\langle.\rangle$ for $s\in\alpha$, it is sufficient to prove that $[\rho]$ semi-commutes with $\{s\}\langle.\rangle$. This can be established by proving that $[\rho]$ semi-commutes with $\{\lambda\}\langle.\rangle$ where $\lambda\in A\cup\{\varepsilon\}$ i.e. $[\rho]|\{\lambda\}\langle P_0\rangle|_i\subseteq |\{\lambda\}\langle P_0\rangle|_{[\rho]\circ i}$.

We have, $q_2\in[\rho]|\{\lambda\}\langle P_0\rangle|_i$ implies $\exists q_1 q_1\rho q_2$ and $q_1\in|\{\lambda\}\langle P_0\rangle|_i$. But $q_1\in|\{\lambda\}\langle P_0\rangle|_i$ is equivalent to $q\models_i\{\lambda\}\langle P_0\rangle$ which means that $\exists q_1'(q_1R_{\lambda_1}q_1'$ and $q_1'\in|P_0|_i)$. Since ρ is a homomorphism,
$q_1\rho q_2$ and $q_1R_{\lambda_1}q_1'$ implies $\exists q_2'(q_2R_{\lambda_2}q_2'$ and $q_1'\rho q_2')$.
Thus, $q_2'\in[\rho]|P_0|_i$ and $q_2R_{\lambda_2}q_2'$. This is equivalent to $q_2\in|\{\lambda\}\langle P_0\rangle|_{[\rho]\circ i}$.

To prove b) it is sufficient to prove that $[\rho]$ semi-commutes with $\{\lambda\}[.]$, where $\lambda\in A\cup\{\varepsilon\}$ i.e. $[\rho]|\{\lambda\}[P_0]|_i\subseteq|\{\lambda\}[P_0]|_{[\rho]\circ i}$.

We have, $q_2\in[\rho]|\{\lambda\}[P_0]|_i$ implies $\exists q_1 q_1\rho q_2$ and $q_1\models_i\{\lambda\}[P_0]$. From $q_1\models_i\{\lambda\}[P_0]$ one can deduce that either $\nexists q_1' q_1R_{\lambda_1}q_1'$ in which case $\nexists q_2' q_2R_{\lambda_2}q_2'$ which implies $q_2\models_{[\rho]\circ i}\{\lambda\}[P_0]$ or q_1 has at least one successor q_1' via R_{λ_1}. Then, ther exists q_2' $q_2R_{\lambda_2}q_2'$ and $q_1'\rho q_2'$..Furthermore, $q_1\models_i\{\lambda\}[P_0]$ implies $q_1'\models_i P_0$ from which one can deduce that $q_2'\models_{[\rho]\circ i}P_0$. Thus $q_2\in|\{\lambda\}[P_0]|_{[\rho]\circ i}$.

Finally, strong preservation of the formulas of RTL(P) by $[\rho]$ can be proved by using b) and the corollary of proposition 4.□

A consequence of proposition 8 is that if ρ is a bisimulation between two transition structures TS_{A1} and TS_{A2} then for any pair of states q_1 and q_2,

$q_1\rho q_2$ implies ($q_1\models_i F$ iff $q_2\models_{[\rho]\circ i}F$ for any formula of RTL(P) on $Im[\hat{\rho}^{-1}]$).

As an application of this fact one can find a generalization of a well-known result [HM] [BR] concerning the strong preservation of the formulas of RTL_{1r} by observational equivalence of CCS [Mil].

Consider the regular trace logic having as models the class of the transition structures $TS_{Ai}=(Q, A, \{R_{ai}\}_{a\in A} \cup \{R_{\varepsilon i}\})$ such that the relations R_{ai} and $R_{\varepsilon i}$ are image-finite and $R_{ai}=(\overset{\tau}{\underset{i}{\to}})^{*}\overset{a}{\underset{i}{\to}}(\overset{\tau}{\underset{i}{\to}})^{*}$. Then, the greatest bisimulation is equal to the observational equivalence relation, $\approx$, in CCS. Thus we have,

$q_1 \approx q_2$ <u>implies</u> ($q_1 \models_i F$ <u>iff</u> $q_2 \models_{[\approx]\circ i} F$, for any formula F of RTL_{1r} on $Im[\approx]$

Another consequence of proposition 8 is that for any pair of transition structures TS_{A1} and TS_{A2} related via a bisimulation ρ, having sets of states Q_1 and Q_2 respectively,

$Q_1 \models_i F$ <u>iff</u> $Q_2 \models_{[\rho]\circ i} F$ for any formula of RTL on $Im[\hat{\rho}^{-1}]$.

That is, if F is a formula globally satisfied by TS_{A1} then F is globall satisfied by TS_{A2} and conversely.

<u>Example 2</u> (continued) : The relation ρ is such that $\rho=\hat{\rho}$. The equivalence relations on Q_1 and Q_2 respectively induced by ρ are defined by,

$(x,y)\rho\rho^{-1}(x',y')$ <u>iff</u> $x+y=x'+y'$ <u>and</u> $0\le x,x'\le m$ <u>and</u> $0\le y,y'\le n$,

$z\rho^{-1}\rho z'$ <u>iff</u> $z=z'$ <u>and</u> $0\le z,z'\le m+n$.

According to the corollary of proposition 4, are strongly preserved all the formulas constructed from predicates representing unions of classes of $\rho\rho^{-1}$. These predicates are combinations of predicates of the general form, $(x+y=k)\wedge(0\le x\le m)\wedge(0\le y\le n)$ where k is a given constant ($k\in\mathbb{N}$). We have,

$[\rho](x+y=k\wedge 0\le x\le m\wedge 0\le y\le n)=(z=k)\wedge 0\le z\le m+n$.

Thus, one can obtain all the formulas of RTL_{1r}, preserved due to the fact that ρ is a bisimulation between TS_{A1} and TS_{A2}. For example, one can obtain that for any $(X,Y)\in\mathbb{N}^2$ and $Z\in\mathbb{N}$ such that $(X,Y)\rho Z$,

$(X,Y) \models^{1r} \forall(in1+out2)^{*}[0\le y\le m\wedge 0\le y\le n]$ <u>iff</u>

$Z \models^{1r} \forall(in1+out2)^{*}[0\le z\le m+n]$.

This equivalence states that if it is almays true that $0\le x\le m\wedge 0\le y\le n$ then it is always true that $0\le z\le m+n$ and conversely. The trace logic considered is RTL_{1r} (with satisfaction relation $\models^{1r}$) since the transition structures considered are models of this logic.

Also, as ρ is a bisimulation between TS'_{A1} and TS_{A2} one can obtain the stronger result ($\models^{1}$ is the satisfaction relation of RTL_1).

$(X,Y) \models^{1} \forall(in1+out2)^{*}[0\le x\le m\wedge 0\le y\le n]$ <u>iff</u>

$Z \models^{1} \forall(in1+out2)^{*}[0\le z\le m+n]$.

IV. CONCLUSION

We have presented some results concerning the preservation of the properties of transition systems when they are related via homomorphisms. The general approach presented, although classical in model theory, has not yet been explored in the specific case of transition systems. The only work, to our knowledge, where a similar method is adopted is [GRS] but the hypotheses on the relation ρ are too strong. Furthermore, our work presents some similarities with [HM] and [BR] where it is shown that properties expressed in a trace logic without propositional variables are strongly preserved by the observational equivalence relation of CCS.

We believe that the problem of property preservation is of foundamental importance from both a theoretical and practical point of view. Its study allows to tackle the following two questions.

1) Compatibility of a logic as a specification and verification tool, with some operational equivalence relation usually expressed in terms of homomorphisms. In fact, if a logic L is to be used as a specification tool for a class of systems then it has to be compatible with some equivalence relation $\overset{op}{\simeq}$ derived from operational semantics in the sense that for any pair of states q_1, q_2,

$$q_1 \overset{op}{\simeq} q_2 \ \underline{\text{implies}}\ (q_1 \models F \ \underline{\text{iff}}\ q_2 \models F \text{ for any } F \text{ of } L).$$

That is, the set of the states satisfying an arbitrary formula F can be expressed as the union of equivalence classes of $\overset{op}{\simeq}$. This is obviously a minimal requirement for the adequacy of L as a specification tool.

If in addition, the logic L is to be used as a verification tool then it is necessary that the converse of this requirement is true i.e.,

$$(q_1 \models F \ \underline{\text{iff}}\ q_2 \models F \text{ for any } F \text{ of } L)\ \underline{\text{implies}}\ q_1 \overset{op}{\simeq} q_2.$$

Thus, the equivalence relation induced from L should agree with the operational equivalence relation. It is surprising that this soundness-completeness requirement has been ignored in numerous works dealing with temporal logics as specification and verification tools.

Results on preservation can contribute to the choice of equivalence relations such that they preserve properties of a certain type. It is noteworthy that observational equivalence of CCS [Mil], although it may be considered too strong from several points of view, does not necessarily preserve properties expressing statements of the form "right after the execution of action a, F holds" or "whenever action a is enabled, F holds".

2) Search for transformations characterized by homomorphisms preserving properties of a certain type. Such transformations may be useful in two cases. The first is derivation by successive refinements of a program such that some specifications be preserved throughout this process. The second is definition of reduction methods [Be] [kw] [Li] [RV] with the aim to prove a given property. In this case transformations should be such that they strongly preserve this property and the resulting systems are of less complexity.

REFERENCES

[BMP] M. BEN-ARI, Z. MANNA and A. PNUELI "The temporal logic of branching time" 8th Annual ACM Symp. on Principles of Programming Languages, January 1981, pp164-176.

[Be] G. BERTHELOT "Vérification des réseaux de Petri" Thèse 3ème cycle, Université Paris VI, Paris, January 1978.

[Br] D. BRAND "Algebraic simulation between parallel programs" IBM research Report RC 7206 (#30923) 6/29/78, IBM Yorktown Heights.

[BR] S.D. BROOKES and W.C. ROUNDS "Behavioural equivalence relations induced by programming logics" to appear in Proc. ICALP83, Barcelona, Spain.

[Gi] A. GINSBURG "Algebraic theory of automata" Academic Press, New York and London, 1968.

[GRS] J.S. GOURLAY, W.C. ROUNDS and R. STATMAN "On properties preserve by contractions of concurrent systems" Proc. Int. Symp. Semantic of Concurrent Computation, LNCS Vol.70, pp51-65, 1979.

[Je] K. JENSEN "A method to compare the descriptive power of different types of Petri nets" Proc. MFCS80, LNCS Vol.88, pp348-361.

[HM] M. HENNESSY and R. MILNER "On observing non determinism and concurrency" Proc. ICALP80, LNCS Vol.85, 1980, pp299-309.

[KM] T. KASAI and R.E. MILNER "Homomorphisms between models of parall computation" IBM Research Report RC7796 (#33742) 8/2/79, Yorktc Heights.

[Kw] Y.S. KWONG "On reductions of asynchronous systems" Theor. Comp. Sci. 5, pp25-30, 1977.

[Li] R.J. LIPTON "Reduction : a method of proving properties of parallel programs" CACM Vol.18, N°12, Dec. 1975, pp717-721.

[Ma] A.I. MAL'CEV "Algebraic systems" Springer Verlag, Berlin Heidelberg New York, 1973.

[Mi] R. MILNER "An algebraic definition of simulation between programs" Proc. Second Int. joint Conf. on Artificial Intelligence BCS, pp481-489, Sept. 1981.

[Mil] R. MILNER "A calculus of communicating systems" LNCS Vol.92, 1980.

[Miln] R. MILNER "Calculi for synchrony and asynchrony" Report TR CSR 104-82, Univ. of Edinburgh, Dept. of Computer Sci. 1982.

[QS] J.P. QUEILLE and J. SIFAKIS "Specification and verification of concurrent systems in CESAR" LNCS Vol. 137, pp337-351, April 82.

[RV] G. ROUCAIROL and R. VALK "Reductions of nets and parallel programs" Net theory and applications, LNCS Vol.84, 1979.

[Si] J. SIFAKIS "Property preserving homomorphisms and a notion of simulation for transition systems" Report RR332, IMAG, Grenoble, Nov. 1982.

From Denotational to Operational and Axiomatic Semantics for ALGOL-like Languages: An Overview*†

B. A. Trakhtenbrot, *Dept. of Computer Science, Tel Aviv Univ.*
Joseph Y. Halpern, *IBM Research, San Jose*
Albert R. Meyer, *Laboratory for Computer Science, MIT*

Abstract. The advantages of denotational over operational semantics are argued. A denotational semantics is provided for an ALGOL-like language with finite-mode procedures, blocks with local storage, and sharing (aliasing). Procedure declarations are completely explained in the usual framework of complete partial orders, but cpo's are inadequate for the semantics of blocks, and a new class of store models is developed. Partial correctness theory over store models is developed for commands which may contain calls to global procedures, but do not contain function procedures returning storable values.

1. Introduction. Despite wide-spread though by no means unanimous acceptance of denotational semantics, the numerous papers developing logical systems for proving assertions about programs in the style of [Hoare, 1969] consistently deviate from a purely denotational approach (cf. [Apt, 1981]). In every case, this ideal approach has been deemed inconvenient and has been compromised in favor of operational formulations, notably in explaining inference rules for calls of recursive procedures and for declarations of local variables. We now realize that at least one reason for past deviations from a denotational approach is that the denotational semantics of local storage for blocks has never, until now, adequately been worked out.

This paper gives an overview of our development of a denotational basis for proof systems concerning ALGOL-like programs. We believe our work demonstrates that the denotational ideal is achievable without excessive complication and with significant benefits, notably, a satisfactory treatment of free (global) variables in commands and formulas, and a semantically sound proof system in which the usual substitution rules naturally hold.

In particular, we have developed a denotational semantics and Hoare-like axiom system for *partial correctness assertions* about an ALGOL-like language we call PROG. PROG is a structured language exhibiting a number of nontrivial features including blocks with local

*A shorter version of this paper was presented by the third author under the title "Understanding ALGOL: The View of a Recent Convert to Denotational Semantics," in *1983 IFIPS Proceedings*, R. E. Mason, ed., North Holland.

†The research reported here was supported in part by NSF Grant MCS80-10707, a grant to the MIT Lab. for Computer Science from the IBM Corporation, and a grant from the National Science and Engineering Research Council of Canada. A portion of this research was performed while the second author was a visiting scientist jointly at the MIT Lab. for Computer Science and the Aiken Computation Lab., Harvard Univ.

variables, nested declarations of recursive procedures, procedure parameters, call-by-name, -value, and -reference parameters, and sharing (aliasing) among identifiers.

2. ALGOL-like Languages. Our focus in this paper is on the family of ALGOL-like languages, since these languages are rich in expressive power, yet are also sufficiently structured to yield a rich algebra and proof theory. Following [Reynolds, 1981], we formulate several of the principles which characterize this class of languages:

(1) There is a consistent distinction between *commands* (or *programs*) which alter the store but do not return values, and *expressions* which return values but have no side-effects on the store.

(2) The only explicit calling mechanism is *by-name*. (Other mechanisms such as *by-value* or *by-reference* are available by simulation (syntactic sugaring).)

(3) The language is fully typed. Higher-order procedures of all *finite* types (in ALGOL jargon, *modes*) are allowed. There is a clear distinction between *locations* and *storable values*.

(4) The stack discipline is an explicit aspect of the semantics. Note that this discipline should be understood as a language design principle encouraging modularity in program construction rather than as an implementation technique for efficient storage management. It is better called the *local storage discipline* to avoid misunderstanding, and we do so henceforth.

As it happens, ALGOL-60 is not ALGOL-like in our terminology, nor are numerous features of ALGOL-68; Pascal and ALGOL-W come closest to being ALGOL-like.

Some comprehensive structural restrictions on ALGOL-like languages are implied by these principles. In particular, a consequence of local storage discipline is that neither locations nor procedures can be freely storable, since otherwise locations allocated inside a block might be accessible after exit from the block via the stored objects.

Types in PROG. We have tried to arrange a syntax for PROG reflecting familiar programming languages, but one place where our denotational perspective persuades us to violate common practice is in maintaining an *explicit* type distinction between locations and storable values (also called "left" and "right" values of expressions), because we feel that using the same syntax both for expressions denoting locations and expressions denoting values is an unnecessary source of confusion. So we consistently distinguish locations from their contents, using the token **cont** for explicit dereferencing. These two *basic* types – storable values and locations – will be called **int** and **loc**, respectively. Thus, $\mathbf{cont}(x^{\mathbf{loc}})$ denotes the element of type **int** which is the contents of x, and assignment commands take the form $LocE := IntE$ where $LocE$ is a location-valued expression and $IntE$ is an **int**-valued expression. Equality tests in PROG can only be between elements of basic type.

The other primitive types are **prog, intexp**, and **locexp**. The domain **prog** is the domain of program meanings, namely, mappings from stores to sets of stores. (PROG has a nondeterministic choice construct. For the partial correctness theory we develop, as opposed to *termination* theory, nondeterminism creates no problems in the semantics or proof theory.) The last two "expression" types provide the semantical domains for expressions whose evaluation yields basic values, viz., the elements of **intexp** (**locexp**) are functions from stores to **int** (**loc**). (Elements of type **intexp** or **intexp** are called "thunks" in ALGOL jargon).

In order to avoid some complications in the partial correctness theory of PROG, we impose two extra un-ALGOL-like restrictions. (None of the semantical properties discussed in §3-5 below depend on these restrictions.)

(5) Declarations of functional procedures which return *basic* values are disallowed.

(6) Expressions of type **intexp** and **locexp** are forbidden as parameters in calls.

A consequence of (6) is that the value of an actual parameter is independent of the store. However, note that while the meaning of a procedure term is a mapping involving stores, *which* mapping the term denotes is independent of the store. Thus we *do* allow arbitrary terms of procedure type in calls, e.g., the procedure term $x := \mathbf{cont}(x) + 1$ appears as an actual parameter in a call of the procedure *iterate*2 of Example 1 below.

Hence, we define the allowable procedure types by the grammar

Procedure types:
Proctype ::= **prog** | *Paramtype* → *Proctype*

Parameter types:
Paramtype ::= *Proctype* | **loc** | **int**

Blocks and Binding in PROG. Procedure identifiers are bound in PROG via procedure declarations occurring at the head of a *procedure block*, e.g.,

$$\mathbf{proc}\, p(x) \Leftarrow DeclBody\ \mathbf{do}\ BlockBody\ \mathbf{end}\,.$$

Identifiers of basic type are bound by either **let**-declarations or **new**-declarations at the head of *basic blocks* of the form

$$\mathbf{let}\ x\ \mathbf{be}\ BasE\ \mathbf{in}\ Cmd\ \mathbf{tel}\,,$$
$$\mathbf{new}\ y^{\mathbf{loc}}\ \mathbf{in}\ Cmd\ \mathbf{wen}$$

where x is a variable of basic type and $BasE$ is an expression of the same type.

Call-by-value is available implicitly through **let**-declarations. A call-by-value of the form $p(BasE)$ can be simulated by the basic block

$$\textbf{let}\, n\, \textbf{be}\, BasE\, \textbf{in}\, p(n)\, \textbf{tel}\,.$$

The **let**-declaration causes the evaluation of the expression $BasE$ in the declaration-time store and causes identifier n to denote the result of the evaluation. Call-by-reference is likewise available by simulation since it is merely call-by-value using location-valued expressions.

There is a fundamental difference between basic and procedure blocks. Namely, *which* basic values are bound to identifiers by basic declarations depends on the store "at declaration time", whereas which procedures are bound to identifiers by procedure declarations is store-independent.

Moreover, basic declarations are not recursive, while procedure declarations are. A reflection of this fact is that bound and free occurrences of identifiers are defined differently for basic and procedure blocks. In particular, in procedure declarations, the declared procedure identifiers bind occurrences of these identifiers in the declaration bodies *and* in the block bodies, while in basic declarations, the occurrences of the declared basic identifier are bound only in the block body (which must be a command). (This is made explicit by their contrasting translations to λ-calculus in the next section: procedure blocks are translated using the **letrec** binding mechanism, whereas basic blocks are translated using λ-abstraction and appropriate constants.)

Example 1 illustrates recursion in procedure declarations, procedures of arbitrarily high finite type, simultaneous procedure declarations (nested declarations are also allowed), and complex expressions as actual parameters in calls, including a procedure abstraction of the form **lam** $p.\,body$ **mal**. The example assumes that the underlying domain **int** is actually integer arithmetic and uses primitive recursion at higher types to define a program which sets the variable x to $A(\mathrm{m})$, where A is a function which grows more rapidly than any function on the integers definable by ordinary (first-order) primitive recursion.

It is convenient to apply higher-order procedure identifiers to varying numbers of actual parameters in calls. In Example 1, procedure *iterate*1 is declared with four formal parameters of respective types $\mathbf{int}, \beta, \alpha, \mathbf{prog}$, but is understood to be of "Curried" type $\mathbf{int} \to \beta \to \alpha \to \mathbf{prog} \to \mathbf{prog}$ rather than $(\mathbf{int} \times \beta \times \alpha \times \mathbf{prog}) \to \mathbf{prog}$. It is called first with three actual parameters corresponding to a call of type $\mathbf{prog} \to \mathbf{prog}$, and is called a second time with one actual parameter in a call of type $\beta \to \alpha \to \mathbf{prog} \to \mathbf{prog}$.

Example 1. Let **prog** denote the objects of type *program*, and let $\alpha = \mathbf{prog} \to \mathbf{prog}$, $\beta =$

$\alpha \to \alpha$, $\gamma = \beta \to \beta$ denote successively higher procedure types.

$$
\begin{aligned}
&\textbf{proc } \mathit{repeat}(q^{\alpha}, p^{\mathbf{prog}}) \Leftarrow q(q(p)),\\
&\quad \mathit{iterate1}(n^{\mathbf{int}}, r^{\beta}, q^{\alpha}, p^{\mathbf{prog}}) \Leftarrow \textbf{if } n = 0 \textbf{ then } p \textbf{ else } r(\mathit{iterate1}(n-1, r, q), p) \textbf{ fi},\\
&\quad \mathit{iterate2}(n^{\mathbf{int}}, s^{\gamma}, r^{\beta}, q^{\alpha}, p^{\mathbf{prog}}) \Leftarrow \textbf{if } n = 0 \textbf{ then } p \textbf{ else } s(\mathit{iterate2}(n-1, s, r), q, p) \textbf{ fi},\\
&\quad A(x^{\mathbf{loc}}) \Leftarrow \textbf{ let } n \textbf{ be } \mathbf{cont}(x) \textbf{ in}\\
&\qquad\qquad \mathit{iterate2}(n, \mathit{iterate1}(n), \mathit{repeat}, \textbf{lam } p^{\mathbf{prog}}.(p;p) \textbf{ mal}, (x := \mathbf{cont}(x) + 1))\\
&\qquad\quad \textbf{tel}\\
&\textbf{do } x := \mathbf{m}; A(x) \textbf{ end}
\end{aligned}
$$

Sharing in PROG. Sharing of locations between identifiers arises naturally from procedure calls. Explicit sharing can also be imposed by a basic block like

$$\textbf{let } x^{\mathbf{loc}} \textbf{ be } y^{\mathbf{loc}} \textbf{ in } \mathit{Cmd} \textbf{ tel}.$$

Example 2 is contrived to illustrate the sharing features of PROG. It includes a declaration of a procedure that swaps the contents of two locations unless they are equal. It also illustrates the new declaration for allocating storage local to a block. The simple idea which underlies local variables in ALGOL-like languages is the *local storage discipline*: execution of a block **new** z **in** *body* **wen** causes allocation of a "new" storage location denoted by the identifier z which is used in the body of the block and then de-allocated upon exit from the block.

Example 2.

$$
\begin{aligned}
&\textbf{proc } \mathit{swap}(x_1^{\mathbf{loc}}, x_2^{\mathbf{loc}}) \Leftarrow \textbf{if } x_1 = x_2 \textbf{ then } x_1 := \mathbf{error}\\
&\qquad\qquad\qquad\qquad\qquad \textbf{else new } z \textbf{ in}\\
&\qquad\qquad\qquad\qquad\qquad\quad z := \mathbf{cont}(x_1);\\
&\qquad\qquad\qquad\qquad\qquad\quad x_1 := \mathbf{cont}(x_2);\\
&\qquad\qquad\qquad\qquad\qquad\quad x_2 := \mathbf{cont}(z) \textbf{ wen fi}\\
&\quad \textbf{do if } \mathbf{f}(\mathbf{a}) = \mathbf{f}(\mathbf{cont}(y)) \textbf{ then } y \textbf{ else } z \textbf{ fi} := \mathbf{null};\\
&\qquad \mathit{swap}(y, z) \textbf{ end}.
\end{aligned}
$$

Note that we are allowing explicit equality testing between locations ("$x_1 = x_2$") in addition to the usual test of equality between storable values ("$\mathbf{f}(\mathbf{a}) = \mathbf{f}(\mathbf{cont}(y))$"). Expressions which evaluate to locations are allowed, as in the "conditional variable" expression to the left of the final assignment command in the example.

In addition to declarations of purely functional procedures which return basic values, other significant language features *compatible* with ALGOL-like principles but *omitted* from PROG include exit control, arrays and user-defined data-types, own-variables, polymorphism, implicit coercion (overloading) and concurrency. These will have to be the subject of future studies.

2. Semantics via Syntax-Preserving Translation to λ-Calculus. The main issue in reasoning about imperative programming languages is that the computer memory or *store* altered by program execution is never mentioned explicitly in programs. A denotational explanation of programs requires that the role of the store be made explicit. This is usually done by, in effect, translating programs into ordinary mathematical expressions which mention stores. Our approach is to formalize the assignment of semantics to programs in two steps:

(1) a purely syntactic *translation* from PROG to a fully-typed λ-calculus enriched with a **letrec**-construct corresponding to procedure declarations, and

(2) assignment of semantics to the λ-calculus in the standard way. Programs simply inherit their semantics directly from the λ-terms into which they translate.

This two step process has also been utilized by [Damm and Fehr, 1980; Damm, 1982]. Our approach refines theirs in that the λ-calculus into which programs are translated is chosen so that its types are the *same* as those of the programming language and its constants correspond to program constructors. (It follows that stores do *not* appear as one of the types of the target language, although they do appear within the definitions of the domains of meaning of various program phrases; in particular there is no λ-abstraction over stores.) In this way, the abstract syntax, viz., parse tree, of the translation of a program is actually *identical* to that of the program; the translation serves mainly to make the variable binding conventions of PROG explicit.

In addition to the binding of free variables, the translation Tr mapping PROG to λ-calculus makes explicit an implicit coercion (the only one) which takes place in PROG. Namely, a store-independent term T of basic type can always be treated as an expression (**Mkexp** T) denoting the constant function of the store identically equal to the value of T. More generally, any function f taking basic values as arguments can also be coerced straightforwardly into a mapping $Mkexp(f)$ taking as arguments functions from stores to basic values. (There is a different constant **Mkexp** for every first-order type, but we usually omit mention of the types of **Mkexp** and similar constants such as **Ifexp** below.) The term (**Mkexp f**) corresponding to $Mkexp(f)$ is abbreviated as $\bar{\mathbf{f}}$.

Procedure blocks are translated using **letrec**, so for example,

$$Tr(\mathbf{proc}\, p(x) \Leftarrow DeclBody\ \mathbf{do}\ BlockBody\ \mathbf{end})$$
$$=_{def} \mathbf{letrec}\, p = \lambda x.Tr(DeclBody)\ \mathbf{in}\ Tr(BlockBody).$$

For a basic block with a **let**-declaration of type **int**,

$$Tr(\mathbf{let}\ x^{\mathbf{int}}\ \mathbf{be}\ IntE\ \mathbf{in}\ Cmd\ \mathbf{tel}) =_{def} \mathbf{Dint}\,(\lambda x.Tr(Cmd))\,(Tr(IntE))$$

where **Dint** is a constant of type (**int** → **prog**) → **intexp** → **prog**. For any element d_1 of type (**int** → **prog**), d_2 of type **intexp**, and store s, the interpretation [[**Dint**]] satisfies

$$[\![\mathbf{Dint}]\!] d_1\, d_2\, s = \begin{cases} (d_1\,(d_2(s)))(s) & \text{if } d_2(s) \neq \bot_{\mathbf{int}}, \\ \emptyset & \text{otherwise.} \end{cases}$$

Note that the binding effect of the block on $x^{\mathbf{int}}$ is reflected in the binding effect of λx on $Tr(Cmd)$, namely, the declaration binds x in Cmd, but does not bind x in $IntE$.

The principal consequence of this syntax-preserving translation is that the basic properties of procedure declarations in ALGOL-like languages – such as renaming rules associated with "static scope" for declared identifiers, declaration denesting rules, and expansions of recursive declarations – can be recognized as direct consequences of corresponding properties of the purely functional λ-calculus.

For example, let E be a system of procedure declarations, and let Cmd_1, Cmd_2 be any commands. The following equivalence holds in *all* models for λ-calculus, viz., all Cartesian-closed models [Barendregt, 1980; Meyer, 1982].

Declaration Distributivity:

$$\mathbf{proc}\, E\, \mathbf{do}\, Cmd_1; Cmd_2\, \mathbf{end} \quad \equiv \quad \mathbf{proc}\, E\, \mathbf{do}\, Cmd_1\, \mathbf{end}; \mathbf{proc}\, E\, \mathbf{do}\, Cmd_2\, \mathbf{end}\,.$$

In particular, this equivalence follows solely from the binding properties of procedure declarations independently of whether declarations are recursive, and also independently of the meaning of constants like the sequencing operation ; . (On the other hand, its validity depends crucially on the fact that procedure declarations, in contrast to let-declarations, have the same binding effect no matter what the declaration-time store.)

The translation for blocks with **new** declarations, is

$$Tr(\mathbf{new}\ x\ \mathbf{in}\ Cmd\ \mathbf{wen}) =_{def} \mathbf{New}\,(\lambda x.Tr(Cmd))$$

where **New** is a special constant of type (**loc** → **prog**) → **prog**. The effect of the translation will be that Cmd runs using a "new" location in place of x. The contents of this new location are initialized to some standard value denoted by the constant $\mathbf{a}_0$ at the beginning of the computation of Cmd and restored to its original value at the end.

In defining the semantics of new declarations, we imagine an ability to generate "new" locations via a *Select* operation mapping any a procedure of type **loc** → **prog** into a new location. We can then define the meaning of [[**New**]]$d^{\mathbf{loc}\to\mathbf{prog}}$ as follows:

$$[\![Tr(\mathbf{let}\ x^{\mathbf{int}}\ \mathbf{be}\ \mathbf{cont}(y)\ \mathbf{in}\ y := \mathbf{a}_0; p(y); y := x\ \mathbf{tel})]\!]e,$$

where e is an environment such that $e(y) = Select(d)$ and $e(p) = d$.

We illustrate the full translation process with

Example 3. Translation of Example 2.

$$
\begin{array}{l}
\textbf{letrec } \mathit{swap} = \\
\quad \lambda x_1^{\mathbf{loc}} x_2^{\mathbf{loc}}. \textbf{Ifexp } \bar{x}_1 \bar{x}_2 \\
\quad\quad (\textbf{Assign } \bar{x}_1\ \overline{\textbf{error}}) \\
\quad\quad (\textbf{New } \lambda z. \textbf{Seq} \\
\quad\quad\quad (\textbf{Assign } \bar{z}(\textbf{Cont } \bar{x}_1))(\textbf{ Seq} \\
\quad\quad\quad (\textbf{Assign } \bar{x}_1(\textbf{Cont } \bar{x}_2)) \\
\quad\quad\quad (\textbf{Assign } \bar{x}_2(\textbf{Cont} \bar{z})))) \\
\textbf{in } (\textbf{Seq } (\textbf{Assign} \\
\quad\quad (\textbf{Ifexp } (\textbf{Mkexp } (\textbf{f a})) (\bar{\textbf{f}}(\textbf{Cont } \bar{y})) \, \bar{y} \, \bar{z}) \\
\quad\quad \overline{\textbf{null}}) \\
\quad (\mathit{swap}\ y\ z))
\end{array}
$$

Constants like **Assign**, **Ifexp**, **Seq**, ..., in λ-terms correspond to the tokens :=, **if**. . .**then**. . . **else**. . .**fi**, ;, ..., of PROG and must be appropriately interpreted.

Note that we have kept our promise that the translation preserves the true syntax of commands: *Cmd* and *Tr*(*Cmd*) have the same abstract syntax.

3. Levels of Understanding. A denotational approach has led us to identify a half dozen levels of abstraction at which aspects of ALGOL-like languages can be understood. The highest level abstracts away all properties except for variable binding; these properties hold in all models of λ-calculus. For example, the fundamental rule:

Procedure-Context Replacement:

$$\frac{\mathit{Cmd}_1 \equiv \mathit{Cmd}_2}{\textbf{proc } E \textbf{ do } \mathit{Cmd}_1 \textbf{ end} \equiv \textbf{proc } E \textbf{ do } \mathit{Cmd}_2 \textbf{ end}}$$

is obvious from a denotational viewpoint, and like the distributing rule, actually holds in all λ-calculus models.

The next level reveals that procedure declarations are recursive; the corresponding proof theory is simply the equational theory of the fixed-point combinator and similar expansion rules for **letrec**.

Properties connecting different fixed-points require the further hypothesis that fixed-points in distinct domains be chosen harmoniously. This is usually captured by imposing an order structure on domains, keeping to order-respecting (monotone) functions on the domains, and choosing *least* fixed points as solutions to recursive equations. At this "monotone" level, we can justify:

Declaration Denesting:

$$\textbf{proc}\,(p(x) \Leftarrow \textbf{proc}\, E\, \textbf{do}\, \mathit{body}\, \textbf{end}), E'\, \textbf{do}\, \mathit{Cmd}\, \textbf{end} \quad \equiv \quad \textbf{proc}\,(p(x) \Leftarrow \mathit{body}), E, E'\, \textbf{do}\, \mathit{Cmd}\, \textbf{end}$$

providing none of the identifiers declared in E occurs in E' or *Cmd*, p is not declared in E or E', and x is not free in E.

At the fourth level of abstraction we entirely account for the procedure mechanism of ALGOL-like languages. Here, the familiar *continuous* models of λ-calculus based on complete partial orders (cpo's) [Scott, 1982; Milne and Strachey, 1976; Stoy, 1977] provide an adequate semantical basis. We refer to properties which are valid for all continuous models as *continuity* properties. The most fundamental continuity property is that every command can be understood as a limit of finite procedure-declaration-free commands.

The original ALGOL 60 report [Naur, et. al., 1963] gave a copy-rule semantics for the language. The equivalence of fixed-point and copy-rule semantics verifies that our choice of denotational "fixed-point" semantics is consistent with the prior operational understanding based on the copy-rule. We give a simplified proof of:

Theorem. In every continuous model, fixed-point and copy-rule semantics assign the same semantics to commands (which may contain global procedures) in PROG.

Still further refined levels are needed to explain the store-dependent aspects of programs, i.e., their side-effects. In particular, continuous models are not adequate to explain local storage allocation, and we must introduce a new class of *store models* discussed in §5.

4. Fixed-point versus Copy-rule Semantics. Copy-rule semantics for ALGOL-like languages have historical precedence over denotational semantics, and are widely regarded as more intuitive for computationally oriented students (cf. [Blikle, 1983]). It seems obvious to us, however, that the tricky and otherwise arbitrary-seeming renaming rules which are part of the definition of the copy-rule, and which are crucial in determining the properties of declarations, spring from a mathematical intuition with an even earlier historical claim. But arguments from intuition are always questionable; putting such arguments aside, we can identify the place where the denotational approach is clearer and more general than an operational approach to be the handling of "global" procedures, i.e., free procedure identifiers.

Reasoning about commands with calls to global procedures is essential in theory and in practice. The need for reasoning about commands containing globals arises, for example, when global procedures denote library procedures. Given assertions about the behavior of the library procedures, one should be able to reason about the behavior of commands incorporating these procedures, without necessarily being given the declarations of the procedures. After all, the code of these library procedures is typically unavailable or written in machine language, and in any case is not what one wants to see. Unfortunately, nearly all the operationally based proof systems apply only to programs without globals, viz., programs in which all procedures are declared.

One can give an operational-style explanation of the range of globals, namely, that global procedures range over textual objects such as "closures". This explanation is clearly unsatisfactory when library procedures are written in another language. Another difficulty with this explanation is that any enrichment of the language enlarges the range of the global procedures, so that all the axioms and rules involving globals must be reexamined for soundness. In contrast, a denotational approach in which *environments* map free identifiers to meanings over a domain of functional objects, smoothly handles commands containing global procedures.

The desire to reason by induction on the structure of programs – which motivates the design of structured programming languages in the first place – also naturally requires reasoning about global procedures, since the procedure identifiers declared in a block inevitably have free occurrences in the body of the block. *Fixed-point induction* is an important instance of a structural inference rule in which free procedure identifiers are essential. The following special case illustrates the essence of the rule when applied to partial correctness assertions of the form $P\{Cmd\}Q$ where P and Q are first-order formulas. (The precise semantics of such assertions is given in §6.)

Fixed-Point Induction: Let p be an identifier and $ProcE$ an expression, both of the same procedure type, such that none of the free *first-order* variables in $ProcE$ are free in P or Q.

$$\frac{P\{[\mathbf{diverge}/p]Cmd\}Q, \quad P\{Cmd\}Q \vdash P\{[ProcE/p]Cmd\}Q}{P\{\mathbf{proc}\ p \Leftarrow ProcE\ \mathbf{do}\ Cmd\ \mathbf{end}\}Q}$$

where $[Expr/p]$ denotes syntactic substitution (with renaming to avoid capture of free variables) of $Expr$ for *free* occurrences of the procedure identifier p.

The soundness of fixed-point induction is an easily proved continuity property.

[Clarke, 1979], extending [Gorelick, 1975], introduced another proof rule for partial correctness of higher-order procedure calls closely resembling the fixed-point induction rule but justified using the copy-rule. Subsequent work [Langmaack and Olderog, 1980; Olderog, 1981, 1983a, 1983b; Apt, 1981] has followed this approach. Our axiom system in §6 includes a version of Clarke's rule called *copy-rule induction.*

[Langmaack and Olderog, 1980] have defended the use of copy-rule induction:

"In soundness and completeness proofs a semantics definition should be employed which yields shortest proofs. The question of equivalence of partly operational and purely denotational semantics should be considered separately."

We remain uncomfortable with this view. It is a useful technical insight that inductive proofs about calls in ALGOL-like languages can be based on copy-rule semantics. Yet this fact seems too coincidental to serve as a justification for postponing denotational arguments. For example, it seems fortuitous that the usual axioms for partial correctness happen not to require the procedure-context replacement rule above. The rule is obvious denotationally, but we know of no justification for it using copy-rule semantics which is any simpler than the proof that copy-rule and denotational semantics are equivalent. We expect that outside the special case of partial correctness proofs, and perhaps even there, it will be disadvantageous to develop proof systems using copy-rule semantics alone.

Of course, whenever there is a nontrivial equivalence between two definitions, there are bound to be facts which are obvious starting from one definition and not from the other, and it should be expected that some important facts about program behavior, possibly such as Clarke's rule, would be seen more easily in terms of the copy-rule. If it were merely the case that the semantical soundness proof was more easily carried out using one of two equivalent definitions instead of the other, we would not be concerned. However, in contrast to the fixed-point induction rule, copy-rule induction is *not sound* in the usual logical sense, although only valid assertions are provable using it.

Namely, copy-rule induction, like fixed-point induction, is formulated in natural deduction style where the *provability* of one assertion from another serves as the antecedent for application of the rule. Because of the reference to the proof system in the antecedent, the meaning of such rules technically changes if we alter the proof system in any way, for example by adding further sound inference rules. This reference to the proof system will be harmless as long as soundness of the rule follows from soundness of the rest of the proof system – as opposed to facts about the detailed structure of proofs. This is what is meant by semantical soundness of a natural deduction style rule (cf. §6). Fixed-point induction is semantically sound in this sense, but copy-rule induction is not because it depends crucially on structural properties of proofs. In fact, we can show that a price to be paid for using copy-rule induction is that adding very simple, obviously sound rules makes the proof systems inconsistent! ([Olderog, 1981] claims to avoid this problem, but he does so by adopting a definition of validity which is not referentially transparent, so that substituting one equivalent command for another cannot be added as a rule in his system without yielding an inconsistency.)

We have not yet worked out as strong a completeness theorem using the fixed-point induction rule or other sound rule in place of Clarke's rule, although we have an idea how to do so. Meanwhile, as a temporary expediency we have included copy-rule induction in our own proof system. Insofar as the remarks of Olderog and Langmaack and others supporting operational semantics for proof systems are intended as a defense of copy-rule induction despite its unsoundness, we disagree with their view. We see no theoretical obstacle to discovering a denotationally sound alternative to copy-rule induction, and we regard developing such a rule as an interesting research problem.

5. Store Models. Although the local storage discipline seems intuitively simple, it raises a number of both practical and theoretical problems.

A well-known practical consequence of the mixture of blocks and recursive procedures is that *run-time* storage allocation is necessary: a block may appear within a recursive procedure which is itself called within the body of the block, so the number of different locations which must be *simultaneously* allocated for nested activations of the block during execution may grow unboundedly, ruling out static ("compile time") allocation.

On the other hand, program schemes with neither free procedure identifiers nor recursive procedure declarations require only a bounded number of locations to be allocated – independent of the interpretation of the scheme – and static allocation is not difficult. The fact that static allocation is possible in this case can be formulated as the theorem that every such program scheme is equivalent to an effectively constructible scheme *without blocks* but with various constants denoting fixed locations. Since copy-rule semantics reduces the meaning of general programs to procedure-declaration-free programs, it follows that the semantics of block storage allocation *in the absence of free procedure identifiers* is easy to explain with the copy-rule. Free procedure identifiers raise problems which have not been dealt with using operational semantics.

From a theoretical viewpoint, the problem is to explain what is meant by a "new" location. Operationally, the "old" locations for a command correspond to the values of the free location variables in it. This is sometimes modeled denotationally by enriching the notion of stores to include with each location an indication of whether the location is "active". Execution of a new block on a store involves selecting the first inactive location as the one to be allocated. The problem with this approach is that the locations designated as inactive by the store may already be accessible to the body of the block, and so the first inactive location may *not* in fact be "new". For example, the block

$$\textbf{new } x \textbf{ in if } x = y \textbf{ then diverge else skip fi wen}$$

ought intuitively to be equivalent to **skip** since the "new" x should never equal the "old" y. But if this block is executed on a store in which (the location denoted by) y happens to be designated as the first inactive location, then the block will diverge. Validity of the expected properties of blocks thus hinges on hypotheses about how the locations designated as active by the store relate to the "old" locations which really are active, and we are in any case still left with the problem of explaining what a new location is.

The denotational meaning of a program is a mapping from stores to stores, and it is not hard to give a purely denotational characterization of what it means to say that such a mapping "reads" or "writes" a set of locations (cf. [Trakhtenbrot, 1979; de Bakker, 1980, Def. 5.9; Meyer and Mitchell, 1982]). The meaning of the body of a **new** block is in turn a mapping from locations to store mappings, and a denotational definition of what locations such a block body "knows about" can also be given with some care. In general, we define a notion of the set of locations which form the *support* of any procedure of finite type. The locations outside the support of a procedure are the "new" ones for it. The support of a command is thus the denotational concept corresponding to the syntactic notion of free location variables appearing in the command. This would appear to provide the desired denotational semantics of block storage allocation.

However, an amusing technical problem arises. Monotonicity is normally required of the functions defining the semantics of λ-terms in order to ensure that the fixed-points necessary to explain recursive definitions exist in the domain of meanings. The operation of allocating and later de-allocating "new" storage turns out not to be monotonic, essentially because of the possibility of running out of new storage locations!

One apparent way out of this difficulty is to admit a new **overflowed** error-object which is maximal in the partial order on programs. This complicates the logic of programs since we now must explicitly reason about the possibility of running out of storage. For example, we might expect that

$$\textbf{new } x \textbf{ in } Cmd \textbf{ wen} \equiv Cmd$$

when x does not occur free in *Cmd*. But this equivalence is only valid providing *Cmd* denotes a program whose support does not contain *all* locations; if it does, then the left-hand side is equivalent to **overflowed**. Similarly, the equivalence

$$(Cmd; \textbf{diverge}) \equiv \textbf{diverge}$$

becomes questionable in the case that *Cmd* denotes **overflowed**. A more serious problem is that although an **overflowed** object circumvents nonmonotonicity, it does not restore continuity. Namely, a command whose support contains all locations is the limit of a sequence of approximating commands with smaller support; allocating new storage is therefore possible for the approximations but yields **overflowed** for the limit. (The discontinuity of new storage allocation is noted in [Milne and Strachey, 1976], with a reference to further discussion in Milne's thesis.)

In general, objects with "large" support force us to face the discontinuity of storage overflow. It would be reasonable to rule out such objects, especially in view of the fact that *definable* objects, viz., objects which are the denotations of phrases in PROG, can be proved to depend on only finitely many locations. Unfortunately, the domain of programs with finite support is not *complete* (closed under least upper bounds) because the lub of a sequence of programs each with finite support may have infinite support.

A simple way around this incompleteness would be to use, for each finite set, L, of locations, a separate domain consisting of those programs with support contained in L. This works as long as no procedure parameters appear, but the mixture of *higher order* recursive procedures and block structure turns out to be explosive. A procedure which takes a program parameter might be called upon recursively within a new block, and might be applied to programs constructed within the block, as in:

$$\begin{aligned} p(q^{\mathbf{prog}}, n^{\mathbf{int}}) \Leftarrow\ & \mathbf{if}\, n \neq 0\, \mathbf{then} \\ & \quad \mathbf{new}\, x\, \mathbf{in}\ p(r(q,x), n-1)\ \mathbf{wen} \\ & \quad \mathbf{else}\ q\ \mathbf{fi}\,. \end{aligned}$$

The domain of such a procedure includes programs with unbounded finite support, and we are no longer able to confine ourselves to the cpo of programs with any particular finite support L.

Difficulties of this sort have led [Reynolds, 1981] and [Oles, 1983] to consider more sophisticated functor categories as domains of interpretation.

Store models overcome these difficulties: they are domains of mappings with *countably infinite* support. Such domains are not complete, but they are ω-complete – closed under *countable* lubs – and it is known that ω-completeness is sufficient to develop the semantics of recursive programs [Meseguer, 1978; Plotkin, 1982].

Allowing elements with countably infinite support is merely a mathematical contrivance to preserve closure under countable directed limits. The countable covering restriction works, despite some intuitively jarring consequences, the oddest of which is that we must hypothesize an *uncountable* number of locations! (But after all, we do not complain about an uncountable set of real numbers even when we compute only with rationals.)

We outline below the main properties of store models and the support notion.

Primitive Domains: Given a set *Loc* (of locations) and a set *Int* (of storable values) we define the domains

$$D_{\mathbf{loc}} =_{def} Loc \cup \{\perp_{\mathbf{loc}}\},\ D_{\mathbf{int}} =_{def} Int \cup \{\perp_{\mathbf{int}}\}$$

to be the flat cpo's.

For the other primitive domains, we select some subset, *Store*, of $Int^{Loc} =_{def}$ the set of *all total* functions from *Loc* to *Int*. *Store* must be closed under finite updates and under permutations μ of *Loc*, i.e., if $s \in Store$, then $s \circ \mu \in Store$. Then

$$D_{\mathbf{intexp}} \subseteq (D_{\mathbf{int}})^{Store},\ D_{\mathbf{locexp}} \subseteq (D_{\mathbf{loc}})^{Store},\ D_{\mathbf{prog}} \subseteq (\mathcal{P}(Store))^{Store}.$$

Here $\mathcal{P}(Store)$ denotes the power-set of stores, so elements of $D_{\mathbf{prog}}$ correspond to nondeterministic mappings between stores.

Higher Domains: The domains $D_{\beta\to\gamma}$ consist of subsets of the ω-continuous functions from D_β to D_γ, and form a Cartesian-closed type-frame with least fixed-points.

Uniformity on Locations: For each type α and permutation μ of *Loc*, the domain D_α is closed under the permutation μ_α induced by μ, e.g., if $\alpha = \beta \to \gamma$, then

$$\mu_\alpha(f) =_{def} \mu_\gamma \circ f \circ \mu_\beta^{-1}.$$

We define a *covering* relation between subsets $L \subseteq Loc$ and elements $d \in D_\alpha$. Let L be a subset of *Loc*. Two stores s, t *agree on* L, written $s =_L t$, iff $\forall l \in L.\, s(l) = t(l)$. Similarly, two sets $S, T \in \mathcal{P}(Stores)$ agree on L if there is a bijection $f : S \to T$ such that $\forall s \in S.\, s =_L f(s)$. Covering has the properties that

(a) if $\pi \in D_{\mathbf{prog}}$, then L covers π iff $\forall s, t \in Store.\,(s =_L t \Rightarrow \pi(s) =_L \pi(t)) \wedge (t \in \pi(s) \Rightarrow s =_{Loc-L} t)$,

(b) L covers $l \in D_{\mathbf{loc}}$ iff $l \in L \cup \{\perp_{\mathbf{loc}}\}$,

(c) if L covers d^α, then $\forall \mu$ fixing $L.\ \mu_\alpha d = d$,

(d) if L_1 covers $d_1 \in D_{\beta\to\gamma}$ and L_2 covers $d_2 \in D_\beta$, then $L_1 \cup L_2$ covers $(d_1\, d_2)$.

Countable Covering Restriction: Every element $d \in D_\alpha$, has a *countable* set covering it.

Interpretability of the Constants: Let

$$Support(d) =_{def} \bigcap\{L \subseteq Loc \mid L \text{ is countable and covers } d\}.$$

There must be elements in the model giving appropriate interpretations to each of the constants used in translating PROG, and these elements must have *empty* support.

We remark that another odd consequence of allowing countable rather than finite covers is that $Support(d)$ may not cover d if no finite set covers d.

Now it is easy to show that all the constants other than **New** are continuous and have empty support. The sole purpose of the covering restriction is to ensure that **New** is interpretable. In particular, a function $Select : \mathcal{P}(Loc) \to Loc$ will be called a *selection function* iff $Select(L) \notin L$ for all *countable* sets $L \subseteq Loc$. As long as Loc is uncountable, selection functions exist, and using *any* selection function as $Select$ in the definition of **New** indicated in §2 yields the same ω-continuous function with empty support. This is the desired denotation for **New**.

Some typical equivalences about **new**-declarations are given below. Support properties of store models are essential to guarantee their validity.

$$\begin{aligned}
\textbf{new } x \textbf{ in } x := \textbf{b wen} &\equiv \textbf{skip}\,,\\
\textbf{new } x \textbf{ in } x := \textbf{a}_0; Cmd \textbf{ wen} &\equiv \textbf{new } x \textbf{ in } Cmd \textbf{ wen}\,,\\
\textbf{new } x \textbf{ new } y \textbf{ in } Cmd \textbf{ wen wen} &\equiv \textbf{new } y \textbf{ new } x \textbf{ in } Cmd \textbf{ wen wen}\,,\\
\textbf{new } x \textbf{ in if } x = y \textbf{ then } Cmd_1 \textbf{ else } Cmd_2 \textbf{ fi wen} &\equiv y := \textbf{cont}(y); Cmd_2\,.
\end{aligned}$$

More generally, we can define an operational semantics for interpreting basic blocks and prove:

Theorem. In every store model, fixed-point and operational semantics assign the same semantics to commands (which may contain global procedures) in PROG.

The natural classes of objects to allow in store models are those with finite support, because PROG-definable programs only read or write a finite number of locations. These objects form a Cartesian-closed type-frame with least fixed-points, but, as we noted, not a cpo. The construction outlined above embeds the desired domains of elements with finite support into (ω-)cpo's. Hence all the requisite properties of cpo's are inherited by the embedded domains, and therefore we are now justified in restricting ourselves to the objects with finite support. In our proof theory in the next section, we in fact restrict variables to range over elements with finite support.

(A closer analysis of the role of limits in program semantics reveals that not all directed sets, but only "algebraic" directed sets $\perp, f(\perp), f(f(\perp)), \ldots$, where $\perp$ is the least element in D_α and $f \in D_{\alpha\to\alpha}$, must have lub's [Guessarian, 1982]. These lub's *do* exist in the frame of elements with finite support. The unexpected peculiarities of countable supports would have been avoided had we developed our semantics using such algebraically closed partial orders instead of cpo's. However, we did not want to take the time to reformulate and prove for algebraically closed partial orders all the well documented properties which make cpo's suitable as semantical domains, so we have kept to the better known cpo framework.)

6. Partial Correctness Theory. Instead of the usual first-order language of storable values, we use a two-sorted first-order language with sorts **int** and **loc**. We also add special atomic formulas for reasoning about the support of global procedures, namely, for each identifier p of **loc** or procedure type and each variable x of type **loc**, there is an atomic formula $\mathbf{Support}(x,p)$ which means that x is in the support of p. This language has the same constructive properties as ordinary (one-sorted) first-order language, e.g., the formulas valid in all interpretations are nicely axiomatizable.

We require assertions about support because we are reasoning about commands with global procedure identifiers. Without global procedure identifiers, one can determine the support of a command by inspection – namely, the support is contained in the denotations of the free location variables. This is obviously not possible for command with global procedure identifiers unless we are told which locations are in the support of the globals.

Any $s \in Store$ provides an interpretation for the contents function denoted by the token **cont**. Thus, given a store model D, a store s, and an environment e to assign values to variables, first-order expressions can be interpreted as elements of $D_{\mathbf{int}}$ and $D_{\mathbf{loc}}$ in the usual way.

We let $P, Q, \ldots$ denote first-order formulas. The satisfaction relation between a first-order formula P and an interpretation D, e, s, written $D, e, s \models P$, is defined as usual.

In defining satisfaction for assertions it is sometimes convenient to ignore the values an environment assigns to basic variables.

Definition. Two environments e, e' are said to *match* iff $e(x) = e'(x)$ for all *procedure* variables x. An environment e *uses finite supports* iff $Support(e(x))$ is finite for each identifier x.

Definition. Let D be a store model. The satisfaction relation $\models$ is extended to partial correctness assertions as follows:

$D, e, s \models P\{Cmd\}Q$ iff (if $D, e, s \models P$ then $D, e, t \models Q$ for all $t \in [\![Cmd]\!]_D e s$),
where $[\![Cmd]\!]_D e \in D_{\mathbf{prog}}$ is the denotation of Cmd in environment

$D, e \models P\{Cmd\}Q$ iff $D, e', s \models P\{Cmd\}Q$ for all e' matching e and all $s \in Store$,

$D \models P\{Cmd\}Q$ iff $D, e \models P\{Cmd\}Q$ for all environments e using finite supports,

$\models P\{Cmd\}Q$ iff $D \models P\{Cmd\}Q$ for all *store* models D.

This notation is also used for formulas, e.g.,

$$D, e \models P \text{ iff } D, e', s \models P \text{ for all } e' \text{ matching } e \text{ and all } s \in Store.$$

It may be helpful to note that by this convention D, e satisfies a first-order formula iff D, e satisfies the first-order universal closure of the formula. That is,

$$D, e \models P \text{ iff } D, e \models \forall x^{\gamma}.P$$

where γ is **int** or **loc**.

Distinguishing locations and their contents becomes particularly beneficial when making assertions about programs. With two-sorted language, our axiom system is able to deal with sharing among program variables explicitly and without excessive complication.

An awkward feature of common programming logic systems which do not allow preconditions to distinguish locations from values is that renaming free variables does not preserve validity. For example, although

$$x_1 \neq x_2\{\, x_3 := x_2 \,\}x_1 \neq x_3$$

is valid in such systems, it fails to be valid if we substitute x_1 for x_3, which can be a source of confusion (cf. [Manna and Waldinger, 1981]). We therefore judge the soundness of arbitrary renamings, which follows routinely for our system, to be a valuable feature.

Definition. A *first-order substitution* is a type-respecting mapping, σ, from *basic* identifiers to first-order terms which *do not contain* occurrences of the token **cont**. Let $\sigma(P)$ and $\sigma(Cmd)$ denote the result of simultaneously substituting $\sigma(x)$ for all free occurrences of basic variables x (renaming bound variables as necessary) in the formula P or command Cmd.

Substitution Lemma: Let σ be a first-order substitution. For any first-order model D and environment e, if $D, e \models P\{\, Cmd \,\}Q$, then $D, e \models \sigma(P)\{\, \sigma(Cmd) \,\}\sigma(Q)$.

This justifies the following:

Rule of Substitution: Let σ be a first-order substitution.

$$\frac{P\{\, Cmd \,\}Q}{\sigma(P)\{\, \sigma(Cmd) \,\}\sigma(Q)}.$$

Another standard source of confusion as a result of sharing occurs in axiomatizing simple assignments. Clearly, no matter what the initial conditions are, after setting $x^{\mathbf{loc}}$ to some constant **a**, the contents of x will equal **a**, namely,

$$\mathbf{true}\{\, x := \mathbf{a} \,\}\mathbf{cont}(x) = \mathbf{a}$$

is a valid partial correctness assertion. But the naive generalization of this example to the case in which x is replaced by some expression whose evaluation yields a location is not valid. For example, let $LocE_0$ be the location-valued conditional expression

$$\mathbf{if}\ \mathbf{cont}(x) = \mathbf{a}\ \mathbf{then}\ y\ \mathbf{else}\ x\ \mathbf{fi}\,.$$

Setting $LocE_0$, rather than x, to **a**, makes the following assertion valid

$$(\mathbf{cont}(x) = \mathbf{a} \wedge \mathbf{cont}(y) \neq \mathbf{a})\{\, LocE_0 := \mathbf{a}\,\}\mathbf{cont}(LocE_0) \neq \mathbf{a}.$$

The problem here is that the meaning of $LocE_0$ depends on the store; $LocE_0$ has different meanings before and after the assignment.

To deal with assignment, we construct for any formula P, a first-order formula $[LocE \leftarrow IntE]P$ such that for each D, e, s, if l, d are the interpretations of $LocE$, $IntE$ in D, e, s, then

$$D, e, s \models [LocE \leftarrow IntE]P \text{ iff } D, e, s' \models P$$

where $s' =_{Loc-\{l\}} s$ and $s'(l) = d$. Now the assertion that after executing the assignment some first-order formula Q holds, is equivalent to asserting that the formula

$$[LocE := IntE]Q =_{def} (LocE = \bot \vee IntE = \bot \vee [LocE \leftarrow IntE]Q)$$

holds in the initial store. (The $\bot$ clauses handle the case that the evaluation of either of the expressions diverges.) Difficulties with assignments are thus completely handled by the:

Assignment axiom:

$$([LocE := IntE]Q)\{\, LocE := IntE\,\}Q\,.$$

Our axiom system AX_D is defined as usual *relative* to an underlying model D. However, it is worth noting that we do not need support predicates in the axioms about D. That is, we only include in AX_D the set $Th(D)$ of all first-order formulas *without* support predicates which are valid in D.

Axioms and rules for the programming constructs **diverge**, sequencing, conditionals, choice, as well as "logical" rules for consequence, conjunction and quantification, along with substitution and assignment above, are as usual. Also familiar is the:

Rule of let-Declarations: If x is a variable of basic type, $BasE$ is an expression of the same type, and y a variable of the same type which is not free in P, Q, $BasE$ or Cmd, then

$$\frac{(P \wedge (y = BasE) \wedge (y \neq \bot))\{\, [y/x]Cmd\,\}Q}{P\{\,\mathbf{let}\; x\; \mathbf{be}\; BasE\; \mathbf{in}\; Cmd\; \mathbf{tel}\,\}Q\,.}$$

A command Cmd is *distributed* iff the block body of every procedure block which occurs in Cmd consists solely of a procedure call. Using rules like declaration distributivity (§2), one can easily transform any command Cmd into another distributed command $DIST(Cmd)$ which is equivalent to Cmd in all λ-calculus models. To ensure applicability of the preceding rules to procedure blocks, we include the:

Distributing Rule: If $Cmd = DIST(Cmd')$, then

$$\frac{P\{\,Cmd\,\}Q}{P\{\,Cmd'\,\}Q\,.}$$

We now enumerate the rules which rely on properties of support.

The usual rules of predicate calculus are applicable to first-order formulas with support predicates, treating $\mathbf{Support}(x,p)$ as a monadic first-order predicate in x for each variable p. We also use the axiom $\mathbf{Support}(x,y) \equiv (x = y \wedge y \neq \bot)$ when y is of type **loc**.

Rule of new declaration: Let $y^{\mathbf{loc}}, z^{\mathbf{int}}$ be variables not free in P, Q, or Cmd.

$$\frac{(([y := z]P) \wedge (\bigwedge_{p \in \mathcal{V}(Cmd) - \{x\}} \neg\mathbf{Support}(y,p)) \wedge (\mathbf{cont}(y) = \mathbf{a}_0))\{\,[y/x]Cmd\,\}([y := z]Q)}{P\{\,\mathbf{new}\ x\ \mathbf{in}\ Cmd\ \mathbf{wen}\,\}Q}$$

where $\mathcal{V}(Cmd)$ is the set of free variables of procedure and location type in Cmd. (Recall that $\mathbf{a}_0$ is the constant used for initialization.)

The two-sorted assertion language also yields descriptions of invariance (noninterference) among programs and properties. For example, if P implies that the truth of Q is invariant under changes to the contents of any of the locations in the support of Cmd, then Q holds before execution of Cmd iff it holds afterward. This gives the:

Rule of invariance:

$$\frac{P \Rightarrow \forall y^{\mathbf{loc}}[\bigvee_{p \in \mathcal{V}(Cmd)} \mathbf{Support}(y,p) \Rightarrow \mathbf{Invariant}(Q,y)])}{(P \wedge Q)\{\,Cmd\,\}Q\,.}$$

Here the assertion $\mathbf{Invariant}(Q,y)$ is an abbreviation for the first-order formula

$$\forall z^{\mathbf{int}}(Q \equiv [y \leftarrow z]Q)$$

where z is not free in Q. This means that Q is invariant under changes to the contents of y. We remark that invariance is the only rule whose soundness actually depends on the fact that environments use *finite*, as opposed to countable, supports.

Given a set of (mutual) procedure declarations E, let

(i) H_E be the first-order formula which asserts that any location which is in the support of one of the procedure identifiers declared in E is also in the support of one of identifiers of procedure or location type which is free in E,

(ii) $Del_E(Cmd) =_{def}$ the result of replacing in Cmd all occurrences of identifiers declared in E by the constant **diverge** denoting the divergent procedure,

(iii) $CpyExp_E(Cmd) =_{def}$ the result of expanding in Cmd all *outermost* calls of identifiers declared in E by the bodies declared for them as usual according to the copy-rule. In addition, actual parameters of outermost calls to global procedures not declared in E are also expanded.

Copy-Rule Induction:

$$\frac{(H_{E_j} \wedge P_j)\{\, Del_{E_j}(Cmd_j)\,\}Q_j \text{ for } j = 1, \ldots, n, \quad (H_{E_j} \wedge P_j)\{\, Cmd_j \,\}Q_j \,\Big|_{j=1}^{n} \vdash (H_{E_j} \wedge P_j)\{\, CpyExp_{E_j}(Cmd_j)\,\}Q_j \,\Big|_{j=1}^{n}}{P_j\{\, \mathbf{Proc}\, E_j\, \mathbf{do}\, Cmd_j\, \mathbf{end}\,\}Q_j \text{ for } j = 1, \ldots, n.}$$

Theorem. For store models D, only D-valid assertions can be proved with AX_D.

In fact, we prove that except for copy-rule induction, the system AX_D is semantically *sound* in the usual logical sense. Namely, an axiom A is sound iff it is valid, and an ordinary inference rule is sound iff, for any store model D and environment e using finite supports, the D, e-validity of its antecedents implies the D, e-validity of its consequent.

Natural deduction style rules of the form

$$\frac{A_1, \quad A_2 \vdash A_3}{A_4}$$

are semantically sound for D iff

if $D, e \models A_1$ for an environment e using finite supports,
and $\forall e'$ using finite supports ($D, e' \models A_2$ implies $D, e' \models A_3$),
then $D, e \models A_4$.

We can show that copy-rule induction is not sound in this sense. (It is sound providing there are no procedure parameters.) We justify the rule instead, following [Olderog, 1981], by showing that if the antecedents are true facts about provability in the particular system AX_D, then the consequent is valid, using special "syntax-directed" properties of AX_D.

It is impossible to find a sound and relatively complete axiomatization for partial correctness assertions about a language as powerful as PROG [Clarke, 1979]. Hence, in our full paper we define PROG′ – a fragment of PROG for which our axiom system is complete in the sense of [Cook, 1978]. Intuitively, this fragment captures commands which generate only a finite number of distinct calls (up to a renaming of first-order variables) when we expand them by replacing a call by its associated body, as in [Clarke, 1979; Olderog, 1981]. We give a direct syntactic condition sufficient to ensure that a program is in PROG′, and demonstrate that our axiom system is complete for as large a class of commands as any other systems in the current literature.

Theorem. AX_D is relatively complete (in the sense of Cook) for PROG′.

7. History. The thesis that λ-calculus underlies programming languages was first extensively argued in [Landin, 1965]. The general denotational approach to semantics which we pursue was developed by Strachey and Scott (cf. [Milne and Strachey, 1976; Scott,

1982]). [Reynolds, 1981a] emphasized the role of typed λ-calculus in explaining the procedure mechanism of ALGOL-like languages. [Damm and Fehr, 1980] and [Damm, 1982] were the first to use explicit translation to typed λ-calculus to analyze ALGOL procedures.

Our proof of equivalence of copy-rule and fixed-point semantics made use of denesting transformations, and seems easier than the corresponding proof in [Apt, 1978], which was for a simpler language (without procedure parameters). [Langmaack, 1973] has used transformations similar to our explicit parameterization and declaration denesting rules to show that a class of ALGOL-like programs can be denested under copy-rule semantics. [Damm, 1982] also contains a proof of the equivalence of copy-rule and fixed-point semantics for denested programs without global procedures.

A comprehensive survey of research on partial correctness of programs is given in [Apt, 1981] to which we refer the reader for a description of the pioneering work of Floyd, Hoare, Cook and Dijkstra. A thorough development of partial correctness for recursive programs with *basic* parameters only is given in [De Bakker, 1980]. De Bakker comes close to achieving the purely denotational approach we propose, though even he compromises in defining the semantics of recursive procedures syntactically. He handles free procedure variables and proves completeness using a fixed-point induction rule. [Harel, Pnueli and Stavi, 1977] keep to a pure denotational approach. However, neither De Bakker nor Harel, et. al. treats sharing (De Bakker requires that his environments be *injections* from identifiers to locations) or procedure parameters, and Harel, et. al. do not even treat blocks; these of course are the source of most of the problems considered in this paper.

Programs with higher-order procedures have been studied in [Langmaack and Olderog, 1980; Olderog, 1981] and more recently in [Damm and Josko, 1982]. Langmaack and Olderog consider an untyped programming language with a copy-rule semantics and independently obtain essentially the same completeness results we described above, restricting themselves to programs without global procedures. (This paper was written well after, and has benefited from, those of Langmaack and Olderog, as well as Damm and Fehr; however, the same ideas were discovered independently by the first author in Novosibirsk.) [German, Clarke, and Halpern, 1983] extend the operational approach to handle globals via closures. Damm and Josko give an axiomatization for a similar typed language with procedure parameters but without basic parameters, local storage, or sharing. They prove a completeness result, but only relative to a higher-order assertion language of uncertain power. Halpern has recently obtained such completeness results for PROG [Halpern, 1983].

[Olderog, 1981] handles sharing using equivalence classes of identifiers. Our approach distinguishing locations and storable values seems technically smoother and more intuitive. [Janssen and van Emde Boas, 1977] also advocate distinguishing locations and their contents, and develop assignment axioms similar to ours. [Schwartz, 1979] also makes the distinction and suggests some axioms for reasoning about sharing; however, he does not justify soundness nor examine completeness of his proposed axioms. Another approach to dealing with sharing is presented in [Cartwright and Oppen, 1981], but their programming language does not allow procedure parameters and places other restrictions on variables appearing in procedures; their assertion language also contains higher-order features such as quantification over sequences.

8. Conclusions. By explicitly translating ALGOL-like programs to expressions in typed λ-calculus with **letrec**, we have clarified the source of a rich mathematical structure of ALGOL-like programs which guides reasoning, both informally and with formal axiom systems, about side-effects.

The denotational approach identifies a half dozen different levels at which successive features of ALGOL-like languages can be explained. It will be interesting to see whether this mathematical classification serves as a useful guide for teaching such languages.

Although the main texts on denotational semantics gave the impression that the local storage discipline had been assigned a denotational semantics, we discovered none of them gave a "correct" semantics capturing the properties desired for the local storage discipline. Indeed, we argued that correct semantics for the local storage discipline could not be constructed using standard continuous models, but we indicated how to construct satisfactory ω-continuous store models for this discipline.

The one place where we have failed to keep to a purely denotational approach is in our use of copy-rule induction. We believe that this failing can be avoided.

Conjecture: Copy-rule induction can be replaced by fixed-point induction supplemented with a few additional semantically sound rules to yield a semantically sound proof system for partial correctness which is complete for at least as large a fragment of PROG as the current AX_D.

We see two natural next steps building on the work we have presented. The most apparent one is to axiomatize side-effect-free function procedures returning storable values, thereby eliminating the need for the two un-ALGOL-like restrictions imposed on PROG. (See [De Bakker, Klop, Meyer, 1982] for a careful development of functional procedures returning storable values in a language without blocks.) The other, more important step in our view, is to develop the partial correctness theory of commands with global procedure identifiers given partial correctness assertions about the globals.

If partial correctness assertions about arbitrary commands are allowed as hypotheses, then the distinction between partial and *total* correctness blurs. For example, if *Cmd* has no free variables, then it is *total* iff **true**{ Cmd }**false** implies **false**. No completeness theory (in the sense of Cook) of total correctness has been developed, and it appears that total completeness can only be proved relative to higher-order theories, e.g., weak second-order. However, it still seems possible to prove (relative) completeness if the assertions allowed as hypotheses are about "pure" procedure calls whose actual parameters contain neither blocks nor commands, and this would be quite interesting (cf. [Meyer and Mitchell, 1982]).

We mention one further open problem of particular interest to us. Note that the obstacles to axiomatizing partial correctness for all of PROG noted by [Clarke, 1979] do not apply if **new** declarations are forbidden.

Open problem: Can PROG – { **new** } be axiomatized (cf. [Damm and Josko, 1982])?

Acknowledgments. The first author benefited from discussions with his colleagues in Novosibirsk, particularly V. Yu. Sazonov, where the approach to using an imperative language and procedure mechanism based on a fully-typed call-by-name λ-calculus was crystallized. Conversations with J. Reynolds significantly influenced our understanding of types and local storage discipline in ALGOL-like languages. We thank W. Damm for many comments and references to related work; B. Josko, who pointed out the definitive counterexample to an earlier "static allocation" approach to **new** declarations; E. R. Olderog, for his meticulous comments and references for an earlier draft; G. Plotkin, for his elegant counterexamples to soundness of Clarke's procedure call axiom; and J. Mitchell, R. Schwartz, and R. Waldinger for comments. We are very grateful to Flavio Rose for expert help with TEX formatting.

References

K. R. Apt, Equivalence of operational semantics for a fragment of Pascal, in *Formal Descriptions of Programming Language Concepts*, E. J. Neuhold, ed., North Holland, 1978.

K. R. Apt, Ten years of Hoare's logic: a survey – part I, *ACM Trans. Programming Languages and Systems* 3, 1981, 431–483.

K. R. Apt, Ten years of Hoare's logic, a survey, part II: nondeterminism, *Foundations of Computer Science IV, Mathematical Center Tracts*, **159**, Mathematisch Centrum, Amsterdam, 1983, 101–132.

H. P. Barendregt, *The Lambda Calculus: Its Syntax and Semantics*, Studies in Logic **103**, North Holland, 1981.

R. Cartwright and D. Oppen, The logic of aliasing, *Acta Informatica* **15**, 1981, 365–384.

E. M. Clarke, Programming language constructs for which it is impossible to obtain good Hoare-like axioms, *J.ACM* **26**, 1979, 129–147.

S. A. Cook, Soundness and completeness of an axiom system for program verification, *SIAM J. Computing* **7**, 1978, 70–90.

W. Damm, The IO- and OI-hierarchies, *Theoretical Computer Science* **20**, 1982, 95–207.

W. Damm and E. Fehr, A schematological approach to the procedure concept of ALGOL-like languages, *Proc. 5ieme colloque sur les arbres en algebre et en programmation*, Lille, 1980, 130-134.

W. Damm and B. Josko, A sound and relatively* complete Hoare-logic for a language with higher type procedures, Lehrstuhl fur Informatik II, RWTH Aachen, Bericht No. 77, 1982, 94pp.

J. De Bakker, *Mathematical Theory of Program Correctness*, Prentice-Hall International, 1980, 505pp.

J. De Bakker, J. W. Klop, and J.-J.Ch. Meyer, Correctness of programs with function procedures, *Logics of Programs*, D. Kozen, ed., Lecture Notes in Computer Science **131**, Springer, 1982, 94–112.

S. German, E. Clarke, and J. Halpern, Reasoning about procedures as parameters, 1983, *this volume.*

I. Guessarian, Survey on some classes of interpretations and some their applications, Laboratoire Informatique Theorique et Programmation, 82-46, Univ. Paris 7, 1982.

G. A. Gorelick, A complete axiom system for proving assertions about recursive and non-recursive programs, University of Toronto, Computer Science Dept. TR–75, 1975.

J. Y. Halpern, A good Hoare axiom system for an ALGOL-like language, 1983, to appear.

D. Harel, A. Pnueli, and J. Stavi, A complete axiomatic system for proving deductions about recursive programs, *Proc.* 9th *ACM Symp. Theory of Computing*, 1977, 249–260.

C. A. R. Hoare, An axiomatic basis for computer programming, *Comm. ACM*, **12**, 1969, 576–580.

T. M. V. Janssen and P. van Emde Boas, On the proper treatment of referencing, dereferencing and assignment, 4th *Int'l. Coll. Automata, Languages, and Programming*, Lecture Notes in Computer Science **52**, Springer, 1977, 282-300.

P. J. Landin, A correspondence between ALGOL 60 and Church's lambda notation, *Comm. ACM* **8**, 1965, 89-101 and 158-165.

H. Langmaack, On procedures as open subroutines, *Acta Informatica* **2**, 1973, 311–333.

H. Langmaack and E. R. Olderog, Present-day Hoare-like systems, 7th *Int'l. Coll. Automata, Languages, and Programming*, Lecture Notes in Computer Science **85**, Springer, 1980, 363–373.

Z. Manna and R. Waldinger, Problematic features of programming languages: a situational-calculus approach, *Acta Informatica* **16**, 1981, 371–426.

J. Meseguer, Completions, factorizations and colimits of ω-posets, *Coll. Math. Soc. Janos Bolyai* **26**. *Math. Logic in Computer Science*, Salgotarjan, Hungary, 1978, 509-545.

A. R. Meyer, What is a model of the λ-calculus? *Information and Control* **52**, 1982, 87–122.

A. R. Meyer and J. C. Mitchell, Axiomatic definability and completeness for recursive programs, 9th *ACM Symposium on Principles of Programming Languages*, 1982, 337–346. Revised as: Termination assertions for recursive programs: completeness and axiomatic definability, MIT/LCS/TM-214, MIT, Cambridge, Massachusetts, March, 1982; to appear *Information and Control*, 1982.

R. E. Milne and C. Strachey, *A Theory of Programming Language Semantics*, 2 Vols., Chapman and Hall, 1976.

P. Naur et al., Revised report on the algorithmic language ALGOL 60, *Computer J.* **5**, 1963, 349–367.

E. R. Olderog, Sound and complete Hoare-like calculi based on copy rules, *Acta Informatica* **16**, 1981, 161–197.

E. R. Olderog, A characterization of Hoare's logic for programs with Pascal-like procedures, *Proc.* 15th *ACM Symp. Theory of Computing*, 1983a, 320-329.

E. R. Olderog, Hoare's logic for program with procedures – what has been accomplished?, *Proc. Logics of Programs*, Carnegie-Mellon Univ., Pittsburgh, 1983, *to appear, Lecture Notes in Computer Science*, Springer, 1983b.

F. J. Oles, Type algebras, functor categories, and block structure, Computer Science Dept., Aarhus Univ. DAIMI PB-156, Denmark, Jan. 1983.

G. D. Plotkin, A Powerdomain for countable non-determinism, 9th *Int'l. Coll. Automata, Languages, and Programming*, Lecture Notes in Computer Science **140**, Springer, 1982, 412–428.

J. C. Reynolds, The essence of ALGOL, *International Symposium on Algorithmic Languages*, de Bakker and van Vliet, eds., North Holland, 1981a, 345–372.

J. C. Reynolds, The Craft of Programming, Prentice Hall International Series in Computer Science, 1981b, 434pp.

J. C. Reynolds, Idealized ALGOL and its specification logic, Syracuse University, Technical Report 1-81, 1981c.

R. L. Schwartz, An axiomatic treatment of ALGOL 68 Routines, 6th *Int'l. Coll. Automata, Languages and Programming*, Lecture Notes in Computer Science **71**, Springer, 1979, 530–545.

D. S. Scott, Domains for Denotational Semantics, 9th *Int'l. Conf. Automata, Languages, and Programming*, Lecture Notes in Computer Science **140**, Springer, 1982, 577–613; to appear, *Information and Control*.

J. E. Stoy, *Denotational Semantics: The Scott-Strachey Approach to Programming Language Theory*, MIT Press, Cambridge, Massachusetts, 1977.

B. A. Trakhtenbrot, On relaxation rules in algorithmic logic, *Mathematical Foundations of Computer Science 1979*, (J. Becvar, ed.), Lecture Notes in Computer Science **74**, Springer, 1979, 453–462.

Cambridge, Massachusetts
October 3, 1983

Yet Another Process Logic

(Preliminary Version)

Moshe Y. Vardi[†]

Stanford University

Pierre Wolper[‡]

Bell Laboratories

ABSTRACT

We present a process logic that differs from the one introduced by Harel, Kozen and Parikh in several ways. First, we use the extended temporal logic of Wolper for statements about paths. Second, we allow a "repeat" operator in the programs. This allows us to specify programs with infinite computations. However, we limit the interaction between programs and path statements by adopting semantics similar to the ones used by Nishimura. Also, we require atomic programs to be interpreted as binary relations. We argue that this gives us a more appropriate logic. We have obtained an elementary decision procedure for our logic. The time complexity of the decision procedure is four exponentials in the general case and two exponentials if the logic is restricted to finite paths.

1. Introduction

While *dynamic logic* [Pr76] has proven to be a very useful tool to reason about the input/output behavior of programs, it has become clear that it is not adequate for reasoning about the ongoing behavior of programs. In view of this, Pratt [Pr78] introduced a *process logic,* that extended dynamic logic with the connectives "during" and "throughout". Parikh [Pa78] chose to extend dynamic logic with quantification over computation paths. His logic, *SOAPL*, is strictly more expressive than Pratt's [Ha79].

At the same time, a different approach was taken by Pnueli, who developed a *temporal logic,* called *TL* [Pn77]. *TL* is oriented towards reasoning about the ongoing behavior of programs, but does not allow programs to be mentioned explicitly. In dynamic logic, on the other hand, the programs are an essential part of the formulas.

---

† Research supported by a Weizmann Post-Doctoral Fellewship and AFOSR grant 80-12907. Address: IBM Research Laboratory, 5600 Cottle Rd., San Jose CA 95193.

‡ Address: Bell Laboratories, 600 Mountain Ave., Murray Hill, NJ 07974.

Nishimura [Ni80] suggested combining the two approaches. The essence of his logic is that computation paths are specified by referring to programs explicitly, as in dynamic logic, and temporal logic is used to specify temporal properties of these computation paths. He showed that his logic, while its syntax is much cleaner than that of *SOAPL*, is at least as expressive as the latter. This approach was continued by Harel et al. [HKP80]. They extended Nishimura's logic by removing his distinction between *state formulas* and *path formulas*. Moreover, their logic, called *PL*, is defined in such a way that it is a direct extension of dynamic logic.

We contend that *PL* is not an adequate logic of processes, since it is at the same time too powerful and not powerful enough. Let us first see why *PL* is not powerful enough.

PL uses Pnueli's *TL* for its temporal part. *TL*, however, is equivalent [GPSS80] to the first-order theory of $(N,<)$, the natural numbers with the less-than relation, and consequently cannot specify arbitrary regular properties. Thus, from that aspect, the temporal part of *PL* is weaker than its dynamic part (see also [Wo81,HP82]). Another weakness of *PL* is its limited ability to deal with non-terminating processes, e.g., operating systems. Such processes often run by repeatedly executing the same program. *PL*, however, cannot specify the infinite repetition of programs, while reasoning about non-terminating processes was a primary motivation for introducing process logics.

Let us now see in what aspects *PL* is too powerful. The interpretation of an atomic program in *PL* is an arbitrary set of paths. But in practice the interpretation of an atomic program is never an arbitrary set of paths but rather a binary relation, i.e., a set of paths of length two, consisting of the initial state and the final state. Even if one wants to consider a higher-level program as atomic, the interpretation of such a program should not be an arbitrary set of paths.

Finally, we believe that the distinction between state formulas and path formulas is inherent to our thinking about processes. A computation path is characterized by the properties of its states, and a state is characterized by the properties of the paths that start from it. The results of removing this distinction are not very intuitive. Consider the *PL* formula $[\alpha]$*someP*, where α is a program and P is an atomic proposition. While we want it to mean that all computations of α eventually satisfy P, it actually is true of all paths that either eventually satisfy P or can be extended by a computation of α that eventually satisfies P. The artificiality of the latter statement is self-evident. This comes as a result of the desire to have *PL* extend dynamic logic in a direct way. In our opinion, any attempt to have a logic for ongoing behavior that directly extends a logic for input/output behavior will lead to artificial results.

The logic that we introduce in this paper, which we call *YAPL* (yet another process logic) for lack of a better name, is an attempt at solving all these problems. Its temporal part is extended to deal with regular properties using the *extended temporal logic* (*ETL*) described in [WVS83] following [Wo81], it can specify the infinite repetition of programs, its atomic programs are interpreted as binary relations, and the distinction between state and path formulas is maintained. Moreover, our logic has an elementary decision procedure. Validity can be decided in two exponentials if we consider only finite paths and in four exponentials if we also consider infinite paths. Our decision procedure is based on a translation from *YAPL* to a variant of *propositional dynamic logic* (*PDL*) [FL79] in the case of finite paths and to a variant of Streett's *ΔPDL* [St81] in the case of infinite paths.

2. Definitions

2.1. Propositional Dynamic Logic with Repeat

We first consider the *propositional dynamic logic of flowcharts* (*APDL*) defined in [Pr81]. It differs from *PDL* [FL79] in having programs specified by automata rather than by regular expressions. It is defined as follows:

Syntax

Formulas are defined from a set of atomic propositions *Prop* and a set *Prog* of atomic programs. The sets of formulas and programs are defined inductively as follows:

- every element $p \in Prop$ is a formula.
- if f_1 and f_2 are formulas, then $\sim f_1$ and $f_1 \wedge f_2$ are formulas.
- if α is a program and f is a formula, then $<\alpha>f$ is a formula
- If α is a nondeterministic finite automaton (nfa) over an alphabet Σ, where Σ is a finite subset of $Prog \cup \{f? \mid f \text{ is a formula}\}$, then α is a program.

Semantics

An *APDL* structure is a triple $M=(S,R,\Pi)$ where S is a set of states, $R: Prog \rightarrow 2^{S \times S}$ assigns binary relations on states to atomic programs, and $\Pi: S \rightarrow 2^{Prop}$ assigns truth values to the propositions in *Prop* for each state in S. The function R is extended to all programs by the following definition:

- $R(f?)=\{(s,s):s\models f\}$.
- $R(\alpha)=\{(s,s')\}$ such that there exists a word $w=w_0w_1 \cdots w_n$ accepted by α and states $s_0,s_1, \ldots ,s_{n+1}$ such that $s=s_0$, $s'=s_{n+1}$ and for all $0 \le i \le n$ we have $(s_i,s_{i+1}) \in R(w_i)$.

Satisfaction in a state s of the structure M is then defined as follows:

- for a proposition $p \in Prop$, $s \models p$ iff $p \in \Pi(s)$.
- $s \models f_1 \wedge f_2$ iff $s \models f_1$ and $s \models f_2$.
- $s \models \sim f_1$ iff not $s \models f_1$.
- $s \models <\alpha>f$ iff there exists a state s' such that $(s,s') \in R(\alpha)$ and $s' \models f$.

Even though *APDL* is exponentially more succinct than *PDL* its validity problem has the same complexity [Pr81,HS83]:

Proposition 2.1: Validity for *APDL* can be decided in time $O(exp(n))$. □

We also use Δ*APDL*, which is to *APDL* what Δ*PDL* [St81] is to *PDL*. That is, a new logical construct denoting infinite repetition is added:

- if α is a program, then $\Delta\alpha$ is a formula,

with the semantics:

- $s \models \Delta\alpha$ iff there exists an infinite sequence $s_0,s_1, \ldots$ of states such that $s_0=s$ and for all $n \ge 0$ we have $(s_n,s_{n+1}) \in R(\alpha)$.

The decision procedure given in [St81] for Δ*PDL* can be adapted to Δ*APDL*. We thus have the following:

Proposition 2.2: Validity for Δ*APDL* can be decided in time $O(exp^3(n))$. □

2.2. Extended Temporal Logic

The temporal part of our process logic will be a propositional temporal logic where the temporal connectives are defined by nondeterministic finite automata (nfa). Note that the logic defined in [Wo81] uses looping automata. Looping automata differ from nfa by not having accepting states. They accepts only infinite words: an infinite word w is accepted by a looping automaton A if there exists an infinite run of A on w. For a more detailed study of these logics see [WVS83].

Formulas of *ETL* are built from a set *Prop* of atomic propositions by means of:

- Boolean connectives
- Automata connectives. That is, every halting automaton A over an alphabet $\Sigma=\{a_1, \ldots, a_n\}$ is considered as an n-ary temporal connective. That is, if $f_1, \ldots, f_n$ are formulas, then so is $A(f_1, \ldots, f_n)$.

A structure for *ETL* is a finite or infinite sequence of truth assignments, i.e., a function $\sigma: m \rightarrow 2^{Prop}$ or $\sigma: \omega \rightarrow 2^{Prop}$ that assigns truth values to the atomic propositions in each state. For a state i of a sequence σ, satisfaction of a formula f, denoted $i \models_\sigma f$, is defined inductively as follows:

- for an atomic proposition p, $i \models_\sigma p$ iff $p \in \sigma(i)$.
- $i \models_\sigma f_1 \wedge f_2$ iff $i \models_\sigma f_1$ and $i \models_\sigma f_2$.
- $i \models_\sigma \sim f$ iff not $i \models_\sigma f$.

For the automata connectives we have:

- $i \models_\sigma A(f_1, \ldots, f_n)$

if and only if there is a word $w=a_{i_0}a_{i_1} \cdots a_{i_m}$ $(1 \le i_j \le n)$ accepted by A such that, for all $0 \le j \le m$, $i+j \models_\sigma f_{i_j}$.

2.3. YAPL

Our process logic (*YAPL*) includes both state and path formulas. Essentially, a state formula is either a formula concerning a single state or specifies that the execution paths of a given program started in that state must satisfy some path formula. A path formula is an *ETL* formula built from state formulas. More precisely, we have the following:

Syntax

We consider formulas built from:

- A set *Prop* of atomic propositions $p,q,r,\ldots$
- A set *Prog* of atomic programs $a,b,c,\ldots$

We now define inductively the set of state formulas, path formulas, and programs. We start with state formulas:

- An atomic proposition $p \in Prop$ is a state formula.
- If f_1 and f_2 are state formulas, then $f_1 \wedge f_2$ and $\neg f_1$ are also state formulas.

- If α is a program (halting or repeating) and f is a path formula, then $\ll\alpha\gg f$ is a state formula.

We now define path formulas:

- A state formula is also a path formula.
- If f_1 and f_2 are path formulas, then $f_1 \wedge f_2$ and $\neg f_1$ are also path formulas.
- If $f_1,\ldots,f_n$ are path formulas, and A is an n-ary ETL automaton connective, then $A(f_1,\ldots,f_n)$ is a path formula.

Finally, we define programs:

- If A is an nfa over an alphabet Σ, where Σ is a finite subset of $Prog \cup \{f? \mid f \text{ is a state formula}\}$, then α is a halting program.
- If A is a Buchi automaton[†] (ba) over an alphabet Σ, where Σ is a finite subset of $Prog \cup \{f? \mid f \text{ is a state formula}\}$, then α is a repeating program.

The notion of program in *YAPL* is more general than in *APDL* or *ΔAPDL*. It can be either a regular (for halting programs) or ω-regular (for repeating programs) set of execution sequences. For simplicity we assume that the words accepted by programs consist of alternations of tests ($f?$) and atomic programs, starting with a test and, for finite words, also ending with a test. There is no loss of generality, since consecutive tests can be merged and vacuous tests can be inserted.

Semantics

A *YAPL* structure is a triple $M=(S,R,\Pi)$ where S is a set of states, $R:Prog\to 2^{S\times S}$ assigns a set of binary paths to atomic programs, and $\Pi:S\to 2^{Prop}$ assigns truth values to the propositions in *Prop* for each state in S.

Note that a *YAPL* structre is essentially a *PDL* structure. However, atomic programs are viewed as sets of binary paths, rather than binary relations. This gives rise to a different way of extending R to arbitrary programs. R assigns to each program a set of paths, i.e., a subset of S^* or a subset of S^ω. Let α be a program, and let $\sigma=s_1,\ldots,s_n,\ldots$ be a path, i.e, a sequence of states of S. The path σ belongs to $R(\alpha)$ if and only if there is a word $f_1?a_1,\ldots,f_n?a_n,\ldots$ in α such that $s_i \models f_i$ and $(s_i,s_{i+1})\in R(a_i)$.

[†] A Buchi automaton [Bu62] over an alphabet Σ is a quadruple $(S,s_0,delta,R)$, where S is a set of states, $s_0\in S$ is the initial state, $\delta:S\times\Sigma\to 2^S$ is the transition table, and $R\subseteq S$ is a set of repetition states. An infinite word w is accepted by A if there is a run r of A on w such that some state of R occurs infinitely often in r.

For state formulas, satisfaction in a state s is defined as follows:

- for a proposition $p \in Prop$, we have $s \models p$ iff $p \in \Pi(s)$.
- $s \models f_1 \wedge f_2$ iff $s \models f_1$ and $s \models f_2$.
- $s \models \sim f_1$ iff not $s \models f_1$.
- $s \models \ll\alpha\gg f$ iff there exists a path $p \in R(\alpha)$ starting in s such that $s \models_p f$.

For path formulas satisfaction in a state s_i on a path $p=(s_0, \ldots, s_i, \ldots)$ is defined as in *ETL*:

- for a state formula f, $s_i \models_p f$ iff $s_i \models f$.
- $s_i \models_p f_1 \wedge f_2$ iff $s_i \models_p f_1$ and $s_i \models_p f_2$.
- $s_i \models_p \sim f$ iff not $s_i \models_p f$.

For the automata connectives we have:

- $s_i \models_p A(f_1, \ldots, f_n)$

if and only if there is a word $w=a_{i_0}a_{i_1} \cdots a_{i_m}$ $(1 \le i_j \le n)$ accepted by A such that, for all $0 \le j \le m$, $s_{i+j} \models_p f_{i_j}$.

3. Translation from *YAPL* to *ΔAPDL* and Decision Procedures

Our goal is to show that every state formula of *YAPL* can be translated into an equivalent formula of *ΔAPDL*. The translation is done in two steps. First, we translate *YAPL* into a restricted version of itself. This version, called $YAPL_*$, does not contain any path formulas except for the formula *true*, which is satisfied by all paths. Then, we show that $YAPL_*$, can be translated into *ΔAPDL*.

To give the translation, we need to show how a *YAPL* formula of the form $\ll\alpha\gg g$, where α is a program and g is an *ETL* formula can be translated into a formula of the form $\ll\alpha\gg true$. The path formula g can describe both finite and infinite paths. Our first step is to separate these two cases. In [WVS83] it is shown how one can construct, given g, a ba A_i, whose size is at most exponential in the length of g, that accepts the infinite models of g. In a similar manner one can construct, given g, a nfa A_f, whose size is at most exponential in the length of g, that accepts the finite models of g. Thus if α is a halting program and β is a repeating program, then $\ll\alpha\gg g$ is equivalent to $\ll\alpha\gg A_f$ and $\ll\beta\gg g$ is equivalent to $\ll\beta\gg A_i$. (Strictly speaking, these are not formulas of the language, since A_f and A_i are not path formulas. However, they can be viewed as such, since they describe paths.) Since nfa and ba have a similar structure, it suffices to consider formulas of the form $\ll\alpha\gg A$, where α and A can either both be nfa or both be ba.

Recall that the words accepted by α are alternations of tests and atomic programs, starting with a test. Thus, we will assume that α is of the form $\alpha=(S_1 \cup S_2, s_0, \delta_\alpha, R)$. The states in S_1 are what we call the test states and the states in S_2 are what we call the atomic program states. The distinction between the two types of states is that all edges leaving a test state are labeled by a test and lead to an atomic program state and all edges leaving an atomic program state are labeled by an atomic program and lead to a test state. The initial state is a test state. If α is a nfa, then the accepting states R are also test states.

Consider now the path automaton A. It is defined over the state subformulas of g. In other words it can be viewed as defined over tests. Let A be (Q, q_0, δ_g, P). What we want to do now is to combine the automata α and A into a single automaton. If the resulting automaton is α', then the translation of $\ll\alpha\gg f$ into *YAPL*, will be $\ll\alpha'\gg$*true*.

The idea of the combination of the two automata, is that we want to incorporate into the automaton α the conditions imposed by the automaton A. The construction proceeds as follows. The states of α' are

$$Q \times (S_1 \cup S_2)$$

To define the transitions, we consider separately members of $Q \times S_1$ and $Q \times S_2$. We denote by s_1 a generic element of S_1 and similarly for s_2.

- There is a transition from a state (q, s_1) to a state (q', s_2) labeled by $test_1 \wedge test_2$ iff there is a transition from q to q' labeled by $test_1$ and a transition from s_1 to s_2 labeled by $test_2$.
- There is a transition from a state (q, s_2) to a state (q, s_1) labeled by an atomic program a iff there is a transition from s_2 to s_1 labeled by a.
- There are no other transitions.

We still have to make sure that the acceptance conditions for α and A are satisfied. Consider first the case that both α and A are nfa. In this case the sets R and P are sets of accepting states. Thus, the set of accepting states for α' is $P \times R$. Consider now the case that α and A are ba. For α, the acceptance condition for a word w is that the intersection of R with the set of states appearing infinitely often when w is fed to the automaton ($inf(w)$) is nonempty. Thus, for α' we require that the intersection of w with the set of states $R_1=\{(q,s) | q \in Q \wedge s \in R\}$ is non-empty. We also have to check that the acceptance condition for A is satisfied. Thus we require that the intersection of

$inf(w)$ with $R_2=\{(q,s)|q\in P\wedge s\in S_1\cup S_2\}$ is non-empty. So, the acceptance condition for α' is that the intersection of $inf(w)$ with R_1 and R_2 is non-empty.

Unfortunately, the condition we have just expressed is no longer a Buchi acceptance condition, so our automaton α' is not a ba. Fortunately, we can transform α' into an ba α'' that is a ba by simply doubling its size. The construction, which improves a construction in [Ch74], is actually general and can be applied to any automaton on infinite strings where acceptance of a word w is defined by requiring a nonempty intersection of $inf(w)$ with many given sets.

Let us consider an automaton $A=(S,s_0,\delta)$ with two repetition sets R_1 and R_2. The construction builds an automaton A'. The automaton A' has two states for every state of S. We will denote its states by $S\cup S'$ where S' is a copy of S. Let R_2' be the corresponding copy of R_2. The transitions of A' are the same as those of A, except that a transition from a state of R_1 is replaced by a transition to a state of S' (rather than to a state of S) and a transition from a state of R_2' is replaced by a transition to a state of S (rather than a state of S'). A word w is then accepted by A' if the intersection of $inf(w)$ and R_1 is nonempty.

So far we have translated formulas of *YAPL* to formulas of $YAPL_*$. Consider now the $YAPL_*$ formula $\ll\alpha\gg true$, where α is a halting program. It is easy to verify that this formulas is equivalent to the *APDL* formula $<\alpha>true$. So it remains to deal with formulas $\ll\alpha\gg true$, where α is a repeating program. Let α be (S,s_0,δ,R), with $R=\{r_1,\ldots,r_k\}$. Let α_i be the infinite program $(S,s_0,\delta,\{r_i\})$. It is easy to see that $\ll\alpha\gg true$ is equivalent to $\bigvee_{i=1}^{k}\ll\alpha_i\gg true$. Furthermore, let β_i be the finite program, $(S,s_0,\delta,\{r_i\})$, and let γ_i be the infinite program $(S,r_i,\delta,\{r_i\})$. Then $\ll\alpha_i\gg true$ is equivalent to the $\Delta APDL$ formula $<\beta_i>\Delta\gamma_i$. This completes the translation.

Let us consider now the complexity of the translation. Translating the *ETL* formula g into an automaton takes exponential time, and the size of the automaton is exponential in the length of g. Thus the translation from *YAPL* to $YAPL_*$ is exponential. The translation from $YAPL_*$ to $\Delta APDL$ is quadratic. It follows that the translation from *YAPL* to $\Delta APDL$ is exponential. Given proposition 2.2, we have proven:

Theorem 3.1: Validity for *YAPL* can be decided in $O(\exp^4(n))$. □

Consider now a restricted version of *YAPL*, denoted $YAPL_t$, that deals with terminating processes. There are no repeating programs in $YAPL_t$. Thus programs are always given as nfa. Hence, we need to consider only finite paths. The result of this restriction is that we never have to deal with ba. The translation given above is now an exponential translation of $YAPL_t$ into *APDL*. We have proven:

Theorem 3.2: Validity for $YAPL_t$ can be decided in $O(\exp^2(n))$. □

4. Results on Branching Time Temporal Logics

In [EH82] a branching time temporal logic called *CTL** was introduced. In *CTL** paths are described by *TL* formulas, and state formulas are obtained by quantifying over paths. That is, if f is a *TL* formula that decribes paths, then $\exists f$ is a state formula that is satisfied in a state s if there is a path p starting at s that satisfies f. We can generalize the definition of *CTL** and define a new logic, *ECTL**, that is similar to *CTL**, but uses *ETL* rather than *TL* formulas to describe paths. *ECTL** (and hence *CTL**) are interpreted over structures similar to the ones used for *YAPL*. The only difference is that for the branching time temporal logics, there is only one (implicit) atomic program. Moreover, *ECTL** can be easily translated into *YAPL*.

Let us call the implicit atomic program in the temporal formulas a. Let α be the halting program a^*, and let β be the repeating program a^ω. It is easy to see that the *ECTL** formula $\exists f$ is equivalent to the *YAPL* formula $\ll\alpha\gg f \vee \ll\beta\gg f$. This gives an exponential translation from *ECTL** to *YAPL*. Combining this translation with the above translation of *YAPL* to *ΔAPDL* still gives us an exponential translation from *ECTL** to *ΔPDL* as the two exponentials do not combine. Given proposition 2.2, it follows:

Theorem 4.1: Validity for *ECTL** can be decided in $O(\exp^4(n))$. □

This also solves the validity problem for *CTL**, which was left open in [EH82].

5. Concluding Remarks

Our results raise some interesting questions about *PL* [HKP]. Let *EPL* be *PL* with two additions. First, instead of using *TL* formulas to describe paths, we use *ETL* formulas. With this addition the logic is equivalent to Harel and Peleg's *RPL* [HP82], so as shown there it is more expressive than *PL*. Secondly, rather than having only regular programs we have both regular and ω-regular programs. We ask:

1. Is *EPL* more expressive than *RPL*?

2. Is the validity problem for *EPL* decidable?

We can answer both question in the affirmative if atomic programs are interpreted as binary relations, and we believe that this is also the answer for the general case.

A more interesting question in our opinion concerns the right interpretation of atomic programs. We have argued that atomic programs should be interpreted as binary relations. One, however, may wish to reason on several levels of granularity, and what might be atomic at one level is not always atomic at a higher level. This motivates interpreting atomic programs as sets of paths. Interpreting atomic programs as arbitrary sets of paths is, nevertheless, still not justified. At the most refined level of granularity, atomic programs are binary relations. Since higher-level programs are (ω)-regular combinations of atomic programs, we should consider only sets of paths that arise from (ω)-regular combinations of binary relations.

From this point of view, an atomic program in the logic is a scheme standing for all (ω)-regular programs. We think this is worth investigating further.

6. References

[Bu62] J. R. Buchi, "On a Decision Method in Restricted Second Order Arithmetic", *Proc. Internat. Congr. Logic, Method and Philos. Sci. 1960,* Stanford University Press, 1962, pp. 1-12.

[Ch74] Y. Choueka, "Theories of Automata on ω-Tapes: A Simplified Approach", *Journal of Computer and System Sciences,* 8 (1974), pp. 117-141.

[EH82] E. A. Emerson, J. Y. Halpern,"Sometimes and Not Never Revisited: On Branching Versus Linear Time", *Proceedings of the 10th Symposium on Principles of Programming Languages,* Austin, January 1983.

[FL79] M. Fisher, R. Ladner, "Propositional Dynamic Logic of Regular Programs", *Journal of Computer and System Sciences,* 18(2), 1979, pp. 194-211.

[GPSS80] D. Gabbay, A. Pnueli, S. Shelah and J. Stavi, "The Temporal Analysis of Fairness", *Seventh ACM Symposium on Principles of Programming Languages,* Las Vegas, January 1980, pp. 163-173.

[Ha79] D. Harel, "Two Results on Process Logic", *Information Processing Letters,* 8 (1979), pp. 195--198.

[HKP80] D. Harel, D. Kozen, R. Parikh, "Process Logic: Expressiveness, Decidability, Completeness", *Proceedings of the 21st Symposium on Foundations of Computer Science*, Syracuse, October 1980, pp. 129-142.

[HP82] D. Harel, D. Peleg, "Process logic with Regular Formulas", Technical Report, Bar-Ilan University, Ramat-Gan, Israel, 1982.

[Ni80] H. Nishimura, "Descriptively Complete Process Logic", *Acta Informatica*, 14 (1980), pp. 359-369.

[Pa78] R. Parikh, "A Decidability Result for a Second Order Process Logic", *Proceedings 19th IEEE Symposium on Foundations of Computer Science*, Ann Arbor, October 1978.

[Pn77] A. Pnueli, "The Temporal Logic of Programs", *Proceedings of the Eighteenth Symposium on Foundations of Computer Science*, Providence, November 1977, pp. 46-57.

[Pr76] V.R. Pratt, "Semantical Considerations on Floyd-Hoare Logic", *Proceedings 17th IEEE Symposium on Foundations of Computer Science*, Houston, October 1976, pp. 109-121.

[Pr78] V.R. Pratt, "A Practical Decision Method for Propositional Dynamic Logic", *Proceedings 10th ACM Symposium on Theory of Computing*, San Diego, May 1979, pp. 326-337.

[Pr81] V.R. Pratt, "Using Graphs to understand PDL", *Proceedings of the Workshop on Logics of Programs*, Yorktown-Heights, Springer-Verlag Lecture Notes in Computer Science, vol. 131, Berlin, 1982, pp. 387-396.

[St81] R. Streett, "Propositional Dynamic Logic of Looping and Converse", *Proceedings of the 13th Symposium on Theory of Computing*, Milwaukee, May 1981, pp. 375-383.

[Wo81] P. Wolper, "Temporal Logic Can Be More Expressive", *Proceedings of the Twenty-Second Symposium on Foundations of Computer Science*, Nashville, October 1981, pp. 340-348.

[WVS83] P. Wolper, M. Y. Vardi, A. P. Sistla, "Reasoning about Infinite Computation Paths", to appear in *Proceedings 24th IEEE Symp. on Foundation of Computer Science*, Tuscon, Nov. 1983.

A PROOF SYSTEM FOR PARTIAL CORRECTNESS OF DYNAMIC NETWORKS OF PROCESSES

(Extended abstract)

Job Zwiers (*)
Arie de Bruin (**)
Willem Paul de Roever (***)

(*) Department of Computer Science, University of Nijmegen, Toernooiveld, 6525 ED Nijmegen, the Netherlands

(**) Faculty of Economics, Erasmus University, P.O. Box 1738, 3000 DR Rotterdam, the Netherlands

(***) Department of Computer Science, University of Nijmegen, and Department of Computer Science, University of Utrecht, P.O. Box 80.002, 3508 TA Utrecht, the Netherlands

Introduction

A dynamically changing network is a set of processes, executing in parallel and communicating via interconnecting channels, in which processes can expand into subnetworks. This expansion is recursive in the sense that the so formed subnetwork can contain new copies of the expanding process. After all component processes of a subnetwork have terminated, the expanded process contracts (shrinks) again and continues its execution. We define a simple language, called dynamic CSP, which can describe such networks. We introduce a formal proof system for the partial correctness of dynamic CSP programs. The proof system is built upon a new type of correctness formulae, inspired by Misra and Chandy [MC], which allow for modular specifications c.q. proof of properties of a network. In the full paper, the proof system is shown to be sound with respect to a denotational semantics for the language.

Acknowledgements

We are indebted to many people for their helpful comments. we would like to thank P. van Emde Boas, J.W. de Bakker and especially R. Gerth for clarifying discussions.

1. The language

First we give the context free syntax of dynamic CSP.
In this syntax, x and u stand for program variables, D and E for channel variables, P for procedure names, s for expressions and b for boolean expressions.

Statements:

$S ::= x{:=}s \mid \underline{skip} \mid b \mid D?x \mid D!s \mid$
$\quad S_1;S_2 \mid [S_1 \,\square\, S_2] \mid \underline{cobegin}\ N\ \underline{coend} \mid$
$\quad P(E_{in-1},\ldots,E_{in-k};E_{out-1},\ldots,E_{out-l};u_1,\ldots,u_m)$

Networks:

$N ::= S_1 \| S_2$

Procedure declarations:

$\quad P(D_{in-1},\ldots,D_{in-k};D_{out-1},\ldots,D_{out-l};x_1,\ldots,x_m)\ \underline{begin}\ S\ \underline{end}$

Programs:

$R ::= T_1,\ldots,T_n : \underline{begin}\ S\ \underline{end}$

The intuitive meaning of x:=s, skip and $S_1;S_2$ should be clear. $[S_1 \,\square\, S_2]$ stands for nondeterministic choice between S_1 and S_2. Boolean expressions are incorporated as statements. They function as "guards": whenever b evaluates to "true", the guard can be passed, i.e. it is equivalent to "skip" in this case. When b evaluates to "false" the guard cannot be passed and the computation is aborted. Because we are only interested in partial correctness ("...if a program reaches (a) certain point(s) then..."), a more familiar construct as if b then S_1 else S_2 fi can be expressed in our language as $[b;S_1 \,\square\, \neg b;S_2]$. We will freely use such "derived" constructs in our examples. A network $S_1 \| S_2$ calls for concurrent execution of S_1 and S_2. In such a network, S_1 and S_2 are not allowed to have "shared" program variables. The two component processes of a network can communicate with each other (only) along named, directed channels. Communication along a channel, say "D", occurs when an output command "D!s" is executed by one of the component processes simultaneously, i.e. synchronized, with an input command "D?x" of the other one. The value of s is then assigned to the program variable x and both processes continue their execution. In dynamic CSP, channels always connect exactly two processes. So a process cannot read from and write to one and the same channel, nor are two processes allowed to both read from or both write to some common channel. A channel from which some process reads or to which it writes is called an external input- or output channel of that process. When two processes are bound together into a network, their common channels, along which they communicate, are said to be internal channels of the network. The concepts of internal and external channels are important to the modularity of our proof system. When dealing with "nested" networks, i.e. networks as $S_1 \| S_2$ in which S_1 and S_2 are themselves (or contain) subnetworks, it is possible that some subnetwork has an internal channel with the same name as some channel of the main network. This is even unavoidable when the subnetwork and the main network belong to different incarnations of the same procedure body in case of a recursive procedure call. Such channel name "clashes" are resolved by introducing a kind of block structure with the cobegin - coend construct, which "hides" internal channels, i.e. no internal channel of $S_1 \| S_2$ is visible anymore for the process cobegin $S_1 \| S_2$ coend.

So in $S \equiv$ cobegin S_1 || cobegin S_2 || S_3 coend coend

with $S_1 \equiv D?x$, $S_2 \equiv D!0$, $S_3 \equiv D?y$,

the S_2 process communicates with S_3 along the D channel internal to $S_2||S_3$, and not with S_1. The D channel of S_1 is an external input channel of S. We note that when no "clashes" arise between the external channel names of processes S_1, S_2 and S_3, then the semantic operator for parallel composition is associative for the network consisting of S_1, S_2 and S_3 executing concurrently, so we can write

cobegin S_1 || S_2 || S_3 coend

without (semantic) ambiguity. In agreement with the modular character of dynamic CSP, we have for recursive procedures a scope concept different from that of Algol like languages. All variables used in some procedure body (which is bracketed by begin - end) are assumed to be local variables, i.e. there are no references to any kind of "global" variables possible. (Correspondingly, there is no explicit variable declaration mechanism needed in dynamic CSP). The parameter list of a procedure consists of input channels, followed by output channels, followed by value/result-variable parameters. To simplify matters technically, we impose the restriction that all names in a (formal or actual) parameter list be distinct. This avoids any kind of "aliasing" that could introduce unwanted sharing of program- or channel variables by two processes.
This section is concluded by an example of an algorithm known as a "priority queue".

```
  Q(in;out;)
  begin
        shrink := false;
        while ¬ shrink
           do
              [ in?val → cobegin
                                      P(in,int1;out,int2;val)
                                   ||
                                      Q(int2;int1;)
                                coend
              □ out!´*´ → shrink := true
              ]
             od
    end,
  P(lin,rin;lout,rout;ownval)
  begin
        shrink := false;
        while ¬ shrink
           do
              [ lin?newval → largest := max(ownval,newval);
                             ownval := min(ownval,newval);
                             rout!largest
              □ lout → rin?ownval;
                             shrink := (ownval=´*´)
              ]
             od
    end :
begin
          cobegin  Q(D;E;) || Userproc(E;D;)  coend
  end
```

The queue can hold an arbitrary number of values: it expands or shrinks into as many processes as are needed. It can be sent a value along an input channel "in", or requested for a value along an output channel "out". In the latter case it sends the least value currently in the queue, if any.

2. The proof method

By now, a number of proof systems has been designed for "static" networks consisting of a fixed number of concurrently executing processes. ([AFR], [SD], [MC]) With the proof systems of [AFR] a specification of a collection concurrently executing processes is derived by means of a "cooperation test" from proof outlines for the component processes. This derived specification is not of the same form as the specifications of the components! Because of this, we cannot repeat the procedure to derive some specification of a still larger network in which the collection processes mentioned above can be handled as just one component. Obviously, such a proof system cannot be used for dynamically evolving networks. Another type of proof system, for example that of [SD], does not distinguish between the form of the specifications of networks on the one hand and of their components on the other. The correctness formulae of the system of [SD] are expressed in terms of the notions "trace" and "state". A state is a function describing the current contents of the program variables of some process. A trace is a sequence of records of communication, indicating which values were communicated along which channel (or with which process in the case of CSP), and also showing the chronological order of these communications. The system of [SD] uses Hoare style correctness formulae and proof rules. A general disadvantage of the Hoare method is, that it is not easy to prove something useful about a nonterminating process. The only way seems to be to resort to proof outlines, i.e. program texts with assertions attached to intermediate control points. However, for a <u>modular</u> set up of a proof system, complete proof outlines are hardly satisfactory as program specifications. For a modular specification of some (possible nonterminating) process, which will execute concurrently with, and communicate with some "unknown" collection of other processes, it seems desirable to include some kind of <u>invariant</u> to describe the interface of the process with its environment. This invariant must then be expressed solely in terms of the (traces of) externally visible channels of the process, and <u>not</u> in terms of the internal state or internal channels. This leads to the following type of correctness formulae:

$$I : \{p\}\ S\ \{q\}$$

where p is a precondition on the initial state and trace, and q is a postcondition on the final state and trace of S. I is an trace invariant for computations of S. The informal meaning of such a formula is:

> If p and I hold initially (that is, p holds for the initial state and trace, I holds for the initial trace), then:
> (1) I is preserved during the computation of S, that is, I still holds after any communication of S.
> (2) If S terminates, the postcondition q will hold for the final state and trace of S.

With this type of formulae, a proof rule for parallel composition can be designed as:

$$\frac{I_1 : \{p_1\}\ S_1\ \{q_1\}\ ,\ I_2 : \{p_2\}\ S_2\ \{q_2\}}{I_1\ \&\ I_2 : \{p_1\ \&\ p_2\}\ S_1\ ||\ S_2\ \{q_1\ \&\ q_2\}}$$

The conclusion of this rule is called an internal specification of the network $S_1||S_2$, because it will mention channels internal (as well as external) to $S_1||S_2$. To turn an internal specification into an external one, we introduce the following abstraction rule:

$$\frac{I' : \{p'\}\ S_1\ ||\ S_2\ \{q'\}\ ,\ I' \supset I \qquad (p\ \&\ I\ \&\ \Pi_{intchan}{=}\Lambda) \supset (p'\ \&\ I')\ ,\ q' \supset q}{I : \{p\}\ \underline{cobegin}\ S_1\ ||\ S_2\ \underline{coend}\ \{q\}}$$

provided that the free channel names, used in I,p and q are included in the external channels of $S_1||S_2$.

$\Pi_{intchan}$ stands for the projection of the trace of $S_1||S_2$ onto the internal channels of $S_1||S_2$, i.e. the subsequence of the trace formed by deleting all records of communication with a channel name not internal to $S_1||S_2$.

Λ stands for the "empty trace".

The merit of the above rule for parallel composition is the simplicity of its form. Moreover, for mere "pipelined" processes, its usage in proofs is also straightforward as the following example shows.

Take the following processes:

$S_1 \equiv$ do IN?x ; if x<0 then D!x fi od

$S_2 \equiv$ do D?y ; OUT!(entier(√y)) od

$S \equiv$ cobegin S_1 || S_2 coend

Denoting by:

- channel names like "D" the corresponding projection of the trace onto that channel.
- D[i]: the i-th element of (projection) D
- |D|: the length of (projection) D
- $trace_1 \leq trace_2$: that $trace_1$ is some initial prefix of $trace_2$
- f(trace) for some function f: the trace formed by applying f componentwise

then, we can write down the following specification for S:

$$OUT = entier(\surd abs(IN)) : \{IN = OUT = \Lambda\}\ S\ \{true\}$$

To prove this from specifications for S_1 and S_2, we can choose these last ones as:

$$D = abs(IN)\ \&\ nonneg(D) : \{IN = OUT = \Lambda\}\ S_1\ \{true\}$$

and

$$nonneg(D) \supset OUT = entier(\surd(D)) : \{D = OUT = \Lambda\}\ S_2\ \{true\}$$

(where nonneg(D) is some predicate expressing that all values occurring in the trace of D are nonnegative ones.)

From these two, the desired specification of S follows easily with the above two

rules.
Heuristically , we can regard the invariants of S and of S_1 as commitments about the behaviour of S and S_1 respectively. The invariant of S_2 is split into a "commitment" OUT = entier($\surd$(D)) which is preserved if and only if the assumption nonneg(D) about the environment is not violated. In the network S, the commitment of S_1 implies the assumption of S_2. This distinction between assumption and commitment will be formalized after our next example. This example shows that the usage of the above rule for parallel composition is rather cumbersome for non-"pipelined" networks, in which information flows back and forth between the component processes rather than in one direction.

We take:

$S_1 \equiv$ x:=0 ; do D!(x+1) ; E?x od
$S_2 \equiv$ do D?y ; E!(y+1) ; OUT!y od
S ≡ cobegin S_1 || S_2 coend

and try to prove:

OUT ≤ (1,3,5,....) : {OUT = Λ} S {true}

from specifications for S_1 and S_2.
(OUT ≤ (1,3,5....) can be written more formally as:
$\forall j\ [\ 0<j\leq|OUT| \supset OUT[j] = 2j-1\ ]$)
Again, heuristically, S_1 has a commitment $C_1 \equiv D \leq (1,3,5...)$
which depends on the assumption $A_1 \equiv E \leq (2,4,6...)$.
For S_2, we have a commitment $C_2 \equiv E \leq (2,4,6...)\ \&\ OUT \leq (1,3,5...)$
which depends on the assumption $A_2 \equiv D \leq (1,3,5...)$

Unfortunately, the specifications:

$A_1 \supset C_1$: {D = E = Λ} S_1 {true}
$A_2 \supset C_2$: {D = E = OUT = Λ} S_2 {true}

will not suffice to deduce the specification for S, as we are stuck on "circular" reasoning when we apply the parallel composition rule:

$$C_1 \supset A_2 \supset C_2 \supset A_1 \supset C_1 \supset ......$$

Some adequate specifications, which are however somewhat difficult to appreciate are:

$D[1] = 0\ \&\ \forall i\ [(1<i\leq|D|\ \&\ E[i-1] = 2i-2) \supset D[i] = 2i-1\ ]$: {D=E=Λ} S_1 {true}

$\forall i\ [(1\leq i\leq|OUT|\ \&\ D[i] = 2i-1) \supset (E[i] = 2i\ \&\ OUT[i] = 2i-1)]$:{D=E=OUT=Λ} S_2 {true}
{D = E = OUT = Λ} S_2 {true}

From the conjunction of the two invariants we can, by inductive reasoning, derive an invariant of $S_1||S_2$ from which the desired invariant of S can be deduced with the abstraction rule; the "circular" reasoning is turned into a "spiral". We can paraphrase the specification for, say S_1, as follows:
Let precondition p1 ≡ {D = E = Λ} and C_1 (as above) hold initially, then if A_1 holds for a prefix of the trace of a computation of S_1, the commitment C_1 holds for that prefix extended with the next communication.

Generalizing this pattern, we now introduce a new type of correctness formulae, inspired by a similar type of formulae used by Misra and Chandy [MC].

Consider the formula:

$$(A,C) : \{p\}\ S\ \{q\}$$

Informally, this means the following:

> Assume p & C holds for the initial state and trace, then the following two conditions hold:
> (1) If A holds after each communication of S up to a certain point, then C holds after each communication of S up to that point and also after the next communication of S, if present.
> (2) If S terminates, then if A holds after each communication of S, then the postcondition q holds for the final state and trace.

The pair (A,C) is called the assumption-commitment pair. the syntactic restrictions on assumptions and commitments are that they only refer to the trace of computations of S, and not to the states S passes through.
Also, the <u>only</u> way to refer to traces in assumptions, commitments, pre- or postconditions is by means of projections Π_{cset}, with cset a set of channel names. Such a projection stands for the subsequence of the trace, formed by deleting all records of communication which do not represent a communication along one of the channels in cset. When cset contains just one channel name, we use this name as an abbreviation for the projection Π_{cset}.

Due to our new correctness formulae, we can formulate a new proof rule which makes the explicit inductive reasoning in the example above unnecessary, as this induction becomes implicit in the soundness proof of the rule. This rule, called the network rule, is a slight modification of a rule proposed by Misra and Chandy [MC], and replaces the rule for parallel composition introduced above.

The network rule is:

$$\frac{\begin{array}{ll}(A_1,C_1) : \{p_1\}\ S_1\ \{q_1\}\ ,\ (A_2,C_2) : \{p_2\}\ S_2\ \{q_2\} & (1) \\ A_{net}\ \&\ C_1 \quad (sp\ A_2 \quad ,\quad A_{net}\ \&\ C_2 \supset A_1 & (2)\end{array}}{(A_{net},C_1\ \&\ C_2) : \{p_1\ \&\ p_2\}\ S_1\ ||\ S_2\ \{q_1\ \&\ q_2\}}$$

with the restrictions:

$$free(A_1,C_1,p_1,q_1) \subseteq free(S_1)$$
$$free(a_2,C_2,p_2,q_2) \subseteq free(S_2)$$

(Where free(X) denotes the free program- and channel variables of X. The free channels of a process are its external channels.)

Example: in the new formalism, we can express specifications for the processes in the example above as:

$$(A_1,C_1) : \{D = E = \Lambda\}\ S_1\ \{true\}$$
$$(A_2,C_2) : \{D = E = OUT = \Lambda\}\ S_2\ \{true\}$$
$$(true,C_1\ \&\ C_2) : \{D = E = OUT = \Lambda\}\ S_1\ ||\ S_2\ \{true\} \qquad (*)$$
$$(true,C) : \{OUT = \Lambda\}\ \underline{cobegin}\ S_1\ ||\ S_2\ \underline{coend}\ \{true\} \qquad (**)$$

with:

$A_1 \equiv E < (2,4,6...)$
$A_2 \equiv C_1 \equiv D < (1,3,5...)$
$C_2 \equiv A_1$ & $OUT < (1,3,5...)$
$C \equiv OUT < (1,3,5...)$

Clearly, (*) can be derived from the specifications for S_1 and S_2 by means of the network rule. Finally, an application of the abstraction rule yields (**).

A formal soundness proof of the network rule can be found in the full paper. A sketch of this proof is as follows:
Assume that C_1 & C_2 & p_1 & p_2 holds initially.
Then we have to prove:

(1) If A_{net} holds after communications up to a certain point, then C_1 & C_2 holds up to that point and also after the next communication.

(2) If A_{net} holds after all communications up to termination, then q_1 & q_2 holds for the final state and trace.

Here, we only show (1). So assume also that A_{net} holds after communications up to (and including) a certain point, say X. We prove, with induction, that for all points Y the following holds:
(*) A_1, A_2, C_1 and C_2 hold after communications up to and including Y.
(**) C_1 and C_2 hold also after the first communiction after Y, say at Y′.

(a) Initially, (*) is trivially fulfilled, since no communication took place. (And we only require something to hold after communication). Now for (**), we know by assumption that p_1 & C_1 and p_2 & C_2 hold initially.
Now there are three cases:

- S_1 communicated along an external channel of the network.
- S_2 communicated along an external channel of the network.
- Both S_1 and S_2 communicated, along an internal channel of the network.

Clause (1) of the network rule guarantees that the commitments of the processes which actually communicated hold after this communication. The fact that we allow references to traces in correctness formulae only by means of projections onto sets of channels can be used to show that the commitment of a process is preserved also when the process did not participate in the communication. So in all cases, C_1 and C_2 hold after the first communication.

(b) Now fix some abitrary point Y after the first communication. By assumption, A_{net} holds for Y. Also, by induction we may assume that C_1 and C_2 hold for Y. But then, with clause (2) of the network rule, A_1 and A_2 hold for Y, which establishes (*). Finally, from (*), the induction hypothesis and the assumption that p_1 & C_1, and p_2 & C_2 hold initially, it follows with clause (1) again that C_1 and C_2 hold after the first communication, for Y′.

3. The proof system

There are several points which deserve attention.
First, since recursive procedures are included in our language, statements and correspondingly correctness formulae, have a meaning only in the context of some environment consisting of procedure declarations. So formulae in our system are of the form:

$$\langle \text{Decl} \mid (A,C) : \{p\}\ S\ \{q\} \rangle$$

(Where Decl is a set of procedure declarations)
However, apart from the recursion rule, we have that for each (axiom or) rule the environments mentioned in premisses and conclusion of the rule are all the same. Therefore, in almost all cases, we do not write down environments explicitly in the formulae, assuming that the environment is clear from context.
Second, although in this abstract we have not defined explicitly the assertion languages to be used in formulae for assumptions, commitments, pre- and postconditions, we remark here that these languages, besides program- and channel variables, also include "mathematical" or "ghost" variables as they are called in the literature. Such ghost variables cannot occur in the program text, so the value they denote is not affected by the computations of the program. Correctness formulae containing free ghost variables are implicitly assumed to be universally quantified for these variables, so:

$$(A,C) : \{p\}\ S\ \{q\}$$

with free ghost variable g, means the same as:

$$\forall g\ [\ (A,C) : \{p\}\ S\ \{q\}\ ]$$

We now discuss in what sense "classical" Hoare style formulae like the normal assignment axiom are incorporated in our system. Notice that if "S" is some noncommunicating statement, then validity of

$$(A,C) : \{p\}\ S\ \{q\}$$

boils down to: if p & C holds for the initial state and trace, then q holds for the final state and trace. So whenever the <u>Hoare</u> formula $\{p\}\ S\ \{q\}$ is valid (meaning that, if p holds for the initial state and trace, then q holds for the final state and trace), then $(A,C) : \{p\}\ S\ \{q\}$ is valid in our system for <u>every</u> assumption-commitment pair (A,C). We therefore introduce axiom <u>schemes</u> $\{p\}\ S\ \{q\}$ in our system, from which normal axioms (schemes) can be obtained by adding some arbitrary (A,C) pair in front of it. It will now be clear that we can incorporate all normal Hoare axioms provided we regard them as schemes in the above sense. For our particular language, we have the following axiom schemes:

$\{p[s/x]\}\ x:=s\ \{p\}$ (assign)

(p[s/x] denotes the assertion p wherein s is subtituted for x)

$\{p\}$ <u>skip</u> $\{p\}$ (skip)

$\{p\}\ b\ \{p\ \&\ b\}$ (test)

However, these axioms are not sufficient if we want a complete proof system! For instance, look at: (true,false) : {true} skip {false}.
This formula is valid, but it cannot be derived from our axioms, since: {true} skip {false} is not valid if regarded as a classical Hoare formula. To correct this we introduce the following rule:

$$\frac{(A,C) : \{p \mathbin{\&} C\}\ S\ \{q\}}{(A,C) : \{p\}\ S\ \{q\}}$$

Now, what about "classical" Hoare rules like the sequential composition rule? Here we introduce proof rule schemes like for example:

$$\frac{\{p_1\}\ S_1\ \{q_1\}\ ,\ \{p_2\}\ S_2\ \{q_2\}}{\{p_3\}\ S_3\ \{q_3\}}$$

which is valid if and only if

$$\frac{(A,C) : \{p_1\}\ S_1\ \{q_1\}\ ,\ (A,C) : \{p_2\}\ S_2\ \{q_2\}}{(A,C) : \{p_3\}\ S_3\ \{q_3\}}$$

is valid for every feasible (A,C) pair.

(notice that the same (A,C) pair is used in all formulae of the premisses as well as of the conclusion of the rule!)
We now claim that the following scheme is sound in our system:

$$\frac{\{p\}\ S_1\ \{r\}\ ,\ \{r\}\ S_2\ \{q\}}{\{p\}\ S_1\ ;\ S_2\ \{q\}} \qquad \text{(sequential composition)}$$

(So the normal Hoare style sequential composition rule can be regarded as a scheme in our system)
We give a sketch of the soundness proof of this scheme:
Take some arbitrary pair (A,C), and assume that p & C holds initially. We prove that if A holds after communications up to some point in the computation of $S_1;S_2$, then C holds after communications up to this point and also after the next communication, if present. (The proof that q holds upon termination if A holds after all communications of $S_1;S_2$ follows similar lines) So assume also that A holds up to some point, say X. The only interesting case is when X lies in the midst of the execution of S_2. In this case, A holds after all communications of S_1, so with the premisse for S_1, we know that C holds after communications of S_1, and that r and C hold when S_1 terminates. But then the premisse for S_2 guarantees that C also holds after communications of S_2 up to X and after the next communication of S_2.

It turns out that many "classical" Hoare rules remain sound when regarded as proof rule schemes in our system. In particular, for dynamic CSP we have besides the sequential composition rule the following rule for the nondeterministic choice construct:

$$\frac{\{p\}\ S_1\ \{q\}\ ,\ \{p\}\ S_2\ \{q\}}{\{p\}\ [\ S_1\ \Box\ S_2\ ]\ \{q\}} \qquad \text{(choice)}$$

We continue with rules for input- and output commands. In these rules, we use substitutions in assertions like: $A[D\langle v\rangle/D]$ denoting the assertion formed from A by replacing terms Π_{cset}, with $D \in cset$, by $\Pi_{cset}\langle D,v\rangle$. As usual, care must be taken that the variable v not becomes bound by some quantifier in A. (In the assertion language, two consecutive trace expressions denote the concatenation of the two corresponding traces. A term $\langle D,v\rangle$ denotes the one element trace, indicating the communication of a value v along the channel D; when the channel is clear from context, the abbreviation $\langle v\rangle$ is also used for such a term.)

$$\frac{\begin{array}{c} C \ \&\ p \supset \forall v\ (\ C[D\langle v\rangle/D]\ ) \\ C \ \&\ p \supset \forall v\ (\ A[D\langle v\rangle/D] \supset q[D\langle v\rangle/D,v/x]\ ) \end{array}}{(A,C)\ :\ \{p\}\ D?x\ \{q\}} \qquad \text{(input)}$$

$$\frac{\begin{array}{c} C \ \&\ p \supset C[D\langle s\rangle/D] \\ C \ \&\ p \supset (\ A[D\langle s\rangle/D] \supset q[D\langle s\rangle/D]\ ) \end{array}}{(A,C)\ :\ \{p\}\ D!s\ \{q\}} \qquad \text{(output)}$$

The first premisse of both rules is clear: we must show that C is preserved for this communication. Since we do not know which value we are going to receive, we must show this for every possible value for the case of an input command. The second premisse for the input rule is also clear: the assumption A can be used to derive some property of the value actually received. This property can be expressed in the postcondition of the command.
The role of the A-term in the second premisse of the output rule is less clear, since the communicated value is not unknown. However, in the next example it is used to fix the <u>channel</u> along which communication occurs:

$S_1 \equiv [\ D!0\ ;\ E!0\ ;\ x:=0\ \Box\ E!0\ ;\ D!0\ ;\ x:=1\ ]$

$S_2 \equiv E?y\ ;\ D?y$

$S \equiv$ <u>cobegin</u> $S_1 \ ||\ S_2$ <u>coend</u>

We can prove: $(true,true)\ :\ \{true\}\ S\ \{x=1\}$

from: $(A_1,true)\ :\ \{\Pi_{D,E} = \Lambda\}\ S_1\ \{x=1\}$

and: $(true,C_1)\ :\ \{\Pi_{D,E} = \Lambda\}\ S_2\ \{true\}$

with: $A_1 \equiv C_2 \equiv \exists v,w\ [\ \Pi\text{subD,E} \le (\langle E,v\rangle\langle D,w\rangle)\ ]$

To prove the formula for S_1 we must show among others that:

$$(A_1, true) : \{\Pi_{D,E} = \Lambda\}\ D!0\ ;\ E!0\ ;\ x:=0\ \{x=1\}$$

Here we can use the assumption A_1 in the output rule to obtain:

$$(A_1, true) : \{\Pi_{D,E} = \Lambda\}\ D!0\ \{false\}$$

The rest of the proof now follows easily.

In the next two rules, for recursive procedure calls, we use the following notation:
- $\overline{D}$ and $\overline{x}$ are abbreviations for lists of channel- and program variables.
- $\overline{E}/\overline{D}$ denotes the substitution of the E-variables for corresponding D-variables.
- ω denotes some special value, used to initialize all local variables of a procedure body.
- var(X) denotes the free program variables of X.
- chan(X) denotes the free channel variables of X.

The rules are:

$$\frac{\langle\ Decl\ |\ \{p\}\ P(\overline{D}_{in};\overline{D}_{out};\overline{x})\ \{q\}\ \rangle\ \vdash\ \langle\ Decl\ |\ \{p\ \&\ \overline{y}=\overline{\omega}\}\ S_0\ \{q\}\ \rangle}{\langle\ Decl \cup \{P(\overline{D}_{in};\overline{D}_{out};\overline{x})\}\ \underline{begin}\ S_0\ \underline{end}\ |\ \{p\}\ P(\overline{D}_{in};\overline{D}_{out};\overline{x})\ \{q\}\ \rangle}$$

Provided that var(p,q) $\subseteq \{\overline{x}\}$, and where $\overline{y}$ denotes the list of local variables of S_0 without the parameters $\overline{x}$. (Notice that we have used a proof rule scheme here)
The essence of the soundness proof for this rule is an induction on the recursion depth of a call of some procedure. A problem is that this recursion depth is not necessarily bounded for a given call. For formulae in which occur such nonterminating calls, the requirement that some postcondition holds upon termination is of course trivially fulfilled, but the requirement for the (A,C) pair is not! The solution to this problem is to remember that the validity of correctness formulae is formulated in terms of (finite) prefixes of the trace of some process, and that each of these prefixes is produced already after the computation has reached some finite recursion depth. See the full paper for a real soundness proof.

$$\frac{(A,C)\ :\ \{p\}\ P(\overline{D}_{in};\overline{D}_{out};\overline{x})\ \{q\}}{(A[\bullet],C[\bullet])\ :\ \{p[\bullet]\}\ P(\overline{E}_{in};\overline{E}_{out};\overline{u})\ \{q[\bullet]\}} \qquad \text{(parameter substitution)}$$

Where $[\bullet] \equiv [\overline{E}_{in}/\overline{D}_{in}, \overline{E}_{out}/\overline{D}_{out}, \overline{u}/\overline{x}]$

And provided that:

$(\overline{E}_{in} \cup \overline{E}_{out}) \cap chan(A,C,p,q) \subseteq (\overline{D}_{in} \cup \overline{D}_{out})$

$\overline{u} \cap var(p,q) \subseteq \overline{x}$

Due to our restriction that all names in a (formal or actual) parameter list must be distinct, and also to the absence of "global" variables, we could keep this rule quite simple.
The rules above can be used to derive something about the changes made to the actual parameters of some procedure call, but they are not sufficient to prove that other variables, not used as actual parameter, are left unchanged by this call. Similar

problems arise when we try to prove that the trace of some channel D is left invariant by the execution of some network of which D is not an external channel. To be able to prove these invariance properties, we introduce an axiom and some rules.

$$(A,C) : \{p\}\ S\ \{p\} \qquad \text{(invariance)}$$

Provided that free(A,C,p) $\cap$ free(S) = $\emptyset$
(free(X) denotes the free program- and channel variables of X)

$$\frac{(A_1,C_1) : \{p_1\}\ S\ \{q_1\}\ ,\ (A_2,C_2) : \{p_2\}\ S\ \{q_2\}}{(A_1\ \&\ A_2, C_1\ \&\ C_2) : \{p_1\ \&\ p_2\}\ S\ \{q_1\ \&\ q_2\}} \qquad \text{(conjunction)}$$

$$\frac{\{p\}\ S\ \{q\}}{\{p[e/g]\}\ S\ \{q[e/g]\}} \qquad \text{(ghost variable substitution I)}$$

Where g is some ghost variable and e is some expression, not containing program- or channel variables.

$$\frac{\{p\}\ S\ \{q\}}{\{p[s/g]\}\ S\ \{q\}} \qquad \text{(ghost variable substitution II)}$$

Where g is some ghost variable and s is some expression, and provided that g does not occur free in q.

We close this section with a restatement of the network rule, a reformulation of the abstraction rule, and the introduction of a consequence rule, which is used in connection with the other two.

$$\frac{\begin{array}{c}(A_1,C_1) : \{p_1\}\ S_1\ \{q_1\}\ ,\ (A_2,C_2) : \{p_2\}\ S_2\ \{q_2\}\\ A_{net}\ \&\ C_1 \supset A_2\ ,\ A_{net}\ \&\ C_2 \supset A_1\end{array}}{(a_{net}, C_1\ \&\ C_2) : \{p_1\ \&\ p_2\}\ S_1\ ||\ S_2\ \{q_1\ \&\ q_2\}}$$

With the restrictions:

free(A_1,C_1,p_1,q_1) $\subseteq$ free(S_1)
free(A_2,C_2,p_2,q_2) $\subseteq$ free(S_2)

$$\frac{(A,C) : \{p\ \&\ \Pi_{intchan}=\Lambda\}\ S_1\ ||\ S_2\ \{q\}}{(A,C) : \{p\}\ \underline{\text{cobegin}}\ S_1\ ||\ S_2\ \underline{\text{coend}}\ \{q\}}$$

Where intchan denotes the internal channels of $S_1||S_2$, and provided that chan(A,C,p,q) $\cap$ intchan = $\emptyset$

$$\frac{(A',C') : \{p'\}\ X\ \{q'\} \quad (\text{with } X \equiv S \text{ or } X \equiv N) \qquad A \supset A' \ ,\ C' \supset C \ ,\ p \supset p' \ ,\ q' \supset q \ ,\ p \,\&\, C \supset C'}{(A,C) : \{p\}\ S\ \{q\}}$$

The normal usage of these rules is as follows:

(1) Use the network rule to derive a formula for $S_1||S_2$.

(2) Use the consequence rule to remove all information about the internal functioning of the network, that is, ensure that no internal channel name remains after the application of the consequence rule, except for a conjunct $\Pi_{intchan}=\Lambda$ (which clearly cannot be removed by means of the consequence rule).

(3) Use the abstraction rule to get rid of the conjunct $\Pi_{intchan}=\Lambda$, and to obtain a formula for cobegin $S_1||S_2$ coend.

4. Conclusion

We introduced a formal proof system for dynamic networks of processes, which has been shown to be sound. Future work will consider the completeness of the system.

References

[AFR] Apt, K.R., Francez,N. and de Roever, W.P.
"A proof System for Communicating Sequential Processes"
TOPLAS 2,3. July 1980.

[CH] Chen, Z.C. and Hoare, C.A.R.
"Partial Correctness of Communicating Sequential Processes."
2nd International Conference on Distributed Computer Systems,
IEEE 1981, 1-12.

[MC] Misra, J. and Chandy, K.M.
"Proofs of Networks of Processes",
IEEE Transactions on Software Engineering, July 1981.

[SD] Soundararajan,N. and Dahl, O.J.
"Partial Correctness Semantics of Communicating Sequential Processes"

ERRATA

Corrections to "A Low Level Language ..." by D. Plaisted

Section 3 last part, definition should be

$$iter^*(\alpha, \beta) \equiv \vee_{k \geq 0}[\alpha \; as \; (T; \alpha) \; as \; (T^2; \alpha) \; as \; \ldots \; as \; (T^{k-1}; \alpha) \; as \; (T^k; \beta)]$$

where T^2 is $T;T$ and T^3 is $T;T;T$, et cetera.

Section 4 paragraph 2

G should be $G_{iter^*(\alpha, \beta)}$.

Vol. 117: Fundamentals of Computation Theory. Proceedings, 1981. Edited by F. Gécseg. XI, 471 pages. 1981.

Vol. 118: Mathematical Foundations of Computer Science 1981. Proceedings, 1981. Edited by J. Gruska and M. Chytil. XI, 589 pages. 1981.

Vol. 119: G. Hirst, Anaphora in Natural Language Understanding: A Survey. XIII, 128 pages. 1981.

Vol. 120: L. B. Rall, Automatic Differentiation: Techniques and Applications. VIII, 165 pages. 1981.

Vol. 121: Z. Zlatev, J. Wasniewski, and K. Schaumburg, Y12M Solution of Large and Sparse Systems of Linear Algebraic Equations. IX, 128 pages. 1981.

Vol. 122: Algorithms in Modern Mathematics and Computer Science. Proceedings, 1979. Edited by A. P. Ershov and D. E. Knuth. XI, 487 pages. 1981.

Vol. 123: Trends in Information Processing Systems. Proceedings, 1981. Edited by A. J. W. Duijvestijn and P. C. Lockemann. XI, 349 pages. 1981.

Vol. 124: W. Polak, Compiler Specification and Verification. XIII, 269 pages. 1981.

Vol. 125: Logic of Programs. Proceedings, 1979. Edited by E. Engeler. V, 245 pages. 1981.

Vol. 126: Microcomputer System Design. Proceedings, 1981. Edited by M. J. Flynn, N. R. Harris, and D. P. McCarthy. VII, 397 pages. 1982.

Voll. 127: Y.Wallach, Alternating Sequential/Parallel Processing. X, 329 pages. 1982.

Vol. 128: P. Branquart, G. Louis, P. Wodon, An Analytical Description of CHILL, the CCITT High Level Language. VI, 277 pages. 1982.

Vol. 129: B. T. Hailpern, Verifying Concurrent Processes Using Temporal Logic. VIII, 208 pages. 1982.

Vol. 130: R. Goldblatt, Axiomatising the Logic of Computer Programming. XI, 304 pages. 1982.

Vol. 131: Logics of Programs. Proceedings, 1981. Edited by D. Kozen. VI, 429 pages. 1982.

Vol. 132: Data Base Design Techniques I: Requirements and Logical Structures. Proceedings, 1978. Edited by S.B. Yao, S.B. Navathe, J.L. Weldon, and T.L. Kunii. V, 227 pages. 1982.

Vol. 133: Data Base Design Techniques II: Proceedings, 1979. Edited by S.B. Yao and T.L. Kunii. V, 229–399 pages. 1982.

Vol. 134: Program Specification. Proceedings, 1981. Edited by J. Staunstrup. IV, 426 pages. 1982.

Vol. 135: R.L. Constable, S.D. Johnson, and C.D. Eichenlaub, An Introduction to the PL/CV2 Programming Logic. X, 292 pages. 1982.

Vol. 136: Ch. M. Hoffmann, Group-Theoretic Algorithms and Graph Isomorphism. VIII, 311 pages. 1982.

Vol. 137: International Symposium on Programming. Proceedings, 1982. Edited by M. Dezani-Ciancaglini and M. Montanari. VI, 406 pages. 1982.

Vol. 138: 6th Conference on Automated Deduction. Proceedings, 1982. Edited by D.W. Loveland. VII, 389 pages. 1982.

Vol. 139: J. Uhl, S. Drossopoulou, G. Persch, G. Goos, M. Dausmann, G. Winterstein, W. Kirchgässner, An Attribute Grammar for the Semantic Analysis of Ada. IX, 511 pages. 1982.

Vol. 140: Automata, Languages and programming. Edited by M. Nielsen and E.M. Schmidt. VII, 614 pages. 1982.

Vol. 141: U. Kastens, B. Hutt, E. Zimmermann, GAG: A Practical Compiler Generator. IV, 156 pages. 1982.

Vol. 142: Problems and Methodologies in Mathematical Software Production. Proceedings, 1980. Edited by P.C. Messina and A. Murli. VII, 271 pages. 1982.

Vol. 143: Operating Systems Engineering. Proceedings, 1980. Edited by M. Maekawa and L.A. Belady. VII, 465 pages. 1982.

Vol. 144: Computer Algebra. Proceedings, 1982. Edited by J. Calmet. XIV, 301 pages. 1982.

Vol. 145: Theoretical Computer Science. Proceedings, 1983. Edited by A.B. Cremers and H.P. Kriegel. X, 367 pages. 1982.

Vol. 146: Research and Development in Information Retrieval. Proceedings, 1982. Edited by G. Salton and H.-J. Schneider. IX, 311 pages. 1983.

Vol. 147: RIMS Symposia on Software Science and Engineering. Proceedings, 1982. Edited by E. Goto, I. Nakata, K. Furukawa, R. Nakajima, and A. Yonezawa. V. 232 pages. 1983.

Vol. 148: Logics of Programs and Their Applications. Proceedings, 1980. Edited by A. Salwicki. VI, 324 pages. 1983.

Vol. 149: Cryptography. Proceedings, 1982. Edited by T. Beth. VIII, 402 pages. 1983.

Vol. 150: Enduser Systems and Their Human Factors. Proceedings, 1983. Edited by A. Blaser and M. Zoeppritz. III, 138 pages. 1983.

Vol. 151: R. Piloty, M. Barbacci, D. Borrione, D. Dietmeyer, F. Hill, and P. Skelly, CONLAN Report. XII, 174 pages. 1983.

Vol. 152: Specification and Design of Software Systems. Proceedings, 1982. Edited by E. Knuth and E. J. Neuhold. V, 152 pages. 1983.

Vol. 153: Graph-Grammars and Their Application to Computer Science. Proceedings, 1982. Edited by H. Ehrig, M. Nagl, and G. Rozenberg. VII, 452 pages. 1983.

Vol. 154: Automata, Languages and Programming. Proceedings, 1983. Edited by J. Diaz. VIII, 734 pages. 1983.

Vol. 155: The Programming Language Ada. Reference Manual. Approved 17 February 1983. American National Standards Institute, Inc. ANSI/MIL-STD-1815A-1983. IX, 331 pages. 1983.

Vol. 156: M.H. Overmars, The Design of Dynamic Data Structures. VII, 181 pages. 1983.

Vol. 157: O. Østerby, Z. Zlatev, Direct Methods for Sparse Matrices. VIII, 127 pages. 1983.

Vol. 158: Foundations of Computation Theory. Proceedings, 1983. Edited by M. Karpinski, XI, 517 pages. 1983.

Vol. 159: CAAP'83. Proceedings, 1983. Edited by G. Ausiello and M. Protasi. VI, 416 pages. 1983.

Vol. 160: The IOTA Programming System. Edited by R. Nakajima and T. Yuasa. VII, 217 pages. 1983.

Vol. 161: DIANA, An Intermediate Language for Ada. Edited by G. Goos, W.A. Wulf, A. Evans, Jr. and K.J. Butler. VII, 201 pages. 1983.

Vol. 162: Computer Algebra. Proceedings, 1983. Edited by J.A. van Hulzen. XIII, 305 pages. 1983.

Vol. 163: VLSI Engineering. Proceedings. Edited by T.L. Kunii. VIII, 308 pages. 1984.

Vol. 164: Logics of Programs. Proceedings, 1983. Edited by E. Clarke and D. Kozen. VI, 528 pages. 1984.